VICKSBURG, 1863

VICKSBURG, 1863

Winston Groom

Alfred A. Knopf   New York   2009

THIS IS A BORZOI BOOK
PUBLISHED BY ALFRED A. KNOPF

Grateful acknowledgment is made to Louisiana State University
for permission to reprint excerpts from *Brokenburn: The Journal
of Kate Stone, 1861–1868,* edited by John Q. Anderson. Reprinted
by permission of Louisiana State University Press.

Library of Congress Cataloging-in-Publication Data
Groom, Winston, [date]
Vicksburg, 1863 / by Winston Groom
p.   cm.
Includes bibliographical references.
ISBN 978-0-307-26425-1
1. Vicksburg (Miss.)—History—Siege, 1863.   I. Title.
E475.27.G794 2009
973.7'344—dc22   2008045984

Manufactured in the United States of America
First Edition

To Wren Murphy

Tireless, scrupulous,
and cheerful all these years
in organizing the many details
of my writing life

The fate of the Confederacy was sealed at Vicksburg.

—Ulysses S. Grant

The opening of the Mississippi River will be to us of more advantage than the capture of forty Richmonds.

—Henry W. Halleck,
general in chief,
Union army

Vicksburg should have ended the war; but the rebel leaders were mad.

—William Tecumseh Sherman

Contents

VICKSBURG, 1863

Preface

The Battle of Vicksburg was the climax of a long, arduous struggle by the Union to regain control of the Mississippi River valley and sever the Confederacy in two. In some ways it resembled a messy chess game, filled with unpleasant and dangerous surprises amid the ruthless grind to capture the rebel king. It was fought from the pestilent swamps of Louisiana to the snow and ice of northern Tennessee. It ranged all along the Mississippi River, with powerful gunboats steaming down from Cairo, Illinois, and immense oceangoing warships coming up from the Gulf of Mexico. It was fought with armies great and small, from Belmont, Missouri, to Fort Donelson, Tennessee; from Shiloh to Memphis and from New Orleans to Baton Rouge.

It was a hard and bloody road, rife with tenacity and indecision, brilliance and stupidity, valor and arrogance, suffering and elation, victory and defeat. When it was over thousands of men, North and South, would be buried along its path, but the death knell of the Southern Confederacy had been struck.

With the Mississippi River valley in Federal hands, the Union could proceed with its plan to carve up the rest of the Confederacy, which it did—though not without setbacks—from middle Tennessee through Alabama and Georgia, in the end leaving the Rebel armies in the Carolinas and Virginia without recourse to food or supplies.

The purpose of this book is to tell the story of the Battle of Vicksburg and the events leading up to it, as well as its aftermath, which, had Southern leaders exercised better judgment, well might have averted the appalling events during the following two years.

It is also the story of Ulysses S. Grant, the unlikely forty-year-old Union general who at the beginning of the war could not even secure a commission but, in the end, fought his army five hundred miles downriver to deliver the coup de grâce that should have ended the Civil War.

Introduction

By no design of my own, in all the earlier war histories I've written, some close relative was involved in the conflict. It's not that my people were professional warriors; they just happened to be of the right age at the right time to be swept up in the fighting. In *Shrouds of Glory: From Atlanta to Nashville; The Last Great Campaign of the Civil War* it was my great-grandfather, who fought with Joe Wheeler's cavalry during the Battle of Atlanta. In *A Storm in Flanders: The Ypres Salient, 1914–1918; Tragedy and Triumph on the Western Front,* it was my grandfather, who went to France with the Thirty-first Infantry (Dixie) Division. In *1942: The Year That Tried Men's Souls* it was my father, who was a captain in the army during World War II. In *Patriotic Fire: Andrew Jackson and Jean Laffite at the Battle of New Orleans,* my great-great-great-grandfather was a major with the U.S. Seventh Infantry Regiment during the War of 1812, and fought with Jackson at New Orleans. I found these direct links with the past particularly gratifying while writing the books, as though I was somehow connected to the events by blood and sinew, however distant.

When I undertook the Battle of Vicksburg several years ago it was with a little trepidation, since there was no known link between that terrific event and anyone in my ancestry. It's not that I'm superstitious but I couldn't help but wonder if I was wandering into uncharted territory of the kind described on old maps as 𝕭𝖊𝖞𝖔𝖓𝖉 𝕳𝖊𝖗𝖊, 𝕿𝖍𝖊𝖗𝖊 𝕷𝖎𝖊 𝕯𝖗𝖆𝖌𝖔𝖓𝖘.

I was conciliated with the fact that a hundred yards or so behind my home at Point Clear, Alabama, on Mobile Bay, there's a small cemetery called Confederate Rest where more than three hundred Rebel soldiers who were wounded at Vicksburg are buried. They had been sent down by rail and steamboat to the Grand Hotel, an elegant resort that still exists today, which in the 1860s had been turned into a Confederate hospital.

The cemetery is a quiet, pastoral place on the edge of a golf course, and the soldiers' graves are marked by row upon row of plain white wooden crosses. That is because their names are unknown, due to a fire at the hotel shortly after the war that destroyed the records. They lie among a grove of tall cedar trees, and when the wind is just right it makes a sound almost like singing.

It wasn't much of a personal connection, but it was the only one I had, till out of the blue came an e-mail from a distant cousin, whom I have never met, who had amassed all manner of genealogical history about the Groom side of the family.

The history of the other sides have been documented almost back to the time of the apes, because those ancestors were inveterate pack rats who collected everything under the sun that had to do with the family for the past two hundred years. It was all kept in neat little packets tied up with blue and pink ribbons and saved in strongboxes that passed from attic to attic until it was finally handed down to me.

Yet on the Groom side, beyond my great-grandparents' generation, the history was always shrouded in mystery, which I assumed was probably because we were descended from criminals, or worse.

This cousin, however, through birth, marriage, census, death, and military records, had traced the Grooms back to 1757, in Virginia and North Carolina, from where in the 1830s they migrated to Wilcox County, Alabama, about a hundred miles up the Alabama River from Mobile, in the heart of the black belt, at that time the greatest cotton-growing region in the nation—maybe in the world.

There, in 1832, at a place named Snow Hill, was born one James Wright Groom, who would become my great-great-grandfather. In 1862, one year into the Civil War, he rode a short distance over to Meridian, Mississippi, and joined the Fourth Mississippi Cavalry Regiment—the so-called East Mississippi Dragoons. Why he chose to enlist in Mississippi instead of Alabama is anybody's guess, but the records show that's what he did.

The Fourth Mississippi had many clashes with the Federal cavalry. At times they rode with Major W. H. "Red" Jackson's bunch, and at others with the legendary Nathan Bedford Forrest. Mostly they did what cavalry was supposed to do: watch and harass the enemy and collect military intelligence. As the fighting around Vicksburg heated up, the Confederates experienced a severe shortage of cavalry, as this book will describe in detail, and the Fourth Mississippi—or at least a part of it—was sent to beef up the beleaguered Rebel army as it fought for its life against the relentless Yankee host under General Ulysses S. Grant.

What role my great-great-grandfather played in this is lost to history; no records show him as being captured or wounded, but he was in a Confederate hospital for three months in the early part of 1863. There is nothing on him in family lore, and I don't have his rebel sword or papers or photograph as I do my great-grandfather on the other side of the family. From all indications, he never rose higher than private, but the records show he wasn't a deserter or a coward, and he fought on till the bitter end.

Afterward, he moved to Mobile, where, according to his obituary in the *Mobile Register,* he died at home of a stroke on May 30, 1906, at the age of seventy-three. It was the same year my father was born, so of course he would not have known him. The obituary described James as "a highly respected citizen of Mobile," and said that he was one of "the best known engineers" in the city, adding that he "won high standing in his profession." He is buried out in Magnolia Cemetery in Mobile, where members of my family have been laid to rest for as far back as anybody can remember.

Whether during the Vicksburg battle James Wright Groom was out there on his horse, dashing through the smoke and the fray, braving cannon fire and clashing sabers with a blue-clad foe, or miles away guarding roads and bridges, cleaning latrines, or stealing chickens, history does not tell us. After all he was just a private soldier.

I'm partial to the more colorful version, first because it's fun to think so, and second because it put me in a receptive mood to discuss the subject at hand. But let me hasten to add that in writing this book at no time did I let the temptation to tell "the better story" overcome my duty to recorded historical material.

Point Clear, Alabama
November 6, 2008

Note on Military Organization, Weapons, and Tactics

The basic Civil War infantry unit was the regiment, consisting of about 600 men, broken down into companies, platoons, and squads and corresponding, roughly, with the modern-day infantry battalion. Regiments were closely knit, had their own colors and identification (such as Fourth Alabama or Sixty-first New York), made reports to higher commands, and were designed to operate as an integrated unit on the battlefield. They were commanded by a colonel. Brigades usually consisted of five regiments (about 3,000 men) and were commanded by a brigadier general. Divisions consisted of three brigades (about 7,000 to 8,000 men) and were commanded by a major general. An army corps consisted of three or more divisions and was commanded by a lieutenant general. "Grand Armies" combined several army corps and could total well over 100,000 men.

Artillery was broken down into batteries of six guns each; in Confederate armies artillery was generally assigned at the brigade level, whereas in Union armies it was usually assigned at division level. It may be added that rarely were any of these units up to book strength, owing to casualties, sickness, leaves of absence, and, of course, desertion.

Infantry parade drill was not merely a quaint traditional formality, as it mainly is in the military today, but a dead-earnest part of nineteenth-century warfare. When troops weren't fighting or tending to other duties, they were drilling—half steps, step-and-a-halfs, obliques, right turns, mark time, close files, left and right flanks—all of it as daintily orchestrated as a French minuet. On large battlefields where thousands of men marched shoulder to shoulder to mass their fire at an enemy, all were expected to arrive at a precise point and a precise time to produce the desired effect. The slightest variation in terrain—a hidden gully, a bramble thicket, or even a fallen tree—could throw the plan out of whack, so attention to marching orders was paramount.

The firepower of an assault could be stunning. With some exceptions in the Confederate army during the early part of the war, both sides were equipped with the standard infantry weaponry of the day, the .58 caliber Springfield, or the .577 caliber British Enfield, or a similar percussion-cap rifle that could fire a conical lead slug a thousand yards (the effective range was three hundred yards) at a rate of about two shots per minute. The slug itself was commonly known as a "minié" ball, after its French inventor. In the full fury of an assault, assuming that one corps had attacked another, it would not be inconceivable that during any given minute sixty thousand deadly projectiles would be ripping through the air toward flesh and bone. The size and weight of the bullet would be sufficient to disable most men no matter where it hit them, even in the hand or foot.

Because they had no munitions factories at the beginning of the war, the Confederates equipped themselves with weapons from state militias or by seizing federal armories, as well as by making large purchases from abroad, principally from Great Britain. As the war ground on they added to their arsenal by collecting Union weapons left upon the battlefield.

More worrisome for the foot soldier, attacks were accompanied by or defended against by artillery fire, which the troops feared even more than rifle bullets because its effects were so ghastly. (Even so, small arms fire caused most of the casualties during the war.)

The artillery pieces had come a long way since the previous major world conflict—the Napoleonic Wars half a century earlier. The standard artillery weapon for both sides was still the smoothbore 12-pound Napoleon but improvements had made it devastatingly accurate at half a mile and more. Ammunition was divided into *shot,* a large spherical solid iron ball, and *shell,* a hollow iron ball filled with gunpowder fused to explode just above an enemy formation, flinging deadly shrapnel as it broke into pieces. Both sides had a variety of other guns as well; rifled Parrots, for instance, could throw a projectile a mile and a half and modern breech-loading Whitworths could crack a shell two miles with amazing accuracy. Any assaulting column could soon expect to come under the fire of these supermutilating weapons that, like the rifle, could fire at a rate of about two rounds a minute.

At that speed, theoretically, the artillery of one army corps—as many as eighty to a hundred guns—could hurl nearly two hundred rounds in any given minute toward the assaulting column. The muzzle velocity of these guns was low compared with twentieth- or twenty-first-century weapons, and soldiers could often actually see the rounds arcing toward them like deadly black grapefruits. One veteran recalled a companion who, watching one of the seemingly slow cannonballs bouncing over the ground near him, stuck his foot out as if to stop the thing and in a split second the foot was ripped completely off his leg. In a battle early in the war a Union general seated on his horse heard a strange sound next to him and, when he turned to investigate, was horrified to see that his chief of staff, still erect in his saddle, had had his head completely taken off by a cannonball. Worse for attacking troops was the *canister* that defenders blew at them when they neared their lines of defense. This consisted of a load of iron balls the size of large marbles that turned a cannon into an enormous shotgun, mowing down ranks of men in a single sweep. Sometimes artillerymen also loaded their cannon with pieces of chain and other scrap metal.

Early in the Civil War most generals still idealized the Napoleonic model as a tactical bible. Set forth most prominently by the French military theorist Antoine-Henri Jomini, this premise held that battles are better won by maneuvering the mass of troops around an enemy than in conducting direct frontal attacks. The notion of entrenching or fortifying was scorned as inducing timidity among the soldiers. Instead, the surprise flank attack or, better yet, an attack on the enemy's rear was the desired ideal. As the conflict wore on, however, "digging in" became so commonplace that by the final year infantry tactics would come to resemble the trench warfare of World War I, still half a century into the future.

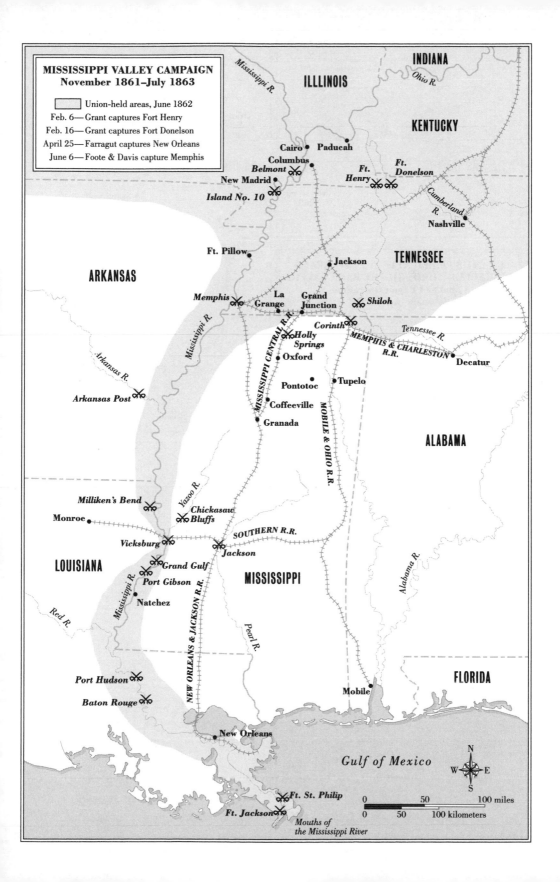

MISSISSIPPI VALLEY CAMPAIGN
November 1861–July 1863

Union-held areas, June 1862
Feb. 6—Grant captures Fort Henry
Feb. 16—Grant captures Fort Donelson
April 25—Farragut captures New Orleans
June 6—Foote & Davis capture Memphis

INDIANA

ILLINOIS

KENTUCKY

Mississippi R.

Ohio R.

Cairo • Paducah
Columbus
Belmont
New Madrid
Island No. 10

Ft. Henry
Ft. Donelson

Cumberland R.

Nashville

TENNESSEE

Ft. Pillow

ARKANSAS

Jackson

Memphis La Grange Grand Junction *Shiloh*

Tennessee R.

MISSISSIPPI CENTRAL R.R.

Corinth
Holly Springs
Oxford

MEMPHIS & CHARLESTON R.R.

Decatur

Arkansas R.

Pontotoc • Tupelo

Coffeeville

MOBILE & OHIO R.R.

Arkansas Post

Granada

ALABAMA

Yazoo R.

Milliken's Bend

Chickasaw Bluffs

Monroe

SOUTHERN R.R.

Vicksburg

Jackson

MISSISSIPPI

Alabama R.

LOUISIANA

Grand Gulf
Port Gibson

Mississippi R.

Natchez

NEW ORLEANS & JACKSON R.R.

Red R.

Pearl R.

FLORIDA

Port Hudson

Baton Rouge

Mobile

New Orleans

Gulf of Mexico

N
W E
S

Ft. St. Philip
Ft. Jackson
Mouths of the Mississippi River

0   50   100 miles
0   50   100 kilometers

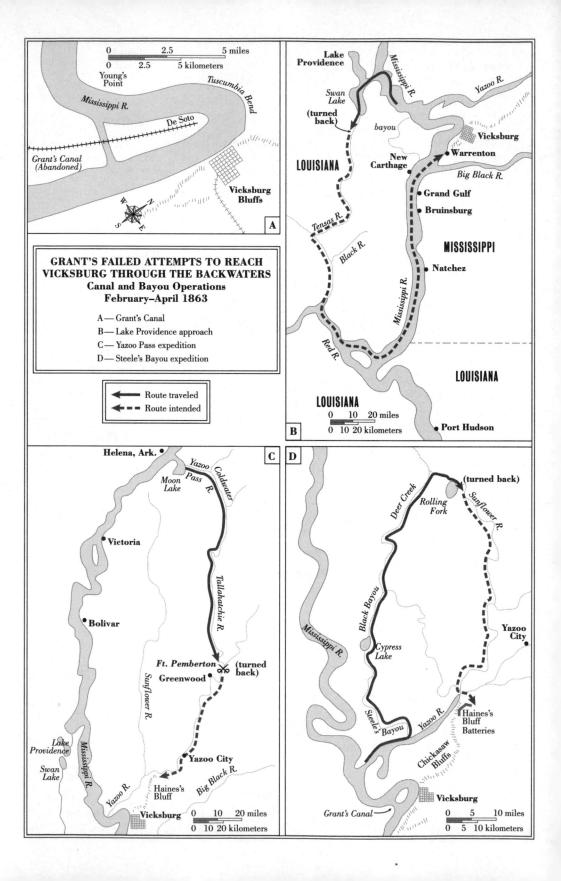

GRANT'S FAILED ATTEMPTS TO REACH
VICKSBURG THROUGH THE BACKWATERS
Canal and Bayou Operations
February–April 1863

A— Grant's Canal
B— Lake Providence approach
C— Yazoo Pass expedition
D— Steele's Bayou expedition

→ Route traveled
→ Route intended

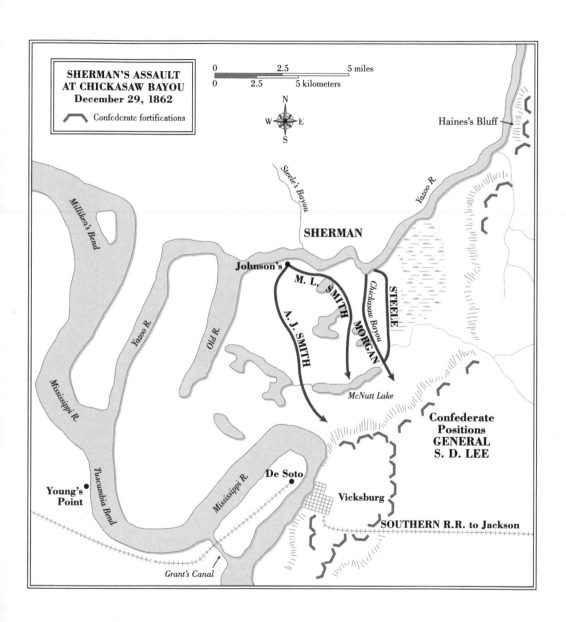

SHERMAN'S ASSAULT
AT CHICKASAW BAYOU
December 29, 1862

Confederate fortifications

0   2.5   5 miles
0   2.5   5 kilometers

N
W   E
S

Haines's Bluff

Steele's Bayou

Yazoo R.

SHERMAN

Johnson's

M. L. SMITH

A. J. SMITH

Chickasaw Bayou

STEELE

MORGAN

McNutt Lake

Milliken's Bend

Yazoo R.

Old R.

Mississippi R.

Confederate
Positions
GENERAL
S. D. LEE

Tuscumbia Bend

Mississippi R.

De Soto

Vicksburg

Young's
Point

SOUTHERN R.R. to Jackson

Grant's Canal

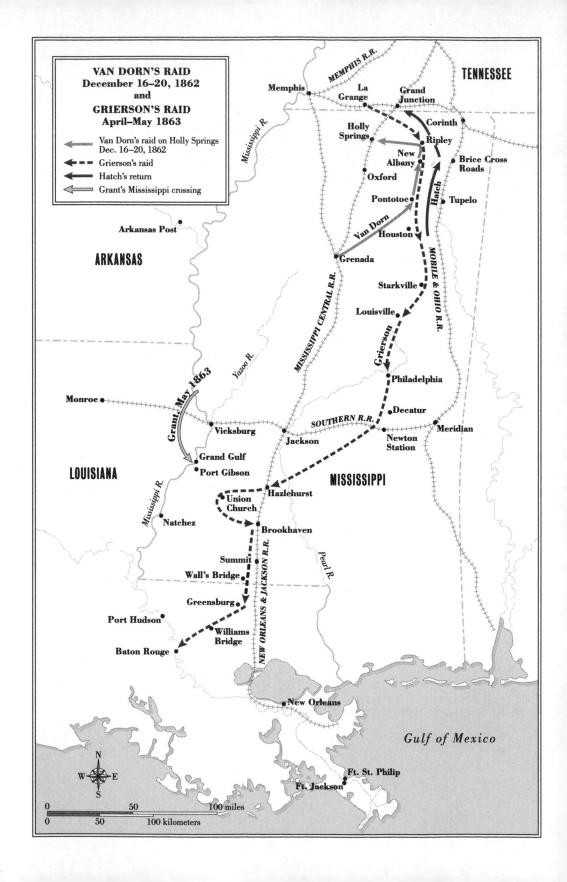

VAN DORN'S RAID
December 16–20, 1862
and
GRIERSON'S RAID
April–May 1863

→ Van Dorn's raid on Holly Springs
Dec. 16–20, 1862
▪▪▪ Grierson's raid
→ Hatch's return
→ Grant's Mississippi crossing

TENNESSEE

MEMPHIS R.R.

Memphis
La Grange
Grand Junction
Corinth
Holly Springs
Ripley
New Albany
Brice Cross Roads
Oxford
Pontotoc
Tupelo
Van Dorn
Houston
Hatch

Arkansas Post
ARKANSAS

Grenada
Starkville
Louisville

MISSISSIPPI CENTRAL R.R.

MOBILE & OHIO R.R.

Grierson

Philadelphia

Yazoo R.

Decatur

Monroe

Grant, May 1863

SOUTHERN R.R.
Vicksburg
Jackson
Newton Station
Meridian

Grand Gulf
Port Gibson

LOUISIANA

Union Church
Hazlehurst

MISSISSIPPI

Mississippi R.
Natchez

Brookhaven

Summit

Wall's Bridge

NEW ORLEANS & JACKSON R.R.

Pearl R.

Greensburg

Port Hudson
Williams Bridge

Baton Rouge

New Orleans

Gulf of Mexico

N
W   E
S

Ft. St. Philip

Ft. Jackson

0   50   100 miles
0   50   100 kilometers

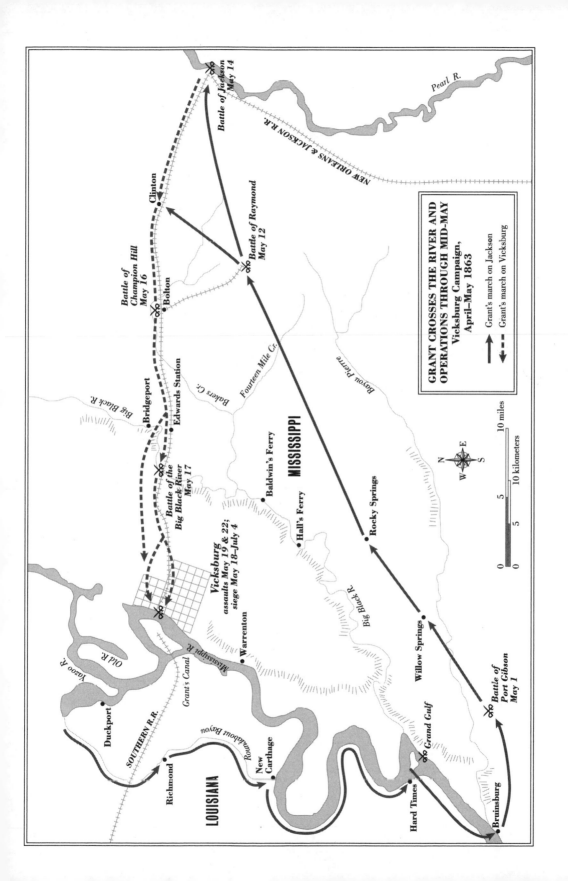

GRANT CROSSES THE RIVER AND
OPERATIONS THROUGH MID-MAY
Vicksburg Campaign,
April–May 1863

Grant's march on Jackson
Grant's march on Vicksburg

10 miles

0   5   10 kilometers
0   5

N
W   E
S

Pearl R.

Battle of Jackson
May 14

NEW ORLEANS & JACKSON R.R.

Clinton

Battle of Champion Hill
May 16

Bolton

Battle of Raymond
May 12

MISSISSIPPI

Bridgeport

Edwards Station

Bakers Cr.

Fourteen Mile Cr.

Bayou Pierre

Big Black R.

Battle of the
Big Black River
May 17

Baldwin's Ferry

Rocky Springs

Hall's Ferry

Big Black R.

Vicksburg
assaults May 19 & 22;
siege May 18–July 4

Warrenton

Willow Springs

Yazoo R.

Old R.

Grant's Canal

Mississippi R.

Duckport

SOUTHERN R.R.

Richmond

Roundabout Bayou

New
Carthage

LOUISIANA

Grand Gulf

Battle of
Port Gibson
May 1

Hard Times

Bruinsburg

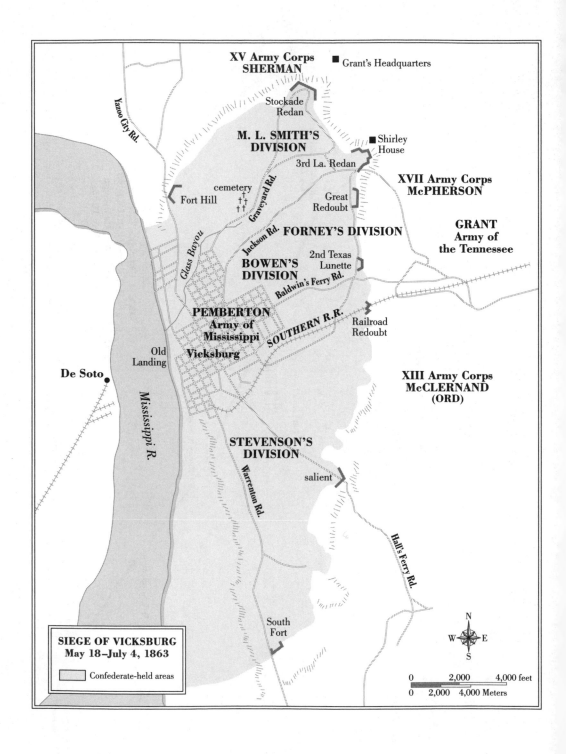

XV Army Corps
SHERMAN

■ Grant's Headquarters

Yazoo City Rd.

Stockade
Redan

M. L. SMITH'S
DIVISION

■ Shirley
House

3rd La. Redan

XVII Army Corps
McPHERSON

cemetery
Fort Hill   † †
              † †

Graveyard Rd.

Great
Redoubt

FORNEY'S DIVISION

GRANT
Army of
the Tennessee

Jackson Rd.

Glass Bayou

BOWEN'S
DIVISION

2nd Texas
Lunette

Baldwin's Ferry Rd.

PEMBERTON
Army of
Mississippi

SOUTHERN R.R.

Railroad
Redoubt

Old
Landing

Vicksburg

De Soto ●

Mississippi R.

XIII Army Corps
McCLERNAND
(ORD)

STEVENSON'S
DIVISION

salient

Warrenton Rd.

Hall's Ferry Rd.

South
Fort

N
W ✦ E
S

SIEGE OF VICKSBURG
May 18–July 4, 1863

Confederate-held areas

0   2,000   4,000 feet

0   2,000   4,000 Meters

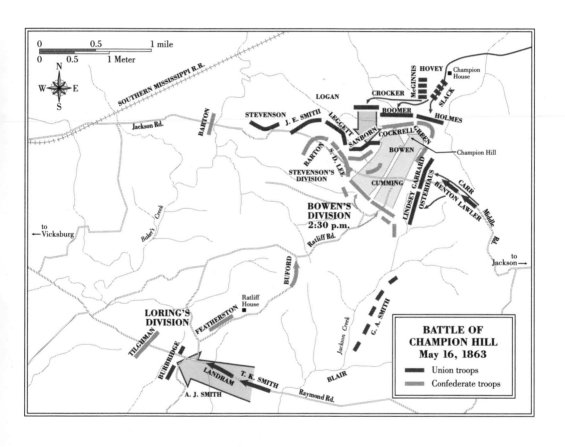

Scale:
0 — 0.5 — 1 mile
0 — 0.5 — 1 Meter

SOUTHERN MISSISSIPPI R.R.

HOVEY
McGINNIS
Champion House
CROCKER
SLACK
LOGAN
STEVENSON
J. E. SMITH
BOOMER
HOLMES
LEGGETT
SANBORN
COCKRELL GREEN
BOWEN
BARTON
Jackson Rd.
BARTON
S. D. LEE
STEVENSON'S DIVISION
Champion Hill
CUMMING
LINDSEY
GARRARD
OSTERHAUS
CARR
BENTON LAWLER
BOWEN'S DIVISION
2:30 p.m.
Middle Rd.
Baker's Creek
to Vicksburg →
to Jackson →
Ratliff Rd.
BUFORD
Jackson Creek
G. A. SMITH
Ratliff House
LORING'S DIVISION
FEATHERSTON
TILGHMAN
BURBRIDGE
LANDRAM
T. K. SMITH
BLAIR
A. J. SMITH
Raymond Rd.

BATTLE OF
CHAMPION HILL
May 16, 1863

Union troops
Confederate troops

PART I

THE WAR MOVES SOUTH

CHAPTER ONE

And So the Ball Was Opened

By mid-1863 a pall of despondency cloaked the Union. In the East, Robert E. Lee's Army of Northern Virginia had fought the Federal armies to a frazzle, with each defeat more stunning and depressing than the last, and after two and a half years of war the North was no closer to capturing the Confederate capital at Richmond than it was in the beginning.

In the western theater some progress had been made, notably by Major General Ulysses S. Grant, a recently promoted captain from the old army whose alleged drunkenness once had caused him to resign in semi-disgrace. Grant had pushed his forces from Illinois down into Missouri and Kentucky and parts of Tennessee, but the grand prize, Union control of the Mississippi River, which would have split the Confederacy in two, still seemed as elusive as a will-o'-the-wisp.

Over the months these glum developments had caused a gradual shift in Northern attitudes. Where once "On to Richmond!" was the rallying cry for enthusiastic Union patriots, now a growing number of these same people looked into a lowering future and were aghast at what they saw. The fighting had touched practically every home, many tragically, and, as the war exploded into proportions beyond anyone's wildest imagination, for some it seemed destined to go on into the eternal forever.

New Yorker George Templeton Strong, a Union observer, wrote in his celebrated diary, "Were the South only a little less furious, savage and spiteful, it could in three months . . . paralyze the nation [so as to] destroy all hope of ever restoring its territorial integrity."

In the South there might have been cause for jubilation over Northern travails, but this was not the case. Naturally, there was relief and celebration over Lee's dazzling victories at Fredericksburg and Chancellorsville, but only because he had saved Richmond from capture. The Confederacy was on the defensive and everyone from the lowest private to President Jefferson Davis understood it. The Union naval blockade of Southern ports along the Atlantic and Gulf coasts now seriously squeezed the South's desperate need for munitions, food, and clothing and anyone in the know realized that the Confederacy could not withstand a lengthy war.

Not by a long shot had the South given up hope, but it had become clear to the Confederate leadership by the bloody, frustrating summer of 1863 that something must be done to force the enemy's hand and bring him to the table with the right of secession, the perpetuation of slavery, or continuous war as bargaining chips.

Both sides read, or more often misread, the other's newspapers, which were notoriously hostile to their own governments, North and South alike, and whomever passed for military intelligence officers in those days frequently interpreted press attacks on Lincoln or Davis as being the sentiment of the whole people. In fact, Lincoln was more determined than ever to pursue the war to its final conclusion, which, by this point, included his Emancipation Proclamation, freeing by executive fiat all slaves in the rebelling states, an edict considered by southerners to be a final throwing down of the gauntlet.

Jefferson Davis also had his agenda, which was to make the Yankee armies pay so dearly in blood and treasure that it would cause a political upheaval come presidential election time in the North the following year that would lead to permanent separation. So for the authorities in Washington, while the eastern theater was becoming a war of attrition, in the West the issue boiled down, as it had from the beginning, to a strategy of controlling the Mississippi and cleaving the Confederacy in two.

What stood in the way was a daunting fortress on enormous bluffs at a critical bend of the river that had so far withstood all Union attempts to conquer it—Vicksburg, deemed by newspaper writers on both sides as the "Gibraltar of the West." Until its capture was accomplished, Northern commerce up and down the river was at a standstill, and the Confederacy remained free to transport infinite amounts of grain, livestock, men, and munitions from its bountiful regions across the Mississippi to provision its armies in Virginia, Tennessee, and elsewhere.

All this in due time, but first let us focus on how America had come to the dark and perilous state of affairs that threatened to shatter the first veritable democracy the world had ever known; of how national progress itself had intervened to create such a wretched schism between nominally peace-loving peoples; of how they lived and what they thought and how things broke apart.

Much had happened in the 250 years since the first colonists arrived on American shores. From rude log huts and stockades, great cities now blossomed along the Atlantic coast and far into the nation's heartland. Almost from its humble beginnings, in which men and women had made their own tools, furniture, and clothing, the country seemed to separate into two distinct patterns. New England and much of the North became a mecca for industry, commerce, manufacturing, and shipbuilding, while the southern regions remained almost exclusively agricultural.

By the time of the Revolution, the American population had reached two and a half million; three decades later, by the War of 1812, it had grown to some eight million, and just fifty years later, as the Civil War broke out, it had exploded to more than thirty million, including nearly four million slaves.

Although slavery had existed in all of the states during the eighteenth century and earlier, by the turn of the nineteenth century most slaves had been confined to the South, many of them cultivating tobacco—at that time, the big cash crop—particularly in Virginia, Kentucky, Maryland, Delaware, the Carolinas, and Georgia. Little cotton was grown in the early years, except along the Georgia seacoast where a unique strain known as long-staple thrived without need of the labor-intensive manual combing of seeds and detritus that were present in the upland short-staple cotton.

But year after year, as the tobacco crops wore out the soil in the Southern border states, fewer slaves were needed to farm the corn and grains that replaced it, and the "peculiar institution," as it had come to be known in the South, seemed doomed to eventual extinction.

Then as the nineteenth century approached, Eli Whitney patented his cotton gin, a device that could pick seeds out of short-staple cotton at a rate fifty times faster than hand labor. This made cotton, which could grow only in warm climates, a spectacularly attractive cash crop, and one for which slaves were ideal in its cultivation, and before long the bondsmen, and the cotton, began first a southward march and then westward into the territories of Alabama, Mississippi, and Tennessee; over time they jumped the Mississippi River into Louisiana, Arkansas, and Texas. Indians no longer posed much threat in these recently wild places because Andrew Jackson had banished many of them after the Creek War of 1813–14 and forced out the rest into what is now Oklahoma when he became president in 1829.

So on the cotton planters came, wearing out the land as they went, then moving on again because it was easier, cheaper, and faster to have slaves cut down virgin forests for plantation fields than it was to fertilize the soil or to rotate crops. Land was dirt cheap at twenty-five cents an acre or less, and within a year or two seas of white cotton bolls were waving under the torrid sun, stretching toward a western horizon filled with riches. Most of these planters came from Virginia, Georgia, and the Carolinas, bringing with them a dozen or more slaves, and as they prospered they bought more land and more slaves and soon set up ever-larger and more palatial plantation homes that replaced the utilitarian houses they had at first built. Behind them came men with one or two slaves, or none, who also hoped to cash in on the bonanza and then buy more slaves to expand their farms. From a total output of just a few thousand bales of cotton at the turn of the century, by the 1820s cotton had become the biggest agricultural crop in the nation and by the eve of the Civil War production had skyrocketed to four and a half million bales, representing two-thirds of all American exports.

At the same time, the South was becoming inextricably bound to Northern industrialists who had begun building textile mills on the New England rivers for finishing the cotton. Northern banking interests financed much of the planters' overhead by taking mortgages on their crops, land, and slaves while New England shipping merchants hauled the bales of cotton to mills in the North and to similar looms in England and France, which distributed the finished clothing to their far-flung empires.

By this time a well-established planter aristocracy had emerged in the South with a few plantations employing thousands of slaves. Most shipped their cotton and other produce down interior rivers to ports along the Gulf and Atlantic coasts such as New Orleans, Mobile, Savannah, Charleston, and Wilmington, and these cities too became wealthy on the cotton trade, shipping back upriver food, implements, and European imports, including fancy carriages, expensive furniture, silver, china and crystal, Oriental carpets, and fine clothing. Principal among these rivers was the Mississippi, but practically the entire

South was tied together economically in the cotton trade: planters, merchants, and the multitudes that worked for them, as well as the slaves themselves. So many were needed: surveyors, lawyers, doctors, preachers, mechanics, cotton gin owners, factors, overseers, editors and printers, druggists, distillers, bar pilots, wagon haulers and boatmen to haul the cotton down and the fine goods up, and later the railroad builders and operators, photographers, and architects for the fine plantations—all of them linked in one way or another to what had become known as King Cotton.

Huge leaps in technology were made in the first half of the century and the North, too, was prospering as both an industrial and an agricultural society. This was the cusp of the so-called second industrial revolution, which Winston Churchill later described thusly: "Every morning when the world woke up, some new machinery had started running. Every night while the world had supper, it was running still. It ran on while all men slept."

The invention of the steam engine gave rise to the steamboats that soon advanced from rudimentary vessels to floating palaces, especially on the Mississippi and its tributaries. Invention of the telegraph made communications almost instantaneous. In New England, armaments factories had evolved into vast enterprises while its shipbuilding industry continued to flourish and its textile mills could now turn out ready-made clothing. As steam railroads began to span the nation, iron-manufacturing foundries arose along the Great Lakes shores and in Pennsylvania, mainly around Pittsburgh. In tiny Delaware, the Du Ponts had long established one of the world's largest munitions factories. In addition, the North abounded with leather-making concerns turning out boots, shoes, saddles, and harnesses, as well as canneries, wagon works, manufacturers of vulcanized rubber, marine yards for constructing warships, and factories capable of producing everything from brass tacks and tools to railroad ties, cars, and engines.

The South had practically none of these but instead purchased what it needed from above the Mason-Dixon Line or from abroad. As a harbinger of things to come, when the nation neared war the South had but a single foundry capable of making cannon.

A few far-seeing and influential southerners realized the implications of this lack and tried to rectify it. They pointed out at meeting halls around the region that it was not only uneconomical but downright foolhardy for southerners to ship their own raw cotton to New England to be finished into clothes, which they were then obliged to buy at Northern prices—and that the same was true with other Yankee manufactured goods. But these men's vision of a diversified Southern economy with its own textile mills and manufacturing industry fell on deaf ears. A visitor to the American South in the 1830s described the relentless cycle of the typical planter's underutilization of his spare capital: "To sell cotton to buy negroes—to make more cotton to buy more negroes, 'ad infinitum.' " What he was describing was the whole of the Southern mind-set.

At the same time in the North, the expansive grain fields of Pennsylvania, Ohio, Indiana, Illinois, and Minnesota became known as the "wheat belt" and the "nation's breadbasket," brought to rich profusion by inventions such as John Deere's steel plow and McCormick's reapers, grain threshers, hay mowers, and binders. Unlike cotton, which was labor intensive because of its long growing season and the concomitant proliferation of weeds and the necessity of hand harvesting, these great mechanical combines often needed twenty mules to pull them, but they could do the work of many scores of slaves. Iowa was famous for its hogs while Wisconsin and Michigan raised dairy cattle and their by-products milk, butter, and cheese, plus vegetable produce crops. Cotton may have been "king" in the Deep South, just as tobacco was in Virginia and Kentucky, but you couldn't eat it, a fact that would eventually be impressed on the southerners to their profound discomfort.

One area in which science had not made appreciable inroads was medicine, which had not progressed much since the turn of the eighteenth century. By the 1850s ether and chloroform had been discovered as general anesthetics, useful in childbirth, during surgery, and, potentially, on the battlefield. However, the accepted treatment for bones shattered by bullets or shrapnel was still amputation to avoid the onset of gangrene, which was almost always fatal. "Bleeding" patients to cure disease was still practiced but falling into disrepute. The various killer fevers—typhoid, scarlet, and yellow—still had no known cause or cure. Potentially deadly smallpox had been treated with a primitive vaccination since the late 1700s but the remedy sometimes killed the patient.

Terrifying diseases that have since been conquered or dramatically reduced, such as typhus, cholera, tuberculosis, diphtheria, dysentery, pneumonia, and tetanus, sent large numbers of men, women, and children to their graves. Even simple infections and ailments such as an abscessed tooth, ptomaine (food) poisoning, mumps, measles, and

chicken pox often had fatal consequences. Few families had not experienced the death of a child, father, or mother at an early age and the
average lifespan, which was about forty years, had not changed much
since the turn of the century. Complications from pregnancy and
childbirth remained the leading cause of death for women of childbearing age.

Despite their links in trade and common nationality, by the mid-1800s
relations had deteriorated steadily between the two sections of the
nation. Slavery, with all of its political and moral ramifications, was
paramount on the list of contentions, but it was intertwined with cul-
tural and hard economic issues that in the 1830s caused a fateful rift
during which the notion of secession first reared its head in the South.
The first of these was the Tariff Act of 1828, which to southerners
soon came to be known as the "tariff of abominations."

In order to finance internal improvements—the building of canals
and roads, the clearing of rivers, and so on, mostly in the North—as
well as to protect Northern and midwestern industrial interests, Congress, during the presidency of John Quincy Adams, a New Englander,
enacted an import tax on European-made goods—more than 50 percent of their value. The enraged southerners—outnumbered by northerners two to one in the House of Representatives and 28 to 20 in the
Senate—saw it as a Northern conspiracy since they had been able to
buy the same type goods from abroad more cheaply than those made
in the North but, under the tariff, they were suddenly obliged to pay
nearly half again more for them. Not only that but, as they predicted,
England and France retaliated by reducing the amount of cotton they
were importing from the South and southerners feared this would
bankrupt their economy. This did not happen, but clearly the tariff
was grossly unfair to the South. Historian Robert Remini, biographer
of both Quincy Adams and Andrew Jackson, characterized it as
"ghastly [and] lopsided." John C. Calhoun of South Carolina, then
vice president of the United States, haughtily announced that his constituents would nullify, or not obey, any law of the federal government
that was not in his state's interests, thus precipitating a crisis solved
only when President Jackson sent warships to Charleston Harbor to
enforce the tariff.

More ominously Calhoun, who was one of the most highly
regarded—though not necessarily beloved—politicians of his time,
asserted in his argument that it was the right of any state that had orig-

inally agreed to become a part of the United States to secede from it if it wished. Some Southern historians have argued that this was the root cause of the Civil War. It wasn't, but it was the beginning of the division between the two sections of the country, and thus the cat, or at least the cat's paw, was out of the bag.*

The controversy left a bitter taste in the mouths of most southerners and the ill will remained over what was perceived in the South as an anti-Southern bias from both Northern members of Congress and northeners in general. Many modern historians have dismissed the impact that the tariff had on the growing schism between North and South, but any careful reading of newspapers and correspondence of those days indicates plainly that here is where the feud began to fester over the years into hatred.

It was further inflamed by the rapid rise of abolitionist groups— originally organized in New England and spreading outward from there—who condemned slavery as immoral and demanded freedom for all American slaves, with the proviso that they be returned to Africa. The abolition movement had begun with only a handful of adherents prior to the American Revolution but expanded in both numbers and power over the years so that by the 1820s all Northern states had abolished slavery for both moral and economic reasons. By then, though, slaves had become a mainstay of the Southern economy.

During the years leading to the Civil War the abolitionists became increasingly militant, establishing the Underground Railroad to spirit slaves northward in contravention of the Fugitive Slave Act, while the authorities in Washington seemed to look the other way. Southerners, for their part, were made ever more anxious by the belligerent tone of abolitionist agitation in light of the depredations against whites during slave rebellions in Haiti and Jamaica and the killing of nearly sixty whites during the Nat Turner slave uprising in Virginia in 1831. The novel *Uncle Tom's Cabin* (1852) by Harriet Beecher Stowe incited Northern passions by depicting the Southern slave's life as a relentless nightmare of sorrow and cruelty, prompting angry southerners to dismiss it practically en masse as an outrageously unfair portrayal.

Then came the John Brown raid, in which the aging and unbalanced white abolitionist tried to organize a slave rebellion in the South

---

* This was not, however, the first attempt made by a state, or states, to secede from the Union. During the War of 1812 the New England states had called a convention to approve an ordinance of secession after their shipping and fishing industries were brought to near ruin by the British blockade of their ports. The convention was in the process of meeting at Hartford when the war ended and so did the crisis.

by seizing the federal arsenal at Harpers Ferry, Virginia. The United States government tried Brown for treason in 1859 and hanged him, but the ever-growing antislavery forces were quick to elevate Brown's stature to martyrdom, infuriating people below the Mason-Dixon Line, slaveholders and non-slaveholders alike. Likewise, abolitionists became enraged and southerners elated at a decision in 1857 by the U.S. Supreme Court in the infamous *Dred Scott* case, in which the Court ruled that a slave was actually not a "citizen," or even a "person," and "so far inferior that they [have] no rights which the white man [is] bound to respect."

By then every decent-sized city North and South had half a dozen or more newspapers, and there were literally thousands of others in smaller towns, most of them vehemently political.* Passions were further exacerbated by the recent invention of the telegraph, which permitted news—say, a speech made in Congress—to be transmitted almost instantaneously to every newspaper in the country, where before it had taken weeks, if not months, for the word to come by regular postal mail. Charges were hurled back and forth between Democratic, Whig, and, later, Republican papers that over the years had become so incendiary that there was precious little middle ground. In the South there arose rabid talk of secession by a group of "fire-eaters," influential orators who insisted that Northern "fanatics" intended to free the slaves "by law if possible, by force if necessary." Hectoring abolitionist newspapers and Northern orators (known as Black, or Radical, Republicans) provided ample fodder for that conclusion.

As all of this spilled into the political mix, America was becoming a magnet for immigration, and by the 1840s the nation was nearly swamped by a deluge of impoverished Irish fleeing the potato famines and Germans fleeing European wars. Many of the Germans moved to the Midwest to set up farms or breweries, but the Irish tended to remain in Northern cities such as Boston, New York, and Philadelphia, where they became ideal candidates for cheap labor in the mills and factories that, for them, were little more than sweatshops. Living in hideous slums, they were derided by southerners as "Northern wage slaves" whose lives were no better, and probably worse, than the average slave on a Southern plantation, or so it was claimed.

However, these immigrants were quickly organized by powerful city

---

* During the Civil War, for instance, the editor of the *New York Times* was also the chairman of the National Republican Committee.

political machines, as well as by the Catholic Church, so that the House of Representatives ultimately became controlled by Northern interests. At the time of the presidential election in 1860 the population of the North stood at more than sixteen million versus approximately nine million southerners, plus their four million slaves—heavy odds in case a war broke out.

The U.S. Senate, however, was different from the House, for in that critical body two members were reserved for each state, and a delicate balance between North and South was retained and at least tacitly observed—that is, until 1820, when the territory of Missouri applied for statehood. Antislavery forces in the North insisted that Missouri be a free state, while Southern legislators demanded that it be slave, owing to the large number of southerners who had settled there with their charges. A compromise was ultimately worked out admitting Missouri as a slave state while prohibiting it in other western territories, and there the issue rested for three decades before another crisis ensued when California asked to be admitted to the Union as free soil.

In the years that followed, crisis seemed to pile upon crisis respecting the vast U.S. territories (especially those acquired after the Mexican War of 1846–48) that were becoming ever more settled. Southerners feared losing their delicate balance in the Senate, while abolitionists envisioned, to their horror, a continuing spread of slavery. In Kansas, heated arguments turned to bloody massacres, filling newspaper headlines for months and arousing furies beyond anything that had gone before. In the halls of Congress debate reached the point where it was barely civilized, if that, sometimes prompting duels and challenges to duels and, in a case that shocked Northern sensibilities, the brutal caning in the Capitol chamber of an abolitionist senator by a Southern congressman.

The 1850s drew to a close in near social convulsion and established political parties began to break apart while new ones appeared in their wake, most notably the Republican Party, which had emerged from a split between the old Whigs (moderates) and the abolitionists. A rupture over the specter of disunion in the Democratic Party created the Northern and Southern Democrats, with each nominating their own slate, virtually ensuring a victory for the Republicans, whose candidate for president was a small-town lawyer from Illinois named Abraham Lincoln.

Led by pugnacious South Carolina, a sentiment emerged in many parts of the South that Lincoln was a die-hard abolitionist and that if he was elected the Southern states should secede. This prompted one Southern woman to lament at the time, "Because of incompatibility of temper . . . we have hated each other so. If we could only separate, a 'separation a l'agreable,' as the French say it, and not have a horrid fight for divorce."

True to its word, when news of Lincoln's election arrived in November 1860, South Carolina promptly voted to secede, followed by eight other Deep South states that were invested heavily in cotton. The Lincoln administration was able to quell secession movements in several border states—Maryland, Kentucky, Missouri, and what is now West Virginia—by a combination of politics and force, including suspension of the Bill of Rights. Many in the North were distressed at the turn of events, especially where there were strong financial ties with the South. New York City, for instance, which had once been the slave capital of the world, had in essence become an enormous bank for the cotton industry, and its lawmakers promptly passed a resolution drawn up by the mayor and approved by the city council to "make common cause with the South," to bar passage of federal government troops through the city, and, in effect, to secede from the Union. Upon the Confederate attack on Fort Sumter in April 1861, the resolution was rescinded.

Even as things began to break apart, most of America remained a land of plenty. Culturally, the nation had blossomed since the turn of the century. In the North, Boston, New York, and Philadelphia remained centers of fashion and social life on the East Coast but cities had also sprung up in what was then known as the "Northwest," where Cincinnati, Chicago, and St. Louis were also becoming places of wealth and society. In the South the old coastal cities of New Orleans, Mobile, Savannah, Charleston, and Richmond now had to share their prominence with towns such as Memphis, Nashville, Natchez, and Vicksburg, barely trading posts a few decades past and now come into their own with the interlacing of all-weather roads, the steamboat, the railroad, and the telegraph.

Americans, who until recently had had no established literature of their own, could now read an abundance of influential books by their fellow countrymen: James Fenimore Cooper and Washington Irving, Hawthorne and Longfellow and Poe, Ralph Waldo Emerson and Walt Whitman. Likewise, in the world of art, Americans could now be proud of having more to offer than their justly famous portrait painters. The Hudson River School, typified by Thomas Cole, produced breathtaking romantic landscape vistas, while realists such as George Caleb Bingham and George Catlin specialized in graceful depictions of Native Americans and other scenes of the American West.

Americans were also, by and large, a deeply God-fearing and religious people but, as the national rift over slavery deepened, organized denominations such as the Baptists and Methodists split into Northern and Southern churches. The Presbyterians managed to keep together, but it was a strain, while the Episcopal church remained a Southern stronghold among the wealthy and planter classes and became a fountainhead of fire-breathing hatred of Yankeeism.* Catholics also maintained their identity, prompting cynics to suggest that it was only because they owed their allegiance to the pope of Rome rather than to any state or country.

In the North a new game called baseball was all the rage while in the South horseracing remained the favorite sport, and those Southern youngbloods able to enjoy a life of leisure often indulged in such pursuits as foxhunting, gambling, drinking, trips abroad, or attending colleges in the North. When, more than two years into the war, the Union general William Tecumseh Sherman was asked by his superior for a confidential assessment of the sorts and classes of men his army was facing in the Deep South, he gave a remarkable evaluation respecting "the sons of planters, lawyers and men about town."

They are, Sherman groused, "good billiard players and sportsmen, men who never did work and never will. War suits them, and the rascals are brave, fine riders, bold to rashness, and dangerous subjects in every case. They care not a *sou* for niggers, land, or any thing. They hate Yankees *per se* and don't bother their brains about the past, present or future. As long as they have good horses, plenty of forage and open country, they are happy. This is a larger class than most men suppose and they are the most dangerous set of men that this war has turned loose upon the world. They are splendid riders, first-rate shots, and utterly reckless. These men," Sherman added darkly, "must all be killed or [imprisoned] by us before we can hope for peace."

---

* As the war drew on it became a practice of some Federal commanders upon occupying a Southern city to arrest Episcopal priests as a matter of course. One of these, Bishop Leonidas Polk, became a major general commanding a Confederate corps until a cannonball disemboweled him at the Battle of Atlanta.

That was all in the future and Sherman's words were not yet ringing in the ears of these young cavaliers (nor their shots in his); for the time being, they were more or less content to defy and threaten the newly elected Lincoln government in Washington.

Young women of the privileged classes were sent to boarding schools or had private tutors to prepare them for careers as educated and well-rounded wives and mothers, and many were treated to the grand tour as a matter of course. Life on a plantation was in many ways like that in a self-contained village or town: there were blacksmiths and carpenters, horse handlers, tool grinders, farriers, canners for preserving vegetables, smokehouses for meat, seamstresses, mule drivers, and of course the field hands—all revolving around the Big House, with its staff of uniformed cooks and servants. It wasn't all moonlight and magnolias in the South but there was plenty enough of that—especially for the slaves, since it was all they had.

The fuse had been lit during the long years before the ascendancy of Lincoln and the Republicans, but now the bomb was about to explode. Typical of the type of Southern youngbloods that General Sherman had alluded to was Charles Colcock Jones, a thirty-year-old Georgian who had graduated from Princeton and held a Harvard law degree and thus had had ample opportunity to observe the Northern abolitionist movement firsthand. He wrote his father, a clergyman: "The Black Republicans may rave among the cold hills of their native states, and grow mad with entertainment of infidelity, heresies, and false conceptions of a 'higher law'; but Heaven forbid that they ever attempt to set foot on this land of sunshine, of high-souled honor, and of liberty. A freeman's heart can beat in no nobler behalf, and no more sacred obligation can rest upon a people than those now devolved upon us to protect our homes, our loves, our lives, our property, our religion, and our liberties, from the inhuman infidel hordes who threaten us with invasion, dishonor, and subjugation."

Returning the compliment, northerners such as the influential abolitionist William Lloyd Garrison had begun branding the South as "the Empire of Satan" while others, including future members of Lincoln's own cabinet, had indulged in such scathing public denunciations of southerners and their way of life as "blood sucking," "studied cruelty," and "wicked and depraved."

Underlying the obvious and real moral and economic questions was a social issue that few, North or South, seemed prepared to grapple with—that of exactly what to do with the slaves if and when

they were freed. Lincoln and a number of Republican middle-of-
the-roaders believed, and so stated, that the Southern slaveholders
should be compensated by the federal government for their monetary
losses, which, in some cases, would be huge. They also called for, as
had many of the early abolitionist societies, the newly freed blacks to
be deported, either back to Africa or to somewhere in Central America. With the exception of higher-minded abolitionists, many influential northerners believed that emancipation would bring on an
unwieldy migration of millions of freedmen across the Mason-Dixon
Line. Northern factory workers likewise felt threatened that such a
diaspora would throw them out of work in favor of former slaves who
would undercut their wages. In the midst of this debate an influential
third political party in the North called the Free-Soilers espoused
their opposition to allowing slavery in the new territories, but their
platform also contained a plank that would forbid blacks to settle
there as well.

In the South, the problem was more acute, especially in those sections where slaves actually outnumbered whites. Conscientious slave
owners truly worried that without the structure of plantation life the
slaves would simply begin dying off, and miserably at that: where
would they go, where would they live, who would nurse them when illness struck, who was to feed and cloth them in lean times; could they
learn to work on their own or would these wretched millions simply
take to the roads, stealing and begging and posing an eternal problem
for generations to come? Other slave owners, less upright and far-
sighted, fretted over who would cook for them and clean their houses
and stables and work their fields and declared that even federal compensation for their initial investment in slaves would not be enough to
compensate for the loss of their lifelong bondsmen.

Deep down, emancipation had become not just a matter of morality
versus economics but one of race, and of the concomitant equality
implied in it. If the black man was no longer a slave, then the dark
implications of the Supreme Court's *Dred Scott* ruling would be rendered moot, and former slaves would be entitled to all the rights of
citizenship—a notion with unsettling overtones that even many northerners were likely to admit. Would they be free to intermarry? To use
the same public accommodations? To sue whites in the courts? To
own firearms? And hovering above all these there remained the old
specter of uprising, of massacre—of slave revenge.

·   ·   ·

In fact, the South had misread Lincoln, at least in the beginning. By tarring all Republicans with the same abolitionist brush, southerners had leaped to the conclusion that Lincoln was hell-bent on abolishing slavery at the earliest opportunity. In fact, the president's attitude fell far short of that, despite his having chosen mostly abolitionists for his cabinet. Instead, he emphasized that his chief concerns were the preservation of the Union and the nonexpansion of slavery into new territories. Right up until the last, including his 1861 inaugural address, Lincoln's public statements emphasized that it was not his intention to interfere with slavery in the states where it already existed, but to let it simply wither on the vine. The southerners either could not or would not believe this.

Nor did they trust a last-ditch effort by Congress to save the Union. On March 2, 1861, two days before Lincoln's inauguration, both houses of Congress passed what, ironically, would have become the Thirteenth Amendment to the Constitution, guaranteeing that no Congress, then or in the future, could pass legislation to disturb slavery in those states where it already existed. Even this did not mollify southerners, either because they recognized that since such an amendment would have to be ratified by three-quarters of the states there were enough Northern states to prevent its passage or simply because, after all the vitriolic rhetoric of the past two decades, they were ready to leave the Union anyway.*

A common Southern mantra was that the North would never fight, and that if they did they would be licked in short order. However, neither the Southern people nor their leaders wanted war; they would have been delighted to be let go in peace. Accordingly, a delegation of commissioners was sent to Washington to see if something could be worked out for a peaceful separation. Lincoln, however, refused to see them and so, as a saying of the day went, "the ball was opened."

Following the Union surrender of Fort Sumter in Charleston Harbor, Lincoln called for volunteers from each state—the South included—to quell the rebellion. At this, North Carolina, Tennessee, Arkansas, and Virginia promptly joined the Confederacy, wanting no part of fighting against their fellow southerners.

---

* Two states, Ohio and Maryland, did in fact ratify this proposed amendment, but after the war began it simply got lost in the shuffle. Ironically, the Thirteenth Amendment in its present form was passed by Congress in 1865, and prohibited slavery in all the states.

While northerners commonly referred to Confederates as "Rebels," the Confederate army did not reflect contemporary images of bomb-throwing anarchists or a rabble of wild-looking malcontents. It was a highly disciplined, proper army in every sense of the term, with skilled military engineers and artillerymen, and counted among its officers more than three hundred West Point graduates, of whom 146 became generals.

The first large battle erupted at Bull Run just a few dozen miles from Washington, where Federal forces suffered a dramatic defeat. Next a powerful Union army under George McClellan tried to get at the Confederate capital of Richmond by coming at it from the sea and moving east, but the Rebels also sent them packing, though with heavy losses on both sides.

In the huge military theater west of the Allegheny Mountains matters were just as unsettled as they were back east, until the Union commanding general, Henry Halleck, determined that the Confederates needed to be driven out of the fortifications that they had been rapidly constructing along the Mississippi River and its tributaries in the upper South. To help accomplish this, Halleck made the unlikely selection of a brand-new brigadier, Ulysses S. Grant, whose casual approach to military discipline and reputation for heavy drinking had preceded him.

Moving his army down the Mississippi from Cairo, Illinois, in November 1861, Grant fought his first battle at Belmont, Missouri, and relentlessly pushed southward in close cooperation with the U.S. Navy, which had assembled a fleet of innovative ironclad warships the likes of which the world had never seen. It took a full year, and five hundred blood-drenched miles marked by savage battles and disheartening setbacks, until at last Grant's Federal army converged on the Confederate stronghold of Vicksburg, Mississippi.

When at last the campaign was over some two years later, the Mississippi River was again open to Northern commerce and the entire western Confederacy had been amputated from the rest. Whatever compelled the South to keep fighting after that point, common sense was not a part of it, for the loss of the river and the West was irredeemable.

The fall of Vicksburg in mid-1863 would have been an excellent time for Jefferson Davis and the Southern leaders to have ended the war. Had they done so, the death and destruction that was prolonged until April 1865 would have been forestalled. Such a concession also would have mitigated the depression and wretched poverty visited on the South after the war, which set the region back nearly a hundred years. Mississippi, for example, in 1860 ranked near the top for per capita income of any state in the Union; by 1865, and ever since, it has ranked the lowest.

CHAPTER TWO

It Was There That War Found Him

As a Civil War general, Ulysses Simpson Grant is a remarkable study. First, he was a most unmilitary-looking officer, often dressing in a plain blue suit and a felt hat and when he wore a uniform it also was plain and unadorned except for his insignia of rank. He left the gold braid and epaulettes to others. His manner was unpretentious and taciturn and, at age thirty-nine, of medium height and slender build, there was little in his bearing or history that suggested he might be destined for greatness, except perhaps for the steady gaze of his piercing blue eyes, which was later interpreted as a determination to succeed. In fact, he projected almost none of the possibilities that mirrored the dynamic young nation into which he was born. That he did not succeed in his early life remained a puzzle to those who knew him, considering that within the span of a decade he rose from failed soldier, hardscrabble wood peddler, lackluster store clerk, and notorious drunkard to the most renowned military hero of the age and president of the United States. In fact, the remarkable thing about Grant was that, by all accounts, he was so *unremarkable*.

Grant was born on April 27, 1822, in the river town of Point Pleasant, Ohio, son of a tanner named Jesse Grant and his new wife, Hannah. The family got by on the father's earnings from working in nearby tanneries and were far from being considered local gentry. It took a month to get the baby named and even then it was by drawing choices out of a hat. As a middle name, Ulysses came out on top, and thus the redheaded, blue-eyed boy became the middle-namesake of the fabu-

lous Greek hero who hid his soldiers inside the giant wooden horse
and conquered the city of Troy. As an homage to Hannah's family,
Grant was given the first name Hiram, after the biblical king who built
the temple of Solomon, thus making his initials H.U.G., apt enough
for a boy but not entirely appropriate as he grew old enough to endure
the barbs of youthful jest.

About the only thing Grant seemed interested in during the lazy and
uneventful 1830s was horses, with which he had reached some kind of
subliminal understanding. By the age of six he was using them to haul
brush for his neighbors and soon was breaking and training them for a
fee, and a few years later he set up his own carriage teams to carry passengers to nearby towns. His equestrianship was such that people
remarked he was "born to the saddle." At the same time, Grant was
known as being shy, indifferent to school, and so absolutely revolted
by the sight of blood that he was unable to stomach even a rare-cooked
piece of meat, a consequence of frequent exposure to his father's tan-
ning operations.

Grant's father was an anomaly for a bootstrap frontiersman and tan-
nery operator; he was a voracious reader of everything from the clas-
sics to contemporary political tomes, and as the 1830s drew to a close
he had taken to writing editorial letters to local newspapers, many
espousing a hatred of slavery that reflected the growing national division over that volatile issue.

As Ulysses grew into his teens his father concluded that an appointment to the United States Military Academy at West Point was the best
chance for his education, first because it was free and second, aside
from Grant's continued fascination with horses, because he was beginning to show some aptitude for mathematics. In due time the appointment was offered and accepted, prompting one of the townsfolk to
profess astonishment that the politician who nominated him "did not
appoint someone with intellect enough to do credit to the district."

Grant's arrival at West Point was inauspicious at best, beginning
with a controversy over his name.

Before he left home, Grant's cousins had engraved his initials,
H.U.G., into his trunk, but having already endured hazing from his
classmates Grant decided to change his name, reversing the middle
with the first, to Ulysses Hiram Grant. However, no sooner had he
arrived at "the gray castle" above the Hudson River than an adjutant
informed him that the only papers he had were filled out for a Ulysses
Simpson Grant. Apparently it was an error made by the appointing

congressman's office (Simpson being his mother's maiden name) but, the army being the army, Grant's explanations were in vain and his choices boiled down to either accepting entry as indicated on the admissions form or clearing out. Thus the legend of U. S. Grant was born, but his fellow cadets did not yet realize this and for some reason they took to calling him "Sam."

Grant was mediocre as a student but became friends with a fellow plebe, Fred Dent of Missouri, a relationship that would have an important impact on his life. He was quite taken with the beauty of West Point, with its statuary and monuments to famous Americans and its fabulous views high above the Hudson. Once he wrote home wistfully, as a seventeen-year-old boy might, "I do love the place, it seems as though I could live here forever if my friends would only come too."

He was mostly lackadaisical in his lessons, nearly flunking French and preferring to sit in the library reading romantic fiction rather than buckle down to hard studies. Only in math and drawing did he excel, and those apparently came naturally to him. Little did he know that the friendships and acquaintances of his West Point days would furnish many, if not most, of the famous officers of the Civil War, including Union generals George B. McClellan, William T. Sherman, and William Rosecrans, as well as Confederate generals Thomas ("Stonewall") Jackson, James Longstreet, and George Pickett.

Despite his academic malaise, Grant was popular with his classmates and was often asked to settle arguments. He was antislavery but believed in gradual emancipation and had little tolerance for radical abolitionists. In most everything, he seemed like just another average cadet, except for his skills at riding, and there he had no peers at West Point. One contemporary recalled that "it was like a circus" to see him ride. Everyone liked to tell the story of Grant's final exercise in the academy riding hall when he rode the giant sorrel York in a jumping contest. It was visitors' day and the stands were packed with parents, of those graduating and those entering the school, as well as most of the Cadet Corps, and York, before Grant got hold of him, was known in equestrian circles as a "killer horse." After various parades and exhibitions the horsemen and their mounts were drawn up into a long line in the center of the horse ring when the riding master moved the bar "higher than a man's head," and announced: "Cadet Grant."

Grant bolted out of line and galloped the length of the hall in front of everyone before wheeling to face the jump and spurring York into a measured dash down the stretch. As he neared the bar, both horse and rider sailed into the air, clearing the obstacle "as if man and beast had been welded together." "The spectators were breathless," according to an observer, and Grant's record in the equestrian high jump stood at the academy for a quarter of a century.

Since Grant had graduated at the middle of his class of 1843 he was denied eligibility for the elite Corps of Engineers and had to settle for the cavalry, artillery, or the infantry. The cavalry would not have him either, owing to no vacancy, so the young second lieutenant was stuck with the infantry, bottom of the heap so far as the army was concerned. Wearing his new dress uniform, Grant went home to Ohio on leave before reporting to his first post, only to discover that people were making fun of him because of his clothes. "From that day forward," Grant biographer Brooks D. Simpson reckoned, "the new brevet second lieutenant never liked wearing a full-dress uniform. The memory of being laughed at . . . never quite faded away."

Grant's first assignment was with the Fourth Infantry Regiment at Jefferson Barracks, near St. Louis, Missouri. In one way this was especially fortuitous because the family of Grant's old pal and roommate from West Point Fred Dent lived there. The Dents were wealthy slave owners who, in addition to their home in St. Louis proper, kept a large plantation outside of town and Dent had urged Grant to pay them a call, which he did. The young lieutenant got along well with his classmate's family, including their four sons and three daughters, the eldest of whom was Julia, who immediately held a fascination for Grant. At nineteen she was not a natural beauty but "was possessed of a lively and pleasing countenance," according to one observer, and had just returned from boarding school and an out-of-town stay with friends when Grant began paying his calls to her family.

It wasn't long before the two of them hit it off, taking to long rides over the twelve hundred acres of White Haven, the name the old "Colonel," Fred Dent, Julia's father, had given the place. Grant must have been impressed by the pleasant countryside of grassy meadows "knee deep in blue grass and clover," where cows grazed and handsome groves of trees graced the tops of hills surrounding the valley through which the sparkling, pebbly Gravois Creek wound its way. Later, Grant and old Colonel Dent would often have intense though good-natured after-dinner discussions, usually about slavery. Both of Julia's parents were impressed with Grant's poised, calm, and logical approach to what was becoming the overarching issue of the day.

These were enchanting times for the handsome lieutenant as

autumn faded into winter and then spring arrived, warm and verdant and, with it, his fancy had turned to love. Then the unexpected happened, which certainly should not have been unexpected by any officer in Uncle Sam's army: Grant and the entire regiment received orders to move their headquarters down to western Louisiana, where they would constitute part of the U.S. Army of Observation. There, on the Texas border, they were to remain as a deterrent force in the ongoing disputes between Texas—which had by then gained its independence from Mexico—and Mexico, which still would not admit it.

Grant was on leave with his family when this sobering news reached him, and he hurried back to see Julia before the regiment pulled out. When he arrived at Jefferson Barracks, however, they had already gone, but he received a few days' extra leave to tidy up personal affairs, which, by then, included asking Julia to marry him. He did this in a sort of offhand (Julia characterized it as "awkward") way: he asked her to wear his West Point class ring. Since this was tantamount to an engagement agreement, Julia demurred, knowing that although she felt the same way, her father, wise in the ways of the world, had spoken to her about the vicissitudes of marrying an ill-paid and low-ranking officer in the United States Army who at any moment might be jerked up and posted hundreds or even thousands of miles away, merely on the whim of the War Department.

Nevertheless, Julia let it be known to Grant that her feelings for him were more than merely passing and there the matter rested for the next two years, with Grant stewing a thousand river miles away in Louisiana until the long-predicted war with Mexico became reality and he was given a brief leave to go to Missouri. Colonel Dent was still opposed to a marriage but softened a bit when Grant told his prospective father-in-law that once the war was over he intended to resign from the army and go into teaching, preferably at West Point, where he hoped his skills in mathematics would stand him in good stead. From then on, as was the custom of the times, Grant was allowed to write "courting letters" to Julia, though the colonel remained skeptical of his suitability.

In the meantime, there was the Mexican War to be fought and Grant received with mixed feelings the information that he had been assigned as quartermaster of his regiment, since the job was conducted for the most part behind the fighting lines. He knew that quartermasters were vital to the operations of any large body of troops because they were responsible for ammunition, food, transportation, quarters, clothing, pay, and other matters vital to keeping troops in the field. And besides, Grant had a fear of going into battle—which most sensible soldiers do—adding in a letter to Julia that, one way or another, it appeared inevitable so she should not worry.

Quartermaster or not, Grant found his way into practically every big battle of the Mexican War. During savage house-to-house fighting in Monterrey the regiment began running out of ammunition and Grant volunteered to ride back and send it forward. Few who were there forgot the sight of the young lieutenant clinging to the neck and one side of his horse as he galloped through the gauntlet of Mexican fire down one street and up another. In his later memoirs he recalled that he had been going so fast that "generally I was past and under the cover of the next block before the enemy fired."

The American victory at Monterrey did not, as Grant had hoped, end the Mexican War; it dragged on for nearly another two bloody years. Grant lost a number of friends and grew unhappy with the continuing carnage. Still, he did his duty when duty called and, as his friend James Longstreet remembered, "You could not keep him out of battle. . . . [He] was everywhere on the field." During the final throes of the battle for Mexico City Grant managed to get behind the enemy with a small cannon, which he and a squad of men hoisted to the bell tower of a church and began to fire into the rear of the Mexican army. Afterward, his commanding general sent another officer, Brevet Major John C. Pemberton—of whom we shall hear much more later—to bring him back to headquarters, where Grant, instead of being bawled out, as he expected, was congratulated and made a brevet* captain for his gallantry.

The fall of Mexico City in September 1847 did not end the Mexican War; instead it lingered another five months, with the American army in occupation of the country while details of the peace were worked out. Soon Grant found himself disgusted by the hordes of "poor and starving subjects who are willing to work more than any country in the world," and yet "the rich keep down the poor with a hardness of heart that is almost incredible," he told Julia. If he made the connection between this and the Southern slaves he never said so, perhaps because of Julia's slaveholding family. Grant also found occasion for socializing with his fellow officers, most of whom would become

* A brevet was a temporary rank usually bestowed for bravery or meritorious conduct. It was not permanent for pay or seniority purposes.

brigade, division, corps, and army commanders on both sides of the Civil War.

During this period Grant's drinking habits were first called into question. Some early historians attempted to downplay them but a family letter written by a superior officer who was from Grant's hometown said that his fellow Ohioan "drinks too much, but don't you say a word on that subject." His stay in Mexico City also provided occasion for Grant to reflect yet again on his dislike of the pomp and circumstance of military life—in particular, fancy uniforms. Of the two commanding generals who led the war, Winfield Scott, a hero of the War of 1812 and soon to become known as "Old Fuss and Feathers," was characterized by Grant as wearing "all the uniform prescribed or allowed by law," while Zachary Taylor, whom Grant most admired, usually dressed himself in a worn old duster and slouch hat.

Grant also found time to reflect on the Mexican War as a whole, which he considered as having been trumped up by President James K. Polk, a southerner, as a cheap way of acquiring territories from Mexico in order to create new slave states. Later, in his memoirs, Grant famously expressed this by branding the conflict "one of the most unjust wars ever waged by a stronger nation against a weaker one."

Grant returned to St. Louis and in August 1848 he married Julia Dent at her family home. Among the army officers present were Longstreet, still recovering from battle wounds, and Cadmus Wilcox, destined to face Grant as a major general commanding a Confederate division.

Grant was assigned to a new quartermaster post at Detroit and Julia, with no housekeeping or cooking experience and no slaves to help her, dutifully tried to fill the role of an army wife. In 1850 she gave birth to a son, Frederick Dent Grant, and she began dividing her time between Grant's post and St. Louis, which only added to his boredom with peacetime military life and the attendant temptations. Whether or not that had anything to do with it, Grant soon joined the Sons of Temperance, with a pledge to stop drinking.

In wasn't long, however, before the Fourth Infantry received orders for the Pacific coast. The notion of Julia going with him was out of the question. With Fred only two and Julia pregnant once again, Grant set out in July 1852 with part of the regiment, on a steamship bound from New York to the Isthmus of Panama. In the days before the Panama Canal and the transcontinental railroad, there were two practical ways to get to the American Pacific coast. The first was the hazardous and discomforting voyage around Cape Horn at the tip of South America. The second was the much shorter but perhaps even riskier route over land and water from the Atlantic to the Pacific across the narrowest part of Panama, and this was the way Grant had been ordered to take several companies of soldiers plus a number of dependents across the isthmus. The passage was nightmarish from beginning to end; the mules that had been requisitioned by the army to carry everyone through the pestilent swamps and jungles never showed up and Grant was forced to hire dugout boats operated by drunken knife fighters who spoke no English. Malaria and other tropical fevers broke out as well as an epidemic of cholera so that by the end of the journey more than a hundred soldiers, wives, and children lay dead and buried in Panama, nearly a third of those Grant had started out with.

All the while, witnesses reported, Grant ministered to the sick and dying, hardly sleeping, pushing things forward as best he could, but when he finally arrived at Panama City he got his first dose of the quirkiness of the press when an English newspaper there blamed him for the disaster. With that behind him, Grant and the remainder of his party reached California, where he was further assigned to the remote outpost of Fort Vancouver, at the mouth of the Columbia River on the Oregon-Washington border. There, Grant learned that Julia had given birth to their second child, Ulysses S. Grant Jr.

It was probably a combination of boredom with the mundane duties of his job and the loneliness of missing Julia, but in any case Grant took up drinking again. By various accounts he either became only a "consistent" drinker or indulged in "sprees," but everyone seemed to agree that only a small amount of alcohol had an out-of-proportion effect on him: a single glass would cause his speech to slur while "two or three would make him stupid." On one occasion when he was to outfit a surveying expedition for his fellow West Pointer George McClellan, Grant "had one too many" at the officers' mess and McClellan apparently made it come back to haunt him when the Civil War broke out.

In the meanwhile Grant tried to supplement his meager army pay by purchasing land on which he planted a crop of potatoes and chopped wood to sell to steamships. Floods wrecked the potato field, however, and the wood also was washed away. He tried to raise livestock and poultry, but this too was a failure, as were his attempts to collect old debts from loans he had made to fellow officers. His letters to Julia were filled with melancholy and boredom and his loneliness was palpable.

In 1854 Grant was reassigned to Fort Humboldt, 250 miles north of San Francisco, and there he first began to think about resigning from the army. But before that could happen an incident allegedly occurred that would follow Grant for the rest of his career. According to various accounts, he was discovered to be drunk while on payday duty and his commanding officer gave him a choice of either resigning from the service or facing court-martial. Some fellow officers insisted that the commander had "had it in for him" since his arrival at the post and that his drinking was no better or worse than anyone else's, but whatever Grant's previous frame of mind regarding the army he made his decision. In May 1854, he wrote Julia that he was coming home.

As the ennui of remote army outposts overtook him, Grant had begun to fancy his future as being that of "a well-to-do Missouri farmer," and he went east to see if he could make the dream come true. He was now thirty-three years old and, with no savings to fall back on, he actually had to borrow money from an old West Point colleague with the imposing name of Simon Bolivar Buckner just to get home. But Colonel Dent had given Julia sixty acres of White Haven as a wedding present and Grant convinced himself that he could farm it at a profit. He was mistaken. Even though he worked long hours in the field alongside slaves provided by Julia's family, he was finally forced into cutting wood and hauling it up to St. Louis, just as he had done as a boy. As the years went by Grant's family grew to two boys and two girls and they all lived in a rude log house that he had built and aptly named Hardscrabble, a considerable comedown for the former Julia Dent, once the belle of White Haven.

Everything seemed to go wrong for farmer Grant. In boom years when the land produced well, prices fell and profits vanished. Then the Panic of '57 spawned a depression so severe that at Christmas he was forced to pawn his gold hunting-case watch to buy presents for the family. A cousin of Julia's helped Grant get a job in a real estate business in St. Louis but, as it turned out, he wasn't very good at that either. He disliked the duty of collecting rents and abhorred the idea of evicting anyone. Still, he tried to make a go of it, finally trading Hardscrabble for a place in St. Louis.

It wasn't a bad house as houses go, but with his family to feed plus four slaves that Julia had owned since childhood—now all teenagers— Grant yet again found it difficult to make ends meet. He applied for the job of county engineer, for which his West Point education had certainly qualified him, but he lost out because of partisan politics. When the new owner of Hardscrabble defaulted on the bank loan, Grant was so strapped for cash that he took the disagreeable step of going to work at his father's leather-goods store in Galena, Illinois, up near the Wisconsin border. Jesse Grant by now had become a prosperous businessman with leather-making enterprises in several Northern states, but he had also become an unbearable blowhard, inserting himself without welcome into local politics and deriding Julia's family as "that tribe of slaveholders."

Nevertheless Grant had few options, since he had just about worn out the largesse of the Dents, and so in the spring of 1860 he rented out the family slaves in Missouri and journeyed up the Mississippi to the little hillside town of Galena, opposite Dubuque, Iowa, to join the family business. People remember him dressed in his worn army greatcoat and a dark slouch hat walking to or from his father's shop, and while at first his spirits seemed to rise at the notion of a secure job it did not take long for the boredom of clerking at a leather-goods store to set in. Customers recalled Grant as merely another apathetic salesman while the South seethed in the wake of Abraham Lincoln's election and rumors of war swirled in the national air. Since he had entered West Point twenty years before, Grant's career seemed shrouded in a haze of indifference and failure, but it was there in Galena, Illinois, that war found him.

The firing on Fort Sumter in Charleston Harbor by the new Confederate States of America did not surprise Grant. To those who derided the notion that war would be the inevitable outcome of the election of 1860, Grant bluntly replied, "The South will fight." He had spent too much time with his wife's slaveholding family in Missouri and among the Southern officers he fought alongside in Mexico to believe otherwise. His personal feelings about slavery had always been that it was bad in general, but that if there was ever to be emancipation it should be brought about very slowly and, somehow, of its own accord. Yet as he grew older, Grant apparently became more ambivalent about the institution when he tacitly became a slaveholder himself with the addition of Julia's bondsmen to the family; in fact Grant even acquired a slave of his own—how is uncertain, but some say as a gift.

One matter over which he was feverently appalled was the prospect of secession. Although the Constitution nowhere specifically forbade states from seceding from the Union, Grant, along with many northerners and southerners, was dismayed by its obvious implications: if one section of the country seceded from the whole, what would prevent other states from doing the same, whether over a actual or a perceived grievance against the central government or, for that matter, even a whim? And should that be allowed to happen, then the seceding states, sooner or later, would likely find cause for trouble with their neighbors, which would inevitably lead to more secessions and possibly to conflicts until, over time, what had once been the United States would reap the fate of Mexico, which seemed to be in a state of eternal war. Thus would the great American experiment in democracy implode into a disastrous, humiliating, and irretrievable third-rate wreckage of what it might have been. At least that's how the thinking went, and was how Grant saw it. He had not, however, voted for Abraham Lincoln for precisely that reason: he was convinced that the Republicans, as the party of abolition, would bring on Southern secession and the consequent civil war that he so feared.

Most northerners had persuaded themselves that even if it came to war it would be a brief and decisive one, and Grant himself held this view until the serious fighting was well under way. In his opinion, despite the Confederacy's confiscation of huge stores of cannon, rifles, ammunition, and other military equipment held in the federal armories of the South, as well as the defection of many West Point graduates to the Southern cause, the manpower and industrial superiority of the North would quickly overwhelm the rebellion. Then, he reasoned in a letter to his father following Lincoln's election, with the Republican abolition party in power, the market for slaves would bottom out until "the nigger will never disturb this country again."

As a military man and West Pointer, Grant felt honor-bound to offer his services, and so notified the War Department of his availability. This communication, for whatever reasons, was ignored. He next petitioned the governor of Illinois seeking a regimental colonelcy, but this also was denied on account of there being so many politicians in the state demanding those same positions. Then he journeyed to Ohio to see his West Point colleague George McClellan, now a general of volunteers, in hopes of securing a job on his staff. Perhaps McClellan remembered the time in California when Grant got drunk while outfitting his expedition, perhaps not, but in any case Grant was left cooling his heels for two days outside McClellan's office before finally returning to Illinois without an interview.

Just as it must have seemed to the thirty-nine-year-old Grant that the war would pass him by, he was overtaken by a stroke of fate. No sooner had he returned to Springfield than an issue arose concerning a new regiment of Illinois volunteers who had revealed themselves as little more than a mob of chicken thieves led by a drunkard. When this information was brought to the attention of the governor, Grant was appointed to take charge of these people and straighten them out— and with the rank of colonel. This he did in a firm, quiet, and persistent way befitting a military academy man, and in less than a month the hooligans were imbibed with drill, discipline, and such liberal doses of the guardhouse that they were rechristened the Twenty-first Regiment, pride of Illinois, and ordered to southern Missouri where secessionist bands were causing trouble.

Thus far Missouri was still in the Union by the slenderest of political threads since, as a slave state, loyalties were decidedly mixed. Small Rebel detachments were burning bridges, reconnoitering, and shooting at Union soldiers, aided and abetted by a large number of Southern sympathizers. Grant's job was to suppress this behavior and, in the days before the conflict turned into "hard war," he chose to do so by offering the carrot instead of the stick, promising protection to those who would profess loyalty to the Federal government. During this period no battles were fought and engaging the Confederates was like chasing ghosts, but Grant performed so well at it that he was given command of three other misbegotten regiments and told to bring them up to snuff. Technically this made him a brigade commander, which ordinarily carried the commensurate rank of brigadier general; nevertheless, he was shocked to learn from the newspapers that he had actually been promoted. This was the doing of an old friend from Galena, the Republican congressman Elihu Washburne, who would figure prominently in Grant's career from time to time.

Now that Grant was a brigadier he not only held more responsibility but some measure of authority, too, since general officers are well set off from the rest in the military hierarchy. In the space of less than two months he had gone from being a has-been former army captain and failed farmer and businessman to a general in command of several thousand infantry soldiers. The question now became what he would do with them.

This was partly answered when he was placed in charge of the District of Southeast Missouri with orders to bring to bay several large Confederate forces operating in that region as well as in nearby Kentucky, on the east side of the Mississippi. Grant had no sooner arrived at his new headquarters at Cairo, Illinois, than he began laying plans for a movement to occupy Paducah, Kentucky, whose citizens were gaily anticipating the arrival of Confederate general Gideon Pillow and his troops. To their dismay, however, Grant got there first, and when the initial shock wore off nervous Paducahans were relieved to hear Grant's proclamation that "I have come among you as your friend and fellow citizen," in which he pledged to respect their "rights and property" (which, as both parties understood, included slaves).

Having occupied Paducah without bloodshed, Grant then turned to a more serious operation across the Mississippi where a Confederate encampment under the Rebel general Sterling Price was building up forces near the little town of Belmont, Missouri, and blocking Union traffic on the river. Grant saw this as an opportunity to bring his troops into a real battle and, with two brigades at hand, he arranged for them to be transported from Cairo on river steamers just to the north of Belmont, with the object of driving the Confederates back into Arkansas.

Even then, Grant seemed to grasp that the overarching strategy in the West should focus on clearing the Mississippi—as opposed to merely capturing cities—thus restoring Federal commerce from the Ohio Valley and Great Lakes to the Gulf of Mexico, while at the same time cleaving the Confederacy in two. This corresponded roughly with the notions of both Abraham Lincoln and the aging Winfield Scott, general in chief of the army. Scott's so-called Anaconda Plan had called for a naval blockade of all Southern ports, including the bottling up of Confederate shipping on the Mississippi, which would deny the South its priceless cotton trade with France and England as well as imports of foreign arms and munitions, "squeezing" the rebelling states into a relatively bloodless economic submission. This was derided in the press, North and South, as being unrealistic—and to some extent it was, without sterner and more immediate measures— but in the end it was the Anaconda Plan that helped bring the South to its knees much sooner than might otherwise have happened.

Lincoln saw it too. In the eastern theater Federal armies had been throttled by Joseph E. Johnston's Rebel army at Bull Run and in the Shenandoah Valley. But the president was slowly coming around to the notion that instead of concentrating entirely on the capture of the Confederate capital at Richmond, the Union might better concentrate on the West. From his youthful days as a flatboatman on the Mississippi Lincoln understood the value of commerce along the great river and its tributaries from both an economic and a political perspective—this last with a canny eye toward the upcoming congressional elections of 1862. As things stood, it was the North that was currently being "squeezed," particularly in the northwestern states (what is now known as the Midwest), which were likewise unable to use the Mississippi to ship their products to foreign and domestic markets—and with the usual results: steamboats rotting at the wharfs, crops rotting in the fields, timber and manufactured goods piling up in storage sheds.* But the more the president pressed for the Union armies to advance downriver, the less it seemed was achieved.

It was not so much the fog of war as it was a haze of obfuscation, obstruction, and excuses. No general in the West seemed anxious to risk his reputation in battle against the Confederates, and the greatest obfuscator of all was the commander of the Department of the West, John C. Frémont, the legendary "pathfinder." Frémont was Grant's boss, elevated to that position partly through his trailblazing exploits in the West and partly because of his political connections. (He had married the daughter of Thomas Hart Benton, a Democratic senator for thirty years.) Frémont had no formal military training but he had published several accounts of his western explorations that had made him a national hero. However, his experience with handling large bodies of troops, let alone whole armies, was nil, and the result was that his department was a mess. Like a self-imposed Prisoner of Zenda, Frémont installed himself in a palatial St. Louis mansion surrounded by a ridiculous coterie of wildly dressed French and Prussian guards and received almost no one in his headquarters, including his own generals. His logistics were utterly chaotic, marked by extravagant government contracts with unscrupulous suppliers, and his chief concern seemed to be an obsession with destroying slavery wherever it existed, a policy that was precisely what Lincoln did not wish to implement for political reasons—at least not for the moment.

It was in this confused setting that Grant set out to do battle at Belmont, which initiated his first serious dealings with the Union navy, which was later to play such a large role in the campaign for Vicksburg. There were plenty of river steamships tied up at docks from Cairo to St. Louis, so Grant had no trouble dragooning captains and crews to

---

* The Mississippi had been blockaded once before, by the British during the War of 1812, with results even more dire, since there were no railroads or canals that midwestern merchants or farmers could use to move their goods and produce.

handle them, but what he now needed were Federal gunboats to escort
his troops twenty-five miles downstream and provide protection while
his force landed. All of this was arranged agreeably by the navy and on
November 7, 1861, Grant shoved off with five infantry regiments, six
artillery batteries, and two cavalry companies, a total of about 3,100
men, accompanied by two wooden gunboats.

The mission was to be in the nature of a raid, rather than an expedition of conquest and occupation. The Confederates had been using
their camp at Belmont to send reinforcements across the Mississippi
to the strong new fortifications they were constructing at Columbus,
Kentucky, on the opposite shore. It had originally been Grant's intention to annihilate both of these positions, but Frémont had not seen fit
to send enough men to do the job, so the best Grant could hope for
was to stem the tide of Rebels crossing the river, if only temporarily,
and deal with Columbus when the time came.

As battles go, Belmont was by no means what Grant had wished for,
though it certainly got him off to a good start. His force landed without
opposition about two miles north of the Confederate encampment in a
landscape of woods and cornfields and marched toward the enemy.
Though the Rebels had been warned at the first sign of Grant's
approach by their cohorts on the Kentucky side of the river, they
were sufficiently surprised so as not to be as ready for battle as the
approaching Yankees. Gray-clad skirmishers and sharpshooters took
potshots at the Union soldiers but withdrew steadily back toward their
campgrounds where the main force was assembling into battle formation. When it was met with a heated fire from Grant's columns of blue,
the Confederates scrambled over the six-foot-tall bluffs that formed
the riverbanks. With their backs thus to the river, Grant lamented afterward, if the Rebels had been immediately pressed he might have
bagged the whole bunch of them and come away with several thousand prisoners.

That was not to be. As Grant sourly described it: "The moment the
camp was reached our men laid down their arms and commenced
rummaging the tents to pick up trophies. Some of the higher officers
were little better than the privates. They galloped about from one cluster of men to another and at every halt delivered a short eulogy upon
the Union cause and the achievements of the command." Worse, while
this foolishness was going on, the Confederates were not just sitting
there like cardboard dummies but instead began working their whole
force upriver, along the bank and out of sight, in an effort to get

between Grant and his critical transport ships. Worse even than that, Grant saw to his horror that coming from the opposite shore were two Rebel steamers filled "from boiler deck to roof" with enemy reinforcements.

With this unnerving development, Grant ordered his men to burn the enemy camp, then retreated back to his transports. But as soon as the fires began to blaze, the Rebel artillery on the Kentucky shore, which had previously held its fire, unsure until then of who was in possession of the encampment, immediately opened up on them. As if that was not bad enough, the Confederates who had worked their way along the riverbank now began to emerge between Grant and his ships, the only route of escape, and the alarm "surrounded" was cried out among the blue-clad soldiers.

Grant, trying to put the best face on it, later remarked, "At first some of the officers and men seemed to think that to be surrounded was to be placed in a hopeless position, where there was nothing to do but surrender. But when I announced that we had cut our way in and could cut our way out just as well, it seemed a new revelation."

Somehow most of his force managed to get back to the transports and haul off to safety upriver, making its escape in an almost comical fashion were it not for the casualties involved. To Grant, Belmont had accomplished at least two things: first, it had proven that his men would fight in a heated battle and, second, it demonstrated to the Confederates that they could no longer operate with impunity in Missouri.

Belmont was a relatively large engagement in the West for that period in the war. Four hundred and eighty-five Union soldiers had been killed, wounded, or taken prisoner and Confederate losses were tallied at about six hundred. Though Grant considered Belmont a victory, he was lampooned in the press, which characterized the action as a Union retreat, "wholly unnecessary and barren of results, nor the possibility of them from the beginning." Nevertheless, the new brigadier general had taken his first major steps down what was to become a long, bloody road.

After Belmont, Grant returned to his base at Cairo and pondered his next move. His strong inclination was always to attack and wrest Columbus away from the Confederates, but by then the thoroughly alarmed southerners had so fortified and reinforced their base that it was impossible with the troops Grant had on hand. Shortly after the Belmont fight, Frémont was fired by Lincoln for delivering a premature "emancipation proclamation" and replaced by the nervous, bug-eyed military whiz Henry Halleck, who had written several admired martial textbooks but never fought a battle. Like Frémont, Halleck was cautious, but he felt compelled to heed Lincoln's frustrated edict that in the western theater a concerted movement southward by Union forces should begin no later than George Washington's birthday in early February.

By then, Grant had under his command two of the three officers who would become his stalwarts in the campaign that would ulti-mately lead to the Battle of Vicksburg, but both were suspect so far as their loyalty to U. S. Grant was concerned.

Colonel James B. McPherson was an energetic young West Pointer who had finished first in his class and been assigned by Halleck as Grant's chief engineering officer, but he was also to act as a spy for Halleck, on whose staff he once served. The object of the spying involved rumors of Grant's drinking, which had not only come to Hal-leck's attention but reverberated all the way up to Lincoln himself from a variety of sources, many of them dubious.*

The second officer was Colonel John A. McClernand, an Illinois congressman and "political general" who had no previous military experience, but he was a friend and political ally of Lincoln's, though he was a Democrat. He was also something of a gasbag who sought to glorify himself at every opportunity and, though Grant had praised him publicly and officially for leadership and bravery at Belmont, it was McClernand who was behind at least some of the rumors that Grant was a drunkard.

With McPherson applying his engineering skills and Grant leaning over his shoulder and puffing relentlessly on his pipe, the two pored through maps and scouting reports and came to an enlightening con-clusion: though Columbus was presently too strong to be taken, it might not be necessary after all. About fifty miles to the east of Colum-bus, near the Kentucky-Tennessee border, the Cumberland and Ten-nessee rivers come within ten miles of each other to join the Ohio, which then flows into the Mississippi. The Confederates had strong fortresses on each of the two rivers near their confluences, Fort Henry on the Tennessee and Fort Donelson on the Cumberland.

Grant and McPherson soon had a plan formulated to capture these

---

* There is no evidence that McPherson engaged in any spying on Grant, and in fact he became one of Grant's most trusted lieutenants.

two bastions by an integrated force of arms, with the desired result of cracking the Confederate stronghold in two where they were least expecting it—right down the middle of Kentucky and Tennessee to the Mississippi-Alabama border. On January 6, 1862, Grant took his plan to Henry Halleck in St. Louis, where both he and it were received with "such little cordiality" that "I was cut short as if my plan was preposterous," according to his own recollection.

Rivers were a main artery of travel in those days but, even so, until the invention of the steamboat, the South would have had little to fear from a Northern invasion in that quarter, since the currents of both the Tennessee and Cumberland flowed north. But by the outbreak of the Civil War the steamboat was in its heyday, with hundreds of them plying rivers all over the West, and immediately upon the outbreak of hostilities the Federal government commandeered as many as it needed for troop transports and gunboats. These last were an especially formidable departure from anything yet devised in riverine warfare.

Aware that the Confederacy was fortifying all strategic points along its rivers, Northern strategists quickly concluded that since the Rebel forts were protected by an array of large fixed cannons, they could be reduced only by the use of powerful steam warships armed with heavy artillery that would be too awkward for an army to lug overland. One of the first men to recognize this was a savvy St. Louis engineer and riverman named James B. Eads, who had made his fortune salvaging submerged wrecks with a small fleet of boats he had tailored especially for the task, including a diving bell named after him. Eads suggested to U.S. secretary of the navy Gideon Welles that several river steamboats could quickly be converted into gunboats by cutting them down almost to the waterline and strengthening them with thick oak planking and arming them with big guns.

While this work was being done, authorities in Washington decided that a fleet of even more powerful warships would be needed, with novel designs suited to the particular needs of fighting on closed, shallow bodies of water. By this time practically all naval warships were powered by the reciprocating steam engine, usually with sailing gear as an auxiliary. That was the "blue-water navy," intended to fight on oceans and not in the treacherous shoals and mud banks of the alluvial Mississippi River bottom. Accordingly, architects in the Naval Bureau of Construction began to draw up plans for an entirely new kind of fighting vessel, the river gunboat.

These were not "boats" in the conventional sense of the term. They were upwards of two hundred feet long and more, weighed as much as five hundred tons, employed crews of up to 150 men, and could bring to bear a concentration of twenty large-caliber cannons at over-the-water speeds of around eight to ten knots. They were self-sufficient except for the coal tenders that supplied their fuel, protected by iron armor plating two and a half inches thick over solid oak planks from twelve to twenty-four inches deep, and carried main batteries of 32-pounder guns as well as huge 42- and 64-pounder Dahlgren guns—far superior to the 12-pounder Parrot guns that were the mainstay of armies in the field.

These became the "City Class" ironclad fleet, named after towns along the Mississippi and its tributaries. In late 1861 and early 1862, the *St. Louis, Carondelet, Louisville,* and *Pittsburg* were completed in St. Louis, and the *Mound City, Cincinnati,* and *Cairo* slid off the ways near Mound City, Illinois.

It was one of the most remarkable feats of shipbuilding in the world, since the authorities in Washington had decreed that the vessels must be commissioned within sixty-four days from laying of the keel to final completion. The man selected to perform this Herculean task was James Eads, who would have finished on time if the government had provided him the funds; as it was, he financed the boats himself until his credit ran out and, even with that, he was only a couple of months late with the whole project.

Two additional ironclads were converted from existing rivercraft: one of Eads's own salvage ships, *Benton,* a monster more than three hundred feet long, and *Essex,* a bit smaller but no less formidable. Furthermore, the U.S. government commissioned construction of a fleet of thirty-eight "mortar boats," each designed as a floating bombardment platform for a 13-inch mortar weighing 17,500 pounds that could lob a 250-pound exploding shell a mile or more into Confederate cities or fortifications.

Then there were the so-called Ellet rams, conceived by a civilian engineer named Charles Ellet Jr., who persuaded Washington that the most effective way to sink an enemy ship in the narrow confines of the western rivers was to tear into it with a fast steamboat fitted with a large iron prow. Fearful that the Confederates might entertain similar ideas, around the time that Grant made his attack on Belmont, the secretary of war, Edwin Stanton, promptly made Ellet a colonel in the army and told him to see to the construction of nine of the ships. Soon Ellet had converted the river steamers *Queen of the West, Lancaster, Switzer-land, Monarch, Mingo, Lioness, Fulton, Horner,* and *Samson* into for-midable ram ships, strengthening their timbers and bulkheads and especially their engine mounts against the inevitable shock of plowing full speed into another ship or boat. Ellet's thinking was that his steam rams would have no need of armaments or heavy guns, which would slow them down, and that their increased speed would provide all the protection needed to avoid fire and sink an enemy. It was a good idea, almost brilliant for the time, considering the confines of the rivers in which operations were intended. Eventually there would be six of the Ellet family—brothers, sons, nephews, and cousins—to join in this novel experiment.

Such was the Union strategy for reclaiming the Mississippi by water: a fleet of nine ironclads, three wooden gunboats, thirty-eight mortar boats, and nine Ellet rams: fifty-nine ships in all, not including tenders, coal barges, transports, signal boats, and other lesser craft.

The Confederacy did not have such complicated naval issues to resolve, mainly because it had no means to solve them. There were no shipbuilding facilities in the southern Mississippi River basin, no large foundries for manufacturing iron plate or for making steamship engines, and the few large-caliber cannons that were eventually mounted had to be taken from existing forts or from captured Union vessels.

Still, the Confederates knew soon enough of the mammoth ship-building enterprises in the making up north, and it had become clear that something must be done to counter them. Accordingly, eight large and fast "river steamers" were commandeered and work was hastily begun for their conversion into fighting warships.

By necessity, lack of armor and armaments dictated that these ships, like Ellet's, would have to be defensive rams, although an attempt was made to give them protective shields by surrounding the superstructures—in particular the pilothouses and engine and mechan-ical compartments—with bales of cotton ("cottonclads") or by wrap-ping them with thick anchor chains or coils of mooring rope. In some cases, "railroad iron" was used and in a couple of instances ship-builders were able to scrounge up enough thin metal sheathing to pro-tect the vessels against rifle fire. These became known as "tinclads."

To make matters more difficult, since the Confederacy had no navy to speak of, civilian riverboat captains and pilots were selected to command the boats, which came to be known as the River Defense Fleet: the *General Lovell, General Price, Little Rebel, General Beauregard, General Bragg, General Sumter, General Van Dorn,* and *General Thompson.* With no uniform specifications to follow, each captain was ordered to equip and outfit his ship as he saw fit, and so, depending on the military knowledge of each officer, these craft began to undergo profound changes from their previous occupations as passenger or freight steamers. Foremost was the installation of large iron rams attached to the bows. Most of these boats were smaller by a third than their Union counterparts and usually carried only one or two guns—fore and aft—but as with Ellet's design it was hoped that their speed (up to twelve knots) would make up for at least some of these disadvantages.

The one matter in which the Confederates did not have to compete with the Yankees was in the organization and composition of crews. From the start, this became a mess for both sides.

Washington could not decide whether the army or the navy would command the gunboat operations in the West. What with the enormous strains of the two-coast naval blockade by the blue-water navy, it was at first concluded that the navy would run the show on the rivers but that the crews would have to be enlisted from the legions of civilian river men in the Department of the West. As it turned out, most of the river men did not wish to get into a shooting war, and so the navy promised that several hundred of its trained sailors would man the gunboats, but this never materialized. In the end, the navy sent some officers and the rest of the crews had to be made of civilians or soldiers from the army, which led one officer to describe them as "a veritable set of landlubbers."

In the South, the same problems arose, made worse by the inevitable shortage of manpower and sheer brass of the Southern riverboat men, who had agreed to serve "with the distinct understanding or condition that they would not be placed under the orders of naval officers." In fact, they *were* placed under a navy officer, but just one, Captain James E. Montgomery, late of the U.S. Navy, who had been given the rank of commodore; still, according to contemporary accounts, these river people were said to be "unable to govern themselves and unwilling to be governed by others."

In the end there were fifty-nine Union ships prepared to reopen the upper Mississippi against eight for the Confederacy to defend it. But whether by water or by land, as Grant moved his army southward, picking up momentum, the battles would be as spectacular as they were decisive.

CHAPTER THREE

U. S. "Unconditional Surrender" Grant

On February 10, 1861, Jefferson Davis, late of the United States Senate, had been pruning rosebushes in the garden of Brierfield, his expansive cotton plantation on the Mississippi River just south of Vicksburg, the city that would eventually become the flashpoint of the Southern Confederacy, when at about noon a horseman from the telegraph depot arrived with an urgent wire. As Davis read the message, "a look of anguish crossed his face," which made his wife, Varina, fear that someone in the family had died. The news was, if anything, more shocking: a convention of the recently seceded Southern states had elected Davis president of the new Confederacy. He reacted, said Mrs. Davis, "as a man might speak of a sentence of death."

Only weeks earlier Davis, fifty-three years old, had resigned from the Senate to take command of the Mississippi state militia, which he hoped eventually would lead to a higher position within the fledgling Confederate army. But this office, the presidency, the most excruciating political challenge of the times, was a thing he neither aspired to nor desired. Like most of the wealthy planters in Mississippi, Davis had strained and pleaded from his chair in the Senate for some compromise to avert the appalling specter of secession, which he feared would bring "a long and bloody war." Ultimately the voices of moderation were drowned out by a cacophony of Southern lawyers, politicians, and other hotheads aggrieved by decades of "Yankee" abolitionist abuse, fanned by a hostile Northern press and antagonized by an equally hostile Southern one.

Whereas Abraham Lincoln would shortly assume office with an entire government in place and an established army and navy to back it up, the new Confederate president would have none of these when he took the oath of office. It was a trial almost too overwhelming to contemplate, and yet Davis's antique sense of duty overrode his personal misgivings. Next day, after "packing a few things," he bade good-bye to Varina and their children and boarded the small weekly paddle wheeler when it stopped at Davis Bend for the trip upriver to Vicksburg; from there the railroad would carry him into the bloodiest crisis in American history. On that same morning, Lincoln said his good-byes to his neighbors in Springfield, Illinois, and got on the presidential train heading for his inauguration in Washington. Neither man could know what the future would bring, only that it would likely be calamitous.

One of Davis's slaves who had rowed his master out to the steamboat was Ben Montgomery, who would wind up owning Brierfield plantation after the war. He would say later, "Jeff Davis was a man you just couldn't tell what he was thinking."

As the war began to crank up in earnest Washington seemed confused as to how to proceed, while the Rebels in Richmond were more sanguine. Yet even if the South believed it was winning, it was also becoming apparent that its problems were as menacing and immense as the land itself.

By mid-1861 a Confederate defensive line had been established all across the South, starting in eastern Virginia at the Atlantic Ocean and stretching southwestward through Kentucky, across the Mississippi River and through Arkansas, into Indian Territory (now Oklahoma), then down to Texas and New Mexico, too, where it finally ended in eastern Arizona, "as a desert stream, in a trickle in dry sand." With more than two thousand miles to protect along those borders, not to mention far larger stretches "in the rear" along the coasts where Federal ships could blockade cities or land troops, and, at this early stage, with no more than 150,000 men in gray uniforms, the problems that loomed must have seemed endless. It was as though no one beforehand had considered the true military implications of secession— which in truth they had not.

At this early point in the war—despite the fighting at Bull Run and the beginnings of the naval blockade, as well as Federal military buildups in the Shenandoah and all along the Southern boundaries—

many southerners, including those in high political places, still hoped that full-scale war was not imminent; that somehow the North would see the error of its ways and let the South go in peace. With Abraham Lincoln in the White House that was, of course, a pipe dream. The simple fact was that the only way the South could win was in the way almost all insurrections are won, if they are won at all: to make the other side pay so dearly in lives, treasure, and energy that it finally gets tired and gives in. Neither the North nor the South fully understood this at the time.

One man who came closer to understanding this than most was Jefferson Davis. For reasons both political and military, it was his strategic policy that the Confederacy would defend itself at all points, contesting every inch of Southern soil from encroachment by Union forces. At his first inaugural in Montgomery, Alabama, he had flung down the defiant gauntlet with the declaration: "All we ask is to be let alone." And by that he meant *everywhere*. The politics involved were both parochial and international. Davis believed that the citizens of the Confederacy would become alarmed and liable to defect if portions of their states were allowed to be overrun by the enemy—even if the reason for it was to concentrate large Southern armies elsewhere to deal a fatal blow at some future date. Internationally, the Confederate leaders clung to hopes that Great Britain and France would give their new nation diplomatic recognition. And further that they would intervene in the war with their powerful navies to lift the Northern blockade of Southern ports, which had thrown nearly half the European textile mill employees out of work (as well as severely hampering the importation of Confederate military supplies). If these powerful countries saw that Union armies were being turned back wherever they were met, Davis reasoned, help would surely flow from that quarter.

At that point, the Confederacy was organized into two large departments—that of Virginia and the East, under Joseph E. Johnston, and across the Appalachian Mountains the Department of the West, under command of Albert Sidney Johnston, whose responsibility encompassed an area of more than a million square miles. Holding it together, or trying to, was the dynamic, rigid personality of Jefferson Davis, cotton planter, intellectual, West Point graduate, hero of the Mexican War, former U.S. senator, and onetime secretary of war. So far, Davis and his generals had done an adequate job, but as they prepared to enter the second year of war cracks began to appear in the seams.

·   ·   ·

Jefferson Davis was born in a Kentucky log house in 1808, not far from the place where Abraham Lincoln was born. As the youngest of ten children, his father, Samuel, fifty-two, and mother, Jane, forty-seven, gave him the middle name Finis, in part to signify that they'd had enough childbearing for one generation. Samuel, a hero of the Revolutionary War, had migrated from Georgia to Kentucky in the mid-1790s, where he set up a sizable tobacco and cotton plantation. But Samuel soon got the migration fever again, this time moving into the Deep South along the Mississippi, where the land was richer and the cotton growing season longer. He settled the family at the little town of Woodville, right below Natchez, and began building a Mississippi planter's (or Creole) cottage whose gardens soon produced an abundance of fruit, vegetables, and most particularly roses, which had become so much Jane's specialty that the place was named Rosemont.

Accounts of Jefferson's childhood seem idyllic, but owing to the lack of suitable education in Woodville, Samuel shipped him off to a private school in Kentucky at the tender age of eight, to be ministered to by a clutch of Dominican monks.* At St. Thomas, Jefferson got an earful of Latin, Greek, and other classical studies and remained there until he was ten, when he was brought home to attend a newly organized local academy with a full curriculum of mathematics, composition, history, and literature.

Once, when he refused to do his lessons and walked away from school, "Little Jeff" was given an instructive lesson by his father, who, instead of whipping him, said this: "It is for you to elect whether you will work with head or hands," then gave him a sack and sent him to the fields along with the slaves to pick cotton all day and see how he liked it. He didn't, and there was no more talk of quitting school.

When Davis was fifteen, in 1823, he was sent off to Transylvania College in Lexington, Kentucky, where he became a first-rate scholar and honor student described by one of his classmates as "the most active, intelligent and splendid-looking young man in the College."

Meantime, Jefferson's father went bankrupt owing to a large debt he had agreed to secure for one of his sons-in-law, lost Rosemont, and

---

* Along the way north on the Natchez Trace, Major Thomas Hinds, late of the Mississippi cavalry during the War of 1812's Battle of New Orleans, stopped off at Nashville for two weeks to visit his old commander, Andrew Jackson. When Hinds introduced "Little Jeff" to the revered hero, Jackson took an immediate liking to the eight-year-old lad, and the experience became one of Davis's most indelible memories.

had to move with his slaves to the large plantation of his eldest son, Joseph, at Davis Bend, just below Vicksburg. He was not there a week before he died at the age of sixty-seven. These developments left the teenage Jefferson with the dilemma of finding a way to afford his senior year of college and then law school or accepting an appointment to the United States Military Academy, which had free tuition. With a certain reluctance that was closer to resignation, in 1824 he chose West Point.

Davis got off to a bad beginning at the Point, by reporting late for admission, and stayed in trouble on and off for his entire four years there. Academically he did not do badly but his deportment was horrible: drinking, missing formations, untidiness, and leaving the post without authorization got him arrested or reported a number of times and once he was court-martialed. His involvement in the infamous "egg-nog riot" of Christmas Day 1826, nearly had him dismissed and it was rumored that he once got into a fistfight with fellow cadet Joseph Johnston over a girl at Benny Havens's notorious off-post drinking establishment. Furthermore, along with many other Southern cadets, Davis developed a distinct aversion to Yankees in the Cadet Corps, as this was about the time that abolitionist fervor in the North was starting to emerge.

Still, he had graduated, even if in the bottom third of his class, and was commissioned a second lieutenant and sent to the infantry training school at Jefferson Barracks, Missouri. From there he saw service on the Indian frontier and participated—as did Abraham Lincoln—in the Black Hawk War, actually capturing Chief Black Hawk himself and escorting him to his boss, Colonel Zachary Taylor, commander of the U.S. First Infantry Regiment. Not only that, but Davis promptly fell in love with Taylor's daughter, Sarah Knox "Knoxie" Taylor. Despite her father's misgivings, the two were married in 1835, six years after Davis had joined the regular army, serving on the hard frontiers among the Indian tribes. At one point he contracted what was probably pneumonia, which nearly killed him and left him sickly for the remainder of his life, a factor that was to weigh heavily during the Civil War years. But with the army now behind him, the newlyweds soon settled in at Davis Bend, at Hurricane, the plantation of his brother Joseph, at a time when cotton truly had become king along the Mississippi River.

Joseph Davis—who was old enough to be Jefferson's father and often behaved as such—had given Jeff some eight hundred acres and sent his slaves to build him a plantation house of his own, Brierfield,

named after the dense thickets of thorny briars that covered the tract.
Joseph also lent him money to buy slaves of his own and other tools
and implements needed for the farm, and soon the young couple settled into the tranquil plantation society of the river. Three months
later their world caved in.

The hot months in the Deep South were the deadly season for "the
fevers," though no one knew exactly why. Most suspected "miasmas"
and other noxious odors emanating from the bogs and swamps. Others pointed to "something in the water," while yet others blamed the
weather itself. In a way, they were all correct, except that it was the
lethal parasite carried by the female anopheles mosquito, which
hatches its young in the warm, putrid swamps that proliferate in delta
country. Planters often made a point of taking their families to
Appalachian Mountain resorts such as the Greenbriar—or even as far
away as Maine. But sometime late that summer both Davis and his
wife were bitten, probably on the same day, and possibly by the same
mosquito, and both came down with either malaria or yellow fever—
"yellow jack," as it was known.

On September 15, while Jefferson lay in a coma near death, Knoxie
Davis passed away. She was twenty-one years old. Davis was disconso-
late during his long recovery from his illness but threw himself into
learning the work of a planter, and by night he devoured every book he
could read from his brother's, and later his own, library—history, law,
poetry, science, literature, politics. His plantation prospered; by 1845
he had some seventy-four slaves working its eight hundred acres and
the bales of cotton began to pile up at the steamboat wharf at Davis
Bend. He became active in state Democratic politics and helped
organize a horseracing track in Vicksburg, as well as an antidueling
society. Nearer home, he was sometimes looked at askance by his
neighbors for banning corporal punishment for slaves at Brierfield;
instead he set up a kind of bondsman's court in which the slaves themselves would hear cases and pass sentence. In his spare time he cultivated a remarkable variety of roses in his garden, just as his mother
had done at Rosemont when he was a boy.

Politics seemed to draw Davis more than he was drawn to it but, like
Lincoln, he developed a reputation as a backwoods stump speaker. He
was a states' rights Democrat, but certainly no fire-eater, and, at the age
of thirty-eight, he found himself elected to Congress. By then he had
taken a new wife nearly half his age, Varina Howell, daughter of a
wealthy Natchez planter, who traveled to Washington for the opening

of his first term only to see him leave his seat six months later when the Mexican War broke out.

Davis was made a colonel in the Mississippi Volunteers and given a regiment to command under his former father-in-law, Zachary Taylor, who had since become the commanding general. The two had eventually reconciled over Knoxie's marriage and death, and Davis earned Taylor's plaudits for distinguished conduct and bravery at the Battle of Monterrey. At the Battle of Buena Vista Davis was seriously wounded in the foot, and again was praised for his gallantry. President James K. Polk offered Davis a commission as a brigadier general of volunteers, but he turned it down to accept an appointment by the governor as the new United States senator for Mississippi, owing to the death of the incumbent.

From the outset Davis warned in his Senate speeches of the dire consequences likely to result from the sectionalism that seemed to be growing exponentially between North and South. In particular, he cautioned his fellow freshman senator Simon Cameron (later to be Lincoln's first secretary of war) that "we have drawn near to that which has been for many years my dread, a division marked not by opinions, but by geographical lines." Patriotism, and only patriotism, Davis asserted, "would save the Republic from the evil consequences so likely to follow from a geographical issue." That was in 1846, and the sectionalism, it would seem, had only just begun.

Throughout his Senate career, Davis's political philosophy revolved around this theme. As his stature in the Senate grew—particularly in the South—Davis never wavered from the belief that some sort of compromise over the slavery issue was vital to the continuance of the nation, and to that end he labored tirelessly to formulate logical arguments against abolitionism, some of them a stretch even for his usually rational mind. One in particular was that the slaves were happier in their condition than they would have been back in Africa: well fed, clothed, Christianized, and free from the horrors of tribal wars. He must have been thinking, one biographer pointed out, of his *own* slaves back at Brierfield, whom he had always treated with the utmost care and respect: making a point of saying good morning, bowing to them in return, tending to them if ill, even bringing them presents when he went out of town. He did not seem to appreciate that other owners might not behave in the same fashion. But the single proposition that seems to have run through all of Davis's political and social makeup ever since his days at the Kentucky school run by monks was that a logical idea, well presented, could never fail—as well as its risky corollary: that he, Davis, could always arrive at the selfsame correct logical proposition. This last was a shortcoming that would often burden him, especially when he found himself leader of the Southern Confederacy.

As war clouds began to gather over the nation, there was little doubt where Jefferson Davis would stand. Until the last he argued in the Senate for what he believed could be permanent solutions to the slavery issue. One was an extension of the Missouri Compromise, drawing the line all the way across the country from Missouri to the Pacific, thus maintaining a political equilibrium in the Senate as new states were added. What he got instead was the Wilmot Proviso, a discordant piece of legislation introduced by a Pennsylvania congressman that would have banned slavery in all territories acquired from Mexico. Although the bill was never passed, it stirred up acrimony on both sides of the ideological spectrum, as though a giant log had been heaved into the political furnace. Davis and other southerners reasoned that a sort of safety valve had been created by the acquisition of the vast Mexican territory that would balance the growing political clout of the abolitionists into the foreseeable future. When this did not occur, sectional feelings were further hardened during the next decade.

In 1853 Davis became secretary of war during the Franklin Pierce presidency, a post at which he excelled, although he developed a considerable reputation as a hands-on administrator whose reluctance to delegate authority often frustrated his underlings.

As war secretary, Davis fought for the so-called Southern Route for a proposed transcontinental railroad to California, arguing (logically, he believed) that it would be easier, cheaper, and safer than the one currently proposed to begin at Omaha, Nebraska, which would have to cross the treacherous Rocky and Sierra mountain chains, which were often snowbound in winter. He lost the argument, but a sidebar developed that explains in microcosm how Davis rarely lost an opportunity to prove himself right.

When he was still a senator, and on the Military Affairs committee, Davis had recommended that the government purchase a number of camels from the Middle East for the army to use in surveying railroad routes and for peacekeeping duties in the arid terrain of the Southwest. He personally conducted a study of the camel and concluded that the latitudes from whence it came were the same as those in which it would be utilized in America and thus worked out a formula showing that a single camel could carry a thousand pounds of freight—versus about a third that for a horse—and that camels needed less than half the water and nutrients horses or mules did. Six camels would be able to do the work of twelve horses in half the time. His colleagues scoffed and the matter was dropped, but when Davis became secretary of war he ordered the project to go forward under his own authority. Accordingly, about one hundred of the strange beasts were purchased in Egypt by the U.S. Navy and, on the afternoon of April 29, 1856, a caravan was paraded before the startled citizens of Indianola, Texas, along with their Arab drivers, dressed in appropriate garb.*

This episode demonstrates two things about Davis's personality: that once he decided on something, no matter how large or small, he was tenacious in seeing it through and, second, he invariably took a direct hand in its implementation. These traits, admirable enough in most people, were to cause trouble when, as president of the Confederacy, he often injected himself directly into the military decision making as the war in the West heated up.

As the 1850s closed and talk of war became more strident, Davis expressed his horror at the notion of civil war, for among all politicians, North and South, he probably knew better than any what modern armies were capable of. He also knew just how ill prepared the South was to fight. The U.S. Army and Navy, though small, at least had arsenals and ships and a solid organization to build on, as well as a wealth of industry and manpower to draw from. The South had none of these, and would have to start from scratch, a fact that did not seem to occur to the fire-eaters who viewed any disturbance of slavery as a threat to their entire way of life.

Davis was a senator again when, one by one, the Southern states began voting to separate themselves from the Union. So it was when Mississippi went out that Jefferson Davis took his leave from the United States Senate. In his final speech he apologized to his Northern

---

* The camels proved something of a mixed benefit for the military surveyors. For one thing, their appearance unsettled herds of cattle, often causing them to stampede, but in general they proved as advertised until the Civil War broke out and surveying expeditions and other western exploits were quickly forgotten. The camels reverted to the wild and their progeny were occasionally seen roaming the southwestern deserts until after the turn of the century. The last sighting of one of the Egyptian camels was reported in 1929.

colleagues for any offenses he might have given to them. "I am sure I feel no hostility to you Senators from the North," he told them, adding, "In this hour of parting, I offer you my apology. Whatever offense there has been to me, I leave here."

That having been said, according to his wife, Davis prayed that "before it is too late, peaceful councils may prevail." Then he left for home and the solitude of Davis Bend, where the fateful message from Montgomery reached him while he pruned his roses in the garden at Brierfield.

Three months after his raid on the Confederate camp at Belmont, Missouri, Ulysses Grant remained anxious for more action. But Frémont's replacement, Henry Halleck, was just as slow and cautious as the Pathfinder had been. He had under him two armies—Grant's at Cairo and another led by Major General Don Carlos Buell based in Cincinnati, right across the Ohio River from Kentucky.

Buell's army had formerly belonged to Brigadier General William Tecumseh Sherman, who had fought admirably but on the losing side at Bull Run, and was then sent west to hold the wavering state of Kentucky in the Union. Sherman hadn't been there long before he was declared "insane" by the secretary of war, then by the newspapers, and then again by the army brass, for insisting to the secretary that it was going to take some 200,000 Union soldiers to put down the rebellion in the upper Mississippi Valley alone—and this at a time when there weren't 200,000 soldiers in the entire Federal army. Sherman was told to go take a rest and Buell was put in charge, but Halleck, rightly or wrongly, suspected that Buell was after his own job and kept him on a tight leash.

Grant was a different matter entirely, and though Halleck felt he had nothing to fear from the taciturn failed soldier–farmer–store clerk he had certainly heard the reports of his drinking habits and was not overjoyed with Grant's attack at Belmont—once the newspapers decided that it had been a defeat. Thus, Halleck, while he had two substantial armies under his control, was reluctant to use them lest they be beaten—or, in Buell's case, be too successful. And so he fiddled while the Confederates fortified and laid their schemes to retake Kentucky and bring the war back to the banks of the Ohio.

Until Grant came along, there wasn't much to speak of in the way of a grand Union strategy in the West. The immenseness of the theater was just as mystifying to the Union generals as it was to the Confederates and at times the plan seemed to be little more than "find the Rebels, fight them and make them run, and capture and hold their cities." This might have worked well enough in a small theater such as Virginia, but with all that open territory out west, while the Yankees were busy capturing or holding, say, Nashville, the Confederates might just march an army up into Illinois and capture Chicago—not that they would have, of course, even if they could have, for the Southern strategy at that point was strictly defensive except for those border states with a large Rebel following. The point is that it was going to take a far-seeing Union oracle to conceive and develop a strategic plan to cripple the huge Southern regions west of the Appalachians, and as it turned out that man was Ulysses S. Grant.

After Halleck's discourteous reception of his proposal to attack Forts Henry and Donelson, Grant proceeded as if the incident had not occurred and went ahead with one of the positive things he could do in the meanwhile, which was to coordinate a plan with the navy for an attack on both Rebel fortifications. Despite the fact that the navy had dumped the operation of the river ironclads into the army's hands, it did agree to furnish officers to man the ships—so long as army soldiers served as the crews. In charge of this considerably powerful flotilla was a stern, teetotaling sailor of the old school, Commodore Andrew H. Foote, who had fought from the China seas to the South Atlantic and was, in fact, the naval officer who had been assigned to purchase Jefferson Davis's camels in Egypt a few years earlier. Foote was a puritanically religious antislavery man who held Sunday school classes for his sailors, abolished the rum ration aboard his vessels, and lobbied for an alcohol-free navy, an endeavor that was ultimately successful. He was also an ardent believer in amphibious warfare—or at best joint army-navy operations—and here was perhaps the most important thing that he had in common with Grant, whose positions on drinking, slavery, and religion were ambiguous, to say the least.

In any case Foote enthusiastically embraced Grant's proposal to have Union gunboats escort his troops on the Tennessee and Cumberland rivers to the Confederate forts and bombard them while the infantry moved overland to finish off the job. It may have been Foote's strident endorsement of this plan or Halleck's skittishness that his supposed rival Buell was planning a move of his own on the Rebel positions in central and eastern Kentucky, but in less than a week after he had dismissed Grant's "preposterous" notion Halleck reversed himself and ordered Grant to go forward with the attack at all deliberate speed.

Both Grant and Foote had realized that the reduction of Forts Henry and Donelson itself was not a matter of much consequence, but the fruits that would flow from it certainly were. First, by outflanking the strong Confederate bastion at Columbus, Kentucky, the Rebels would be forced to either withdraw or surrender, thus opening the Mississippi down to their next important fortification, a bristling little obstruction on the Tennessee-Kentucky line called Island Number 10, which plugged the way to Memphis like a cork in a bottle. Second, and equally as important, by removing the enemy forts on the Tennessee and Cumberland rivers, the powerful Union gunboats could follow the paths of these two major streams almost at will, blasting Confederate railway bridges into matchsticks and otherwise disrupting communications in the enemy's rear. The significance of this can hardly be overstated. The Tennessee River not only ran the length of that state, but it bisected the main Confederate railroad connection between Memphis and Virginia, before turning well into the Deep South states of Mississippi and Alabama and then back northward again through Chattanooga and on up to its source at Knoxville. Likewise, the Cumberland offered a river highway straight into Nashville, the Confederates' most vital staging and communications center in the theater, as well as the site of the Confederacy's second largest iron and steel foundry.

Thus Grant was already prepared when he received word of Halleck's change of mind on the project, which, perhaps coincidentally, had occurred right after Halleck got word that Buell's army had defeated the Confederates in a battle at Mill Springs, in the southern part of Kentucky about 150 miles to the east, and was also threatening the Confederate army headquarters at Bowling Green. With Grant's attack on the forts, this would constitute a general Union movement southward all across the Confederate front from the Cumberland Gap to the Mississippi, a distance of more than three hundred miles—a measure that Grant had been pressing for Halleck to order all along.

For its part, the Confederacy knew it was in trouble in the West, but Jefferson Davis had scant troops or armaments to send to his old friend and comrade-in-arms Albert Sidney Johnston. When on the eve of the Federal thrust he received an almost frantic message conveyed through one of Johnston's subordinates, he replied, "My God! Why did General Johnston send you to me for arms and reinforcements, when he must know that I have neither?"

So Johnston was on his own. He was an able, impressive-looking officer whom Davis had looked up to at West Point, but his task was almost impossible. First, he was outnumbered by Federal forces by about two to one; second, many of his soldiers were armed with nothing but shotguns and old flintlocks left over from the War of 1812, and uniforms in many units were often a matter of personal taste.

His situation, in fact, illustrated the almost complete unpreparedness of the Confederacy at this stage of the war. When Johnston informed Davis soon after taking over command in mid-September 1861 that he desperately needed rifles for 30,000 men, a cadre of engineers, and other military necessities, the president had his secretary of war inform the general that the Richmond government could spare but one thousand rifles and, further, that the whole available Confederate engineer corps at the time consisted of only six captains and three majors, "of whom one is on bureau duty." Johnston did, however, manage to increase his force slightly by cajoling state governments to send him a few militia units, including a regiment of Texas Rangers, who crossed the Mississippi River with their horses.

By late winter Johnston had several large Yankee armies bearing down on him all across his line in southern Kentucky, and one place he was desperately worried about was Fort Henry, on the Tennessee. After months of urging the bishop warrior General Leonidas Polk to fortify a base there, he was bitterly disappointed to learn that the outpost had been sited on poor ground. First, it was situated below heights from which it could be taken under plunging fire. Worse, it was found that when the river was running high the place flooded right up to the cannon barrels, and the river now was fourteen feet above normal and rising. Worse yet, the fortifications remained uncompleted. "It is most extraordinary," Johnston lamented. "I ordered General Polk four months ago to at once construct those works. And now with the enemy on us, nothing of importance has been done!"

It must have been with apprehension, if not foreboding, that he immediately ordered General Lloyd Tilghman, a West Point graduate and engineer, to rush to the scene and do whatever he could to prepare Fort Henry and its 3,400 men for an assault he was certain was coming.

Whether or not Grant knew of these shortcomings, the plan he had worked out to reduce the fort consisted of a flotilla of four of Commodore Foote's ironclads, as well as three older wooden gunboats, followed by nine transport steamers carrying some 15,000 infantrymen in two waves—two full divisions and a better than three-to-one advantage over the Confederates.

The troops would embark at Paducah in the late afternoon of February 3, 1862, fifty miles downstream from Fort Henry, and arrive about eight miles below the fort before dawn on the fourth. Then the big black-painted ironclads would move forward in line to test the defenses. Once they established the range they'd retire to wait for the transports to go back to Paducah and pick up the remaining division, so that by February 5 all was in place. The gunboats would move forward and bombard while the troops disembarked and marched overland to the undefended heights overlooking the works.

It might have looked easy, but the Confederates had at least two artillery pieces capable of doing great harm to the gunboats—a 6-inch Whitworth rifle and a huge columbiad smoothbore that could hurl a hundred-plus-pound projectile. Just these two did considerable damage as Foote's flotilla steamed nearer and nearer to the fort. The other cannons, though fairly large, were either flooded out by the swollen river that now flowed freely through the fortification itself or weren't powerful enough to inflict much injury. Foote's flagship was struck thirty-two times and the other ironclads faired about the same, but little major damage was done except for the luckless *Essex,* which had already received a shell in her steering apparatus when she was struck in the boiler, scalding to death many in the engine crew. That, however, was the high tide, as it were, of the Confederate fight, for the Whitworth soon exploded, knocking her crew out of action, and the columbiad—ten feet long and weighing some fifteen thousand pounds—was accidentally spiked by a broken primer.

By then the Union ships were blasting away at point-blank range while Grant's 15,000 soldiers floundered their way through the marshes in hopes of bagging the whole Confederate force. In this, however, they were disappointed. Tilghman had called to Fort Donelson for reinforcements even before the Federal assault began, but when none were forthcoming he decided that, rather than lose both the garrison and the fort, he would send away the bulk of his army overland to Fort Donelson, where they could make a stand with the troops there. When it became apparent that further resistence was futile, Tilghman surrendered Fort Henry and was made a prisoner along with his skeleton crew who had manned the guns.

Thus victorious, Grant wired Halleck that Fort Henry was in Union hands and that he was sending his army behind the retreating Confederates while the ironclads returned to the mouth of the Ohio at Paducah; after hasty repairs, they would then steam into the Cumberland for an assault on Fort Donelson. While the ironclads were thus employed, the three wooden gunboats continued on up the Tennessee, blasting bridges, fortifications, trestles, and Southern steamboats unlucky enough to get caught in their path. They continued on this 150-mile joyride all the way down through Tennessee, cutting into northern Mississippi and Alabama, destroying as they went, and panicking a population that had been assured the dreaded Yankees would never get that far south.

Grant's prediction that a move against Fort Henry would cause the Confederates to withdraw from Columbus had proven correct, and the 11,000 Rebels who had blockaded the Mississippi River there were soon in full retreat into Tennessee. Not only that, but coupled with the defeat at Mill Springs, in the far eastern part of the state, General Johnston now concluded that his army at Bowling Green was in peril from a renewed thrust by Buell. Accordingly, he ordered them to retreat as well, giving up not only his well-established line across southern Kentucky but much of Tennessee too, since without reinforcements from the East he could not protect Nashville and his vital supply base there.

With the fall of Fort Donelson, the onus now fell on fifty-six-year-old Confederate brigadier John B. Floyd, another "political general" who had served as U.S. secretary of war following Jefferson Davis's term in that office. A man with little military experience, Floyd not only had been removed from his command in the Shenandoah Valley at the insistence of Robert E. Lee, he was also under federal indictment in Washington for malfeasance stemming from some shady manipulations with Indian Trust bonds belonging to the Department of the Interior. And as if that weren't enough, he was also roundly excoriated throughout the North for allegedly using his position as secretary of war to transfer large numbers of arms and munitions to Southern arsenals on the eve of the conflict.

Floyd's second in command was better, but not by much; he was fifty-six-year-old Brigadier General Gideon Pillow, a bombastic Tennessee lawyer who had been given a prominent military appointment by his friend and fellow Tennessean President James K. Polk during the Mexican War, in which he was twice wounded; his record was marred, however, by an acrimonious dispute with his commanding general, Winfield Scott.

Third in command was the thirty-nine-year-old Kentucky brigadier Simon Bolivar Buckner, a West Point classmate of Grant's who had been cited for bravery in the Mexican War. In fact, he was the very one who, years earlier, had lent money to Grant so that he could get home to St. Louis.

Knowing that Fort Donelson could probably not withstand Grant's onslaught, Johnston's charge to Floyd was to at least hold him off long enough until the army at Bowling Green, some seventy miles to the northeast, could be safely evacuated toward Nashville. With this in mind, and with some 17,500 men—including the cavalry command of Nathan Bedford Forrest, already well on his way to living up to his well-earned sobriquet the "Wizard of the Saddle"—Floyd determined not only to hold off Grant but to defeat him, and save the West.

Grant started his army overland on the twelve-mile march toward Fort Donelson on February 12, nearly a week later than planned. By then his army had grown considerably, owing to reinforcements being rushed to the scene by an elated Halleck, who saw in Grant's success a jewel in his own crown. When all was said and done, Grant could count on about 27,500 men against Floyd's 17,500—but all was not said and done. Harking to Floyd's persistent demands, Johnston had been sending him whatever Confederate reinforcements he could and Grant would not now enjoy the textbook formula of a three-to-one majority recommended for attacking fortified positions.

The march from Fort Henry began on a balmy morning, which at that time of year can be deceiving. Anyone familiar with the South in winter knows that the weather is subject to sudden and dramatic changes and, not understanding this as the day wore warmly on, Grant's soldiers began shedding their heavy overgarments and blankets until the roadside was littered with them. The officers, who should have known better, did nothing to stop them.

By the time he reached the outskirts of Fort Donelson and his army encountered the first line of Rebel pickets, Grant sent out his disposition orders. The division under sixty-year-old C. F. Smith, the white-haired former commandant of cadets while Grant was at West Point, was told to peel off north and anchor the Union line on a bend in the river, while the hatchet-faced Illinois politician John McClernand would hold the right on Grant's line to the south, preventing a Confederate escape.

Exactly what Grant had been expecting when he reached Fort Donelson is not recorded, but what he found there late that afternoon was a six-mile-long crescent-shaped line of Rebel rifle pits and field artillery positions stretching on both sides of the river bend with the fort to the north and the little town of Dover to the south. Grant's plan at the time was to invest the Rebel line and wait for Foote's ironclads to arrive and shell the fort into submission, as they had back at Fort Henry. Accordingly, he gave instructions to set up and wait for orders, but it wasn't long before McClernand became embroiled in a fight with a Confederate battery to his front and was repulsed after several bloody and wasted charges. This should have given Grant pause that McClernand needed close supervision, and he probably ought to have attached himself to the inexperienced general for the duration of the campaign. But instead Grant rode off to the north end of his line and found a comfortable farmhouse in which to spend the night.

As expected, the next morning Foote's gunboats began to move on Fort Donelson, but unlike his earlier success the lone ironclad that was then on the scene, *Carondelet,* was driven off with significant damage and many casualties and a simultaneous attack by Smith's division proved futile and costly. Not only that, but as night fell so did a drizzling rain, which turned into sleet, ice, and snow that covered everything, sent the temperature plummeting to 12 degrees, and froze to death a number of Union wounded, causing the others to curse their own stupidity in throwing away their cold-weather gear.

At this point Grant decided to wait for Foote's full ironclad fleet, as well as his reinforcements coming by transport steamers and overland from Fort Henry, and so while the icy weather continued the next day the two sides huddled in their respective lines content to take potshots at each other across no-man's-land.

By morning Grant's reinforcements began to arrive: 2,400 from Fort Henry and 7,500 sent by Halleck from Paducah. The former he assigned to Smith's division, which needed replacements after the abortive assault on the previous day, and the latter he placed under the command of Lewis "Lew" Wallace, a tall, multitalented, thirty-five-year-old Indiana lawyer who would go on to write *Ben-Hur,* to hold the center with this full new division. Now Grant felt ready and, with Foote's ironclads finally in place, he waited for the sound of ships' guns to complete his victory.

Instead he got a rude surprise. The Confederate guns at Donelson were much better situated than those at Henry and soon Foote's gunboats, which had engaged the fort from nearly a mile away, suddenly went reeling backward down the river with smokestacks shot off, pilothouses blown apart, timbers splintered, iron plate dented, and, perhaps worst of all, Foote himself seriously wounded. This unsettled but did not unnerve Grant and he wired Halleck that the place could probably be taken only by a "protracted siege." Accordingly, he told McClernand to crab around to his right, southward, to cut off any Confederate escape route, instructed everyone else to hold their ground, and before dawn on February 15 went off downriver to meet with the navy commodore, who had been shot in the foot.

Just after sunrise Grant may or may not have heard the dim rumble of artillery fire from the far south end of his line where McClernand's division was posted, but as he rode away from the conference with Foote he was met by a frantic messenger with the disquieting news that the Confederates were attacking McClernand in force and had thrown the whole division back in disarray. This was the last thing Grant had expected, having assumed that Pillow and Floyd were merely bumblers who would have surrendered sooner or later. As he neared his beleaguered positions, Grant was further informed that wounded and dead Confederates were found to be carrying extra rations in their haversacks. Unlike some of his subordinates, who interpreted this as proof that the Rebels were planning a prolonged assault, Grant concluded that it was instead a sign that they were trying to escape, and he busied himself trying to rally McClernand's demoralized troops.

Grant's intuition had been correct. After their repulse of Foote's ironclad attack, the Rebel soldiers were jubilant and Floyd, who had forecast the worst as the Federal gunboats closed in, had decided to go for a breakthrough of the Union lines at the southernmost point, near the village of Dover, which was occupied by McClernand's division. Pillow made the initial assault at dawn the next day, while Buckner brought his division down from the northern sector to cover the flanks as the whole of the garrison made good its escape.

Fortuitously for the careworn southerners, another fierce snowstorm came whipping in from the west, hiding the sights and sounds of the Confederate movement, and as day broke regiment after regiment of gray-clad infantry charged through McClernand's lines killing and scattering men and horses and capturing artillery. Bloodstains on the freshly fallen snow proved how hot the fight had become as Grant rode into the melee about three hours on, urging men to refill their cartridge boxes and get back into the fighting. Seeing their commander in chief at the front, they did it with a cheer. "The one who attacks now will be victorious!" Grant declared to whomever would listen, an axiom that he followed, rightly or wrongly, throughout the war. Presently he came upon a traumatized McClernand, who was overheard to mutter, "This army wants a head." Taken aback by this impolitic remark, Grant replied, "It would seem so," and rode on. The snowy ground all around him was littered with crumpled bodies of the wounded, dead, and dying, Union and Confederate alike, and after a while Grant, repelled by the bloodshed, told his staff, "Let's get out of this dreadful place."

Instead of pressing the Yankees harder, Floyd managed to snatch defeat from the jaws of victory by stopping to assess his situation. After sending a telegram to Johnston prematurely, claiming, "The day is ours," the Confederate general got cold feet and the usually sanguinary Pillow did the same while Buckner, known for his caution, ironically insisted on pushing forward for a complete breakthrough.

Floyd's original orders from Johnston had been to protect the west flank of the Bowling Green army as it withdrew southward—and this he had accomplished by delaying Grant for more than a week—but the other part of his instructions called for him to get his army safely away from Donelson if holding the fort proved untenable, and this now became the tricky part. Listening to Pillow's and Buckner's increasingly heated argument, Floyd vacillated first one way, then the other, before agreeing with Pillow to return his divisions to their original lines. For all intents and purposes this ended the Battle of Fort Donelson, except for several curious footnotes.

First was the behavior of Floyd and Pillow with respect to the inevitable surrender. Floyd was afraid that his previous indictment by the U.S. government—as well as the charges that he illegally transferred government arms to Southern arsenals while he was secretary of war—would land him in jail, or worse. And Pillow, for his part, had made such a boisterous habit of publically proclaiming "Give me liberty or give me death" that he was too chagrined to surrender lest he become a laughingstock. Therefore the two senior generals passed along the onerous duty of capitulation to their subordinate, Buckner, while they cravenly made their escapes by night to safety across the river.

Meantime, there was at least one Confederate officer at Fort Donelson who had no intention of capitulating, and that was Nathan Bedford Forrest, who declared, "I did not come here for the purpose of surrendering my command." With Buckner's acquiescence, Forrest and his cavalrymen waded all night through swamp water sometimes rump-high on their horses and by sunup had delivered themselves out of harm's way, taking along a number of infantry soldiers who felt likewise.

Finally it was Buckner's turn to perform his repugnant duty. He sent a letter to Grant alluding to his "present state of affairs" and asking for the appointment of commissioners to "agree upon the terms of capitulation," signing it, "Respectfully, your obedient servant, etc."

Awakened from his sleep by the arrival of this message, Grant sent a terse reply to his former friend and benefactor, stating, "No terms except an unconditional and immediate surrender can be accepted. I propose to move immediately upon your works." History has not recorded Buckner's personal reaction when he received this rude answer to his pointedly civil request—after all, it was the first surrender of an entire Confederate army. But if he expected Grant to let his men march out of Fort Donelson as the Confederates had when Fort Sumter capitulated the previous spring—under arms and with the Union flag flying to board their ships for home—he was sorely mistaken. Buckner sent Grant a grumbling response complaining about "the ungenerous and unchivalrous terms which you propose," then hauled down his flag and made himself a Union prisoner.

In the North, Grant became a hero almost overnight. When word got out about the "unconditional surrender" part of his reply to Buckner, he was heralded in the press as U. S. "Unconditional Surrender" Grant. Learning from newspaper reports that the general had been seen smoking a cigar during the height of the battle, people sent him cigars by the box load, and he thus began a habit that would eventually kill him. With Donelson out of the way, Grant was all for pushing on immediately to Nashville but, inexplicably, Halleck held him up. Nevertheless, in taking Donelson Grant had swept up an entire enemy army of 12,000 prisoners and inflicted some 2,000 casualties—at a cost of some 3,000 casualties of his own—and the capture of Fort Donelson was trumpeted as the first great victory for the Union.

For its part, the Confederacy's entire strategic plan had been set on its ear. From just west of the Cumberland Gap to the Mississippi, the Southern defensive front across Kentucky had collapsed, and with the fall of Nashville now imminent Johnston ordered it evacuated too. At least Nathan Bedford Forrest was there when he was most needed to try and bring order out of the chaos. While panicked mobs threatened to break into Confederate stores and warehouses, Forrest oversaw the loading and disposition of hundreds of wagons filled with munitions, food, and clothing, which were then put on railroad cars and headed toward Atlanta and other Southern cities. Likewise, Forrest had his men dismantle entire weapons factories and sent their precious machinery south to be reassembled. For a forty-year-old former slave trader and cotton farmer with no formal military schooling—in fact, little formal schooling at all—Forrest was already becoming a legend in the annals of cavalrymen. He worked his way up from private to general by dint of courage, ingenuity, and raw military horse sense, and it has been suggested, more than once, that if he had held higher command sooner—that, say, of an army—the war in the West may have had a different outcome.

Now that Johnston's Kentucky front had actually caved in, most of Tennessee would have to be abandoned as well and a new line established across the entire southern part of the state—gateway to the Confederate heartland of Louisiana, Mississippi, Alabama, Georgia, Florida, and the Carolinas, stretching more than three hundred miles from Chattanooga to Memphis and with one-quarter fewer troops to defend it—thanks to Grant and the fiasco of Fort Donelson.

CHAPTER FOUR

I Will Do the Best I Can

U. S. Grant became a public hero because of the conquest of Forts
Henry and Donelson, yet in the process he managed to get most
of his superiors angry at him, in particular Halleck, who suddenly perceived Grant's newfound popularity as a threat.

After all, while Grant had captured an entire Confederate army at
Donelson—the first significant Union victory of the war—the so-called
commander of the West had been seated squarely behind his desk in
St. Louis and receiving no credit for it—try as he might. To make
things worse, Halleck's impulse in the days that followed was to slow
Grant down by ordering him not to press on and take Nashville, which
was within easy reach. While the bewildered Grant felt duty-bound to
obey these orders, he saw nothing wrong with ordering the 12,500
men Buell had sent as reinforcements (when it appeared that a siege
would be needed to force Donelson's surrender) forward to capture
Nashville on their own—which they did, bloodlessly, a few days later.
This in turn caused Buell to become angry at Grant, too, because it
had been his ardent desire to ride into that important Southern city at
the head of his troops, and not have them ordered there under another
general.

Not only that, but Halleck also embarked on a campaign to discredit
Grant to Halleck's own boss, George McClellan, charging that Grant
had failed to communicate with him (Halleck) after taking Fort Donelson and had gone without permission to Nashville. He accused Grant
of "neglect and inefficiency," concluding, "It is hard to censure a suc-

cessful general immediately after a victory, but I think he richly deserves it." A few days later Halleck added a postscript. "A rumor has just reached me," he wrote, "that since the taking of Fort Donelson General Grant has resumed his former bad habits [the drinking]." McClellan, who possibly remembered Grant's insobriety a decade earlier in California, replied, "Do not hesitate to arrest him at once if the good of the service requires it."*

So now it seemed that everybody was mad at Grant—including the commanding general of the army—except for Abraham Lincoln, who recognized a winner when he saw one, and successfully submitted Grant's name to the Senate for confirmation as a major general of volunteers. Such was Grant's naïveté that in the midst of all this backstabbing, he wrote to his wife, "There are not two men in the United States who I would prefer serving under than Halleck and McClellan."

But Halleck had further ideas for Grant's undoing and relegated the new major general to the backwaters of Fort Donelson. Being anxious—as was Grant—to capitalize on the present disarray of the Confederate army, Halleck ordered an expedition of nearly 10,000 in fifty transport ships to proceed amphibiously along the Tennessee River, laying waste to bridges, railroads, telegraph lines, and other war-aiding communications and infrastructure; then to establish an advance base near the northern Mississippi border from which the entire army could operate. To lead this important mission Halleck selected one of Grant's division commanders, C. F. Smith, and though Grant respected, even loved, his old former West Point commandant of cadets, the humiliation of being grounded by Halleck actually brought him to tears. It was just one step above being relieved of command, and Grant wrote sadly to Halleck saying that he would resign, if it was in "the interests of the service."

Then fate played into Grant's hands without him knowing why at all. The unpleasant rumors about him and his drinking and "neglect" and "inefficiency" had finally reached Lincoln, who probably saw them for what they were and ordered Halleck, in effect, to "put up or shut up" regarding those charges. This alone must have given the general a start when another bombshell landed. Tiring of McClellan's unremitting pomposity and posturing at his command headquarters in

---

* As it turned out, a Confederate sympathizer or outright disloyal civilian telegraph operator at the relay station at Cairo had failed to deliver many of Grant's timely reports to Halleck. As to his drinking, there were those on his staff at that time who swore the rumors were untrue.

Washington, Lincoln ordered "Little Mac" to get out from behind his desk and go to the field to personally take charge of the Federal army in Virginia, which was supposed to be moving on Richmond.

With McClellan gone as general in chief of the Union army, Lincoln put Halleck in command of all the forces in the West, the very position he'd been angling for all along.

Now that he needed strong fighting generals—such as the one he'd just been trying to sabotage—Halleck immediately realized that, in particular, he needed to rehabilitate Grant. Accordingly, he informed the War Department (and, tacitly, Lincoln) that the problems with Grant had been the result of confusion and misunderstandings, all to the effect that Grant was now—and had been all along—an upstanding example of proper soldiering. To Grant himself, Halleck wrote unctuously, "You cannot be relieved from your command. There is no good reason for it. Instead of relieving you, I wish you as soon as your new army is in the field to assume the immediate command and lead it on to new victories."

As the glow of approval once again shined upon him, another quirk of fate now threw Grant into contact with the man who would ultimately become his closest confidant and best friend, within the army or without, William Tecumseh Sherman. In the months and years that followed, the two of them would be largely credited with winning the Civil War.

Yet Sherman arrived on the scene beneath a cloud worse than the one that Grant had just escaped from under, for it was widely believed that Sherman was "crazy." But crazy or not, Halleck ordered him to take a division of raw recruits up the Tennessee and join Smith in the destruction of Southern rails and bridges, following which, Grant believed, the Federal army would set up for a final showdown with the Confederates in the West.

Sherman was born February 8, 1820, in Lancaster, Ohio. His father, a prominent lawyer and state supreme court justice, died when Sherman was nine, leaving behind a wife, nine children, and a mountain of debt, and the family was forced to rely for subsistence on the kindness of friends and relatives. Accordingly, Sherman was parceled out to the wealthy Ewing family down the road and treated as one of their own. As a teenager Sherman grew into a tall, awkward redhead with a somewhat nervous disposition, whose foster father, Thomas Ewing—by now a United States senator—got him an appointment to the U.S. Military Academy in 1836 when he was only sixteen. At West Point, Sherman stood out as a model student, ranking high in the class of 1840. In his last year another Ohio boy entered the academy with the unlikely name of U. S. Grant and Sherman later claimed he was instrumental in bestowing upon him the nickname "Sam."

Sherman's first assignment was to the Seminole Wars in Florida, where the Indians were resisting their removal to Oklahoma along the Trail of Tears; from there he was posted to Savannah and Mobile, where, through the wealthy connections of his influential foster father, he mingled easily and well among the local gentry and developed an abiding fondness for the Southern people. But when the Mexican War broke out, instead of being ordered into battle, Sherman found himself relegated to supply duty in California, which galled him almost to distraction and nearly led to his resignation. He sailed around the Horn in the summer of 1846, stopping at Rio de Janeiro, where he went to the opera, and Valparaiso, Chile, which did not impress him, finally reaching Monterey, California, where he found the state in an uproar known as the Bear Flag Revolt, involving General Stephen Kearny and his recent boss, the Pathfinder, (then) Colonel John C. Frémont.

A further uproar was caused by the discovery of gold at the mill of German-born John Sutter, which touched off the California gold rush and, typically, Sherman found himself embroiled in all these zany events.* By then he was engaged to be wed to his foster sister Eleanor "Ellen" Ewing, who was four years his junior.† In 1850 he went back east long enough to marry her and, since her father had recently been named secretary of the interior, their wedding was attended by practically every political luminary of the day, including the president of the United States.

Because of the astonishing monetary inflation caused by the gold rush, Sherman had found that as a married man he could not survive in California on army pay, and requested, and received, orders posting him to billets in the eastern United States. Meantime, as he acquired a growing family, investors persuaded him to return to the West Coast not as a military officer but as president of a bank. Sherman accepted, resigning his commission, but, as in so many booming economies that

---

* By virtue of his West Point–acquired knowledge of minerals, Sherman was the first official to certify that the ore found at Sutter's Mill was in fact gold.

† Uncustomary as it is today, it was not unusual in the nineteenth century and earlier to marry within the same family—siblings excepted.

are based on a single, crucial feature, the California market went bust, and so did Sherman's bank. Finding himself back in Ohio with a family to support, he wound up, much to his chagrin, at his foster brother's law firm as a sort of glorified bill collector.*

This did not last long, however, for after applying for reinstatement in the army he learned from the (then) secretary of war, John Floyd, that a new military academy in Louisiana was looking for a superintendent and Sherman was soon appointed to the job, supervising fifty-six students at an annual salary of $3,500, at what would one day become Louisiana State University.

Sherman went to the campus near Baton Rouge alone, to organize the budding college, which at that point consisted of only some barracks-type buildings, an armory, and a few classrooms. He threw all his energies into making the school a model of excellence and got on famously with everyone involved with it, from the governor on down. On New Year's Day 1860, the Louisiana Seminary of Learning and Military Academy officially opened, but Sherman was increasingly disheartened as war loomed in the wake of the John Brown raid and its aftermath, the election of Lincoln, and the secession of South Carolina.

Sherman typified many Northern men of his day. Although his brother John Sherman, a lawyer, had risen to the U.S. Senate as a Republican and was considered an abolitionist, Sherman was pointedly not in that camp. "I would not, if I could," he told his foster brother Thomas Ewing, "abolish or modify slavery. Negroes in the great numbers that exist here [in Louisiana] must of necessity be slaves. All the congresses on earth cannot make the negro anything else but what he is. He must be subject to the white man, or he must amalgamate or be destroyed."† And again: "As to [the wrongness of] Slavery in the abstract and Slavery in the territories, I do not particularly take issue—but as to abolishing it in the South or turning loose 4 Millions of Slaves, I would have no hand in it."

However, Sherman, like Grant, was adamantly hostile to the very

---

* One day while on business in St. Louis, Sherman was walking down the street when he recognized the shambling figure of U. S. Grant approaching. He never could remember what the two of them spoke about except that "West Point and the regular army were not good schools for farmers [or] bankers."

† By "destroyed" Sherman apparently meant die out as a race. What Sherman meant by "amalgamate" is uncertain. The word has several meanings, among them "unite," "join together," "integrate." Or did he mean "intermarry"?

notion of secession. He considered the United States to be a single entity and that individual states could not simply make off with themselves without the express consent of the majority of states, and therein, of course, was the very grit of the argument. "On the question of secession I am an ultra. I believe in coercion and cannot comprehend how any Government can exist unless it defend its integrity. . . . However the question of the national integrity and slavery should be Kept distinct," he wrote to his brother, "for otherwise it will gradually become a war of Extermination without End."

To one of his instructors at the Louisiana military school, whom he considered a friend, Sherman warned: "You, you people of the South, believe there can be such a thing as peaceable secession. You don't know what you are doing. . . . The country will be drenched in blood. You mistake the people of the North. They are a peaceable people, but an earnest people and will fight too, and they are not going to let this country be destroyed without a mighty effort to save it. . . . The North can make a steam-engine, locomotive or railway car; hardly a yard of cloth or shoes can you make. You are rushing to war with one of the most powerful, ingeniously mechanical and determined people on earth—right at your doors. You are bound to fail."

Having delivered these harsh but prophetic words of wisdom, Sherman began preparing to extricate himself from Louisiana. At that point the state had not yet seceded, but he had no trouble seeing what was ahead and was determined to leave the academy in as proper shape as possible before he turned it over, tidying up books, paying the bills, writing memos. By early February 1861, as other Southern states began leaving the Union, Sherman felt his position in Louisiana was being compromised. In advance even of an ordinance of secession, the Louisiana governor suddenly ordered Federal forts seized and their arms distributed throughout the state. As a last straw for Sherman, some of these—rifles "still in their old familiar boxes, with the 'U.S' scratched off"—were delivered to him for safekeeping in the armory of his military academy. "Thus I was made the receiver of stolen goods," he said indignantly, and with that he turned in his resignation and headed north, up the Mississippi River.

Sherman wasn't sure what he was going to do next, but as late as mid-March 1861 he was fairly certain that "there would be no employment for me" in the national crisis and wrote that "I was extremely anxious about the future. It looked like the end of my career." Shortly after he

returned north, however, he was offered the presidency of the Fifth
Street Railroad, a mule-drawn streetcar service in St. Louis, but he had
no sooner accepted and moved his family to Missouri when events
overtook him. As state after Southern state left the Union, Lincoln was
content to sit back and await developments, and these were not long in
coming. When the president called for 75,000 volunteers supplied by
every state to put down the rebellion inspired by Beauregard's firing
on Fort Sumter, it was an almost unheard-of number of men, and the
reaction of Southern states that were expected to contribute to this
force showed precisely how far sectional feelings had deteriorated.

Here, Sherman's family political connections paid off. Within a few
days he was notified by his brother-in-law, Charles Ewing, that he had
been appointed colonel of the U.S. Thirteenth Infantry, and was to
report immediately to Washington, whose inhabitants were hysterically anticipating a Confederate attack at any moment. When this
failed to materialize, Sherman was put on inspection duty and within
three months was promoted to command an infantry brigade at the
Battle of Bull Run, where he turned in a creditable performance during the disgraceful Union defeat.

An example of Sherman's style of command is revealed by an amusing anecdote. As he was trying to reorganize his brigade after the
retreat from Bull Run, one of his officers, a lawyer, informed him that
he was returning to New York because his three-month term of enlistment had expired. Sherman, in the presence of a number of men, told
the officer, without flinching, "Captain, if you attempt to leave without
orders, it will be mutiny, and I will shoot you like a dog." Later that
afternoon Lincoln himself appeared in his carriage to help buck up
the troops. As he and Sherman were sitting in the carriage, the same
officer approached and said, "Mr. President, I have a cause of grievance. This morning I went to see Colonel Sherman, and he threatened
to shoot me."

"Threatened to shoot you?" Lincoln inquired. Then, looking at
Sherman, and then back to the man, the president said to him in a loud
stage whisper, "Well, if I were you, and he threatened to shoot, I would
not trust him. I believe he would do it!" The red-faced officer disappeared into the crowd to the tune of laughter by his fellow soldiers.

A month had barely passed after the debacle at Bull Run when
Sherman received yet another promotion. He was made a brigadier
general and selected to become second in command to General Robert
Anderson—the man who had endured the mortification of surrender-

ing Fort Sumter and who was now in charge of the Department of the Cumberland, which included Kentucky and Tennessee. Sherman arrived in Louisville amid a thoroughly confused state of affairs. Not only was the Kentucky legislature contemplating secession and Confederate officers raising troops from all over the state, but the Rebel general Albert Sidney Johnston was then occupying Bowling Green in the south, while General Felix Zollicoffer had entered in the east near the Cumberland Gap and General Leonidas Polk occupied Columbus, on the Mississippi River. Worse, it was reported that a Confederate force under Simon Buckner was moving on Union headquarters at Louisville itself.

It seemed to Anderson, and to Sherman when he got there, that everything bad was happening at once, and that they had not the troops in their command to prevent it. Anderson, aging and worn down by the ordeal at Fort Sumter, felt himself under an unbearable strain while Sherman was rushing around trying to put out fires. Then, according to Sherman, Anderson "said he could not stand the mental torture of his command any longer, and must go away, or it would kill him." Thus, scarcely a month after he arrived, Sherman found himself commanding the most volatile military department in the country, and the most critical as well, and this is where the assertion that he was crazy entered the picture.

As bad luck would have it, Secretary of War Simon Cameron had been on a fact-finding trip to the western theater* and decided to look in on Sherman at Louisville. At first Sherman said he was "delighted to have an opportunity to represent the true state of affairs," but then became wary when Cameron not only showed up with an entourage of newspaper reporters but insisted that they remain in the room while Sherman made his private assessment of the military situation.

At one point during the briefing Sherman offered his opinion that before the war was over it would take upwards of 200,000 Union soldiers to subdue the southerners in his sector, by which he meant the entire Mississippi Valley. This early in the war, such a prophecy naturally elicited "alarm" by the secretary of war, but nothing further was said about it during his visit and Sherman justifiably assumed that his opinion would be kept confidential.

It wasn't. Shortly afterward, Cameron asked U.S. Army adjutant

* It was as a result of this same fact-finding mission that Frémont was relieved and Halleck put in his place.

general Lorenzo Thomas—who had been at the meeting—to submit a memorandum of what was discussed, and in particular to address what he called Sherman's "insane" suggestion that 200,000 troops would be needed. According to Sherman's information, Cameron's communication was somehow leaked to the press, and within a week newspapers throughout the North were reporting that Sherman was "crazy, insane, mad," and that he had "demanded two hundred thousand men for the defense of Kentucky." Likewise, it was reported that an assistant secretary of war had muttered something about Sherman being "gone in the head, looney." By Sherman's own account his position became "unbearable," and, he remembered, "It is probable that I resented the cruel insult with language of intense feeling."

Sherman tried to straighten out the misunderstanding with his superiors—in particular with McClellan—but to no avail. Like Anderson before him, he began to feel the intense pressure of administering a department more than twice as large as the ones in Virginia and Missouri put together and with only one-tenth of the troops that the other two department commanders had. With all the talk of insanity, Sherman actually began to wonder about such things himself. After all, two close relatives had been placed in mental asylums and he even told his wife that he felt he might be going crazy. He had been in command at Louisville a little over a month when, on November 5, he wrote to McClellan asking to be relieved.

After returning from his restorative leave, Sherman was a different soldier altogether. He was ordered by Halleck to Paducah to organize Grant's supply lines during the battles of Forts Henry and Donelson. Like Grant, Sherman had experience in military supply from his California days, and Grant was profoundly grateful for his constant solicitations, which arrived along with each day's supply boat, offering to send down anything within reason that Grant might need: "surgeons, nurses, officers' wives, laundresses"—even himself, with the caveat that though he was senior to Grant in grade he would happily serve under him, no questions asked.

With Grant still at Fort Donelson, on the Cumberland, Sherman was given a fresh, reinforced division of about 9,000 men to go up the Tennessee and meet there with the rest of Grant's command, now under C. F. Smith. It was by now a formidable force consisting, in addition to Sherman, of the divisions of Stephen A. Hurlbut, Lew Wallace, John A. McClernand, and Benjamin M. Prentiss. Smith's division was now under the command of W. H. L. Wallace, owing to a freak accident so common to the times. Smith had scraped his leg on something rusty getting into one of the small boats and the wound turned septic. Modern medicine could have cured it easily, but within weeks the gallant old soldier would be dead of blood poisoning. At any rate Grant steamed deep into Tennessee to resume his command, which was now 42,000 strong, with Buell's army of 35,000 marching overland from Nashville to join them as swiftly as it could—enough combined, it was assumed, to overwhelm anything the disorganized Confederates might throw at them.

With Sherman's division spearheading the invasion, the expedition began disembarking in mid-March 1862 at a small steamboat wharf called Pittsburg Landing that would gain terrible immortality under a new name: Shiloh.

Grant rejoined his army on March 17, making his headquarters in the mansion of a Union sympathizer near the village of Savannah, on the Tennessee River, about six miles north of Pittsburg Landing. There, under strict orders from Halleck, he would wait for Buell to arrive and in the meanwhile put his army through drilling exercises. He had given no instructions for them to fortify their positions because, as he said later, he thought fortifications were a demoralizing factor—especially for the newer troops, whom he feared would then become reluctant to fight out in the open if the situation required it. At first, Sherman didn't like it, and he confidentially told newspaper reporters, "We are in great danger here," but as the days went by, and except for a few cavalry patrols the Confederates showed no intention of coming out from their lair in Corinth, Sherman's worries began to vanish.

In his mansion at Savannah, Grant paced and smoked his cigars and waited for Buell, confident not only that his army was safe from harm but that any upcoming battle with the Confederates would be easier than the victory he had just presided over at Fort Donelson. In the mornings he would take a steamboat south to Pittsburg Landing to watch the men drill. Intelligence indicated that the Confederates were gathering men to defend Corinth—rumors had placed their numbers as high as 150,000—but Grant put little stock in this. After all, he had seen Albert Sidney Johnston's Rebels retreat almost without a fight all across Kentucky and Tennessee and now down into Mississippi, and saw no reason to believe they would behave differently now.

In this he was mistaken.

Johnston was gathering a force at Corinth, but not to defend it. He was planning nothing less than a battle of annihilation and, as things were shaping up, he might just have the wherewithal to pull it off.

The alarming reversals in the West had finally shaken Jefferson Davis from his delusion of contesting every inch of Southern soil. It simply could not be done and now, with an entire Yankee army poised to invade his home state, Davis concluded to meet desperate times with desperate measures. He stripped the Gulf Coast of its defenses, consisting primarily of 10,000 Confederate soldiers under Braxton Bragg, who was headquartered at Mobile. Also ordered up to Corinth were the 5,000 troops at New Orleans under General Daniel Ruggles, who had been in position to defend the South's largest and most important city. Next he directed Bishop Polk to take 10,000 of the men he had evacuated from Columbus, Kentucky, and head south for Corinth on the double, even though that would leave precious little to impede a Federal advance straight down the Mississippi River. Finally, the 15,000 troops across the river in Arkansas under Earl Van Dorn— who had just lost the Battle of Elkhorn Tavern—were ordered to move to the ferries at Memphis and pile on the boxcars for Corinth, even though that meant uncovering the state of Arkansas to the Union army.

If all went as planned, when combined with Johnston's 15,000 who were retreating from Bowling Green ahead of Buell's army, burning bridges as they went, it would give the southerners an army of 55,000 men—enough, it was believed, to whip Grant's 42,000 and then turn on Buell's 35,000 and whip them, too, provided the Union commanders didn't link up first—and even if they did 55,000 southerners against 77,000 Yanks weren't bad odds, all things considered, or so it was believed in Richmond. Still, it was a dangerous gamble, and failure could have dire, even fatal consequences. This would be the Confederacy's first great roll of the dice, though there would be many more before the war ended.

Until Johnston arrived, the man in charge at Corinth was the Creole general Pierre Gustave Toutant Beauregard, who had made it one of his military callings to commit to memory Jomini's *The Art of War* and who became convinced that he had found the perfect prospect for a Confederate victory. As Beauregard saw it, with the exception of Lew Wallace's division posted about three miles north, Grant's army languished at Pittsburg Landing, confined between its seventy-five-foot-high bluffs along the river and surrounded elsewhere by deep murky creeks and swamps; this was an army without fortifications, without patrols, just sitting there, drilling and housekeeping and waiting for

Buell to show up. Hit them now and hit them hard, Beauregard reasoned, and their destruction was at hand.

Johnston, still in overall command, agreed with Beauregard in principle but wanted to wait until all his troops arrived, most especially the 15,000 under Van Dorn, who—though Johnston could not know it—didn't receive his order to join him until March 25, six days after it had been sent. Van Dorn hurried by himself across the river and met with Johnston and Beauregard at Corinth and assured them he would do everything possible to cross his army into Mississippi, but in the end it proved not enough, due in part to insufficient shipping. Fearing that Grant was about to turn west and attack undefended Memphis or that Buell might soon rendezvous his forces with Grant's, Johnston decided to fall on Grant immediately, concluding that surprise and Southern ferocity would overcome the absence of Van Dorn's force.

On Thursday night, April 3, 1862, the Rebel army set out from Corinth, twenty miles to the southwest, intending to launch the attack by midmorning the next day, but things quickly began to go wrong. A terrific wave of thunderstorms and the resulting mud slowed the column's advance; wagon roads became clogged; artillery bogged down; regiments got lost, whole divisions got lost—even guides got lost—and when all was said and done it was Sunday, April 6, when the Confederates were finally in place to begin their assault.

At least the rain had stopped and by Saturday evening the skies were clear and the stars shone hard and bright. The weather had warmed from the previous week and a Southern springtime was in the air. Oaks were tasseling and there were the beginnings of green shoots on other trees, but the woods were still bare except for the flowering of dogwoods and redbuds. In an open clover field a peach orchard was in full pink bloom. Grant's men were a western army, boys from Iowa and Indiana, Ohio and Illinois. Back home it was planting time across the broad, grain-rich plains that soon would wave in oats and wheat and corn enough to feed the entire Union population. For the Southern boys, who slept fitfully beside their rifles in the thickets and woods that night, it was planting time, too, but there wasn't much to boast about now. In days gone by the cotton, tobacco, and sugarcane would have gone in after the last freeze, but not this year. Because of the war and the Federal blockade it would rot in the fields or on the wharfs, and though the government in Richmond had pleaded for farmers to grow produce that would help the war effort not everyone did, for nobody yet knew quite what to expect.

.   .   .

During the time between the Rebel army's departure from Corinth and its arrival at Pittsburg Landing, Beauregard began to argue against the attack, having convinced himself that the delays not only had cost the Confederates the element of surprise, but that Buell had probably come up in the meantime to make the Yankee army over 70,000 strong, but the Creole general was wrong. Grant was still alone.

The forwardmost Federal force—consisting of Sherman's division—was in fact reporting Rebel activity in its front, but the reports were not credited by headquarters. One Union colonel sent back word that there were Confederates in his front "as thick as fleas on a dogs back," but no one at headquarters seemed concerned.

After breakfast on Sunday morning Sherman himself rode up to find out what the fuss was about and immediately saw his orderly get shot dead off his horse right next to him. "About 8 a.m.," Sherman recalled, "I saw the glistening bayonets of heavy masses of infantry to our left front in the woods beyond the small stream . . . and became satisfied for the first time that the enemy designed a determined attack on our whole camp."

Some of Sherman's regiments simply ran off across the hills and fields toward the river; others tried to stand up against the onslaught but finally caved in and fled too; still others rallied behind Sherman and other officers and put in a more determined resistance. But by 10 a.m. the Confederates had worked their way around Sherman's positions and got their artillery firing into his rear, at which point the whole force gave way. McClernand had come up with his own division, and so had Prentiss, but both were appalled by the power of the Confederate charge and slowly gave way. Sherman rallied what was left of two of his brigades and his artillery next to a little wood-planked Methodist chapel, where he had made his headquarters. It was named Shiloh, a Hebrew word meaning "place of peace."

On the Rebels came, overrunning Union positions and on many occasions stopping to eat the still-warm breakfasts of Yankee soldiers who had fled, since they themselves had long since devoured their own rations on what was supposed to have been a one-day march. That delay, plus the very speed of their attack, caused many Confederate regiments to become as entangled as the brush and brambles they were charging through, and soon the fighting broke down into scores of smaller battles within the whole.

By this time Sherman had been twice wounded and had three horses shot from under him; a bullet had grazed his hand, which he wrapped in a handkerchief, and another ripped off his shoulder strap, but when a courier from headquarters arrived to ask about the situation the Ohioan simply replied, "Tell General Grant if he has any men to spare I can use them. If not, I will do the best I can."

About this time Grant himself appeared on the field. He, too, had been having his Sunday breakfast at the mansion at Savannah when he heard the uproar to the south and ordered a steamboat to carry him there posthaste. On the way, he slowed down at Crump's Landing long enough to yell to Lew Wallace to get his division prepared to march immediately, and then he proceeded toward the sound of the guns.

During the same thunderstorm that had deluged the Confederates two nights earlier, Grant's horse had slipped in mud and landed on top of his ankle, which left him walking on a crutch and unable to mount without help. Now, with the crutch strapped to his saddle, Grant debarked at Pittsburg Landing dismayed at the seemingly endless line of stragglers and fugitives retreating from the fight to safety beneath the tall bluffs along the river. The situation was clearly critical, but Grant somehow managed to remain calm where other men might have faltered. He rode into the eye of the battle to each of his division commanders and to some, such as Prentiss, another "political general" who was fairly new to the game, he gave orders—"maintain your position at all hazards"—and to others—Sherman in particular—he simply indicated for them to do the best they could.

Although they were winning, the Confederates were faced with a different, but no less difficult, prospect: the confusion that results from an army outstripping its objectives. To sort this out, Johnston and Beauregard told all four corps commanders to align themselves in a southeast-to-northwest axis and to continue pushing the Yankees toward the river and the swamps.

In fact, the Federals had been pushed back to within less than a mile of the river along a line anchored in the south by a peach orchard and on the north by a particularly vicious clump of brambles that the Confederates dubbed the Hornet's Nest, connected, roughly, by a half mile or so of an old wagon rut known as the Sunken Road. To clear the Hornet's Nest, Daniel Ruggles, the old Rebel general from New Orleans, dragged up sixty-two cannons and proceeded to blast the Union soldiers out of their positions and back toward the bluffs and the river, killing in the process General W. H. L. Wallace, whose division quickly joined the rest in flight.

Down at the Peach Orchard things were not going quite as well for the attackers. The fighting was so heavy and the day had become so hot that soldiers from both sides, including many wounded, found sustenance at a small body of water in a clearing just next to a copse of woods. As the afternoon wore on this became known as the Bloody Pond, where both Yankees and Rebels filled their canteens and washed and tended their wounds, adhering to an unspoken pact not to fire on each other.

Successive charges on the Peach Orchard finally dislodged the Yankee defenders, but not before a Confederate tragedy occurred. Seeing that his officers were having difficulty getting their soldiers to rush yet again into that deadly tumult, Albert Sidney Johnston rode among them, shouting, "I will lead you! I will lead you," and did just that, returning to the cheers of his finally victorious men, his uniform torn by bullet holes, including one in his boot. It seemed a slight wound at first but suddenly he began to collapse in his saddle, and when he was helped to the shelter of a ravine to discover the reason, it was found that a minié ball had severed an artery just behind the knee and that he was rapidly bleeding to death. Tennessee governor Isham Harris, who had fled the capital at Nashville when Union forces arrived, was serving as Johnston's aide-de-camp. He tried to stem the flow of blood but within a few minutes the commanding general of the Confederate Department of the West was dead.

By then it was midafternoon and command devolved to Beauregard, who ordered the fighting to go on with renewed fury. So far the Confederates had pushed the Federals out of the Hornet's Nest, the Peach Orchard, and finally, as the afternoon sun began to wane, from the Sunken Road as well. In that last action the Rebel attack was so fast and furious that it completely surrounded Prentiss's division, and its commander was forced to surrender what was left of the nearly 6,000 men he had started the day with, as well as all his artillery. With Sherman's, McClernand's, Hurlbut's, and H. W. L. Wallace's divisions pushed back nearly to the Tennessee River, and Prentiss surrendered with his 2,200 survivors, all that was left, it seemed, was one final, concerted, slashing bayonet charge by the whole Confederate force and Beauregard would have had Grant's army bag and baggage. But it did not turn out that way.

Like the Federals, the Confederates were exhausted, used up by the exertion and constant horror of a full day's battle that had begun at sunrise and hadn't let up, even at sundown, and the Rebel charges became feebler because of casualties and straggling. In the gathering darkness Beauregard figured it was enough for today. He was content that his army had sent Grant's men reeling with their backs to the river, captured two score of their guns, and took as prisoners the remnants of an entire Union division, including its commander. There would be time enough tomorrow to finish off the job.

Beauregard's greatest fear at this point was that Grant's army might escape on the steamboats during the night; what he did not know, however, though he ought to have anticipated or at least suspected it, was that Buell's army had finally appeared, and with it the salvation of Grant. As well, Lew Wallace, whom Grant had shouted at from his steamboat as it passed Crump's Point that morning, had at long last arrived with his fresh division, after spending most of the day floundering around lost in the Tennessee River swamps.

Grant had given over his field headquarters for a hospital and spent the night under a tree down by the bluffs in a driving rainstorm that had come up from the west, heartened no doubt as Buell's troops— some 20,000 of them by daybreak—arrived by ferry from across the river.

Just across the way, Beauregard's men slept next to their rifles and the bodies of the dead of both sides, which, it was said, now covered the battleground so thickly a man could walk across it using them as stepping-stones. But the general remained confident that sunrise would see the destruction of the Yankee invaders. Just before going to sleep, he telegraphed Richmond that the fighting had ended in "a complete victory, driving the enemy from every position." When dawn finally came, however, the noise of battle resumed not from the Confederates, who were still awaiting orders, but from their enemies. Grant's army was coming on.

The startled Confederates at first gave way as the Yankee brigades recaptured places now memorialized in histories of the Civil War: the Peach Orchard, the Hornet's Nest, Bloody Pond, the Sunken Road. But the Rebel disorganization soon was rectified and just before the blueclads reached the Shiloh chapel, now serving as Beauregard's headquarters instead of Sherman's, Confederate artillery began to blast away at the oncoming Federals and the lines of Rebel infantry began to murder the Union ranks with rifle fire.

By midafternoon both sides were again worn out and Beauregard had to face the reality that Buell's men were now arriving in force. There was no choice, he said afterward, but to order the army back into the fortifications of Corinth. For their part, the Federals had had enough as well; having retaken their camps and what was left of their possessions, the fight was out of them. All, that is, except Sherman, who, as revenge for his humiliation the previous day, decided to give chase. He might as well not have bothered because he was about to be taught a lesson by a man who knew how to teach them well.

On Tuesday, April 8, the day after the major fighting had ended, Sherman took most of his division and a regiment of cavalry to see if further damage could be done to the Confederates, who had been retreating all night in a violent sleet storm that had turned the weather icy again. All he found along the Corinth road were Rebel hospital tents filled with the dead and dying and those too injured to be moved. About six miles out Sherman encountered a Rebel encampment at an old logging site that had been clear-cut and, seeing gray-clad cavalry milling around inside it, ordered an attack. An infantry regiment was sent out as skirmishers, flanked by the cavalry regiment, while a brigade marched up behind. If Sherman had known who was inside the Rebel camp, he might have had second thoughts, or at least proceeded more cautiously, because the man in charge of the Rebel cavalry troop was Nathan Bedford Forrest.

Instead of doing the prudent thing and galloping off, Forrest ordered his three hundred troopers to charge directly at Sherman's oncoming soldiers, who numbered at least several thousand. At this audacious performance, Sherman's skirmishers threw down their rifles and ran away, followed by the cavalry regiment, as Forrest's men tore into them. Sherman quickly found himself in the position of a man who has cornered a beast in the woods, only to find that it is meaner than he is. Known for his almost unimaginable personal courage and daring, Forrest had galloped so hard that at first he did not realize he had outraced his own men, and suddenly he found himself alone among the disorganized but still dangerous enemy, who closed in, shouting, "Kill him! Kill him!" With saber in one hand and blazing pistol in the other, his horse rearing and plunging, Forrest demonically lashed out until one bluecoat pushed the barrel of his rifle against Forrest's side and pulled the trigger, sending a bullet tearing into his back. Enraged, Forrest reached down and snatched one of his tormentors by the collar and hoisted him up behind him on the horse; then, employing this startled passenger as a shield, he galloped through the tumult of gunfire and bayonets back to his own lines, where he unceremoniously dumped the amazed enemy soldier to the ground.*

* Surprisingly, while Forrest's wound was painful it was not disabling.

After that, Sherman, too, decided he had had enough and the Battle of Fallen Timbers became the final engagement of the Shiloh campaign. The American public, North and South, was shocked, then outraged, as news of the deadly struggle became known. Approximately 20,000 men had been killed and wounded—in about equal numbers for each side. Moreover, the Union had lost nearly 3,000 captured and the Confederates some 1,000. Nothing like it had ever happened before in the Western Hemisphere; indeed, more men fell at Shiloh— and most of them on one day—than the entire number of American dead and wounded during the Revolutionary War, the War of 1812, and the Mexican War combined. Based on the conduct of the Confederates at Forts Henry and Donelson, and their flight from Kentucky and Tennessee, Grant, like so many others, had convinced himself that victory in a single great battle would cause the Confederacy to dissolve. However, after Shiloh he reached the conclusion that the only way to restore the Union was the total subjugation of the South.

CHAPTER FIVE

The Anaconda Squeezes

E ven though Grant had saved the army at Shiloh and driven the
Confederates from the field, it seemed now that practically *every-one* was mad at him, including the general public, which had so
recently proclaimed him a great Union hero after the Fort Donelson
victory.

News reports of the fighting published in Northern papers, alongside the horrendous casualty lists, began to accuse Grant of allowing
his army to have been "completely surprised" by the Rebel attack; that
men in blue had been bayoneted to death while sleeping in their tents;
that Grant had so little control of his troops most of them ran off at the
first signs of battle; that Grant had been dallying in a mansion far away
when he should have been with his army seeing to it that his men were
protected and alert against a surprise attack; that he had been saved
only by the miraculous arrival of Buell at the last moment; that he was
negligent in not pursuing and destroying an enemy army after it was
clearly in retreat.

Worse, soon came the usual charges of drunkenness, incompetence,
and sloth; references were made to his unmilitary bearing, of carelessness and indifference to his soldiers. Ohio even sent down its lieutenant governor, who reported back to the Cincinnati *Commercial
Appeal* that there existed in Grant's army "an intense feeling of indignation against Generals Grant and Prentiss, and the general feeling
amongst the most intelligent men with whom I conversed, is that they
ought to be court-martialed and shot."

Grant was denounced from the halls of Congress to the White
House as a hopeless and inept blunderer and alcoholic, and a chorus
arose for his removal. The buck, as always, stopped with Lincoln. Popular lore has it that he told the critics: "Find out what kind of whiskey
Grant drinks and send a barrel of it to my other generals." There is no
direct evidence that he actually said this, but there is evidence that he
responded: "I can't spare this man. He fights."

The furor, however, nearly unhinged Sherman. In a volcanic letter
to the Ohio lieutenant governor, Benjamin Stanton, Sherman stopped
just short of challenging him to a duel. In a point-by-point refutation,
Sherman accused Stanton of prefering "camp stories to authentic data
then within your reach," and "circulating libels and falsehoods," and
concluded that Stanton had deliberately sought to undermine the
morale of the entire United States Army.

Sherman reserved his most pungent scorn, however, for the
reporters and their editors, whom, he claimed in a letter to his wife,
"are the chief cause of this unhappy war—they fan the flames of local
hatred, and keep alive those prejudices which have forced friends into
opposing hostile ranks. In the North the people have been made to
believe that those of the South are horrid barbarians, unworthy of
Christian burials, whilst at the South the people have been made to
believe that we wanted to steal their negros, rob them of their property,
pollute their families [an allusion to miscegenation], and to reduce the
whites below the level of their own negros.

"If the newspapers are to be our government," he wrote, "I would
prefer Bragg, Beauregard . . . or any other high Confederate officer
instead." "The American press," he complained to his brother Senator
John Sherman, "is a shame and a reproach to a civilized people. When
a man is too lazy to work & too cowardly to steal he turns Editor &
manufactures public opinion."

Without mentioning McClernand by name, Sherman reserved a
special loathing for those reporters who he believed attached themselves for pay to particular high-ranking officers in return for giving
them favorable mention in news stories. Of these, Sherman wrote,
"My rule is now well understood, and they keep clear of me. If one
comes into my camp, I will arrest him as a spy & have him tried by
court-martial & if possible shot or hung."

In the midst of this uproar, Halleck arrived to personally assume command of the army, or, more precisely, three armies—Grant's, Buell's, and
another belonging to the newly promoted major general John Pope,

presently expected to arrive at Shiloh. This would give Halleck a total of 120,000 men with two hundred guns divided into four corps, commanded by Buell, Pope, McClernand, and Major General George H. Thomas, a forty-five-year-old Virginian and West Point graduate who had sided with the Union and whom his men called "Pap." Grant, however, received nothing for his troubles during the Battle of Shiloh, except perhaps a demotion—at least he viewed it that way—to become Halleck's second in command, a position that, considering Halleck's egomaniacal personality, amounted to little more than a sinecure. Grant rarely complained, but Sherman could see that his old friend plainly "felt the indignity, if not the insult, heaped upon him."

When Grant finally did protest, Halleck slapped him down, saying, "For the last three months I have done everything in my power to ward off the attacks which were made upon you. If you believe me your friend you will not require explanations; if not, explanations on my part would be of little avail." This was mostly a gratuitous falsehood, but in Halleck's favor Sherman did recall that when Lincoln had demanded a reason for the shocking casualty rate at Shiloh, Halleck at least did not lay the blame on Grant, but instead placed it on "the Confederate generals and their soldiers."

Meantime, on Friday, April 4—the same stormy night that Union and Confederate soldiers had experienced the day before Shiloh—some 150 miles to the northwest, one of Commodore Foote's Federal ironclads, the *Carondelet,* pushed off quietly from its berth three miles above a low-lying island smack in the middle of the Mississippi River. This was Island Number 10, so marked on navigation charts because it was the tenth such river island in a chain beginning at the mouth of the Ohio.

When the Confederates evacuated Columbus, Kentucky, after the fall of Fort Donelson, they planned to make a stand at Island Number 10, which was fast becoming the South's last, best hope to control the Mississippi from southern Kentucky all the way down to Vicksburg— a three-hundred-mile-long stretch that included the critically important city of Memphis.

On February 28, two weeks after the surrender of Fort Donelson, a small army under Brigadier General John Pope, a forty-year-old West Pointer with strong connections to the Republican Party as well as to the Lincoln family, began a march southward from Commerce, Missouri, to New Madrid, Missouri, taking ten days to cover the approximately seventy miles. New Madrid was across from and a couple of miles north of Island Number 10, where the river curves in a reverse S bend like a sidewinder rattlesnake in motion.

When he got there, Pope received a much ruder reception than he'd reckoned on. Upon the evacuation of Columbus, there had been 17,000 Confederate troops on hand, as well as sixty pieces of artillery, many of them of large caliber. But during Johnston's withdrawal from Kentucky a few weeks earlier Beauregard, in temporary command, began stripping the Western Department of any troops he could find to meet the impending crisis that was building up with the Yankee army now before Corinth. Therefore he had ordered the "fighting bishop" Polk to bring 10,000 Confederate soldiers from Columbus to the Corinth fortifications, and send only 7,000 down to defend New Madrid and Island Number 10, taking with them all the big guns. Thus Pope had figured that taking Island Number 10 was going to be a cinch.

Leaving the island so poorly defended was a damned-if-you-do, damned-if-you-don't choice for the Confederates, but Beauregard reasoned that if his army could defeat the Yankees at Corinth, and the forces he had left at Island Number 10 could merely hold on, then the Rebel armies would sweep northward and drive the Yankees one and all before them to the Ohio River and beyond.

It was in this setting that Pope encountered the Confederates in early March, snug in their fortifications at New Madrid. What he saw he did not like. First, the Mississippi was in its springtime flood, which had inundated much of the countryside. Second, the enemy lines were surrounded by marshes and protected in their rear by the river. Third, his intelligence had not been able to discover the strength of the Rebel garrison, which, in fact, totaled 1,400 men and fourteen guns. Fourth, a small flotilla of wooden Confederate gunboats had arrived to support the defense.

The first thing Pope did was order a "reconnaissance in force," which amounted to an attack by 7,000 troops. This was almost immediately called off when the blue-clad soldiers came under a withering fire from both the New Madrid guns and those of the little Rebel gunboats, which, because of the high condition of the river, could blast the countryside for more than a mile in any direction. Now Pope did what he thought was the prudent thing and settled in for a siege.

He ordered large-caliber siege guns, which soon arrived from St. Louis; as well, Halleck began sending him more men until toward the end his army had grown to about 30,000. He captured the little hamlet of Point Pleasant, downriver from New Madrid, from which his artillery could drive off any Confederate attempt to supply Island Number 10 by water. Finally, he asked for, and received, the aid of Commodore Foote's fleet of seven large ironclads, towing ten odd-looking mortar boats, which could each lob a 13-inch projectile more than a mile.

Having watched this formidable buildup, the Confederate commanders agreed that New Madrid was untenable, and under cover of a horrendous rainstorm they evacuated their soldiers to Island Number 10 on the night of March 13. Two days later the siege began in earnest, when Foote anchored the mortar boats, sixty feet long by twenty feet wide, just out of range of the Rebel guns and began a round-the-clock bombardment of Island Number 10. This noisy business continued for two weeks, without observable effect, while Pope became vexed nearly to distraction by the lack of cooperation from Foote's big ironclads, which lay at anchor out of danger, doing nothing.

Pope had devised a scheme for the undoing of Island Number 10 by sending a large body of his men across the river below the island near Point Pleasant; once on the Tennessee side, they would be able to completely cut off supply lines to the besieged enemy outpost. Trouble was, at least one of the ironclads needed to get below the island to blow the little Confederate flotilla out of the water so that Pope's troops could cross unimpeded. Then it would be just a matter of time.

Yet Foote would not hear of it. In the navy, then as now, loss of a ship—especially something so large as an ironclad—was a very serious matter, one that would be examined by boards and even courts-martial, so that blame could be laid. In the navy, careers were made or broken by such choices, and Foote wasn't ready to stick his neck out. After examining the situation, he concluded that trying to pass the large Confederate batteries that bristled along Island Number 10 and the Kentucky and Tennessee shore would subject his ships to almost certain destruction. Almost as bad was the prospect that one or more of his ironclads would be disabled by enemy fire and—unlike operations at Forts Henry and Donelson where the rivers ran northward— the boat and its crew would be swept helplessly southward by the flood current, right into the waiting arms of the Rebels. Possibly the commodore's decision was also clouded by his physical condition; the wounded foot he had received during the Battle of Fort Donelson had not healed and showed no signs of doing so, and he could scarcely move from his berth aboard the flagship.

The army therefore loitered in inert frustration, punctuated only by a continuous booming from the mortar boats, until Pope finally asked Halleck to solve the problem, which he did, by asking Foote if there was not some way to find willing volunteers to run the gauntlet below. Foote called a war council of his captains and, of the seven, all said the task was impossible—but one. He was Commander Henry Walke, the man who had led the navy flotilla during Grant's attack at Belmont, and Foote told him to get ready.

The preparations took four days. First Foote put fifty volunteers from an Illinois regiment into boats that, with muffled oars, sneaked up to a Confederate battery of eleven big guns on the Kentucky side of the river and discovered to their relief that high water had led to the position being manned only for fire missions. The Yankee infantrymen gleefully spiked what guns they could and heaved others from their mounts, rendering the battery unserviceable for the time being. Then, the next day, April 1, every mortar boat in the fleet concentrated fire on a large Rebel floating battery anchored at the northern tip of Island Number 10. The fire was so intense that the defenders cut the moorings and let the battery drift downstream, where it became harmless.

Walke had been busy preparing his ship, *Carondelet,* for the dangerous passage. He heaped every piece of iron he could scrounge onto the portside top decks, including huge lengths of anchor chain that he wound around the pilothouse. His engineers rerouted the steam that normally escaped from the smokestacks back to the paddle-wheel housing to avoid the *puff-puff* noise of the ship. Toward dusk on the day of the effort, he took on a company of riflemen to protect against a boarding attempt and, as well, the entire crew was armed with cutlasses, pistols, pikes, and hot-steam hoses connected to the boilers. At 8 p.m., under cover of a fortuitous thunderstorm, Walke steamed down the river, stopping after about a mile to pick up a coal barge packed with bales of hay that he lashed on to protect the vulnerable side of the vessel.

Carondelet came quietly and steadily through the murky night—obscured by the storm from moonshine but frequently lit up by flashes of lightning. On her bows was an experienced river pilot, taking soundings and relaying them back to the pilothouse. All was going just according to plan, and it was even hoped by some aboard that the ironclad might just slip by the Confederate batteries sight unseen, when the unexpected happened, as it often does.

In rerouting the exhaust line from the smokestacks, the soot from the boiler fires that were normally dampened by the escaping steam suddenly caught fire, shooting up a continuous blaze of flames five feet high from both stacks. This peculiar phenomenon caught the Rebels' attention, and immediately illumination rockets began bursting above the river. At this, Walke ordered full steam ahead, and *Carondelet* shot forward. According to an observer, "vivid flashes of lightning lit up the hurried preparations of the rebels," who were scurrying to their guns, "while peal after peal of thunder reverberated along the river, and the rain poured down in torrents." Now all the Confederate batteries within range were firing, causing the shoreline to burst into an orange sheet of flame. From his place in the bows, the river pilot stood "in a perfect shower of cannon balls and musket balls," as he tried to discern the course by dropping lead lines or make out banks or shoals in the lightning flashes.

For all their efforts, the Rebels' long, difficult fortifying of Island Number 10 had come to naught. A reporter from the *St. Louis Dispatch* recorded that "the judgment which we were able to form from the shrieking of their shot, was that they flew from five yards to thirty yards over our heads." This was because Walke had decided that rather than do the expected—which was to steer the boat way over to the Missouri side of the river—he would hug close in to the Kentucky-Tennessee shore, and to Island Number 10, where the Confederate batteries—being located on high bluffs—would have to depress their guns to get at him. Thus they overshot, and thus Pope had his ironclad down below, which made quick work of the Confederate wooden flotilla, chasing it downstream and out of the action.

Now, according to plan, Pope ferried his army across the river, while the Confederates, acknowledging that their situation was hopeless, began evacuating Island Number 10 and its environs. Pope caught up with them a few miles south at the little town of Tiptonville—just as Grant was fighting for his life at Shiloh—and bagged what he claimed was the whole force of 7,000 Rebels. Some historians discount this and place the actual figure at a little more than half that (the remainder having escaped through the swamps), but, in any case, Pope enhanced his reputation and earned a fine new promotion that dramatically revealed how overrated he was.

When Island Number 10 fell, Pope was told to bring practically all his army to Pittsburg Landing to join Halleck in the movement against Corinth, leaving Foote and the navy with only a few regiments of infantry to deal with Rebel defenses along the river, the immediate prize of course being Memphis. On April 13 Foote's fleet had reached Fort Pillow, a Rebel bastion named after the Confederate general who had disgraced himself at Fort Donelson, which was well fortified with long-range, heavy artillery. As at Island Number 10, the ailing commodore was content to stand off and bombard the position until some better plan for its reduction took shape in his mind—and this he did for more than a week, when momentous news reached him.

After a tedious struggle that had begun six months earlier, the Union navy had captured its greatest prize yet in the war: New Orleans.

With a population of about 170,000, New Orleans was not only the Confederacy's largest city, it was larger than the rest of the South's major cities combined and had been a major commercial hub for the Southern states. By the eve of the Civil War it accounted for nearly a third of the nation's exports, including some 2.2 million bales of cotton, as well as rice, timber, sugar, and other commodities and goods, finished or unfinished. But by late 1861 much of the trade had vanished, due to the drying up of commerce with the states of the Midwest and to the Federal blockade patrolling the mouth of the Mississippi. Actually, the river had several major "mouths," and numerous smaller ones, as it drained through the ponderous, marsh-choked delta into the Gulf of Mexico. While the Union navy was able to close some of these outlets, it was never able to completely shut them off, and therein lay the Yankees' need to take and hold New Orleans, where all river traffic must pass before it reaches the channels and swamps below.

Conventional wisdom in Washington, however, held that taking New Orleans by sea—that is, by the deep-draft, blue-water navy—was not feasible, first because the fleet's largest warships would be unable to cross over the many shoals and bars at the Gulf passes, and, second, even if they could, two formidable obstacles lay in their way. These were Confederate Forts St. Philip and Jackson, situated across from each other about seventy miles downriver, brandishing a total of 126 big guns between them, all commanding the approaches from downriver. Unfortunately for the Confederates—and the hapless New Orleanians—the authorities in Richmond for once concurred with Washington.

As a stopgap measure to plug the hole, in the autumn of 1861 the Union navy patrolling off the various river passes concluded that if it could get a squadron of large ships up the river about fifteen miles to what was known as Head of Passes, it could cut down considerably on blockade running, since all large boats and ships would have to pass through there to reach the Gulf outlets. Accordingly, on October 3, 1861, four U.S. warships—aided by information provided them by local oysterers and fishermen—managed (barely) to scrape across the bar of Southwest Pass and stationed themselves in fairly deep water to await any enemy craft seeking to exit the river.

They found few or none, but a week later, in the inky early morning hours of October 11, this large and powerful Federal flotilla received an unwelcome surprise. At 3:30 a.m. Captain John "Honest John" Pope (no relation to General Pope of Island Number 10 fame) was awakened in his cabin aboard the flagship *Richmond*—a brand-new 225-foot-long, twenty-two-gun, 2,600-ton steam screw sloop—by a sailor crying, "Captain, there's a steamer alongside of us!" Pope rushed topside to find what he later described as "an indescribable object" approaching his ship. This turned out to be the *Manassas*, a Confederate ram hastily fashioned out of an old tugboat and covered with iron boiler-plate variously said to look like "a sharp-pointed egg," "an eggplant," a "potato," or a "turtleback."

The Rebel vessel shivered *Richmond*'s timbers with a mighty blow but, as luck would have it, had not struck the ship proper but instead a coal barge moored alongside. Panic, however, prevailed upon the *Richmond* and Captain Pope signaled his other three ships: "Enemy present. Get under way," while his guns began firing broadsides into the blackness in all directions. The Confederate arrangement had been that once *Manassas* had struck and disabled *Richmond,* she would fire off a rocket that would launch the main attack. This consisted of towing three fire rafts toward the Yankee ships, which would be followed by five converted river tow boats armed with various calibers of guns and which would begin blasting away at the lit-up targets. Unfortunately the fire rafts drifted away, as did the *Richmond* and the *Preble,* which had dropped their anchor cables in their haste to "get under way" and were now caught in the four-knot current without enough steam to steer, promptly running fast aground on a sandbar. The other two Federal ships, *Vincennes* and *Water Witch,* managed to flee over the bar and into the Gulf as the Union navy debated whether or not to scuttle the remaining vessels, while the ragtag Rebel flotilla smugly retired, marking the end of that phase of the Union effort to blockade the Mississippi.

Not long after this disgraceful episode, an ambitious Yankee navy commander named David Dixon Porter thought he had arrived at a way to get big ships into the river and past the formidable defenses of Forts Jackson and St. Philip and up to New Orleans itself. His plan was this: it was already proven, or so he thought, that if the tides were right deep-draft naval warships could be gotten over the sandbars and shoals of the Southwest Pass. Once into the river, if a fleet of mortar boats could be constructed, they could move up within range of the two Rebel bastions. Theoretically, by bombarding around the clock from a range of a mile or so, each day the mortar boats could lob upwards of three thousand explosive shells—weighing 250 pounds apiece—into the Rebel forts, blasting them into oblivion within forty-eight hours while the rest of the fleet waited out of danger. Then, Porter informed the secretary of the navy, New Orleans would be theirs for the taking.

It all sounded good to Gideon Welles because capturing New Orleans would be by far the most important action so far in the war, and he immediately ordered work to begin on twenty-one of the mortar craft. The question then became who would lead such an expedition, since it was obvious that Porter, as a mere commander, did not have the rank. Porter had a solution to that, too; he offered up his foster brother, Captain David Glasgow Farragut, a sixty-year-old salt who had served in the War of 1812 and who was presently languishing on a navy retirement board at the Brooklyn Navy Yard. Stunned and delighted to be snatched out of mothballs, Farragut energetically began to assemble his fleet, which was formidable: two steam frigates—the largest in the navy—five steam screw sloops, a dozen gunboats, plus the twenty-one mortar boats, as well as various tenders, towers, and barges—243 guns in all—in fact, the largest American war fleet ever assembled.

In addition, for operations against New Orleans proper, Farragut would have some 18,000 infantrymen under General Benjamin Butler of Boston, another of the political generals, who had raised his own army in New England and was now impatiently waiting for orders on Ship Island, an isolated sand dune in the Mississippi Sound twenty-five miles south of Biloxi.

There were delays and foul-ups, to be sure; critical supplies and munitions were missing, there were Rebel snipers to contend with, and the crucial element of surprise was lost when it was discovered that shifting sands had reduced the depth from twenty to sixteen feet and the bigger ships had to be scraped inch by inch across the bar, losing two weeks of time. As if all this wasn't bad enough, unbeknownst to Farragut, he was being stabbed in the back by, of all people, his foster brother David Dixon Porter, who had recommended him to lead the expedition in the first place.*

When Porter first concocted the plan to seize New Orleans and took it to the Navy Department, he knew that he would not be appointed to lead it himself. His actions thereafter suggest an almost diabolical scheme to set Farragut up as a straw man by first recommending him to lead the assault, then knocking him down with surreptitious communications to his bosses in order to obtain command for himself. Accordingly, just as the New Orleans operation was getting started, Porter wrote the assistant secretary of the navy disparaging Farragut's abilities, concluding that "men of his age in a seafaring life are not fit for important enterprises, they lack the vigor of youth. He [Farragut] talks very much at random at times and rather underrates the difficulties before him without fairly comprehending them."

Whatever impression this ugly letter had, by April 14, 1862, five months after Porter had laid out his original plan, Farragut—the knife still sticking from his back—was coming up the Mississippi, ready or not.

Both the citizens of New Orleans and the Confederate authorities there greeted these developments with mounting alarm. Things had seemed relatively secure only six months earlier when the little River Defense Fleet repulsed the big Yankee warships at Head of the Passes—so much so that in Richmond it was perceived that the real danger to the city would come from above, from those Union ironclads that had been constructed along the Ohio River. In desperation, the Confederacy had begun building four ironclads of its own, two at New Orleans and two at Memphis, each designed to be more powerful than those of the Federals.

* In addition to Farragut, Porter's lineage included his father, David, a hero of the War of 1812; an infamous brother, William "Dirty Bill" Porter, also a naval officer; and a cousin, Major General Fitz John Porter, who was cashiered from the army in disgrace after the second Battle of Bull Run. In his famous diary, Gideon Welles tended to tar them all with the same brush, describing David Dixon thusly: "Like all the Porters, he is a courageous, daring, troublesome, reckless officer." And again: "He [is] . . . not over-scrupulous [in] ambition, is impressed with and boastful of his own powers, [and] given to exaggeration in relation to himself—a Porter infirmity."

But then came Shiloh, draining away most of the manpower that had been assembled to protect New Orleans. Not only that, but as the Yankee war machine ground down the river toward New Madrid and Island Number 10, most of the hastily assembled River Defense Fleet was sent north to operate against it. Now that the Federals were into the Mississippi in force, authorities in New Orleans urgently wanted their small flotilla back, but in a perfect example of the squeaky wheel getting greased the Confederate secretary of the navy refused. The boats that had been built in New Orleans to defend New Orleans, he decreed, needed to stay above Memphis, for the enemy was already there, and Forts Jackson and St. Philip would simply have to hold their own against the Union armada.

Ever since the war opened, New Orleanians had been told that the forts were impregnable; that their big guns were more than a match for any wooden warships the Union could throw at them; that land defense batteries up and down the river would blast the enemy to splinters; that a rebel army was on hand to repel any Yankees who ventured ashore. But now that the hour was at hand things were looking much chancier. The new commander of Confederate forces at New Orleans wasn't so confident either.

He was Major General Mansfield Lovell, a thirty-nine-year-old West Point quasi-Yankee from the District of Columbia whose prior occupation had been deputy street commissioner of New York City and who, with everyone else, had recently turned out for the funeral cortege of Albert Sidney Johnston as it wound through the streets of New Orleans toward a marble crypt. Lovell had been dealt a cruel hand for a newly arrived commander, because Grant's army—now Halleck's—was inching toward Corinth, and there would be no bringing back of the thousands of soldiers from New Orleans who had been sent northward against the Federals at Shiloh.

Laying that aside, Lovell set about strengthening Forts Jackson and St. Philip, improving their overhead casements against plunging bombardment, positioning shore or "water batteries," stocking rations and ammunition, installing more than one hundred pieces of artillery, and beefing up their compliments to more than a thousand to serve the guns. After consulting with his commanders, Lovell ordered what everyone hoped would be the saving feature of the fortifications: a raft, or boom, across the river, held up by large floating cypress logs, that would cause the Federal ships to stop or at least slow them down so that Rebel guns could blow them into eternity.

Only now did the Confederate authorities seem to come to grips with the age of steam-powered warships, when in fact steam power had been prevalent for several decades. Fort St. Philip had been around since the days of the French, but after the Battle of New Orleans during the War of 1812, Andrew Jackson recommended rebuilding it, as well as another bastion, Fort Jackson, on the west bank opposite. Designed on Vauban's pentagon model, by the time they were completed during the 1820s the forts presented formidable obstacles indeed, for in those days an enemy would have come in slow sailing ships, subject to fickle winds and currents that provided gunners an excellent opportunity to sink them. But in the age of the modern steam engine all had changed. Now warships could ascend the river at will against winds and currents, presenting hard-to-hit moving targets, especially at night.

Thus a boom across the river seemed the only answer, and work on it had begun in March, but a spate of spring storms sent the river rushing down higher than ever and with more than the usual content of "deadheads"—large trees uprooted by erosion for hundreds of miles along the riverbanks above—that hung up in the boom until it broke. Another boom was hastily built, this one held up by the hulks of old sailing vessels. In addition, a number of fire rafts were constructed, set to be released upon the Union fleet when it approached the forts. Moreover, one of the two big ironclads in the works at New Orleans was readied to be sent downriver in case of emergency, even though its engines did not work. That being done, the Confederates and the citizens of New Orleans anxiously awaited what would happen next. They did not have long to wait.

By April 15, the beginning of Holy Week, the first of Farragut's ships began arriving at a point just south of the forts and two days later his mortar boats were anchored along the west bank behind a large stand of forest that the Confederates negligently had forgotten to cut down. Two days later Farragut opened the bombardment at a range of about a half a mile from Fort Jackson and somewhat longer for St. Philip. It took a while for the mortar boats to function as designed, because the crews were new and untried, and the same was true of the Confederate gunners. But by the next day, Good Friday, both sides had improved and a perfect duel began, with hundreds, and then thousands, of the massive projectiles striking the forts, dislodging guns, threatening to set powder magazines afire, and killing and wounding a few men. For the most part, the Confederates simply huddled beneath their heavy overhead casements to ride out the storm and fired their guns from beneath these shelters. A few mortar boats were hit, but little damage was done.

Also, on the day that the bombardment began, Rebel soldiers were observed making repairs on the boom and, after sending up a night reconnaissance party for a firsthand look, Farragut devised a plan to break it. On the night of April 19, during a tremendous thunderstorm and furious shelling by the mortars, two of the smaller Union gunboats sneaked up to the cable. An engineer from one of them attached an explosive charge connected by two electrical wires. The idea was that the boat would then be allowed to drift downstream, and when a safe distance was reached, the wires would be stuck together to produce the explosion. Unfortunately, an ill wind blew the boat away too fast and the wires broke. Another party from the second gunboat approached the problem in a more conventional manner. Yankee sailors got aboard one of the hulks and went at the cable with hammers and chisels, and within half an hour the boom parted. The Confederates caught on to this only after the damage had been done, and despite heavy firing the Federal gunboats got away.

For the next two days the bombarding went on but, to Farragut's supreme displeasure, no appreciable damage was done to the forts, which continued to return fire obstinately and in kind. Finally he could stand it no longer and, despite Porter's protests to the contrary, on Easter Sunday Farragut declared that all the mortaring had not produced the desired effect and that his fleet would run the gauntlet before the enemy could repair the boom.

Because of unfavorable downriver winds that would have slowed the ships, Farragut waited until the early morning hours of the twenty-fourth to launch his assault. Then, at 2 a.m., his fleet shipped anchor and headed upriver, into they knew not quite what, but when Farragut's clerk, a man named Osborn, optimistically predicted that they would lose "not more than a hundred men" the expedition commander responded darkly, "I wish I could think so."

At first, everything went even better than "according to plan." Farragut had arranged his seventeen-ship fleet into three divisions, intended to be spaced about a quarter mile apart. The testy old captain had planned to lead the first division himself, until his staff talked him out of it on the grounds that if he were killed or wounded the movement might fall into disarray, and so he led the second division in his flagship, *Hartford*.

Preparations had begun several days earlier. The big ships were smeared with mud as camouflage and their decks painted white to reflect whatever starlight there was for easier navigation; powder, shells, and shot were piled by each gun; and the grisly practice of sprinkling the decks with sand to keep the gun crews from slipping in blood was completed. The 2 a.m. castoff of the first division was not flawless; the twenty-two-gun *Pensacola* could not free up her anchor and delayed the start by an hour while the other ships milled around in the stream. The assembly, however, went totally undetected by the Confederates, who at the least should have had lookouts posted close to the shores to give warning, and the entire first division passed through the open part of the boom before being spotted. Even then, the alarm was sounded not by the Rebel lookouts but by the Federals themselves, when Porter had every one of his twenty mortar boats open up on Fort Jackson, as well as blast away at the Confederate water batteries that were located below the forts.

A major aspect of the Rebel defense plan had been to unleash a torrent of burning fire rafts that were expected not only to illuminate the Federal ships but, it was hoped, to set at least some of them on fire. But for some reason this did not materialize as planned, and only a few of the rafts went downstream.

However, the Confederates did manage to set off huge bonfires of cordwood and driftwood laid along the banks, which provided some lighting for their gunners, whose artillery was trained on the area around the boom. By 3:45 the six ships of the first division not only had reached the cut in the boom but were through it when this storm of shot and shell smashed into them, splintering masts, spars, and superstructure, dismounting guns, crushing topside timbers, and killing and wounding sailors.

By then the Rebels' scraped-up "mosquito fleet" went into action, including the egg-shaped ram *Manassas*. It consisted of eight aging river steamers and tugs that had been jury-rigged with pieces of iron to give some slight protection; some carried bow rams and a few medium-heavy guns. They weren't much to stand up to Farragut's ships (24 guns to 374) but apparently the thinking was they might serve to slow them down enough for the big guns from the forts to do real damage. In any case, when the alarm first sounded the Confederate fleet sallied out to meet the enemy in one of the most desperate and unequal naval battles of the Civil War. The experience of the Confederate gunboat *Governor Moore* provides an example.

The *Moore,* named after the governor of Louisiana, had already tangled with three of Farragut's big ships, and most of the ninety-three-man crew had been killed or wounded, including half of those on deck serving the guns. However, the commander, a former U.S. Navy officer named Beverly Kennon, was determined to fight on. He had only two guns, both 32-pounder rifles, one astern and one on the bow, and with these he launched an attack on the Federal twenty-two-gun *Varuna,* manning the bow gun himself. His first shot riddled *Varuna*'s decks, killing and wounding a dozen men, and then, with his own gun knocked off its mounts, Kennon backed off, took a broadside from *Varuna* that "swept his decks of nearly every living object," and plowed into *Varuna*'s starboard side, crushing her planking and ribs. *Varuna* then fired another round of shot at point-blank range into *Governor Moore* and, with seventy-four of his crew now either killed or wounded, the plucky Rebel skipper headed toward shore to abandon ship. *Varuna,* meantime, staggered away downstream, where it ignominiously sank in mud.

"I ordered the wounded to be placed in a boat," Kennon said, "and all men who could, to save themselves by swimming to the shore and hiding themselves in the marshes. I remained to set the ship on fire" (to keep her from falling into the hands of the enemy). Then he scrambled on deck to save himself, "but found wounded with no one left to take care of them, I remained and lowered a boat, and got through just in time to be made prisoner. The wounded were afterwards attended to by the surgeons of the *Oneida* and *Eureka.*"

Lit up by the illumination fires on the riverbanks and the lightning-like flashes of artillery-shell explosions, ferocious little battles like these ranged up and down the river for the better part of an hour and a half in the area of the forts. A few of the fire rafts got into action, flaming mast-high and pushed by the tugs. One of these, the CSS *Mosher,* saw *Hartford* enter the gap in the boom and began nudging its flaming pyre toward Farragut's flagship. *Hartford*'s helmsman tried to evade the fire but in the process promptly ran his ship aground, with her bowsprit stuck out over the Louisiana marshes. *Mosher* shoved the raft against *Hartford*'s side, prompting Farragut to cry out, "My God, is it going to end this way?"

Flames were scorching *Hartford*'s decks and licking up toward her masts as her gunners poured shot and shell into *Mosher* and Farragut's clerk began dropping twenty-pound artillery shells down into the burning raft. When they exploded they blew out the fire, but the big warship was badly burned and a number of sailors singed. Still, *Hartford* was able to back out of the mud and rejoin the fight, which continued unabated until around sunrise amid great clouds of gun smoke and the booming of more than five hundred big guns that produced a continuous flashing and racketing that reminded one sailor of "a vision of hell," while to the crusty old admiral himself, "It was as if the artillery of Heaven were playing on earth."

Most of the Confederate boats were sunk, crippled, abandoned, or run aground. The *Manassas* was left a flaming hulk that floated downriver past the anchored mortar fleet. The little *McRae,* however, refused to give up, according to the commander of the Rebel riverine forces, Colonel Edward Higgins, who watched her continue the battle alone. "At daylight," Higgins said, "I observed the *McRae,* gallantly fighting at terrible odds, contending at close quarters with two of the enemy's powerful ships. Her gallant commander, Lieutenant Thomas Huger, fell during the conflict, severely, but I trust not mortally, wounded."

A little after that it was all over. The smoke that had lain over the river like a deep Louisiana fog was soon peeled away on a fresh spring breeze, revealing that most of Farragut's fleet was now above the forts and the big danger had passed. Missing were *Varuna,* which had been sunk downriver; *Itasca,* disabled by a shot in her boiler, failed to make it through the boom, and *Kennebec,* which got tangled up in it and couldn't move; *Winona,* last in line, had tried to get by just after daylight but was turned back when fierce fire from the forts threatened to sink her.

Several theories of naval warfare had been dispelled that morning, most notably Porter's notion that a heavy bombardment by large mortars would reduce any fortification to ruins in a matter of days. The forts were indeed heavily wrecked, but the damage to Farragut's fleet was testimony enough that they could continue to function— especially during daylight, when the *Winona* quickly found the going too hot to handle. Another maxim that called for rethinking on both sides was the concept that wooden ships could never force passage between heavily reinforced modern land batteries.

Searching for a reason, Jefferson Davis proclaimed that it was only because Farragut had made his move at night, instead of in the daytime, reinforcing his opinion with a statement from the Confederate commander on the scene, who declared that "except for the cover afforded by the obscurity of darkness, I shall always remain satisfied that the enemy would never have succeeded in passing Forts Jackson and St. Philip." That was true as far as it went but raises a cardinal rule of military warfare, which is: always expect the unexpected.

Why the Confederates allowed the broken boom to go unrepaired remains a mystery. Large as the gap was, any cursory inspection would have revealed the cut. With a powerful enemy fleet just below, it would seem to be negligence of the highest order, yet no one was ever charged. Likewise, the use of underwater torpedoes (what are now called mines) was well established by then, and it would seem that such obstacles would have been of immeasurable value in conjunction with the boom. None were laid, however, possibly owing to the fast-rushing current at that point and the constant influx of debris and deadheads that flooded the river. Who can tell the results if the Rebels had placed a number of these destructive devices right within the gap the Federal navy had cut in the boom?

Farragut had his fleet reassembled that morning at a point six miles above the forts called Quarantine Station. There he took stock and began cleanup and repairs. Thirty-seven sailors lay dead and 147 were being tended by the surgeons. While this was going on, crews washed the mud camouflage from the topsides, decks were cleared of debris and swept clean, and shell holes were hastily covered and the fleet made as shipshape as possible for the next item on the agenda, which was New Orleans itself. The infantry force of 10,000 under Butler had followed in shallow-draft transports through the bayous and would march into New Orleans within the week, but Farragut's fleet, with its powerful guns, would reach the city first.

After daybreak on April 25, the sounds of heavy cannonading wafted up toward the city from Chalmette, where Farragut's ships were easily knocking out the last Rebel shore batteries. By midmorning, angry cries and curses rang out from atop the great city levee as the tall masts of the Yankee fleet were seen coming upriver. Early editions of the newspapers had carried headlines touting GLORIOUS NEWS FROM THE FORTS, before the awful truth was learned. The day was gloomy, overcast with rain, and the mood of the people matched the weather.

As soon as the news of the Yankee passing of the forts reached New Orleans, the citizens burst into a frantic uproar. The city had known this kind of anxiety five decades earlier when it came under attack by a large British army and naval force during the War of 1812. In the final superb action of that conflict, a determined defense by a ragamuffin force of Louisianans and backwoodsmen from Tennessee and Kentucky led by Andrew Jackson had destroyed a 10,000-man British professional army on the plains of Chalmette, and the great British war fleet had been turned back by the guns of Fort St. Philip. At the time, it was the stuff of which legends are made, but that was then and this was half a century later.

Now, as Farragut's ships began rounding Slaughterhouse Bend, the sight of their black silhouettes sent a shudder of fright and indignation through the beleaguered and defenseless city. Women wept and men shook their fists and brandished pistols and shotguns. The levee was choked with agitated mobs burning cotton by the hundreds of bales, and dumping into the Mississippi barrels of rice, sugar, molasses, and everything else in the warehouses along the wharfs that might be of use to the Yankees, including—in what must have been painful for some to watch—casks of whiskey, wine, and rum.

There was little else they could do. They had sent their soldiers away to whip the Yankees at Shiloh, only to have them defeated; they had counted on the forts to make them safe, but these, too, had failed. The River Defense Fleet that had been constructed for their protection had been sent up to Memphis. Their last hope had been the powerful ironclads *Louisiana* and *Mississippi,* but almost at this very moment *Louisiana* was floating down the river seventy miles to the south, a burning hulk scuttled by her own crew, and now, to their astonishment and dismay, came the *Mississippi* before their very eyes, cast adrift in flames to save her from capture. Nothing was left save wrath and despair as "the crowds on the levee howled and screamed with rage."

The Rebel commander, Lovell, had clearly seen the end once Farragut had gotten past the forts and he evacuated his few remaining troops so that the civilian authorities could declare New Orleans an open city. This, it was to be hoped, would deprive the Yankees of any moral excuse to bombard the town into a pile of bricks and rubble. Farragut's ships were lying right off the crowded levee when the admiral demanded a surrender. What he got instead was defiance.

Two of his officers, bold men if ever there were, rowed in, braving epithets from the mob, and marched up to the City Hall, where they presented Farragut's terms to the mayor. These included a formal declaration of surrender as well as the order to replace the Confederate flag with the Stars and Stripes atop all public buildings.

But the mayor, presumably speaking for his people, rebuffed them.

As to a document of surrender, he told the two Federal officers, "This satisfaction you cannot obtain at our hands." He went on to say in his reply to Farragut that "this city is without the means of defense [against the] overpowering armament before it," and, therefore, to acknowledge a formal surrender would be "an idle and unmeaning ceremony." So far as replacing the Confederate flag was concerned, the mayor rose on his highest political horse, declaring, "I could not find in my entire constituency so wretched and desperate a renegade as would dare to profane the sacred emblem of our aspirations," adding that merely occupying New Orleans "does not transfer allegiance from the government of [the citizens'] choice to one which they have deliberately repudiated."

Farragut digested this news with equanimity; to him, merely having possession of the largest and most commercially important city in the Confederacy was satisfaction enough. Next day, a Sunday, he ordered that services be conducted on the open decks on each of his ships, hoping it might help defuse some of the hostility. If that were so, it was short-lived, for any day now General Butler and his 10,000 Yankees would arrive in New Orleans to take over.

As this event transpired, Commodore Foote was still stewing above Memphis while his ships lobbed shells into Fort Pillow. He was elated by the news of the fall of New Orleans, but his physical condition from the wound at Fort Donelson had only grown worse. Finally he asked to be replaced, and Washington granted the request by placing in charge Commodore Charles Henry Davis, a fifty-five-year-old Boston Brahmin who, until now, had been strictly a saltwater sailor.

Davis had no better idea than Foote did about how to get at Fort Pillow, except to wait for the return of the Federal infantry to storm the position. Meantime, the best he could do was continue Foote's practice of stationing a mortar boat a mile or two downriver to toss shells into the fortification at half-hour intervals. That vessel was guarded by one of the large ironclads, which rotated the duty with the other six that waited about three miles above at a spot in the river known as Plum Point Bend. This week it happened to be the *Cincinnati*'s turn when, on May 10, the unexpected again became the reality.

At the same time that Foote was preparing remarks for his departure ceremony a council of war was being held at Memphis among the captains of the Confederate River Defense Fleet. It had been sent up from New Orleans a month earlier before it was apparent that the real dan-

ger to the city lay not from Foote but from Farragut below. Now that
this bitter fact had revealed itself, the question weighing heavily on the
mind of Captain James E. Montgomery, the Rebel commander, was
what to do next.

None of the options was pretty. Sixty miles to the north, gathered
near Fort Pillow, sat the enemy—seven huge ironclads, as well as the
mortar boats and various tenders and support vessels, all fresh off their
victories at Forts Henry and Donelson and Island Number 10. To the
south was Farragut's armada of oceangoing steam warships, working its
way north after conquering New Orleans. If Vicksburg fell, or if Farragut's fleet somehow got past it, the eight scantily clad and armed Confederate rams would likely find themselves in the unenviable position of
having to fight both enemy fleets at once, with predictable results.

The one thing Montgomery and his Rebel skippers had in their
favor was surprise. If Foote's (now Davis's) fleet began steaming south,
Rebel scouts at Fort Pillow and along the river would be able to sound
the warning, while the Yankees enjoyed no such intelligence system
along the riverbanks. A vote was taken, and the decision was, quite literally, to sink or swim.

At 7 a.m. on May 10, a Union sailor who had been holystoning decks
aboard *Cincinnati* began hollering that there were eight Rebel steamboats coming around the bend, bearing straight down on them from a
mile away. Clearly Montgomery had achieved his surprise. *Cincinnati*
was roped to trees alongside the riverbank while most of her crew
enjoyed a leisurely Saturday morning, drinking coffee, washing
clothes, and preparing for inspection. Her steam was so far down she
hadn't the power to hold herself in the current or even turn her wheel
when the alarm was first sounded. Gun crews rushed to their stations
as general quarters was called but—with the exception of the engineers down below who were throwing oil and everything else burnable
into her fires—the men aboard *Cincinnati* could only wait and watch
with dismay as the Rebel steamers bore in on them at full speed, great
plumes of black smoke billowing from their stacks and pushing ten-
foot-tall waves—or "bones in their teeth"—at the bows.

These were the so-called cottonclads, though each was also protected by whatever scrap iron and tin their skippers had managed to
scrounge—the "General's Fleet," some called it, as most of the boats
were named after Southern generals. Leading the pack was the *General Bragg,* described by one participant as "a powerful Gulf steamer,
built full in the bow and standing up twenty feet above the surface of
the river."

When the Rebel ram was scarcely fifty yards off, *Cincinnati* loosed a blast from her starboard battery that sent cotton bales and splinters flying into the air, but on *Bragg* came until she struck *Cincinnati* a glancing blow with her cast-iron prow that produced "a fearful crash," tearing a hole twelve feet long and six feet deep in the Union ironclad, flooding her magazine and "knocking down everything from one end of the boat to the other." This was indeed a mighty collision but, unfortunately for the *Bragg,* she was left with her iron beak stuck securely in *Cincinnati*'s topsides, whereupon the Federal gunners unleashed another broadside that blew *Bragg* out and away and "tore an immense hole in her from side to side," according to an Ohio newspaper reporter who claimed to have been aboard the Union ship.

The elation of the Yankee gun crew was palpable but momentary, owing to the sudden appearance of the *Sumter,* which "under a full head of steam, then struck *Cincinnati* in the fantail, cutting into her three feet, destroying her rudders and steering apparatus and letting the water pour into the hull of the boat." Next in line came the *General Lovell,* which smashed into *Cincinnati*'s port quarter, and holed there too. That settled it, in more ways than one, as *Cincinnati* began to sink to the bottom—which, fortunately for her, was only wheelhouse deep. Her survivors scrambled to the top deck, only to be met by a hail of bullets from *Sumter*'s Rebel sharpshooters, who brought down a considerable number of them, including the captain, who was shot in the mouth.

Meantime, racket from the battle had rumbled back upriver and while the Yankee fleet scrambled to get into the action it, too, was caught with its steam down and came into the battle disjointedly, with *Mound City* well ahead of the pack. As soon as she rounded the bend, *Mound City* found herself face-to-face with the *General Van Dorn,* which plowed into her almost head-on, forcing her to make for the bank, where she sank ingloriously stern-first into the Mississippi mud.

Next to arrive was the USS *Benton,* which came into the fray like a bear beset by hornets. Sailors stranded on the sunk Yankee ships gawked at the spectacle through the thickening gun smoke "like so many turkeys on a corn-crib," while *Benton*'s pilot put her helm so hard over that she began spinning around in midstream like a revolving door, blasting alternately with her forward, side, and stern batteries of 9-inch Dahlgrens at the fierce little Confederate rams. As other ships of the Yankee fleet began to appear, Montgomery decided that enough good work had been done for one day and hoisted the signal to retire beneath the guns of Fort Pillow. Davis was relieved to let them go unmolested while he contemplated the significance of the morning's events; with two of his most powerful ships sitting on the bottom, it was clearly a defeat for the Union navy.*

Commodore Davis was still trying to adjust to the import of the bold Rebel attack when a few days afterward he was bewildered by another surprise. One afternoon while his fleet lay at anchor off Plum Point, six peculiar-looking vessels of war, flying the Stars and Stripes, appeared from upriver, steamed past his ships, and anchored off to themselves without so much as a hello. Confederate scouts along the riverbanks had seen the boats earlier but thought they were some kind of trans-ports. When a gig was sent over to investigate, Davis was even more perplexed to learn that this little flotilla was commanded by, of all things, an *army* lieutenant colonel named Alfred Ellet.

Presently, the officer in charge of this new force arrived with three more of the strange craft and introduced himself to Davis as Colonel Charles Ellet, brother of Lieutenant Colonel Alfred Ellet, and carrying papers from the War Department signed by Secretary of War Edwin Stanton authorizing him to conduct naval operations against the enemy "with the concurrence" of the senior naval officer present. Here was a weird animal indeed, a navy run by the army—and not only that, but apparently by an army of Ellets as well, six of them in all: cousins, brothers, nephews, etc., who commanded most of the boats.

These, of course, were the elusive Ellet rams, earlier alluded to, the concept for which had initially been rejected by both the army and the navy before finally being taken on as an army project, supervised by its creator, Colonel Charles Ellet, with the express blessing of Stanton himself. The crews were a hodgepodge of volunteers from infantry regiments and civilian riverboat men who not only received the going rate for seamen's wages, which was much higher than equivalent mili-tary pay, but also were in line for bonuses akin to the old custom of prize money for each Rebel craft sunk or captured.

Ellet's initial meeting with Davis did not go well. The commodore was vaguely aware that some plan for adding rams to his fleet was in the works, but he had not understood the nature of the relationship.

---

* In fact it was the worst defeat that a Federal fleet took during the entire war, but to his superiors in Washington Davis put an entirely different face on it. He informed Navy Secretary Welles that a great Union victory had been won, with three enemy gun-boats destroyed—which was untrue, since all were quickly repaired—and that he was left holding the field, or, more precisely, the stream, which was true far as it went except that a third of his force had been outclassed by the Rebel boats.

Now, however, he was confronted by an audacious army colonel who wanted the navy's cooperation for an immediate joint attack on the Confederate fleet at Fort Pillow, or Memphis, or wherever they were. Davis, who had just tangled with this bunch, insisted it was impractical, not only because it would bring the Union warships under the guns of Fort Pillow but—as Foote had argued earlier at Island Number 10—should any of his valuable ironclads be damaged, they might well be swept downriver into the hands of the enemy.

Since Ellet's charge from the War Department had been to secure the concurrence of the senior naval officer on hand, he asked Davis if it would be all right for his rams to give it a try. Though Davis considered such a mission suicidal (and privately confided that the rams "were not worth much"), the commodore agreed, oddly, to "concur" but not to "cooperate," and with that Ellet departed to make his preparations for engaging the Confederate navy.

His task was not without its trials. First, in addition to the regular scuttlebutt about dangers from the fort and the Rebel gunboats, the river men also got wind that the Confederates were hard at work building two large ironclads of their own at Memphis. This was true enough so far as it went. Work was indeed being pushed forward at the Memphis docks on the *Arkansas* and the *Tennessee,* a pair of 165-foot behemoths armed with columbiads, Dahlgrens, and long-range 6-inch rifles, but they were far from completed. Nevertheless, some of Ellet's jittery civilian crewmen asked for their pay and departed, causing temporary delays.

After reshuffling his personnel to suit these developments, Ellet prepared his attack for June 5 but, as a precaution, sent his brother Alfred ahead the night before in a light yawl to reconnoiter the fort and its environs. After drawing near to Pillow in the early morning hours, Alfred noticed no visible activity and, on closer inspection, found to his astonishment that it had been abandoned. Accordingly, he had his men row over to shore and land, while he personally "planted the national colors upon the ruins of one of the magazines and sat down to await the coming of daylight and the rams."

The situation was likewise at Fort Randolph, a much smaller Confederate installation some twelve miles farther south, which was also found deserted. By now the whole Federal fleet had been alerted and Davis got up steam on his ironclads, following Ellet and his rams down the winding river course toward Memphis, another grand prize in the winning of the West.

CHAPTER SIX

Mississippians Don't Know, and Refuse to Learn, How to Surrender

Until the war came Vicksburg and its genteel environs were like a land in a storybook. Passengers aboard steamboats plying the Mississippi could look with awe and envy upon broad lawns and green pastures surrounding the elegant mansions that lined both sides of the river. Beginning in early spring the white blossoms of apple, peach, pear, and citrus trees perfumed the air and by midsummer an ocean of white cotton boles stretched as far as the eye could see. On Sundays, along the great River road, which was shaded by magnolias and moss-draped oaks, fashionable carriages carried families for visits to nearby plantations or other outings, accompanied by men on thoroughbreds dressed in stylish suits with velvet trim and wearing felt or beaver top hats.

In the town itself, Saturday nights were a time for formal dances in stately homes that lined the gas-lit streets along the bluffs, while on Sunday afternoons after church, picnics were held beneath the oak, sycamore, walnut, and dogwood trees that topped the scores of grass-covered hills surrounding the city. In the town park, a smartly dressed militia company might be conducting marching drills, while out at the racecourse dandies and their ladies cheered the action.

On weekdays the city was a hive of commerce, its wharfs crowded with steamboats up from the Gulf states and down from the Great Lakes unloading passengers, foodstuffs, machinery, furniture, barrels of whiskey, and manufactured goods. On fancier passenger craft there

was often lively music from a steam calliope, and occasionally a show-
boat would arrive, accompanied by a brass band and performing acts.
And then there was the cotton; there was always the cotton, arriving in
five-hundred-pound bales from the interior, some by mule wagon,
some by rail, some by smaller riverboats on nearby streams emptying
into the Mississippi. Black stevedores hauled it to the boats and
stowed it in the holds; bale after bale, there was always the cotton. Of
course, it hadn't always been that way.

Like all cities, Vicksburg emerged from humble beginnings and was
especially typical of the way important river ports developed in the
cotton states. It was located on the cutbank side of the Mississippi,
where the river doubles back on itself in a 180-degree horseshoe bend
nearly half a mile across. The fast current in the horseshoe had carved
out a channel deep enough for steamboats as the river lashed against
steep, two-hundred-foot-high bluffs of limestone and shale that had
formed hundreds of millions of years before. This meant that Vicksburg and its countryside didn't flood each winter and spring like surrounding areas, when the river could easily rise fifty or sixty feet in a
matter of weeks and inundate the land for hundreds of square miles.
The advent of the railroad in the 1840s provided another reason
for the town's rising importance since, being located on the east side
of the river, it was connected in one way or another to all of the bur-
geoning web of America's rail system.

The first settlers were, naturally, Indians who, as early as Neolithic
times, gravitated to what were later called the Walnut Hills, later
known as Chickasaw Bluffs, which would become an ominous factor
in the Civil War era. They were attracted by the abundance of food:
deer, bear, small game, waterfowl, berries, nuts, and roots as well as
plentiful varieties of fish from the Mississippi and its dozens of tributaries. Originally they were mound builders who later separated into
tribes such as the Natchez, Yazoo, and Tunica, who over time evolved
into farmers as well as hunter-gatherers, raising corn, gourds, and
other vegetables and domesticating wild turkeys, ducks, and geese.

The first would-be white settlers appeared in 1686 when Jesuit
priests established a mission known as Fort St. Pierre, but it was short-
lived owing to the Indians' aversion to being converted to Catholicism.*
A decade later French soldiers occupied the place, strengthened the for-

---

* The form of this aversion was harsher than that of most potential Catholic con-
verts. After destroying some idols at an Indian temple, a Father Davion was forced to
flee for his life in a hail of arrows, spears, and stones.

tifications, and by 1721 there were approximately three hundred Europeans living in its environs. Eight years later this experiment also failed, when Indians angry over a long forgotten incident massacred two hundred French planters and soldiers in a similar conclave at Natchez, then turned on the Vicksburg settlers and killed them, too. There things stood for the next forty years until European wars forced the French to cede their Mississippi Valley territories to Spain, which soon established its own outpost at Vicksburg in 1790.

The Spanish ruled the area for the next fifteen years until, with the establishment of the new United States of America, settlers quickly spread westward into the cotton belt. A few years later a Virginian named Newit Vick arrived and began laying out plots of land for a development on the bluffs overlooking the river. In 1825 Vicksburg was incorporated as a city under the laws of Mississippi, and five years later President Andrew Jackson engineered the ejection of all Indian tribes from the South to what is now Oklahoma, paving the way for massive white immigration to the outlying areas.

Vicksburg had become an important stopover port well before the introduction of the steamboat in the first decade of the nineteenth century. For years, merchants and settlers had used flatboats, arks, and keelboats to carry their goods and themselves downriver from the Midwest, as well as Pennsylvania and other states of the East, ultimately offloading at New Orleans for shipment around the world. But the steamboat added an entirely new dimension, since no boat without an engine could navigate back *up* the river against the strong current flow. By 1835 Vicksburg had become the seat of Warren County and a thriving city of 2,500 citizens—and many times that in slaves—with a compliment of banks, cotton factors, merchants, sawmills, foundries, and insurance businesses, as well as cobblers, saddlers, gunsmiths, clothiers, jewelers, druggists, lawyers, doctors, and men of the cloth, all in one degree or another connected to, and affected by, the raising and transportation of cotton.

It also naturally attracted its share of riffraff and, like Natchez, down the river, a collection of gamblers, thieves, forgers, prostitutes, swindlers, smugglers, murderers, con men, and other unsavory characters soon formed a little "city within a city" of saloons and whorehouses beneath the Vicksburg bluffs. Things came to a head in 1835, when one of these denizens staggered drunkenly up the hill and disturbed a fashionable Fourth of July picnic being given by the local militia company. He was seized by a mob of indignant citizens, tied to a tree, given twenty lashes, then tarred and feathered and ridden out of town on a rail. With their ire now whipped up, the mob formed a committee of about four hundred vigilantes and began destroying gambling houses and saloons along the waterfront. When they reached the notorious Kangaroo Club, the angry owner shot and killed a physician, who was also an elder of the Presbyterian church. The mob grabbed the shooter and four of his associates and without further ado hanged them publicly in the middle of town and, in a particularly spiteful twist, cast a sixth man adrift on the Mississippi in a rowboat with his hands tied behind his back. After that, most gamblers left town and things quieted down in the under-the-bluffs community.

In 1836 the beginnings of a rude railway connecting Vicksburg with the state capital at Jackson were laid down by slave labor, with the cars drawn by horses and mules. Two years later the steam locomotive was introduced and by midcentury Vicksburg was connected by rail and by river to most of the rest of the country. Meantime, many of the cotton farmers had replaced their original rough plantation houses with palatial mansions, mostly in the then-popular Greek style, and were living a life of luxury and ease, attended by staffs of house servants while hired overseers rode herd over the platoons of slaves who toiled to make them rich.

By the late 1850s, Vicksburg had established itself as one of the premier cities of the South and, like New Orleans and Natchez, had shed much of its frontier aura for a more cosmopolitan image. Along with American settlers from Virginia and the Carolinas came immigrants from Great Britain, France, Spain, Italy, and Russia. As well, there were still a few Indians around who had abandoned their tribes to become "civilized." Churches had been erected for Methodists, Baptists, Presbyterians, Episcopalians, and Catholics, including a convent of nuns. Jews, who had become a rising merchant class, worshipped in their homes. There were schools, both public and private, and a magnificent four-story county courthouse with an imposing golden dome, which had just been completed as war broke out.* The city boasted six newspapers, each aligned with a political position, if not a political party, but being an editor in those days was a hazardous occupation. Several were killed either in duels or fights, including the editor of a Unionist paper who was shot dead by the editor of the states' rights paper.

.   .   .

* It was distressing to the townspeople that during the siege Union warships used the courthouse as an aiming point, since it was the most visible object in the city.

For generations, at lavish barbecues and dances or on the church steps after Sunday services, the wealthy class had spoken confidently, even smugly, of the superiority of the Southern way of life, of their home of sunshine and plenty, as opposed to the frigid land of immigrants, rude "mechanics," do-gooders, and busybodies above the Mason-Dixon Line, sentiments that, in time, filtered down to the working classes as well.

But for the past decade, from Natchez to Mobile, from Memphis to Vicksburg, there had been darker talk still. In saloons and hotel bars men began speaking openly of defiance, of outright resistance, even of disunion, while newspapers prominently ridiculed the rhetoric of Northern abolitionists that threatened their livelihoods, their social order, and indeed their entire way of life.

If they were dispossessed of their slaves, they said, who would grow the cotton that fed the world's textile mills? (In nearby Madison Parish, Louisiana, for instance, according to the census of 1860 there were 1,293 whites and 9,863 slaves.)

And they said: "If the government can take our slaves, what else will they take from us?"

And they said: "It was they in the North who brought the slaves here to begin with, and reaped their great fortunes from it. How can they now propose to take them away?"

And they said: "We agreed to join the Union. Why won't they now let us leave it in peace?"

In fact, these sentiments were deceptive. Unlike much of the Deep South, Vicksburg—and Natchez, as well—was conservative, with most of its political power resting in the old Whig Party. Talk of rebellion and secession disturbed them since, as a river town, there were strong connections with the North and its valuable commercial trade. The wealthier planters were fearful, too, for no one knew what war would bring, and there was of course a real chance they could lose everything. In the face of all the secessionist hoopla, during the stress-filled election of 1860 Vicksburgians and residents of the county in which they lived voted hopefully for John Bell, a Whig senator from Tennessee whose Constitutional Unionist Party had formed to keep the South from seceding.

They said: "The Union Party is founded upon a rock, and the gates of hell shall not prevail against it!"

And they said: "Let us wait and see what happens. Rashness may be fatal to everything for which we have striven."

And they said: "Will you see the Constitution torn in tatters by bands of secessional agitators and traitorous fanatics?"

When the results of the election came in and Lincoln had won, the Unionists were profoundly disturbed, because they, too, saw the Republicans as avowed enemies of the South. But still they urged caution. "What is our duty in this crisis in our national affairs?" they asked. "We do not mean to rebel against the government because an obnoxious man has been made president."

Soon after the firing on Fort Sumter the state legislature called for an election of delegates to a convention on whether or not to secede as well. Vicksburg, as expected, sent two Unionists to the meeting, but the best they could do was offer an amendment to the overwhelming secessionist vote, which called for "an Ordinance providing for an adjustment of all difficulties between the free and slave states by securing further Constitutional guarantees within the present Union." Their amendment was defeated.

In the end, the old-line conservatives were either shouted down or converted as their sons rushed to the tailors for gray Confederate uniforms. Many loyal Vicksburg men—as did many other moderate southerners—began to change their minds after Lincoln called for Mississippi to supply troops to fight against the other Southern states in open rebellion. This, coupled with his order suspending the right of habeas corpus, had convinced them that the president and his radical Republican Party were proving to be quite as despotic as the fire-eaters had predicted.

"If we submit to Lincoln's rule no matter how unjust it might be," said one, "then in four years we shall have no rights worth fighting for. We cannot see it that way. We should make a stand for our rights—and a nation fighting for its own homes and liberty cannot be overwhelmed. Our cause is just and must prevail."

Perhaps the most vociferous Unionist in town was the editor of the *Vicksburg Whig*, a man with the resounding name of Marmaduke Shannon, who summed up the general feeling when he wrote, "We do not think there can be any doubt as to the duty of patriots at this crisis. It is to follow the destiny of the State and abide its fate. We are Mississippians. Our State has spoken. We, too, take our position by its side." In Shannon's case, it was a costly decision, for five of his children would die during the war.

As in cities and towns all over the South, young men rallied to the call. In Vicksburg the Old Guard and the King Cotton Guard were formed of prosperous lawyers, doctors, businessmen, and others of social prominence; so were the Jeff Davis Rebels, the Hill City Cadets, and the Vicksburg Sharpshooters. As well, a company nicknamed the "Foreign Legion" was composed of French, Irish, Germans, and other nationalities, many of whom did not speak English but who wanted to join the fight anyway.

U.S. postage and currency was suspended in favor of Confederate bills and stamps. Women went to work sewing uniforms and other dry goods needed by the soldiers. Subscriptions for Confederate bonds were taken, including $250 worth of certificates purchased by two former slaves. Terrible as the prospect of disunion was, a certain exhilaration was attached to it as well—they were forming a whole new government, a whole new nation, out of practically nothing, just as their forefathers had done. At least that's how they saw it at the time.

Now they had their government and their war, though, for the past six months it had not gone well. True, in the East, Confederate armies had held their own in Virginia, though it had become clear that a major Union push would soon be in the works. But in the West it was as if an endless cataract of failure was inundating them: New Orleans gone, defeat in Arkansas, Kentucky, Nashville, and at Shiloh, and now Federal forces working their way down the river toward Memphis.

At first, when the excitement of the rush to war had died down, things returned fairly much to normal in Vicksburg. There was ample food and a number of new jobs were created, including the expansion of local foundries to make cannons and other implements of war. Business, at least for a while, went on as usual. But as summer turned to autumn and autumn to winter a noticeable change came over the city. The steamboats that regularly arrived from Pittsburgh, Cincinnati, Louisville, and St. Louis had stopped coming altogether and their commerce was lost. Likewise, steamers from New Orleans that bore goods from the East Coast, England, and continental Europe—everything from clothing to needles to shoes, hats, candles, books, and the myriad other items sold in the shops along Washington Street—these stopped coming too.

Worse, the cotton crop of 1861, one of the most prosperous in recent memory, was going nowhere. In March 1862, just as New Madrid was falling to the Yankees, the Vicksburg authorities passed an ordinance that forbade storing or bringing cotton into the city and ordering any cotton already there to be moved out, so that it "may be

Safely burned, should it be necessary to do so, to prevent it from falling into the hands of our Enemies." So the wharves were empty and many people were out of work and some were already becoming destitute; food was becoming scarcer and there was a money shortage—and not much to buy with it anyway.

Still, there remained a certain spirit of *c'est la guerre* among the white residents, who by now consisted mainly of women and children, the military-aged men for the most part having been sent to the fighting fronts. They began by growing vegetable gardens in their backyards and, since there was at least no shortage of cotton, dusted off their grandmother's old spinning wheels to produce homespun—the rough, rude cloth used to make clothing back in frontier days. One woman observed with amusement that of the few men left in Vicksburg, many "thought nothing of calling on ladies dressed in homespun suits," whereas it would have been unthinkable before the war. The same lady noted in her diary in a mixture of dismay and pride, "Finished the ugliest calico dress I ever possessed, and without assistance, too." Another recalled that her friends would make hats fashionable enough to wear by plaiting bleached palmetto palm leaves, "And if they were going to church or to a party and wanted a trim for a hat, they went out in the garden, cut a flower, and stuck it on." Little did they know how much worse things were going to get.

By the late spring of 1862 the people of Vicksburg began to comprehend with devastating clarity that they might soon be next on the list—the veritable bull's-eye, as it were—and that if their fortress city fell the Confederacy would be sheared in two, then carved up like a Sunday turkey, and who among them could tell what lay ahead: Yankees striding insolently through the streets, slaves run amok, homes and property confiscated, wives and daughters molested. It was not a pleasant notion to contemplate, and even harder to digest. But one thing the Vicksburg citizens decided—if not unanimously, then at least collectively—was that they weren't going to be a pushover like the folks in New Orleans.

News of the Union victory downriver hit Vicksburg like a thunderclap. Until now the war had been far away, and though the outcome at Shiloh had made the residents uneasy, they took a measure of comfort knowing that the Yankee army was still some three hundred miles to the northeast at Pittsburg Landing and facing a powerful force gathering at Corinth under Beauregard to hold them in check.

New Orleans, however, was about half that distance from Vicksburg, and there was no Rebel army to bar the way. Worse, should the
Yankees come on steam transports up the river, they could be there
any day.

Equally ominous was the enemy progress down the river from the
north. First Columbus, Kentucky, then New Madrid and Island Number 10, and now Union ironclads were laying siege to Fort Pillow, just
above Memphis. If those two bastions went, Vicksburg would lay
plainly in the crosshairs—the lone impediment to Yankee control of
the Mississippi.

It wasn't just the people of Vicksburg or the authorities in Richmond who understood this; Lincoln himself had taken an abiding personal interest in the subject, according to Commodore Porter, the
mortar-boat commander who had devised the plan to take New
Orleans. When at the end of 1861 Porter had gone to Washington to
present his scheme, he wrote later that he had been shown into a meeting with Lincoln, Secretary of the Navy Gideon Welles, army commander in chief George McClellan, and others, during which the
president had the following to say: "See what a lot of land these fellows hold, of which Vicksburg is the key." Running a bony finger over
a map, Lincoln continued: "Here is the Red River, which will supply
the Confederates with cattle and corn to feed their armies. There are
the Arkansas and White Rivers, which can supply cattle and hogs
by the thousand. From Vicksburg, these supplies can be distributed
by rail all over the Confederacy. Then there is the great depot of supplies on the Yazoo. Let us get Vicksburg and all that country is ours.

"The war can never be brought to a close until that key is in our
pocket. I am acquainted with that region and know what I am talking
about," said the president, alluding to his youthful trips down the Mississippi on flatboats. "As valuable as New Orleans will be to us, Vicksburg will be more so. We may take all the northern ports of the
Confederacy, and they can still defy us from Vicksburg. It means hog
and hominy without limit, fresh troops from all the States of the far
South, and a cotton country where they can raise the staple without
interference."

Porter later recalled that Lincoln impressed on those present to
make the capture of Vicksburg a strategic aim of the utmost importance, and remarked that "a military expert could not more clearly
have defined the advantages of the proposed campaign."

Unaware of being discussed in such exalted circles, the people of
Vicksburg still had good reason to suspect as much, and while there

was no panic there was certainly anxiety, and an apprehensive resignation that the war was upon them, or about to be. Those unable to join the fight pitched in any way they could, including burning their own cotton. For many the experience was unforgettably painful, watching their very livelihood consumed by flames.

It had been Beauregard's idea, a sort of quasi-mandate after the fall of New Orleans, when it was clear the Federal gunboats could roam the river at will, at least up to Vicksburg. Cotton had become as good as gold and it had already been proven that the Federals did not stoop to scruples when it came to taking people's cotton to sell on the lucrative open market. Rather than allow that, Beauregard told local officials to see to it that cotton was burned, whether in the bale or in the field, so that soon the whole river valley looked as though it was a land afire.

Kate Stone was a tall, handsome twenty-year-old who lived with her widowed mother, three younger brothers, and a sister on the family plantation, Brokenburn, across the river a little north of Vicksburg. Two older brothers were off at war. She was spirited, educated in Shakespeare and the novels of Walter Scott, and wholly devoted to the Southern cause. In 1861, Kate had been looking forward to a long sightseeing trip to the North—which she had never visited—and then on to Europe for the summer, but that was disarranged when war broke out. Instead, she stayed to help her mother run Brokenburn and kept a diary, to which she confided a few days after the momentous news of the fall of New Orleans reached her: "Fair Louisiana, with her fertile fields of cane and cotton, her many bayous and dark old forests, lies powerless at the feet of the enemy. Though the Yankees have gained the land, the people are determined they shall not have its wealth, and from every plantation rises the smoke of burning cotton. The order from Beauregard advising the destruction of the cotton met with a ready response from the people, most of them agreeing it is the only thing to do. As far as we can see are the ascending wreaths of smoke, and we hear that all the cotton of the Mississippi Valley from Memphis to New Orleans is going up in smoke.*

"We have found it hard to burn bales of cotton. They will smoulder

---

* It was assumed that the government in Washington would confiscate Southern cotton as contraband and sell it to British and French textile mills, both to ease the strain on international relations caused by the blockade and to reap profits with which to finance the war. But in fact not all cotton was being destroyed. A number of planters, most owning smaller farms in the interior, hid their picked cotton for a rainy day, which would soon become a bone of contention for both sides, as we shall see.

for days. So the huge bales are cut open before they are lighted and the old cotton burns slowly. It has to be stirred and turned over, but the light cotton from the lint room goes like a flash. We should know, for Mamma has $20,000 worth [more than $400,000 in today's money] burning on the gin ridge now; it was set on fire yesterday and is still blazing."*

It was money her mother had intended to use in part for their European summer vacation—the inestimable grand tour—but in Kate Stone's diary there is no hint of despair; instead, there is outrage and defiance.

"The Yankee gunboats are expected to appear before Vicksburg today," she wrote, "and every effort is being made to 'welcome them with bloody hands to hospitable graves.' We only hope they may burn the city if they meet with any resistance. How much better to burn our cities than let them fall into the enemy's hands."

As soon as it became apparent that New Orleans would fall, General Mansfield Lovell began evacuating what troops and military stores he was able to save via the railroad up to Jackson, and thence to Vicksburg. These were substantial: cannons—light and heavy, gunpowder, rifles, ammunition, food, wagons, livestock, tents, and all manner of related supplies. As the artillery arrived in Vicksburg it was emplaced as quickly as possible. Batteries of heavy guns were located on the river below the town to guard against the enemy ships when they made their approach. On the bluffs directly above the city, more big guns were placed to deliver plunging fire. Vicksburg was seething with military activity, soldiers working alongside slaves to strengthen the fortifications. Bombproof emplacements were dug into the cliffs and ridges with thick overhead protection against mortar fire. The railroad from Jackson brought ammunition and stores in continuous runs, and plans were being drawn in Richmond to hurry more soldiers to the city.

Meantime, General Benjamin Butler was making his presence felt downriver at New Orleans, and when news of this reached Vicksburg many of its citizens became convinced that their earlier fears were all too true.

* The figure is indicative of the fantastic profits to be made growing cotton. Brokenburn had 800 of its 1,200 acres under cultivation, at a rate of return of $500 per acre (in today's money), year after year—when they had bought it for one dollar per acre or less.

Butler was an odd sort of duck, and looked it. At forty-four, he was rotund, slightly cross-eyed, with a puffy face, a beaked nose, and long stringy hair dangling to his neck from the back and sides of a bald head. He was a Massachusetts Democrat who, at the convention of 1860, had voted—fifty-seven times, no less—for Jefferson Davis as candidate for president of the United States. When that nomination failed he supported the candidacy of Senator John Breckinridge, a former vice president of the United States, who was presently a Confederate general and later served as Jefferson Davis's secretary of war. However, when Southern states began to secede, Butler cast his lot with the Union, and he was rewarded with the position of brigadier and, later, major general. His military career both before and after New Orleans was anything but stellar, but during the occupation he managed to invite the enmity of practically everyone.

Before Butler had even arrived to officially take over the city of New Orleans, an indignant citizen named William Mumford had torn down the American flag that Farragut had ordered hoisted over the Federal mint. Hearing of this, Butler had Mumford seized, tried by a military court, convicted of "high crimes and misdemeanors," and hanged in the mint's courtyard. His rationale was that if southerners wouldn't respect the U.S. flag, they could at least learn to fear it, but the act provoked more outrage than fear in the rest of the Confederacy.

Next Butler told New Orleanians that they needed to sign a loyalty oath to the Federal government. He didn't require it, but soon enough it became apparent that those who didn't were in for a hard time. Outlying plantation owners had their slaves and cotton confiscated and sold as "contraband," a term he coined, while Butler's brother, Andrew, quickly became rich off the trade. Wealthy New Orleans citizens who did not sign the loyalty oath were unceremoniously evicted from their homes and Butler's officers, "down to and including mere lieutenants," were ensconced there in their stead. Butler himself shortly gained the dubious sobriquet "Spoons," an allusion to people's silverware that allegedly disappeared under his supervision.

But the general's most infamous nickname in the South soon became "Beast Butler," following a run-in he had with the ladies of the city. Shortly after his occupation began, reports reached Butler that many women were behaving discourteously toward Union soldiers— glaring at them hatefully, averting their eyes, gathering their skirts when they passed them in the street, singing Confederate songs, and so forth. When Butler got wind of this he told his adjutant to issue an order stating that if any woman "shall, by word, gesture, or movement, insult or show contempt for any officer or soldier of the United States, she shall be regarded and held liable to be treated as a woman of the town, plying her trade."

Whether the general intended it or not, the order was interpreted in the South and elsewhere to mean that women so regarded were fair game for rape and other "indignities too disgraceful to mention." This set off a firestorm of vituperation that flared not only throughout the Confederacy but across the Atlantic, where the British prime minister, Lord Palmerston, vilified Butler by declaring, "Any Englishman must blush to think that such an act has been committed by one belonging to the Anglo-Saxon race." For his part, Jefferson Davis characterized Butler's behavior as "revolting" and issued a proclamation branding him an outlaw and not a soldier, to be hanged if captured. Learning of the order from the *Vicksburg Whig,* Kate Stone consigned the general to her diary's anti-Yankee wish list, praying that "he may not long pollute the soil of Louisiana."*

Many prominent New Orleans businessmen and planters asked their friends in Washington to appeal directly to Lincoln for relief from Butler's harsh measures, but the president was unmoved. Even to those who claimed to be pro-Union men, Lincoln replied that they should not hope "to be merely passengers . . . on the ship of state," implying that before they received respite the southerners would have to take positive action on behalf of the Federal government. He further stated that he intended to prosecute the war "by any available means," leaving the unhappy Louisianans to contemplate just what that might mean.

As expected, as soon as Butler and his army took over New Orleans, Farragut began pushing his fleet upriver to complete the conquest. His commanders caused the surrender of Baton Rouge, on the western bank, by threatening to destroy the city by cannon fire; then they steamed upriver and cowed Natchez into capitulating for the same reason without a shot being fired. Having accomplished that, Farragut's ships forged farther north, arriving within sight of Vicksburg on the morning of May 18, 1862, a little over three weeks after the victory at New Orleans.

---

* It has been said for years that after Butler moved on to other atrocities, a potter in New Orleans fashioned a line of chamber pots featuring his likeness on the bottom— in color, no less; but to the author's knowledge this has never been confirmed.

The Union force consisted of five big warships, *Oneida, Kennebec, Winona, Sciota,* and *Itasca.* The flotilla also included two transports filled with 1,400 infantry under General Thomas Williams to occupy the city.

By now, spring was in its full glory along the Mississippi; the trees were leafed out, jonquils and irises were blooming in the lawns and gardens, and the smell of clover was in the air. It was a clear, bright day and the sun dazzled on the river rushing past the city on its springtime flood. From atop the bluffs, some twenty stories high, the Federal ships seemed small, even tiny, as they steamed slowly toward the town, but they were larger than anything Vicksburgians had seen this far upriver, slender and graceful with tall sailing masts that seemed completely out of place on the Mississippi, as did the great black 11-inch cannons that lined their gun decks. Powerful as these ships were, one can only imagine the emotions of the sailors as they rounded the last bend and saw Vicksburg's hulking bluffs, daunting as a medieval fortress.

At straight-up noon the ships dropped anchor. Ordinarily it would have been the time church bells were rung to mark the close of services, but the citizens had long since gone out to see the show. At twenty minutes past twelve, a longboat from the *Oneida,* displaying a white flag of truce, put out toward the city. Halfway there a cannon shot from the direction of the Vicksburg wharfs disturbed the tranquillity. Watchers on the bluff could see the warning shot plunge into the river across the longboat's bow. The Union longboat hove to and waited as a Confederate steamer pulled away from the wharves and headed toward it.

A message sent by the captain of the Yankee fleet, Commodore S. Phillips Lee, was handed to the steamer and the two boats returned from whence they came. The message was directed to "The Authorities at Vicksburg" and read: "The undersigned, with orders from Flag-Officer Farragut and Major-General Butler, respectively, demand the surrender of Vicksburg and its defenses to the lawful authority of the United States, under which private property and personal rights will be respected—Respectfully Yours, S. Phillips Lee, Commanding Advance Naval Division."

It had been agreed upon by the officer of the longboat and the captain of the steamer that the two boats would meet at the same spot in the center of the river at 3 p.m. Promptly at three the longboat arrived at the appointed place. The steamer did not, and it kept the boat's crew at their oars for two hours, trying to maintain their place in the rushing stream. When the Rebel steamer finally showed up at about five, it carried not one but three answers to Commodore Lee's demand, each a variation on the same theme.

Colonel James L. Autry, the military governor of Vicksburg, informed the Yankee commander that "Mississippians don't know, and refuse to learn, how to surrender." He referred Lee's demand to Brigadier General Martin Luther Smith, commanding the Vicksburg defenses, who was even more to the point. "Having been ordered to hold these defenses," he said, "it is my intention to do so as long as it is in my power." The mayor of Vicksburg also got into the act, stating, "Neither the municipal authorities nor the citizens will ever consent to a surrender of the city."

How Commodore Lee digested this information is unrecorded, but just before sundown he ordered his fleet to drop down below the city, apparently to digest it further. There he remained the following day, and most of the next, until about sundown when his lookouts spied Confederate troops along the bluffs and opened fire on them, with negligible results. Lee then sent in his gig under another flag of truce, this time giving notice to the mayor that he would begin bombarding the city within twenty-four hours. This was ample time, he said, to remove the women and children, "as it will be impossible to attack the defenses without injuring or destroying the town, a proceeding which the authorities of Vicksburg seem to require."

Next afternoon, the bombardment began. As the great 166-pound shells began smashing and bursting into the city, many civilians fled to the countryside. Those lucky enough to have friends or relatives with surrounding plantations had a fairly easy time of it; others could move only a couple of miles inland, out of range of the cannons, and pitch tents or other rude shelters and make do as best they could. Before they left they boarded up their homes and buried their silver or took it with them, along with their house slaves. Factory owners dismantled machinery and sent it east to Jackson, to be distributed in safer areas. Stores were closed or closing, and last-minute purchases were on a cash-and-carry basis. Property transactions assumed land office proportions, with one wealthy resident complaining darkly in a letter to Jefferson Davis that "the Jews in Vicksburg are buying up real estate . . . and other property has fallen into their hands."*

---

* There is no evidence recorded in the county records to suggest that this was true.

As such things go, the bombardment was not particularly heavy since the ships' guns could not be elevated enough to do much damage, either to the Rebel artillery batteries on the bluffs or to the town itself. Still, some shells struck the city, one blasting a hole in the Methodist church and another landing in someone's kitchen. A few days later, when Farragut arrived on the scene, he did not like what he saw. Plainly the shelling was not going well. He called a conference with the army commander, General Williams, as to the feasibility of his storming the city with his brigade, but the answer was no, unless the fleet could reduce the Rebel batteries, which it could not. With that, Farragut sourly ordered the bulk of the flotilla back down to New Orleans, leaving a handful of gunboats to keep a watch on developments. It was Farragut's fervent intention to take his fleet out of the shallow, muddy confines of the Mississippi River and back into deep blue water, where it belonged. Thus the first attempt to capture Vicksburg ended in failure.

The developments in which Farragut was interested did not take long to materialize. Trains could be heard arriving night and day carrying Confederate troops to the city. More cannons and munitions were delivered. Furious digging could be observed on the heights as line after line of entrenchments were thrown up and bulwarked. Vicksburg was fast becoming what Jefferson Davis and others had always claimed it was: the Gibraltar of the West.

Meantime, most of the residents began to return to their homes and were relieved to find that few were damaged. They tried to resume normal lives but found it impossible. The city became choked with troops, many without shelter and begging to sleep on people's verandas, or even on their lawns. Stores tried to reopen but with little to sell, and what was on hand assumed grossly inflated prices. Salt, for instance, which before the war had sold for about a dollar a sack, was now a precious commodity and sacks sold for upwards of $100— nearly $2,000 in today's money—if it could be had at all. Men who otherwise lived lives of leisure now found themselves "hewers of wood and drawers of water," according to the diarist Kate Stone, who recorded that "one gentleman I saw walking down the street had a fish in one hand, a cavalry saddle on his back, bridle, blankets, newspapers and a small parcel in the other hand. And nobody thought he looked odd."

If the departure of Farragut's warships led Vicksburgians to believe the danger was over, however, they were quite mistaken. Soon as word got back to Washington that Farragut had left for the Gulf of Mexico, the Navy Department was livid. Secretary Welles ordered a dispatch sent to intercept Farragut at New Orleans, invoking not only his personal displeasure at the abandonment of the thrust, but Lincoln's as well: "It is of paramount importance that you go up and clear the river with utmost expedition," the message read, adding that all other naval operations "sink in comparison to this."

For Farragut, "orders was orders," and so he began assembling a new and much larger fleet to attack the city. This time he brought along Commodore Porter and his mortar squadron, which had wreaked such havoc on Forts Jackson and St. Philip, as well as 3,200 soldiers he had managed to pry away from Butler, which effectively doubled the infantry force of General Williams.

For the Mississippians it became apparent all too soon that these people were not going to go away.

CHAPTER SEVEN

Sometimes Now We Can Get the Papers

The Confederate evacuation of the Mississippi River forts had resulted from more bad news at the fighting front. On May 30, four days before Ellet discovered the forts had been abandoned, Beauregard—to the dismay of the Richmond authorities—had sneaked out of Corinth when General Halleck orchestrated a glacial pincers movement to corner him.

After Shiloh, and despite the terrible casualties, Halleck found that he had on hand an army of some 120,000 Union soldiers and two hundred guns, and with these he intended to move on Beauregard's stronghold, but—to the surprise of many—with no sense of urgency whatever. It took Halleck three weeks simply to reorganize his force at Pittsburg Landing and on April 30 he wired Secretary Stanton, "I leave here tomorrow morning, and our army will be before Corinth tomorrow night." What prompted him to make this boastful prediction is puzzling because, given that he had so thoroughly worked out his plan of attack, it took the diminutive general a full month to move his columns twenty miles south to the Rebel bastion, which, at the beginning, he had estimated to contain some 70,000 Confederate defenders. By the time he arrived that figure had been reassessed to as many as 200,000 when Beauregard actually had no more than 52,000 men who were fit for duty, owing to diseases and the heavy casualties at Shiloh.

To Halleck, the wilderness of northern Mississippi was filled with ghosts and shadows and a Rebel behind every tree, and he had no intention of duplicating the misfortune of Grant by letting himself get caught surprised and unprepared. Accordingly, Halleck approached Corinth with the mentality of a man conducting a portable siege. Moving out of Pittsburg Landing, he would creep the army forward for less than a mile, then set it to digging and fortifying, while engineers corduroyed* the road ahead for another short distance and hacked out laterals in the forest along the entire eight-mile front, so that men from one unit could quickly reinforce those in another if they were attacked. It continued thusly, day after maddening day—march forward for less than an hour and then start excavating entrenchments. When it became apparent that this was the procedure by which the army would advance on Corinth, many of the men began complaining—what with all the digging and fortifying they were saddled with under the hot Mississippi sun. But Halleck, like Grant before him, still envisioned a final conflict that would settle the fate of the war in the West and was taking no chances.

Neither, for that matter, was Beauregard. Crammed into every spare inch of living space in Corinth were diseased, wounded, and dying soldiers and, as reinforcements arrived, sanitation reached such crisis levels that the water supply became tainted. Even though his army was well entrenched in a good defensive position, Beauregard knew he could not long stand a siege by Halleck. That, coupled with the realization that his force represented the South's last best hope of holding off the Yankees in that theater of war, led the Creole general to a distasteful and desperate measure.

Just as the Federal armies began to concentrate before Corinth, Yankee scouts heard the sounds of train whistles and the noise of cheering men within the city, a sure sign that the Rebels were being reinforced. They also reported the existence of large siege-type guns bristling from embrasures around the enemy fortifications, and "deserters" who walked into Union lines reported the arrival of a number of regiments from other Southern commands. General Pope reported to Halleck: "The enemy is reinforcing heavily, by trains, in my front and on my left. The cars are running constantly, and the cheering is immense every time they unload in front of me. I have no doubt, from all appearances, that I shall be attacked in heavy force at daylight."

---

* Corduroyed roads, a feature that goes back to Roman times, consist of tightly abutted logs laid perpendicular to the direction of the road, allowing heavy traffic over swampy or soggy areas.

Meanwhile, the Union soldiers could clearly detect the music of military bands behind the Rebel lines, and during pauses in their patriotic Southern tunes, buglers played various calls to action. Not only that, but they could see in the distance Rebel soldiers at the parapets, backlit by campfires, although these particular sentries seemed strangely impervious to sharpshooters' bullets, leaving the Yankees to wonder just what kind of men they were facing.

Beauregard, of course, was pulling off the greatest con of the war and saving his army in the process. Military manuals stress that withdrawal in the face of a large and prepared enemy is among the most dangerous of combat maneuvers, and the little Creole did it with such precision and aplomb that when the Federals finally entered Corinth the next morning they found that the Rebels had practically cleaned up after themselves before departing. Not a sick or wounded man was left behind—only two or three civilians out of the entire population of the town remained—and all of the stores and most of the munitions were gone too. The arriving "troop trains" were discovered to have been the work of a single locomotive running up and down the network of tracks that converged on Corinth, stopping every so often to blow its whistle to stimulate the orchestrated cheers heard by the Yankee troops. The Rebel "sentries" were nothing more than cornfield scarecrows dressed in worn-out Confederate uniforms and the big defensive guns were "Quaker" artillery—stripped-down tree trunks painted black with tar pitch and set on broken-down artillery caissons. The Confederate "deserters" who reported heavy reinforcements were plants sent by Beauregard. It is ironic that, aside from his joint command with Joseph E. Johnston at the first Battle of Bull Run, the Corinth hoax became, arguably, Beauregard's greatest achievement during the war.*

Halleck assessed this development with mixed emotions. He must have felt relief at not having to fight a battle he could possibly have lost, but on the other hand the entire Rebel army had escaped his grasp and the "battle to decide the fate of the war in the West" had come to

---

* Grant claimed to have known that the Confederates were evacuating. He wrote later that General John A. Logan, who had a number of railroad men in his division, told him that the old-timers, by putting their ears to the rail running through Corinth, not only had distinguished between trains that were coming and going, but knew that the departing trains were full and the arriving trains were empty. What Grant did with this information vis-à-vis Halleck is not reported, but in his memoirs Grant said he was convinced Corinth could have easily been taken a few days after the Battle of Shiloh.

naught. In order to save face, he informed Stanton that his army had captured 10,000 prisoners and 15,000 stands of arms, which was nowhere near the truth. Halleck had taken those numbers from a message provided by Pope—who had chased after Beauregard with his Army of the Mississippi—and claimed with his customary braggadocio that there were "not less than 10,000" Confederate stragglers scattered in the woods, "who will come in within a day or two." The fact that this never materialized did not prevent Stanton from publicly congratulating Halleck for his "glorious victory," adding, "The whole land will soon ring with applause at the achievement of your gallant army and its able and victorious commander."

This was not exactly the truth either. Northern newspapers accused Halleck of having let the Rebels slip through his fingers when a decisive victory might have ended the war. "A barren triumph," said one; "tantamount to a defeat," cried another, but in any case, after Beauregard withdrew, Forts Pillow and Randolph were flanked and cut off from the rail junction at Corinth, which is why they were vacant when Colonel Ellet got there, and why the road to Memphis now lay wide open.

On the morning of June 6, 1862, just after sunrise, Commodore Davis's ironclads anchored about a mile above Memphis near a bend called Paddy's Hen and Chickens, in plain view of Colonel Montgomery's River Defense Fleet, which was drawn up before the city in line of battle. Given that the day might turn out to be a long one, Davis had decided to feed his crews breakfast and began rounding up his ships before attending to the work at hand, whereas the Confederates, feeling no need of such luxuries, straightaway opened fire.

Except for the ram fleet, Memphis itself was completely defenseless, having relied for its safety on the forts upriver and the prowess of Johnston's (now Beauregard's) army, which was now, of course, out of the picture. Nevertheless, most the city's 22,683 citizens held a misbegotten hope that their little seven-ship wooden navy—carrying a total of twenty-eight light guns to the sixty-eight heavy guns of their Union ironclad adversaries—would pull off another Plum Point Bend–style triumph. Early that morning many expectant thousands had lined the tall bluff overlooking the river. Women waved their handkerchiefs and men cheered while "Negro boys carried wine and lunches in baskets," adding a circus atmosphere to the grim proceedings as the first Rebel shots rang out. They shared the common knowledge that their fate, and the fate of their city, depended entirely on the results of this encounter.

The Confederate rams began moving steadily forward, when suddenly from around the bend above the Federal fleet another group of boats appeared and, passing swiftly through the ironclads, made straight for them. To spectators on the heights of the Memphis bluffs, the scene must have appeared as a tableau in miniature, as if toys were being moved around in a children's playroom. These fierce-looking little craft that were flying the Union flag and closing with such astonishing speed were, of course, the Ellet rams, previously identified by Confederate spies as mere "transportation vessels."

Having anchored a few miles above Davis's ironclads when the fighting opened, Colonel Charles Ellet came out of the pilothouse waving his hat and shouted, "It is a gun from the enemy! Round out and follow me! Now is our chance!" Ellet led the way in *Queen of the West* while his brother Lieutenant Colonel Alfred Ellet followed in *Monarch*. As it turned out, the *Queen* and the *Monarch* were on their own, though Ellet did not then realize it, for the rudder on *Lancaster* had broken and *Switzerland,* which was supposed to follow *Lancaster,* dawdled in uncertainty, as did the rest of the rams following her. However, it turned out not to have mattered.

By now the scene below the bluffs was obscured by dense battle smoke, lit by dim flashes of cannon fire and punctuated by explosive booms and the throbbing racket of steam engines pushed to their limit. All that anyone could clearly see were the tall smokestacks of the two Yankee rams rising above the white billows as they plunged into the clash. Below, however, on the river, the action was chaotic, dramatic, and decisive. *Queen of the West* and *General Lovell* spotted each other simultaneously and bore in straight on. At the last moment, when a direct collision at full speed probably would have sunk both vessels, one of *Lovell*'s engines failed and *Queen* crashed into the side of the Rebel ram, mortally wounding her. Then, before the *Queen* could extricate herself from *Lovell*'s innards, the Confederate ram *Sumter* smashed into *Queen*'s wheelhouse, forcing Colonel Ellet to rush outside, where he was promptly shot in the knee by a Confederate pistol.*

---

* Though the wound did not appear to be particularly serious, in two weeks the persistent old engineer was dead from complications, a fate all too common in Civil War days.

Alfred Ellet arrived on the scene in *Monarch* to give the *General Lovell* her final death crush, while the *Queen* limped off toward the Arkansas shore, looking for shallow water to settle in. *Monarch* thus found herself alone in the fight against the remaining vessels of the River Defense Fleet, and what ensued was akin to slapstick comedy. Two Confederate rams, *General Beauregard* and *General Price,* came at *Monarch* from opposite sides, intending to mash her in between them, but at the last second *Monarch* gunned her engines and slipped forward, leaving the two Rebel vessels to crash violently into each other—which they did—while *Monarch* rounded and came back to ram *Beauregard,* which was also struck by gunfire from the ironclads and sank near the Arkansas shore. The *General Price* staggered off to do the same.

By now the big Yankee ironclads had closed in for the kill and the Confederates knew their only chance was to head south. This precipitated a running gun battle for ten miles, during which *Sumter* and *General Bragg* were both disabled by shots from the ironclads and their crews captured. *Little Rebel,* Montgomery's flagship, took an unlucky shot in her boiler and was abandoned while her crew escaped into the woods. The *General Thompson* was grounded and set afire by her captain, while her crew also clambered up the banks and got away. Only the *General Van Dorn,* which had sunk the Union ironclad *Mound City* a few weeks earlier, managed to flee downriver unharmed. The sun had not risen half high in the sky when the whole affair was ended, and the anguished spectators on the bluff saw the tide of their own future drift away with the gun smoke and debris of the River Defense Fleet which, ironically, had been built to defend New Orleans.

Meantime, Ulysses S. Grant had become thoroughly fed up with his treatment at the hands of Halleck. In fact, he had made arrangements to depart from Halleck's command and even possibly to resign from the army. After Corinth, Grant received permission for a thirty-day leave, and when Sherman got wind of it and went to visit his friend he found Grant's camp desks and trunks packed and stacked for shipping out next morning. "Sherman, you know that I am in the way here," Grant said resignedly. "I have stood it as long as I can." When Sherman asked where he was going, Grant told him St. Louis, and when Sherman inquired if he had any business there, Grant replied, "Not a bit."

Sherman argued that Grant would be miserable sitting on the sidelines while other generals fought the war. And he further managed to persuade Grant that all his troubles were caused by Sherman's personal nemesis, the press, which, he reiterated, was "dirty, irresponsible, corrupt, malicious etc.," and would soon "drop back into the abyss of infamy they deserve." He even used himself as an example, noting that just a few months earlier he had been dismissed as crazy, whereas now, after the Battle of Shiloh, his reputation was in ascendancy again. So if Grant remained in the army, Sherman concluded, "some happy accident might restore him to favor and his true place."

Grant canceled his plans, and just as Sherman had predicted the "happy accident" soon occurred, when George McClellan suffered a humiliating defeat at the gates of Richmond by Robert E. Lee, and Halleck was called to Washington to replace him as general in chief. This in turn restored Grant as commander of the Army of the Tennessee and, ultimately, led him onto one of the larger pages of history. Grant's recollection of the incident years later, after he had served as president, is as good an illustration as any of his immutable taciturnity: "General Sherman called on me as I was starting [to leave] and urged me so strongly not to think of going, that I concluded to remain."

The long, hot Mississippi summer weather lingered late into autumn while the war in the West languished almost as a backwater compared with great events in the East. Before he left for Washington, Halleck, rather than striking out with his entire Federal force on hand for Vicksburg, Mobile, or even Atlanta, as Grant had suggested, instead dismantled his grand army piecemeal. To the War Department he explained his actions on grounds of sanitation, saying he feared the onset of crippling epidemics associated with keeping so many troops close together in the sweltering Southern climate. This was not an unreasonable assessment given the problems Beauregard had reported. Even Lee had predicted that Northern armies could not operate in the Deep South during the hot season. In retrospect, with both New Orleans and Memphis now in Federal hands, a quick move on Vicksburg with this powerful force likely could have, at that point, taken the city from the rear.

In any case, Buell and his Army of the Ohio were peeled off east toward Chattanooga, repairing the Memphis and Charleston Railway as it went. Grant and his Army of the Tennessee were detailed west to occupy Memphis and its environs, while Pope's Army of the Mississippi was called back to garrison and defend Corinth itself, except that

Pope was no longer with it. After McClellan's disheartening performance during the Seven Days' Battles around Richmond, Pope was
selected by Lincoln and Halleck to command the Federal Army of Virginia, where his reputation for imprudence soon resulted in one of
the most decisive whippings of the war by Lee at the second Battle of
Bull Run.

So divided they went, per Halleck's instructions, everywhere it
seemed except after Beauregard, who had massed his still-intact Rebel
army at Tupelo, Mississippi, some fifty miles south of Corinth. Shortly
after the affair at Corinth, however, Beauregard placed himself on two
weeks' sick leave, which in retrospect was probably the wrong thing to
do if he wished to retain his position in the army. If he believed his
evacuation ruse was a clever demonstration of retrograde operations,
some of his superiors at Richmond were clearly unhappy about it—
including Jefferson Davis, whose aversion to retreat was well known.
Thus it did not come as a complete surprise when Beauregard was
summarily relieved of command even as he packed for his medical
leave and his army given over to Braxton Bragg. At the same time,
Davis hacked a separate command away from Beauregard's (now
Bragg's) army—consisting of the 20,000 troops under Earl Van
Dorn—specifically to deal with the rising crisis at Vicksburg.

For his part, Grant spent the rest of the summer and the fall wondering what his role would be. Under Halleck, his job appeared to
consist of nothing more than consolidating gains and holding western
Tennessee against any incursion by Rebel forces. But Grant had an
army of 50,000 and his personal inclination was to go and fight somebody with it. It had become obvious that the navy couldn't take Vicksburg alone. Memphis was captured, New Orleans was gone, but those
cities had been unarmed. Vicksburg, though, was heavily fortified and,
as Lincoln had astutely observed, remained the key. Grant believed
that he was the man with the men to unlock it.

Back in Washington, though, Halleck was still worried, as he was
always worried about something—or anything. Now he feared that
Beauregard's host was lurking out there somewhere, ready to attack
without warning, and against that eventuality he kept Grant in place. It
galled Grant from the moment he woke up in the morning till the time
he went to sleep, but until he could figure out a way to use his army the
way he thought it ought to be used, he would have to live with babysit-
ting western Tennessee.

·   ·   ·

From the diary of Kate Stone, 1862: "*June 25:* Well, we have seen at last what we have been looking for for weeks—the Yankee gunboats descending the river. The *Lancaster No 3* led the way, followed by the *Monarch.* We hope they will be the first to be sunk at Vicksburg. We shall watch for their names."

To the planters along the river it was a nightmare incarnate. The loss of Memphis had opened the country along the river to the Federals right down to Vicksburg, and they wasted no time in coming. "We all ran out on the gallery for the first sight of the enemy," wrote Kate Stone, "and soon we saw one craft bearing rapidly down the river, dark, silent, and sinister. . . . Oh, how we hated them deep down in our hearts." Kate and her sisters and mother "rushed back into the house, each person picking up any valuable in the way of silver, jewelry or fancy things he could find, and away we ran through the hot, dusty quarter lot, making for the only refuge we could see, the tall, thick cornfield just beyond the fence. We could see the spyglass leveled at us."

And four days later: "We hear today that the Yankees are impressing all the Negro men on the river places and putting them to work on a ditch which they are cutting across the point opposite Vicksburg at DeSoto. They hope to turn the river through there and to leave Vicksburg high and dry, ruining that town and enabling the gunboats to pass down the river without running the gauntlet of the batteries at Vicksburg. They have lately come up as far as Omega, four miles from us, taking the men from Mr. Noland's place down."

As indeed the Yankees were. The emergency rush of big guns into the Vicksburg fortifications and Rebel troops arriving daily to thwart a land attack had stymied Farragut, whose fleet was once more below the city. General Williams, even with his force doubled to more than 3,000 men, would still not attempt an assault on the city and other plans were needed. One scheme called for construction of the canal that Kate Stone described. To say the least, it was a daunting task, and more than 1,200 slaves, many going willingly, others taken at gunpoint, came from nearby plantations to assist in the project.

The DeSoto peninsula pointed at the Vicksburg bluffs like an accusing finger from the west. It was formed by the hairpin curve of the river and was the western terminus for the Vicksburg, Shreveport and Texas Railroad. The canal proposed by Farragut and Williams, simple-looking on paper, turned out to be a stupendous piece of military engineering. It required a mile-and-a-half-long cut, forty feet wide and fifteen feet deep, to be made across the peninsula's gloomy cypress swamps beginning three miles above the city and ending a mile or so below it. If successful, the Mississippi would rush through, leaving DeSoto Point as an island, while forming a new western channel that would not only doom Vicksburg forever as a river port but allow commercial and military vessels to pass unmolested by the big guns on the bluffs. But it was easier said than done.

By day and by night thousands of slaves and soldiers toiled amid dangerous snakes and alligators in the fetid, swampy muck, beset by the July heat and clouds of disease-carrying mosquitoes—as well as occasional shells that the Confederates tossed over just to ramp up the discomfort. This soon began to take its toll, not just on morale but on the very lives of those involved, as fresh grave sites began to multiply along the route of the excavation.

At the same time, Farragut was not only mired in a quandary as to his next move, but he was again betrayed by his ambitious foster brother, Commander Porter, who never scrupled to undermine the man he had grown up with.

Ever since Vicksburg's hostile reception to Commodore Lee's overtures back in May, Farragut had worried about bringing his big ocean-going ships this far up the river. Now Porter took it upon himself to send a letter to Gustavus Fox, who was Gideon Welles's assistant secretary of the navy, that said: "I never expect to hear of Farragut again. I have an idea he will ground on the bars of the Mississippi, and remain there the rest of the season. He went up without good pilots in those large ships where gunboats was all he wanted. He went up at a high stage of the river, and if the water falls he is done for and you can make up your mind to fit out a new squadron. If you can get one without having an old fogy in it, what a blessing it will be to the country. When I think of what a splendid thing we had of it here, I collapse."

Soon Farragut was roundly chastised by Fox, Welles, and the president himself for his alleged inaction, and he stood below fortress Vicksburg with no better notion of how to conquer it than the excavation of the DeSoto canal, which was not going as planned anyway. In addition to all the other vicissitudes, the river was falling to a level where it could not slash through the cut and form the new channel. Finally, after studying the stream of unhappy communications from Washington, Farragut determined that among the objectives the Navy Department sought was a linkup between himself and Davis's ironclad fleet, which lay above the city, out of range of Vicksburg's guns. What end this rendezvous might achieve was uncertain but, at least to the old commodore's mind, it would fulfill some of the expectations of his superiors. Therefore, Farragut sent an order that in the predawn hours of June 28 three of his five big warships, *Hartford, Richmond,* and *Brooklyn,* followed by eight of his gunboats, would run the gauntlet of Vicksburg's Rebel batteries.

He had made this maneuver successfully before, of course, between Forts Jackson and St. Philip, below New Orleans, and now decreed that the same tactics would apply. Promptly at 4 a.m. Porter's mortar boats—a number of which were "dressed as bushes" to disguise them for what they were—opened full blast on what was assumed to be the enemy's artillery atop the Vicksburg bluffs. If nothing else, the fight that followed was spectacular.

The Confederates manning the Vicksburg guns had figured something like this would happen and tried to plan accordingly, but it was impossible to presight their weapons on moving ships, even more so when their movement would likely come in darkness, as it had below New Orleans. Nevertheless, after Porter began his preliminary mortar barrage the defenders stood on full alert, resting their hopes on the fact that Farragut's ships would be slowed considerably against the current and that plunging fire from the heights could easily penetrate their exposed wooden decks and superstructures.

Porter ceased his mortaring at about 10 p.m. on June 27, and, with little better to do in the eerie stillness that followed, most residents blew out their candles and went to bed. Six hours later all hell broke loose. Porter's guns came alive with a fury so far unexperienced, and as Farragut's ships drew near they, too, began blasting away with enormous 9-inch guns until the whole of the bluffs seemed awash in orange fire. It reminded a Rebel gunner of a great lightning storm, with unbroken flashes and thunders, "one upon the other," while out on the river a sailor described the fire from batteries on the heights as "a continuous sheet of flame."

Residents rushed out into the streets and fled toward the woods behind town, hoping to get beyond the terror of the explosions. In his newspaper the *Whig,* Marmaduke Shannon related a scene of "men, women and children, both black and white, some dressed and others almost nude. . . . One man [was holding] his wife in his arms—she having fainted with fright."

The Confederates, however, were giving as good as they got, and the

Federal ships had to endure the ordeal for nearly two hours, until the sun finally came up and the smoke cleared away. Van Dorn, who had just arrived in Vicksburg the day before, sent a telegram apprising Jefferson Davis of the situation: "Bombardment heavy yesterday and this morning. No flinching. Houses perforated; none burned yet. All sound and fury and to brave men contemptible."

Once in safety around the bend of the river, Farragut was alarmed that not only were two of his gunboats missing but also the *Brooklyn*, one of his powerful deep-water men of war. A messenger was sent through the swamps of DeSoto Point to ascertain the whereabouts of the ships and when he returned Farragut was both relieved and annoyed to learn that *Brooklyn*'s captain had been delayed by towboats servicing Porter's mortars until, as the sun rose, he was subjected to such punishment from the Confederate batteries that he had decided to retire.

Most of the fleet, however, had successfully, if not safely, passed the formidable enemy bastion, having sustained fifteen killed and thirty wounded, along with considerable damage from Confederate cannon fire that narrowly missed Farragut himself. At the very moment he had leaped from his habitual spot on a spar aloft, a shot passed right through the rigging that surely would have blown him to kingdom come. Now, having achieved the objective mandated by Washington— that of uniting with Davis's ironclads—the quandary that had dogged him since capturing New Orleans remained: What to do next?

A solution did not take long to materialize, though it appeared in an unwanted and unsuspected fashion.

For nearly a year unsettling rumors—which were quite true—had reached the North that the Rebels also were constructing powerful ironclads. Confederate navy secretary Stephen Mallory was seeking ways to relieve the Union blockade, which was threatening to strangle the economy. While blockade-runners took up some of the slack, they could not come near to replacing the lost commerce. Since the Confederacy couldn't possibly match the Yankees in shipbuilding, Mallory concluded the only hope was to produce a few ships that would be overpowering. Ironclads seemed to be the answer.

The Federals, of course, had had the same idea, and on March 9, 1862, a clash between two of the weird-looking, revolutionary vessels occurred off Hampton Roads, Virginia, when the USS *Monitor* and the CSS *Virginia* (ex-*Merrimack*) fought to a draw that would soon render wooden warships obsolete. Both sides also understood that control of the rivers was just as critical as that of the open seas—especially so for the Confederacy, since rivers were the South's lifeline. Accordingly, the Richmond government had authorized construction of four big shallow-draft ironclads—the *Louisiana* and the *Mississippi* at New Orleans and the *Tennessee* and the *Arkansas* at Memphis. The first two, as we have seen, were destroyed during the Battle of New Orleans, and when Memphis fell the *Tennessee,* which was far from completion, was set afire and scuttled by the Confederates. The *Arkansas,* however, was moved from her slip soon after the fall of Island Number 10 and towed south, far up the Yazoo River, north of Vicksburg, where she underwent a transformation that was nothing short of miraculous.

In the haste and confusion of moving the *Arkansas,* she was left little more than an uncompleted derelict, which was the way her first commander, forty-six-year-old Lieutenant Isaac N. Brown of the Confederate navy, found her on May 28, 160 miles up the Yazoo, where the spring floods had left her stranded four miles from the nearest dry land. According to Brown, "Her condition was not encouraging," which might have been one of the preeminent understatements of the war: her engines were in pieces, guns strewn about the decks with no gun carriages, rail-iron armor sunk beside her at the bottom of the river, and not a blacksmith's forge in sight. Owing to the anticipated falling of the river during summer, and the large Federal fleet on the Mississippi that might appear at any time, Brown had little better than a month to get his hulk seaworthy and in fighting trim.

Within a week of his arrival, Brown had fished up *Arkansas*'s armor from the river bottom and towed her down to Yazoo City, where he set up shop under the sweltering summer sun with two hundred workers, both laborers and mechanics, and fourteen blacksmith's forges scavenged from local plantations going day and night. Foraging parties brought in tons of railroad iron that Brown had bent and bolted onto the bare hull. Private contractors built the gun carriages at record speed, and the guns were hoisted upon them. When the armor ran out, boilerplate was laid on the hull to give at least the appearance of protection. A mud-brown paint was applied to the finished product but it was defective and within a few weeks the ship took on a patina of burnished rust.

For crew, Lieutenant Brown had rounded up a hundred or so local river men, most of whom were fugitives from the remnants of Colonel

Montgomery's River Defense Fleet, which was wrecked at Memphis, and the army provided Brown with a company of sixty infantrymen from the Missouri Orphan Brigade.* As a further complement, Brown had a dozen officers, engineers, and midshipmen, most from the old U.S. Navy. The finished product consisted of a craft 165 feet long and thirty-five feet in beam that drew about twelve feet of water. A great iron ram had been fashioned to her bows and she carried ten heavy guns of all descriptions, three at each broadside and two at either end. Except for her engines—one of which tended to shut down at inopportune moments—the *Arkansas* was a match for any Federal ironclad on station above Vicksburg. Whether she would prove a match for all of them, plus Farragut's big men of war and gunboats, remained to be seen.

The Federals had gotten wind that something big and sinister was brewing in the swampy reaches of the Yazoo but, like Beowulf, they had not yet seen the monster, only heard tell of it. On the morning of June 27, the day before Farragut made his run past Vicksburg, Colonel Alfred W. Ellet, commanding the ram fleet in place of his now deceased brother, hauled off up the Yazoo for a look-see. It was bold business, considering that his rams were unarmed and that he had no earthly idea what he might find there, be it Rebel artillery batteries, mines, gunboats, or other disagreeable things.

With his nephew, nineteen-year-old Lieutenant Charles R. Ellet, leading the way in *Lancaster,* Ellet steamed in the *Monarch* some fifty miles upstream until he came to a Rebel defensive boom that had been placed across the river below Yazoo City. There lay three Confederate gunboats, the *General Polk* and the *General Livingston* as well as the *General Van Dorn,* which had escaped destruction at Memphis. Contrary to instructions, the three boats had not kept up steam, and as soon as they saw the Yankee rams approaching, their commanding officer panicked and ordered them set afire, leaving the Ellets to steam back out of the river with the satisfaction of having achieved one of the cheapest victories of the war. Still, they had not seen the elusive ram, but they were about to.

Meantime, as his ships swung at anchor in the Big Muddy, five hun-

* Missouri and Kentucky contributed organized units to both sides during the war. Because the Union soon occupied both states, the Confederate brigades became known as "orphans," because they had no home.

dred miles from deep blue water, Farragut fretted over his predicament. Without a far larger infantry force—an army, really—capturing Vicksburg was out of the question. And though the navy might be able to make costly dashes past the batteries on the bluff, the river was certainly not open for commercial traffic so long as the guns of Vicksburg were operating. In the intervening time, Farragut watched with growing alarm as his coal supply and provisions dwindled, his sailors increasingly turned up on the sick list in the unhealthy climate, and the level of the river fell dangerously lower in the summer heat.

About the only break from these sweltering doldrums came at straight-up noon on the Fourth of July when Farragut ordered the ship's band to play the "Star-Spangled Banner," accompanied by a celebratory twenty-one-gun salute that startled people for miles around, including Kate Stone at Brokenburn, who, after acknowledging the Yankee gunfire, told her diary: "Another Fourth of July has come and gone by without any festivities, not even dinner for the Negroes, but they have the holiday."* On July 13, Farragut took the extraordinary step of warning the Department of the Navy that "in ten days the river will be too low for the ships to go down. Shall they go down, or remain up the rest of the year?" It was an imposing question, soon to be solved.

In the predawn hours of July 14, the Confederate ram began to stir. As the *Arkansas* reached the confluence of the Yazoo and Sunflower rivers, it was discovered that a leaky valve had sent steam into her forward powder magazine and Lieutenant Brown ordered the vessel tied up to the banks at a sawmill clearing and the wet powder spread out on tarpaulins and turned and shaken in the sun. Having done that, and with her powder dry, the *Arkansas* lumbered downstream toward the Federal fleet.

Coincidentally, at about the same time, the ironclad *Carondelet,* the gunboat *Tyler,* and the Ellet ram *Queen of the West* raised steam and entered the Yazoo† in search of the mysterious Rebel Grendel that had

* It would be a long time before Vicksburg celebrated another Independence Day. In fact, the occasion was not officially recognized in the city again until 1945, during World War II.

† In the decade prior to the war, a minstrel composer from Pennsylvania named Stephen Foster was looking for a bucolic Southern river to feature in a song. His first inclination was to use South Carolina's Pee Dee River, but he didn't like the ring of it. Then he settled on the Yazoo, until his brother told him the name sounded peculiar. Foster agreed, and thus "Way Down upon the Swanee River" (also known as "Old Folks at Home") entered the American musical culture.

been so much on people's minds of late. As "the sun rose clear and fiery," the *Arkansas* gained Old River, a large lake formed by a cutoff where the Yazoo flows into the Mississippi ten miles above Vicksburg, and there she spied the Federal flotilla dead ahead.

The *Arkansas* was cleared for action. "Many of the men had stripped off their shirts," a Rebel crew member remembered, "and were bare to the waists, with handkerchiefs bound round their heads, and some of the officers had removed their coats and stood in their undershirts. The decks had been thoroughly sanded to prevent slipping after the blood should become plentiful. Tourniquets were served out to division officers by the surgeons with directions for use. The division tubs were filled with water to drink; fire buckets were in place; cutlasses and pistols strapped on; rifles loaded and bayonets ready."

With her U.S. ensign waving above her stern, the powerful ironclad *Carondelet* was in the lead, captained by the ubiquitous Henry Walke, of Island Number 10 and Memphis fame. Ironically, he had been a friend of Brown's in the old navy, as well as his messmate on Commodore Matthew Perry's celebrated voyage to Japan.

Brown got up full steam and headed straight for the big ship, intending to ram her, ordering his bow gunners to hold their fire lest the recoil slow their speed. For some reason, however, the usually pugnacious Walke suddenly decided he wanted no part of *Arkansas* and, as the distance closed to half a mile, he fired one "wildly aimed bow shot," then turned tail and ran downriver, firing from his stern guns as he went, while the *Arkansas* gave chase.

Soon the *Carondelet*'s fire began to tell, and the *Arkansas*'s crew felt the heavy shot plaster the iron plating of their bow. The sole casualty at this stage of the action was an unlucky Irishman who had stuck his head out of a port to see what was going on, "and was killed by a heavy rifle bolt that had [narrowly] missed the ship." Lieutenant George W. Gift, in command of the bow guns, ordered the nearest bystander to help push the Irishman's body into the river, "fearing that the sight of the mangled corpse and blood might demoralize the gun's crew. 'Oh, I can't do it sir,' the poor fellow replied, 'it's my brother.' The body was thrown overboard," Gift remembered.

Arkansas gained steadily on *Carondelet* and Brown, from his position on the shield directly over the bow guns, could actually see the big iron shells arcing out of his enemy's rear battery. "While our shot always seemed to hit his stern and disappear," Brown reported, "his missiles, striking our inclined shield, were deflected over my head and lost in air." A fragment of one of these, however, gave Brown a bad cut on his scalp and moments later a shot from *Tyler* crashed through the pilothouse, cut through the wheel, and killed one pilot and wounded another. The wounded man, it turned out, was the more serious loss because he was the only one who was familiar with the Yazoo River.

Just as *Arkansas* closed in, Brown was struck in the head by a rifle bullet fired by one of the *Tyler*'s sharpshooters, and when he awoke and resumed command he discovered that his ship had "entered the willows" that marked a dangerous sand bar. By then *Carondelet* had wobbled off toward these shallows, her steering damaged, and *Arkansas* pursued, closing enough to unleash a devastating broadside at close range "that caused her to heel to port, then roll back so deeply as to take water over her decks." At that point, Brown himself went out on deck, a move that under normal circumstances would have been suicidal. But the *Carondelet* had buttoned herself up tight as a turtle, so the Rebel skipper was able to walk around on his own decks, "within easy pistol shot, in uniform, uncovered, and evidently [to them I was] the captain of the *Arkansas.* Their ports were closed, no flag was flying, neither a man nor an officer was in view, not a sound nor a shot was heard," Brown said.

"Our last view of the *Carondelet,*" recalled the acting master of the gunboat *Tyler,* "was through a cloud of enveloping smoke with steam escaping from her ports, and of her men jumping overboard."

Until now, *Tyler* and *Queen of the West* had hung around trying to assist *Carondelet,* but upon seeing her disabled and aground they concluded that discretion was the better part of valor—but not before Lieutenant William Gwin, skipper of the *Tyler,* hollered out for the *Queen* to use her ram against *Arkansas.* "His only answer to this, however," said *Tyler*'s master, "was to commence backing vigorously out of range, while Gwin was expressing his opinion of him through the trumpet [bullhorn]."

There ensued a running gun battle for the ten miles it took for the Yazoo to empty into the Mississippi, with the Union boats getting the worst of it. The two wooden vessels were no match for the armor and big guns of *Arkansas* and soon "blood was flowing freely on board the *Tyler* as shot-after-shot from the Rebel ironclad found its mark." *Tyler* and *Queen of the West* finally turned into the big river, with *Arkansas* close at their heels.

"The code signals were run up in warning of the character of the company we were keeping," reported *Tyler*'s master, but the fleeing

Yankee sailors were astonished that, with all the cannon fire that had preceded them, not a ship in either Farragut's or Davis's fleet was ready for action, but instead "swung at their anchors as if this day was to be as placid as the last."*

But soon as they saw the rust-colored ironclad with her big Rebel flag, the blue-clad sailors scrambled into action. By then, conditions aboard *Arkansas* had nearly arrived at the limits of endurance; Brown reported that temperatures in the engine and boiler rooms had reached up to 130 degrees, and new men had to be rotated in every fifteen minutes to service the fires. When the Federal fleet finally came into sight, the impression it left on Brown was awe-striking: "Six or seven rams, four or five iron-clads, without including the one accounted for a hour ago, and the fleet of Farragut generally behind or inside of this fleet." He also had time to ponder that so many of the officers on these ships "had been valued friends," who now would have killed him just as cheerfully as he would them.

Brown would have used his ram on the enemy ships but was dissuaded by the *Arkansas*'s cranky engines. Instead, he told his pilot to "shave that line of men-of-war close as you can," in order to forestall the Federal rams—which were only now gathering steam—from plowing into him. *Arkansas* ran the gauntlet through the entire Union fleet, spitting fire fore, aft, and from both sides. First to receive punishment was the *Hartford,* Farragut's flagship, as Brown steamed his vessel straight into what he felt at the time was "a real volcano," with fire and explosions closing in from all sides, while his gunners blasted away "to every point of the circumference, without fear of hitting a friend or missing an enemy."

Inside the Rebel ship the din was nearly unimaginable as hundreds of "sledge-hammer blows were delivered to his armor plate" by cannon fire that was "literally continuous." At one point the colors were shot away, but a courageous midshipman scrambled through "a hurricane of shot and shell" to replace them. A ball from one of Farragut's large ships smashed into the forward gunroom, killing and wounding sixteen men and singeing the hair and beard of Lieutenant Brown. No sooner was that absorbed than another shot from one of Farragut's big 11-inch naval guns came through amidships and killed or wounded everyone at the columbiad gun, then continued across the gun deck and killed eight and wounded seven at the starboard broadside station.

---

* They had heard the firing, all right, but assumed that their little flotilla had merely been shelling the banks at suspected Confederate positions.

Still the *Arkansas* came on, her cannon fire blowing up one of the Ellet rams with a shot and wreaking havoc with the Yankee fleet in general. Prostrated firemen had to be dragged out of the boiler room and laid on decks covered with blood while others went down to replace them. As they neared the lower line of ships, Brown stuck his head out of the shield and saw the ironclad *Benton,* which was flying Davis's admiral's colors, just about to cross his bows. He shouted for his pilot to ram her, but at the last instant *Benton* squeezed up enough steam to slide out of the way—though not before receiving Brown's parting shot, "a starboard broadside which probably went through him from rudder to prow."

At last Brown and his ship got clear, and few if any in the Federal fleet mourned his going, let alone wished to give chase. But if the crew of the *Arkansas*—or what was left of it—thought they were home free, they were mistaken. As they made the hairpin curve of the river at Vicksburg, the Rebel sailors were amazed to see yet another Union fleet drawn up below the city to meet them. This was Porter's squadron, mostly mortar boats—one of which had grounded and was set afire to keep from being captured—and a handful of gunboats. Brown was relieved, however, to note that they kept a respectful distance from the batteries on the Vicksburg bluffs. His situation was such—with so many wounded and dead—that rather than pitch into this new enemy threat he put into the city wharf at the foot of the bluff to take stock.

Arkansas had been terribly mangled in the day's fracas. Sailors counted more than a hundred holes in the smokestack. One old tar said it reminded him of "an immense nutmeg grater." This had also drastically slowed the ship's speed because it ruined the draft from the flues. Cannon fire had broken the big ramming beak, all the lifeboats had been shot away, and a whole section of railroad iron had been torn from the side. Lieutenant Gift, Brown's second officer, described the scene aboard ship: "A great heap of ghastly slain lay on the gun deck, with rivulets of blood running away from them. There was a poor fellow torn asunder, another mashed flat, whilst in the 'slaughter-house,' brains, hair, and blood were all about. Down below, fifty or sixty wounded were groaning and complaining, or courageously bearing their ills without a murmur. All the army stood on the hills to see us round the point. The flag had been set up on a temporary pole, and we went out to return the cheers the soldiers gave us as we passed."

If Farragut still harbored doubts of "what to do next" the appearance of the *Arkansas* dispelled them once and for all. First, his wooden mortar boats and gunboats would now be easy prey for the Confederate iron monster and, second, there was the monster itself, which needed destroying. Finally, there was the nagging issue of the falling river that threatened to strand his ships if he didn't move them into deeper water. Time, too, was crucial. Farragut knew that the *Arkansas* had been injured in the run through his fleet; how seriously could not be determined, but every day she was allowed to sit at Vicksburg was another day for her to be put back in fighting shape. Farragut did not wait for orders from Washington; his fleet would run the Vicksburg batteries at sundown, and so furious was the old commodore that he diabolically hoisted the *Hartford*'s heaviest anchor high on the port yardarm, meaning to drop it on the Rebel ram and crush her with it if he got close enough.

Vicksburg's elation at *Arkansas*'s triumphant arrival turned to horror when a mob of citizens rushed down to the docks to cheer and congratulate the crew, then recoiled when they saw the carnage. Thus the sailors were left to remove their dead and wounded themselves, as well as stockpile more coal and get ready for another fight. As Farragut's ships began to steam into sight, it had been Brown's intention to go out and give battle, but just as he was preparing to shove off one of the Federal ships "sent a 120-pound wrought-iron bolt through our armor and engine room," killing a number of the crew and disabling the port engine. Nevertheless, the *Arkansas* gave a good account of herself, firing broadsides as fast as her remaining gun crews could load and fire at the passing ships, "so close that we could hear our shot crashing through their sides, and the groans of their wounded."

For the next week Farragut and his people were content to bombard Vicksburg in general, and the *Arkansas* in particular, from the safety of their downstream positions. But though neither the citizens nor the Confederates knew it, yet another "What next?" question would lead to their temporary relief.

The canal being dug by General Williams was now admittedly a failure, the water having fallen so low that the river would not fill it. Worse, illness and disease among all the soldiers and sailors had reached crisis proportions and, finally, Brown's ruse of constantly raising steam from his smokestacks had caused the entire fifty-ship Union fleet to keep up their steam also, which in turn was causing them to run dangerously low on coal. Still, the Federal bombardment kept up, sometimes with as many as 150 big shells landing in the city on a given day. Many of the townspeople had reburied their silver and gone to the countryside, while others stayed at home and dug rude caves in the surrounding hills to use for shelter when the shells fell thickly.

On July 21, sailors aboard the *Arkansas* saw a disturbing sight. A fresh Federal ironclad, the *Essex,* and the redoubtable ram *Queen of the West* began heading for them at full steam.* Lieutenant Brown was by now in desperate straits. His port engine was still disabled and he was helplessly moored at anchor; his crew complement of one hundred was now down to twenty-eight, and when word got round of the sort of bloodbath that could happen aboard a warship his efforts at recruitment had failed. Brown saw one last chance and took it, somehow maneuvering the bow of *Arkansas* around at the last moment so that she would receive the blow of *Essex* on her ram, impaling her. This caused *Essex* to sheer away and promptly run aground, but not before she fired several shots that killed or wounded a dozen of Brown's men.†

The Rebel skipper then used the same tactic on the *Queen,* which managed to strike a glancing blow but also ran aground. The two Union ships somehow extricated themselves and escaped downriver, but that was the end of Farragut's attempts on the *Arkansas,* as well as his third and final try to take Vicksburg. A week later, on July 27, his blue-water fleet hauled anchor and steamed south to where he thought it belonged, and Davis's ironclads, north of the city, disappeared upriver toward Arkansas and Memphis. With the departure of the Union navy and with the *Arkansas* still on the loose, Williams and his canal-digging infantry were forced to abandon their project and were removed by ship to Baton Rouge, where they would soon face another trial.

With the naval siege now raised, many citizens who had fled Vicksburg began to return. The destruction caused by the sixty-seven-day Union bombardment was considerable. Some twenty-five thousand shells fell on the city, but on closer inspection most damage was superficial, or at least repairable. No major fires had started. It was also remarkable that only a few residents had been killed or wounded, despite the sad death of Mrs. Patience Gamble, who was decapitated by a Union shell while trying to lead her little boy to safety, as well as

* *Essex* was commanded by William D. "Dirty Billy" Porter, brother of Commander David Dixon Porter, who detested him and had not spoken to him for at least a decade.

† After the action had ended, the crew of the *Arkansas* was astonished to find that the *Essex* used, in one of her guns that day, projectiles that were probably never used before, to wit: "Marbles that boys used for playing," Lieutenant Gift said. "We picked up hundreds of unbroken ones on our forecastle. There were 'white allies,' 'chinas,' and some glass marbles."

the death of a little girl who had inadvertently played with an artillery shell. Just seven Confederate soldiers had been killed, and twenty-five wounded, in addition to the carnage aboard the *Arkansas*. Foodstuffs were still in short supply, but much of this was because it had been difficult to bring them into town from the outlying plantations during the bombardment.

The recent news from the East of Robert E. Lee's victory over George McClellan at Richmond had left some clinging to the false hope that the war might soon be over. Most Vicksburgians, however, understood that their ordeal was far from finished. Still, this was a welcome respite, and Kate Stone, acerbic as ever, wrote in her diary, "The Yankees have called off their gunboats and quit the river in disgust. Sometimes now we can get the papers."

Part II

VICISSITUDES

CHAPTER EIGHT

Grant Begins to Stir

Major General Earl Van Dorn was characterized by Dabney H. Maury, one of the Confederacy's most beloved generals, as "The most remarkable man the state of Mississippi has ever known. He used to ride a beautiful bay Andalusian horse, and as he came galloping along the lines, with his yellow hair waving and his bright face lined with kindliness and courage, we all loved to see him. He gave assurance of a man whom men could trust and follow."

Nevertheless, General Maury's sentiment was not universally shared. A Kentuckian with the Orphan Brigade apparently spoke for others when he painted a portrait of Van Dorn as "a coxcomb, dandy, fop, ball-room beau and [a] thing of perfume, paint and feathers." And while many Vicksburgians at first welcomed Van Dorn's arrival as the brave handsome native son and West Pointer sent by Beauregard to save the city from infernal Yankeedom, others deplored his well-earned reputation for "whoring and drunkenness," vices that were especially frowned upon in that Victorian age. Moreover, whatever goodwill Van Dorn had accrued as a native son who grew up right down the road in Port Gibson quickly evaporated when he declared that he would see Vicksburg "reduced to ashes" before letting the Yankees have it. As if that wasn't enough, there was the appalling matter of Order No. 9.

When Van Dorn arrived to take command of the Mississippi District he was vexed by what he considered "disloyal" behavior by many citizens of the state. Foremost, this consisted of an illegal trade in cot-

ton across enemy lines between many Mississippi and Louisiana
planters and Northern "commerce agents." It was believed in Richmond that this activity was undercutting the Confederate government's hopes of bringing England and France into the war to break up
the Union blockade, once they discovered they could get the needed
cotton anyway. In addition, many southerners were refusing to accept
Confederate scrip except at a harsh discount, which had led to runaway inflation. Last, but not least, the Southern press felt justified in
printing just about anything it damn well pleased, including sensitive
information such as troop strengths and movements and other order-
of-battle secrets, often accompanied by disparaging remarks about certain Confederate commanders.

In a nutshell, Van Dorn saw all these acts as recklessly interfering
with the government's ability to conduct the war, undermining troop
morale, and giving the enemy valuable military intelligence. Thus he
issued General Order No. 9, which placed most of Mississippi under
martial law. Severe penalties, including death, were prescribed for
violators, and many citizens, some of them prominent, found themselves thrown into the stockade, without remedy of bail or habeas
corpus. Half a dozen were actually hanged. Price controls were im-
posed, newspapers suppressed, and other disagreeable measures put
into place, prompting an outrage that echoed all the way back to
Richmond.

In the meantime, Van Dorn oversaw a program of defensive construction that rivaled any in the Confederacy. The departure of the
Union naval fleet bought Vicksburg time to install a powerful line of
fortifications that curved around behind the city in a nearly ten-mile
arc anchored on the river above and below. Using the natural strength
of the steep ridges and sharp ravines that surrounded Vicksburg on
the east, Major Samuel Lockett, an 1859 West Pointer and chief engineer for the Department of Mississippi, oversaw the creation of this
bastion. When complete, it would include 172 artillery positions,
redoubts, redans, lunettes, and other forts and strongpoints connected
by a continuous line of trenches designed to be manned by 30,000
troops. This, it was believed, would make Vicksburg all but impregnable from a land attack coming from the east.

As for the river side, cannons were sent to the city from all points of
the Confederacy, making Vicksburg practically invincible from attack
in that quarter and, it was still hoped, impassable to Union warships.
This having been done, by the autumn of 1862 Vicksburg truly began

living up to its billing as the Gibraltar of the West: the great river remained closed to Federal traffic and the vital Confederate supply line to the trans-Mississippi was sustained.

As the days grew hotter, the armies in the West lapsed into a kind of mutual malaise, as though they were two panting beasts struggling to restore themselves from the shock and horror of Shiloh. There was scheming aplenty on the part of the Rebels, of course, and a few battles, which gained them little in the long run.

First, after Farragut left Vicksburg, Van Dorn decided it would be a good time to recapture Baton Rouge, an important port about two hundred miles south that had been critical to the trans-Mississippi trade before it fell to Farragut's fleet. For this enterprise, he selected Brigadier General John Breckinridge, a former vice president of the United States, to command an expeditionary force of 4,000 of his Kentuckians downriver. Breckinridge concurred, provided that Van Dorn send the by now patched-up *Arkansas* to engage the Federal gunboats and keep their heavy artillery out of the fight. That having been agreed to, Breckinridge put his men on the march while Van Dorn ordered the *Arkansas* to get up steam.

The problem—or at least one problem—was that Lieutenant Brown, who had taken a few days' leave in Grenada while the ship was being repaired, had fallen violently ill, and Van Dorn had ordered the ship's first officer, Lieutenant Harry K. Stevens, to take command. Hearing of this, Brown hauled himself out of his sickbed and threw himself on a train, hoping to stop the departure, but he arrived too late. *Arkansas,* as Brown had predicted, was in no condition to make a journey of that length. First, her chief engineer had undergone an emotional breakdown from the strain of the recent fighting, and the only available replacement was an army man who knew little or nothing of the *Arkansas*'s type of engine. She was also short of other crew from casualties and illness, and replacement positions still had not been filled.

Nevertheless, the ship cast off on August 3 but, after passing the mouth of the Red River 150 miles downstream, the engines "had grown so contrary" a stop had to be made for repairs, and then another, until the scheduled rendezvous to coincide with the attack was missed. At dawn on August 4, the noise of Breckinridge's assault was heard by the crew aboard the *Arkansas,* which lay by then just off Baton Rouge. And there they also found their old enemy the ironclad

Essex, plus one or two wooden gunboats, whose fire had caused Breckinridge's infantry to withdraw, even after successfully driving the Union forces from their positions and right down to the river's edge.*

Destruction of the *Essex* and her companions should have been short work for the big Confederate ironclad, allowing Breckinridge to resume the recapture of Baton Rouge, but as soon as it rounded the bend the cranky starboard engine gave out and the Rebel ship veered into a grove of submerged cypress stumps where she grounded herself. Engineers worked furiously on the machinery "with files and chisels," but it took all day to get the thing running again. Meantime, the crew could see Breckinridge's frustrated army in plain sight, waiting for something to happen, as well as the Union army huddled on the bluffs. To complete the picture, hundreds of residents had lined the bank to watch the proceedings, including "many ladies in carriages [who] had come to see our triumph. They waved us on with smiles and prayers, but we couldn't go," the ship's second officer, Lieutenant Gift, recalled bitterly.

The frustration lasted until well after sundown, when the balky engine was finally fixed and the ship refloated by heaving over a large quantity of railroad iron that had been lying on the decks. No sooner had they got under way, however, than the same engine quit, and it took the exhausted mechanics all night to get it started again, including setting up a forge on deck to fabricate a large metal pin that had broken.

At sunrise the Federal flotilla, sensing a kill, began moving in on the crippled Rebel ship. Stevens determined to fight it out then and there, but just as steam was raised to get under way the port engine conked out for good. Seeing that his demise was inevitable, Stevens did not even consult the other officers before setting fire to the main cabin and wardroom. As the sailors jumped into the water to make shore, flames burst out through the ports and huge explosions tore the ram apart, scuttled by the live artillery rounds left in her guns. Thus ended the saga of the *Arkansas,* only twenty-three days long, but in that short period she had caused two large Union fleets to withdraw from Vicksburg and nearly captured Baton Rouge.

As summer drew to a close, Confederate strategy in the western theater was ephemeral and murky. Breckinridge, after the aborted Baton

---

* These consisted of the brigade of General Thomas Williams, late of the canal-building project across from Vicksburg. Williams was killed in the action, reportedly decapitated by a cannonball.

Rouge expedition, accomplished what was probably the most important operation by marching his men fifty miles upriver and, on August 12, occupying the tiny town of Port Hudson, which was soon turned into a powerful fortress so that it effectively closed the Mississippi to enemy commercial traffic all the way to Vicksburg, some three hundred river miles to the north.

Meantime, Bragg took the main Confederate army from Tupelo, where it had languished since the Battle of Shiloh, and sent it by roundabout rail through Atlanta to Chattanooga, from where he intended to launch a northward invasion he hoped would regain Tennessee and Kentucky, before moving on Ohio itself. Opposing him was Buell's Army of the Ohio, which had earlier been detached from Corinth. In northern Mississippi another army, led by the Rebel general Sterling Price, had been ordered to support Bragg by keeping Grant's troops from reinforcing Buell.

It was then that Van Dorn, calculating that Vicksburg was safe for the time being, proposed a linkup with Price and a joint attack to regain the important railroad junction at Corinth, the seat of so much grief and suffering to the Southern cause. A victory there, he thought, would force Grant to pull back north, from whence he had started long months ago, or be picked apart piecemeal by Van Dorn's combined army. Price agreed, and on September 29 Van Dorn marched out, 22,000 strong, to meet Major General William Rosecrans, who held Corinth with about equal numbers.*

The battle began auspiciously for the Confederates on the morning of October 2. It was a violent collision in which the Federals defending the old Rebel outer fortifications northwest of town were overrun and by the end of the day the Yankees were fighting from enclaves on the edge of the city; thus, by nightfall, it appeared that a Rebel victory was in the offing.

Next morning the Confederate artillery opened up full blast, followed by a headlong infantry charge in which one of Price's brigades broke straight through Union lines and found itself in the streets of Corinth proper. Trouble was, they were the only ones; the rest of Van Dorn's army had failed to make significant advances, and so the astonished Rebels had no choice but to turn around and fight their way out.

---

* Van Dorn and Rosecrans both graduated in the West Point class of 1842, which produced eleven Civil War generals. Rosecrans had finished at the top of his class and Van Dorn at the bottom, and each was anxious to prove whatever meaning might be associated with it.

All morning under a sweltering sun the Confederates charged and were repulsed until the ditches outside the Federal positions were piled high with Rebel dead and dying. When the sun was straight overhead, Van Dorn had to concede that, aside from getting his men killed, no further results were likely to be produced and he called the operation off.

The fury of the Confederate attack is plainly reflected in the numbers: 4,222 Rebel soldiers were killed, wounded, or missing, while Rosecrans lost about half that, at 2,520.

At almost the same moment Van Dorn was canceling his assault on Corinth, Braxton Bragg, some four hundred miles to the north—and a mere two-day march from the Ohio River—was in the middle of Courthouse Square at Frankfort, Kentucky, installing a new Confederate governor, having chased off the pro-Union man. So far, most everything had gone according to plan in his cherished notion of marching an army right into the heart of Yankeedom. According to the conventional Confederate wisdom, this would cause every Union soldier in the West to be withdrawn northward from Southern soil and reduce their gains to naught.

Whether such a dream come true was dancing through Bragg's mind as the new governor, Richard Hawes, began his inaugural address is not recorded but, if so, it was rudely interrupted by the blasts of Union cannon shells that panicked the Southern dignitaries and scattered them in the streets of the Kentucky capital. The untimely arrival of Buell's army not only made Hawes Kentucky's shortest-lived governor but put Bragg's expedition in danger of destruction. His last best hope lay with his four divisions—about 20,000 men—temporarily under the venerable Bishop Polk, which he had parked about fifty miles southwest at Bardstown, and which he now ordered to proceed at once straight east to Harrodsburg, from where they might try to fight their way out of this unexpected mess.

Buell, with 77,000 men under his command, began closing on Bragg as fast as he was able, which in fact was not very fast at all. A drought had dried up most streams along his route of march and thirst was a powerful retardant when it came to moving infantry. This was no less true, however, for the Confederate army, and when Bragg's men reached Perryville, about seventy miles south of Frankfort, the grizzled Rebel commander decided he'd had enough of running and drew up for battle against a force nearly four times his size.

Buell might have had the numbers but many of them were raw and untested in battle, like the so-called Squirrel Hunters from Indiana, recently enlisted to deal with the emergency of Bragg's approach. Buell was coming at Bragg in three widely separated columns, about twenty miles apart, but they began to merge when word got back that the Confederates were in force at Perryville. In fact, they were not in force there—at least not full force. One division under Kirby Smith was still ten miles northeast at Harrodsburg, giving Bragg a total of about 16,000 infantry in three divisions to face a vanguard of 55,000 of Buell's men in eight divisions.

Buell posted his army in a six-mile front north to south on the western approaches to Perryville, largely along a ridge called Chaplin Heights, a wise enough alignment, considering that he believed Bragg's force was about twice the size that it actually was. Bragg, for his part, had no idea he was facing most of Buell's army, believing instead that he was contending only with an advance contingent of about his own strength. With this in mind, at 1 p.m. on October 8, he told the good bishop Polk and Major General William J. Hardee, who, in the old army, had authored the standard infantry tactics manual, to proceed with an immediate assault on the Federal divisions opposite them at the northern end of Buell's line.

The Rebels' ferocious charge took the Yankees completely by surprise, coming as they did screaming the Rebel yell out of a dark stand of trees, accompanied by a shocking artillery barrage. Those bluecoats who didn't throw down their arms and run away were quickly swept up or brushed aside in the Confederate attack as it rolled westward across a little valley. Because of an acoustic gap in the hilly terrain, most Federal commanders didn't even know an attack was taking place. Buell himself did not know it until three hours after the fact, which accounts for why five of his divisions never got into the fight at all.

By then it was getting dark and the Confederate and Union outfits were so intermingled that people on both sides were firing on friend and foe alike. At one point Polk, whose uniform jacket was of a dark, almost blueish gray, actually rode into a Federal stronghold and ordered a Union colonel to quit shooting at his troops. When he suddenly became aware of where he was and who he was talking to, the bishop-general providentially managed to bluff his way back to Rebel lines by passing himself off as a Yankee general. In any case, the fact that scenes like this were being played out across the battlefield indicated to everyone that the time had come for a halt.

By midnight Buell had finally figured out what was going on in his front and issued orders for a general assault on the Confederate lines the next morning. Somehow these orders were misunderstood by Union major general Thomas L. Crittenden, who did not advance his three divisions at daylight, per instructions.* In the end, it did not matter, for during the night Bragg, too, had taken stock of what he was facing and headed south.

For the Confederacy, the autumn of 1862 was not a harbinger of promising things to come. Although the Battle of Perryville might have been counted a victory if measured by the fact that of the 1,350 men lying slain most were wearing blue uniforms, Braxton Bragg's northern invasion had still come to an embarrassing close. After all the fighting and killing and angst and destruction and broken promises, the Southern mind remained outraged that from Kentucky to Missouri, from Tennessee to Arkansas, from Virginia to South Carolina, and from Louisiana to Mississippi, Yankee soldiers still occupied their sacred soil.

Back east, at least on paper, it had been going well for the Confederacy until recently. In late August after Robert E. Lee had humiliated the supercilious John Pope at Second Bull Run, he then undertook an invasion of Maryland that ended very badly at the drowsy village of Antietam, where Lee's army suffered more than 10,000 casualties. As in Bragg's fight at Perryville, more Northern boys had been killed, but in the end Lee's offensive was turned back and had to be counted a failure. Worse, he couldn't easily replace those kinds of losses, whereas the North could.

Antietam was also the catalyst for which Abraham Lincoln had been waiting to issue his Emancipation Proclamation, threatening to free all slaves in the seceded states if the Confederates did not lay down their arms by January 1, 1863. If Lincoln thought this would achieve the desired effect, he was emphatically proven wrong. The southerners immediately accused him of having been an abolitionist all along, and the indignation generated by the proclamation all but extinguished hope for a negotiated settlement at that point.

In the Deep South, there was also the unavoidable truth of the fail-

* Crittenden was the brother of Confederate major general George B. Crittenden, who was accused of drunkenness and negligence in the Rebel defeat at Mill Springs, Kentucky, nine months earlier. He himself was accused of misbehavior at the Battle of Chickamauga a year later and resigned his commission shortly afterward.

ure at Corinth. Brave and daring as it might have been, by the time
Van Dorn returned to Vicksburg many dead cats were already being
flung his way. By then, the Richmond government had peremptorily
rescinded his Order No. 9, and his enemies, of which there were now
many, began a campaign to have him removed. Upstanding citizens
sent letters to Jefferson Davis condemning Van Dorn for "intemper-
ance and other vices," the last likely a veiled reference to a widely
known affair the general had conducted with a certain Miss Martha
Goodbread in Texas, as well as other juicy grist from the rumor mill.
Mississippi senator James Phelan chimed in with a letter to the Confederate president denouncing what he called "the universal opprobrium which covers [Van Dorn] and the lower than lowest deep to
which he has fallen in the estimation of the community. . . . He is
regarded as the source of all our woes and disaster." Still not content,
Phelan continued: "The atmosphere is so dense with horrid narratives
of his negligence, whoring and drunkenness that an acquittal by a
court-martial of angels would not clear him of the charge."

Worse, perhaps, one of Van Dorn's own officers, the highly
respected brigadier general John S. Bowen, preferred formal charges
against him for neglect of duty and failure to care for his wounded at
Corinth.

Though an army court indeed soon cleared Van Dorn of all these
accusations, including drunkenness during battle, the firestorm of
malediction that now swirled about him caused Jefferson Davis to
send a new officer to command the department; thus replaced, however, Van Dorn would still have one final, brilliant act to play out in
Mississippi before being sent to Bragg in Tennessee, carrying his vices
with him, where his death warrant was fated to be signed.

The officer who arrived as Van Dorn's replacement seemed to many an
unlikely choice for the tremendous responsibility of defending what
was now the South's most crucial strongpoint in the western theater.
He was Lieutenant General John Clifford Pemberton, the forty-nine-
year-old scion of an old Philadelphia family who, like General Mansfield Lovell, his fellow northerner and failed defender of New Orleans,
aroused suspicions in the clannish Southern community because of
his birthplace.

Pemberton was born on August 10, 1814, into a gentrified family of
good Quaker stock. His paternal ancestors had immigrated to America
a century and a half earlier, along with William Penn, to escape reli-

gious persecution in England. While retaining their Quaker heritage, the Pembertons over generations became relaxed in their devotion to the austere dictates of Quakerism, so that by the time young John came along dancing, fashionable clothes, elegant parties, and city mansion style–living had become their norm. John's father, for whom he was named, even became a soldier during the War of 1812, an avocation particularly frowned upon by the peace-loving Quaker meeting. John's mother, Rebecca Clifford—with whom he was particularly close—was likewise descended from old Quaker bloodlines and saw to it that he was educated in the best private schools.

After a year at the University of Pennsylvania, John made a career leap that at first must have surprised his family. By now almost six feet tall, slender and with dark hair and brown eyes, he had decided he wanted to go to West Point and become an army officer and civil engineer. Years earlier, his father, a wealthy merchant, had met future president Andrew Jackson during the course of his travels south, and the two of them became friends. Still, Pemberton senior was reticent about asking Jackson, who by then was in his second term in the White House, for an appointment for his son, on grounds that it might smack of favoritism.* Rebecca, however, felt no such scruple and wrote a letter to the president pleading for intervention on her son's behalf. It seemed to do the trick, because on May 15, 1833, John C. Pemberton received his appointment to the U.S. Military Academy from the president himself.

Thus Pemberton, like so many other players in the drama, entered West Point, class of 1837, where, for reasons unexplained, his up till then satisfactory level of deportment and academic achievement took a turn for the worse. It started out with throwing rolls in the dining hall; at least that's what earned him some of his first demerits. During his years at the Point, Pemberton seemed satisfied with the "gentleman's C," and by the time he graduated he had racked up a disagreeable 163 demerits, graduating twenty-seventh out of fifty-one in his class.† He also became acquainted with cigars and chewing tobacco, as well as whiskey, which almost caused him to be expelled his senior year. Pemberton, it seems, while on orderly duty, was accused of a number of charges involving liquor in his barracks, placed under arrest, and made to live in a local boardinghouse until a court-martial

---

* By then, the Jackson administration was under heavy fire from the press on charges of political cronyism, nepotism, and other forms of string pulling.

† By comparison, George Armstrong Custer accumulated an appalling 726 demerits during his tenure at West Point. Robert E. Lee accumulated none.

could be convened. Like Jefferson Davis before him, however, he out-
lasted his accusers and was allowed to graduate with his class, which
included future generals Braxton Bragg, Jubal Early, and W. H. T.
Walker on the Confederate side and Joseph Hooker and John Sedg-
wick, who stayed with the Union.

Math, as it turned out, had not been Pemberton's strong suit at the
academy and, with his aspirations of becoming a civil engineer now
dashed, he somehow managed to get assigned to the artillery, which
itself requires no small knowledge of mathematics. This took him
south to Florida to fight the Seminoles, where, he predicted to his
brother, he would probably "get scalped by those damned Indians or
die a natural death in some of the swamps." While he did chase Seminoles through the swamps of southern Florida, he returned with his
scalp intact, only to be posted to the mountains of western North Carolina, where he chased more Indians—the Cherokees. During the next
several years Pemberton was sent to a number of stations from Maine
to the Canadian border in Michigan, mostly frontier outposts where
duty consisted of dealing with a variety of native uprisings. Finally, in
1842, after nearly five years of service, he was promoted to first lieutenant and sent to Fort Monroe, Virginia, where he met a girl who
would change his life.

Thus far in his career, Pemberton had indulged in a seemingly endless series of dalliances with young women that left him unsatisfied
and unfulfilled, but then in 1844 he met Martha "Pattie" Thompson,
the attractive daughter of a Norfolk shipping tycoon. Romance blossomed into wedding plans and by all accounts the thirty-one-year-old
officer seemed blissfully happy when, as it often does in the military,
war intervened. This time it was the Mexican War, which became the
proving ground for so many future Civil War officers, and when Pemberton shipped out in early 1846 it was with the understanding that
marriage with Pattie was in the offing when he returned.

Pemberton participated in most of the big battles and campaigns of
the war, being wounded and breveted to major on the staff of General
William Jenkins Worth. During the Battle of Mexico City he came into
contact with Captain Ulysses Grant, whose pending marriage had also
been postponed by the war. On one occasion Grant remembered that
Pemberton had walked his horse, painfully footsore, while other junior officers, against orders, had ridden, and in his memoirs Grant rec-
ollected of the Pennsylvanian: "A more conscientious, honorable man
never lived."

John and Pattie married in early January 1848 at Christ Episcopal

Church in Norfolk. His parents did not attend the wedding but in time became affectionate toward her. By then he had been in the army for a decade and longed for a post where he could settle down, preferably near Philadelphia. Instead, after a long period of uncertainty when Pattie became pregnant, but lost their first child, a daughter, Pemberton was posted to Florida again, and then to New Orleans. There Pattie had another daughter, named after her, and she and Pemberton settled into army life at Jefferson Barracks. In the next ten years, more children would follow, and more assignments, which would take Pemberton to the far-flung frontiers of the growing nation, from Washington to Kansas to Utah. In the army his star rose steadily, but not meteorically, and always there was the longing to go home to Philadelphia.

All this while political tensions had been building that would soon tear the country apart. What Pemberton thought about it is anybody's guess, since he left his opinions unshared, on paper or otherwise. When Fort Sumter was attacked in the spring of '61, Pemberton was on duty in the nation's capital. On April 19, four days after Lincoln declared the South in a state of rebellion and called for 75,000 troops to put it down, Pemberton was ordered to go with his regiment and seize all steamboats along the Potomac to ensure they did not fall into Confederate hands. This he did, although he had told his brother, Israel, that if Virginia seceded he would resign his commission.

This is somewhat of a puzzle, if you don't count his wife into the picture. Various historians have asserted that Pemberton had "adopted Virginia as his native state" before he'd even met his wife, but there seems little evidence to support this, given his long-standing penchant to return to Philadelphia. Pemberton's brother rushed to Washington to try to dissuade him from going against the Union, arguing that it would bring pain and shame to the family. On the other hand, Pattie, now back in Norfolk with the children, wrote him, "My darling husband, why are you not with us? Why do you stay!" Wrenched between two worlds, Pemberton vacillated a few more days, then resigned his commission and headed south to join the 146 other West Point graduates who went on to become generals of the Confederacy.

In Richmond, Governor John Letcher appointed Pemberton a lieutenant colonel of Virginia troops, with orders to organize training camps. During the next two months his official rank bounced around between the Confederate States Army and Virginia's army until an astonished Pemberton found himself a brigadier general. After a brief stint overseeing the emplacement of shore batteries around Norfolk, he was summoned by Robert E. Lee, then a major general, to assist him with the coastal defenses around Charleston, South Carolina. It was here that controversy found him, and so shadowed him for the remainder of his life.

Lee had a soothing way about him that appealed to the hotheaded Charlestonians, who were no less sanguinary now than they had been when they started the war. The long, undefended coastline between Charleston and Savannah inspired well-founded fears of a Northern invasion in that quarter, and there was much work to be done on the fortifications. During this time Union amphibious forces were frequently raiding and reconnoitering along the marshy coast, and Pemberton's initial reaction had been to send his men to the scene of action. Lee, however, made a point of explaining to Pemberton that it was more important to secure his own lines and troops than it was to risk losing them by trying to defend a particular spot. This instruction later led to harsh misunderstandings between Pemberton and the South Carolina civil authorities.

When, in the early spring of 1862, McClellan's grand army landed below Richmond and began working its way up the Yorktown peninsula, Lee was sent to Richmond, and Pemberton, who was then promoted to major general, found himself in charge of all the waterfront defenses of South Carolina and southern Georgia. He soon found it to be a Herculean task, complicated by a reluctance of some planters to lend their slaves for the extensive fortification projects required, as well as having to find sufficient troops, artillery, iron, and other materials for building interconnecting railroads, and the funds to pay for it all. A particularly nerve-racking period occurred when he was called upon by Richmond to send a large body of his troops west to support Beauregard's much anticipated defense of Corinth.

It was at this stage that animosity began to fester between Pemberton and the civilian leadership of Charleston, as well as the state's irascible governor, Francis Pickens. Recalling Lee's admonition not to risk losing his army in order merely to defend a particular place or point, Pemberton sized up the situation and began consolidating and condensing his lines, abandoning many of the waterfront strongpoints that had previously been considered essential to keep the Yankees at bay. Pickens, in particular, was troubled by this, and after corresponding with Pemberton he concluded that Pemberton would likely be willing to sacrifice Charleston without a fight, if it meant saving his army. Thus Pickens and other prominent Charlestonians wrote to Jefferson Davis that it was their intention to "see the city in ruins" before allowing it to fall into enemy hands undefended, in the process casting a vote of no confidence in Pemberton.

These disagreeable communications finally got back to Lee, who, though he certainly had his hands otherwise full in Richmond at that point, took time to countermand his original admonition to Pemberton about not losing his army. He suggested to the Pennsylvanian that critical places, even symbolic places such as Charleston, must be defended "street by street, house by house as long as we have a foot of ground to stand upon." Pemberton took Lee's new edict to heart and began a strenuous program of installing defenses in and around the city and its outlying areas, but it came too late for the picky Charlestonians, who had begun to view Pemberton's Northern roots with suspicion. Women whispered behind his back and wrote in their diaries about possible Yankee treachery, while a number of prominent men conducted letter-writing campaigns to their influential friends in Richmond. In the end the consensus in the Confederate capital was that, no matter how unfair and unfounded the accusations against Pemberton were, he had lost the confidence of his constituency and had to go.

Pemberton thought so too, and would have been glad to get leave, but finding an acceptable replacement took time. Then someone remembered that Beauregard, who had been languishing on sick leave ever since his ignominious departure from Corinth, might now be available. This having been decided, Pemberton departed, out of the proverbial frying pan and into the ineluctable fire.

Though he had hoped for a command in Virginia, Pemberton's new assignment called for him to take charge of the military district of Mississippi and that part of Louisiana east of the river. It must have come as a surprise, if not a shock, but after receiving the blessings and promised support of Jefferson Davis, Pemberton arrived in Jackson, the Mississippi capital, on October 9, 1862, and established his headquarters there. What he found could scarcely have been encouraging. Van Dorn's aptitude for day-to-day administration of military affairs had been sorely lacking, and by most accounts he had showed no interest, save for the disastrous Order No. 9. Pemberton promptly began to reorganize the department, laying especial emphasis on the support services: engineers, quartermaster, and ordnance.

The problems he faced both tactically and strategically would probably have been enough to make Lee himself cringe. Vicksburg, of course, had become the supreme prize, and Pemberton was well aware that Grant would soon be coming for it. With the Confederate navy out of the picture, and Federal gunboats now controlling the river above and below, the very topography that made the city seem impregnable was also its Achilles' heel, leaving it vulnerable to a surprise amphibious assault. Grant commanded an active army estimated at some 60,000, while Pemberton could muster fewer than half of that, and there was also the very real prospect that the Federals would marshal a landward campaign out of Tennessee to come up behind the city, or perhaps some combination of both.

Another matter that would dog the defense of Vicksburg until the end was the awkward, even conflicting, command structure that Jefferson Davis had set up. Before Pemberton left for Mississippi, he was promoted to lieutenant general, the Confederacy's highest rank, which was reserved for army commanders, and was told to report directly to Richmond—and to Davis, personally. This did not matter for the present, but there would come a time when it would.

Pemberton's strong suit—at least he thought so—was in planning and organizing, not in direct field command, and this also soon led to problems. When he arrived in Mississippi, both the press and the public welcomed him as a relief from the overbearing Van Dorn. Stories ran about his meticulous restructuring of the chaotic organization he had inherited from his predecessor, and though there was a predictable undercurrent of griping over his Northern origins it was soon dispelled by Pemberton's courtly manners toward prominent ladies and gentlemen of the state, which was duly reported in the newspapers.

Unfortunately this did not extend to the ordinary foot soldiers, who lived a life of hardship and danger. In those days, perhaps more than now, men who were expected to lay down their lives for cause and country wished to know exactly who was leading them. They wanted to get a look at the man and size him up, hear him talk and watch him ride, and see how he behaved in battle, or, absent that, at least be able to talk to someone who had.

From Pemberton they got precious little of this, as he preferred to stay in his headquarters in Jackson, working on plans with his staff, and the visits to Vicksburg, the northern front at Holly Springs, or Port Hudson, in the south, were too few, too short, and too far between, causing one cavalryman, in a letter to his wife, to characterize the new commanding general as an "insignificant puke."

Nevertheless, Pemberton continued apace to develop plans to

counter whatever Grant had in store for him. In the South, military campaign seasons were the reverse of what they were in the North, where armies often went into winter quarters. And as soon as November arrived along the Mississippi, with its riot of autumn foliage and splendid bracing days, Grant began to stir.

CHAPTER NINE

Until It Pleases God to Take Me . . .

S ince his return to army command, Grant had dwelled in a twilight of monotonous "guard duty" in western Tennessee and Kentucky. His problem was not so severe as Pemberton's, for there was little fear after Shiloh and Corinth that the Confederates would try to attack him in force any time soon. But Halleck had dispersed Grant's army over a 150-mile front and required that he also protect the 250 miles of rail supply lines leading from the north. With Nathan Bedford Forrest on the loose, that was a tall order. To Grant, it must have seemed that Forrest was everywhere at once—raiding, tearing up track, burning bridges, attacking small outposts, capturing wagon trains, and disrupting things in general—in the process earning for himself Sherman's sobriquet "that Devil Forrest," which he flaunted defiantly until the end of the war.

Meanwhile, Grant placed Sherman in charge of Memphis, with two divisions of about 14,000 men. It was the irascible Ohioan's first taste of control over civilians, and he exercised it with a stony harshness tempered by a chilling logic. When Sherman entered the city he found it all but closed down, and immediately he ordered everything—businesses, schools, churches, theaters, and saloons—to begin operating again. What he did about the galaxy of prostitutes that descended from points north upon Memphis and other Southern cities in the wake of the Union occupation is not recorded. (In Nashville, for instance, a delegation of concerned citizens badgered the Federal commander into deporting the prostitutes back to Ohio, but once the boat landed it was turned back yet again, prostitutes and all, by an equally concerned group of citizens in Cincinnati.) From the records available, Sherman's policy seems to have been focused more on practical lines. He rounded up all the fugitive slaves he could find and set them to work on his fortifications, restored the city council to its functions, and organized a civil police force so that "very soon Memphis resumed its appearance as an active, busy, prosperous place."

This proved to be an oversimplification, and premature as well. It wasn't long until Sherman discovered that most citizens were still unhappy with the turn of events that had led to his arrival. Whenever they showed it, however, he showed them back. First, he threatened to close any church—and this included virtually all of them—whose minister or priest refused to offer a Sunday prayer to the president of the United States, whom they reviled. Next he began expelling from their homes the wives and families of rebel soldiers and sympathizers in reprisal for Confederates shooting at Union gunboats operating on the Mississippi.* Predictably, he arrested a number of newspaper reporters, both local and Northern, whose stories displeased him. On September 24, he ordered the town of Randolph, Tennessee, burned to the ground in retaliation for people firing on U.S. vessels and also, for the same reason, commanded the immolation of all homes, farms, and outbuildings for fifteen miles down the Arkansas side of the river opposite Memphis.

These seem to be the earliest of Sherman's pyromaniacal urges in connection with Southern civilians and their property, but by a long shot they were not his last. He had by now refined his philosophy regarding the civilian population of the South, and expressed it bluntly to Treasury Secretary Salmon P. Chase three weeks after taking over Memphis. The war, he said, had thus far been "complicated with the belief that *all* [southerners] are *not* enemies." Sherman branded this assumption a great mistake and declared, "The Government of the United States may now safely proceed on the proper rule that all in the South *are* enemies." This was a leap for Sherman, perhaps even an epiphany of sorts, because he had spent so much time in the South before the war and made so many friends he still held dear. In his mind

* His orders read that for every incident of Confederates firing on Union or civilian boats, ten Southern families would be expelled from their homes in Memphis. When four Federal gunboats were fired upon shortly afterward, Sherman expelled forty Memphis families, and as the expulsions increased the legend of Sherman's cruelty began to fix itself in Southern lore.

it led to only one solution, and that was hard war—total war—where the conflict would no longer be confined to the battlefield alone but would consume everything and everyone around it and devil take the hindmost. It was ruthless policy, but he did not shrink from it.

Ironically, a problem that vexed Sherman particularly was the same one that bedeviled Van Dorn when he issued his Order No. 9—what to do about the cotton trade between the lines. The U.S. Treasury had recently adopted a policy encouraging such marketing on the premise that the bales of cotton purchased from Southern planters would be sent north and then sold to England and France for gold specie, which was much needed at the time. Sherman, however, contended that this was antithetical to the Union cause, since the southerners took the gold received from the Northern cotton traders and used it to buy arms, munitions, medical supplies, and other military goods from those same foreign countries, in fact *prolonging* the war in a vicious cycle of contraband trade. "We cannot carry on war and trade with a people at the same time," he famously announced.

Sherman insisted that Federal troops should simply go into Mississippi and seize the cotton for nothing, and to that end he outlawed all gold, silver, and Federal treasury notes in his department outside Union lines, hoping it would put a stop to the practice. It didn't. Instead, he complained to Chase, "The commercial enterprise of the Jews soon discovered that ten cents would buy a pound of cotton behind our army; that four cents would take it to Boston, where they could receive thirty cents in gold. That translated into a 300 percent net profit over what they paid the Southerners.

"The bait was too tempting," he continued, claiming that the cotton traders had now begun to barter with southerners for "salt, bacon, powder, percussion caps, etc. etc., worth as much as gold."

Grant concurred in this assessment, writing Chase himself that the cotton traders' "love of gain is greater than their love of country." Accordingly, he issued orders that all "speculators" were to be searched and, if found carrying gold or silver, turned back. If on the other hand they were caught with contraband items that might be bartered with the Confederates, they were to be arrested. "Jews should receive special attention," Grant added—a notation that was destined to lead him into trouble and embarrassment, but that was in the future.

For now, Grant felt strongly that his army ought to be doing something other than pacifying civilians and guarding railroad bridges and track, and he wired Halleck that he wanted to organize a big push south. His problem, he noted, was that Washington's expectation that he hold every position in his large department was unrealistic and he proposed consolidating his troops and invading Mississippi, with the aim of taking Vicksburg. The tracks of the Mississippi Central Railroad ran straight south in the center of the state and Grant planned to use them as a guide and a road, provisioning his army from trains coming down from the Federal supply dumps in Kentucky. His first objective was the state capital at Jackson, some two hundred miles south, then he would turn due west to Vicksburg, less than fifty miles distant.

To beef up his army, Grant ordered most of a division based at Helena, Arkansas, to cross the river, which would involve help from the navy—namely Admiral Porter, a sailor who was skeptical of the army in general and West Pointers in particular, and who had been waiting impatiently in Cairo following the navy's retreat from Vicksburg. For their first meeting aboard his flagship, Porter dressed in his spit-and-polish with about as much gold braid as a French admiral and was therefore perhaps understandably startled at the appearance of his counterpart, Grant, who arrived in a slouch hat, gray pants, and a dingy brown coat that was buttoned wrong. Nevertheless, Porter, or so he said later, was impressed by Grant's "calm, imperturbable face" and, after a lengthy conference, came away convinced that Grant was the man—and not a slick politician like McClernand, whom he had met earlier—to lead the Union to victory on the Mississippi River.

Grant's was a bold plan, and somewhat dangerous, because he would be taking his army deep into enemy territory, far from his base of supply, to where the Confederates had no doubt set up formidable defenses that could be quickly reinforced by rail. Even his friend Sherman was against this, arguing, "I am daily more convinced that we should hold the river absolutely and leave the interior alone. With the Mississippi safe, we could land troops at any point." But Grant was determined to grind it out on land and began organizing a huge supply base at the former Confederate stronghold of Columbus, Kentucky, where a rail line ran down through Tennessee and into northern Mississippi. With this in place, and after receiving only noncommittal replies from Washington about his intentions, Grant decided to strike out on his own.

Under his plan, by the end of November he would have marched some 30,000 men across the Tennessee-Mississippi border, taking Holly Springs, while Sherman, with another 20,000 from Memphis, would be on the way to link up with him at the university town of

Oxford. But then events began to come to Grant's attention that suggested a change of plans might be in order. These had to do with the machinations of his most troublesome subordinate, Major General John A. McClernand.

McClernand had been a trial for Grant since Belmont, where he had stopped to give speeches before the battle was won, and especially since Fort Donelson, where his division had been driven from its position by the Confederates and he'd tried to blame it on Grant. McClernand was an Illinois political general, with a face like a hatchet and a mind just as sharp—a lawyer, a newspaper publisher, and an anti-abolition Democrat who nevertheless remained on good terms with Lincoln and had received his rank accordingly. No one ever questioned McClernand's bravery, but his military judgment and political posturing were another matter entirely. At the least, Grant knew McClernand bore close watching when in the field; what he didn't realize was that he needed watching all the time.

It is probably safe to say that McClernand harbored aspirations for the presidency, likely as early as 1864. It was well established in American political circles that a record of high-ranking military service had won many a presidential election before the war—as it would afterward—and McClernand was apparently determined now to pitch-fork himself into the ranks of the stellar commanders by proposing a secret win-the-war-quick scheme to Abraham Lincoln himself.

In September, under the guise of a leave of absence, McClernand, who hated West Pointers as much as Admiral Porter did, traveled to Washington, carrying with him the inflated notion that he was "tired of furnishing the brains for the Army of the Tennessee." He told Lincoln that he wished to be temporarily detached from Grant's command for a recruiting campaign through Illinois, Iowa, and Indiana. He insisted to the incredulous president that he could raise at least 60,000 new troops, given his own popularity in the Midwest and the fact that the governors of those states were desperate to reopen the Mississippi for trade. In exchange, McClernand wanted command of this new army, which would take Vicksburg with an amphibious assault down the Mississippi. After thinking it over, Lincoln apparently decided that it couldn't hurt, since new recruits were getting hard to come by, and also he was all too aware of the discontent—not to say desperation—of the midwestern states.

If the account given later by Porter is accurate, and there is some reason to suspect it might not be, Lincoln soon became enthralled

with the plan. Porter had seen the president shortly after McClernand's visit and was told that he would replace flag officer Charles H.
Davis as commander on the Mississippi River. After assuring Lincoln
that he intended to capture Vicksburg "with a large naval force, a
strong body of troops, and patience," Porter was asked by the president who he thought would be the best general to command the army
operations. When Porter replied that it should be either Grant or
Sherman or both, Lincoln shocked him by saying, "Well, Admiral, I
have in mind a better general than either of them; that is McClernand,
an old and intimate friend of mine."

When Porter professed not to know who McClernand was, Lincoln
declared that he had been the savior of Shiloh when Grant had failed
and that McClernand was "a natural-born general." The president
wrote out a letter of introduction for Porter to give to McClernand and
asked him to visit the Illinoisian before he left for the Mississippi.
Porter did, and found McClernand at the Willard Hotel, laying plans
for his upcoming wedding to his dead wife's sister, who was twenty-
four years his junior. Vicksburg, McClernand told the astonished
admiral, would be taken in one week!

Thus, with the lukewarm consent of Halleck, McClernand went on
his way to assume the recruiting stump, and Porter to assume command of the river fleet. The newest expedition to conquer Vicksburg
was under way.

McClernand's enlistment campaign proved quite successful;
although not exactly what he had promised Lincoln, he did in fact persuade some 40,000 midwestern boys to sign on for cause and country,
and he was in the process of recruiting still more when word of his
activities reached Grant. Early on, Grant had selected as his chief of
staff a lawyer named John Rawlins, who had been a neighbor and
friend in Galena, and who watched over the general with more than
just canine-like loyalty. He was a savvy political adviser, as well as
Grant's keeper when it came to matters of his alcohol delinquency.
Rawlins, himself a teetotaler, was perfectly suited to the job, because
as a child he had been obliged to peddle firewood and coal on the
streets of Galena when his alcoholic father could not provide for the
family.

It was at about the time Grant was preparing to march his army into
Mississippi that Rawlins saw a disturbing report from a commander
up in Cairo, mentioning that a large number of midwestern recruits
were beginning to arrive there, destined downriver for Memphis,

"with a sort of loose order to report to Gen. McClernand." This was the first that Grant had heard of it, and to make matters worse a muddled communication arrived from Halleck suggesting that he push no farther south at that point, but instead wait for a decision from Washington as to Sherman's role in the thing. Clearly agitated, Grant wired back, "Am I to have Sherman move subject to my orders, or is he and his forces reserved for some special services?" Halleck replied, "You have command of all troops sent to your Dept., and have permission to fight the enemy where you please." No sooner had Grant interpreted this to mean he could proceed with his plan than Halleck sent another message leaving Grant more puzzled than before: "The enemy must be turned by a movement down the river from Memphis as soon as a sufficient force can be collected."

What did this baffling declaration mean? Grant wondered. Was he to be in charge of this new force? Was Sherman? Was McClernand? Did it foreclose his advance through central Mississippi? Was Halleck somehow in cahoots with McClernand's scheme to usurp part of his command? It was maddening.

Grant decided to put the question to the test. He told Sherman to put his troops in motion from Memphis and, on November 20, 1862, cross into Mississippi and link up with him. A few days later Grant had taken Holly Springs, some twenty miles below the state line, and by December 5 he had captured Oxford. The Confederates obligingly fell back before his superior force, and with Sherman's linkup now imminent Grant had his 50,000 troops in Mississippi, heading south.

However, the more that Grant thought about it, the more he became concerned that something extraordinary and threatening was afoot with respect to McClernand and the army of new recruits who were arriving daily at Memphis. Therefore, he decided to take a different tack. Since Confederate resistance to his invasion had thus far been lighter than expected, Grant now reversed himself and told Sherman to march his divisions back to Memphis and organize a new force consisting of his own troops plus the "McClernand men" and, while Grant continued fighting his way south to invest Vicksburg by the landward side, Sherman would load this new army on steamboats for a surprise attack on the city's northern flank, via the Mississippi and the Yazoo rivers.

To the letter, at least, this would square neatly with both Halleck's authorization for Grant to fight the enemy where and when he pleased as well as his directive that "the enemy must be turned by a movement down the river." The interesting part is that if Grant was congratulating himself for slyly circumventing what he feared might be a connivance between Halleck and McClernand, he was as wrong as could be. Halleck had no more use for McClernand than Grant did, but he was loath to communicate it because Lincoln himself was said to be solidly behind the plan. All Halleck could do—or rather all the canny old army bureaucrat in him *would* do—was continue making vague recommendations that were subject to enough interpretation by everybody to keep his own nose clean.

Such was the strategy for taking Vicksburg as the year of 1862 came to a close. So far as it went the plan seemed well laid, but well-laid plans in war have a way of turning sour for the simple reason that it is always dangerous to assume an enemy is going to sit there and let you bowl him over like a dummy made of straw.

By now, Pemberton was thoroughly alarmed at the events unfolding before him in northern Mississippi. For the time being, he perceived no threat from the south but, just in case, he had ordered Port Hudson reinforced and restrengthened yet again, in case the Federals decided to mount an offensive from New Orleans.

As November wore on, however, repeated messages from Van Dorn, who commanded at Holly Springs, foretold of an impending invasion by Grant's army, which finally prompted Pemberton to leave his paperwork in Jackson and go up to the front and see for himself. At once he ordered Van Dorn to pull out of Holly Springs and fall back to the Tallahatchie River north of Oxford, and soon afterward, when Grant began his advance, Pemberton told Van Dorn to withdraw again and set up a deep defensive line behind the Yalobusha River at Grenada, midway between Jackson and the Mississippi-Tennessee border. Grant followed, stalking.

Pemberton's position was clearly in peril. He was outnumbered by about three to one—too weak to attack—and sooner or later Grant could simply keep maneuvering him out of his positions by flanking movements until he was ultimately left helpless, or useless, or both. Several weeks earlier, as soon as Pemberton began to divine Grant's intentions, he began telegraphing Braxton Bragg in Tennessee to send him some troops; Bragg refused, saying it was too dangerous. Pemberton then contacted Richmond, asking authorities there either to order Bragg to dispatch reinforcements or perhaps to bring them from the trans-Mississippi, where Lieutenant General Theophilus Holmes was said to command a large army at Little Rock doing little or nothing at present. In fact, not only was Holmes doing nothing, he wasn't even intending to do anything except stay there and make his presence known for the sake of Arkansas citizens who felt that the Richmond authorities had deserted them. He replied with a disrespectful letter saying as much, and branding Pemberton as a man who "has many ways of making people hate him, and none that inspire confidence."

In response, Jefferson Davis concluded that because of the distances involved the western theater needed a single commander to coordinate movements and allocate forces, and for this job he selected General Joseph E. Johnston, who was recovering from wounds suffered during the Federal advance on Richmond. For Davis it was a practical solution to a sticky problem. First, a high place for Johnston, the hero of Bull Run, had to be found, and it was out of the question to let him resume command of the Army of Northern Virginia in place of the victorious Lee. Second, Davis didn't like Johnston (the feeling was mutual) because he considered him difficult, condescending, and a prima donna, and sending him out west would solve at least part of that problem.

Johnston agreed to go, but he went reluctantly, which was not a good sign. He brought with him a pessimistic attitude surpassed, perhaps, only by that of his wife, who had come along with him. Shortly after arriving in Tennessee, she'd written a friend back in Virginia of her new surroundings: "How dreary it all looks and how little prospect there is of my poor husband doing ought than lose his army. Truly a forlorn hope it is."

There was also a major flaw in Davis's plan that had all the earmarks of being fatal, and it had to do with the authority that Richmond bestowed upon Johnston to conduct the war in the West as he saw fit. Johnston's mandate extended from the Alleghenies to the Mississippi, but no farther. This meant that he would be able to request, but not order, assistance from the considerable Confederate forces across the river, including those of the dilatory Theophilus Holmes. With a shortage of troops and control of the river in the balance, this seems incredibly shortsighted on Davis's part.

If that wasn't bad enough, when Johnston came on board he naturally assumed that Pemberton would report directly to him and no one else. Pemberton, however, understood that Johnston would be his immediate superior, but, still, there was Davis's instruction that he should report straight to Richmond. So Pemberton did both, which led to no end of trouble when advice from the two headquarters began to conflict. Around this time Mary Chesnut, the acknowledged doyenne of Richmond insider gossip, ruminated in her famous diary on Davis and the uneasy command situation in the West, closing with a queer notation from Euripides: "Whom the Gods would destroy, they first make mad."

Joseph Eggleston Johnston at first impression seemed to be an ideal military commander for the new Southern nation. He had graduated in the top half of his West Point class of 1828 (the same class as Jefferson Davis), was wounded and breveted twice during the Mexican War, and at the age of fifty-three had become the youngest general in the United States Army. Despite his short stature, Johnston's bearing was always impressive: dapper, handsome and trim, with sideburns, mustache, and Vandyke, and the courtly manners of a Virginia gentleman that he learned from his father, a circuit judge who had fought in the Revolutionary War. He was the highest-ranking officer of the old army to resign in favor of the Confederacy.

But when the occasion arose, Johnston could also be petty, jealous, spiteful, secretive, defensive, and resentful, which in time of crisis were certainly not assets to his personality. The occasion arose most prominently with respect to Jefferson Davis. If one leaves out the rumor of his altercation with Davis during their West Point days, the ill feelings seem to have been triggered in the late 1850s when Davis, then secretary of war, held up Johnston's promotion, and again right after secession, when Davis appointed Johnston to the rank of full general—which under most circumstances would have been received as an honor, except Johnston resented the fact that three other generals had been appointed before him, giving them seniority. His complaint was that he had outranked each of them in the old army, which might have had some merit but Johnston chose to exacerbate things by distributing his feelings all over Richmond, prompting Davis to conclude that he was a troublemaker.

For his part, Johnston was further annoyed by the fact that Davis, who was of course himself a West Pointer and Mexican War hero, let alone a former secretary of war, tended to meddle not only in the organization of the army but in its operations as well, right down to strategy and sometimes even tactics.

During the first Battle of Bull Run, or First Manassas, Johnston, along with Beauregard, was in charge of the army that defeated the first big Federal invasion of Virginia. Though he was the senior officer on the field, he relinquished command on grounds that Beauregard was more familiar with the terrain, but much of the credit for the victory attached to Johnston, and rightly so. After Beauregard fell from favor, Johnston was given command of the Army of Northern Virginia as McClellan began his ill-fated Peninsula Campaign, but he retreated nearly a hundred miles from Yorktown, to within five miles of Richmond, before finally standing up to the Federals at what became the Battle of Seven Pines. The fight itself was inconclusive, but there the Union advance stalled until the entire campaign was finally hurled back in disgrace by Robert E. Lee, who took over after Johnston was wounded.

For most southerners, in the years right after the war Johnston remained one of the great heroes. Even his hardest adversaries, Grant and Sherman, noted in their memoirs that they considered him one of the Confederacy's most formidable strategists. But the light that history has cast upon his career has been less kind. In retrospect, Johnston seems to have been the Confederacy's answer to McClellan: beloved by his soldiers (they called him "Uncle Joe"), admired for his military bearing, praised for his ability to organize an army and prepare it for battle—everything, that is, but the battle itself. There his shortcomings were revealed: "timid," some called him; "prudent" was a more charitable word. Throughout the war Johnston always seemed to be preparing for attacks that never came off—maneuvering, delaying, testing, and feinting—waiting for the golden opportunity to deliver a crushing blow that would not risk his army in the process.

An acquaintance of Johnston's recalled an incident from many years earlier that provides some insight. Hearing that Johnston was reputed to be a fine wing shot, he invited him to go quail hunting in the Virginia coutryside. Most times when a covey rose up, Johnston declined to fire, and when asked what was wrong he would reply that the birds were too far away, or screened by brush or trees, or that the sun was in his eyes, leading the friend to conclude that he was afraid to take a shot unless it was perfect. In short, he wasn't a gambler or a killer like Robert Lee.

While Pemberton continued to bombard the War Department with requests for more troops, Davis was receiving pleas from Mississippi governor John J. Pettus and Senator James Phelan to pay a visit to the beleaguered state and reassure the population and the soldiers that they were not forgotten. Davis was well aware of the importance of Vicksburg and the probable calamity to the Confederate cause if the city was lost, and he decided to go even though the military situation in Virginia was becoming critical with a large Union army threatening Fredericksburg. Moreover, the governor not so subtly reminded Davis of his own local connection. "You have visited the army of Virginia," he wrote. "At this critical juncture could you not visit the army of the west?" And Phelan told him: "The present alarming crisis in this state, so far from arousing the people, seems to have sunk them in listless despondency.... Enthusiasm has expired to a cold pile of damp ashes. If ever your presence is needed . . . this is the hour."

To avoid speculation that the government was abandoning Richmond in the face of a huge Federal buildup on the Rappahannock, Davis sneaked out of Richmond on a night train to Chattanooga, where he would see General Joseph Johnston, who had just established his headquarters there. He continued on to Murfreesboro, only thirty miles southeast of Nashville, where General Braxton Bragg's army was encamped. After a conference with Bragg, and over the strenuous objections of Johnston, Davis secured from Bragg's army a reinforced division, of about 9,000 men, to aid Pemberton during the present emergency. Having accomplished that, he returned to Johnston's headquarters, where he learned that Lee, with a force half its size, had hurled the 120,000-man Federal army back across the Rappahannock, leaving behind them 13,000 dead and wounded on the heights of Fredericksburg. Davis was of course greatly relieved, but Johnston received the report in a way that only underscored his resentments. "What luck some people have," he remarked. "Nobody will ever come to attack me in such a place."

Since Johnston had never visited the Mississippi front under his command, Davis asked him to come along to Vicksburg, and when "Uncle Joe" balked the president nearly had to order him to go. In any case, armed with the good news of Fredericksburg, the president and the commander of the western theater went on to the bluff city, arriving on December 19, 1862, where more news, good and bad, awaited them.

The good news was that a few days earlier one of Admiral Porter's most powerful ironclads, the *Cairo,* had ventured up the Yazoo River, never to return.

Several months before, Beverly Kennon, the Rebel navy officer previously stationed in New Orleans, arrived at Vicksburg with plans for an underwater explosive device he had been tinkering with. The torpedo, or mine, was not unknown to the Confederates; indeed, it had been used in Charleston and, as we have seen, might have been employed to great advantage during Farragut's attack on New Orleans. But the early ones had been activated by a percussion primer—that is, when a ship struck the mine a bullet in its nose would set off the explosion—and they were too often defective after exposure to the water.

The contraption Kennon had in mind would be electrically detonated, with copper wires suspended beneath the surface running to a camouflaged "torpedo pit" hidden on shore, where the mine would be manually set off with an electric battery. A number of these devices were assembled with the notion of protecting the Yazoo from further Yankee incursions, and the man selected to lead the mining enterprise was Lieutenant Isaac Brown, presently a captain without portfolio since the demise of the *Arkansas*. It was a deliciously wicked scheme and worked to perfection as the *Cairo* steamed insolently up the Yazoo. As her bow crossed over one of the five-gallon glass demijohns—large jugs used to store whiskey or make wine—that were filled with black powder, it exploded with such fury as to actually lift the huge warship right out of the water, and, just as she settled down again, a second mine blew up directly beneath her. Within ten minutes the pride of the U.S. Navy's Mississippi River fleet was lying on the bottom in thirty-six feet of water, earning her the dubious distinction as the first warship in history to be sunk by an electric underwater mine.*

That was the good news. The bad news was what the *Cairo* was doing there in the first place. She had arrived a few days earlier with a flotilla of gunboats and other vessels, the first to darken Vicksburg's waters since Farragut had abandoned his designs the previous summer. Reports by Rebel spies at Memphis produced the ominous news that a large riverborne attack by Yankee infantry was in the making.

With the bulk of his force menaced by Grant's army north of Grenada—more than 150 miles away by rail—this new threat left Pemberton facing twin swords of Damocles. He had been forced to leave fewer than 6,000 men to defend Vicksburg itself and desperately

* The wreck of the *Cairo* was discovered in 1956 by the Civil War historian Edwin Bearss, who was then employed by the National Park Service. In 1964 she was raised in three pieces from the mud bottom and in 1977 hauled to the Vicksburg National Battlefield. Over the years *Cairo* has been painstakingly restored until today she remains among the most fascinating, and certainly the largest, Civil War artifacts.

needed relief. To that end he summoned the unpopular Earl Van Dorn for an important mission.

It seemed that a colonel of the Texas Brigade, which had recently been remounted as cavalry, had been ruminating on how the cause could best be served by men on horseback. His conclusion was that a great surprise raid employing most of the available cavalry in the department—about 4,700 sabers, including irregulars—could be staged far behind Grant's lines to cut him off from his base and force the Federals to retire. The notion became all the more attractive when Bragg decided to unleash Forrest around Memphis and, most especially, along the rail line from Columbus, Kentucky, that had become Grant's lifeline.

It was the Texas colonel's proposal that Holly Springs should be the target of this raid, since reports had arrived indicating that Grant was stockpiling enormous stores of food, ammunition, clothing, and other material there.

Pemberton heard the officer out, then sent for Van Dorn and appointed him to lead this delicate operation. The little Mississippian was profoundly grateful to accept the challenge, since he continued to remain in the doghouse because of the odious Order No. 9, the abortive Baton Rouge expedition, and most especially the failure at Corinth. Recently he had written his wife in frustration and disgust, "Until it pleases God to take me . . . I shall fight this war if I am left with no friends but my family."

The first thing Van Dorn insisted upon was utmost secrecy and only a few high-ranking officers were told of the ultimate destination. In fact, the rank and file was not even told that he was to lead the expedition. Van Dorn handpicked the regiments that were to participate and made the decision not to bring along artillery, which would slow the column down. Instead he would rely on the shock and awe produced by 2,500 Confederate cavalrymen—the number finally settled upon—dashing out of what he hoped would be a misty dawn onto an unsuspecting enemy.

An additional advantage was that, until recently, Van Dorn and much of the cavalry had been posted in and about Holly Springs and knew their way around. Kickoff time for the raid was Tuesday, December 16, and, as usual for that time of year, the weather had turned horrible—rain and bone-chilling cold—but, even so, it might mask the noise of the advance. If everything went as planned, they would attack Holly Springs in four days. As the troopers rode out two abreast from their bivouac in the early hours, their column stretched nose to tail for more than three miles along the south bank of the Yalobusha. A member of Van Dorn's staff recalled that the controversial general "rode straight as an Indian, sitting astride his horse like a knight, and looking every inch a soldier."

Practically from the moment Davis and Johnston arrived in Mississippi, they had engaged in anxious conferences and inspections of the Vicksburg defenses from the riverfront batteries, to the Walnut Hills above the city, to the little town of Warrington, about fifteen miles downriver, where the southern end of the Vicksburg fortifications were anchored. Johnston did not approve of Pemberton's disposition of batteries, arguing that the way the lines were laid out required an entire army to man them and constituted a trap, rather than employing lesser fortifications that would allow the army to maneuver against the enemy in the field. Next they traveled by train north to Grenada, where Pemberton's front was established, and where Johnston later claimed that he also disagreed with Pemberton's plan of defense, which he believed was "so extensive" as to be worthless.

In particular, Johnston said he preferred an offensive-defense strategy that would rely on movement and opportunity rather than the static defense favored by Pemberton. In other words, Johnston was willing to give up as much ground as necessary to make that perfect shot he always had in mind. Pemberton, on the other hand, was trying to square the admonition Robert E. Lee had given him back at Charleston not to risk losing an army just to defend a particular point of ground with Lee's later reversal of that maxim, when he had counseled that if it came to defending Charleston, the city must be held "street by street and house by house." Also there was Davis's charge that Vicksburg be retained at "all costs."

There was something else, too, that in the end might have dramatically changed the outcome of the campaign. Across the river in Arkansas sat the Rebel army of Theophilus Holmes, said variously to contain between 35,000 and 50,000 men. Presently there was no Yankee force of any size in Arkansas, and both Johnston and Pemberton had been urging Davis to transfer at least some of these men over to Vicksburg, which seemed to them the obvious solution to counter Grant's invasion. That would have given Pemberton 50,000 men, including cavalry, and one of the rare opportunities for the Confederates to meet the enemy on more than equal terms.

The problem was, Holmes wouldn't budge. The secretary of war had written him a letter, which he believed constituted an order, to join Pemberton in Mississippi. No movement had been forthcoming, however, and the only thing accomplished was the resignation of the secretary of war, which he tendered after Davis chided him for sending an order to an army without clearing it with him first. Finally, while visiting Vicksburg, Davis himself wrote Holmes, who was in Little Rock, asking him to provide 20,000 men for Pemberton's aid. "We cannot at all points hope to meet the enemy with a force equal to his own," Davis explained, "and must find our security in the concentration and rapid movement of troops." That was all well and good, but then Davis added two sentences that sealed the fate of the enterprise. "I have thus presented to you my views, and trusting alike in your patriotism and discretion, leave you to make the application of them when circumstances will permit. Whatever may be done should be done with all possible dispatch."

Holmes, a half-deaf fifty-eight-year-old North Carolinian and West Pointer, had, like so many ranking officers of both armies, served with distinction in the Mexican War. But he had been criticized by some for apathy, and was later appraised thusly: "Although undoubtedly the possessor of many soldierly qualities, it is apparent that he was unequal to his high rank." He appeared to be one of those unfortunate commanders who recognizes all the problems lying before him but can never figure out a solution. At any event, Holmes seemed to take Davis's plea to heart, especially the part about "Whatever may be done should be done with all possible dispatch." He immediately did nothing.

With all these things to consider, Pemberton decided to maintain his defensive front behind the Yalobusha River and await the results of Van Dorn's raid.

North of the Yalobusha, Grant peered through the misty rain contemplating how to eject Pemberton from his entrenchments. Even with Sherman and his men now back in Memphis Grant still outnumbered the Confederates three to two, but he was in no great hurry to bring on a fight. As soon as Sherman got downriver and began the assault on Vicksburg, Grant was certain that Pemberton would be forced to redeploy a significant portion of his army—or even the whole of it—to deal with that situation. When he did, Grant would be ready to pounce.

It was also about this time that Grant issued an odious order of his own, which would dog him all the way to the White House years after the war ended. Reports had continued to pile up that the cotton speculators were ignoring his warning about trading with the enemy in gold specie and greenbacks and, worse, actual contrabands of war (i.e., slaves). By December 17 Grant had heard enough and told Rawlins to issue the following decree, styled "General Orders No. 11": "The Jews, as a class having violated every regulation of trade established by the Treasury Department and also department orders, are hereby expelled from the department within twenty-four hours from the receipt of this order."

It went on to say that his post commanders would "see that all of this class of people . . . be required to leave," and that any who didn't would be arrested and made prisoners, adding that no appeals would be heard by his headquarters or by anyone else within his authority.

The effect of the order was to banish not only the Jewish cotton traders and speculators who had come from all over the North, but also the numerous Jews who had long resided in Tennessee and Kentucky, from Memphis to Paducah, and all points in between.* And that was not to mention the Jews who were in Grant's own army. The results were immediate and devastating. Whole families were uprooted, some in the dead of night, and sent packing either up the Mississippi by steamboat or across the Ohio to Cincinnati and other cities. Many Union-loyal Jews who had nothing to do with cotton speculating were swept up in the dragnet when overenthusiastic officers rousted them out of house and home, carrying only the bare necessities. Horror stories were circulated, including that of a baby tossed bodily into a boat bound for the far side of the Ohio; many Jews who for one reason or another did not get the word in time were arrested and put in stockades.

Reaction by the Jewish community was not long in coming. A delegation of Jewish leaders from Kentucky sent a telegram of protest to Lincoln, and when that did no good one of them, Cesar Kaskel, took it upon himself to go to Washington and see what could be done.† Eventually, Kaskel received an audience with the president, who denied

* Aside from the Indian removal by Andrew Jackson, it was the largest expulsion of a particular race of people under authority of the U.S. government until the relocation of Japanese and Japanese Americans from the West Coast in 1942.

† Whether the telegram reached Lincoln has been a subject of discussion over the years. It did in fact reach Washington, but where it went from there remains a matter of controversy among some historians.

knowing anything about the matter. When it was explained, however, the following colloquy was said to have ensued.

"And so the children of Israel were driven from the happy land of Canaan?" Lincoln asked, to which Kaskel responded, "Yes, and that is why we have come unto Father Abraham, asking protection."

"This protection they shall have at once," was Lincoln's reply, and he sent Kaskel away with a note instructing General Halleck to cancel Grant's order—which he finally did a full month and more after it was issued. Later, Halleck wired Grant: "It may be proper to give you an explanation of the revocation of your order expelling all Jews from your department. The President has no objection to your expelling traitors and Jew peddlers, which, I suppose, was the object of your order, but as it proscribed an entire religious class, some of whom are fighting in our ranks, the President deemed it necessary to revoke it."

As mentioned, the matter did not rest there but continued to ferment in the political cauldron until it arose again as an issue when Grant ran for president in 1868. What followed was an unseemly string of denials by several of Grant's old staff cronies to the effect that he was unaware of the order, and that subordinates had written it without his approval.

Of course Grant suspected nothing of those repercussions as he bided his time north of the Yalobusha, waiting for Sherman to shove off for Vicksburg and lure Pemberton's men away from his front. Later he would remember: "My action in sending Sherman back was expedited by a desire to get him in command of the forces separated from my direct supervision [McClernand's recruits]. I feared that delay might bring McClernand, who was his senior and who had authority from the President and the Secretary of War to exercise that particular command—and independently. . . . I doubted McClernand's fitness."

If Grant indulged himself in daydreams, it must have been doubly satisfying to picture McClernand standing on the dock at Cairo, furious as a bride left at the altar, when news of Sherman's departure came his way.

It was a little better than one hundred miles from Grenada to Holly Springs by the circuitous route Van Dorn had plotted out. The cavalrymen would skirt far to the east—some thirty miles—from the main line of the Union advance down the Mississippi Central Railroad. Still there was always the danger that a Yankee cavalry patrol would spot them, and so the Rebel outriders were double-posted and hard on the lookout.

The first day they made a remarkable forty-six miles before stopping to rest around midnight. At dawn they were on the road again before bedding down for a few hours in a cold drizzle, and without fires so as to avoid detection by Yankee patrols. Passing through the village of Pontotoc they were treated to a lively reception by the townspeople, who lavished them with food and drink, but the urgency of the mission prompted Van Dorn to keep on pressing northward. It was near Pontotoc that they were spotted by a column of Federal cavalry. Its commander tried to warn Grant but, through some mix-up of the "I told him to do it" and "I ordered it done" variety, headquarters was not notified of this valuable information until the morning of Van Dorn's proposed attack.

On Thursday, December 18, both men and horses were near exhaustion and many troopers slept in their saddles as they went slip-and-stumble through the flooded bottomlands. Next day, as the unsuspecting Union garrison at Holly Springs was preparing for a Christmas holiday dance, Van Dorn's men were a mere thirty miles away. The weather had broken and turned snappy cold and they were now under the direction of local guides, who brought them down a little-known road that led into Holly Springs.

By midnight on the nineteenth, they had closed in on the town. As luck would have it, three Yankee cotton speculators turned up on the outskirts of town, and Van Dorn's men quickly relieved them of their clothing and their "trading passes," and soon afterward three disguised Confederate cavalrymen entered Holly Springs bold as you please for a look around. They returned with good news: nobody suspected anything and the coast was clear.

Grant in fact had about 4,000 infantry posted in the vicinity, but only 1,500 in the town itself—and of these only about half were fighting troops, the rest being detail men. The fighting men were in several encampments ranging from half a mile to a mile from one another. Still, they were infantry, and infantry was considered an abomination to cavalry, owing to what massed rifle fire could do to horses. Be that as it was, Van Dorn decreed that the attack would begin at dawn.

Meantime, an orgy of blundering was under way between Grant's headquarters and the commander at Holly Springs. Just about the time that Van Dorn and his party were arriving outside town, alarming reports began to come in to Grant's nerve center down at Oxford. A slave had told Union scouts of a large body of Confederate cavalry on its way north. Then the commander of the original Federal scouts who had seen the gray raiders arrived in person to add his news. Other

details followed rapidly over the telegraph, all pointing to an impending Rebel attack on Holly Springs.

Grant began sending messages ordering his available cavalry to get
cracking against this dangerous intrusion behind his lines. Foremost,
he sent a telegram to the post commander at Holly Springs, Colonel
Robert Murphy, a Wisconsin lawyer and "political officer," warning,
"Jackson is moving north with a large force of cavalry . . . send out all
the cavalry you can to watch their movements. I am sending the cavalry
from the front."* What Murphy made of this is unknown, but after
alerting his cavalry as directed he went to bed.

The nervous slave informant was taken to the Holly Springs mansion in which Colonel Murphy was sleeping. It was now 5 a.m. Murphy heard out the slave and sent him on his way. The amazing thing is
that the slave had carried Van Dorn's plan to Murphy as sure as if it
had been handed over by Van Dorn himself. But instead of immediately rousting the garrison Murphy wrote out a telegram for Grant, saying, "Van Dorn only 14 miles from town, 5,000 cavalry, intending to
destroy stores and dash on to Grand Junction. He is on the Ripley
Road and expected to be here by daybreak. Have ordered out my cavalry, but my force is only a handful."

And as if that was not amazing enough, Murphy then went *back* to
bed, which is where he was found right after sunrise when all hell
broke loose.†

From their concealment a mere two hundred yards from the edge of
town, Van Dorn's men, nearly all 2,500 of them, burst forth at a gallop,
battle flags flying and pistols firing above the shrieking Rebel yell.
They dashed right through one of the infantry encampments, where
the startled and disbelieving occupants emerged from their tents in all
manner of dress and undress before scattering up and down streets
and alleys and across lawns and fields, including the town cemetery.
Some ran all the way to Memphis, or so it was said. A brief, vicious
sword fight broke out between part of an Illinois cavalry regiment and
a Confederate detachment from Mississippi, but the Yankee horsemen
were quickly subdued.

---

* Colonel William "Red" Jackson was nominally the commander of Confederate
cavalry in northern Mississippi. Grant had not yet learned that Van Dorn himself was
leading the raid.

† Murphy claimed in his official report that he had been captured running from the
rail depot to rejoin his command but, judging by the reaction of Grant to the surprise
attack, he does not seemed to have been believed.

Half-dressed women came rushing from their homes to cheer the Rebels on, shouting, "Kill them! Kill them!," some weeping with elation and relief. Children also appeared, clapping and waving small Confederate flags. The unfortunate Murphy was paraded before Van Dorn covered only with his humiliation and his nightshirt. Local lore has it that Ulysses Grant's wife, Julia, was likewise rousted from the comfortable home she had been occupying with the general before he went south, and Van Dorn ordered that a guard be posted at her door so that she would not be molested.*

The raiders found much of what they had come looking for on Depot Avenue.† Here were the mountains of Federal stores that Grant's army depended upon to exist deep in enemy territory—warehouses filled with uniforms, shoes, food, rifles, pistols, ammunition, tents, saddlery, wagons—as well as a generous supply of whiskey and cigars, which were appropriated in no time at all by the jubilant raiders. Of course, this last became a concern to Van Dorn and his officers since the main purpose of the raid was to carry off or destroy all the Yankee supplies, and drunk soldiers do not make good stevedores. But after the arduous and scary march the raiders were not to be denied, and they set out to prove that drunk men *do* make good stevedores, with mixed results.

By midmorning, Confederate officers had distinguished between what could reasonably be carried away and what needed to be destroyed. There was so much that it staggered the imagination of the average trooper, who, under the Confederate system, had brought to the war his own horse, tack, pistol, saber, and uniform—and here all these things were for the taking. Many Rebels were seen stuffing half a dozen or more pistols into their blouses, and carbines were gathered, too, and handfuls of cigars and bottles of whiskey and tinned oysters and fruits. Some raiders helped themselves to fresh Yankee horses found in the Federal corrals.

On sidings adjacent to the depot warehouses were boxcars lined end upon end and packed to overflowing with untold riches. These were set afire, as were the stores in the warehouses themselves (and with the blessing of their owners, it might be added), since there was no time to carry the booty into the street for fear Union forces would soon be upon them. It was not an idle concern, for as soon as Grant

* Other accounts say she was down in Oxford with Grant at the time of the raid.

† Afterward renamed Van Dorn Avenue, and remains so today.

discovered he no longer had telegraph contact with Holly Springs he would realize what had happened, and Van Dorn was well aware of that as well.

In midafternoon a pall of smoke hovered above Holly Springs and the surrounding countryside. Several homes and their outbuildings had inadvertently caught fire, including one containing Mrs. Grant's handsome new carriage. Van Dorn had detailed scouts in all directions to warn of approaching danger, while others were responsible for tearing up track so that a Federal relief force could not get at them by railroad. At 4 p.m., he decided that enough had been accomplished and it was best to git, while the gittin' was good.

To dispose of the large number of Yankee prisoners, which he obviously could not take with him, Van Dorn demanded that Murphy sign a document of surrender, including the provision that all Federal soldiers would be paroled, meaning that they would agree not to fight again until properly exchanged. Murphy was stupid enough to sign the paper, ensuring that if by chance a Union relief party suddenly arrived on the scene his 1,500 men would have been of no use to aid them.

With that, Van Dorn and the Holly Springs raiders rode out of town, heading north toward Tennessee, where they hoped to link up with Bedford Forrest and inflict even more mischief. That they did not succeed hardly mattered. As it was, they had destroyed some $1.5 million of Union supplies—worth $50 million today—and gave Grant a setback from which he was hard-pressed to recover. As usual, his enemies—including, naturally, the Northern press—were waiting in the wings with shrill cries and mean whispers.

CHAPTER TEN

I Reached Vicksburg, Landed, Assaulted, and Failed

Back at Memphis, Sherman knew nothing of the situation unraveling at Holly Springs when he set out with four divisions— some 32,200 men—to assault Vicksburg by the river route. His main body embarked on December 19, the day before the raid, and arrived off the mouth of the Yazoo on Christmas Day, anticipating that he would take the 6,000 Confederates by surprise while Grant was pinning down Pemberton's army along the Yalobusha River. He was wrong on both counts.

At the same time Van Dorn's raid destroyed the stockpiles of supplies for Grant's invasion of Mississippi, Forrest had so thoroughly wrecked the trestles, bridges, telegraph lines, and rail tracks across Tennessee and up into Kentucky that it ensured no more supplies would be forthcoming. It was all the more remarkable since most of Forrest's 2,100 troopers had been green recruits riding jaded horses and armed with shotguns or squirrel rifles. By the time the raid ended, the brigade was mounted admirably, well armed, and larger in strength than it was in the beginning.

When he considered the hard facts, Grant was forced to a painful conclusion: he must withdraw his army back toward Memphis or starve. It is the only time during the entire war that a cavalry action alone had turned back a major campaign. Even as he began trying to communicate his decision to Sherman and to Halleck in Washington, Grant realized that there was no way to know for sure if they got the word. In fact, they didn't for a critical eight days.

However, Pemberton knew through reports from his scouts and spies that Grant was in full retreat, leaving him free to redeploy his own troops to deal with the threat everyone suspected was brewing upriver. If Sherman actually believed he was going to sneak up on the Confederates at Vicksburg, then sending the *Cairo* into the Yazoo to reconnoiter and bombard Rebel gun batteries the week before was a strange way of going about it. By the time his full force had gathered at the mouth of the Yazoo—the Indian name meant "river of death"—the defenders were ready for them, or at least soon would be.

With the departure of Grant's army, Pemberton transferred three infantry brigades from the Yalobusha line down to Vicksburg to defend the city's northern flank. This was defined by the meandering Yazoo, which was protected on its southern bank by a series of tall bluffs known collectively as the Walnut Hills, or Chickasaw Bluffs, beginning at the Mississippi and ranging up to Haines's Bluff, nearly twenty-five tortuous miles by water and about twelve miles by land. The terrain in between the Yazoo and this line of bluffs was an infantryman's nightmare—possibly his worst nightmare. Most of it was utterly impassable, cut through and through by marshes, cypress swamps, cane brakes, shallow lakes, snaky bayous, bogs, old river cut-offs, and dense, tumbledown old-growth forest. As if that weren't enough, large stands of trees had been chopped down and their branches skinned and honed to make a thorny abatis. It might have been marginally negotiable for the occasional bear hunter, but to bring a large military formation across most of it in any order—or, for that matter, at all—was a practical impossibility.

Only three approaches lent themselves to a waterborne assault from the Yazoo, and the Confederates knew where they were. They were located about four miles from Vicksburg in an area of relative open fields and bottomlands near the racetrack, which had once been part of a cotton plantation, but still there were swamps and bayous an enemy had to cross to reach the bluffs and high, level ground. Rebel batteries, entrenchments, and rifle pits covered them nicely.

The immediate problem for the Confederates, however, was that the present 6,000 men left to guard the city still weren't enough to hold off the 32,000 Yankees converging on them with artillery and gunboats. The fate of Vicksburg would depend on whether the 10,000 troops that Pemberton had recently entrained at Grenada could get there in time, and possibly another 9,000 from Bragg that Davis had finally ordered sent over Johnston's protest. If not, the next best thing would have been simply to hole up in the formidable defenses of the city itself, but that would have created consequences that were more far-reaching, as Major General Martin Luther Smith, who commanded at Vicksburg proper, explained.

"The inquiry naturally arises," General Smith wrote in his after-action report. "Why meet the enemy outside of our fortification and on a line so extended? The Yazoo," he said, "drains a section of the country of great wealth and fertility, has its source in the heart of the state, and is navigable to the Mississippi Central [Railroad]." Not only was it important to protect the agriculture of the Yazoo Valley, Smith wrote, but it was even more critical to keep the enemy from controlling the river, seizing the many Southern steamboats operating there, and setting up a base of operations "that would be most dangerous to our success."

The main impediment to Union control of the Yazoo, Smith pointed out, were the powerful gun batteries on the bluffs at Snyder's Mill, near Haines's Bluff, which the Confederates believed were impregnable from direct assault from the river, by either ironclads or infantry, or both. But, he went on, if Sherman could break the Rebel line along the Chickasaw Bluffs, he could come up behind Snyder's Mill, and the Haines's Bluff defenses, taking them from the rear, then proceed to break the Jackson–Vicksburg trunk of the Mississippi Central. This would isolate Vicksburg from the rest of the Confederacy and make its capitulation a short matter of time.

As Sherman's armada steamed downriver from Memphis, the Rebel spies and scouts kept tabs as best they could, but the ultimate destination could not be predicted for certain. On the twenty-first, Sherman put in on the Arkansas side of the river and began embarking Federal troops from Helena, then proceeded south again. There was a possibility, of course, that the landing was planned for some place far above Vicksburg, from where the Yankees would move eastward to cut into Pemberton's flank and rear on the Yalobusha. Nobody knew for sure until a dark, rainy Christmas Eve, and the revelation alone was the stuff of a theatrical melodrama.

On a gloomy night in a lonely outpost way across the Mississippi, about twenty miles north of Vicksburg, two Confederate officers were playing cards in a small building on a cotton plantation near the river when a little black girl came in and told them she had heard a steamboat coming. That far north of Vicksburg it was bound to be the enemy, so the two men went out on the porch to have a look. To their astonishment, a Yankee ironclad appeared, then another, and another, seven in all, and interspersed between was a seemingly endless line of transport steamers—they counted fifty-nine—packed to the gunnels with Federal troops.

One of the officers, Major Lee L. Daniels, had been a telegraph operator in Vicksburg before the war and, coincidentally, was the messenger who had delivered the telegram to Jefferson Davis at Brierfield, telling him he had been elected president of the Confederacy. Daniels jumped on his horse and rode three miles back to the Rebel telegraph station and began frantically tapping out a warning to his corresponding lookout down on DeSoto Point, just opposite Vicksburg. Nobody answered, and Daniels tried again, and again, growing panicky as the minutes ticked off.

At last a response came through from an officer at the other end, Colonel Philip H. Fall, who wanted to know: "Golly, old fellow, what's up?"

"Great God, Phil, where have you been," Daniels tapped out. "I have been calling, and the river is lined with boats. Almost a hundred have passed my lookout. I can see lights as far as the eye can reach up the river. God speed you. Rush across and give the alarm."

There was a momentary pause, and Daniels's key began to tap again: "God bless you. Bye, bye. We may never meet again."

Incredulous as he wrote out Daniels's message, Fall dashed to a skiff and shoved off into the stormy river, bucking waves, wind, and current as he struggled for Vicksburg, burning a red light to show the batteries at the base of the bluff that he was friend not foe. It was past midnight when Fall, bedraggled and dripping water, made his way across the dance floor at the home of Vicksburg socialite Dr. William Balfour, who, with his wife, Emma, was hosting a Christmas ball that included most of the prominent officers of the army and their ladies. The band fell silent and the guests parted as Fall approached Martin Luther Smith and gave him the message, whereupon the general turned "ashy pale" and announced to the startled guests, "This ball is at an end. All noncombatants leave the city," or words to that effect. If nothing else, it was a splendid example of how telegraphy had changed the face of modern warfare.*

---

* This account is taken from a letter Daniels wrote to General Stephen Dill Lee in 1904, which Lee, then president of Mississippi State University, used in composing an article on Confederate telegraph operators for the Mississippi Historical Society.

Now that the Confederates had divined Sherman's intentions, they rushed every fieldpiece and infantryman they could lay their hands on to the Chickasaw Bluffs front. Fields of fire were cleared, rifle pits dug, entrenchments excavated; more abatis were laid into position. Guns were sighted and ammunition brought up by the wagonload. Arrangements were made by the quartermaster to regularly feed the troops hot meals; hospitals were organized; the ladies of the city ripped up petticoats to make bandages and cloth wadding for bullets. Martial law, so unpopular under Van Dorn's administration, was again declared to discourage spies, and anyone entering the city was required to obtain a pass from the provost marshal. Pemberton published a strongly worded bulletin recommending that all residents leave town, and he warned those who stayed that they could be subjected to hardships, or worse, as the army went about its tasks.

Operational command of the bluffs was delegated to Brigadier General Stephen Dill Lee, a twenty-nine-year-old artillerist and Charlestonian who had graduated seventeenth in his West Point class of 1854. Lee sized up the ground before him, with the bluffs running roughly southwest to northeast parallel to the river, and concluded that the Federals would probably land at the Johnson plantation or a bit northwest of there near the racecourse. Once ashore, there were three likely approaches close in to the bluffs; the first came to be known as the Sandbar, the second was near an old Indian mound, and the third ran along a fork of Chickasaw Bayou, which wandered along in front of the bluffs for a mile or so before draining out into the Yazoo.

Lee had at his disposal at that time only a single infantry brigade of 2,500 with which to face Sherman's ten brigades of about 25,000, and only four Rebel artillery batteries of twenty-six guns against Sherman's ten batteries of sixty guns. To say that a timely arrival of the men Pemberton had sent down from the Yalobusha and those on the way from Bragg's army was paramount would be a gross understatement.

The Confederates knew the stakes were high. Sherman thought he did, too, but was about to find out just how high during the next week. It was his first independent field command and obviously he wanted to do well. A few days before leaving Memphis he wrote his brother John, the senator, about his aspirations for the invasion, closing with the mention of a little house in Ohio that he wanted to buy, he said, for Ellen and the children after the war, "if I survive, which of course I do not expect...."

Early morning the day after Christmas found Sherman's armada at the mouth of the Yazoo, where he remained while an infantry brigade debarked on the Louisiana side to wreck a few miles of the railroad that ran from DeSoto Point toward Shreveport and on into Texas. Why Sherman did not proceed immediately up the Yazoo to his objective remains a mystery, for by giving the now totally unsurprised Confederates another day to fortify, reinforce, and organize, he certainly did himself no favor. But on the second day Sherman moved and, just as Lee had surmised, began to debark at Johnson's plantation, as well as a couple of miles upriver near the racecourse, north of where Chickasaw Bayou emptied into the Yazoo.

That same morning, which was the day after Christmas, Jefferson Davis was delivering a speech to the Mississippi legislature at the Capitol building in Jackson, forty miles from Vicksburg. It was, in effect, a State of the Union address—or State of the Confederacy, as it were—a sort of compilation of all the things he had been saying since his formal inauguration as president the previous February.

Why he chose this occasion to unburden himself of these ruminations was no doubt in part because of the adjurations of Governor Pettus and Senator Phelan, who had warned of Mississippians' flagging spirits and the suspicion that they were being ignored by the Richmond powers that be. Also, of course, Mississippi was Davis's home state and, in particular, Vicksburg was his hometown. When the Federals under Farragut first came up from New Orleans to take the city, they had put in at Davis Bend, where a detachment of Yankees burned Hurricane, his brother Joseph's magnificent plantation, then descended on Brierfield and ransacked it. Thus Davis was probably feeling doubly incensed when he told the legislators that the North was waging a war "for the gratification of the lust of power and aggrandizement, for your conquest and your subjugation, with a malignant ferocity and with a disregard and a contempt of the usages of civilization entirely unequaled in history.

"Such, I have ever warned you, were the characteristics of the northern people," Davis told them. "After what has happened during the last two years, my only wonder is that we consented to live for so long a time in association with such miscreants and have loved so much a government rotten to the core. Were it ever to be proposed again to enter into a Union with such a people, I could no more consent to it than to trust myself in a den of thieves."

Davis then launched into a novel excoriation of the hated Yankees that was becoming more popular—to brand them, like blacks, as a separate race entirely.

"There is indeed a difference between the two peoples. Let no man hug the delusion that there can be renewed association between them. Our enemies are a traditionless and homeless race. From the time of Cromwell to the present moment they have been disturbers of the peace of the world. Gathered together by Cromwell from the bogs and fens of the north of Ireland and England, they commenced by disturbing the peace of their own country; they disturbed Holland, to which they fled, and they disturbed England on their return. They persecuted Catholics in England, and they hung Quakers and witches in America."

It was a thought-provoking argument, so far as it went. Previously, southerners had railed against Northern abolitionism, commercialism, and sharp business practices, such as the so-called Tariff of Abominations. But labeling them as an entirely different race—and a lower one at that—was to ratchet up the unpleasantness to a new level. In making his case, Davis was echoing the dreaded Confederate sea raider Admiral Raphael Semmes and a number of other southerners who contended that the North was populated by the descendants of the Puritan Roundheads, of Oliver Cromwell, who in 1649 had overthrown and executed the king of England, before being forced to flee to Holland and finally settling at Plymouth Rock, Massachusetts.

On the other hand, so Semmes's argument went—and by implication it was almost tribal in nature—southerners were the hereditary offspring of Cromwell's enemies, the "gay cavaliers" of King Charles II and his glorious Restoration, who had settled at Jamestown, Virginia, with their easygoing, chivalrous, and honest ways (omitting, in a possible lapse of memory, that the original settlers of other Southern states, such as Georgia, had been convicts or, in the case of Louisiana, deportees, and that in his own case his wife was a Yankee).

In any event, if Davis sought to beastify the Northern people with his rhetoric, he probably couldn't have picked a more receptive audience, since news of Sherman's pyrotechnics in and about Memphis had preceded him downriver. "The issue before us is of no ordinary character," the president informed the legislature. "Will you be slaves or will you be independent? Will you transmit to your children the freedom and equality which your fathers transmitted to you, or will you bow down in adoration before an idol baser than ever was worshipped by Eastern idolaters?

"Those men who now assail us," he continued, "who have been associated with us in common Union, who have inherited a government which they claim to be the best the world ever saw—these men, when left to themselves, have shown that they are incapable of preserving their own personal liberty. They have destroyed the freedom of the press; they have seized upon and imprisoned members of state legislatures and of municipal councils, who were suspected of sympathy with the South; men have been carried off into captivity in distant states without indictment, without a knowledge of the accusations brought against them, in utter defiance of all rights guaranteed by the institutions under which they live. These people, when separated from the South and left entirely to themselves, have in six months demonstrated their utter incapacity for self-government. And yet these are the same people who claim to be your masters."

There might have been a certain persuasiveness to that line of reasoning until one considered that, on this very morning, it was Davis himself who issued the order declaring martial law in Vicksburg. Notwithstanding, the president hoisted himself even higher on the soapbox, sprinkling his oration with Shakespearean and biblical allusions. The war had grown "so gigantic," he asserted, that neither side could stand it much longer, but he reassured his audience that "it is impossible with a cause like ours, that we can be the first to cry, 'Hold, enough!' " Then he made a remarkable admission.

"In the course of this war our eyes have often been turned abroad. We have expected sometimes recognition, and sometimes intervention, at the hands of foreign nations. Never before in the history of the world have a people so long a time maintained their ground, and shown themselves capable of maintaining their national existence, without securing the recognition of commercial nations. I know not why this has been so, but this I say: 'Put not your trust in princes,' and rest not your hopes on foreign nations. This war is ours; we must fight it out ourselves. And I feel some pride in knowing that, so far, we have done it without the good will of anybody."

It was a striking disclosure, since a keystone of Confederate foreign policy had been that England and France would intervene to lift the Union blockade, a notion to which the Southern people had clung from the beginning, and which to some was becoming the last best hope. To dash it now, when he knew his speech would be reprinted in newspapers throughout the South, would surely come as an unwanted revelation that can be explained only by Davis's desire to stir up Southern patriotism. But even if it might have inspired some renewed defiance back east where Robert E. Lee at Fredericksburg had just whipped the Yankees again, here in the West, with its long string of disappointments and defeats, it must have been received as harsh music.

Yet it was all too true. Just as Southern pundits had predicted, two years of war and Union blockade had achieved at least part of the desired effect. In Great Britain alone, most mills were closed or operating only part time and two and a half million loom operators were out of work and their families impoverished. What the Rebel pundits had not anticipated, though, was that rather than blaming the Yankees for their misery many British blamed *them*, for starting the war in the first place, and over the cause of slavery on top of that. In Manchester, England's premier cotton-mill city, the out-of-work laborers sent Lincoln a message of encouragement, commending him for trying to rid the world of the evil institution.

France, which was more pro-Southern, had offered to mediate the conflict but was quickly rebuffed by the Lincoln administration, which deigned to tolerate not even a whiff of the notion that the South should be internationally recognized as anything other than a rebellious section of an autonomous United States.

Confederate diplomats did manage to score what they thought was a victory in that regard when a French investment company agreed to float a bond issue (at an exorbitant interest rate) of some $25 million to help finance the war. Among the Richmond hierarchy it was felt that this amounted to recognition by the French establishment—at least tacitly—that the Confederacy existed as a serious entity and not merely as a figment of disgruntled minds. Even this small hope fizzled, however; after a brief success the prices began to drop on negative war news and fear that the Confederates would repudiate their debts, and soon the bonds plummeted off the charts.

Davis did not reveal the intricacies of all these matters to the Mississippi legislators that morning in the rotunda of the marble and brick state capitol building; it was enough for him to remind them they were on their own. After recounting the victories of the Army of Northern Virginia and reasserting that the Confederate capital at Richmond was inviolate, Davis admitted that he had come to Mississippi with serious doubts about the course of the war in the West. However, he told the lawmakers, after inspecting the troops and their defenses, he would return to Richmond "anxious, but hopeful" that they would "meet and turn back these worse than vandal hordes."

If Davis had pronounced himself satisfied and hopeful with military prospects in the West, Joseph Johnston was anything but. When called upon to speak after Davis had finished, Johnston stood and gave this brief remark: "My only regret is that I have done so little to merit such a greeting. I promise you, however, that hereafter I shall be watchful, energetic, and indefatigable in your defense." Then he sat back down to thunderous applause, looking forward to a moment when he could speak with Davis privately.

When the moment arrived, Johnston began to unburden himself of frustrations that had been building ever since Davis ordered him west, which of course had foreclosed his overriding hope of regaining command of the Army of Northern Virginia. He complained to the president that his "command was a nominal one merely, and useless; because [of] the great distance between the armies of Tennessee and Mississippi; and the fact that they had different objects and adversaries, made it impossible to combine their action; so there was no employment for me unless I should take command of one of the armies in an emergency, which, as each had its own general, was not intended or desirable."

Davis replied that it was for this very reason that Johnston had been sent west—that because both Bragg's and Pemberton's armies were so far away from Richmond, it was imperative to have a senior officer closer to the scene of action with the authority to transfer troops and coordinate movements between them.

Johnston protested that both armies were "too weak for [their] object[ives], that neither could be drawn upon to strengthen the other," and that "the distance between them was so great as to make such transfers impracticable." (In Johnston's account, for some reason they did not discuss the 10,000 men that Davis had just ordered sent from Bragg's army—over Johnston's fervent opposition—to reinforce the Vicksburg garrison during the present crisis.) Johnston recorded only that "these objections were [by Davis] disregarded."

With that, the president boarded a train to Richmond and the reluctant Johnston prepared to return to his preferred headquarters with Bragg's army in Tennessee. Pemberton was already down at Vicksburg, where things were becoming graver by the hour.

Sherman's flotilla had come steaming up the muddy Yazoo River in a great fire-belching parade the likes of which had not yet been seen in the history of war. The big ironclads led the way, blasting anything and everything ahead and on both banks that looked like it might contain a

Rcbel; next came the troopships—120 of them in all, containing more than 32,000 men—interspersed with "tinclad" gunboats, which were blasting away too. Farragut's attack on New Orleans, with its 10,000-man assault force, must have looked puny in comparison.

That first day, December 26, was devoted to landing the invasion force and its accompanying gear, from artillery and ammunition to food and officers' horses. Transport steamers carrying the Fourth Division, commanded by Frederick Steele, tied up along the banks north of where Chickasaw Bayou emptied into the Yazoo and debarked its troops. South of that, on the opposite side of the bayou, the Third Division under Major General George Washington Morgan was offloaded near the Johnson plantation house, which had been fired upon and burned by the gunboats sometime earlier. South of them, Morgan Smith's Second Division debarked at a point opposite the Indian Mound at the base of the Chickasaw Bluffs and that night A. J. Smith's First Division arrived, after retrieving its brigade from the railroad wrecking enterprise, and was put in at the southernmost point, opposite the Sandbar. Thus was Sherman's army arrayed on the following morning, December 27, on a front of about five miles running roughly north to south, facing the Chickasaw Bluffs, just as Stephen D. Lee had predicted.

Over the next two days various reconnaissances were made to test the Rebel positions, and the results were disappointing. The ground upon which Sherman had chosen to deploy his forces was essentially an island, bounded on the south and west by the Mississippi, on the north by the Yazoo, and on the east by Chickasaw Bayou. In hopes of diverting Confederate troops away from the bluffs, the navy had cooperated with Sherman by sending the ironclad *Benton* up toward Snyder's Mill to feign an attack there and destroy a Rebel battery. Instead, Confederate cannoneers inflicted so many hits on the ship that an estimated thirty shells came through the portholes alone, mangling many crewmen and mortally wounding the captain, whose right arm was ripped off and his side split open, exposing the lungs.

Years after the war, Stephen Lee wrote that if Sherman had immediately attacked at the Indian Mound, or the Sandbar, he probably "could have gone into the city," as two of the three regiments occupying the defenses there had been rushed north to shore up Chickasaw Bayou. Morgan Smith had his entire division in line, but made only a demonstration, and Smith himself was seriously wounded. Sherman put his division under the supervision of A. J. Smith, who, after Sherman concluded that "he could not cross the intervening obstacles [in his front] under heavy fire," was moved to a new attack position at the bayou.

Meantime, Steele's Fourth Division, which was the farthest north, had become mired in mud, quicksand, swamps, and bayous and found it impossible to reach the bluffs under any circumstances, Rebel fire or not. Steele was first ordered to move his men farther south, but when that also proved impossible he was told to retrace his steps back to the Yazoo and reembark on the transports, which would carry him downstream to the desired location. What Sherman was finding out was what all infantry commanders find out sooner or later, which is that having a map of a place is one thing, but it often becomes quite something else when the actual ground is encountered.

The situation, then, on December 29, was that Sherman's front had shrunk considerably both north and south, and his line of attack had essentially become a triangle, with Lee's Confederates occupying the base and parts of both sides, while Sherman occupied the apex. Fortunately for the Confederates, the three brigades that Pemberton had sent from the Yalobusha had finally arrived and were hurried into the line. This now gave Lee about 10,000 men, but they still had to be spread out—in greater and lesser concentrations—along a thirteen-mile front, all the way from Vicksburg up to Snyder's Mill, whereas Sherman could pinpoint the spot where he wanted to break through. All the while they had been there, Sherman listened in vain for the sounds of gunfire that would signal that Grant had arrived with his army behind Vicksburg, which would have caught the Rebels in a large pincers. But by early morning Sherman had decided he was on his own.

His plan was to have both divisions on the flanks begin a heavy fire as a diversion, then smash through the Rebel center by moving across a shallow part of Chickasaw Bayou, near where Chickasaw Creek cut through the bluff, and then up the bluffs themselves and on to open, level ground. For this task he selected the Third Division, led by General George Morgan, a forty-two-year-old Pennsylvanian who had flunked out of West Point in his third year and become a lawyer, then a much decorated regimental commander in the Mexican War. Sherman later said that Morgan had promised him, "General, in ten minutes after you give the signal I'll be on those hills."

The night before, Morgan had ordered a pontoon bridge to be built over the bayou to his front, but in the dark the engineers put the span over the wrong body of water. When the mistake was discovered at daybreak, Morgan ordered them to replace it in the correct spot but, as soon as they began, Rebel artillery and sharpshooters drove them back into the woods.

All morning a chorus of cannon and rifle fire had punctuated the battle area while Sherman's troops moved into jump-off positions and Lee emplaced his men correspondingly along the bluffs. Morgan had decided upon three brigades to spearhead the attack: the Ohioans and Indianans of Colonel John F. De Courcy from his own division and, from Steele's division—over which he now exercised operational control—the Missourians of Brigadier General Francis P. Blair, another political general who was a brother of the postmaster general, and the Iowans of Brigadier General John M. Thayer. When orders reached De Courcy, who had been up close to the front with his men, he went back to Morgan and asked, "General, do I understand that you are about to order an assault?" After Morgan replied in the affirmative, De Courcy—whom Morgan described as "an officer of skill and experience"—replied, "with an air of respectful protest: My poor brigade! Your order will be obeyed, General."

The day had been gray, cold, and overcast, typical December weather for northern Mississippi, and Morgan was supervising some last-minute preparations when Sherman's assistant adjutant general rode into his camp saying that he had orders from the boss, which he repeated verbatim: "Tell Morgan to give the signal for the assault; that we will lose 5,000 men before we take Vicksburg, and may as well lose them here as anywhere else"—to which the startled Morgan replied, or so he claimed later, "We might lose 5,000 men, but that his entire army could not carry the enemy's position in my front; that the larger the force sent to the assault, the greater would be the number slaughtered."

Having got this off his chest, Morgan ordered the signal, which went off at noon.

A furious cannonade broke out between the two armies as Sherman's men moved forward into a perfect hail of artillery and rifle fire. To people who had remained in Vicksburg, it was as if they were in an earthquake; the concussion carried all the way across the Mississippi to Kate Stone's Brokenburn plantation, and far back into the interior on the Jackson road, where many residents had fled.

As the brigades of De Courcy and Blair began picking their way through the abatis they "came under a withering and destructive fire.

All formations were broken; the assaulting forces were jammed together, and, with a yell of desperate determination, they rushed to the assault and were mowed down by a storm of shells, grape and canister, and mini-balls, which swept our front like a hurricane of fire. Never did our troops bear themselves with greater intrepidity. They were terribly repulsed, but not beaten."

Such was the description of General Morgan, who was there to see it. Most of Thayer's brigade somehow became misdirected and blundered off to the right; his lone regiment that crossed to the bluffs correctly was also routed. Many of De Courcy's men made it across Chickasaw Bayou, but the fire of two Confederate regiments from Louisiana was so terrible that they could not stand it. "Balls came zip-zip into the trees and the ground around us," said an Ohio company commander. "Occasionally, thud, a bullet takes some poor fellow, and he is carried to the rear." Similar treatment was in store for Frank Blair's Missourians when they came against some boys from Tennessee and Louisiana, sending them pell-mell back across the bayou, leaving behind a hundred Union dead and more than five hundred wounded or captured.

It was the same from one end of the line to the other. About half a mile to the right, at the Indian Mound, the Sixth Missouri also managed to get across Chickasaw Bayou but then found themselves in a horrible predicament. Faced with a relentless fire from above, they were pressed against the base of the bluffs, unable to move forward or backward. Sherman's account details how they "actually scooped out with their hands caves in the bank, which sheltered them against the fire of the enemy, who, right over their heads, held their muskets outside the parapet vertically, and fired down. So critical was the position, that we could not recall the men till after dark, and then one at a time."

Meantime, as the battle reached its most pitiless intensity, Pemberton, who was directing the overall defense of the city, received a weird telegram from Johnston, who had stayed in Jackson despite the fight that was raging for control of the city he was charged to save. Johnston informed Pemberton that at last the 10,000-man reinforced division from Bragg's army had begun to arrive in Jackson and the question Johnston asked must have staggered Pemberton: did he want these troops forwarded to Vicksburg immediately or, as Johnston was recommending, detained in Jackson as some kind of reserve? Pemberton wasted no time in answering: "Yes, I want all the troops I can get. The service in the trenches is exceedingly exhausting to most of the men."

They began to arrive just after sunset, in command of Major General Carter Stevenson, and the noise of locomotives and the cheering from the Vicksburg train depot echoed all the way out across the Yankee lines. As if that wasn't enough, to add to the misery a hard cold rain began to fall, and the Northern men had been ordered before they embarked from the transports to leave behind everything "that could impede our movements in any way." That included tents, blankets, raincoats, haversacks—even overcoats. Not only that, but orders had gone out that no campfires were allowed lest they give away their positions, and so they hugged the ground, quivering, watching their breath smoke up the winter twilight. "A night commenced, such as God forbid, I may never have to live through again—exposed to the merciless cold and howling wind," wrote a Missourian in Steele's division. Far worse was the condition of the hundreds of wounded, who lay wet and freezing, screaming and groaning at the base of the Chickasaw Bluffs.

The attempt had been a dismal failure, as Sherman reflected sourly: "Our loss had been pretty heavy, and we had accomplished nothing, and had inflicted little loss on our enemy." In fact, his losses had been a lopsided 1,779 against the Confederate's 187. Worse, they were almost out of ammunition, and Sherman had to ask Admiral Porter if he could send a transport up to Memphis to bring back four million rounds.

One would have thought that would have been the end of it, but Sherman was not to be outdone—at least not yet. Likely, he was pulled by two forces: first, a fervent desire to do something positive for the war effort and, second, to do something—anything—to avoid the criticism and humiliation he knew was in store if he pulled out now.

What he settled on was risky, but not as risky as what he had just been through. The Confederate batteries up at Snyder's Bluff—variously referred to by each side as Haines's Bluff, Haynes's Bluff, or Drumgould's Bluff—were the key impediment to control of the Yazoo River valley. Once they were neutralized or seized, his army could move right up the Yazoo and land at will, inflicting mayhem in the interior of Mississippi, destroying the railroads that were providing Pemberton with reinforcements and supplies, and even turn on Vicksburg via a different inland route and invest it by siege. As he sat in his tent with the rain drumming down the idea began to appeal to him more and more, especially in light of the alternative, and so he laid out his plan, asking Porter for cooperation.

Basically the scheme was this: Sherman would load 10,000 of his best infantry on the transports and Porter would sneak them up to

Snyder's Bluff under cover of dark. At daylight, all twelve of Porter's big ironclads and other gunboats would open bombardment to numb the defenses of the Rebel fortifications, and under cover of this the infantry would take the forts by storm. The rest of the army could then pass by unmolested and go upriver for points undisclosed. The only further obstacle that would have to be overcome was the boom that the Confederates had laid across the river upstream of the bluff, which was rumored to be protected by underwater mines of the ilk that had sent the *Cairo* to Davy Jones's locker. To counter this, Porter called upon Colonel Charles Ellet, of Memphis ram fame, to solve the problem, which he did, at least in theory, by constructing a giant rake— forty-five feet long, it was said—that would be worked from the bow of his lead boat to sweep the channel clear of these obnoxious devices. History does not tell us who was supposed to operate this rake, but presumably Ellet believed there were such bold men among his sailors.

While Ellet's· men worked on constructing the rake and other staff members, army and navy, fiddled with the myriad details of the project, Sherman was confronted by another problem requiring his immediate attention. The night after the battle, General Morgan had asked Sherman to agree to send out a delegation to see about retrieving his wounded from in front of the Confederate lines. At first Sherman refused on the grounds that it would be a sign of weakness, but as the rains beat down and the pitiful cries of the wounded grew fainter and less frequent he softened his position. Through some misunderstanding, however, probably having to do with the dark and the jitters, this truce party was compelled to return, but two days later Sherman sent a personal note to General Carter Stevenson, who by virtue of seniority had now been designated Confederate commander on the Chickasaw Bluffs front. With Stevenson's assent, on December 31, Union medical parties ventured out to retrieve their wounded and bury their dead, and even after the truce ended four hours later, at sundown, not a shot was fired by either side.

It was New Year's Eve, with the fateful year 1863 on the cusp. Americans North and South, whether drinking in a low, dark tavern, dancing at a brilliant ball, or simply lying in bed, or, for that matter, trapped in a swamp along the Mississippi River a thousand miles from home, must have had their moments of solemn wonder at what the next year would bring.

Scarcely anyone did not have a family member or a friend, or a friend of a family member, or a friend of a friend of a friend who had not been killed or wounded in the war. In cities across the North so-called mourning stores were established, wherein widows could purchase the latest styles of dresses and ladies' apparel in black; in the South, because of shortages, such fashionable niceties were problematic. It had started out in '61 almost as a lark, Fort Sumter and some skirmishing in the Shenandoah Valley. But then came Bull Run and Ball's Bluff, where the carnage began in earnest, and men were shot down by the thousands; then the Peninsula Campaign and the Seven Days, where it ran into the tens of thousands; then Second Bull Run, Shiloh, Antietam, and Fredericksburg, where it ran nearly into the thirty thousands. For those who could afford them, lead-encased coffins had become a popular item for returning the remains of soldiers killed in battle; some featured a small glass window so that the face of the deceased could be viewed.

On both sides the disruptions had been far-reaching and in many places ordinary life had come to a standstill. In the South conditions had gone from bad to worse. The Union blockade had already created shortages of food in an economy oriented to producing an inedible commodity. While farm labor was not yet affected because of the slaves, a far greater proportion of Southern boys had gone off into the service, leaving women to do work to which they were unaccustomed. In the North—especially the Midwest—closure of the Mississippi and exorbitant railroad freight fees had put a dramatic crimp in commerce. Whether any of these thoughts crossed the minds of Sherman's soldiers huddled around their fireless camps in the rainy, soggy bottoms, or those of Pemberton's men on the bluffs above them, celebrating New Year's Eve with a victory drink, one thing was for sure—neither side had shown the least inclination to cry, "Hold, enough!"

Sherman's 10,000 picked men were already aboard the transports and waiting to go. Midnight came, and the new year with it, and still they waited in a driving rain and a soupy fog that began to boil in off the river. Through the darkest hours before dawn they waited still, while the fog swirled so thickly that a man could not have seen a horse if he was standing ten feet from it. Porter was the first to bear ill tidings. It was nearly 5 a.m. and the ironclads and gunboats had been unable to navigate through the fog to their rendezvous point. At this rate it would be broad daylight before they arrived at the enemy batteries, when all surprise would be lost and the attackers easy prey for the Rebel guns.

Sherman received the news dejectedly but in the end was stoic.

With the rain still coming down and no telling when it would end, the Yazoo was already running over its banks. High-water marks on the trees around them foretold that a major flood might drown the army. Furthermore, Sherman recalled that, all night, "we could hear the whistles of the trains arriving at Vicksburg, could see battalions of men marching up toward Haynes's Bluff, and taking post at all points at our front." He realized that this was no Beauregard sleight of hand like that of Corinth, and that settled it. With everything conspiring against him, Sherman ordered a full withdrawal of everyone and everything, down to and including the giant rake. In his official report, he made his summary of the operation brief. "I reached Vicksburg at the time appointed, landed, assaulted, and failed," he said. Thus came to an end the third attempt to take Vicksburg.

For his part, Pemberton was thoroughly satisfied. He had whipped two large Federal armies and sent them reeling out of Mississippi, and he confidently told Jefferson Davis: "Vicksburg is daily growing stronger. We intend to hold it."

By the next morning a clammy mist still covered the river, and the Union flotilla was making its way back down the Yazoo when Porter sent Sherman a final piece of bad news. During the night General McClernand had arrived by steamboat off the mouth of the river, mad as hell and ready to take command of his army.

CHAPTER ELEVEN

If You Can't Smile, Grin!

It had been a harrowing Christmas at Brokenburn, the Stone family plantation across the river from Vicksburg. First, Kate's younger brother Jimmy was dying of pneumonia. Then word came that her older brother, William, had been reported killed at Fredericksburg. Next, her littlest brother, Johnny, was captured by some of Sherman's men who had gone to break up the railroad, and they were threatening to hang him as a spy.

In many respects, the art of medicine by 1862 had progressed only slightly since the Revolutionary War and the practices of "bleeding" and "blistering" represented two supremely ignorant applications of Hippocrates' dictum, "First, do no harm." Kate had just returned from a holiday ball in Vicksburg to learn that Jimmy was near death.

The fourteen-year-old was slowly strangling in his own fluids. Two doctors prescribed blistering, the application of a searing iron or other device to burn the skin on the outside of the chest, producing large blisters that were somehow believed to exorcise congestion in the lungs. As the boy's condition worsened, the doctors announced they could do no more, and the family gathered round for what they believed would be his final hours. A third physician showed up and prescribed an eggnog laced with brandy every half hour. This proposal was superseded by yet another attempt at blistering—this time by placing a turpentine-soaked cloth between his shoulder blades and pressing it flat with a scalding iron.

When the "exquisitely painful" application was completed, and

Mrs. Stone returned, Jimmy murmured, "They have killed me, Mamma. Don't leave me anymore." Despite everything, the eggnog at least seemed to have some effect and Jimmy began a slow recovery. Kate was looking forward to a merry Christmas, when the devastating report of her brother William's death was brought in by a neighbor who had read it in a newspaper. Coming as it did on Christmas morning, and just as Sherman had arrived with his fleet off the mouth of the Yazoo, this heartbreaking news plunged everyone into "despair and the wildest grief." The large Christmas dinner was ruined; messengers were sent after the newspaper and to the telegraph office, and thirteen-year-old Johnny Stone, Kate's youngest brother, "started for Vicksburg to get full particulars." A copy of the newspaper was soon brought back to the house, where, to everyone's relief, it was discovered that the officer who had been killed was a different William Stone, but no sooner had that revelation been digested than it was discovered that young Johnny was missing.

Three days passed while the "incessant" noise of the battle raging at Chickasaw Bluffs racketed back to Brokenburn. The brigade that Sherman had left on Kate's side of the river had been busy wrecking rail tracks, burning plantations, and confiscating mules, horses, and slaves and arresting citizens suspected of disloyalty. Johnny was swept up in these proceedings while he was trying to cross the river to Vicksburg and made a prisoner aboard one of the Union gunboats. There he was interrogated by the Federals, who were "trying to find out what he knew of troops, guns, government stores, etc., but he refused to tell them anything."

Then a Yankee colonel "privately told him that the men were anxious to hang him," pointing out that "they had hanged men at several points coming down the river for not talking." The threats, however, "had no effect on Johnny," and in the end he "became quite a favorite with the soldiers." Three days later they released him, completing the joyous season.

There remained one snag, and it was that with so many bluecoats now patrolling the west side of the river Kate had told her most trusted slave to take her horse, Wonka, and hide him in the deep woods across the bayou. This he did by tying him up in a canebreak, which would cause trouble later on.

On the last day of 1862, just as Sherman decided to withdraw from Chickasaw Bluffs, a colossal battle convulsed the Confederacy, which had a significant bearing on the course of the Vicksburg campaign and the war in the West.

Since Braxton Bragg's aborted excursion into Kentucky and planned invasion of Ohio in early October, his Army of Tennessee had sat unmolested at Murfreesboro, just thirty miles southeast of Nashville, and Lincoln had told Henry Halleck to have the commander of the Army of the Ohio, William S. Rosecrans, who had replaced Buell, do something about it. Rosecrans was reluctant until Halleck wired him, "If you remain one more week in Nashville, I cannot prevent your removal."

What resulted was the Battle of Stones River, or Murfreesboro, as it came to be called, a tragic and epic struggle that left a shocking butcher's bill of nearly 25,000 casualties out of 80,000 men on both sides—more than either Shiloh or Fredericksburg and nearly as many as Antietam.* In the end Bragg's army made an orderly withdrawal forty miles south and the men defiantly planted their battle flags at their old stomping grounds near Tullahoma.

The only good that came from it was that Lincoln had demanded a general push south by all his armies from Virginia to the Mississippi in hopes of impressing the British Parliament, which would be meeting in January. His concern was that without some clear-cut Union victories, the pro-Confederacy politicians might yet push the body toward official recognition of the South, if not outright intervention in the war. Unfortunately, his plans were foiled that very month by Lee in Virginia, who had handed General Ambrose Burnside such a decisive beating at Fredericksburg, and by the Van Dorn–Forrest raids, which caused Grant to retreat out of Mississippi.

So if in a military sense the Battle of Stones River served little other than enriching the Tennessee soil with thousands of dead bodies, it at least gave the Lincoln administration something to crow about to the British diplomats in Washington. For the Confederacy it was not a wooden stake through the heart, but more akin to a stake through the hand, since it did nothing to relieve Vicksburg, whereas a Rebel victory obviously would have given Grant pause about future downriver movements.

---

* The night before the battle the weather turned freezing, and as the men sat around their campfires bands on each side began serenading with familiar tunes, closing with "Home Sweet Home," which left men both blue and gray misty-eyed as they sang along before going to sleep.

Perhaps just as important, the outcome at Stones River gave Lincoln renewed support and resolve, both of which had been steadily eroding from his political base ever since Bull Run, and it certainly offset Sherman's precipitous retreat at Chickasaw Bluffs. Many of Lincoln's own people—including some in his cabinet—were turning against him, and the Republican Party had lost heavily in the midterm elections. Alluding to "administrative imbecility," *Harper's Weekly* opined: "Disgust and despair . . . are rapidly filling the hearts of the loyal North . . . the Government is unfit for its office." Former secretary of the navy and noted historian George Bancroft branded Lincoln as "incompetent," and he further described him as "ignorant, self-willed and surrounded by men some of whom are almost as ignorant as himself," while abolitionist William Lloyd Garrison declaimed him as "nothing better than a wet rag."

This last barb had as much to do with the president's ambivalent policy on slavery as it did with his conduct of the war. His position had always been that although disapproving of the practice he had never intended to disturb it in the states where it already existed—at least until now. Even on the eve of his Emancipation Proclamation, Lincoln sought some way to ease the wrath he knew it would provoke by proposing that the government offer owners $300 for each slave they set free by the year 1900, providing, of course, that the seceded states stop fighting and return to the Union. Also, he continued to press for some sort of deportation system whereby the freed slaves would be removed to colonies in African or Central American countries, in order to appease Southern apprehension over the consequences of emancipation. (When he was chided for making the $300 offer, Lincoln observed that the war had already cost more than the value of the entire slave population.)*

In December 1862, just before the Emancipation Proclamation was set to take effect, and just prior to his trip downriver to Vicksburg, General McClernand approached Lincoln on a secret mission. It seems that the ubiquitous Illinois Democrat had remained on friendly terms with many leading Confederates who had been among his prewar political cohorts, and some of these were now inquiring what terms the administration would offer if the South sued for peace. Lincoln's answer was vague, veiled, and unarticulated, but the gist of it

---

* In this he was doubtless correct. By then the war was costing $2.5 million per day, "Sundays included," while government revenues were less than 20 percent of that.

seemed to be that emancipation would still go forth as advertised, but that if the Rebels would lay down their arms then some modification of the proclamation and its repercussions would be forthcoming, e.g., gradual freedom instead of immediate, government compensation to the slaveholders, and forgiveness for rebellion instead of punishment. In any event, the president wrote, "if the friends you mention really wish to have peace upon the old terms they should act at once." Whatever became of his suggestion notwithstanding (and nothing did), Lincoln's conciliatory approach merely inspired fury from the northern abolitionists, who demanded total war, "hard war," and full emancipation *now*, not in some distant future of the next century.

The president even got into trouble with famed abolitionist Harriet Beecher Stowe, author of *Uncle Tom's Cabin*, over the response he gave to newspaper editor Horace Greeley's most recent denunciation of him.* In it, Lincoln had said that if he could save the Union by freeing all of the slaves, he would do it; that if he could save it by freeing none of the slaves, he would do that too; and that if it took freeing some and leaving the rest as slaves, that was on the table as well.

Mrs. Stowe countered in a parody, asserting the president had gotten it precisely backward; a man of respectable moral values, she insisted, would have announced that he would free the slaves if it meant saving all of the Union, none of the Union, or some of the Union, and letting the rest of it go south. In any event, these were the kinds of things that dogged Abraham Lincoln as the portentous year of 1863 rolled in. A congressman reported Lincoln's having complained that "if a worse place than Hell existed, he was in it."

The heart of the problem, of course, was patience, and the Americans were an impatient people, a direct consequence of the political system they themselves had invented. That was the conclusion of the astute observer of America, Alexis de Tocqueville, who gave it as his opinion that while the world's other civilized nations continued to be ruled by monarchies, oligarchies, or other strongman arrangements, the democratic principle of electing leaders by popular vote was particularly vulnerable in time of war.

"Democracy," de Tocqueville had famously written in 1835, "appears to me to be much better adapted for the peaceful conduct of society . . . than for the hardy and prolonged endurance of the storms

---

* Upon meeting Stowe for the first time, it is said that Lincoln remarked, "So you're the little lady who started this great war."

[wars] which beset the political existence of nations. The reason is very evident; it is enthusiasm which prompts men to expose themselves to dangers and privations, but they will not support them long without reflection."

The reflection of which the Frenchman spoke was self-evident. War taxes, disruption, defeat, and death were overburdening the population, and as the reality of the conflict pressed ever more upon them, the stream of army volunteers had dwindled to a trickle, resulting in contentious proposals for military conscription that exploded into bloody riots when a national draft measure was enacted a few months later. Already a faction within the Democratic Party, calling themselves "Peace Democrats," was gathering a movement to oust Lincoln in the next year's election and fashion some sort of truce with the Confederate states. None other than Lincoln's newfound nemesis General George B. McClellan would lead it.

What the president needed, what the Republicans needed, what the North needed, was a quick, solid victory—a big one at that—and Stones River fit the bill nicely.

That aside, Grant and Sherman were of course excoriated in the press after their defeats at Holly Springs and Chickasaw Bluffs. All the old charges were dredged up—Sherman was crazy, Grant was drunk, and both campaigns were marked by "repulse, failure and bungling." Particularly galling for Sherman were news stories that directly connected his being replaced by McClernand after the debacle at Chickasaw Bluffs, when in fact it had been preordained by McClernand's seniority; Sherman's relief was simply bad timing. Sherman rebuffed accusations that he had bungled by protesting, "I never worked harder or with more intensity in my life," but later he did something uncharacteristic. He blamed one of his subordinates for the failure before Vicksburg, stopping just short of accusing the officer of cowardice.

He was Brigadier General George W. Morgan, who on the morning of December 29 had not only commanded his own Third Division but maintained operational control over the First Division of A. J. Smith. While visiting him earlier that day, Sherman claimed that Morgan had promised him he would lead his men, personally, onto the Chickasaw Bluffs within ten minutes from the time the signal was given. In his memoirs, Sherman pointed out that Morgan did neither, and blamed him for "failure to obey his orders or to fulfill his promise made in person"—serious charges indeed.

Morgan, however, wound up with the last word. In the late 1880s the editors of *Century Magazine,* which was enormously popular in that era, began to assemble accounts by well-known military figures who had fought in the war, before their recollections were claimed by time or death. This was eventually published as *Battles and Leaders of the Civil War,* a multivolume compendium of the war's significant events as told by the participants, which became both influential and controversial, and remains so today.

When he was asked to write an account of the battle, Morgan used the occasion to defend himself. Not only did he deny and refute the allegations in Sherman's memoirs, but he produced a letter from Stephen Dill Lee saying that Sherman could easily have taken the bluffs by a vigorous attack at the Indian Mound or the Sandbar. "Had Sherman moved a little faster," the Confederate commander wrote Morgan, "he could have gone into the city."

Be that as it may, there was still plenty of finger-pointing and acrimony going around when Sherman and McClernand finally met up on a steamer in the Mississippi. Sherman attempted to salvage his embarrassing defeat by promoting yet another attack—though this time not on Vicksburg.

A few days earlier a Yankee ammunition boat named the *Blue Wing,* steaming down from Memphis to Vicksburg, had suddenly vanished up the Arkansas River without so much as a howdy-do. As it turned out, this vessel had been hijacked by a large Rebel force operating out of Fort Hindman, a mysterious structure also known as Arkansas Post that was reported to be well fortified and defended by some 5,000 Confederate soldiers. In Sherman's opinion, until these people were eliminated, Federal traffic on the Mississippi would be unsafe along the several hundred winding miles of river between there and Vicksburg and he persuaded McClernand to take the 30,000 veterans from Chickasaw Bluffs and clean it out.*

McClernand agreed and the expedition got under way immediately. The troop transports steaming out of the Yazoo were instructed to keep going upriver until they reached the offending Rebel outpost. Admiral Porter, who did not like McClernand, hadn't liked him when they met in Washington, and liked him now even less, agreed to escort the attacking force with three of his ironclads, but only after Sherman

---

* McClernand and his supporters argued that it was McClernand who first had the idea to go after Arkansas Post; others say he and Sherman arrived at the notion simultaneously. By the most solid accounts Sherman gets the credit.

"begged him for the sake of harmony." On January 8, the flotilla reached the White River and, at dawn on the tenth entered the Arkansas, where, finding themselves a few miles below the fort, the infantry was disembarked.

After what amounted to token resistance in the countryside, the 5,000 Confederates retreated inside their fort, which by several accounts looked something like a medieval castle, complete with parapets, moat, and drawbridge. McClernand got wind of this withdrawal and reported it to Sherman, who led one corps, and to Sherman's erstwhile scapegoat George Morgan, who led another. These two men quickly marched up to surround the bastion amid desultory rifle and cannon fire that nevertheless killed or maimed about 1,000 men in both armies. Meantime, after fighting their way up the Arkansas River, Porter's big ironclads shoved in to Fort Hindman so close that their bows were actually on shore and the U.S. flags on their tall masts fluttered above the Rebel ramparts—startling Sherman and his men on the far side of the stronghold. From point-blank range the Yankee gunboats proceeded to blast away, flinging chunks of bricks, timbers, and men into the air until the Confederate gunners fled their posts and sought refuge in the moat, which at least was dry.

Soon a large white flag appeared on one of the parapets, followed by a number of smaller ones, and the Federals ceased fire. The large flag had been raised by a colonel named Robert R. Garland, who claimed he had done so on the instructions of a staff member of Fort Hindman's commanding officer, Brigdier General Thomas J. Churchill, a thirty-nine-year-old Kentuckian who had practiced law in Little Rock before the war. Churchill, however, denied ever giving such an order, and the feelings against Colonel Garland ran so high among his fellow officers that he asked to spend the night with Sherman, during which, by Sherman's account, the two of them sat up till the early morning hours in a little log cabin that had been used as a Rebel hospital, drinking coffee, breaking stale bread, and talking politics amid the gore of the surgeons' tables.

As for McClernand, he had remained much of the time aboard his headquarters steamer, the *Tigress,* which was where Sherman found him after the battle. Sometime that morning McClernand had ordered one of his officers to climb up a tree and report on Rebel movements, which is how he discovered that the Confederates were removing themselves back into the fort. When Sherman boarded McClernand's flagship he found the general almost beside himself, repeatedly singing

General Ulysses S. Grant, often derided as a drunk, pressed on from Illinois to Vicksburg, until the Mississippi Valley was retaken. He then went east to fight Robert E. Lee. (Union)
National Archives and Records Administration (NARA)

President Abraham Lincoln said the capture of Vicksburg was "the key" to winning the war. Library of Congress (LOC)

General William T. Sherman, Grant's friend, became a famous advocate for "hard war." (Union) NARA

Commodore Andrew H. Foote, who commanded the original Federal ironclad fleet as it fought its way downriver from Cairo, Illinois. (Union) NARA

Admiral David Dixon Porter commanded the Federal ironclads during the battle at Vicksburg. (Union) LOC

General Henry "Old Brains" Halleck was the Union army's timid commander in chief. (Union) NARA

Admiral David Glasgow Farragut, crusty and always ready for a fight, wondered why his big oceangoing warships were sent 400 miles upriver. (Union) NARA

General John A. McClernand, the Illinois "political" general who gave Grant trouble at every turn. (Union) LOC

General Benjamin "Beast" Butler, whose harsh rule of captured New Orleans earned him international opprobrium. (Union) NARA

General James B. McPherson was prophesied to one day become the head of the U.S. Army "if he lives." (Union) NARA

General John Rawlins, Grant's long-suffering chief of staff, worried constantly about his boss's drinking problem. (Union) NARA

General James H. Wilson, Grant's engineering officer, was a keen observer of the battle. (Union) NARA

The earliest photograph of Vicksburg from across the river. Old Courthouse Museum (OCM)

General Benjamin Grierson led the celebrated deceptive Union cavalry raid through Mississippi, despite being afraid of horses. (Union) LOC

CUTTING THE CANAL OPPOSITE VICKSBURG.—SKETCHED BY MR. THEODORE R. DAVIS.—[SEE

Slaves digging the first cutoff canal in 1862 at DeSoto Point. The Federals hoped to isolate Vicksburg from the Mississippi River. So many slaves and soldiers died on the project that it was abandoned. *Harper's Weekly*

Kate Stone kept a vibrant journal of the conflict. Louisiana State University Special Collection

Emma Balfour kept a diary during the siege. OCM

A powerful Brooke rifle, part of the Confederate defenses. OCM

Brierfield, the plantation home of Jefferson Davis, near Vicksburg. OCM

The Marine Hospital Battery at Vicksburg. OCM

The USS *Cairo,* one of eight powerful Union ironclads that wrested control of the Mississippi, was sunk by a Confederate mine but raised 100 years later and restored. Naval Historical Center (NHC)

Commander Isaac N. Brown miraculously completed the construction of the CSS *Arkansas,* then fought her through the Federal fleet. (C.S.A.) NHC

Colonel Charles River Ellet, one of six Ellet family members to serve in the "army's navy" during the campaign. (Union) NHC

The CSS *Arkansas* terrorized the Federal fleet on the Mississippi River. NHC

"Black Terror," from an 1863 *Harper's Weekly* sketch. Admiral David Porter, angry at Confederate successes on the Mississippi, had this fake ironclad constructed in one day at a cost, he said, of $8.63, and decked out with bogus smokestacks and a big "Quaker gun." When he floated it downriver, Rebels fell for the hoax and scuttled their recently captured Union ironclad *Indianola,* making themselves laughingstocks in the Northern press. *Harper's Weekly*

Confederate president Jefferson Davis, who lived near Vicksburg, believed the bastion could be held. NARA

General Joseph E. Johnston, the Rebel commander in the West, was known as a great strategist, but he was reluctant to attack. (C.S.A.) NARA

General John Pemberton, the Philadelphia Yankee who commanded the Rebel army at Vicksburg. (C.S.A.) LOC

General Earl Van Dorn, the controversial Rebel commander who led the great raid against Grant's army at Holly Springs. (C.S.A.) Alabama Department of Archives and History (ADAH)

General Stephen Dill Lee commanded the Rebel army during the Confederate victory at Chickasaw Bluffs. (C.S.A.)
Mississippi Department of Archives and History

General Carter Stevenson commanded a Rebel division. (C.S.A.) ADAH

General William Wing Loring, who disappeared with his division from the battlefield at Champion Hill, bears a striking resemblance to the image of William Shakespeare. (C.S.A.) LOC

General John Stevens Bowen, a friend of Grant's before the war, died right after the siege ended. (C.S.A.) ADAH

General Nathan Bedford Forrest led raids in Tennessee that took pressure off the Confederates. (C.S.A.) ADAH

General Lloyd Tilghman was killed at the battle of Champion Hill. (C.S.A.) ADAH

Caves dug by beleaguered Union soldiers near the Shirley House. OCM

HEAD OF THE CANAL OPPOSITE VICKSBURG, MISS, CUT BY ORDER OF GENERAL GRANT.

The canal that Grant ordered dug in 1863 to avoid the guns of Vicksburg.
This excavation also proved to be an abject failure. *Frank Leslie's Weekly*

The terror of the siege, as illustrated by *Harper's Magazine*. *Harper's Magazine*

The Eighth Wisconsin mascot, Old Abe, a bald eagle that the Confederates referred to as a "buzzard." OCM

A Confederate veteran in front of a typical Vicksburg cave, some years after the war. OCM

Captured Confederate artillery after the surrender. OCM

The U.S. flag flying over the Vicksburg courthouse after the battle. OCM

WOMEN OF THE SOUTH COMPELLED BY HUNGER TO APPLY TO THE FEDERAL COMMISSARY FOR FOOD.

After the surrender, Vicksburg's nearly starving women endured the humiliation of asking their Yankee conquerors for food. *Frank Leslie's Weekly*

out, "Glorious! Glorious! My star is ever in the ascendant! I had a man up a tree!, etc.," and boasting of the "splendid report" he intended to make. As Sherman anticipated, McClernand's splendid report failed to credit the role of Porter and his ironclad navy, which had in fact defanged Fort Hindman by reducing its guns to scrap metal and its portals to brickbats. After sending the 5,000 Confederate prisoners—minus their dead and wounded—up the river to prison at Alton, Illinois, McClernand's army returned to the boats in a snowstorm and headed back down toward Napoleon, a little village where the Arkansas met the Mississippi, there to be met by the wrath of Grant.

By then Washington had articulated its own plans for the reconquest of the Mississippi, and these included a march up to Vicksburg from New Orleans by the army of forty-seven-year-old Major General Nathaniel Banks, yet another political general, who had been, among other things, Speaker of the U.S. House of Representatives and governor of Massachusetts. Somewhere along the way the handsome, debonair Banks had picked up the nickname "Bobbin Boy" for his early employment in a New England cotton mill, an occupation that might have given him at least limited knowledge of the overwhelming problem he would face when he replaced "Beast" Butler as the military commander of the Department of the Gulf.

Word of Butler's reign of malfeasance and mismanagement had reached too many important ears in Washington to be tolerated any longer. When Banks had arrived in December, just as Grant and Sherman believed they were closing in on Vicksburg, what he found in New Orleans was a military situation that resembled a criminal enterprise.

Corruption was rampant at practically all levels and the evil, as usual, was cotton and its economic cousin sugar. "Everybody connected with the government has been employed in stealing other people's property," Banks told his wife. "Sugar, silver plate, horses, carriages, everything they can lay their hands on. There has been open trade with the enemy. No attention has been given to military affairs."

The military affairs that Banks was charged with consisted in the main of his orders to march his army up from the south through Louisiana and Mississippi to meet up with Grant to capture Vicksburg. To accomplish this, enough reinforcements had been sent with him to bring his total force up to nearly 36,000, with the expectation in Washington that Banks would proceed immediately. After taking stock, however, he discovered that three obstacles stood in his way, and foremost was the civil administration that he had also been charged to straighten out.

The between-the-lines trade in cotton, and to a lesser extent sugar, was scandalous. Corruption was so rife that Banks had hardly set foot in New Orleans when he was offered a $100,000 bribe to look the other way by a consortium representing New England textile merchants run by none other than General Butler's own brother. "I thank God every night that I have no desire for dishonest gains," Banks wrote his wife.

Even so, Banks was acutely aware of the need for cotton in the New England mills—after all, he was a New Englander and they didn't call him the Bobbin Boy for nothing. Two-thirds of the Northern mills were now shut down, but the Federal government more or less discouraged cotton trading with the enemy. The only way to choke off the illegal trade involved stationing troops throughout the state, wherever the activity was taking place, but that in turn resulted in a loss of manpower for Banks's projected military advance on Vicksburg.

Not only that, but Banks soon decided that an incalculable source of *legal* cotton, so badly needed in the Northern textile mills, remained untapped—cotton that, in fact, was as yet ungrown. The reason was that as soon as U.S. troops began to occupy Louisiana, most of the slaves had run away from the plantations. Never mind that Louisiana was one of the states excluded from the Emancipation Proclamation because it was deemed to be under Federal control; they ran off anyway, and nobody seemed able to do anything about it.

Banks decided that putting blacks back to work should be a paramount objective—whether they considered themselves to be slaves or not—and to that end he got the plantation owners to agree to pay the blacks a small stipend to return to the fields while, for his part, the New Englander promised to use the Union army to make sure they went there and stayed there.

Satisfied that these measures would get the legal cotton business up and running, Banks now had to tackle another unexpected problem caused by the activities of Major General Richard "Dick" Taylor—the son of former president Zachary Taylor and brother-in-law to Jefferson Davis—who, after his graduation from Yale, had served as his father's military secretary during the Mexican War. Taylor had been a successful sugar planter in Louisiana until the war broke out and, after serving with distinction in the Virginia theater, arrived back in his adopted state shortly before Banks, charged with causing as much trouble for the Yankees as possible.

With an army of barely 2,000 men, most dressed in homespun or worse and with no artillery, few standard firearms, horses, or other military equipment, Taylor organized one of the most effective military forces in the Confederacy, starting with a series of hit-and-run attacks on Union garrisons in Louisiana that compelled Banks to detail even more of his soldiers to cope with the new threat.

If this wasn't enough, when Banks took command he believed that the march up to Vicksburg would be relatively straightforward until he encountered Pemberton's army at or near the fortress city. What he didn't know was that a very large part of Pemberton's army was some 150 miles *south* of where he believed it to be, at a heavily fortified bastion on the Mississippi called Port Hudson, which Banks had not even heard of until after his arrival in New Orleans.

As it had been for Buell in Tennessee, Burnside in Virginia, and Grant in Mississippi, the pressure on Banks from Washington was to *do* something. But Banks was not to be rushed. Equipment had not arrived as promised, troops needed more training, civil affairs needed attending, and a significant obstacle now was manpower. Because of all the detailing of men to intercept the illegal cotton trade, enforce the return of the blacks to the plantations, and deal with the depredations of the Rebel general Taylor, Banks was now down to about 12,000 to 15,000 men who could be made available for the Vicksburg operation. Since intelligence had correctly estimated that the Confederates at Port Hudson had an army of about 11,000, and were defended by a complement of heavy guns that Banks could not match, it was his studied opinion that an attempt to take the fort by storm would be ill-advised. Likewise, if he attempted to march his army around Port Hudson, he would risk being caught in the open between the Port Hudson army and Pemberton's larger forces, which could easily come down from Vicksburg by rail to confront him. Therefore, Banks informed Halleck, he must seek other strategies if he was to get in on the Vicksburg adventure.

Jefferson Davis was in high dudgeon when he returned to Richmond from Vicksburg and the western defenses. Rarely did he miss an opportunity to make a public speech, not because he was a political hack or hog but because he was thoroughly convinced that as president of the Confederacy he owned a unique pedestal from which to coax, rile, reason, and, when necessary, plead or beg with his chosen people to summon another dose of intestinal fortitude. This was not always an easy task of late, for despite their recent defeats the Federal armies were as ever-pressing as some perverse tide that had suddenly become oblivious to the phases of the moon.

The Confederates had for nearly two years been whipping Yankees in Virginia, but Southern independence seemed no closer than a mirage on a desert horizon. In the western theater it was even worse; there had been dramatic reverses, including the loss of most of Tennessee and the lost hope of regaining Kentucky and Missouri, and now Grant and Co. had set their designs on Vicksburg. In Virginia, where the theater was small and the field of maneuver narrow, Robert Lee had worked wonders against superior Union armies led by inferior generals. In the West, though, the expanses were so much greater, the rivers navigable to anyone with a navy—which of course left the Confederates out—and the Northern armies still maintained at least a two-to-one advantage.

Still, much had been accomplished in two years' time, as Davis was always eager to point out. Where at the beginning there were few facilities to produce arms, ammunition, gunboats, clothing, leatherwear, uniforms, salt, canvas, and all the myriad goods and paraphernalia needed to keep armies in the field, now there were many; where before the war cotton took precedence above all agriculture, many Southern farmers now produced corn, rice, beans, peas, cane, cattle, and hogs. It wasn't a perfect economy by any means—in the counties and parishes surrounding Vicksburg, for instance, many growers cravenly raised cotton for the Yankee cash in it—but all in all, the transition had been better than expected.

By comparison with the North, however—whose main insufficiency was Southern cotton—the shortages were staggering and inflation beyond control. In Vicksburg, the benchmark seemed to be the price of a barrel of brandy or whiskey, which was selling for upwards of $60 as compared to its prewar price of $5; at least this is what many diarists of the day saw fit to emphasize. In most places, food staples had shot up five or ten times their prewar value because supply had simply not caught up with demand and showed no signs of doing so. But somehow, some way, southerners were muddling through it and nobody was actually starving. With the exception of a few short-lived food riots in large cities, the people endured the shortages, if not cheerfully at least with patriotic resignation. As one of them advised, "If you can't smile, grin!"

On the night he made his speech to the citizens of Richmond, Jefferson Davis came to the balcony of the Confederate White House fully replenished and waving an explosive device certain to fill the

Southern heart with fire and brimstone. This was Lincoln's detested Emancipation Proclamation, which had taken effect a few days earlier and which, at least for Davis, marked the point of no return.

Lincoln would always claim that he issued the proclamation as a war measure against those states in rebellion (the slave states outside the Confederacy were not affected; nor was it enforceable except in those areas of the South under Federal control), but if that were so, he also must have realized that if he carried through with it such a measure might well foreclose any negotiated settlement of the kind he had been seeking.

Viewed strictly as a war ruling, the best Lincoln could hope for was that the proclamation would cause the slaves to revolt and leave the southerners without field hands to grow their crops or build military fortifications. As it turned out, this did not occur until Union armies drew close by, and then they themselves became nearly swamped by the flood of black refugees, as the Federals at Vicksburg would soon find out. It also caused furious political dissent in the slave states that had remained loyal to the Union, whose citizens feared, correctly in many cases, that their slaves would abandon their plantations too. Nevertheless, Lincoln felt duty bound to go through with it. When he announced the proclamation in September 1862, he gave the southerners a hundred days to think it over; it was the ultimate stick in his carrot-and-stick approach to Civil War diplomacy. But if he thought it would put the fear of God into the Rebels and bring them back to the fold he had badly miscalculated. What it put into them instead was more like the wrath of God.

On that particular torch-lit night in Richmond Jefferson Davis addressed the Confederate nation with his typically vigorous outrage, yet he began his sermon on a curiously humanitarian theme. It had always been his position to equate the plight of the slaves with that of the Indians, who were now apparently fading away because of their inability to assimilate to the white man's ways. Thus he characterized Lincoln's proclamation as "a measure by which several millions of human beings of an inferior race, peaceful and contented laborers in their sphere, are doomed to extermination." Davis no doubt believed this; he had written and spoken on the subject at length over the years. Yet one must wonder if such statements weren't made as much to demonize the Yankees in the international arena as out of heartfelt concern over the fate of the black man.

For the majority of southerners—slaveholders and nonslaveholders alike—Lincoln's order was simply a form of highway robbery. The Richmond *Dispatch* probably spoke for many when it recommended to northerners that they "dismiss from their minds at once the miserable delusion that the South can ever consent to enter again, upon any terms, to the old Union. [Even] If the North will allow us to write the Constitution ourselves, and give us every guaranty we ask, we would sooner be under the government of England or France than under a Union with men who have shown that they cannot keep good faith. . . . The only terms on which we can obtain permanent peace is final and complete separation from the North. Rather than submit to anything short of that, let us resolve to die like men worthy of freedom."

Not that the proclamation was roundly popular north of the Mason-Dixon Line either. Orville Browning, Lincoln's old friend and confidant, warned that the recruiting of new volunteers would slow to a trickle and any attempt to draft soldiers "would probably be made the occasion of resistance to the government," predictions that turned out all too true. In Congress, Democrats who favored making peace with the South became ever more shrill, led by an Ohio congressman with the nearly unpronounceable name of Clement Vallandigham. "Ought this war to continue?" Vallandigham bellowed, "a war for the negro? No—not a day, not an hour!"

Likewise, there were objections at the grassroots level. In many regiments—and not just those from the border states—soldiers had enlisted on the premise that they were fighting for restoration of the Union, not for the freeing of slaves, and yet that was where Lincoln's proclamation was now taking them. A midwestern soldier wrote home, "I am for anything that will cause Union and peace," but added, not untypically of many others, "If I had thot that it was the idea to set the Negroes all free they would not have got me to act the part of a Soldier in this war."

Of course not everyone felt that way; in fact most probably didn't. Suffice it to say that the Emancipation Proclamation was not roundly greeted with approval as it went into effect upon the new year of 1863.

Grant had returned to Memphis on January 10 in an understandably bleak mood. Everything seemed to be working against him; his best-laid plans had gone astray and once again his name was mud in the Northern press. Because he was unable to punish Van Dorn and his Confederate raiders for the shameful defeat at Holly Springs, Grant reserved a special place on his list of iniquitors for the scapegrace Colonel Robert Murphy, whom he blamed for the fiasco. Murphy was summarily cashiered from the army for what Grant branded "disloyalty or gross cowardice"—Grant was unable to say quite which—without a court-martial or even a hearing, possibly because Murphy was a lawyer with political connections and Grant wasn't taking any chances.

Next he had to confront the twin problems of Sherman's defeat at Vicksburg and the disagreeable fact of McClernand's arrival there to take command of the army. To cap it all came a startling report from McClernand that he intended to lead the army on what Grant complained to Halleck was a "wild-goose chase" several hundred miles up the river to Arkansas Post. Grant's objection was that McClernand's escapade would constitute no more than a sideshow and a distraction from what he rightly saw as the one and only objective of the Army of the Tennessee, which was Vicksburg. He conveyed this to McClernand in a stern message on January 11, saying, "I do not approve of your move on the Post of Arkansas. . . . It will lead to the loss of men without a result. You will immediately proceed to Milliken's Bend [across from Vicksburg] and await the arrival of re-inforcements." But it was too late; McClernand had already gone.

Grant's instructions did not catch up with McClernand until he stepped victoriously from his flagship at Napoleon, where he was further dismayed by rumors that Grant himself was on his way downriver. The reports were true. Not only was Grant furious that McClernand had apparently disobeyed his direct order, but he had received disturbing messages from both Sherman and Porter alleging that McClernand was "unfit" to command an army.*

For Grant, this was unwelcome but not surprising news, since his opinion of McClernand was about as low as Sherman's. But now that the Illinois politician had arrived on the scene, he was already spreading disharmony among the senior commanders. "It was made evident to me," Grant wrote later, "that both the army and the navy were distrustful of McClernand's fitness to command [and] it would have been criminal to send troops under these circumstances into such danger."

---

* Sherman was particularly incensed at McClernand's ascension, writing that it appeared that Lincoln was deliberately trying "to insult me." At one point later on he described McClernand as "the meanest man we ever had in the west—with a mean, gnawing ambition, ready to destroy everybody who could cross his path."

Accordingly, Grant decided to invoke his authority as commander of the Department of Tennessee and its army to personally assume control of the Vicksburg campaign. Given Lincoln's and Secretary of War Stanton's endorsement of McClernand, Grant no doubt understood this might be a political hot potato but was willing to take the chance.

As per Grant's orders, McClernand took the army down to Milliken's Bend and Young's Point, which was where Grant found him on January 29, still smarting from the reprimand over Arkansas Post. McClernand seemed to be pacified after Grant conceded—in retrospect—that wiping out Arkansas Post had been a good idea, but when Grant finally set him straight over who was going to lead the Vicksburg campaign from now on the ambitious general flew into such a towering rage that Grant characterized him as "insubordinate." "I over looked it," Grant added later, "as I believed, for the good of the service." For his part, McClernand wrote to Lincoln, "I believe my success here is gall and wormwood to the clique of West Pointers who have been persecuting me for months. . . . Do not let me be destroyed, or what is worse, dishonored, without a hearing."

At this point the president was having about as much trouble with his political generals as he was with the professional ones, and he responded to McClernand with one of his famously placating rejoinders: "I have too many *family* controversies already on my hands to voluntarily take up another. You are doing well—well for the country, well for yourself. . . . Allow me to beg, that for your sake, for my sake, for the country's sake, you give your whole attention to the better work." There it might have rested, except that it was not in McClernand's nature to let anything rest for very long, especially where there was a personal slight involved, be it real or perceived.

CHAPTER TWELVE

When We Can Do No Better
We Will Blow Them Up

The month of December 1862 had been a near disaster for the Army of the Tennessee. About the only good thing to come out of Grant's Vicksburg campaign was an epiphany, which visited him after the misfortune at Holly Springs.

"Up to this time," he wrote in his memoirs, "it had been regarded as an axiom in war that large bodies of troops must operate from a base of supply which they always covered and guarded in all forward movements." But facing a long retreat and with rations for his army virtually wiped out by Van Dorn, Grant had ordered his wagon teams to form foraging parties and confiscate southerners' food along a thirty-mile-wide swath east and west of the Mississippi Central tracks, all the way back to Memphis, where he could be reprovisioned by steamboats from the North. Still, it was a two-week march, and Grant was never completely sure that such a measure could feed so large an army for that long.

"News of the capture of Holly Springs and the destruction of our supplies caused much rejoicing among the [citizens]," Grant remembered. "They came with broad smiles on their faces . . . asking what I was going to do now without anything for my soldiers to eat." When Grant informed them of his foraging expeditions, the smiles changed to frowns, and when they cried, "What are *we* going to do?," Grant laconically informed them that if they wanted food, they'd best head out fifteen miles in either direction "and assist in eating up what we had left."

What amazed Grant, and inspired his epiphany, was the amount of food his men collected, since his army was at least ten times larger than the resident population along the route of march. "It showed that we could have subsisted off the country for two months instead of two weeks," he said. "This taught me a lesson which was taken advantage of later in the campaign." As indeed it would. "Our loss was great at Holly Springs," Grant admitted, "but was more than compensated for by [the provisions] taken from the country, and by the lesson taught."

For the time being, however, Grant was faced with a military dilemma that has confounded many a general before and since—how to cope with an enemy who has just defeated you.

At present he had McClernand's, formally Sherman's, 30,000 men spread out on the wrong side—the west side, the Louisiana side—of the Mississippi from Young's Point, just opposite the Yazoo, up to Milliken's Bend, about twenty-five miles upriver. Within a few weeks he would have 50,000 strung out on the riverbanks all the way to Lake Providence, some seventy miles from Vicksburg. (He had left one corps back in Memphis to hold the city.) If he was to capture Vicksburg, he needed his main force on hand to take advantage of any weakness in Confederate defenses, and also to remain strong enough to discourage—or at worst withstand—an enemy attack in his rear from the trans-Mississippi.

Because of the terrain, the high conditions of the river in winter, and the necessity of resupplying by steamboat, the only places the troops could encamp were right upon or behind both the natural and the man-made levees abutting the banks. In other words, Grant's army was living between a river and a swamp where outdoor life in the dampness of winter was by definition unhealthy if not perilous. It wasn't long before the sick lists began to swell with pneumonia, smallpox, dysentery, typhoid, and "other malarial diseases," and lonely burial parties of half a dozen men became an unnerving sight, digging graves in the rain and cold atop the waterlogged levees. Deaths averaged about eighty-five a day, an ominous prelude to what would likely befall this great congestion of men if they remained during the blistering summer months.

Grant's problem, of course, was to get from the wrong side of the river to the right one, where he hoped to subdue the Confederates and the city. A northern approach was not practical, as Sherman had recently found out. As for a western movement across the river, there were no suitable places for an amphibious landing opposite Vicksburg for ten miles in either direction—the Rebels had seen to that—and above the city there was endless swamp. A full-scale assault on the bluffs themselves would have been suicidal, and Grant admitted as much.

Getting his men across the river onto high ground far enough below the city for an attack was the ideal solution, but in order to accomplish it one of two things would have to occur. Porter's ironclad fleet, along with enough transports to ferry the army and all its supplies across the river, would somehow have to steam south, past the formidable Vicksburg batteries; or Farragut's fleet at New Orleans would have to run beyond the now equally formidable batteries that the Rebels had installed way down at Port Hudson. The navy was skeptical that either could be done.

Another option—one that Sherman had reversed himself on and now favored—was to return the entire army to Memphis and start all over again down the Mississippi Central route, making sure this time that the rear supply bases were well protected. It was, Grant admitted, probably the smartest move from a military perspective, but he declined to do it—not for military reasons but for political ones.

"The North had become very much discouraged," he reflected. "Many strong Union men believed that the war must prove a failure. The elections of 1862 had gone against the party that was for the prosecution of the war to save the Union if it took the last man and the last dollar. Voluntary enlistments had ceased throughout the North, and the draft had been resorted to to fill our ranks. It was my judgment at the time that to make a backward movement as long as that from Vicksburg to Memphis, would be interpreted . . . as a defeat. There was nothing left to be done but to go forward to a decisive victory. This was in my mind from the moment I took command in person at Young's Point."

So he said, but there may have been another factor at play in Grant's mind besides politics, and that was ambition, and it had to do with Nathaniel Banks. Banks's mandate from the War Department had included marching his army north from New Orleans and joining Grant at Vicksburg, where, by virtue of seniority, he would assume command of the campaign and, if it was successful, get the lion's share of the glory too. Even though Banks had no military training, his powerful political standing had prompted Lincoln to commission him a major general right after the war began, believing that he could have a positive effect on recruitment and secure cooperation by the industrialists of his native Massachusetts. Therefore, if Grant had pulled the army back to Memphis and started again with a long land march, there was a good chance that Banks would already be before Vicksburg when Grant arrived, and possibly force its surrender without him.

Apparently that annoying prospect was also on Grant's mind when he decided to leave his army at Vicksburg, even if he was on the wrong side of the river, and during the cold and rainy flood season at that. At least Sherman thought so, for he wrote to his wife on January 24, shortly after the Arkansas Post expedition, "Grant, fearing that Banks might reach Vicksburg from below, was uneasy, and hurried us back here, and here we are again. . . ." Greater generals than Grant often instilled their own ambitions into the mix, and occasionally allowed it to subordinate sound military judgment. Personal drive is usually an asset to a commander, so long as it is not the only thing, and in Grant's case, history shows that it wasn't.

Still, having made the decision to fight it out, Grant was now confronted with another familiar quandary: what to do next? As usual, when military minds begin to churn—as frequently they do on generals' staffs—solutions begin to present themselves.

The first was resumption of General Thomas Williams's cutoff canal at DeSoto Point, across from Vicksburg, the one that had been abandoned the previous year. The notion was that the ironclads could pass the enemy batteries at night—this had already been proven—but the dozens more wooden troop transports and supply steamers would be torn to pieces. Grant hadn't known much about the canal but Lincoln remained keen on the enterprise and kept inquiring about it. That was enough for Grant and he ordered McClernand to look into it, whereupon McClernand, being senior, passed the buck to Sherman.

About 4,000 men and thousands of confiscated slaves worked on the DeSoto ditch during this period, which was also a time of incessant rain that sent the Mississippi over its banks and threatened to drown the men at their campfires and in their tents. When they weren't digging on the canal, from their perches on the levee they looked apprehensively between the water inundating the land behind them and the steamboats tied up to it on the other side, which might prove their only salvation if the great flood materialized. Sherman reported that if the river rose another eight feet, which was entirely possible, his men would "have to take to the trees."

The revised ditch was to be sixty feet wide and thirteen feet deep and more than a mile long—for its time a colossal excavation. Giant steam dredges and pumps ordered by Lincoln himself had been brought down from Cairo, but still the canal refused to accept the river's current. Engineers determined that large river eddies at each end of the ditch were flinging the water away from the desired channel; nevertheless, Grant ordered the men kept to their picks and shovels "day and night until its completion." Dams were erected at either end to make the digging easier. Later Grant would say that he did it only to occupy the men's time while a greater scheme was developed, but his official correspondence indicates otherwise.

As the excavation emerged from the cypress swamps of DeSoto Point to the low marshes nearer the river, Confederate cannoneers on the upper bluffs of Vicksburg made the workers lives' miserable, if not horrifying. Their principal tormenter was a large-caliber cannon nicknamed "Whistling Dick," which compelled one Federal soldier to remember: "It would shoot big shells in on us. We would sit down under the bank until they got in better humor, and then we would get up and go to work again." In particular, "Whistling Dick" played havoc with the steam dredges.

What had once been called Williams's Ditch, after Brigadier General Thomas Williams, now became Grant's Canal. As the original architect of the undertaking, Williams might have been interested in its progress—or lack of it—but that was not to be. Two weeks after he had abandoned the original canal project, Williams's brigade had been sent to Baton Rouge, where he was killed.

In any event, more than half the men in Sherman's and McClernand's corps were at some point working on the canal; illness and deaths mounted; the river continued to rise; Rebel shells continued to fall. Captain William Capers of the First Louisiana Heavy Artillery, who was the operator of "Whistling Dick" and other guns, remembered, "I found that two dredge boats had well-nigh succeeded in cutting through. I commenced day and night, and finally drove the dredge boats away and put a quietus to all work on the 'canal.' " In Vicksburg, citizens had taken to climbing an eminence called Sky Parlor Hill in their spare time to watch the show across the river and the Confederate cannon fire upon it. One woman scanning the river as her spyglass swept across the canal to the Yankee gunboats and back mused, "Was it a dream? Could I believe that over this smiling scene the blight of civil warfare lay like a pall?"

No sooner had Grant telegraphed Halleck in jubilation—"The canal is near completion . . . I will have Vicksburg this month or fail in the attempt"—than the dam on the northern end collapsed. To every-one's frustration, rather than rushing through the ditch to scour out a new channel the Mississippi simply caved in its walls and filled it with mud and debris, then began spreading out in all directions over such dry land as remained. Just before they "took to the trees," most of Sherman's men, and McClernand's too, were evacuated by steamboat twenty-five miles upriver to Milliken's Bend, which marked the end of the DeSoto Point ditch-digging scheme, as well as the fifth attempt to take Vicksburg.

An Illinois soldier remarked, "When the last of us got away there was not a bit of ground to be seen and the water was running over our shoes when we stood on the levee."

Sherman wrote in disgust, "We must get on dry land to fight. . . . On this side of the river we do no good whatever, for the Mississippi is an ugly stream to ford at this season of the year."

As an early spring came on, Kate Stone reported in her diary, "The plums and sassafras are in full bloom and the whole yard is fragrant. The hardy garden violets and the quaint little heartsease have been perfuming the winter wind for weeks, and the garden is gay with jon-quils and narcissus."

Still, with the breaking up of the Shreveport railroad during Sher-man's Chickasaw Bluffs campaign and resumed Federal gunboat patrols along the river around Vicksburg, many things had become scarce or nonexistent. "We all drank sassafras tea for a while but soon got tired of it," Kate wrote. "Okra coffee is now the favorite drink. Mamma had several bushels of the seed saved. After experimenting with parched potatoes, parched pindars, burned meal, roasted acorns, all our coffee drinkers decided on okra seed as the best substitute."

While the Army of the Tennessee sat idle on the levees—wet, brood-ing, stultified, and ready for action—a carnival of looting and arson ensued on Kate's side of the river. By then her mother had packed up all the jewelry, silver, china, crystal, Persian carpets, and other valuables—even Kate's diary—so that in the event a Yankee "foraging party" turned up nearby they could be carried to hideaways down in the swamps. Kate's horse, Wonka, was also frequently concealed in a canebrake, but as late February broke with occasionally warm days, mosquitoes emerged in swarms. Tied up and unable to move or bite at his tormentors, the animal became edgy and unmanageable.

In a letter to his brother, Sherman seemed to deplore the soldiers' misconduct, which contrasted somewhat with statements he made a short while afterward, in which he seemed to condone it. "Our armies are devastating the land and it is sad to see the destruction that attends our progress," he wrote two weeks after the army had arrived opposite Vicksburg. "Farms disappear, houses are burned & plundered and every living animal is killed and eaten. General officers make feeble efforts to stay the disorder but it is idle. Our soldiers are lawless and will turn upon our own country." And again, in a letter the same day to General Ethan Allen Hitchcock, grandson of the Revolutionary War hero, who, as head of the new Board for Revising Acts of War, sought Sherman's advice on administrative and civil matters: "Houses are fired under our very feet & though hundreds know why & who did it, yet the comd'g Genl. cannot get a clue. Soldiers in plundering & burning make no discrimination between friends or foe. Even Negroes are plundered of their blankets, chickens, corn meal & their poorest garments."

On the other hand, his private approach to the marauding seems to have been of the "boys-will-be-boys" variety, as indicated in a defense to Secretary of War Stanton after one of Sherman's units was accused of vandalism. "The regiment in question," Sherman opined, "is one of the best & most disciplined in our service & being composed mostly of younger & energetic men from St. Louis, is somewhat famous for its acts of fun, frolic & mischief & even crime, with a perfect skill in evading detection & pursuit. They are lawless and violent & have for years been taught [that they] can do no wrong. They . . . come to us filled with the popular idea that they must enact war, that they must clean out and destroy the Secesh, must waste & not protect their property, must burn waste & destroy."

Isolated incidents of pillaging, vandalism, and other unmilitary conduct are difficult if not impossible to prevent during any war. But along the Mississippi in the opening months of 1863 the practice seems to have been both widespread and out of control, with the victims being mostly women, children, old men, and, as Sherman noted, even slaves. Such wholesale misconduct within a military organization implies, almost by definition, a tacit complicity by officers of all ranks, from the lowest lieutenant to the commanding general. In short, if they had wanted to, the leaders could have had it stopped.

While work on the ill-fated DeSoto Point canal was still in progress, Grant's advisers had presented him with another option to get the army below Vicksburg without having to run past the river batteries.

This involved a dramatic proposal to connect—yet again by a sort of canal—no less than five different rivers and bayous leading out of Lake Providence, seventy miles north of the city. There, by a tortuous five-hundred-mile waterborne roundabout deep through the swamps and jungles of northeast Louisiana, the army ultimately would turn out into the Mississippi thirty miles above impassable guns of Port Hudson, either to head south and reduce that place with the cooperation of Banks or to steam back north along the 250 winding miles of the Big Muddy and land on dry ground within marching distance of Vicksburg itself.

Lake Providence was an old "horseshoe lake" that the Mississippi had cut off during one of its myriad changes of course over the years. The first order of business was to create an entranceway connecting it with the river, which called for blowing up the levee so that the water would rush in and deepen the lake. Then an antique stream known as Bayou Baxter would have to be routed out. That in turn would link the lake with Macon Bayou, which connected to the Tensas River, which joined the Black River, which emptied into the Red River, which flowed into the Mississippi. Not only would some of these streams need to be deepened where necessary, but underwater snags and tree overhangs had to be removed to let the troop transports and supply boats—as many as two hundred of them—pass without ripping out their bottoms or knocking over their smokestacks and superstructures.

For this daunting task Grant chose one of the up-and-coming young officers of the wartime army, Major General James B. McPherson, who a scant ten months earlier had been a mere lieutenant colonel of engineers on Grant's staff (and a proposed spy on him at that). He was appraised thusly by an observer: "He was one of the best officers we had. He was but thirty-two years old at the time, and a very handsome, gallant-looking man, with rather a dark complexion, dark eyes, and a most cordial manner." McPherson was an engineer officer of fine natural ability and extraordinary acquirements, having graduated number one in his class at West Point, and was held in high estimation by Grant and his professional brethren. So high in fact had McPherson risen in the esteem of his fellow officers that Grant had recently remarked of him, "One day he could go all the way," meaning that McPherson could become commander in chief of the U.S. Army. To this Sherman concurred, but added darkly, "If he lives."

McPherson now commanded the XVII Corps in the Army of the Tennessee, most of which was conveniently posted on the levees around Lake Providence. He immediately ordered a thirty-ton steam tug to be dragged overland by mules from the Mississippi to Lake Providence, so as to reconnoiter his assignment. He didn't like what he saw.

However it may have appeared on Grant's maps, Bayou Baxter was little more than a silted-up slough that dead-ended in a shallow cypress swamp as dismal as Milton's hell. In order to cut a channel it would be necessary not only to clear the cypresses but to cut the stumps off so close to the bottom that the flotilla could pass over them.

A lesser man might have reported back to headquarters that the job was impossible, but McPherson was a go-getter, undaunted by such challenges. First he secured a number of newfangled underwater steam saws that could slice off the cypress stumps nearly flat with the bottom. At the same time he organized press-gangs to round up runaway blacks and the slaves from nearby plantations to do the heavy lifting. The steam dredges from the DeSoto Point operation were brought up too. Meantime, McPherson had commandeered Arlington, a splendid plantation on the lake that was home to a Confederate senator from Louisiana, who reportedly kept a fabulous wine cellar. There, according to local recollection, McPherson, his staff, and top commanders used the first floor as stables for their horses while occupying the upper stories as living quarters. In the evenings they entertained themselves by turning the little steam tug into an excursion boat, in which they tooled around the six-mile-long lake on sunset cruises to the accompaniment of a regimental band.

As the winter wore on the levees became honeycombed with Union graves and the men continued dying of diseases. Grant finally visited the site and was also discouraged by what he found. Even with the blacks doing much of the work (it was said that the majority of soldiers spent their time on the banks fishing or playing horseshoes) the sheer magnitude of the undertaking seemed overwhelming. Worse, as Grant himself pointed out in his memoirs, there were so many narrow and twisting places along the proposed five-hundred-mile route that even small parties of Confederate raiders could blockade the streams and ambush transport and supply ships, which called into question the feasibility of the whole enterprise. Why Grant hadn't figured this out at the beginning is anybody's guess, but afterward he offered a somewhat lame hint in trying to silence critics, explaining that the plan "served as a cover for other efforts which gave a better prospect of success."

In any case, as at DeSoto Point, Old Man River himself proved to be the final arbiter. This time, instead of rising to drown out Grant's Canal, the water began to fall, making passage from the river into Lake Providence impassable for military craft, and thus rendering the canal worthless. The project was therefore abandoned, and with it the sixth attempt to take Vicksburg. The steam dredges were left to rot in the cypress swamp and the men returned to their fishing and horseshoes—but not for long.

Admiral Porter had his own ideas for the Rebels' undoing, which presently had nothing to do with armies or canals or amphibious landings. Instead, after correctly identifying the two main objectives of the Mississippi campaign, he just as correctly proceeded to separate them. One, of course, was to reopen the river to commercial traffic from the Midwest to the Gulf and thence to ports far and wide. Desirable as this was, it would still require the reduction of Vicksburg and Port Hudson, which only the army could accomplish, and they weren't getting anywhere fast. From a purely military standpoint, however, the second goal was even more vital, and that was to sever the Confederate connection between the bountiful lands of the trans-Mississippi, since the ultimate destination of their bounty was the Rebel armies of Virginia, Tennessee, and Mississippi.

In sheer size, the trans-Mississippi was nearly as large as the rest of the Confederacy east of the river. Up until then it had provided the South with more than 100,000 soldiers, about 30 percent of the number presently serving under arms. Perhaps even more significantly, the trans-Mississippi was an inexhaustible granary that supplied much of the beef, corn, hogs, rice, wheat, and staples that filled stockpiles in Atlanta and Richmond. Not only that, but because of the blockade it also was a major conduit of European arms, munitions, and medical supplies through supposedly neutral Mexico. Cut off the supplies, Porter reasoned, and the enemy armies would begin to wither and starve. His view was later shared by no less an authority than the Harvard historian and philosopher John Fiske, who wrote in 1900, "To sever from the Confederacy its three trans-Mississippi states was an object of paramount importance. It would destroy nearly half its resisting power."

This Confederate pipeline had already suffered a major blow with the fall of Memphis, and Sherman, before going up the Yazoo to attack Chickasaw Bluffs, had seen to the destruction of the Shreveport and Vicksburg Railroad. While these actions went a long way toward cutting the connection, it still left almost three hundred miles of the Mississippi under Rebel control all the way down to Port Hudson, and it was upon this stretch that Porter cast his nautical eye.

He already knew he could get his ironclads past the Vicksburg batteries—albeit with the inevitably heavy damage—and once below there would be no sustainable source of coal, and the fireboxes of the ironclad ships were not designed for burning wood. Porter was still trying to figure a way to solve that problem when a catalyst arrived in the shape of a big Confederate riverboat named *City of Vicksburg* that steamed up from the South laden with supplies and tied up at the town docks. The brazenness of this prompted the admiral to summon his newest charge, Colonel Charles Rivers Ellet, who a scant six months earlier had been a nineteen-year-old medical cadet. Following the death of his father during the Battle of Memphis, young Ellet now commanded the army ram fleet, which, over the protest of Secretary of War Stanton, had just been turned over to the navy. Porter now wanted to know if Ellet thought it was possible to send in one of his rams to sink the *City of Vicksburg*, which, to his eternal annoyance and disgust, was lying in plain sight of his flagship.*

Ellet replied that it was not only possible but, with himself in command, it was as good as done. Thus in the early hours of February 2, 1863, Ellet began sneaking downriver in *Queen of the West,* his best ram, which could burn either coal or wood. Elaborate preparations had been taken according to Porter's instructions, or so the admiral believed. Double bales of cotton had been placed around the decks to fortify against Confederate cannon shot, a nighttime attack had been ordered to minimize the danger from Rebel batteries, and Ellet had been told to strike the *City of Vicksburg* just aft of her wheel, then blast her with turpentine-encased shot in order to set her ablaze.

Everything was going according to plans until Ellet decided to change them. Told to attack while it was still dark, he dallied around with last-minute preparations so that it was after sunrise before he got into position, and by then the Vicksburg guns were on full alert. As in the ill-fated attempt to ram the *Arkansas,* a big river eddy caught *Queen of the West* just as she was bearing in and her blow glanced off. She fired her turpentine balls, setting *Vicksburg* afire, but the Rebel guns began exacting a stern toll. The cotton bales Ellet had layered

---

* Porter might have sunk her himself with gunfire, but that would have meant bringing his own ship within range of the Vicksburg batteries.

around the superstructure caught fire and all hands were ordered out into the hail of enemy fire to shove them overboard. By then it was apparent no more could be done and, while hundreds of Vicksburgians ran onto the bluffs to watch, the *Queen,* still ablaze and being shot at by every gun in the batteries, bore off toward the western shore where Sherman had some batteries of his own.

After putting out the fire and looking things over, Ellet decided his damage was slight and Porter told him to push on downriver in search of Confederate supply ships. He was accompanied by the unarmed river steamer *De Soto,* which Sherman had lent him as a support vessel and safety valve, if trouble should occur. The first Rebel boat he caught up with was typical of the haul that was crossing on a daily basis from the trans-Mississippi. She was the steamer *A. H. Baker,* carrying 110,000 pounds of barreled pork, some five hundred live hogs, several tons of salt, and other sundries, bound for Port Hudson and points east. Thus encouraged, Ellet continued on his rampage.

By then the Confederates had put out the alarm but, even so, a number of their transports failed to get the word and were taken captive, including one boat with a party of women from New Orleans aboard, whose destination seemed to be Port Hudson. Porter floated down a barge of coal for Ellet, which he recovered and hid up a bayou, then began a campaign of pillage on the smaller streams feeding into the Mississippi. At one point he stopped at a plantation near Grand Gulf that had belonged to former president Zachary Taylor and appropriated its cotton. He sent parties of his "marines" ashore with orders to destroy enemy wagon trains and, if fired upon from the banks, burn the plantation homes nearby. After two weeks of this he made his first reckless mistake, violating Porter's orders to stay near the mouth of the Red River.

Full of as much steam as his boilers, Ellet took the *Queen* eighty miles up the Red River to see about a big gun the Confederates were rumored to be landing there. On the way he captured a steamer with 4,500 bushels of corn, a number of Confederate soldiers, and a German with $32,000 in his pocket. When he arrived at the place the gun was supposed to be delivered to, Ellet not only found himself bracketed and shot through and through by Rebel guns, but he got stuck on a sandbar and had to abandon ship, leaving the *Queen* in enemy hands. He and most of his crew escaped on the *De Soto,* which was following close behind, but she also ran aground and they were forced to re-escape on the captured Confederate corn boat.

For two days Ellet and his men desperately eluded a host of angry Rebel steamers that were now looking for him in every part of the river system. Out of food and fuel, the crew fed the corn into the engine's fireboxes and ate what was left, and it seemed only a matter of time before their unarmed boat would be apprehended. Then salvation appeared out of a Mississippi River fog in the form of the new ironclad *Indianola,* which Porter presciently had sent downriver when communications with Ellet were lost. After conferring with *Indianola*'s captain, and explaining what had happened, Ellet and his people went north toward Vicksburg, assuming their mission had been accomplished. In Porter's eyes, it was nothing of the sort, for he viewed the loss of *Queen of the West* as a major defeat. "I can give orders, but I cannot give officers good judgment," he telegraphed the secretary of the navy. "The *Indianola* is now there by herself. Whether the commander will have the good sense not to be surprised, remains to be seen."

It did not take long for Porter to find out. *Indianola*'s captain hung around for two extra days, by which time the Confederates had not only repaired and manned *Queen of the West* but also sicced upon him the formidable *William H. Webb,* a converted steam ram. On the moonlit night of February 24, these two caught up with the Yankee gunboat about twenty-five miles south of Vicksburg. In the ensuing battle, the mighty *Indianola* got herself sunk in ten feet of water and her crew made prisoners, and Porter's humiliation was complete, or so it seemed. But then there occurred one of those weird and wonderful incidents, which on the rarest of occasions can make war actually seem like fun.

Next morning, after Porter recovered from his fury over losing the *Indianola,* he concocted a delicious plot to keep her from falling into Rebel hands. First he commandeered a large river flatboat and set a veritable army of carpenters to work, dolling her up like a Union ironclad. By late afternoon, the barge had been extended to more than three hundred feet long, with forty-foot-high enclosed paddle wheel–houses made out of a cabin hauled from a nearby plantation, two tall smokestacks of nailed-together barrels set upon smoldering tar pots, and a big "Quaker gun" that poked menacingly forward. To conceal the hasty work, the dummy ship was plastered with tar and christened "Black Terror," complete with the Stars and Stripes flying from a flagstaff. As a finishing touch, some wag nailed a sign on its side: DELUDED PEOPLE, CAVE IN! The finished cost of the hoax ship, Porter claimed, had been $8.63. Just before midnight a Union towboat dragged the creature around to the bend above Vicksburg and cut it loose downriver.

When the Confederate batteries sighted it in the moonlight they assumed it was real and opened fire, but the current carried "Black Terror" rapidly past with no observable damage. It hit a sandbar just off DeSoto Point, but Sherman's people rowed out and shoved it off. Meanwhile, Confederate headquarters at Vicksburg had fired off a warning that a big Yankee ironclad was on the loose south of the city and ordered the salvage parties attempting to raise *Indianola* to demolish her, rather than let her be retaken. Just as the sun was setting, Rebel scouts reported "Black Terror" lying off the western shore not far above where the recovery operation was in progress. Actually she was aground again, but that was all it took; *Queen of the West* and the *William H. Webb,* which had been standing by, promptly came about and took off downriver, while the Rebel salvage party blew up *Indianola* with her own gunpowder. For a while, Pemberton and his army became laughingstocks, not just in the North but throughout the Confederacy as well.

For his part, Porter had partially redeemed himself by the dummy ironclad trick, but the fact remained that two of his fleet's most powerful ships, *Queen of the West* and *Indianola,* were either sunk or in the hands of the enemy, and thus ended the U.S. Navy's forays into the Rebel-held part of the Mississippi until further notice.

While that was taking place, another scheme for conquering Vicksburg had captured Grant's imagination, promising the "better prospect of success" that he craved. This entailed an expedition through the wild, snake-infested swamps and bayous on the "right" side of the Mississippi across the river from Helena, Arkansas. There, a body of water with the romantic name Moon Lake connected with a number of inland streams before emerging through more than four hundred miles of scummy water into the Yazoo, *above* the dreaded Rebel batteries at Haines's Bluff. By dispatching most of a full infantry division for the mission, it was hoped that a foothold—or at least a toehold—would be secured on the high and dry land behind Vicksburg to break the railroad linking the city with Jackson to prevent Confederate reinforcements. At the same time a continuous stream of Federal troops—some 30,000 in all—would pour into the watery pipeline and assemble themselves into a force formidable enough to take the Yazoo forts from the rear, invest the town itself, or meet the Rebels on an open battle-field.

These prospects, however, depended on a certain amount of coop-eration by the Confederates; namely, that they would have to be surprised by the movement, at least to the extent that they couldn't mount a timely, solid defense at the point of invasion. Grant had become convinced that, without the big guns of the Yazoo forts to con-tend with, Porter's formidable ironclads could provide more than ade-quate artillery fire to support a beachhead and a landing. Still, the most inexplicable aspect of this plot was the notion that a full division of Yankee troops on sixteen transport ships escorted by six gunboats could traverse four hundred winding miles into the Rebels' own terri-tory without them finding out about it.

The man Grant sent as his liaison to coordinate between the army and the navy was Colonel James H. Wilson, a twenty-six-year-old engineering officer with a goatee and a bright outlook on life, who was "nervous in temperament, plain and outspoken on all subjects" and destined to become one of Grant's workhorses. On February 3, he was on hand to see 1,500 pounds of Yankee gunpowder blow up the levee at Yazoo Pass. The Mississippi River at that point was nine feet higher than the countryside behind the barrier, and Wilson reported that the water rushed in "like a perfect Niagara," flooding everything before it. The Confederates had thoughtfully chopped down a number of large trees to impede just such an enemy incursion, but these were carried off in the frothing water that soon covered every spot of low-lying ground for many hundreds of square miles.

Everything that could took to high ground, and whatever couldn't took to the trees. Cattle, hogs, and other livestock that weren't swept away by the flood bunched forlornly on little hillocks as the water rose around them. Snakes and other disagreeable creatures invaded houses. Chickens and turkeys perched on the eaves of outbuildings up to their rooftops in water. Many residents of the river plantations fled inland, and most of those who stayed dutifully burned their cotton, if it hadn't already been drowned out.

By now thoroughly alarmed, Pemberton ordered General William Wing Loring to see what could be done to stop a back-door invasion through this maze of rivers. After conferring with the still-shipless Confederate naval lieutenant Isaac Brown, it was decided to construct a fortification on a low but relatively dry piece of land in the fork between the Yalobusha and Tallahatchie rivers, where they joined to form the Yazoo. Eight pieces of artillery, some of them large, were hauled to the site, and slaves from nearby plantations were conscripted to assist the couple of thousand Rebel soldiers in constructing trenches and breastworks that included more than two thousand bales of cotton and thousands of sandbags for casemates and parapets. The place was promptly dubbed Fort Pemberton.

More big trees were felled along the upstream banks to impede the passage of the Yankee flotilla, but why underwater mines were not employed has never been explained. As a finishing touch, the Confederates sank the captured steamer *Star of the West* to block the channel just north of the fort, thus ending the career of that historic ship.*

Once it left the Mississippi and crossed Moon Lake, the invasion force was swept violently into the Yazoo Pass. An Iowa soldier aboard one of the transports compared his ship's entry from the Mississippi with being "whirled round and round like a toy skiff in a wash tub." The steamer, carrying a five-hundred-man regiment, was heaved into the lake backward as it joined the mighty wash of logs, debris, and other transports in the swirling maelstrom.

The levee cut had rendered Yazoo Pass deep enough, but years of disuse had made it so congested with overhanging trees that the going was agonizingly slow, and as if that wasn't enough the Rebels conscripted slaves to fell hundreds of huge trees, so that they lay thickly bank to bank across the channel. Yankee working parties of five hundred men and more were rotated day and night to clear the path, which had to be done manually by chopping the boughs away, then sawing the trunks and hauling them to the banks on ropes. It took the convoy the rest of February just to navigate twelve miles of Yazoo Pass and into Coldwater River, from where, it was hoped, they would soon enter the Tallahatchie and then emerge into the Yazoo above the Confederate batteries at Haines's Bluff.

Despite the slowdowns, Grant seemed thoroughly satisfied with the progress, and he ordered McPherson to stand by with his whole corps ready to move as soon as he gave the word. And he wrote his congressman, "The Yazoo Pass expedition is going to prove a perfect success."

---

* *Star of the West* had been the supply ship designated to provision the Federal troops manning Fort Sumter in Charleston when the war broke out. In the attempt she was driven away by a warning shot over her bow that is generally conceded as being the first shot of the Civil War. Later sent to the Gulf of Mexico, she was captured by Confederate cavalry under Earl Van Dorn—another story in itself.

When they got into the wider Coldwater the steaming became smoother and, led by two ironclads, six tinclads, and two steam rams, the flotilla entered the Tallahatchie and was more than a hundred miles down it when they encountered Fort Pemberton.

At first glance, the place didn't look like much. For one thing, it was barely above water, much as Fort Henry had been a long year earlier when Grant and the ironclads had first approached it. Second, from what they could see of its armaments, there was little to fear. The most dangerous weapon in Fort Pemberton was a 6.4-inch Whitworth rifle—hardly a match for the 11-inch Dahlgrens that the ironclads carried—but, along with a 32-pounder, the Rebel guns happened to be sighted straight downriver on a mile-long stretch that the Yankee gunboats would have to navigate. When the first ironclad appeared they cut loose and the battle was on. At the height of the fray, Confederate general William Loring stood on the mud ramparts of Fort Pemberton hollering at his men, "Give 'em blizzards! Give 'em blizzards!," thereby earning for himself the moniker "Old Blizzards," which stuck with him throughout his long and controversial career.

The Union naval officer in charge was Lieutenant Commander Watson Smith, a man clearly beyond his capacity for this sort of adventure. Already shaky after the weeks of cutting through the Confederate obstructions and dealing with narrow rivers and sometimes shallow channels that had actually stove in the bottom of his command boat, *Chillicothe,* Smith seemed to come apart when Rebel shells began to fall. And he completely broke down when a shell flew right into an open port where two big Federal guns were about to be fired, exploding not only itself but the two live shells in the *Chillicothe*'s guns, killing or maiming thirteen of the gun crew. Upon fainting and being revived, Smith started issuing orders "in the most complete gibberish," the gist of which was an immediate withdrawal of the Federal gunboats behind the river bend.

After a day Commander Smith composed himself and tried once again, but with the same results. The ironclads were, basically, at the wrong end of an artillery funnel, and the Confederate gunners were pouring it on. Even inside their armored hulls, men were killed and wounded when bolts, rivets, and pieces of wood flew around as deadly splinters whenever a Rebel shell exploded on the plate outside. After two days of this, Smith again called the whole thing off, much to the disgust of Colonel James Wilson, who complained to Grant that the navy had no "backbone."

Shortly after the Federal flotilla turned back, it met up with troop transports carrying the division of General Isaac Quinby, who, by virtue of his rank, assumed command and insisted on having a second look. He decided that an infantry attack on Fort Pemberton would solve the problem, but after floundering around in the muck for more than a week Quinby concluded that the expedition had been foiled by its own designs: the same water that had rushed in when the Federals blew the levee to allow passage into the rivers had so flooded the land that the infantry became useless. A suggestion was then taken to blow a second break in the Mississippi levee to let in so much more water that Fort Pemberton and its occupants would be drowned.

So Quinby went back up the river and blew a levee about six miles north of the first one, but the only thing it accomplished was flooding more of the countryside and, when he returned, there sat Fort Pemberton, high, dry, and waiting for him. Not only that, but an ominous report from the rearward boats stated they could hear the Confederates again hard at work chopping trees across the narrower streams, apparently in an effort to trap them in from behind.

That ended the seventh attempt to take Vicksburg.* As for Commander Watson Smith, when he returned from the expedition he was declared a mental case by a surgeons' board. Porter relieved him of command and sent him north, where, as if to prove a point, he died shortly thereafter of "brain fever."

It was now the middle of March and Grant, as yet uncertain about the fate of the thousands of men he had sent down Yazoo Pass, found himself "much exercised for [their] safety." He had heard about the trouble with Fort Pemberton, but nothing concrete about the result there had reached him. Being a man of action, Grant decided to see for himself if there was another way to prevail, for Porter had come up with his own bizarre proposal for attacking Vicksburg from the rear. It involved yet another amphibious expedition that would take advantage of the now thoroughly flooded bayous and rivers that the admiral asserted would not only get the troops above the Confederate batteries at Haines's Bluff but get them past Fort Pemberton as well.

---

* The others were: Farragut's attempt to bombard the city into submission; General Williams's failed canal project; Grant's foiled march to take Vicksburg from the rear; Sherman's abortive attack at Chickasaw Bluffs; the failed Lake Providence expedition; and the abandonment of Grant's renewed canal scheme.

The plan was to steam up the Yazoo to an obscure stream opposite Vicksburg called Steele's Bayou, then follow it north, away from the city, through Cypress Lake, Black Bayou, and Deer Creek to the Rolling Fork, where, a hundred miles later, they would then turn southward again into the Sunflower River and then another hundred miles down to the Yazoo. It was a tortuous loop of two hundred miles, but it left Fort Pemberton about thirty miles to the east, before reentering the Yazoo twenty miles above the Confederate batteries at Snyder's, Drury's, and Haines's bluffs.

As luck would have it, Sherman got tapped for the duty, along with one of his divisions, and on March 16 he embarked his men on transports that were to follow close behind the van, which consisted of five ironclads, four mortar boats, and four tugboats, commanded by Porter himself. They had no sooner shoved off than things began to go awry.

Surely it was one of the strangest wartime expeditions in naval history. Because of the levee break the water was so high that in many places the big ironclads found themselves steaming above drowned roads and houses and even entire forests, with only the very tops of their tallest trees showing. Keeping in the channel became a major project. The ironclads drew seven feet of water, whereas in normal times, according to Porter, these streams "did not contain enough water to float a canoe." But the flood had put at least fifteen feet under them, provided they did not sail off into an underwater hill or vale.

Almost immediately another problem presented itself, similar to the one encountered by the Yazoo Pass expedition—only worse. The twisting narrowness of the streams and the rise in water level often put the boats right in the path of overhanging trees and limbs that, when struck, carried away almost everything on deck, especially on the river steamers with their tall smokestacks, elevated pilothouses, and ponderous loading tackle. Not only that, but the trees and branches were inhabited by all species of swamp creatures that had sought refuge from the flood. Whenever a boat crashed or bumped into one of these natural obstacles, its decks were immediately inundated with a perfect shower of live zoological specimens: 'coons, possums, snakes of all descriptions and temperaments, rats, mice, lizards, wildcats, cockroaches, and a host of other insects so varied and plentiful that their identification could only be guessed at. Sailors manned brooms to sweep these startled visitors overboard, but some refused to go, which made life aboard ship more interesting.

After a few days Sherman's flotilla began to look like a moving shipwreck. By then, most smokestacks had been torn off the transport boats or bent beyond use. Wheelhouses, booms, ships' boats, masts, sometimes entire superstructures had been demolished, and whenever the steamers hit a dead or damaged limb it would come crashing straight onto the deck, smashing skylights and framework, adding to the chaos. As with the Yazoo Pass expedition, smoke from burning cotton billowed from whatever high ground there was and often obscured navigation. Porter was appalled by the "wicked[ness]" of such wanton destruction, and shouted to a grizzled old overseer, "Why did those fools set fire to that cotton?"

"Because they didn't want you fools to have it," was the equally discourteous reply.

At one point, pyres that blazed along Cypress Bayou actually threatened to roast Porter's gunboat crews alive. As he described it, the bayou "was exactly forty-six feet wide. My vessel was forty-two feet wide." On both sides of the stream some six thousand bales of Confederate cotton were aflame. After learning from a slave that the cotton would burn for two or three more days, Porter was determined to push through. "All the ports were shut in and the crews called to fire quarters, standing ready with fire-buckets," he said. A tugboat that was in the lead disappeared into the inferno after soaking everything down, and when it emerged on the other side all the paint was blistered and many of the crew scorched. On the deck of *Cincinnati,* Porter was forced to jump into a small iron-plated closet, followed by the captain, while the helmsman "covered himself with an old [wet] flag that lay in the wheelhouse."

"Just after we passed through the fire," Porter reported, "there was a terrible crash, which some thought was an earthquake. We had run into and quite through a span of bridge about fifty feet long, and demolished the whole fabric, having failed to see it in the smoke."

And that was just the beginning. Cypress Bayou was so crooked, Porter said, that "at one time the vessels would all be steaming on different courses. One would be standing north, another south, another east, and another west through the woods. The tugs and mortar-boats seemed to be mixed up in the most marvelous manner." It was also filled with huge soggy logs with their ends pointing upward, "presenting the appearance of *chevaux-de-frise,* over which we could no more pass than we could fly." All this had to be cleared by hand, and no sooner had it been done than the sailors heard the sinister racket of chopping from the dismal swamps ahead.

The ironclads, which had no tall masts or booms, managed to weather the damage better than the transports, and as a result Sherman and his infantry fell farther and farther behind the armored van. By March 20 Porter's naval force had reached the head of the Rolling Fork, the pass that would take them into the wide and deep Sunflower River. From there, the sailing promised to be fast and smooth all the way back down to the Yazoo River and victory. But just then a combination of bad luck, misapprehension, and Rebel ingenuity brought the operation up short.

Right at the entrance to the Rolling Fork was a small collection of houses, and along the banks a number of slaves stood watching "Mr. Linkum's gumboats" as they gathered to enter the pass.* Suddenly Porter looked out over his bridge and saw "a large green patch extending all the way across. It looked like the green scum on ponds," he said. When he asked the slaves what it was, one of them replied, "It's nuffin but willers, sah. When de water's out ob de bayou, den we cuts de willers to make baskets wib." As Porter was digesting this, the man added, "You can go troo dat like a eel."

It was not so. As Porter's new flagship *Carondelet* entered the strange patch of vegetation "full-steam-ahead," it first slowed abruptly, then came to a complete halt. "The little withes caught in the rough iron ends of the overhangs and held us as if in a vice," Porter reported. "I tried to back out, but t'was no use. We could not move an inch, no matter how much steam we put on."

The men brought out large hooks and tried to snag off the willow branches, but to no avail. Porter looked to the banks for the man who had originally advised him about the willows and received a sobering reassessment. "All I could find out from them was that 'dey was mo' tougher than ropes.' " Presently the crew produced "saws, knives, cutlasses and chisels" and went over the side, but as soon as the little wil-

---

* In 1862 a Connecticut musician and Union patriot named Henry Clay Work published a minstrel song popularly known as "The Year of Jubilo," a verse of which goes like this:

> *Say darkeys hab you seen de massa,*
> *Wid de muffstash on his face,*
> *Gos long de road sometime dis mornin'*
> *Like he gwine to leab dis place?*
> *He seen a smoke way up de ribber,*
> *Where de Linkum gumboats lay,*
> *He took his hat an' lef' berry sudden*
> *An' I spec he's run away!*

low switches were cut away "others sprang up from under the water and took a fresher grip on us, so we were worse off than ever." But even that was wishful thinking.

Suddenly from ahead came a boom of artillery fire, along with the chilling crack of a Whitworth rifled gun—possibly the same one that had helped thwart the Federals at Fort Pemberton—which had a dead-on accurate range of more than a mile. Earlier, as the flotilla was waiting for the other ironclads to catch up, a Lieutenant Murphy, who commanded one of Porter's boats, pointed out that there was an old Indian mound ahead and that it might be a good idea to fortify it—just in case—while they were waiting. Porter agreed, wondering why, if it was such a desirable strong point, the Confederates had not occupied it themselves. "It must have been because they thought it worthless," he recalled thinking. "They showed themselves to be poor judges in such matters."

As Rebel shells began bursting all about them, Porter quickly came to appreciate why the enemy hadn't occupied the Indian mound: it was indefensible. "Suddenly I saw the sides of the mound crowded with officers and men. They were tumbling down as best they could; the guns were tumbled ahead of them. There was a regular stampede," he said. Just as he was taking that in, scores of Rebel sharpshooters abruptly opened up on them from the swamps, behind trees, stumps, and hummocks, and worse—if such a thing was possible—"We could not use our large guns; they were way below the banks, and lying so close to it that we could not get elevation enough to fire over."

Porter was in a fix for sure. His boats were stuck fast in the willows and surrounded by enemy sharpshooters who made any attempt to free them up suicidal; he was powerless to return fire and Sherman's infantry, his only salvation at this point, was somewhere back down Deer Creek, oblivious to his predicament. For all Porter knew, there may have been Confederates behind him as well as ahead and on both sides, and if they could obstruct the creek, and keep his crews pinned down inside the boats, then a boarding attack was probably imminent. A shiver of fear must have run over him when he realized what would happen if the Rebels actually seized his ironclad fleet—in a nutshell, the whole face of the war on the Mississippi would instantly be changed.

Porter was determined that this would not happen on his watch, however, and took preventive measures. First, even if he could not elevate his own guns, the four mortar boats he'd brought along had no such problem, and he immediately set them into action lobbing their big 13-inch shells. It took a while to get the range, but finally the mortars managed to silence the Rebel batteries, at least temporarily. Next Porter sent out riflemen of his own to try to deal with the sharpshooters and when their fire had slackened—also temporarily—he "set to work again to overcome the willows." As the gunfire stopped, the slaves again began to gather on the bank and one of them overheard Porter grumble to himself, "Why don't Sherman come on? I'd give ten dollars to get a telegram to him." According to the admiral, the following colloquy ensued.

"I'm a telegram-wire, Massa," said one of the slaves. "I'll take him for half a dollar. I'm de county telegraph, sah. I does all dat bizness."

Astonished, Porter asked the man, "Where's your office, Sambo?"

"My name ain't Sambo, sah. My name's Tub, an I run yer line fer yer half a dollar."

With nothing much to lose at that point, Porter handed him the half dollar and scribbled out a message: "Dear Sherman: Hurry up for heaven's sake . . . ," which Tub tucked into his hair, then vanished into the swamps. No sooner had this hopeful measure been set into motion than word reached Porter that Rebel steamers were in the process of debarking 2,000 troops at a landing up ahead. As if to emphasize how unpromising the situation had become, the Confederate artillery opened up on them again from a different location. As night came on, Porter was constrained to issue a general order steeped in gloom: "Every man and officer must be kept below, ports kept down, and guns loaded with grape and canister and only fired when an attempt is made to board us or rush upon us. Put all hands on half rations. No lights at night. Men to sleep at the guns. . . . Every precaution must be taken to defend the vessels to the last, and when we can do no better we will blow them up."

But then, right at sundown, providence smiled on Admiral Porter and his beleaguered flotilla. The crews suddenly began to notice that the water in Rolling Fork "had begun to run rapidly, and large logs began to come in, and pile up on the outside of the willows." The water continued to rush in almost like a rising tide—although they were hundreds of miles from the ocean—and soon began to lift the boats free of the accursed willows. It was, Porter realized afterward, the torrent from the second levee that General Quinby had blown up a day or so earlier in hopes of flooding out Fort Pemberton. Somehow the wall of water did not reach that place, but it did pile up enough under the Yankee boats in Deer Creek for Porter to give the order to ship all rudders and try to back out down into the fraternal embrace of Sherman's 7,000 infantrymen. As an added bonus, the new flood lifted the ironclads high enough to employ their big guns against the Rebel tormentors in the swamps.

Sherman, however, knew nothing of this when the telegrapher Tub found him late that night and handed him Porter's note, which he had thoughtfully concealed in a cigar wrapper. "The admiral stated," Sherman recalled, "that he had met a force of infantry and artillery which gave him great trouble by killing the men who had to expose themselves outside the armor to shove off the bows of the boats, which had so little headway that they would not steer. He begged me to come to his rescue as quickly as possible."

Immediately Sherman dragooned a regiment of Missouri infantrymen and sent them forward down a swampy river road, then set off himself in a canoe after more reinforcements, which were farther back down the river. Presently he located a brigade on a steamer and off they went to Porter's rescue, "crashing through trees, carrying away the pilot-house, smoke-stacks, every thing above deck, but the captain was a brave fellow, and realized the necessity," Sherman wrote. "The night was absolutely black, and we could only make about two and a half of the four miles. We then disembarked, and marched through the canebrake, carrying lighted candles in our hands."

After this Druid-like procession had slogged till nearly dawn, Sherman rested the men in a plantation field and, at daylight, began marching again toward the sound of Porter's guns, which they could now hear distinctly in the distance and which, Sherman remembered, told him that "time was precious." Still they waded through miserable mires where "the smaller drummer boys had to carry their drums on their heads," and they had actually come twenty-one miles by noon, when they met up with a detachment of the Missouri troops. Porter had sent these men back downriver to prevent the Confederates from blocking in his gunboats from behind, and not a moment too soon, for the Rebels were already at work with their axes. Finally Sherman and his soldiers came in sight of the gunboats, which the rising tide had lifted enough to "occasionally [fire] a heavy eight-inch gun across the cotton fields into the swamp behind."

Somewhere along the way Sherman had acquired an old horse that he rode bareback with a rope bridle, and when he approached the stricken gunboats the sailors came out and cheered him "most vociferously," as his bluecoats "swept forward across the cotton-field in full view." When Sherman found Porter, "He was on one of his ironclads, with a shield made from a section of a smoke-stack, and I doubt if he was ever more glad to meet a friend than he was to see me. I inquired of Admiral Porter what he proposed to do, and he said he wanted to get out of that scrape as quickly as possible."

It was now March 21, five days after the invasion force had entered Steele's Bayou. Now the boats and men were backing out single file, thwarted, rudderless, dejected, caroming off the banks in place of steerage, and with Vicksburg no closer to capture than it was when they first arrived there in December.

For Pemberton, it was no time to gloat, since only a fool of a general would relax his guard with a whole enemy army still within his sight. But for the Confederates, the repulse of all these Yankee efforts—this was their eighth fiasco—suddenly began to assume an ironic and unintended aspect.

Joseph Johnston, from his headquarters with Bragg in far-away Tullahoma, was so delighted by the turn of events that he began asking Pemberton to return the 9,000 troops on loan from Bragg's army that had been lent during the Chickasaw Bluffs crisis. He was also full of praise for Pemberton and his splendid defense. "I believe your arrangements at Vicksburg make it perfectly safe," he told the Pennsylvanian in a congratulatory message. What Pemberton couldn't know at the time was that Johnston would apparently cling to that assessment even in Pemberton's gravest hour of need.

As for Confederate officers who were in the know, their impressions were more sober, and probably best summed up by Pemberton's engineering officer, Major Samuel Lockett, who recalled, "Though these expeditions all failed, the desperate nature of most of them convinced us that General Grant was in deep earnest, and not easily discouraged."

CHAPTER THIRTEEN

I Fear Grant Won't Do

More than Grant knew or even suspected, horrible gnashing sounds had begun to resonate around Washington. General in chief Henry Halleck informed Grant that Lincoln had become "rather impatient" about the lack of progress at Vicksburg, adding, "In my opinion, the opening of the Mississippi will be to us of more advantage than the capture of forty Richmonds."

For more than ten weeks, failure had piled upon failure, and the press was again on a harangue, insisting that Grant was habitually drunk, incompetent, and irresponsible. Worse, some of Grant's own generals shared those sentiments, not only among themselves but with their powerful friends in Washington. Secretary of War Edwin Stanton had become so alarmed that he began drawing up an order to replace Grant with, of all people, Benjamin Butler.

What would have been most hurtful, had Grant known it, was the appraisal given by a general who had always been sympathetic to him and whom he counted as a friend. He was Brigadier General C. C. Washburn, who complained to his brother Elihu, Grant's staunchest patron in Congress, that both the army and the campaign were being "badly managed," and concluded, "I fear Grant won't do." And in a case of the pot calling the kettle black if ever there was one, even old "Rosy" Rosecrans, Grant's colleague from West Point days, couldn't resist dropping a hint of Grant's reputed inebriation to a newspaper reporter.

Much of the backbiting stemmed from jealousy, resentment, ambition, or frustration on the part of a few angry souls, chief among them the ever-troublesome McClernand, whom Colonel Wilson, of Grant's staff, characterized as "a man of hasty and violent temper," and who Sherman, never one to mince words, assessed as "a dirty dog." On March 13 the backstabbing McClernand wrote Lincoln, "Genl. Grant I am informed was gloriously drunk and in bed sick all next day. If you are averse to drunken Genl's I can furnish the name of officers of high standing to substantiate the above." Also, unlike Grant's other generals, the Illinois politician maintained a salon of newspaper reporters around his headquarters. From there, it was easy to plant stories of his commander's alleged debauchery and ineptitude, which the newsmen dutifully sent back to their editors in Chicago, Cincinnati, and New York, who were uniformly angry at Grant for restricting their correspondents' access, especially after Sherman brought court-martial charges against one of them and threatened to have him hanged.*

In private correspondence to members of Lincoln's cabinet, Grant was disparaged as, among other things, "a poor drunken imbecile," "a foolish, drunken, stupid . . . jackass," and "much of the time idiotically drunk." These unflattering appraisals, and others, predictably found their way into the president's hands and compelled him to contemplate action of some sort. As one newspaper correspondent put it: "Public opinion had set so strongly in this direction because of the great length of time spent at Young's Point and Milliken's Bend, fruitlessly as it seemed to the nation, that his [Grant's] friends found it difficult to defend him."

The extent of Grant's drinking is harder to assess because, at the time, his friends all swore that he didn't, and his detractors all swore that he did. That he had problems with alcohol in the past there is no doubt, and there is good evidence that he did during the Vicksburg campaign as well. A newspaper reporter remembered that the general liked his whiskey straight, and had come wandering into a tent one night after word had circulated that a barrel was available, swilling down three army-issue tin cups of the stuff before retiring. Later there

* He was Thomas W. Knox, of the *New York Herald,* who had defied Sherman's orders by smuggling himself aboard a boat during the Chickasaw Bluffs expedition. Knox escaped hanging but was banished from the department, whereupon he went to Washington and secured permission to return from Lincoln himself. Upon his arrival he was taken aside by Grant, who informed him that, despite the approval of the president, things might happen in a wartime situation that were "beyond his control." Knox "took the hint, and removed himself on the first steamer upriver."

would be other, more damning corroborations, but it is probably safe
to say that Grant still knew his way around the bottle at this stage of
the campaign.

Grant's affliction appears to have been a combination of low tolerance for alcohol—often referred to as "not being able to hold one's
liquor"—and binge drinking, in which the drinker does not stop until
the liquor is gone or he simply passes out. In other words, Grant did
not seem to fall into the category of what is presently defined as a
"functioning alcoholic." Over and again, witnesses referred to his
"becoming stupid" after only a drink or two.

A correspondent for the Chicago *Times* with the delightful name
Sylvanus Cadwallader became one of the few reporters who was close
to Grant during the war and saw him on a daily basis during the Vicksburg campaign. Years after the war, when Grant was dead, he gave the
following appraisal of the general's relationship with alcohol in order,
he said, "to set to rest the conflicting statements which have at various
times been published about Gen. Grant's habits.

"The truth was that Gen. Grant had an inordinate love for liquors.
He was not an habitual drinker. [But] he could not drink moderately.
When at intervals his appetite for strong drink caused him to accept
the invitation of some old classmate or army associate . . . he invariably
drank to excess. Though absolutely refusing to drink on one day, there
was no certainty that he would not be inebriated on the next."

There is no evidence that Grant ever drank—to excess or otherwise—
during a battle or when some important movement was afoot. His
sprees appear to have been confined to periods of military inactivity and
possibly arose from boredom or loneliness. It has been suggested—
not just by historians coming afterward but by contemporaries who
were there—that Grant tried to keep Julia nearby whenever possible,
because he made a point of abstinence when she was around, which
possibly accounted for her presence at Holly Springs and/or Oxford,
around the time of the Van Dorn raid. However, Colonel Wilson, upon
first reporting to Grant's headquarters two months earlier, was
shocked when the chief of staff, John Rawlins, told him, "Now, I want
you to know what kind of man we are serving. He's a goddamn drunkard, and he's surrounded by a set of goddamned scalawags who pan-
der to his weakness."

Another incident, perhaps more telling than the others, occurred
when Rawlins handed Grant a letter saying that if he ever again
touched so much as a drop, he (Rawlins) would resign his commission

and leave. Even though it was a promise not to be kept, Grant and the Union itself should probably be thankful that he stayed, for Rawlins served throughout the war as Grant's mentor, counselor, and conscience, making every effort to keep his boss on the straight and narrow.

For his part, Grant was stoic, dismissive, and noncommittal about the reports, or so he said later. "Visitors to the camps went home with dismal stories to relate; Northern papers came back to the soldiers with these stories exaggerated. Because I would not divulge my ultimate plans to visitors, they pronounced me idle, incompetent and unfit to command men in an emergency, and clamored for my removal. I took no steps to answer these complaints, but continued to do my duty, as I understood it."

Meantime, back in Washington, as the rumors and informal complaints began to pile up against Grant's record of failures on the Vicksburg front, the consensus of Lincoln's cabinet was that he should be fired. The president, however, did not concur. "I think Grant has hardly a friend left, except myself," he remarked to John Hay, his secretary. "I rather like the man. Let us keep him a little longer." For added emphasis, to others seeking Grant's removal he repeated his earlier appraisal, "I can't spare this man. He fights."

It was a reprieve, if nothing else, but at the same time it was decided by Stanton to send out what amounted to a spy, to hang around Grant's headquarters and see if the bad reports were true. Actually, Stanton sent two spies, just to make certain. The first was Lorenzo Thomas, the army's adjutant general, whose cover story was to be an inspection of black regiments that the administration was now trying to enlist as a new experiment. The second was Charles A. Dana, Harvard graduate, former Horace Greeley newsman, and resident for some years of the socialist Brook Farm commune, who was to be investigating various complaints against army paymasters in Grant's department. To disguise his true mission Dana was even given his own cipher or telegraph code, which would be read by no one but Stanton, but having been forewarned nobody at Grant's headquarters was fooled.

In the case of General Thomas, it hardly mattered because he became so infatuated with the recruiting and military organization of ex-slaves that he was still far upriver when Grant began his final attack on Vicksburg. Dana, however, presented a different problem, for he was due any day and Rawlins called a special staff conference to deal with the matter. When he revealed that a Washington spy was coming to live with them, several staff officers "could hardly be restrained from open manifestations of their hostility"; to wit, the chief of artillery was all for throwing young Mr. Dana into the Mississippi River.

The ever-practical Rawlins, however, managed to settle things down, calling such sentiments "discourteous and unmilitary." He informed one and all that Dana was to be treated with the utmost civility; that he was to be given his own tent right next to Grant's, a seat was to be reserved for him at the mess table, and a horse, tack, and anything else he needed or wanted would be made available, so that Dana would feel as comfortable and at home as possible. As it turned out, this is probably what saved Grant's head from the block and his reputation from obscurity.

If Grant still had qualms about Nathaniel Banks marching his army up from New Orleans and stealing his thunder, he needn't have worried. Not only would Banks not beat him to Vicksburg, he wasn't coming at all.

In early January 1863, Banks set about fulfilling the part of his mission that involved the joint attack on Vicksburg. Immediately he discovered that because of the depredations of Dick Taylor and his ragtag Rebel force, he felt compelled to spread out his 36,000-man army to protect everything from New Orleans to Baton Rouge and points in between. That left Banks with at most 15,000 men for an overland campaign, which should have been enough, except for the guns and garrison of Port Hudson, which lay between him and his objective. After convincing himself that this was too tough a nut to crack, Banks then floundered his army through the swamps of the Atchafalaya basin in hopes of finding a way to get above Port Hudson and cross to high ground on the Mississippi side of the river. But like every place else along the lower river that time of year, the Atchafalaya was immersed in floodwaters, and the expedition was, quite literally, a wash.

To Banks's rescue—or so it seemed at the moment—came Admiral Farragut, who had become furious over the Confederates' control of the Mississippi between Port Hudson and Vicksburg, and especially at the capture of the *Indianola* and *Queen of the West.* According to several accounts, Farragut sent an invitation for Banks to join him for a nightcap after dinner in his cabin aboard the *Hartford,* where he spoke his mind, or rather gave a speech: "We have more men and more resources than these traitors and five times as much money. By God, shall a United States ship of war hesitate to go in and destroy a dozen of these wretched Mississippi steamers? I am sick of hearing my officers complain of cotton-clad boats and impregnable rams. They should pitch in and destroy them!"

Warming to his subject, the old admiral poured another glass of wine and waxed heroic. "What matters it, General, whether you and I are killed or not? We came here to die. It is our business and must happen sooner or later," he informed the startled Massachusetts politician. "We must fight this thing out until there is no more than one man left and that man must be a Union man. Here's to his health!"

To Farragut's mind, three important things could be accomplished by a joint army-navy assault on Port Hudson. Foremost was the fall of the fortification itself. If Banks could launch a land attack simultaneous with Farragut's ships running past the Rebel batteries, between the two of them they just might succeed in distracting and dividing the Confederates to reveal a soft spot in their defenses that Banks could exploit. Second, with his powerful warships above Port Hudson, Farragut could cut off Confederate commercial traffic from the Red River, and certainly discourage it from lesser outlets, which had always been a priority in the Mississippi River valley campaign. Finally, even though his large ships drew too much water to be used as transports, they could provide invaluable firepower when, and if, Grant decided to cross the river. With these considerations weighing in the balance, the sixty-two-year-old admiral set about assembling his force in preparation for running the big guns of Port Hudson on March 14, 1863.

The rub was that during the seven months since Farragut first went up the Mississippi past Port Hudson—and came down again in ignominy the previous July—great changes had been wrought at that Confederate bastion. In fact, when Farragut steamed past it the last time, it wasn't even a bastion, but an outpost manned by an agglomeration of field artillerymen with peashooters. Yet after Breckinridge's failed attempt to retake Baton Rouge, and his subsequent retirement from there to Port Hudson, it was recognized by the Confederate authorities on the scene and in Richmond that here was a natural strongpoint only fools could ignore.

Before the war, Port Hudson was a small Southern town that, because it was near the mouth of the Red River, became a important commercial link between the two southern halves of what had since

become the Confederacy. A railroad spur was built in the 1850s, connecting it with other roads and tracks to facilitate trade across the river.
Like Vicksburg, it had a natural bluff—though, at sixty to eighty feet,
not as high by far—that ran several miles along the Mississippi before
leveling out to swamp on both the northern and southern ends, and,
again like Vicksburg, the terrain behind it was cut up with ravines,
hills, bayous, and pestilent swamps that would go far to impede an
attacking army.

When Farragut and Banks got around to the notion of attacking it,
Port Hudson had a steamboat landing, a number of cotton, sugar,
grain, and tobacco warehouses, stockyards and various stores, and
saloons and hotels, as well as fifty or more residences. Plantations dot-
ted the surrounding countryside wherever the landscape permitted.
And by then Port Hudson had become a military citadel second in
strength and importance only to Vicksburg itself.

Around the time Banks had arrived in New Orleans, Major General
Franklin Gardner, a New Yorker who had been a member of Grant's
West Point class of 1843, took command at Port Hudson. Like so many
others, he had been breveted for gallantry in the Mexican War, and
he'd done good service at Shiloh before commanding a brigade in
Polk's corps during Bragg's invasion of Kentucky.

Gardner immediately began to expand and revamp the existing fortifications at Port Hudson, and when he finished a two-and-a-half-mile
stretch along the river was dominated by forty-three Rebel guns, ranging from gigantic 10-inch columbiads and rifled 32-pounders—some of
which were not yet mounted—to field batteries of 12- and 6-pounders.
To complement these, Gardner had around 10,000 troops under his
command to counter the 15,000 that he expected Banks might hurl
at him.

But Banks wasn't going to hurl anything at anybody. Instead of
marching his army up to Port Hudson to be ready to attack from the
rear as soon as Farragut's ships began passing in front, he decided to
hold a grand review on the parade ground at Baton Rouge. He sent a
couple of regiments up toward Port Hudson to "feel out" the defenses,
but that was all. Finally Farragut got tired of waiting and gave the order
for his force to weigh anchor.

His fleet consisted of three steam-screw oceangoing ships of the
line—*Hartford,* his flagship, *Monongahela,* and *Richmond,* as well as
the older sidewheeler *Mississippi,* which had been Commodore
Matthew Perry's flagship during his visit to Tokyo a decade earlier,

when he had famously opened Japan to Western trade.* Farragut also had four smaller gunboats, as well as six mortar vessels, with which to bombard the Rebel fortifications. In all, this amounted to ninety-two guns, against the Confederates' forty-three, but only the starboard half of the flotilla's batteries could be fired during the passage.

Moreover, two additional elements worked against Farragut: the river current was about five knots against him, so he would have to run the Confederate gauntlet upstream making no more than three knots— about the speed at which a man walks—and, second, the enemy batteries on the bluffs would be able to direct plunging fire onto his ships, while his own guns would have trouble elevating to the level of the topmost Rebel batteries.

As the fleet gathered downstream at Profit Island on the morning of March 14, the regular precautions were taken, all under the watchful eyes of Confederate spyglasses at Port Hudson: heavy chains were warped over the starboard sides of the ships to deflect enemy shot; cotton, wood, boilerplate, and other protective materials were banked around vulnerable machinery; anything that might get blown into deadly splinters was removed and stowed below. A civilian chaplain who happened to be aboard for the ride was first puzzled, then startled, when "I saw them place little square, shallow wooden boxes filled with sawdust, like the spittoons one used to see in country barrooms, behind the great guns and asked what that meant. I was told that it was to have an absorbent ready to be thrown upon any blood that splashed the deck."

Having already lost the element of surprise by assembling in broad daylight, Farragut brazenly ordered the fleet to fire about a hundred shots at the Port Hudson bluffs that afternoon in order to gauge the range to the batteries. As an innovative finishing touch, he had three of the four smaller gunboats lashed to the port, or nonfighting, side of the big ships to serve as backup power in case of damage to their engines. Although this proved a useful experiment, the historic *Mississippi*, because of her side-wheel paddle boxes, could not carry a supporting gunboat and so went up on her own.

When the sun went down it was the eve of the Ides of March, and the night became dark as a dungeon. About 10 p.m. two red lights appeared on *Hartford*'s stern "like glowing coals," signaling that the

---

* A steam-screw ship was driven by a propeller rather than side or stern paddle wheels.

ships should get under way. Second in line was *Richmond,* followed by *Monongahela,* with *Mississippi* bringing up the rear. Their rate of speed against the current meant that each ship would be in range of the Confederate guns for more than an hour. They had not been under way long before a Rebel rocket whooshed into the air from the west side of the river, warning of their approach. Still, even as they beat upriver in the inky night and came within the range of the enemy guns, no shots were fired. Some aboard the ships came to believe that the Rebels could not see them in the dark, but that was wishful thinking.

Without warning, from the west side of the river opposite Port Hudson, a great bonfire suddenly exploded straight up toward the sky, the dry pine crackling like a house afire, and then another, and another, until the whole Yankee fleet was backlit. Right afterward, a Confederate battery roared out, and then all hell broke loose. "It was the most terrible and sublime display of human power that I had then ever or have since seen," marveled the civilian chaplain, who was aboard *Richmond.* Lieutenant A. Boyd Cummings, executive officer of the ship, gave the order to return fire: "You will fire the whole starboard battery, one gun at a time, from the bow gun aft. Aim carefully at the flashes of the enemy's guns—*fire!*" Nearly a hundred guns were roaring and flashing by then, illuminating the night in a spectacular display that called to mind a relentless lightning storm, complete with thunder.

Hartford was hulled several times. More Confederate bonfires were lit under the bluffs. The tricky river current suddenly swung *Hartford* around as she reached the upper batteries by the hairpin curve. That she had come through at all was something of a miracle but now, having passed Port Hudson proper, she was being swept by the current right back toward the Rebel batteries. To avoid this, the captain deliberately ran her aground on a sandbar, where, with the aid of the gunboat *Albatross,* which was lashed to her port side, she was able to back off, straighten herself, and escape from the seething cauldron. So far, so good, but that was as far as it went.

When it came *Richmond's* turn, she steamed into a soup of gun smoke that obscured almost everything but the water lapping at her bows. For the next three-quarters of an hour a ferocious artillery battle ensued, with gunners on both sides aiming only at the flashes of the other's guns, which was all they could see in the murky distance. But the Confederates were getting the better of it; a solid shot tore through *Richmond's* hull into the engine room, where it struck a main steam valve and twisted it open, sending scalding steam throughout the engine room, the fire room, and the berth deck and causing the steam pressure to drop to almost zero. At the same time another shot ripped off the leg of Commander Cummings, who had first given the order to fire, killing him. Other Rebel guns began to find their mark, and the *Richmond*, unable to proceed upriver even with the aid of her lashed-on gunboat, came about and retired.

Worse, on deck, the *Richmond*'s gunners, "working in furious haste" and obfuscation because of the smoke, had not realized that their ship had turned around and, thinking they were still firing at the enemy on the bluffs, began pouring shot and shell into the hapless *Mississippi*, which was firing as the two ships passed. Time and again *Mississippi* was hit and finally went aground on a sandbar, where she lay stuck as in cement, a sitting duck for the Confederate guns.

Monongahela had only just entered the fray when a Rebel shot promptly jammed her rudder post, and she too ran aground. The force of the grounding was such that her lashed-on gunboat, *Kineo*, ripped free of her lashings and plowed even deeper into the mud. *Kineo* managed to get free and pull *Monongahela* off, but just as she did an overheated crankshaft pin gave way that stopped *Monongahela* for good, and she, too, began drifting back downriver under the ruthless fire of the Confederate batteries, which killed or wounded twenty-seven of her crew.

Meantime, *Mississippi* was being slowly blasted apart. She was now afire and her decks thick with wounded, dead, and dying. Her executive officer Lieutenant George Dewey—later Admiral Dewey of the Battle of Manila Bay in the Spanish-American War—remembered hearing the long, chilling echoes of the Rebel yell from the steep bluffs, which, he said, "was not pleasant to the ear," and at almost the same time another chilling thought came to him: "How they must hate us!"

Dewey was commended for saving the lives of many of *Mississippi*'s wounded crew by organizing a lifeboat relay, but ultimately the old vessel—now "a dying ship manned by dead men," Dewey wrote, "with guns still going off from the heat of the fires"—was dislodged from the bar by the current and swept in flames downriver past the forlorn anchorage of failed contenders, where she exploded spectacularly on a shoal.

Only Farragut had made it, and Port Hudson still loomed above the river strong as ever. The other five of his ships, including the gunboats, had been turned back with severe casualties. Farragut remained convinced that if only Banks had attacked Port Hudson from the rear at the same time his fleet was trying to pass the place would have fallen. Now he would never know and was left to drink the bitter wine of defeat.

At Vicksburg, Grant had had enough. He'd tried everything except for crossing his whole army over the Mississippi proper, below the city, and now he was determined to do just that. The winter floods were subsiding and the roads on his "wrong" side of the river were becoming, if not fully functional, at least passable, with some Herculean efforts from his engineers. The decision to cross the river was Grant's alone. Sherman, who had tangled with the Confederate army during his amphibious assault at Chickasaw Bluffs, was dead set against it, and he reiterated this in a lengthy letter to Grant, recommending that he take the army back upriver to Memphis and start out again, overland, into the heart of Mississippi. But by then Grant had his mind made up.

His first move was to contact Porter about running past the Vicksburg batteries with his ironclads and escorting a number of troop transports and barges—the latter not containing any troops, which was considered too dangerous—so that Grant would have them on hand to ferry the army across south of the city. Seeing that nothing else was working, Porter agreed—with private reservations—that, on April 16, he would send seven ironclads and their unarmed charges on a night passage past the formidable Rebel artillery positions. At the same time Porter gave Grant a dire warning that must have given the commanding general pause. If either the attempt to pass the Vicksburg batteries or the cross-river assault failed, Porter said, it would be the end of it all. There was no way he could get his slow gunboats back upriver against the six-knot current once they passed the city; Farragut's debacle at Port Hudson had demonstrated they would be too long exposed to the much strengthened Confederate batteries to survive.

Ten days earlier, on the Louisiana side of the river, Major Isaac F. Harrison, commanding a battalion of Confederate cavalry (which along with the small infantry brigade of Colonel Francis Marion Cockrell had been harassing the Yankees), had become puzzled when scouts reported a large column of blue-clad infantry, accompanied by artillery and cavalry, moving from Milliken's Bend through the back-river bayous out of sight of the river, to the far south of Vicksburg. He dutifully reported this to General John Bowen, who was commanding the Confederate defenses at Grand Gulf, Mississippi, about forty miles south of the city. Bowen first assumed that it was either a raid or a foraging party. But the next day, more Yankee infantry appeared, pushing farther and farther south. When news of this reached Pemberton, who maintained his headquarters at Jackson, forty miles from Vicksburg, he reckoned it was merely an attempt to cut off Confederate supplies from the rich Louisiana plantations, or possibly even a move to transfer troops to Banks down in Baton Rouge for another go at Port Hudson.

Still, it was clear that the Yankees were up to something; in the past three months they had failed at Chickasaw Bluffs, the DeSoto Point canal, the Lake Providence canal, the Yazoo Pass expedition, and the Steele's Bayou–Deer Creek fiasco, and Pemberton was inclined to believe that Grant was preparing to evacuate his army back to Memphis. He had convinced himself by then that Vicksburg was so strong nothing could get past it on the river. Therefore, so he reasoned, there was nothing for the Yankees to do but retreat and perhaps once more try to come up in his rear. That view was soon reinforced when Rebel scouts informed him that many Union troop transports had begun heading toward Memphis. Next, from far above Vicksburg, came reports that Grant had landed an entire division at Greenville, Mississippi, which was even more puzzling, since to get at Vicksburg from Greenville would have been an extremely roundabout march, and easily countered.

More puzzling still were reports that the Yankees continued to press farther south below Vicksburg, out of sight in the sloughs and bayous on the Louisiana side, and in greater and greater force. Major Harrison could do little more than fight running gun battles with their cavalry or small hit-and-run actions, all the while keeping his superiors informed. Bowen had by now become alarmed and sent first two and then three of his Missouri regiments under Colonel Francis Cockrell across the river in supply steamers. But after a series of swamp sniping and queer running gunfights—some of which were conducted from scows and flatboats armed with small cannons—even this could not stop the rising tide of blue.

Grant had been facing a make-or-break situation and by now he knew it. Dana, the erstwhile Stanton spy, had been quickly charmed by the courtesies—artificial or not—shown him by Rawlins and other high-ranking officers as well as by Grant himself. What he saw convinced him that, far from being a habitual drunkard and inept administrator as he had been portrayed, Grant was a solid and worthy commander. At the same time, his people had been able to draw out of Dana something of the malediction against Grant in Washington and this no doubt inspired additional impetus for his resolution to attack Pemberton by crossing the river here and now.

In his memoirs Grant states that all the other attempts—the canal building, bayou routes, and so forth—had been doomed to failure, and he always knew it, but he'd allowed them to proceed on grounds that it gave the men something to do. But a reading of his reports in the official records, as well as his many private letters to Halleck and others, makes this claim seem disingenuous. In any event, he was now faced with one last throw of the dice, and there is no doubt he was determined to make the most of it.

His closest friends and advisers were aghast when Grant announced that the man who would lead the amphibious assault across the river would be none other than his eternal nemesis McClernand, commander of the XIII Corps. They tried to talk him out of it but to no avail. Sherman, who now commanded the XV Corps, had already gone on record as opposing the enterprise; McPherson, who commanded the XVII Corps, was still way up north near Lake Providence, and Stephen Hurlbut remained in Memphis with his XVI Corps. Of all these generals, McClernand had been the most enthusiastic when the operation had been proposed and, furthermore, Grant had something more devious in mind for Sherman when he put his scheme into action.

As a matter of fact, Grant had other things in mind than merely getting his army over the river, and at this point he played his cards quite close to his chest—even with his closest friends. What he proposed to do was not simply risky; it was perhaps the most hazardous Federal operation of the entire war, unless one assumes that going up against Robert Lee was reckless just on the face of it. What Grant had to accomplish was a successful amphibious landing on a hostile shore—arguably the most difficult and dangerous of military operations—and then a successful movement inland with no significant base of supply, since he had already conceded there was no way to bring a continuous chain of wooden transport vessels past the Vicksburg batteries.

Worse, he had no sure way of knowing what the Confederates might throw at him once they determined his design. East of the river, Vicksburg was still connected by railway to most of the South and it was always possible that the Confederates would rush reinforcements to

Mississippi and hurl division after division of Rebel infantry upon him just as he tried to establish a beachhead. Rosecrans, up in Tennessee, couldn't help, other than to threaten Bragg at Tullahoma and to make him think twice before sending reinforcements. And the failure of Banks and Farragut at Port Hudson proved that help from that quarter would probably not be forthcoming.

On the other hand, there was some hope that Joseph Hooker's massive spring campaign in Virginia would at least occupy if not defeat the Confederate army in a campaign that was headed for a showdown at the hamlet of Chancellorsville on the same day that Grant planned to send his army across the Mississippi. If successful, that would at least keep reinforcements from Virginia off Grant's back, or so it was hoped.

But here again one of the great ironies was that the abject failures of all the canal digging and river expeditions were actually now working in Grant's favor. Richmond—and most especially Joe Johnston, who had made his headquarters with Bragg's army—had begun to assume that Vicksburg was secure, at least for the moment, and in fact kept pestering Pemberton to return the troops earlier borrowed from Bragg. In response, Pemberton had almost cavalierly agreed to send off four of his brigades, consisting of some 8,000 infantry, but no sooner was this done than he discovered to his shock and dismay that Grant was *not* evacuating his army back to Memphis but instead bringing more troops downriver in anticipation of an attack on the city.

On April 14 Rebel scouts confirmed that sixty-four Federal transports loaded with troops had departed Memphis, headed south. If that wasn't warning enough, what happened two days later certainly was; it was the night that Porter sent his ironclads to run the Vicksburg batteries.

Meanwhile, the Federals continued their push southward on the Louisiana bank, with the division of General Peter Osterhaus, a thirty-nine-year-old German who had received his education in Prussian military schools, spearheading the attack for McClernand. Osterhaus had intended to occupy the town of New Carthage, opposite Davis Bend and Brierfield, as a possible staging area for the cross-river assault, but he found it already occupied—by the Mississippi River; only the roofs of its buildings were showing above water. He skirted around it, continuing to march south, harassed but not thwarted by Harrison's Rebel cavalry and Cockrell's infantry. On the other side of the river, Bowen was beginning to fear for their safety, and he telegraphed Pemberton that these troops should be withdrawn while there was still time.

Meantime, Porter was preparing to run the Rebel batteries at Vicksburg. He was well aware of the dangers involved and took all the precautions. Seven ironclads and three transports would make the run. The ironclads were the *Benton,* with Porter himself commanding, *Lafayette, Louisville, Mound City, Pittsburgh, Tuscumbia,* and *Carondelet,* now repaired from her earlier drubbing by the *Arkansas.* The transports *Forest Queen, Silver Wave,* and *Henry Clay* would tow coal barges to fuel the fleet afterward. For protection, a coal barge was lashed to each of the warships as well; logs, wetted bales of cotton, and hay were positioned on the port sides to absorb the impact of Rebel shells. Sacks of grain and hay had also been stored below as fodder for horses and men, assuming the gunboats made it below.

For some inexplicable reason, the Yankees had still not gotten it through their heads that surprising the Confederates in such a riverine enterprise was well-nigh impossible. Thus orders went out that the fleet was to proceed single file with lights out. To avoid chimney sparks, steam was rerouted from the smokestacks to the paddle wheels, and to mask engine noise the ships were to run at almost idle speed, barely enough for steerage, and to ride with the six-knot current. It was calculated that the boats would be under the Rebel guns for approximately two and a half hours. At 10 p.m. the fleet shoved off.

The night was villainously dark. Aboard the steamer *Von Phul* Grant watched them pass from a grandstand seat on the top deck. His wife, Julia, was present, as was McClernand's new bride, both of whom had come down two weeks earlier. Julia had also brought two of the children, including twelve-year-old Fred, who would stay on with his father through the campaign. Charles Dana recalled the scene as Porter's fleet weighed anchor. "First a mass of black things detached itself from the shore, and we saw it float out toward the middle of the stream. There was nothing to be seen but this big black mass, which dropped slowly down the river. Soon another black mass detached itself, and another, then another. They floated down the Mississippi darkly and silently, show neither steam or light, save occasionally a signal astern, where the enemy could not see it."

It wasn't long, of course, before the enemy *did* see them; they had been watching them all along. First came a few rifle shots, warnings from scouts posted on the opposite side of the river, then the boom of the Confederate signal gun thundered out. "There was a flash from the upper forts," Dana said, "and then for an hour and a half the cannonade was terrific, raging incessantly along the line of about four miles extent." The newsman in Dana quickly came out. "I counted five hundred and twenty-five discharges," he said. Grant's aide James Wilson recalled that one of Grant's children "sat on my knees with its arms around my neck, and as each crash came it nervously clasped me closer."

As the enemy fleet approached, the city of Vicksburg twinkled along the great bluffs like a miniature galaxy. At the hillside home of Major William Watts an elegant ball was in progress when the floors and windows began to tremble and the night was rent with an earsplitting roaring of guns. A woman who was at the dance recorded that one young girl, "trimmed in silk and lace, clasped her hands and exclaimed to the brigadier general" she'd been dancing with, "Where shall we go!"

"To the country for safety," the officer replied in jest, but the girl, along with three of her companions, immediately ran shrieking into the night as the Yankee shells began to fall on the town. A guest from the dance ran after them, trying to bring them back, "and as a shell would be heard coming, he would cry, 'Fall!' and down they would drop in the dust, party dresses and all." Finally they were rounded up and brought back to the ball. "If you could have seen our party dresses and our hair, and the flowers, full of dust, you would never have forgotten us," one girl exclaimed.

As the head of Porter's fleet approached the river's hairpin turn at the city, the Mississippi River suddenly became "lighted up as if by sunlight," as a chain of fires was touched off by the Confederates on both sides of the river: bonfires, old houses, straw piles, tar barrels— anything that would burn. As at Port Hudson, it backlit the Yankee fleet, thus canceling out both the cover of night and the element of surprise. In theory this should have signaled the death knell for Porter's fleet, but it did no such thing. All of the ironclads and transports got through, save one, the transport *Henry Clay,* which had been set afire, then abandoned and sunk. Though most had been struck multiple times by Rebel shot and shells, not a life had been lost and the vessels remained functional and intact as they steamed out of range.

The Confederates blamed this failure on defective artillery fuses recently received from Richmond, which had not been tested beforehand. In any case, Grant had turned the tables on Pemberton. Not only had he marched most of his army below Vicksburg, out of the range of

the Confederate guns; he now had most of the transportation necessary to ferry it safely across downstream at a place of his choosing. If
that was not bad enough, while Pemberton was pondering his newfound state of affairs, Grant reached into his bag for two more tricks
that went far to seal the fate of Vicksburg and the Confederacy.

CHAPTER FOURTEEN

So Thick a Snake Couldn't Wriggle Through It

As McClernand's XIII Corps began its southward advance, Brokenburn was right in its path, and Kate Stone and her family finally cleared out. Her older brother William was home on leave from Virginia and was first to see the handwriting on the wall. He moved the majority of the Stone family's slaves and the rest of its baled cotton westward, then set about helping the Confederate forces on that side of the river.

As McClernand's divisions marched below Vicksburg to rendezvous with the transports, widespread depredations became manifest among the plantations along the way. Since Brokenburn had been situated between Sherman's corps to the south at Young's Point and McClernand's to the north at Milliken's Bend it had so far escaped the ravages visited on other homes near the Union encampments, but now the bluecoats were on the move.

"The place looks deserted now with its empty cabins and neglected fields, and the scene is the same wherever we go," Kate wrote in her diary. Her problems began during the last week in March when her horse Wonka was finally taken. Previously when Yankee patrols or "foraging parties" were known to be in the neighborhood, the family's trusted servant Webster would hide the animal in a canebreak, but this time he brought him back into the yard, saying that "he would die if he was kept where the mosquitoes could get at him any longer." Just at that moment "two villainous-looking Yankees rode up to the gallery where we three ladies and two children were standing. They had pistols in their hands and proposed a 'swap,' but we all refused and begged them not to take the horse." Instead the bluecoats went after him and, when Kate ran to open the gate so the horse could escape, one of them pointed the pistol to her head and threatened to kill her, while the other caught the animal and took it away. "The life we are leading now is a miserable, frightened one," she told her diary, "living in constant dread of great danger, not knowing what form it might take, and utterly helpless to protect ourselves."

A week after her horse was taken Kate and her sister walked to a neighboring plantation to see if they had any news. "As we approached the house," she said, "it struck me that something was wrong."

A party of Federal troops had just ransacked the place, Kate wrote, and no sooner had she learned that than more looters reappeared. They were blacks, newly enlisted into the Union army, who roamed through the house pointing guns at people, terrifying the women and threatening to kill the elderly man who owned it. They kept the women penned in a room for several hours while they took anything of value and destroyed what was not, and at last "leisurely took themselves off, loaded with booty." When Kate and her sister returned home, they found the slave quarters occupied with a milling gang of strange blacks from neighboring plantations who "did not say anything, but they looked at us and grinned and that terrified us. It held such a promise of evil."

That was enough for Amanda Stone, Kate's mother. She gathered the brothers and sisters and an elderly aunt, dug up the silver and other valuables from the backyard, and stole away at night, headed west, to Texas. They rode all night on horseback, hauling a cart with all their clothing and family treasures, photographs, and portraits, headed for a bayou where they hoped to find skiffs to take them far enough west to catch the train at Monroe. They found the skiffs all right, but when they returned to get the cart with their clothes and valuables they found that it had been taken by Webster, their once most trusted servant.

The little town of Delhi seemed to be a funnel for all those escaping west, and as Kate encountered it, "the scene there beggars all description: such crowds of Negroes of all ages and sizes, wagons, mules, horses, dogs, baggage, and furniture of every description, very little of it packed. It was just thrown in promiscuous heaps—pianos, tables, chairs, rosewood sofas, parlor sets, with pots, kettles, stoves, beds, and bedding, bowls and pitchers and everything of the kind just thrown pell-mell here and there, with soldiers drunk and sober, combing over it all, shouting and laughing. While thronging everywhere were refugees—men, women and children—everybody and everything try- ing to get on the cars, all fleeing from the Yankees or worse still, the Negroes."

In the midst of all this, more terrible news finally caught up with the Stone family. Kate's little brother Walter, who had joined the army just months before, when he'd turned eighteen, had died of a fever seven weeks earlier at a place called Cotton Gin, Mississippi. "Poor little fel- low," she wrote, "he was not used to strangers. It wrings my heart to think of him suffering and alone. We have no likeness of him. He has only a memory and a name."

Truth was, there would be a lot more suffering before this war was finished, and in particular before the end of the coming battle at Vicksburg—suffering both physical and emotional and upheaval on a scale unseen on the American landscape before or since. "Mamma regrets coming away as she did," Kate told her diary, "but what else could she do. So passes the glory of the family."

The two ploys Grant had concocted to bamboozle Pemberton in his hour of crisis worked like a charm. First was an extensive cavalry raid in his rear to disrupt his communications, and the second was a division-sized feint by Sherman up the Yazoo River to make the Con- federates worry that the danger would be coming from that quarter.

The cavalry raid was launched by Grant from Memphis under the command of Colonel Benjamin Grierson, a thirty-seven-year-old for- mer Illinois music teacher who, ironically, had an excessive mistrust of horses after being kicked in the face by a pony when he was a child. Grant's orders were simple and unwritten: go into the heart of Missis- sippi and "do all the mischief" you can. To Grierson this meant the destruction of Confederate property and stores, burning railroad tres- tles and bridges, tearing up rail track, toppling telegraph poles and rip- ping down wire, and anything else to upset and distract Pemberton's forces.

As in the East, Yankee cavalry had usually gotten the worst of it when tangling with its Southern counterpart. This can be explained in part by tradition: in the South, riding and horseracing were the princi- pal sports and the horses there were blooded and far superior to the farm and dray animals found in the North. Since it was calculated that it took two years to turn out a seasoned cavalry trooper, the North had been far behind at the start of the war, but now the Federals were beginning to catch up. As we have seen, the most prized items taken by Northern soldiers were usually the Southern planters' horses; for the ordinary soldier it was tantamount in modern terms to stealing a car, but for the cavalry it involved the serious business of remounting themselves on better-quality stock.

In any case, Grant—a first-rate horseman himself—having been embarrassingly foiled in his first attempt to take Vicksburg by Van Dorn's and Forrest's cavalry raids, now proposed to turn the tables. On April 17, the same morning Porter's fleet dropped anchor below Vicksburg after running the Rebel gauntlet, Grierson and 1,700 of his troopers rode out of La Grange, Tennessee, headed for the Mississippi state line. Their loads were light: minimum baggage, six small artillery pieces, wrecking tools, forty rounds of ammunition, and five days' rations for both horses and men—after that they would have to live off the land. Grierson's additional equipment consisted of a pocket copy of Colton's map of Mississippi, which could be purchased at any sundries store, a small compass, and a Jew's harp, which he liked to play in the saddle. He also carried with him something more useful: an unsigned report by a Mississippian who had presumably remained loyal to the Union documenting "the locations of well-stocked plantations, Confederate warehouses, the varying loyalties of the people in different sections of the state" and other valuable information.*

Grierson's command was styled the First Brigade, First Cavalry Division, XVI Army Corps (Hurlbut's) of Major General Ulysses S. Grant's Department of the Tennessee. It consisted of three regiments: the Sixth Illinois, the Seventh Illinois, and the Second Iowa, plus the artillery battery. Nobody knew where they were going except Grierson, and he had only a vague idea of what he was going to do when they got there—all he had been told was to use his own discretion, wreck things, and try to escape back through the wilds of Alabama. Richard Surby, a sergeant in the Seventh Illinois, kept a diary, into which he confided that when they rode out of camp, "[There was] a gentle breeze from the south. The fruit trees were all in full bloom, the

---

* It is presumed by most historians that the provider of this information was an altruistic Unionist, but the principal documenter of the raid records that "among his [Grierson's] military papers for that month is a mysterious receipt for fifty dollars paid to one Vernon Joniean."

gardens were fragrant with the perfume of spring flowers, the birds sang gaily, all of which infused a feeling of admiration and gladness into the hearts of all true lovers of nature." This seems in ironic contrast with the mission they had been given; in any case the morning Grierson left, his immediate superior, Hurlbut, dispatched a message to Grant from Memphis: "God speed him, for he has started gallantly on a long and perilous ride."

By the third day the raiders had traveled eighty miles into Rebel territory and encountered little or no opposition, but they were well aware that their presence had become known. At the town of Pontotoc Grierson took stock and weeded out nearly two hundred troopers with various ailments, complaints, or indications of timidity and sent them back to La Grange with a number of prisoners, instructing them to ride in a column of fours obliterating the column's previous tracks to make the Rebels think that all the raiders had returned to Tennessee. Next day he conjured an even more ornate ruse by sending out the Second Iowa to tear up the Mobile & Ohio Railroad. Afterward, all six hundred were to proceed back to La Grange, making sure to eradicate the southward hoofprints of the main raiding party.

Grierson then marched southward to Newton Station on April 24, a little more than halfway between Jackson and Meridian, and made short work of the Southern Railroad there. Not only did his men tear up track, they captured and blew up two locomotives, a store of arms, and thirty-eight boxcars packed with supplies and munitions bound for Vicksburg, including 300,000 percussion caps and 30,000 pounds of gunpowder. This having been accomplished, they left town at a quick pace in midafternoon, when word came down that Confederate cavalry were on their trail. It was reported that many of Grierson's troopers were reeling in their saddles after "liberating" a supply of Rebel whiskey from a local warehouse.

By then Pemberton was frantic, and he made everyone else frantic in turn. The enemy to his front was still well across the river, but the enemy in his rear was, well, in his rear right now, creating all manner of destruction and alarm. The crux of Pemberton's distress was that he had no cavalry of his own to speak of. There were a few militia troops here and there—one in fact was chasing Grierson, or so he thought; actually, they had fallen for the ruse and was now pursuing the Second Iowa back toward La Grange.

Pemberton's cavalry problem had begun when Richmond ordered Van Dorn's magnificent horsemen—some 6,000 troopers in all—away to Tennessee to assist Bragg, leaving Pemberton essentially blind in most of his department. It wasn't a crucial matter until recently, since most of the action had been confined to Grant's attempts to get at Vicksburg through swamps where cavalry wasn't of much use anyway. But now, just when he needed Van Dorn and his people most, they were unavailable. A month earlier he had telegraphed Joseph Johnston, "urgently requesting that the division of cavalry under Major-General Van Dorn . . . might be returned to me." The answer came back from one of the department commander's aides that Van Dorn and his men were "more needed" in Tennessee than in Mississippi, and that the infantry Bragg had sent during the Chickasaw Bluffs crisis was "more than a compensation" for the mounted force.

In subsequent communications, Pemberton was nearly forced to begging. As the Grierson raid developed, he wired Richmond: "I have so little cavalry here that I am compelled to direct a portion of my infantry to meet raids in Northern Mississippi. If any troops can be spared from other departments, I think they should be sent here." And again to Johnston: "The little [cavalry] that I have is on the field [opposing Grierson] but totally inadequate. Could you not make a demonstration with a cavalry force on their rear?"

The answer to all of this was no. The reason involved another ruse that Grant had pulled from his grab bag, this one designed to keep Bedford Forrest off his back. Forrest had been making life miserable for Yankee outposts along the Tennessee-Mississippi-Alabama border, when Grant made—and unlike Pemberton was granted—a request that a diversion be created from Rosecrans's department to occupy Forrest while Grierson carried out his Mississippi adventure. This was the infamous mule-cavalry raid of Colonel Abel Streight, in which 1,700 troopers, riding mules (thought to be hardier than horses in rough terrain), plunged into northeast Alabama on the same day and on the same mission of destruction as Grierson's caper.

Outnumbered three to one, Forrest gave chase before catching up with Streight's band near the Georgia line, where he finally captured them with a trick. Wanting to avoid an out-and-out fight, Forrest approached Streight with a flag of truce and demanded his surrender. The colonel met him between the lines and said he would give up only if Forrest could convince him that he had a completely superior force. Not wishing to reveal his weakness by having his men come out into the open, the wily Forrest had arranged for his soldiers to haul the only two pieces of artillery he possessed around in a circle, across and behind a high cut in the road, so that it would appear to Streight that whole batteries were being brought up to the front.

Finally Streight could stand it no longer. "Name of God! How many guns have you got?" he demanded. "There's fifteen I've counted already!"

"I reckon that's all that's kept up," Forrest replied nonchalantly.

That was enough for the Yankee colonel, who handed over 1,466 soldiers with all their mounts, artillery, and equipment, the victims of a cruel hoax. When Streight finally saw that Forrest had barely four hundred men, "He demanded that he should have his arms back, and that we should fight it out," Forrest said. "I just laughed at him and patted him on the shoulder and said, 'Ah Colonel, all is fair in love and war, you know.'"

This was the kind of story that made Forrest's reputation, but it hardly did anything for Pemberton's. Grierson continued tearing up things in his rear while Grant was threatening to cross the river below Vicksburg and Sherman was apparently looking to cross above it, and Pemberton had no cavalry worth mentioning to help do anything about any of it. But since Grant was still on the wrong side of the river, where he could not be got at, and Grierson was at least somewhere where he could be got at, Pemberton began dispatching infantry eastward where, though they could not actually catch Grierson, they might at least protect the rail lines, communications, and other vital components of his war machine.

Grant had first decided to launch his amphibious assault against Warrenton, about ten miles below Vicksburg. But when he got to calculating he discovered that the only viable launching point on the Louisiana side of the river would take five hours of transport time going against the Mississippi current, which would give the Confederates plenty of time to rush large bodies of troops from Vicksburg proper to greet him as his soldiers reached the banks, a prospect that was unacceptable.

He then concluded to go farther downriver opposite Grand Gulf, some forty miles south of Vicksburg, where the Rebels had established a battery of eight heavy guns, and land there after Porter had silenced the enemy artillery. This would put him much farther away from the city than he originally planned, but at least there would be no large Confederate army on hand to contest the landing. At the same time he realized that, being so much farther from his objective, his army would have to be fed and provisioned to a greater extent than first thought, and on April 22, five days after the first run past the Vicksburg batteries, a second flotilla consisting only of unarmed wooden transports loaded with provisions each towing barges filled with the same was organized to run the gauntlet.

It was such hazardous work that of the six steamers only two captains and one crew volunteered to accompany their boats on the trip, but army volunteers—composed mostly of former river men from prewar days—made up the difference. As before, the transports, each loaded with 100,000 rations, steamed down past the batteries at night and, miraculously, five of them got through.

Still reeling from the humiliating passage of Porter's armored fleet the previous week, the Confederates were positively shocked at this turn of events. Major Samuel Lockett, the Rebel engineer in chief, remarked that although ironclads passing batteries without serious damage was no surprise, "No one dreamed that ordinary river steamboats could do so."

In any case, now Grant had in place the means for his cross-river assault; his only question now was where? With Warrenton out, Grand Gulf seemed the logical place, once Porter had put the Rebel cannons out of business, and this he attempted to do on April 29, after much delay. The delay was caused in part by McClernand, who was required to march his corps farther downriver to a plantation named Hard Times, where he was to embark. If witnesses—including Charles Dana—can be believed, the trouble was McClernand's new wife, Minerva.

For some reason, the general had determined to bring her along on the cross-river assault, despite Grant's strict orders that everyone travel as lightly as possible. But McClernand, who had avowed to be the first man ashore on the Rebel side of the Mississippi, apparently decided that his bride of four months should be allowed to see her husband in action. Thus her wagonloads of baggage and accompanying entourage of servants had to be brought up to the head of the column on roads so greasy and overwashed that sometimes entire teams of horses and hub-deep guns would simply disappear into the mire without a trace. To make matters worse, McClernand had also invited his fellow politician Illinois governor Richard Yates, along with his cronies and hangers-on, to come along for the ride. Finally, with everything in place, Porter's ironclads set out to put the quietus on the guns of Grand Gulf.

While the first assault wave of 10,000 of McClernand's troops waited anxiously aboard the transport steamers, Porter's seven iron-clads, each carrying a crew of 200, lay off in front of Grand Gulf at about 10 a.m. and opened fire with a mighty broadside blast. One would think that the combined weight of eighty-four heavy naval guns versus the eight guns of the Confederate land batteries would have quickly sealed the fate of the Grand Gulf Rebels. Grant certainly thought so, and Porter did as well, but before the first smoke had cleared the Confederate batteries began to reply in kind. One shot tore into the *Benton*, Porter's flagship, and started a fire. Another flew through one of *Tuscumbia*'s gunports and killed or injured most of the artillerymen. A second hit the same port and jammed its shutters closed, while yet another exploded in the wheelhouse. When a shot wrecked one of *Tuscumbia*'s engines she began drifting backward downriver, out of the fight.

The other Yankee gunboats suffered to a lesser extent but in the three hours that it lasted they took a collective two hundred hits, leaving sixty-four of their crews as casualties, including eighteen dead, as compared with three Confederates killed and fifteen wounded. Boarding the *Benton* to confer with Porter, Grant found himself "sickened by the sight of the mangled and dying men" and decided that a landing at Grand Gulf would not do. Porter had his ironclads lay off at a distance and as soon as the sun began to sink he opened fire again, creating enough of a diversion to allow the transports and barges to squeeze by the Rebel batteries.

At daylight on April 30, McClernand's army was again packed aboard the transports at De Shroon's plantation, ten miles below Grand Gulf. During the night, scouts had brought before him "an intelligent Negro" who told Grant that there was a steamboat landing at the hamlet of Bruinsburg, right across the river, and that there were good roads from there to the interior of the country. Though it would put the army farther away from Vicksburg—which was forty miles north, and with two defensible streams in between—Grant saw no other alternative. He had to act quickly because Pemberton must certainly be fully alarmed and laying plans for his arrival. Getting McClernand across the river to establish a strong foothold before the Rebels could march an army down to meet him now became paramount.

Remarkably, Pemberton had no such thing in mind. All of Grant's distractions, from Grierson's raid to the aborted attack at Grand

Gulf—compounded by his lack of cavalry reconnaissance—had the Confederate general thoroughly flummoxed, and he was about to be flummoxed again.

Right before the attack on Grand Gulf, Grant had asked Sherman, whose corps was still up at Milliken's Bend opposite the Yazoo, if he could create a feint to keep the Confederates guessing where the main landing would come. Knowing that Sherman, like himself, was excoriated in the newspapers for every perceived misstep, Grant told his friend that he "did not like to order me to do it, because it might be reported in the North that I had been 'repulsed,' etc.," but the Ohioan sneered at the very notion: "Does General Grant think I care what these newspapers say? You are engaged in a hazardous enterprise, and for good reason wish to divert attention; that is sufficient for me, and it shall be done."* Sherman immediately ordered two of his divisions on the long slog downriver toward Hard Times, and prepared the third for his "feint."

Accompanied by a ten-boat flotilla of ironclads, tinclad gunboats, and mortar boats, Sherman's force steamed up the Yazoo to the vicinity of his previous mortification at Haines's Bluff, where corpses of his soldiers still rested beneath the river overflow. His final instructions to Frank Blair and his ten regiments were for "every man to look as numerous as possible."

While the gunboats engaged the Confederate batteries, Sherman had his men disembark "with much pomp and display" and behave like they were preparing to attack the Rebel installations, at least until night fell, when he withdrew them back to Milliken's Bend. Union observers soon recorded "great activity being seen in Vicksburg," among which—although they could not know it at the time—was an urgent telegram sent by the Confederate commander, Major General Carter Stevenson, to Pemberton, who was still directing operations from Jackson: "As it is not known what [Union] force has been withdrawn from this front, it is not improbable that the force opposite [meaning Grant's army at Hard Times] is . . . a feint to [make us] withdraw [our] troops from a main attack here [at Vicksburg]. I venture to hope that the troops will not be removed far until further developments below render it certain that they [Union forces] will cross in force."

---

* Privately, Sherman remained dead set against Grant's plan, describing it in a letter to his wife as "one of the most hazardous and desperate moves of this or any other war. I tremble at the result." Nevertheless, he carried out every command and suggestion made by Grant with an alacrity as remarkable as it was commendable.

This was in response to Pemberton's order to Stevenson that he "hold 5,000 men in readiness to move . . . and, on the requisition of Brigadier-General Bowen move them" to Grand Gulf. At that point Bowen was convinced that he would need all the help he could get. Even if the Yankees had decided not to attack Grand Gulf, he was certain they would invade somewhere south of there at any time. To thwart this, Bowen had concluded that "it would require from 15,000 to 20,000 men to insure our success," and forwarded that assessment, with the concurrence of chief engineer Lockett, to Pemberton. As it happened, Bowen's evaluation turned out to be prophetic. Since the Yankees would be traveling in steamboats, it would be difficult if not impossible to march an army overland fast enough to meet them, but at least Bowen thought that with a little help from Pemberton he could assemble enough force to resist their initial advance and, with any luck, throw them back on the river.

John Bowen, thirty-three, was among the most talented and courageous young generals of the Confederacy. He had earned a Phi Beta Kappa key at the University of Georgia before entering West Point, where he graduated near the top of his class in 1853. He served on the frontier fighting Indians before resigning from the army to become an architect in St. Louis, which was where he and Grant became good friends. He was badly wounded leading his brigade at Shiloh the previous year, and Pemberton probably could not have picked a better officer to meet the threat that Grant now presented.

When it became evident that Grant was probably going to cross the river below Vicksburg, Pemberton began pulling back infantry units he had sent into the interior to ward off Grierson's raiders and funneling them to Bowen. But as Pemberton saw it—or at least as he tried to explain it later as an answer to why he did not throw his whole force against Grant immediately—his problem was one of logistics. "The only means of subsisting my army south of the Big Black [the river at Grand Gulf] are from Vicksburg or Jackson," he said, noting that both cities were more than forty miles from Grand Gulf, by poor dirt roads. "Without cavalry," he added, "I could not have protected my own communications, much less cut those of the enemy."

Meantime, Grierson's cavalry raid continued to occupy Pemberton's time and energy. After wrecking the railroad at Newton Station, Grierson continued south, sending out decoy parties of raiders from his main body to destroy telegraph lines, rolling stock, track depots, stores, and anything else of use to the Rebels. He also continued his practices of deception, which were so good that at least one of his own companies got lost and stayed lost, unable to catch up because Grierson was burning his bridges behind him. These multiple raids, branching off in all directions from the main body, expanded and prolonged the Confederates' confusion, since Grierson was frequently reported as being at two or more places at the same time. For instance, on the day that McClernand was loading his corps aboard the transports to cross the river, Pemberton dispatched a telegram to Major James Chalmers, his cavalry commander in northern Mississippi, ordering him to intercept Grierson's force at Okalona as it headed back to Tennessee. But at that very moment Grierson "was less than thirty miles south of Pemberton's own headquarters at Jackson, almost 200 miles from Okalona!"

By then, Pemberton had ordered anyone who could ride a horse or mule out looking for the destructive Yankee will-o'-the-wisp, but to no avail. Grierson put even more distance between himself and his pursuers when he bluffed a ride on a Confederate ferryboat across the Pearl River by claiming to be Rebel cavalry in search of conscripts. After crossing his force, Grierson burned the ferry, then sent a fake telegram to Pemberton's headquarters stating that the Yankee raiders had headed off in the opposite direction from which they were going, which was southeast, toward Baton Rouge.

As the days went by the picture became clearer, however, and Grierson's activities now seemed to indicate his route of escape. Pemberton told Bowen to send Wirt Adams's cavalry regiment out after him, a wonderful irony since Adams and his men were presently stationed at Port Gibson, very near Bruinsburg, where Grant would soon be in the process of landing. Even Adams, a Vicksburg banker and cotton broker before the war, and as competent a soldier as ever there was, got conned by Grierson whose men, posing as Confederates, convinced an actual Rebel to lay out Adams's plan to ambush the main column. Then, while Adams cooled his heels waiting for Grierson to turn up at the ambuscade, the foxy cavalryman doubled back and burned a number of rail trestles and boxcars, further disrupting Confederate communications. At that point Grierson estimated that he was being chased "by 20,000 men, sent out from various points to intercept and destroy us."

It might not have been quite that many, but in fact two Rebel forces, about equal in numbers to Grierson's own, were converging on him not twenty miles behind. One belonged to Adams and the other to a fierce, belligerent, and reckless Tennessee colonel named Robert V. Richardson commanding so-called partisan rangers, whose reprehensible behavior had resulted in arrest warrants being issued for him by both Pemberton and Johnston.* Nevertheless, Richardson turned up in Jackson at the height of the Grierson invasion and somehow persuaded Pemberton to assign him to the chase. He proceeded to load his troopers and their animals on rail cars headed south and, along with Adams, rapidly began closing in on Grierson, who was having problems of his own. It seems that after a peaceful ride into the village of Summit, Mississippi, on a lovely spring afternoon, Grierson's men discovered hidden in the swamp some thirty barrels of rum, which they promptly began to abuse. "I discovered them before it was too late to save my men," Grierson recorded, and the raiders pushed on, or reeled on, as it were, with Adams and Richardson in pursuit.†

As they neared the town of Osyka, the Yankee horsemen for a change fell victim to a Confederate ruse. Because of its remoteness, the little village had been selected as a great Rebel supply depot, but it had only a few guards since no one expected enemy raiders so far south. When the Confederate commander got wind of Grierson's presence in the neighborhood, he sent out one of his officers, a lieutenant named Wren, to purposely let himself get captured. Upon interrogation by Grierson's men, Wren described Osyka as heavily guarded by infantry, cavalry, and a battery of artillery—disinformation that persuaded Grierson to steer clear of that place and continue on to refuge at Baton Rouge.

By now such Confederate telegraph wires as remained were humming with up-to-date information on Grierson's whereabouts and a force was sent out from the large garrison at Port Hudson to join in the manhunt. Aware that their time was wearing short, Grierson's men pushed forward in forced marches marked by absence of food and sleep until the Rebel cavalry at last caught up. A series of running gun-

---

* Richardson seemed to believe that he was a "law unto himself," not unlike William Quantrill and a few other renegade Confederates. He stood accused of various strong-arm tactics, including stealing from conscripts and citizens, bushwhacking, and other questionable behavior. Grant's corps commander Stephen Hurlbut branded him an outlaw and vowed to hang him.

† By then Grant's army was becoming adept at ferreting out hiding places where southerners hoped to save their belongings. Gardens were almost always assumed to contain the buried family silver and many a rosebush met its fate under the Yankee spade. In Mississippi, along the river, swamps were a favorite location to stash larger items including, as we have seen, favorite animals, cotton bales, whiskey barrels, etc.

fights ensued until the Yankee raiders at last escaped across a bridge before an inept guard could torch it and entered into the stuff of legends, riding into the safety of Baton Rouge "under the ghostly moss-hung trees, past shadows of plantation houses and sugar mills," followed by a joyful coterie of slaves who ran forward with flowers crying, "The Yanks come to free the black folks."

Grierson later calculated that they had marched over six hundred miles in sixteen days, "killed or wounded about one hundred of the enemy, captured and paroled over 500 prisoners, many of them officers, destroyed between fifty and sixty miles of railroad and telegraph, captured and destroyed over 3,000 stand of arms. . . ." All this in exchange for three killed, seven wounded, and fourteen captured.

It was a truly remarkable adventure, but its overarching consequence, as Grant had always intended, was to produce a significant distraction for Pemberton while the ever-delicate Federal amphibious landing was taking place. That aside, however, one of the raiders, Sergeant Stephen Forbes of the Seventh Illinois, later provided one of the classic appraisals of cavalry operations in general, with particular respect to Grierson's undertaking.

"A cavalry raid at its best," he wrote, "is essentially a *game* of strategy and speed, with personal violence as an incidental complication. It is played according to more or less definite rules, not inconsistent, indeed, with the players' killing each other if the game cannot be won in any other way; but it is commonly a strenuous game, rather than a bloody one, intensely exciting, but not necessarily very dangerous." Grant's infantry tended to agree, at least in part, gleefully provoking their mounted counterparts at every opportunity with the sarcasm, "Who ever saw a dead cavalryman?"

Even if McClernand was not the first man ashore on the Mississippi side of the river he wasn't far behind. History does not tell us whether Mrs. McClernand was with him at the time, but the landing had been completely unopposed and the men disembarking from the transports and barges entered into a springtime landscape of bluebirds, dogwoods, ripening blackberries, and the gaping faces of a few slaves who had remained after their masters had fled.

By noon, April 30, there were some 17,000 infantry ashore and in the process of fanning out toward the town of Port Gibson when someone discovered that before McClernand ordered the men to board the transports he had forgotten to have anyone issue them their three-day ration of food and ammunition.

Combat operations had to be suspended until the oversight could be rectified, but if during those four critical hours Pemberton had assembled a larger defensive force, it might have meant the difference between winning or losing the campaign.

What Grant thought about this latest delay went unrecorded, but he could not have been pleased, especially since he had just finished drawing up a reprimand against McClernand for failing to provide tents, food, and other welfare for the more than a thousand troops of his corps that he had left behind sick at Milliken's Bend. In any case Grant, who had come across that morning on Porter's flagship, *Benton,* did state for posterity's sake, "I felt a degree of relief scarcely ever equaled since."

By 4 p.m. the errant rations and ammunition had been ferried across the river and McClernand got his corps marching toward Port Gibson, about twelve miles inland. That was where everyone expected the Confederates to make a stand, since the rain-swollen Bayou Pierre emptied into the Mississippi just above Bruinsburg and was unfordable until it reached a bridge just west of Port Gibson.* Sure enough, the Rebels were there in force; more than 5,000 of them under John Bowen who had come rushing down from Grand Gulf when the invasion was spotted.

Unfortunately for the Confederates, the "force" that was available to Bowen was not nearly equal to its task. By nightfall of the Yankee D-day, Grant recorded that there were on Mississippi soil some 20,000 infantry, with more pouring in every hour. Thus Bowen was outnumbered four to one, even including 3,000 of the 5,000 men that Pemberton had ordered Stevenson to "hold in readiness" in Vicksburg. These had in fact been ordered by Stevenson to go to Bowen's assistance, but they had arrived wretched after a two-day forced march. Sherman gloated afterward that those soldiers were "later recalled and sent back to Haines Bluff" to defend against his feint, adding that with all this Confederate relief force's marching and countermarching, by the time they got back to the city "the men were perfectly exhausted, and lay along the road in groups, completely fagged out." The marching and countermarching turned out not to be true, for Stevenson had sent them along when Bowen called, but it was a good story anyway, and Sherman enjoyed telling it over the years.

---

* McClernand had brought over no cavalry in the initial landing, presumably because he wanted all the infantry he could get to occupy the ground and prepare the way for others. But this left him even blinder than Pemberton, so far as knowing where the Rebel army was.

As McClernand's skirmishers finally pushed out toward Port Gibson across "a pleasant glen full of green grass and abounding in shade trees," they began to encounter enemy resistance. Soon they passed by the Windsor plantation, said to be the most splendid mansion in the state. It was there that McClernand made his headquarters. As they pressed forward along the dust-choked road the unnerving sounds of gunfire began to racket across what was once a tranquil countryside. It swelled all through the long sunset and the muted twilight till well past twelve, when it seemed to fade of its own accord in what Grant belittled as "nothing rising to the dignity of a battle."

Perhaps that was so, but not to Charles Dana, who arrived on foot the next morning after hitching a ride with a quartermaster. "I got out of the wagon as we approached, and started toward a little white house with green blinds, covered with vines," Dana recalled. "The little white house had been taken as a field hospital, and the first thing my eyes fell upon as I went into the yard was a heap of arms and legs which had been amputated and thrown into a pile outside. [It] gave me a vivid sense of war such as I had not before experienced."

When the avalanche of unwelcome events began sliding toward Pemberton, among the first things he did was contact Joe Johnston in Tennessee, Jefferson Davis in Richmond, and Edmund Kirby Smith in Alexandria, Louisiana, pleading for reinforcements. Davis promptly assured Pemberton that troops would be sent forthwith from Mobile and from Charleston, where Beauregard had just defeated a Yankee attack. Johnston, on the other hand, served up nothing but advice. "If Grant's army lands on this side of the river, the safety of Mississippi depends on beating it," he said. "For that object you should unite your whole force." At least that was something; from Kirby Smith, who had replaced the indecisive and unpopular Theophilus Holmes as commander of the trans-Mississippi, Pemberton received no reply at all.

There is much to be considered in Johnston's admonishment that Pemberton unite his whole force, the most important feature being that it was not delivered until *after* Grant had landed on Mississippi soil. At that time, Pemberton's available strength numbered as many as 50,000 troops, but these were spread out across the entire state of Mississippi and part of Louisiana. The largest concentration, some 26,000, was in and around the Vicksburg defenses—from Haines's Bluff to Warrenton. In addition there were by now 16,000 at Port Hudson, right below the Louisiana border. The others were scattered in various capacities: at Grand Gulf, at Fort Pemberton up in the bayous, guarding railroads and bridges, posted along the Yalobusha at Grenada, cavalry operating in the northern part of the state, as well as individual bands of "partisan rangers," or militia, acting as a sort of home guard in their own towns and villages. Moreover, by no means were all of these combat troops; a portion served as quartermasters, telegraphers, engineers, couriers, doctors, clerical staff, ordnance personnel, teamsters, blacksmiths, signalmen, munitions bearers, and so on.

Assuming that Pemberton had united his whole force, he actually could have met Grant on the field with a superior army, but the dangers in doing so were manifest. If, for instance, he had stripped Port Hudson of all its defenders, there would be nothing to keep Banks and his army from marching straight up to Vicksburg and combining his army with Grant's. Similarly, if the Vicksburg garrison had been sent fifty miles downriver to stem the Yankee onslaught, what was to prevent Grant from ordering his remaining corps—15,000 strong under Hurlbut at Memphis—from boarding steamboats and invading the defenseless city from the north along Chickasaw Bayou? And then of course there was the likelihood of more cavalry raids in the Confederate rear that might delay or even foreclose the arrival of reinforcements by destroying the railroad. The possibilities were complex, urgent, and not easy to contemplate, but Pemberton had to contemplate all of them. The fate of the Confederacy would hang on his decisions, and here converged the fatal flaws in the strategy for saving the western states, which is to say approximately one half of the whole.

As we know, back in Pemberton's days as commander of the South Carolina district, Robert E. Lee had admonished him that some points or cities, such as Charleston, would have to be defended "street by street and brick by brick," if for no other reason than that they were either critical strategically or symbolic to the cause. Jefferson Davis had reiterated the same notion: Vicksburg was so important it must be held "at all extremities," including "house-to-house" fighting, if necessary.

On the other hand Pemberton's immediate superior, Johnston, was inclined by training and disposition toward an entirely different vision. Like many officers of his time, Johnston's perceptions had been shaped by lessons gleaned from the Napoleonic Wars, where the battlefield was epitomized as a fluid, ever-changing encounter, with the advantage going to the side that quickly massed its troops for a strike at the enemy's weakest point. If the weak point was not immediately apparent—so Johnston's reasoning went—then ground (cities and strongpoints included) should be given up in order to maneuver until the mortal blow could be delivered.

These conflicting strategies—especially as concerned the predicament of Vicksburg—were almost mutually exclusive. If Pemberton had uncovered the city to challenge Grant in the field, he would have violated what Lee and, more significantly, Davis had told him. And if he did not he would of course be going against Johnston's instruction to concentrate his army and beat Grant before he got enough troops on the Mississippi side of the river to take the city.

This is where the break in the chain of command became dangerous. Johnston had been sent west to correct a serious Confederate command problem that emerged when the Federals penetrated the Department of the West on two different fronts—Rosecrans in middle Tennessee, threatening Alabama and Georgia, and Grant down the Mississippi, aiming to retake the river with all of its decisive implications. Around the same time, Pemberton had been sent to Mississippi to rectify the perceived mismanagement by Van Dorn, but Pemberton's channels of communications—and authority—had been made fuzzy when Davis told him to report directly to Richmond. Although Pemberton certainly understood that Johnston was his superior, he believed he also reported to an even higher authority, none other than the president of the Confederacy.

Johnston certainly didn't help matters; advice was one thing, assistance was quite another. "Uncle Joe" seemed content to remain with Bragg's army in Tennessee, four hundred miles away, and let matters in Mississippi take care of themselves the way they had in the past. Even when Pemberton pleaded with him for reinforcements Johnston ignored him, thus reinforcing the Pennsylvanian's inclination to rely instead on Jefferson Davis in his times of trouble.

Ulysses Grant's problems at this point were tactical, not strategic, but no less real and just as dangerous as Pemberton's. He had a tenuous foothold on Mississippi soil with 20,000 troops and sixty field guns, backed up by Porter's formidable ironclads. But no one was more aware than Grant that, until his entire army was across the river and organized to meet a Confederate threat, he faced the possibility of a humiliating defeat such as the one Sherman suffered at Chickasaw Bluffs. Far worse was the ominous prospect that his army could be annihilated, should the Rebels sucessfully press him with his back to the river.

In the predawn hours of May 1, the battle for Port Gibson commenced in earnest. McClernand had sent his corps on two roads that converged about five miles outside Port Gibson—the Bruinsburg road, which was the shorter of the two, and the Rodney road, which met up with it near the Magnolia church. The first shots of the battle may have been fired when Confederate brigadier general Martin Green rode into the yard of a house occupied by a group of terrified women who were hastily throwing their valuables into a wagon for evacuation. Green was in the process of reassuring them that no enemy advance was likely before dawn when out of the blackness came a volley of Yankee bullets that smashed into the ladies' wagon, prompting them to leap aboard and charge off hysterically into the night.

Green had posted his brigade of Mississippians and Arkansans astride the road near the church, while a brigade of Alabamians under Brigadier General Edward D. Tracy had taken position to block the Bruinsburg road. During the night a division of McPherson's corps arrived from across the river and was sent forward. As dawn broke on a lovely May Day morning the air around the Magnolia church became foul with gun smoke and whirring metal, and for almost five hours until the sun had nearly reached its zenith the two Confederate brigades of about 1,200 each held their own against a Yankee army now numbering more than 23,000. Inevitably, the Rebels were beaten back by sheer numbers. As the bluecoats pressed forward, many of them passed by a grime-covered Grant sitting astride a nag with only the wooden tree of a leatherless saddle for comfort. "Push right along. Close up fast," he urged them.

Early that afternoon, as Tracy was engaged in conversation with a sergeant of a Virginia artillery battery, "a ball struck him on back of the neck passing through. He fell with great force on his face and in falling cried, 'O Lord!' He was dead when I stooped to him," the gunner said. By then the day had become oppressively hot and men on both sides were near exhaustion. Bowen, wondering desperately when Pemberton would send him help, tried to maintain his composure, but there was something frantic in a midday wire he sent to headquarters: "Losses very heavy. The men act nobly, but the odds are overpowering."

As Green's brigade and Tracy's (now under the command of Colonel Isham Garrott) fell back, they passed two fresh brigades—the Missourians of Francis Cockrell and the Mississippians and Louisianans of William E. Baldwin—that Pemberton had finally managed to get into the battle. With these new troops the Confederates were able to contest the Federal advance along the Rodney road for the rest of the afternoon, but it was obvious to Bowen that unless much heavier reinforcements arrived he would soon be overwhelmed. Therefore he did what the Yankees least expected: he counterattacked. Cockrell's Missourians were chosen for the task. After marching southwestward around McClernand's far right, they crept stealthily through a jungle of ravines, then slammed furiously into the flanks of half a dozen Federal regiments "with great slaughter" and sent them flying helter-skelter into the woods. But the blue-clad juggernaut proved irresistible, just as Bowen knew it would be, and McClernand's line was restored by sundown. According to a Rebel captain, double lines of Yankee riflemen began to pour bullets into them "thick and fast as hailstones from a thundercloud or raindrops in an April shower . . . almost sufficient to obscure the sunlight."

Early that evening Bowen telegraphed Pemberton that superior numbers compelled him to retire across Bayou Pierre, a stream that ran perpendicular to the battle area just north of the Confederate positions. In his reply, the commanding general wondered rather plaintively to Bowen if he could not "retain your present position, if possible," adding, "You must, however, of course be guided by your own judgment. You and your men have done nobly." By then Bowen had already pulled back, still hoping for further reinforcements, which came too little and too late. The battle for Port Gibson had been lost, and Grant had secured his beachhead. It must have given him a supreme satisfaction to note that he was finally "on dry ground and on the same side of the river with the enemy."

By next morning Grant had even more troops on the field. McPherson's second division had come across the river, bringing the total to more than 28,000. Except for the division that remained north of Vicksburg to continue its diversion, Sherman's corps was slogging as fast as it could down the Louisiana side for its crossing. The diversion, however, seemed to be working, because the meager reinforcements sent by Pemberton brought Bowen's strength up to only 9,000, barely enough to make up his losses for the day. The Battle of Port Gibson had cost 1,662 casualties, divided almost evenly between the two sides.

For Grant, there had been an unpleasant lesson learned. Even though the Rebels had been outnumbered three to one at their full, reinforced strength, they were still able to hold off Grant's army for nearly a full day. Though it had cost them dearly—Confederate casualties were proportionately three times higher than Grant's—at this rate the southerners might be able to delay the Yankees in time to rush enough men to Mississippi to tip the scales in their favor. Grant identified the problem immediately—the terrain had become his worst enemy.

"The country in this part of Mississippi stands on edge," he observed, "[with] the roads running along the ridges except when they occasionally pass from one ridge to another. The sides of the hills are covered with a very heavy growth of timber and with undergrowth and the ravines are filled with vines and canebrakes, almost impenetrable. This makes it easy for an inferior force to delay, if not defeat, a far superior one."

It was all too true. As in all war, when an army begins to move it usually finds itself in an evolving situation. Aside from land that had been cleared for cotton growing, the countryside near the river was jungle as thick and tangled as any in darkest Africa, the domain of bears and wild pigs, and cane so thick a snake couldn't wriggle through it.* It compelled an advancing army to travel on the roads, limiting the fighting front they could present to the roadway itself. The rest of the army could only remain stacked up for miles in columns one behind the other, while the Confederates chose the most favorable ground for defense. Grant had maps, but the maps had not told him about this.

---

* This part of Mississippi is legendary for its wild bear. William Faulkner famously depicted the scene in his novella *The Bear*. But it was President Teddy Roosevelt who captured the country's imagination when, in 1902, he went on a bear hunt near Vicksburg. After an all-day chase, Roosevelt's party at last caught up with the creature, but the president declined to shoot it. When the story got out, a Brooklyn man named Morris Michtom patented a brown toy bear that he called a "Teddy Bear" and presented it to the president, creating a fad that continues to this day and making a fortune in the process.

Part III

THE CORPSE FACTORY

CHAPTER FIFTEEN

The Enemy Will Soon Be upon Us

G rant was quick to grasp that speed and maneuver were the only tactics that could extricate him from this hellish topography and into a landscape favorable for fighting on his own terms. If it's true that a cat has nine lives, and if Grant had been a cat, then adding up all the previous failures to take Vicksburg would make this the last one.

Thus, when he reached the now-vacated town of Port Gibson, Grant at once set to building a bridge upstream across Bayou Pierre that could quickly take his columns farther north and east into open country. An old bridge at Port Gibson had been burned by the Confederates when they withdrew, but what Grant needed now was a new larger, sturdier bridge that could carry his entire army across, heavy guns, wagons, and all. He nominated his staff engineer James Wilson for the task, owing to Wilson's prior experience constructing bridges on the Louisiana side of the river. In retrospect, it was an extraordinary feat, since the water was high and running fast and there was quicksand in the bottoms. Wilson and the brigade that had been assigned to him plunged into the work that morning, tearing down "houses, stables, fences, etc.," and by that same afternoon Grant had his bridge, fifty yards long and fifteen feet across—with side rails, no less—strong and safe enough to support a marching army.*

* The project was not without its setbacks. Engineers decided to test their original handiwork by sending across a cannon drawn by four mules. The bridge tipped over and the gun and mules sank to the bottom, prompting one of the workers to remark, "Better [that] than a column of infantry."

Meantime, Grant was faced with another problem that he alone was confident would be solved. The lead divisions of the army had crossed the river on April 30. It was now May 2, and their three-day rations were nearly exhausted. Grant ordered foraging parties to fan out for ten miles on either side of the advance, which developed into what was surely one of the oddest-looking military operations of the war. Since the army's supply wagons had yet to cross the river, it was decided to procure the necessary transportation vehicles from the citizens of Claiborne County, with which to rob them of their food. Yankee quartermasters, escorted by cavalry, soon were roaming the countryside in cotton wagons, buggies, gigs, carriages, oxcarts, fringed surreys, hansom cabs, goat wagons, buckboards, even logging sleds, and the booty they brought in was beyond even Grant's imagination: barrels of bacon and cured pork, flour, cornmeal, molasses, salt, and sugar; wagonloads of corn, hogsheads of cheeses and butter, herds of cattle, sheep, swine, and goats; flocks of geese, chickens, and ducks; jars of put-up vegetables and fresh ones if they had matured; plus the inevitable larders of whiskey, rum, and, from the finer plantations, vintage wines. All these things, so dear in the city, were found in abundance in the countryside, leaving one to conclude that hoarding had become commonplace.

About the only items Grant's people could not procure from the good residents of Mississippi were coffee, as Kate Stone eloquently attested; hardtack, which no self-respecting Mississippian would eat anyway—at least, at that point, of his or her own free will—and soap. Accordingly, Grant ordered ample supplies of these items, including 150,000 bars of soap, hauled down along the single-lane, jerry-built road through the Louisiana swamps, then ferried across the river from Hard Times to supplement the abundance of meat and groceries that the foragers were bringing in.

Sherman, who was presently marching his corps south along that very road, was appalled. He sent a message telling Grant, "This road will be jammed sure as life if you attempt to supply 50,000 men by one road." To the Ohioan, Grant's response came like a bolt from the blue. "I do not calculate . . . supplying the army . . . from Grand Gulf," Grant said. Hardtack, coffee, and salt was all he intended to bring over, adding that he would "make the country furnish the balance." To Sherman—who had written to his wife, "No place on earth is favored by nature with natural defenses as Vicksburg, and I do believe the whole thing will fail"—it seemed like madness, but by then Grant already knew it could be done.

The foragers also left their usual calling cards or, as an Illinois soldier put it, "proofs of their customary lack of respect for the property of rebels," in which the troops lolled about, "eating their bacon and hardtack from marble-topped tables and rosewood pianos." As McClernand's and McPherson's divisions marched deeper into the interior of the state, these plantation homes, which Dana compared with "the finest villas on the Hudson," were stripped of anything valuable, and often as not what couldn't be carried away was smashed or left to rot in the rain. Then, when Sherman's corps finally came across and found nothing left to loot, they reacted spitefully by burning down the houses.

Meantime, as well, Grant was surprised when his twelve-year-old son, Fred, accompanied by Charles Dana, walked into his headquarters house in Port Gibson. Grant had left the boy asleep aboard one of the steamers at Bruinsburg but, awakened by the distant rumble of the battle at Port Gibson, he had set out alone and on foot to find his father. Along the way he met up with Dana, and the two of them somehow acquired "two enormous horses, grown white with age," Grant recalled, "each equipped with dilapidated saddles and bridles." Grant was chagrined that he had "no facilities for even preparing a meal," but they all managed to get by until the headquarters wagon trains were ferried across. Grant himself had endured the hardships with his men, "sleeping on the ground without blankets or covering of any kind, and having no baggage but a toothbrush," according to the journalist Cadwallader.

By afternoon on May 2, McPherson's corps had marched all the way to Hankinson's Ferry on the Big Black River some twenty miles northeast of Grand Gulf, while McClernand's corps rested for a day in Port Gibson after the battle. By now not only had Grant's army flanked Grand Gulf but, by crossing Bayou Pierre upstream, they also threatened to cut off and capture Bowen's whole force. When this distressing news reached Pemberton, who had at last moved his headquarters from Jackson to Vicksburg, he reluctantly ordered Bowen to evacuate Grand Gulf. This was carried out in a timely, orderly, and effective fashion, with the men spiking the guns, blowing up the magazines, and making off with almost all the stores and baggage in the middle of the night to link up with Pemberton's army.

Grant had suspected as much but had no way of proving it, so on the morning of May 3 he rode off to find out for himself, with only a small cavalry escort. This certainly might have meant trouble if he had stumbled across Bowen's 9,000 men on their march from Grand Gulf, but as luck would have it he didn't. Porter, meantime, had taken notice of the explosions when the Confederates set off their magazines and decided to investigate. With several of his ironclads he steamed cautiously up to, then past, the Grand Gulf fortifications that had caused him so much grief a few days earlier. When nothing happened, he put in at the once formidable bastion and, discovering it deserted, hoisted the Star-Spangled Banner over its battered ramparts.

It wasn't long before Grant himself showed up, only to receive another perplexing surprise. It had been the expectation in Washington that once Grant crossed the Mississippi he would send at least a part of his army south to cooperate with Banks against Port Hudson. Grant understood this, and had already earmarked McClernand's corps for the assignment. It was a sound strategy too, at least on paper, because with Port Hudson taken the combined armies, as well as the navies under Farragut and Porter, could then converge on Vicksburg with an irresistible force. But as we have seen, Banks did not seem to appreciate this design, or felt he had greater priorities.

Back in March, instead of advancing his available force against Port Hudson, he had detailed more than half of it to chase after Dick Taylor's little army and to protect strongpoints in the wilds of Louisiana. Now Grant learned to his amazement and disgust—from a letter that Banks had sent three weeks earlier, but that only now had caught up with him at Grand Gulf—that Banks had taken his remaining 12,000 men deep into the Red River country, some 150 miles *away* from Port Hudson, to deal with Rebel problems there and would not be available at Port Hudson until May 10. Given this turn of events, Grant decided it would be better to leave the Massachusetts politician flopping around in the Louisiana bayous than to wait for him.

"The news from Banks forced upon me a different plan of campaign from the one intended," Grant recalled. "To wait for his co-operation would have detained me at least a month. The reinforcements [Banks could bring] would not have reached ten thousand men after deducting casualties . . . [meanwhile] the enemy would have strengthened his position and been reinforced by more men than Banks could have brought. I therefore determined to cut loose from my base, destroy the Rebel force in rear of Vicksburg and invest or capture the city."

Those were bold words but Grant meant every one of them, given that each tick of the clock magnified his vulnerability. It also might have crossed his mind that with Banks out of the picture he would be the senior general on the field and wouldn't have to share credit for the victory with anybody else. On the other hand, if there wasn't a victory, Grant was willing to take the blame for that, too.

In Pemberton's headquarters the mood seemed to vacillate between anxiety and elation. As Grant was landing, Pemberton wired Davis that Port Hudson was being evacuated, "and the whole force concentrated for a defense of Vicksburg and Jackson." But Davis wired back that it was necessary to hold both Vicksburg *and* Port Hudson, as "a connection with the Trans-Mississippi," and told Pemberton to countermand the order. Pemberton did so in a kind of compromise that could have turned out to be one of his better decisions of the campaign, but didn't, through no fault of his own; he ordered Gardner to hold Port Hudson with 2,000 men and send the rest (about 8,000) to Jackson, from where they could be distributed as needed.

On May 2, during the Battle of Port Gibson, Pemberton again telegraphed Davis, "It will require 6,000 cavalry to prevent heavy raids and to keep railroad communications, on which our supplies depend. Vicksburg and Port Hudson have each about thirty days' subsistence at present." This final sentence was freighted with meaning, although no one seemed to grasp it at the time. If Davis and the War Department expected Pemberton to hold Vicksburg and Port Hudson to the last, and if enough reinforcements could not be rushed in quickly to help defeat Grant's army in the field, or to lift a siege if it came to that, then Pemberton's estimate of thirty days of supplies spelled with clockwork precision how long those garrisons could last.

But as the desperate hours passed it appeared the urgent reinforcements might indeed arrive on time. From Beauregard's South Carolina command 5,000 were already boarding the trains, with 4,000 more set to follow. Likewise, Johnston was at last sending more than advice, telegraphing Pemberton that Forrest's cavalry was finally moving to his assistance. It was only a quarter of the 6,000 Pemberton had asked for but it was *Forrest's,* and to most minds that would make up the difference.* Meanwhile, other untapped sources of manpower were being

* In requesting the 6,000 cavalry, Pemberton undoubtedly meant the force under Earl Van Dorn that had been on loan from him to Bragg's army. While these would not be coming, Van Dorn himself could not have come if he'd wanted to. On May 7, a doctor named George Peters, of Spring Hill, Tennessee, walked into Van Dorn's headquarters and blew the general's brains out after becoming upset over Van Dorn's alleged "undue attentions" to his wife. An interesting sidelight is that before firing the fatal shot Peters had secured a pass from Van Dorn to go through the lines, thus enabling him to escape into Union-held territory.

set in motion, including 600 recently exchanged prisoners—a full regiment—whom Pemberton ordered to be rearmed and returned to the army. Hundreds more who had been guarding bridges on the Big Black River and other points on the railroad were told to come to Vicksburg.

Not only that, but Davis personally ordered Johnston to remove himself from Tennessee posthaste and go to Mississippi to supervise the defense of Vicksburg, taking with him 3,000 "good troops" from Bragg's army. The Virginian complied with alacrity, but with his usual caviling. "I shall go immediately, although unfit for service," he replied, alluding to continued discomfort from his wounds at Seven Pines.

All this, coupled with the revelation that Sherman's corps had pulled out opposite the city's northern defenses, led Pemberton to wire Davis that even though Grant's army had established a foothold below, "With reinforcements, and with [Forrest's] cavalry promised in North Mississippi, [I] think we will be all right."

This must have come as sweet music to Jefferson Davis, given that on that same day the Rebel Army of Northern Virginia had inflicted on the Yankees one of the most decisive beatings of the war at Chancellorsville, about fifty miles southwest of Richmond. Outnumbered two to one, Robert E. Lee had surprised, and then routed, the Federal army under Joseph Hooker. The only cloud over the triumph had come when Lee's most valuable lieutenant, Stonewall Jackson, had been mortally wounded. Nevertheless, with this almost miraculous victory, and with Pemberton's reassuring words from Vicksburg, Davis must have rested not only easier but supremely confident that the star of the Confederacy was again in the ascendant.

Pemberton might not have been so sure, but there was no panic at his headquarters as he evolved a plan of defense. There was no stopping Grant from landing the rest of his troops; Bowen's defeat at Port Gibson had seen to that. But landing was one thing; beating a sizable Confederate army on its own turf was another.

As Pemberton saw it, Grant's vulnerability lay in what would become an ever-lengthening line of supply. From its present position the Federal army was still about forty to fifty miles southeast of Vicksburg, and its base of supply was way up at Milliken's Bend on the Louisiana side of the river. There were only two ways to keep that supply line going. One was the rickety, tortured path through the swamps down to Hard Times that Sherman had complained about, and the other was to carry the provisions downriver by steamboats. This last had worked well enough the first two times, but when Grant had ordered a third fleet of transports to run the Vicksburg batteries they had fared poorly, with a number being sunk or inflamed, owing to much-improved gunnery by the Confederates, now that they had gained experience shooting at live moving targets.

Pemberton reasoned that the only way Grant could keep his army supplied was to establish a base north of Vicksburg, on the same side of the river, somewhere up the Yazoo, and to do that he would have to conquer the Rebel batteries at Haines's Bluff. Thus he concluded that he would have to keep Haines's Bluff fully manned.

At the same time, when Pemberton reviewed his maps in light of Grant's likely route of march, he saw before him an almost perfect defensive position in the rear of the city. This was the line of the Big Black, a deep river wide enough for steamboats that ran from the Mississippi at Grand Gulf and arced around his fortifications about ten miles east of the city. Its western banks—those on *his* side—were lined with bluffs, not as tall as Vicksburg's, of course, but formidable for any army that planned a cross-river assault.

If the Big Black had formed a complete arc back into the Yazoo, Vicksburg's rear defenses would have been immeasurably improved, especially if it had intersected with the Yazoo right on the east side of the Haines's Bluff bastion. But it did not, and there was the rub. Pemberton was convinced that Grant would hurry his army along the far side of the Big Black, using it as a shield, until he reached the spot where it began to narrow and turned off north. There, he predicted, Grant would try to force a crossing and secure his base on the Yazoo, with Porter's ironclads cooperating. And it was there that Pemberton intended to be waiting for him, if he didn't spot a better opportunity along the way.

Then Grant threw another curve. Instead of moving north along the Big Black, Grant's army made a beeline northwest, away from Vicksburg, and toward the Jackson–Vicksburg railway, with the object of cutting off Pemberton's lifeline for reinforcements and supplies. For a critical few hours Pemberton didn't know what to make of this, and he proceeded with his plan to concentrate his troops behind the Big Black. Accordingly, when William Loring and his division finally reached the area, as senior commander he ordered Bowen to march his division west alongside his own.

On May 10, the day Stonewall Jackson died, Grant gave his three corps commanders their order of march; it was to be a three-pronged attack. McClernand, on the left, was to hug the east bank of the Big Black, advancing toward the Confederate railroad and posting guards at river crossings to warn if Pemberton was coming out. McPherson, on the right, was to move toward Raymond, a town about ten miles west of Jackson, to guard against a Confederate movement from that direction. Sherman would march in the center toward Edwards Station, ready to lend support to either of the other corps, should they need it.

Grant knew that the ever-cautious Halleck never would have approved of his cutting loose from his base of supplies on the river, but he had a solution for that, too. He waited until right before the march to inform the general in chief of his plan—a message that would have to be carried by horseback to one of the transports, ferried across the river, hauled up the sloggy bayou road to Milliken's Bend, and placed on another transport bound all the way up to the telegraph depot at Cairo, Illinois, before it could be wired to Halleck. "I knew the time it would take to communicate with Washington and get a reply would be so great that I could not be interfered with," Grant said laconically.

At that point, Grant was so confident of success that he ordered Hurlbut to send downriver a full division from his command at Memphis, plus another brigade to hold the base at Milliken's Bend. It was his intention, if necessary, to throw his entire command into the fight at this juncture, a risk he was willing to take, even though the politician in Grant was fully aware of the ramifications if he failed. These included, among other things, risking the defeat of the president and the future course the war would take, and upon these two subjects rested the fate of the United States. Whether Grant had read de Tocqueville or not, he had certainly read in the newspapers of the impatience with the war effort. It was one of the prices you paid for democracy.

At 3 a.m. on May 11 the Rebel general John Gregg, whose brigade had been one of those recently ordered up from Port Hudson, was in camp near Jackson when he received an urgent telegram from Pemberton, ordering him to take his troops to Raymond immediately. Reports had come in that a large column of Yankee infantry was marching in that direction from Utica, a town about twelve miles southeast. Pemberton's message said that Wirt Adams's cavalry would be at Raymond for scouting purposes, but when Gregg arrived that afternoon all he found "was a single sergeant and 4 men," plus a local mounted company composed "of youths of the neighborhood."

Gregg, a native Alabamian turned Texas lawyer and politician, sent a message to Adams, who had made his headquarters at Edwards Station, about twenty miles west, telling him to come at once to Raymond, then began placing his brigade in position to meet the Federal advance. From the scanty intelligence he had received, Gregg believed the enemy was nothing more than a brigade about his own size "on a marauding excursion." In fact, what he would soon be facing was McPherson's entire corps, 12,000 strong, but unequal as the fight was Gregg's men would give more than they got for the better part of the day.

The clash began about 11 a.m. when the division of John "Black Jack" Logan, another political general, ran into the Rebel front and were heavily and bloodily repulsed. A vicious attack by Gregg threw Logan off balance, but when he recovered and reinforced he launched a counterattack of his own, which likewise failed. By then, however, as Gregg watched regiment after regiment of bluecoats begin wrapping around his flanks, he realized he was up against a leviathan and somehow managed to disengage before he was crushed.

As Gregg's soldiers retreated through the tree-lined streets they found no time to stop and partake of the elaborate picnic dinner that the ladies of Raymond had prepared for them in honor of their anticipated victory. While Gregg formed his men in defensive position five miles northeast of Raymond to have another go at McPherson, the blue-clad victors arrived in town and helped themselves to what they considered a well-earned hot meal. It had been a nasty little fight, with the Rebels suffering 515 killed, wounded, or missing and McPherson losing 442. As at Port Gibson, the Confederate losses were far greater in proportion to the number of troops they had on the field.

Anne Martin, a daughter of the *Vicksburg Whig* editor Marmaduke Shannon, watched indignantly as "that immense army pour[ed] into [Raymond], flaunting their star spangled banner, playing Yankee Doodle, and, oh, the desecration! The Bonnie Blue Flag . . . All night the fife and drum was heard as fresh regiments passed . . . we could hear them tearing down fences, shooting cattle, shouting and going on and we expected every minute to be broke in on . . . the doors were locked but they broke them open and took everything but one sidesaddle, even pulled the curtains down and tore them in strings. The remaining sidesaddle was taken by one of these fancy yellow [mulatto] girls, an especial pet of one of their officers. . . . We could see them bringing all kinds of plunder, showing around silverware and jewelry they had stolen. If you are ever invaded, Emmie, don't bury anything. . . . Hearing that Mrs. Robinson had buried her silverware, they dug up every foot of her garden until they found it. Mrs. Durden's baby was buried in the yard and would you believe it: that child's remains were dug [up] no less than three different times in search of treasure. This is how we fared at the hands of the Yankees."

These unfortunate episodes made little or no impression on the commanders of the two opposing armies, although Pemberton had officially, and in writing, expressed concern that by defending Vicksburg and its immediate environs he would, by necessity, be leaving the rest of the state beholden to the tender mercies of the Yankee army. For Grant, the favorable results of the battle for Raymond provoked a quick shift in strategy. Rather than simply settle for breaking the rail line to Vicksburg, he now decided to order a ninety-degree wheel to the east and assault Jackson itself, clearing the city of enemy troops and rendering it useless as a Rebel reinforcement center and operating base.

That same day, Johnston arrived in Jackson as Jefferson Davis ordered. What he found there was a total of 6,000 troops, with Gregg as senior commander, and news that Sherman's 16,000-man corps was astride the Jackson–Vicksburg railway about ten miles west of the city. The fact that it was actually McPherson's corps, not Sherman's, along the rail tracks did not matter; Sherman was in the area in any event, down toward Raymond.

Despite the fact that Johnston was also told that some 5,000 reinforcements were scheduled to arrive either the next day or the day after, the Virginian straightaway decided that the cause was hopeless and ordered an evacuation of the city. *"I am too late,"* he wailed in a telegram to Confederate secretary of war James Seddon, as if to absolve himself of blame in case a disaster occurred. It was strange that he was able to reach this conclusion, given that he had no way of knowing whether the Yankee force on the railroad was coming after him, holding still, or going in the opposite direction. Stranger yet, he sent off a dispatch to Pemberton, telling him to bring up all his forces and fall on the enemy's rear, offering to "cooperate" with the troops he had on hand at Jackson.* "To beat such a detachment," Johnston

---

* The dispatch to Pemberton was sent by three separate couriers to make sure that at least one copy got through. However, one of the couriers was a Union spy who immediately delivered the secret message to McPherson. Armed with this information, Grant ordered McClernand's corps to "about face" and prepare to protect the Federal rear.

advised, "would be of immense value." Finally, Johnston ordered Gregg to oversee the defense of the city by a delaying action until the evacuation could be accomplished.

While Johnston retired to his room at the Bowen House hotel, Gregg began marching his two brigades out of Jackson at night toward the Yankee host that had been reported gathering to the west at Clinton. In the meantime, the Rebel general John Adams, who was commanding the district of Jackson, was assembling rail and wagon trains for removing all the military stores and munitions in preparation for taking them northward. (Earlier in the week Pemberton, in anticipation of a possible attack on the capital, had advised Governor Pettus to move all vital state records and documents to a place of safety.)

Gregg's defense of Jackson was just as courageous and just as futile as his defense of Raymond. Early that morning it had begun to pour rain, turning the roads to glue, slowing the Union advance. But by noon a full-fledged engagement was in progress, with the Rebels giving ground foot by surly foot to allow Johnston's evacuation to proceed.

About that same time, Pemberton received Johnston's message of the previous night. It placed him in a quandary, but apparently not one that included Johnston's admonition to march his army into Grant's rear and start a fight. Pemberton had assembled some 23,000 men at Edwards Depot, located on the rail line about twenty miles due west of McPherson's Yankee corps at Clinton and thirty miles from Jackson, leaving another 7,500 to hold Vicksburg and 3,000 more to guard various bridges and crossroads.

Later, he summed up his appreciation of the Virginian's strategy thusly: "The 'detachment' General Johnston speaks of in his communication consisted of four divisions of the enemy, constituting an entire army corps, numerically greater than my whole available force in the field." This of course was untrue. McPherson had only two divisions at Clinton, totaling about 11,000 men, but Pemberton went on to reiterate the superior numbers of Grant's army, concluding that "the movement expressed by General Johnston was extremely hazardous." Then he did what any commander of his limited combat experience would do under such vexing circumstances: he called a council of war. When the council disagreed with him, though, he ignored it.

Half a dozen generals were assembled for Pemberton's pitch. He told them of Johnston's order to march the army into Grant's rear, and of Johnston's proposal to cooperate with his force at Jackson. Even though Pemberton had reluctantly answered Johnston's dispatch by agreeing to comply with the order, he now opposed the idea. He told the council that he was now convinced it was best to pull back to the robust positions on the west side of the Big Black and let Grant break his army apart on the Rebel defenses when he tried to attack them.

From what he knew at this stage, Pemberton argued, not only was a full Union corps before him at Clinton, but to the southeast McClernand's corps was ready to attack him as well, as soon as he moved forward. He stated that he considered it his solemn duty to first defend Vicksburg itself, even if it meant leaving Grant's army to ravage the rest of Mississippi. Jefferson Davis had personally ordered him to "hold Vicksburg at all costs," he said. It is over this clash of opinions that a war of words has roiled discussion of the Battle of Vicksburg from that day to this.

A majority of the generals disagreed with Pemberton. They had an army that wanted to fight, they argued; the Yankees were on Mississippi soil, and they wanted to get at them here and now. Johnston's order should be obeyed, they said. However, the minority, led by Loring, felt the best move would be to attack Grant's rear between Jackson and Grand Gulf and cut off his supply line. This, it was maintained, would force the Federals to retreat.

It was an alternative with both merits and disadvantages, chief among the latter being that, unbeknownst to the Rebels, Grant's army *had* no supply line but was "living off the land." At least that's the way Grant liked to tell it in the years to come. In fact he did have a very important supply line that consisted of the munitions trains that kept his army in bullets, powder, shot, and shell, without which it would be useless, as well as the pipeline for Union reinforcements. If that line could be cut, and the landing spots at Grand Gulf and Bruinsburg retaken, Grant would be forced to either fight the Confederate army at a place of their choosing or cut his way out of Mississippi any way he could.

Pemberton preferred to stick to his own strategy, convinced that major reinforcements would be coming from other parts of the Confederacy—enough to outnumber and beat Grant with a superior army. Nevertheless, with the vote of the others strongly in favor of going on the offensive now, he reluctantly opted for Loring's proposal.

Since Loring had championed the idea, Pemberton sent him off first, in the direction of Dillon's plantation, about seven miles to the southeast. Then he scribbled a message to Johnston, informing the commanding general that his order to attack was not to be obeyed, and that he was going to go after Grant's supply line. He closed this missive almost plaintively, saying, "I wish very much I could join my reinforcements," making several suggestions as to how this could be accomplished. What he didn't know was that there would be no reinforcements. Joe Johnston had sent them all away.

Ever since Grant's army began moving inland, Confederate authorities at Jackson had been digging earthworks and rifle pits, using slave labor as well as civilian volunteers. This was to be the last-ditch line of defense, after Gregg moved his army out toward Clinton to meet and stall the Yankees. The Union force consisted of the two divisions of McPherson's XVII Corps, aligned on the Vicksburg–Jackson railway northeast of the city, as well as two divisions of Sherman's XV Corps, which was approaching from the southwest. Owing to a lack of good reconnaissance, Gregg had been prepared to meet McPherson, but Sherman's appearance was news to him, until it was too late.

During the early hours of May 14 it began to rain heavily and by sunup the roads were a sea of paste as McPherson's men trudged their way toward Jackson. Skirmishers from the two forces met at about 9 a.m. as the skies began to clear, just west of the deaf and dumb asylum on the Clinton road. At first sight of the enemy main force, the Confederates attacked amid a furious cannonade by a Mississippi battery that sent the Yankees scattering. But the bluecoats quickly regrouped and re-formed with a series of well-coordinated regimental maneuvers that slowly began to outflank the Rebel force. As planned, Gregg gave ground obstinately until about 2 p.m., when word came that the last evacuation trains were on their way out of Jackson. He then ordered his men to withdraw and join the rest of Johnston's retreat northeast toward the town of Canton.

Good order and a spirited defense had been the hallmarks of Gregg's command, but a comparable analogy could not be made with the defenders of the city's southwest approaches. Because Sherman's attack there had not been anticipated, the Confederates had posted only a single brigade plus some assorted detail units and a group of civilian volunteers. At the first roar of Sherman's artillery batteries, these frightened men absconded without even burning their bridges behind them, and Sherman moved easily into town, capturing three Rebel field batteries—nine cannons in all—and several hundred prisoners of war.

The Battle of Jackson had cost 1,000 or so casualties, and though it got better play in the press because it involved a Rebel state capital it was nonetheless considered a minor engagement, at least to those with no personal stake in it. As with Port Gibson and Raymond, the Confederates suffered the most casualties, having used two brigades to defend against four enemy divisions—odds of six to one. The long-term effect of this was summed up dramatically by Lieutenant Colonel Arthur Fremantle, a British officer of the famous Coldstream Guards, who had come to America to observe the Civil War. He later told some Rebel officers, "Don't you see your system feeds upon itself? You cannot fill the places of these men. Your troops do wonders, but every time at a cost you cannot afford."

That evening Grant, Sherman, and McPherson parleyed at the Bowen House hotel, opposite the Mississippi capitol building, with Grant occupying the room Johnston had just vacated. There, the commanding general laid out his plans for Pemberton's undoing, based on the intercepted orders from Johnston that the Union spy had betrayed to McPherson. The corps of McClernand and McPherson, Grant said, would deploy to intercept and destroy Pemberton's army as it marched toward Clinton. Meantime, Sherman was to linger in Jackson another day to "destroy [it] as a railroad centre, and manufacturing city of military supplies," which, Grant delicately added, "he did most effectually."

Along those lines, earlier that day Grant and Sherman had visited a Jackson cloth factory, which had continued to operate throughout the battle, its machinery manned "mostly by girls." They stayed long enough to see tent cloth bearing the letters "C.S.A." coming off the looms, whereupon Grant told Sherman, "I think they have done work enough" and ordered the girls sent home, "taking with them as much cloth as they wanted." Then, over the pleas of the owner, who pointed out that the girls were impoverished and would have no jobs, Sherman had the place torched.

Likewise he had his troops destroy all the rail tracks leading in and out of Jackson,* blow up an arsenal, incinerate a foundry, and wreck

---

* Sherman's people probably destroyed more rail tracks, before or since, than any army in the history of the world, and it was here that they developed and refined their famous recipe for "Sherman's neckties." A regiment would line the track and at a given signal heave up a section of rail, which was then detached from its cross ties. The ties were placed in a pile and set on fire with the rails placed atop them until the iron glowed red in the center, whereupon strong men at each end would twist the rail around a tree until it was bent useless.

or burn any other public property that might "contribute to the enemy war effort." This last Sherman interpreted most liberally and his corps, which had already developed a particular flair for arson, was only too happy to participate. In the process of carrying out their mission, his men managed to burn down the Catholic church, two hospitals, a carriage factory, the public stables, an entire city block of private and public buildings near the capitol—even the state penitentiary, which Sherman later protested was done by the convicts themselves.

Colonel Fremantle, the British observer, had joined Johnston around the time of the evacuation and said of the Union occupation, "During the short space of thirty-six hours, in which General Grant occupied the city, his troops . . . had gutted all the stores, and destroyed what they could not carry away." By the time Sherman departed the next afternoon, half the town was in flames, including whole blocks of private homes, with only their smoldering chimneys still standing, leaving Jackson with the sorrowful nickname "Chimneyville." As he rode away Sherman declared that Jackson "can be of little use to the enemy for six months," later blaming most of the looting, vandalism, and arson on the unauthorized use of liberated whiskey and rum. Then he marched his corps westward toward Vicksburg to join McPherson and McClernand for what they were now certain would be a quick and decisive end to the campaign.

Joe Johnston said that he was furious at Pemberton for disobeying his orders to attack Grant's rear, but if he had been sincere in his desire to unite their two forces he had an odd way of showing it. As soon as Johnston heard that reinforcements were within just a few hours' reach of Jackson, he sent urgent messages for them to halt and move off in the opposite direction. First to receive these alarming instructions was Brigadier General Samuel B. Maxey, West Point graduate and veteran of the Mexican War, aboard a train from Port Hudson with his 3,000-man brigade, which had stopped at a depot thirty miles south of Jackson. There, Maxey was handed a wire stating, "Halt! Don't come any farther. Fall back on your wagons. . . . Go in the direction of Port Hudson."

Maxey suspected the message might be a Yankee trick, so he detached the engine from the rail cars and sent it and one of his aides toward Jackson to see what was going on. A few miles south of the city the aide encountered a man coming toward him on a handcar carrying another message from Johnston's headquarters directing Maxey to "take measures to save your command by crossing the Pearl River," which was in the opposite direction from Jackson. Bewildered that instead of being the savior he himself was now in need of being saved, Maxey obeyed instructions and took himself out of the fight.

A similar warning was sent to a brigade coming from South Carolina, commanded by Brigadier General States Rights Gist, a thirty-two-year-old Harvard-educated lawyer and son of the former governor of that state whose given name was the very epitome of the Lost Cause. Gist was within ten miles of Jackson when a courier intercepted him with orders to divert his leading elements—1,500 men—fifty miles away from the city. Likewise two brigades from Bragg's Tennessee army under Brigadier Generals Evander McNair and Matthew Ector were halted at Meridian, just a few hours from Jackson by rail.

Having thus sent away all these hard-to-come-by reinforcements—more than 10,000 men—Johnston sent a curt message to Pemberton saying: "Your dispatch of yesterday just received. Our being compelled to leave Jackson makes your plan impracticable. The only mode by which we can unite is by your moving directly to Clinton, informing me that we may move to that point with about 6,000." Then Johnston proceeded with the rest of his command toward Canton, which was about twenty-five miles northeast of Jackson, instead of swinging them around southeast to effect the union with Pemberton's army he said he desired.

The whole affair was handled poorly on the Confederate side, with Johnston dithering Hamlet-like on the outskirts of Jackson while Pemberton vacillated between there and Vicksburg like a rat trapped in a maze. If Pemberton had taken out his adding book on May 14, he would have discovered that with the 23,000 troops he presently had in the field, and the almost 10,000 he had left behind at Vicksburg or elsewhere on guard duty, he could have assembled a 33,000-man army that would have been at least the equal to anything Grant could have thrown against him at that point, given that Sherman's corps was in Jackson. Rarely had any Confederate general been offered such favorable numerical odds.

The fact that Pemberton felt compelled to leave nearly 10,000 infantry in Vicksburg is testimony enough to the conflict of command between his ultimate superior, Davis, who had told him to hold Vicksburg and Port Hudson at all costs, and the instructions of his immediate superior, Johnston, who had told him when the Federals began their invasion, "If Grant crosses unite all your forces and beat him." Pemberton interpreted these orders to be mutually exclusive, and thus tried to accommodate both, which usually results in bad consequences, as it did now.

Moreover, if Johnston hadn't panicked and decided to retreat from Jackson, but instead told Gregg to pull back to the entrenchments around the city and hold on "at all costs"—and had he not sent his new reinforcements away—Johnston's army by the afternoon of the fourteenth should have numbered more than 17,000. And even if Johnston couldn't hold Jackson, if he had looped his 17,000 men around to the northwest and united with Pemberton, then a concentrated Rebel army—combined with those still in Vicksburg—would have numbered some 50,000, again, enough to deal with Grant on an equal basis. This also would have given Johnston the advantage of a direct supply line to the provisions and munitions stored at Vicksburg, not to mention vastly superior knowledge of the terrain.

But Johnston did not do these things, and Pemberton did not do these things, and now each was marching off in a different direction, one from the other.

Jefferson Davis was understandably alarmed by the news from Mississippi—at least from what he could get of it, now that the telegraph from Jackson and Vicksburg had been cut by the Yankees. In Richmond, the surge of elation following Lee's brilliant victory at Chancellorsville was dampened by grief over the death of Stonewall Jackson, and on its heels came intense anxiety over the fate of Vicksburg and the war in the West, which Davis considered one and the same, even if others did not. Johnston, for one, complained to the authorities in the Confederate capital, "The near danger appears to be much greater than the distant one."

Davis, however, was doing all he could. When it became clear after Chancellorsville that the menace from the Army of the Potomac had passed, at least temporarily, the president went to Lee to see if he could send some of his troops to Mississippi to assist Pemberton. After all, Longstreet and most of his large corps was still down in North Carolina, having missed the Chancellorsville fight entirely. If these troops could be rushed to Vicksburg in time, then Grant might well be destroyed in a powerful pincers movement between Jackson and the river.

Lee was not amenable to the idea. What he had in mind, he told the president, was to go on the offensive and march his entire army north through Maryland and into Pennsylvania. Among other things, he said, this would likely create a diversion to keep Grant from being reinforced. As to Longstreet, the general continued, if the Yankees discovered he had gone to Mississippi, they would probably launch another attack on Richmond. Besides, he said, Longstreet's corps would be sorely needed in the Pennsylvania invasion to make up for the 13,000 casualties his army had suffered at Chancellorsville.

Abraham Lincoln was likewise apprehensive over the situation then developing in the West. The catastrophe at Chancellorsville had hit him particularly hard—like a "thunderbolt," according to his friend the California journalist Noah Brooks, who described the president when he got the news as pacing his office in the White House, groaning, "My God! My God! What will the country say! What will the country say!"

Lincoln simply could not seem to find proper leaders for his armies; either they were outgeneraled like Hooker, Burnside, and Pope or they were dilatory like Rosecrans, McClellan, Buell, and Banks. Now, having just been handed another humiliating defeat in the East, the pressures were building, not only against Lincoln's war policy but also against his administration in general, following enactment of the Emancipation Proclamation.

In fact the nation was growing war weary, just as de Tocqueville had prophesied, and the so-called Peace Party, composed of Democrats, was gaining popularity. And from the Midwest reports had begun to filter back about a secretive antiwar organization called the Knights of the Golden Circle, said to be planning to overthrow the government.

General Burnside solved part of the problem, or so he thought, right after he was named the new head of the Department of the Ohio following his defeat at Fredericksburg. Upon arriving in Chicago, Burnside learned that the obnoxious Clement Vallandigham was stumping around Illinois preaching against the war in general and Lincoln in particular. The former congressman's remarks so incensed Burnside that he had Vallandigham arrested in the middle of the night and thrown in jail for treason. When Vallandigham asked for a writ of habeas corpus, Burnside himself denied it. Not only that, but when the antiwar *Chicago Tribune* objected in its pages that Vallandigham's arrest was unconstitutional Burnside had the newspaper closed down.

One could easily see Burnside's point: if Vallandigham's tirades did not constitute treason, what did? On the other hand, there were many thousands in the North—perhaps hundreds of thousands—who felt exactly the way Vallandigham did. Was it now against the law to express one's opinions about the war? The notion was a sticky one to contemplate, and the Vallandigham affair immediately created a furor, mainly with the press, which is always by nature sensitive to such things as the First Amendment, but also among civil liberties advocates. Lincoln felt compelled to overrule his Indiana general, but with Solomon-like perspective. He had Vallandigham released from jail but then banished him south, inside Rebel lines, where he could rant and rave all he wanted. Then the president ordered Burnside to let the *Tribune* reopen, and not to fool with it again, thus letting word get out to the other departmental commanders that newspapers were sacrosanct.

Nevertheless, Lincoln knew the situation at Vicksburg was dicey, with Grant down there all by himself and no fast way to get him help. If Grant's army somehow got gobbled up, Lincoln would be in political trouble and he knew it, and yet he managed to appear optimistic throughout the battle. Despite the continuing hubbub regarding Grant's alleged drunkenness, the president wrote his old friend the Illinois congressman Isaac Arnold, "Whether or not Gen. Grant shall or shall not consummate the capture of Vicksburg his campaign from the beginning of this month up to the twenty-second day of it, is one of the most brilliant in the world."

When the telegraph to Jackson went dead, the citizens of Vicksburg became suspended in a limbo of rumor and uncertainty. One, however—Lida Lord, daughter of the Episcopal minister Dr. William Wilberforce Lord—did not "doubt either the valor or wisdom of our generals, but felt confident [of] the speedy surrounding and utter annihilation of Grant's army."

That was wishful thinking, since Pemberton, whether or not he knew it, was dancing on the sharp edge of a knife. As he maneuvered south to cut off the enemy supply line, the last thing he wanted was to tangle with Grant's army, but that was exactly what Grant had in mind.

Since it had originally been Loring's idea to attack Grant's supply line, Pemberton had him lead off the march before daylight on May 15, followed by the divisions of Bowen and Stevenson and, lastly, the four-hundred-wagon supply train. From the beginning things began to go sour.

First, someone at Pemberton's headquarters had forgotten to order up food and munitions from Vicksburg, and that caused a delay of six or seven hours. Then Loring reported that a ford across Baker's Creek about two miles from Pemberton's headquarters at Edwards Station was unusable owing to high water from a torrential downpour the night before. That prompted another delay of several hours while the lead elements took an awkward detour. There was no excuse for these lapses other than sloppy staff work. Pemberton and Loring both should have sent scouts and engineers to reconnoiter the route of march, and the failure to bring up provisions was plainly unforgivable.

The result of these two blunders was that instead of hitting the Yankee supply route with an irresistible force at sunrise the next morning, the army was forced to stop in its tracks and camp for the night with Loring's lead division no farther than three miles from the original starting point on the railroad line. Nevertheless, the men were in fine spirits and spoiling for a fight. A Tennessee officer in Stevenson's division enthused just before his men marched out that they were "fighting for their properties, for their families, for their rights [and] can't be subjugated," adding that they were "all joyful and full of glee marching perhaps into the jaw of death." That may well have been so but, before the army could resume its march the next morning, the courier that Johnston had sent from Jackson finally arrived with his message informing Pemberton that his plan was "now impracticable" and again ordering him to march east to unite the two forces.

Pemberton at this point considered such a tactic suicidal, but orders were orders. He immediately issued instructions for the army to turn around and march the other way, which, by itself, was a difficult maneuver; first, all those four hundred wagons would have to be turned around so that they'd become the head of the column instead of the tail and it was while this was being done that a most fateful collision of the campaign at Vicksburg began.

Ever since first light the ominous thuds of artillery fire had sounded in the distance, indicating that some kind of contact had been made with the enemy. As Pemberton and his staff rode forward to see what the matter was, he encountered Loring, who advised the commanding general that "the sooner [Pemberton] formed a line of battle the better, as the enemy would soon be upon us." Pemberton concurred and sent word to all division commanders. So after first having faced south to cut a Federal supply line, then reversing itself to face north for the union with Johnston, the Confederate army now turned east to face U. S. Grant.

. . .

Unlike Pemberton, Grant had moved with alacrity after leaving Sherman to tend business in Jackson. Armed with the revelations in Johnston's purloined order telling Pemberton to move forward and attack Grant's rear at Clinton, Sherman now had *his* army do an about-face and march west to meet the Confederates. McClernand's and McPherson's corps marched toward Vicksburg on parallel roads until dark when they went into bivouac. Ironically, as the men of both armies bedded down that night they were a mere four miles apart, though no one on either side knew it. The fact that Pemberton had first disregarded Johnston's order to move on Grant's base of supplies, then reversed himself again and was turning east to link up with Johnston, was not just immaterial; instead, it played right into Grant's hands. As luck would have it Grant caught the Rebel army at a most vulnerable time: strung out on the march for three miles, just when it was trying to change directions.

The earlier firing that Pemberton had heard resulted when the ubiquitous Wirt Adams and his cavalry ran into a brigade from McClernand's corps that was advancing down the Raymond road. Eventually it swelled into a constant, unsettling noise, but a major battle had not been joined. It was a little after 10 a.m.

Even though Pemberton had not wanted a fight at this point, the good thing was that the route of march his army had been following lay along a low ridgeline beginning at Champion Hill, the cotton plantation of Sid and Matilda Champion, and extended southward to the Raymond road. Champion Hill itself sloped gently down some seventy feet to the same kind of countryside Grant had found so nightmarish when he had first landed on the Mississippi side of the river: cut up by steep ravines, streams, ridges, canebrakes, thick timber, and underbrush fit only for the bears, wild boars, panthers, and other creatures that inhabited it. It meant that Grant's army would have to travel on the three available dirt roads that ran east to west, and on these Pemberton had set up roadblocks. That was the good news. The bad news was that Grant outnumbered him by about two to one.

Stevenson's division, which had been last in the original line of march, now became first and set up defensively on Champion Hill, unlimbered its artillery, established field hospitals, and waited for the Yankees to appear. To their immediate south the Missourians and Arkansans of Bowen's division did the same and, farther south still, Loring's men followed suit. They would not have long to wait.

Part of McClernand's corps had come up opposite Loring's and Bowen's divisions but, because Grant had instructed the commanders to "move forward cautiously," they did not attempt to bring on a general attack but contented themselves with engaging each other in an artillery duel. The Confederates ran their guns out in front to provide a lively exchange, but before long the rifled Yankee Parrot guns began to take their toll on the Rebel smoothbores and they were slowly forced back to the main battle line. This, however, led Pemberton to assume that Grant's attack would fall on his right, while just the opposite was true.

In fact, something very sinister was afoot in the deep woods in front of Stevenson's division on Champion Hill, which lay near the Vicksburg–Jackson road about half a mile from the rail tracks. Brigadier General Alvin P. Hovey, a contentious Indiana lawyer who took to soldiering "just as if he expected to spend his life in it," had marched his division down the Jackson road until he came upon a skirmish line sent out by the Rebel general Stephen Dill Lee, who had performed so well during the Battle of Chickasaw Bluffs. Eager to get at his enemy, but wary of Grant's instruction to proceed with caution, Hovey sent a message to McClernand asking if he should attack. McClernand, who was farther south with the main body of his corps, passed the decision on to Grant.

Grant decided to have a look-see and rode to the front, but he was not pleased with what he found. The ground the Rebels had picked to defend, he wrote later, "whether by accident or design," was well chosen, and he opted to wait until McPherson's corps was up before launching an all-out assault. Meantime, Hovey reported that scouts had found Champion Hill full of Rebels, and that Confederate artillery fire had become so heavy that he would have to either move his men forward or retire. When the first of McPherson's divisions—that of John Logan—arrived, Grant sent it around to the right, hoping to flank Carter Stevenson's division, but the latter shifted Stephen Lee's Alabama brigade to conform to the Yankee movement.

By "refusing" his flank, Stevenson had prevented an almost certain disaster, but in doing so he left a dangerous gap between Lee and Brigadier General Alfred Cumming's brigade of Georgians. Now Cumming was faced with a dilemma, because if he shifted to conform to Lee it would leave a six-gun battery that had been covering a vital crossroads unprotected, and if he did not it would leave the unacceptable gap. The situation perfectly illustrates the problem of being outnumbered by an enemy, who can simply keep extending around until you are left too thin to effectively resist. Cumming eventually decided to divide his force, sending half into the gap and the other half to defend the guns. It wasn't a perfect solution but it would have to do. There wasn't any perfect solution.

With Logan's division now in line with Hovey's and the artillery and long-range rifle fire getting hotter by the moment, Grant was confronted with the choice of going forward to attack now or waiting for McPherson's other division under Brigadier General Marcellus Crocker to come up. That would have provided him an overwhelming superiority of three divisions against Stevenson's one, but it would also allow the Rebels time to improve their defenses. At 10:30 Grant gave the go-ahead and the bluecoats began moving forward.

It was very rough going to reach Champion Hill. An Indiana soldier reported that his company had to "pull ourselves up the sides of the ravines by the bushes." All the while the Confederate artillery was playing on the Yankee line, but because it was shielded behind the cut-up terrain little damage was done. Within the hour the bluecoats had reached the foot of the hill two hundred yards from the Rebel line, and McPherson gave the order to storm the heights. From Stevenson's horrified perspective—and probably Pemberton's, too, since he was in a position to watch it—the double-rank Yankee formation had added at least two brigades that had not been spotted previously, so that along the Confederate front the enemy line appeared as a giant door, about to be swung shut, overlapping Stevenson's extended left flank.

At 11:30 the Federal attack exploded out of the woods directly up the face of Champion Hill led by Hovey's Indianans, bayonets fixed and glinting in the springtime sun. The section of the line they happened to fall upon was manned by Cumming's thinned-out Georgians. Despite a murderous fire from four Rebel guns just below the crest of the hill, the Federals braved the double-shotted canister and overwhelmed the position in five minutes, capturing the Confederate guns in the bargain.

Meantime, Lee had managed to repulse successive charges by Black Jack Logan's division, but Cumming's collapse to his right compelled him to withdraw. For the better part of an hour and a half the battlefield was consumed in desperate and bloody fighting, at times involving gun butts, bayonets, fists, knives, and artillery sponge staffs. The din was at once breathtaking and terrible, as the nonstop roar of scores of cannons offered an earsplitting backdrop to the incessant musketry, which, to a young girl trapped in her home during the battle, sounded "like the crackling of a canebrake that is on fire." A lieutenant in an Ohio regiment watched as the first man in his company to die was shot in the head going up Champion Hill, then the lieutenant gasped in horror as his own brother was shot through the heart.

"He had his gun at the ready, about to aim, and as he fell in death, he pitched his musket toward the enemy; it fell with the bayonet stuck in the ground, the stock standing up," the soldier wrote after the war.

Back in the rear, the sawbones in the field hospitals were attending to their grim work. One of them, Dr. William Beach of London, Ohio, who had set up his surgical station at the Champion House—which was also Grant's headquarters—remembered seeing Grant and his staff dismount at the gate of an abandoned farmhouse he had set up as a surgical station for Logan's division. "The steady roar of battle had rolled from Hovey's front by this time to that of Logan's, which was steadily advancing, and where the sound of the conflict was now simply *terrific*." Beach remembered the commanding general "leisurely taking his cigar from his mouth, he turned slowly to one of his staff and said, 'Go down to Logan and tell him he is making history today.' "

For the Confederates, by midafternoon the battle was in danger of deteriorating into a rout, but about 2 p.m. Pemberton took a desperate chance. The large Union force on his right (McClernand's corps) that had seemed so threatening earlier that morning had shown no inclination to attack, and so he ordered Bowen to abandon that front and come to Stevenson's assistance at Champion Hill. The fact that the Yankees, not Stevenson, now occupied the hill served only to inspire Bowen, and his men came on the run to pitch into Hovey's exhausted soldiers just at their moment of triumph.

Led by the brigades of Colonel Francis Marion Cockrell and General Martin Green, not only did Bowen's Missourians chase Hovey's Indianans off Champion Hill, recapturing eleven Rebel cannons, they chased them at the point of the bayonet all the way back to Grant's headquarters, half a mile behind the fighting line, punching a huge gap in the Federal front. "We ran, and ran manfully," recalled one of Hovey's men, who characterized the action as "the most desperate hand-to-hand fighting." Joining in this devastating offensive was Lee's brigade, which had rallied after its retreat off the hill. In the midst of all this, a group of women from the Isaac Roberts plantation manor, where Pemberton had made his headquarters, and which was smack in the middle of the battlefield, poured out into the yard and began cheering the Rebel soldiers and singing "Dixie." General Cockrell provided his own notion of inspiration by riding among his troops "with a magnolia flower in one hand and a sword in the other."

Bowen's bold attack, according to no less an authority than James B. McPherson, the Federal corps commander, "turned the tide of the battle in favor of the Confederates." All during this crisis, witnesses recalled, Grant stood unperturbed with his back resting against his horse, a bay mare, giving occasional orders and smoking his eternal cigar. Fortunately for Grant, Crocker's division came up in the nick of time to slow Bowen's rampage. If Pemberton could have sent Bowen reinforcements, it might have won the day for the Confederates, but because of an extraordinary turn of events reinforcements were not forthcoming. As it was, Bowen's troops had stripped the dead and wounded of their ammunition and now were fighting for their lives.

Loring had been instructed by Pemberton to keep contact with Bowen's division, so when Bowen began his double-time march north to reinforce Stevenson, Loring should have shifted as well, or at least inquired of Pemberton if this was what was wanted. Instead he did nothing.

William Loring was a peculiar soldier with a difficult personality, whose photograph bears a striking resemblance to the familiar likeness of William Shakespeare. Born in North Carolina in 1818, his family moved to St. Augustine, Florida, where as a boy of fourteen he participated in the Seminole Wars. In 1846, as a member of the Florida legislature, he received, without benefit of a West Point education, a direct commission to the regular army and was breveted lieutenant colonel after losing an arm during the Battle of Chapultepec in the Mexican War. When the Civil War broke out he was the youngest line colonel in the U.S. Army and was immediately commissioned a brigadier general after siding with the South.

No sooner had Loring joined the Confederate army than he became known as a troublemaker. When in 1861 a force he commanded in western Virginia came under the command of Robert E. Lee, Loring and Brigadier General John B. Floyd—of Fort Donelson notoriety and disgrace—began a campaign of backbiting and insubordination against Lee that caused the Virginian much embarrassment. Assigned to Stonewall Jackson's army later that year, Loring also began a feud with that formidable officer, culminating with the infamous "Romney petition," in which he sponsored a list of grievances against Jackson

for demanding "undue hardships" on his command. Jackson threatened to resign over Richmond's handling of the affair and the situation
was defused only when Loring was transferred out of the department
to the West.

Now, at the height of the fighting on Champion Hill, only Loring's
division could provide the reinforcements needed to make Bowen's
attack a success, but neither he nor his division could be found.

As Bowen's men prepared for their assault, Pemberton sent Loring
instructions to bring his men up in support. When no response was
forthcoming, Pemberton sent his inspector general, Major Jacob
Thompson, to reiterate the order. Loring shook his head, "asking me
[Thompson] if General Pemberton knew that the enemy was in great
force in his [Loring's] front." "The order I delivered," Thompson
informed Loring, "was that General Pemberton desires you to come
immediately, and with all dispatch, to the left, to the support of General Stevenson, whatever may be in your front."

Thompson returned to Pemberton's headquarters and repeated the
conversation he had had with Loring. Just then two of Stevenson's
regiments broke and Pemberton went out to rally them. When he
returned, he again asked, "Where is Loring?" Again, Thompson was
sent to find him, along with Pemberton's adjutant general, Thomas H.
Taylor, and when they did not return promptly Pemberton himself
rode off in a fury toward Loring's last known position, but all he could
find were two forlorn regiments, while the whereabouts of the rest of
Loring's division remained a mystery.

Meanwhile, things were beginning to fall apart on the Confederate
left. A series of assaults on Stevenson's northernmost flank had caused
him to fall back and try to re-form at about 4:30 p.m., and at five
Bowen sent back word that his division was out of ammunition, under
increasing pressure, and "could no longer hold its position." Still finding no trace of Loring, Pemberton returned to the Roberts plantation,
where a short time before the ladies of the house had serenaded his
soldiers with "Dixie" and learned from an exhausted Bowen that his
division had been forced all the way back to the original line. Upon
this bleak news Pemberton was left with little choice but to retreat to
Vicksburg. Aside from saving the army and defending the city, his
options had run out.

CHAPTER SIXTEEN

Shut Up as in a Trap

At last Loring turned up, and in the nick of time, but only to help prevent a complete collapse of the army. His disappearance during the battle was explained by the fact that instead of rushing to Bowen's assistance when he might have helped to drive an irreparable wedge between the Federal forces, he led his division on a circuitous march through dismal back trails and paths rather than using an obvious route along the plantation road that would have brought him into the fight when he was needed most. As a result, when he finally arrived, the Battle of Champion Hill was over, and it fell to Loring to hold off the Yankee army until Pemberton could get his men to safety across the Big Black River.

Crucial to this maneuver was to fend off McClernand's large and dangerous Yankee corps, which had at last begun to stir, and for this task Loring selected the brigade of General Lloyd Tilghman, the gallant defender of Fort Henry in the winter of '62. The Marylander and his men put up a stiff fight to keep the bluecoats at bay, holding off two entire divisions, during which Tilghman was killed by a cannon shell that ripped through him, front to back.*

By then it was getting dark and Grant decided his men had had

---

* Witnesses said the shot that killed Tilghman hit about fifty yards ahead, bounced, then passed straight through the general before killing a horse belonging to his adjutant. Tilghman's staff brought his body back to Vicksburg for burial the next day, accompanied by his son, Lloyd Tilghman Jr., who was an officer with the army.

enough for the day. While they rested, Pemberton tried to hustle his dispirited Rebel army across the Big Black railroad bridge and entrench them in the defenses that had been prepared on the landward side of Vicksburg before Grant's host could fall on them once more.

Meanwhile, Loring disappeared again—this time for good. After assisting in the escape of Pemberton's army, he had begun looking for a way to join the others behind the Big Black but became lost in the dark. A local doctor offered to guide him, but the route was so rough that Loring had to abandon most of his artillery and supplies. Finally, knowledgeable civilians in the neighborhood informed him that strong Federal forces were nearby and, unless he wanted to fight his way through them, he couldn't reach the Big Black bridge. Given that option, Loring chose to head off to the southeast, away from the action and away from Vicksburg, and turned up with his division several days later at Johnston's headquarters near Canton.

Champion Hill was an appalling battle; McPherson called it "one of the most murderous of the war," and Hovey, who had left a third of his division dead or wounded there, branded it "the hill of death." More than 6,000 men were killed, wounded, or missing—and missing often meant dead—on both sides, not counting Loring's "missing" division. Grant had lost 2,363; Pemberton, 3,840 plus an embarrassing thirty pieces of artillery.

Afterward, the mournful sights on the battlefield were recorded by a number of people in Grant's victorious army, including Charles Dana, who remembered riding over the bloody, torn-up ground with Grant's chief of staff, John Rawlins, and some other officers. When they reached Champion Hill, "We stopped and were looking around at the dead and dying men lying all about us, when suddenly a man, perhaps forty-five or fifty years old, who had a Confederate uniform on, lifted himself on his elbow, and said, 'For God's sake, gentlemen, is there a Mason among you?'

" 'Yes,' said Rawlins, 'I am a mason.' He got off his horse and kneeled by the dying man, who gave him some letters out of his pocket. When he came back Rawlins had tears on his cheeks. The man told us he wanted to convey some souvenir—a miniature or a ring, I do not remember what—to his wife, who was in Alabama. Rawlins took the package, and some time afterward he succeeded in sending it to the woman."

Another officer who walked the ground where the fighting had been the most terrible remembered that the hill had been covered by grass, but afterward, because the rifle and cannon fire had been so thick, the entire crest "looked as though it had been cut down by a hoe."

Because he was unaware that Loring had departed, Pemberton ordered Bowen and his 5,000 Missourians to occupy a line of rifle pits and fortifications hastily dug out on the east side—the Jackson side— of the Big Black, just twelve miles east of Vicksburg, in order to protect Loring's anticipated crossing. Meantime, the rest of the army was withdrawing over the river any way it could—on the railroad bridge and by walking over a steamboat that had been placed athwart the river for use as a bridge. Once on its western side, Pemberton hoped to reorganize his command and use the Big Black as a moat to keep Grant away from Vicksburg.

Even though Bowen had the river to his back, his position on the east bank was a fairly strong one and covered the only crossing for miles around. His perimeter was about fifteen hundred yards long, north to south, with a sluggish bayou in front for a barrier and anchored at both ends by impassable cypress swamps. The line itself had been built of logs and cotton bales and was protected by abatis in the northern sector. The ground in front was flat, with mostly open cotton fields for half a mile that were thoroughly covered by Bowen's artillery batteries, which contained eighteen guns. Thus ensconced, Bowen and his exhausted soldiers sat down to await Loring's arrival.

Meantime, Pemberton found time to scratch off a message to Joe Johnston, wherever he was, telling him of the defeat at Champion Hill. He added that if the army was driven back into Vicksburg it would be necessary to evacuate the vital strongpoints on the Yazoo that centered on Haines's and Snyder's bluffs. Almost as a postscript he told Johnston, "I have about sixty days provisions at Vicksburg and Snyder's." He communicated the same news to General John Forney, in command at Snyder's Bluff, whose responsibility it would be to get the troops, stores, and munitions into the city.

As the dark hours ticked away, both Bowen and Pemberton were becoming apprehensive over Loring's whereabouts. As the sky in the east brightened to pink, Pemberton remained convinced that Loring would turn up sooner or later and decided to wait a few more hours in case "Old Blizzards" had somehow got lost in the dark.

What turned up instead was McClernand and 15,000 Yankees, accompanied by Grant, who did not like what he saw. To assault such a narrow, fortified front, full of infantry and artillery, might be suicidal—at least for those doing the assaulting—but already he had in mind a greater plan.

Sherman's corps, having finished its pyromaniacal handiwork at Jackson, was now hurrying west, north of the Jackson–Vicksburg rail tracks, in order to keep Johnston's little army from uniting with Pemberton. But Grant knew that if Sherman crossed the Big Black at Bridgeport, seven miles above, he could then swing south along the west side of the river and slam into the flank of the divided Rebel army and destroy it, while McClernand kept Bowen's men penned up on the near side of the river. It was a comforting thought, but apparently before Grant could express it to anybody a big redheaded Irishman commanding one of McClernand's brigades took it upon himself to upset Grant's rational and humane strategy for bagging the Rebel army.

He was Michael K. "Mike" Lawler, an Illinois farmer whom the newspaper correspondent Cadwallader described thusly: "General Lawler was a large and excessively fat man—a fine type of the generous, rollicking, fighting Irishman. His cherished maxim was the Tipperary one: 'If you see a head, hit it.' I cannot say positively that he acted in this case without orders, but I always supposed he did."

Charles Dana had a take on him too, and it is worth repeating: "Lawler weighs two-hundred-fifty pounds, is a Roman Catholic and was a Douglas Democrat and served in the Mexican war. He is brave as a lion and has about as much brains, but his purpose is always honest and his sense is always good. He once hung a man of his regiment for murdering a comrade, without reporting the case to his commanding general, but there was no doubt the man deserved his fate."

At the first pale streaks of dawn, from his position opposite the northernmost part of Bowen's salient, Lawler sized up the disposition of Martin Green's Rebel brigade and thought he saw a chink in the armor. First, the Confederates had placed no artillery at that end of the line, having chosen instead to position it in the center and southern sectors. Second, even though the narrow bayou would be an obstacle, Lawler's scouts told him it was fordable. Third, his brigade was partially hidden in a small copse of trees only a few hundred yards from the Rebel line. If it could be rushed en masse, and the enemy taken by surprise, the thing just might be doable. As Lawler was considering all this, a scout came in and reported that there was a long swale, or depression, running parallel to the enemy line and just fifty or so yards away from it. That settled the matter. At 8 a.m. Lawler stripped off his jacket, rolled up his sleeves, slung his sword belt over his shoulder—which he was obliged to do because of his extraordinary girth—and gave the order to charge.

When Bowen's men saw 2,000 Yankees burst out of the trees and come rushing toward them, they were shocked, then mystified after firing only a volley or two, when the entire enemy brigade appeared to become swallowed up by the earth. It had, of course, dived into the swale, sheltered and concealed, which was worrisome enough, but right about then their attention was drawn to the southern end of the line, where Federal troops were now making threatening gestures. All the while the artillery of both armies kept up a thundering fire that was enough to rattle the nerves of anyone within the salient or without, and the disappearing act that Lawler's brigade had pulled seems to have been forgotten by everyone—except Lawler.

An hour later, at precisely 9 a.m., the Rebels manning the northern-most sector of the salient were staggered to see the colossal Irishman and his 2,000 men suddenly rise up as one and make a mad dash for that part of the line between the brigades of Green's Arkansans and John C. Vaughn's Tennesseans. From the swale, Lawler had been able to distinguish the different regimental battle flags and selected that point on the theory it might cause the Confederates the most confusion.

It was but a short distance from the swale to the Rebel line but there was also the bayou, or moat, to contend with. Lawler's bluecoats, however, plunged in enthusiastically, "where the mud ranged from the men's knees to their armpits," according to Cadwallader, who called it "the most perilous and ludicrous charge that I witnessed during the war. They scrambled through and out of it, stormed the rebel rifle pits and swarmed over their cotton-bale breastworks with irresistible impetuosity," he wrote, "suffer[ing] severely from the musket fire on their advance, and from the rebel batteries on the opposite shore of the river."

As Lawler's soldiers bulled their way into the Confederate lines in the far north of the salient and began "hitting heads," a number of grayclads surrendered, but most escaped. The rest of the Union line was astounded by what they were witnessing, but soon they recovered and also began a rush at the Rebel parapets, each brigade moving forward in echelon, one guiding on the other, north to south.

This proved too much for the weary Confederates who had been beaten so badly at Champion Hill. Leaving their sixteen guns behind, they made a dash of their own toward the planked-over railroad viaduct and the river steamboat–turned–floating bridge.* As the last of them passed across to the west bank of the Big Black, Pemberton's engineering officer Samuel Lockett fired incendiaries he had preset on both structures and within moments they became infernos in the otherwise soft May morning.

As for Pemberton, who had hoped from the beginning to hold off the Yankees along the westward line of the Big Black, he was now forced to the painful conclusion that this was no longer possible. Between casualties and the disappearance of Loring, his field army had been reduced by half during the past two days. It was demoralized, disjointed, and badly in need of reorganization and that could be done only behind the formidable buttresses of the Vicksburg defenses. So Vicksburg it was, despite the Philadelphian's agonized misgivings about the Confederacy's future there, which he knew was bleak.

As he headed back toward the city, Pemberton was joined by Lockett, who recalled the gloomy ride. "I was the only staff officer with him," Lockett said. "He was very much depressed by events of the last two days, and for some time after mounting his horse he rode in silence. He finally said: 'Just thirty years ago I began my military career by receiving my cadetship at the U. S. Military Academy, and to-day— the same date—that career is ended in disaster and disgrace.' "

Since dawn on Sunday, May 17, the citizens of Vicksburg had listened in dumb apprehension to the cannon fire in the east, knowing that it signified the Yankees were drawing nearer. At that distance the noise of artillery sounded less like distant thunder than it did the muted grunting of some enormous animal, but the people of Vicksburg knew exactly what it was when they heard it.

News about the Yankees taking Jackson had come to Vicksburg only the night before, right after Emma Balfour told her diary, "All has been uncertainty and suspense. No news from any quarter—not a word from our army. It is terrible when we know that events, so fraught with deep interest to us, are transpiring." Then, while the fight for the Big Black was taking place, Lieutenant S. M. Underhill, an aide to

---

* No less an authority than Major Samuel Lockett described the Confederate retreat as "a disgraceful stampede."

Stephen Lee and a family friend of Dr. Balfour and his wife, arrived with a shattering account of the Confederate defeat at Champion Hill. He wept as he related the events and his mistaken impression that Lee had been killed in the battle. "I wept too," Emma Balfour said, "but not only for [Lee]; indeed all individual feeling seems merged in grief and interest for my country. Oh, will God forsake us now! I cannot believe it. He may chasten us, and though cast down, I will not be disheartened or discouraged!"

Later, her self-professed confidence was dispelled as the bedraggled Rebel army began pouring into the streets of the city at the end of a lonely and terrifying day. "I hope never to witness again such a scene as the return of our routed army! From twelve o'clock till late in the night the streets and roads were jammed with wagons, caissons, horses, men, mules, stock, sheep—everything you can imagine that appertains to an army.* Nothing like order prevailed, of course, as division, brigades & regiments were broken and separated."

The residents, she told her diary, "poured forth all [they] had to refresh them," carrying water buckets to the street corners and putting out as much food as they had. "Poor fellows," Emma wrote. "It made my heart ache to see them, for I know from all I saw and heard that it was want of confidence in the Gen. commanding that was the cause of our disaster. I cannot write more—but oh! There will be a fearful reckoning somewhere. This had been brooding & growing—and many feared for the result. Gen. Pemberton has not the confidence of officers, people or men."

After stating that "I cannot write more," she proceeded to do so anyway, doubtless impelled by a fuller recognition of the magnitude of events unfolding around her. "What is to become of all the living things in this place when the boats commence shelling, God only knows. Shut up as in a trap, no ingress or egress, are thousands of women & children who have fled here for safety," was her dire conclusion.

Mary Loughborough was one of the last who had been able to gain ingress, only to regret it. The day after Porter's fleet passed the Vicksburg batteries, she took her two-year-old baby daughter and boarded a train for the safety of Jackson, where she'd been invited to stay with

* Knowing that Vicksburg would likely be besieged, Pemberton had ordered the army to round up all eatable livestock in the surrounding countryside and herd the animals into the city, at the same time denying them to Grant's army.

friends. Two weeks later, as Grant closed in around the capital city, Mary had made the decision to flee back to Vicksburg, where her officer husband was stationed, rather than "take the cars" to Mobile, as Mrs. Pemberton did.

The morning of the Battle of the Big Black, she and some friends walked to the Methodist church, while the distant rumble of the guns mingled with the ringing of church bells to provide a surreal backdrop for an otherwise lovely Sabbath day. All of the city's regular clergymen and physicians had gone out to minister to the wounded and the service at Mary's church was conducted by a "traveler," who afterward "requested that the ladies meet and make arrangements for lint and bandages for the wounded."

As they left the church, the disastrous results of the past several days were revealed in the streets of Vicksburg. At first, "there seemed no life in the city; sullen and expectant seemed the men—tearful and hopeful the women" but then "the stir of horsemen and wheels began, and wagons began . . . soon, straggler after straggler came by, then groups of soldiers worn and dusty with the long march."

" 'There has been many a life lost to-day,' " one soldier told her, " 'many an officer and man.' " " 'Ah! truly, yes,' I said; for the ambulances had been passing with the wounded and the dead," she remembered, "and one came slowly by with officers riding near it, bearing the dead body of General Tilghman, the blood dripping slowly from it."

Vicksburg's women lined the streets and asked the dejected soldiers, "What can be the matter? Where on earth are you going," and when they replied that they had been beaten, the women cried, "Oh, shame on you!" When the men responded that "it was all General Pemberton's fault," the women told them, "It's all your own fault. Why don't you stand your ground? Shame on you all!"

The women fixed the soldiers dinner anyway for, like Mary Loughborough, they could see that "they did seem indeed heartily ashamed of themselves. And where these weary and worn out men were going, we could not tell. I think they did not know themselves."

By night the city had fallen quiet again. Fresh soldiers from the Vicksburg garrison had been hustled into the outer fortifications, but Grant did not come. Officers had succeeded in herding the defeated troops into staging areas and restoring some semblance of their former organization, in hopes that they would be ready when Grant's army made its appearance.

As the lamps began going out in Vicksburg's windows, "the streets

were all but deserted," Mary wrote, except for the occasional clatter of
a wagon or an officer's horse. "And what will the morrow bring forth?"
she asked, wondering if when she awoke the streets would echo with
the tread of the Yankee army. "But the heavens above so calm,—so
soothing, the quiet glide of the silent river and the wind swaying
the trees with a monotonous wave—quelled and laid [to rest] these
thoughts of evil." Now, she wrote, "It was in God's hands."

"Shut up as in a trap," as Emma Balfour had so tartly observed, was
precisely the situation in which Pemberton found himself—a trap of
his own making, although Grant preferred to see it otherwise. About
noon on Monday, the eighteenth, while Pemberton was inspecting the
city's outer defenses along with several of his generals, an exhausted
courier arrived after an all-night ride through Yankee-infested territory. He brought with him Johnston's reply to Pemberton's desperate
message of the previous evening. "If you are invested in Vicksburg,"
Johnston said, "you must ultimately surrender. Under such circumstances, instead of losing both troops and place, we must, if possible,
save the troops. If it is not too late, evacuate Vicksburg and its depend-
encies, and march to the northeast."

By now, marching the army northward was out of the question, with
Sherman's corps coming up across the Big Black from that direction.
He might, of course, have tried to cut his way out south as Loring had,
leaving the 10,000 men who had been holding Vicksburg to try to
stave off the Federals until he could link up with Johnston's 10,000,
then come up behind Grant for another go at it. But Pemberton knew
that this was merely a wishful, foolish pipe dream, as engineer Lockett
said later when he suggested to his commander that the troops still had
a lot of fight and energy left in them: "He [Pemberton] replied that my
youth and hopes were parents of my judgment."

And even if that were possible—which it wasn't—it would still be in
direct disobedience of Jefferson Davis's instructions that Pemberton
should hold Vicksburg "house by house" if necessary. His only hope
at this point was that Davis would somehow manage to send a large
enough force from the east, or from Bragg's army, to defeat Grant and
lift the siege he knew was coming. On the other hand, for all Pemberton knew, Davis might have changed his mind about holding Vicksburg after the events of the past two days, but there was no way of
knowing. With the Yankee army coming up before the city Pemberton
could barely communicate with Johnston, let alone Richmond.

And there was another reason against following Johnston's orders that Pemberton surely must have contemplated. Being a Yankee himself, if he had marched his army out of the city and let the Federals have Vicksburg without a struggle, he would have been branded the biggest traitor in the South.

Still, there were many things he did do at this juncture that had a direct bearing on keeping Grant out of Vicksburg. In fact, given the short and trying circumstances, the Philadelphian had arranged a surprisingly warm welcome for his old Mexican War comrade when the Yankee army emerged on the scene.

Most important, the smoke had hardly lifted from the Big Black battlefield when Pemberton sent Lockett hurrying back to Vicksburg with orders that whatever instructions Lockett might give for development of the defense of the city were to be considered as having come from Pemberton himself. And history cannot deny that, within a matter of a few days, Lockett had used this carte blanche to improvise one of the most formidable defensive positions of the entire Civil War, which— had it not been for the Union navy's control of the Mississippi River— might have lasted indefinitely.

It will be remembered that a year earlier Lockett had been ordered by Van Dorn to begin work on the landward, or eastern, defenses of the city, and that he had used his military engineering skills to lay out a line of continuous fortifications anchored on the river about two miles south of the city and extending in a shallow arc to another river-anchored fort about two miles north of it. After a month of surveying, the plan that Lockett conceived was a kidney-shaped arc extending one to two miles beyond the city proper. His own description is illuminating.

"No greater topographical puzzle was ever presented to an engineer. The difficulty of the situation was enhanced by the fact that a large part of the hills and hollows had never been cleared of their virgin forest of magnificent magnolia-trees and dense undergrowth of cane. At first it seemed impossible to find anything like a general line of commanding ground surrounding the city; but careful study worked out the problem.

"The most prominent points I purposed to occupy with a system of redoubts, redans, lunettes and small field-works, connecting them by rifle-pits so as to give a continuous line of defense. The work began about the 1st of September with a force of negro laborers hired or impressed from the plantations of the adjacent counties."

Well and good, but events of the passing months, including torrential rainstorms, had taken their toll when Lockett found himself trying to usher the army into its new, last-ditch position. The main works were protected in front by trenches six to ten feet deep with ramparts, parapets, and banquettes for infantry and embrasures and platforms for artillery.* Not having been occupied, they were much washed and weakened by the winter's rains. The rifle pits connecting the main works had suffered in the same way, while on many parts of the line these pits had never been finished.

"All the field artillery, Parrot guns and siege pieces on the river front were moved to the rear line, platforms and embrasures being prepared for them, and ammunition was placed in convenient and protected places," Lockett said. "The field artillery brought in by our retreating army was likewise put into position as it arrived, and the morning of the 18th found us with 102 guns ready for service. Some portions of our front were protected by abatis of fallen trees and entanglements of telegraphic wire. The river batteries were still strong, having lost none of their sea-coast guns."

In the meanwhile, the Confederates employed themselves in the necessary but lamentable enterprise of home burning. "Last night," Emma Balfour wrote, "we saw a grand and awful spectacle. The darkness was lit up by burning houses all along our lines. They were burnt [so] that our firing would not be obstructed. It was sad to see. Many of them we knew to be handsome residences put up in the last few years as country residences—two of them very large and handsome houses—but the stern necessity of war has caused their destruction." One that should have been destroyed, but was not, was destined to become famous.

This was the Shirley House, an elegant white-frame manor of the Creole-cottage design. It was owned by two transplanted Yankees, James and Adeline Shirley—he from New Hampshire and she of the notable Quincy family of Boston—who were longtime residents of Vicksburg, where James was an attorney and judge. The house stood a quarter mile outside of the Rebel line, where it would provide convenient cover for the enemy, but just as a Confederate soldier

---

* The French nomenclature used in the U.S. military engineering lexicon derived mainly from the work of the famed seventeenth-century French military engineer Sébastien de Vauban, who, after conducting fifty-three successful sieges for Louis XIV, was put in charge of constructing all major fortifications for the French army. Thus nicknamed "the poacher turned gamekeeper," Vauban built dozens of forts along the French borders, most of which remained impregnable until subjected to the high-explosive gunpowder used in World War I.

approached it with a burning torch a Yankee sniper shot him. According to Adeline's daughter Alice, "The poor fellow crept away under the shelter of some planks where he died alone, where his body being found next day was buried under the corner of the house." Meantime, McPherson's men came running down the road and began shooting at the house. Adeline stuck a white flag of truce on a broomstick out the window, but when Federal soldiers entered they cared not a whit about her Yankee accent or her Boston upbringing and looted and savaged the place. Subsequently it became a Union hospital, a billeting area for Federal troops, and an observation post for Grant and his generals.

The Confederate army was put into positions from right to left, south to north, as follows: in the south was Carter Stevenson's cut-up division, John Forney's fresh troops occupied the center, and defending the northern sector was the garrison division of Major General Martin Luther Smith. John Bowen's exhausted Missourians and the Texas Legion of Colonel Thomas N. Waul were held in reserve. Thus was the Rebel army arrayed for Grant, who, as expected, was not long in coming.

Ulysses S. Grant was quite pleased with himself and rightly so. In just under three weeks he had managed to get his army across a formidable river, fought and won five battles, and finally brought the Confederate army to bay in Vicksburg, where he planned to crush them without delay. He seems not to have given much consideration to the fact that a wounded animal cornered in its own lair can often be very dangerous.

All in all, things had gone as Grant had wanted them to, except for McClernand's performance at Champion Hill, which in Grant's opinion had been dilatory. With the exception of Hovey's division, which had been operating separately to the north and attached to McPherson when the action began, the rest of McClernand's corps had remained maddeningly inert as the fighting reached its most pitiless intensity, despite Grant's orders for McClernand to attack. "Had McClernand come up with reasonable promptness," Grant reported sourly, "I cannot see how Pemberton could have escaped with any organized force." For his part, McClernand insisted that he received no orders to attack until late in the afternoon, but his inactivity at Champion Hill was yet another black mark against him in Grant's book of reckoning.

An amusing sidelight occurred during the Battle of the Big Black when a brigadier general from Banks's staff arrived with a week-old message from Halleck in Washington, ordering Grant to abandon his attack on Vicksburg and go downriver to join Banks in the defeat of

Port Hudson. Grant informed the courier that "the order came too late," and the man had just started to argue with him when General Lawler in his shirtsleeves burst out of the ditch with his troops and fell upon the Confederate line. "I mounted my horse and rode in the direction of the charge," Grant recalled long afterward, "and saw no more of the officer who delivered the dispatch; I think not even to this day."

Because the Confederates had burned their bridges behind them, it took a day to get the Union army over the Big Black on crossings improvised from planks and pontoons and even rolled logs. When they at last came up before Pemberton's final bastion, not a few Yankee veterans were dismayed by what they saw. A Rebel soldier probably described it best in suggesting that when God created the earth "he had a lot of scraps and pieces left over and dropped them down on Vicksburg."

Lockett was ingenious enough to utilize these scraps and pieces to the fullest so that, as regiment after Union regiment arrived before the city, the Rebel defenses reared up at them, forbidding as the serrated walls of a medieval castle. The approaches were all uphill and into the gaping iron maws of row upon row of enemy cannons, loaded with double-shotted grape and canister. What was more, Lockett's designs were such that most of these projecting ravine spurs and sinuous promontories gave the Rebels interlocking fire, which meant that anyone trying to take them would be exposed to getting shot in the back or side as well as in the face. A Yankee officer noted, "The approaches to this position were frightful—enough to appall the stoutest heart."

On the other hand, this was now a victorious Yankee army, Grant's army, full of fire and brimstone, and with the confident pulse of triumph coursing through it. This was felt most supremely in Sherman's corps, which had suffered such a humiliating defeat at Chickasaw Bluffs six months before. As they had had no part or share in the glory of the Union conquest at Champion Hill and the Battle of the Big Black, they now sought retribution and vindication as they once again marched on the same formidable Rebel works along the lower reaches of the Yazoo at Haines's Bluff—only this time from the landward side, the back door, so to speak.

While McPherson and McClernand were pushing toward Vicksburg along the Jackson road and the railroad tracks, respectively, Sherman's men had forced a crossing upstream on the Big Black on a makeshift pontoon bridge of India-rubber boats, and after brushing aside some nominal Rebel opposition their lead elements came in sight of the Confederate fortresses on the Yazoo.

Along the way Sherman rode into the yard of a log cabin to get a drink of water from a well where other soldiers were drinking. On the ground he saw a book and asked one of the soldiers to hand it to him. "It was a volume of the Constitution of the United States," he said later, "and on the title page was written the name of Jefferson Davis." He was further startled upon being told by one of the slaves that "the place belonged to the then President of the Southern Confederation." He learned on additional inquiry that Davis's brother Joseph had a place nearby, and that after the Yankees had looted and burned his home at Davis Bend during Farragut's expedition the previous year he had moved his belongings, including slaves—along with those of his brother Jefferson—to these places inland where he hoped they would be safe. This was soon confirmed by a member of Sherman's staff who had just returned from the elder Davis's plantation, where he had confiscated a pair of carriage horses. "He found Joe Davis at home," Sherman said, "an old man, attended by a young and affectionate niece; but they were overwhelmed by grief to see their country overrun and swarming with Federal troops."

The night that Sherman's corps crossed over the Big Black, he and Grant had sat on a log by the roadside as the troops passed by. "The whole scene was lit up with fires of pitch-pine," Sherman wrote in his memoirs, "the bridge swayed to and fro under the passing feet and made a fine war picture." Next morning, as the church bells rang in Vicksburg and the troops appeared before the city Sherman, according to Grant's recollection, "was equally anxious with myself. Our impatience led us to move in advance of the column, and well up with the advanced skirmishers." There along the Yazoo, as "the bullets of the enemy whistled by thick and fast for a short time . . . Sherman had the pleasure of looking down on the spot coveted by him the December before where his command [had] lain so helpless."

With the Confederates quickly evacuating the Haines's Bluff–Chickasaw Bluffs fortifications as per Pemberton's orders, Sherman turned to Grant in astonishment and awe and exclaimed: "Until this moment I never thought your expedition would be a success. I never could see the end clearly; but *this* is a campaign—this is a success if we never take the town."

Next day, May 19, Grant ordered an immediate assault on the Confederate works that he was convinced would bring the campaign to a decisive conclusion. It was a notion based in sound military science. An army that has just lost a battle is at its most vulnerable: baffled, disorganized, frightened, insecure. Such, Grant reasoned, was the condition of the Rebels, who had just retreated into Vicksburg. "The enemy had been much demoralized by his defeats at Champion Hill and the Big Black," Grant said later, "and I believed he would not make much effort to hold Vicksburg."

The Rebel commanders had anticipated an onslaught and were preparing to meet it. In addition to the pick and shovel, Colonel Winchester Hall of the Twenty-sixth Louisiana remembered, "I had ordered out the band, and intended to give our opponents 'Dixie' at daylight, but Brigadier General Francis Shoup, who now commanded our brigade, considered it untimely to make overtures to the enemy." Instead, every available man was told to redouble his work with the pick and the sandbag to strengthen their positions and ready all the guns for defense of the line.

At 2 p.m. that warm afternoon, all three Federal corps made a concerted charge at the Confederate line. The men undertook this almost cheerfully, believing like their commanding general that they had only to rush the Rebel works and it would all be over, the grand prize taken, the Confederate army bagged—even the end of the war. In this spirit they marched forward out of the tangled woods and thickets, shoulder to shoulder, cheering and shouting, then broke into a mad dash to sweep over the enemy fortifications and drive the Rebels back into Vicksburg, maybe right into the Mississippi River.

Just as they appeared within range of those self-same fortifications, from beneath the headlogs placed along the parapets came a withering, stabbing, continuous sheet of yellow flame and gray rolling rifle smoke the result of which, Sherman wrote, was that "the heads of columns [were] swept away as chaff thrown from the hand on a windy day." His men were shot down in clumps, and it was the same all along the six-mile-long Rebel front; bullets zinged and whizzed, raining down leaves, twigs, and small branches on the blue-clad army as it struggled through the storm of fire. Sometimes above the incessant din the audible thud of a ball striking flesh was heard, often followed by a yelp, grunt, or scream. An Illinois officer whose company was pinned down in canebrake recalled the enemy bullets neatly slicing off the stalks one at a time, so "they lopped gently upon us," until, after a while, the men were practically buried under the stalks of cane.

Many of the Federal soldiers turned and ran as the full fury of the Rebel fire made itself felt, while many others—perhaps even most—

found themselves in a horrifying predicament. They had rushed to the base of the Confederate parapets where Lockett had ordered six-foot-deep trenches dug, and there they lay trapped, unable to scale the walls of the ramparts in the face of such fire yet unable to flee without the very real probability of getting shot in the back. "These miserable men were compelled to huddle in the ditches below the fortifications for nearly five hours, until dark came and they were able to sneak away," Lockett said.

Some anxious but curious Vicksburgians had gone out to see what they could see of the battle, which was miles or more east of the city proper. These included Mary Loughborough, who was staying with family friends, and whose husband, Major James Loughborough, was on the staff of General Carter Stevenson. "They stood on every available position where a view could be obtained of the distant hills, where the jets of white smoke constantly passed out from among the trees," she told her diary. "Looking out from the back veranda, we could plainly see the smoke before the report of the gun reached us." To Mary, the rifle fire sounded "irregular," probably owing to massed volleys that the Confederates were firing as the Union soldiers charged, were repulsed, then re-formed and charged again. "[It] sounded to us, in the distance, like the quick, successive droppings of balls on sheet iron."

After a while, some of Mary's friends "suggested going for a better view up on the balcony around the cupola of the court house. The view from there was most extensive and beautiful," she wrote. "Hill after hill arose, enclosing the city in the form of a crescent." From their perspective, four stories high in the middle of town, the battle seemed to rage most ferociously in the center of the Rebel line where Stephen Dill Lee's Alabamians were tearing apart the charging Yankee columns. "What a beautiful landscape lay out before us!" Mary marveled. "Far in the distance lay the cultivated hills—some already yellow with grain, while on other hills and in the valleys the deep green of the trees formed the shadows in the fair landscape."

Down on the smoky, flashing, crashing battlefield, Colonel Hall, who had wanted to serenade the arriving Yankees with "Dixie," was watching the action of his regiment, "when I felt something strike the calf of my right leg, as though a clod had been thrown against it. In a moment I became dizzy. I sat down on a bank of earth near to me. A deathly faintness came over me."

An orderly gave Hall a drink of whiskey and he was put on a

stretcher, but because of the galling fire it was too dangerous to carry him to the rear, so he was left in a wagon rut in the road, where he was hit in the side by a spent minié ball. Hall had to lie there till after dark when it was finally safe to move him, "with bullets whistling all around us," first to a field hospital, then back to a house where his wife and children were staying.*

Near sundown it became clear that the dreaded Yankees were not going to come into Vicksburg that day. "So twilight began to fall over the scene," Mary reported in all her panoramic innocence, "hushing to an occasional report the noise and uproar of the battle field—falling softly and silently upon the river."

The fiasco cost Grant nearly 1,000 men and many of his best junior officers, but he tried to put the best face on it by ignoring the outcome and reporting that the attack "resulted in securing more advanced positions for all troops where they were fully covered from the fire of the enemy." For his part, Pemberton was admirably astonished by the ferocity of his so-called defeated army. In fact, what astounded him most was that although he had lost confidence in them and they in him, they had not lost confidence in themselves. Here, behind the ramparts, they would not have to rush around under fire, dancing to the orders of generals they did not trust and orders they did not understand. Here, behind the ramparts, they could be what they were most comfortable being—namely, a bunch of squirrel shooters, out for bigger game.

Grant could be pardoned for miscalculating the morale of the Confederate army, but now he decided to test its strength, which was another thing entirely. The day after that abortive first assault he called together his corps commanders and all agreed that the attack had failed because it had been concentrated on the strongest positions of Pemberton's defenses. This in turn had been necessary because the nature of the terrain and thickness of vegetation had made the roads that led into the city the only suitable avenues for approach, a fact that was certainly not lost on the Confederates.

Grant now determined to make a second offensive in two days' time, in hopes of finding weak spots in the enemy entrenchments. He made

---

* Hall had to listen while two surgeons debated whether to try to save his leg or saw it off. The former was decided upon, and during the operation they discovered the minié ball had split in two and shattered the tibia in a compound fracture. He kept the leg but was left with a lifelong limp.

this decision despite the military axiom that troops assaulting strong enemy fortifications should enjoy at least a three-to-one numerical superiority, while he had fewer than two to one. The assault was set for May 22 at 10 a.m., the precise moment of push-off confirmed when all three corps commanders synchronized their watches with that of their commanding general—said to be the first such occasion in warfare that this modern time-coordinating technique was used.

Next morning at dawn, the Federal artillery opened the party. Nearly two hundred guns, including some sixty pieces captured from the Confederates in the past weeks' battles, began making a shambles of the Rebel fortifications up and down the line, splintering headlogs, unseating cannons, and blasting packed-earth embrasures, overhead "bombproofs," and other field works. When Union artillery spotters with spyglasses indicated an effective hit, the Yankee gun crews would cheer and redouble their efforts at the cannons.

What is more, Admiral Porter had ordered his ironclads on the river to open fire on the city in hopes of hitting some installation, and for good measure he had several mortar boats towed into range. These began lobbing their 13-inch shells into the town, blowing buildings apart and terrifying and injuring the citizens. Lockett used the occasion to measure the depth of a crater blown out by one of these behemoths and found it to be eleven feet deep. Being on the receiving end of all this, the Confederates hugged ground—or "ate dirt"—and waited for their chance.

When the "softening up" was deemed sufficient the Federal regiments, who had watched the proceedings thus far in astonishment, now began to move forward across the half mile of no-man's-land toward the Rebel lines, banners flying, drums beating, and bayonets glistening. If anyone realized that they were being funneled into a trap, they didn't show it. A Northern newspaper reporter offered this purple account of the scene: "At exactly ten o'clock the whole Federal army was transformed into a monster serpent, which began to writhe and twist and turn and undulate . . . the earth began to shake and tremble—the curtain had gone up on the tragedy of war."

The Confederate artillery, which had so far been employed in trying to silence the Union batteries, now turned its attention to the lines of advancing bluecoats. Shot and shell tore through the ranks, opening gaping holes that quickly filled in as junior officers repeatedly ordered "close ranks." These were men who now considered themselves veteran soldiers, having fought through all the battles of the past several weeks. They had heard the cannons roar and the bullets moan and emerged victorious in every encounter. They feared not and they marched on.

As the Federals drew nearer, the Rebel officers held their lines in check. Their artillery could reach out and take a life or limb a mile or so distant, and the British-made Enfields with which most of the men were armed had an effective range of about three hundred yards. But the officers still held fire. They wanted the Yankees to come right into the hard killing zone, the area that began at half that distance, where these Southern squirrel shooters, these frustrated and embarrassed men, could take revenge for their recent humiliations. The Rebel commanders determined to wait until they could hardly miss.

Somebody on Grant's staff—and, for that matter, Grant himself—should have seen it. They had watched the enemy burning houses and chopping trees to make clear fields of fire. They had observed the ground and knew there was no way to cut through the tangled thickets or climb the often vertical-walled ravines without being shot down. They knew that the only viable approaches to the Rebel line were still along the several roads leading into the city, and that the Confederates had not been out there clearing away obstacles in order to make it easier for them to get into town. But the men still feared not and they marched on.

For their part, the Confederates had on their minds not another Cannae-like annihilation, though the Yankee army bearing down on them certainly might have seemed like the furious Romans of yore. While these southerners had neither the manpower nor the discipline of Hannibal's Carthaginians to trick and trap the enemy, they didn't need it. The plan they had in mind was as simple as organized warfare itself: build a strong enough fortification and let the enemy break himself upon it.

Sherman, whose corps held the northern end of the Union line, did not want a repeat of the disastrous pell-mell charge of the first attack three days earlier. He therefore called on 150 volunteers to go in ahead with a portable bridge to span the deep ditch the Confederates had dug below their works. These men promptly dubbed themselves the "Forlorn Hope," and before dawn they began dismantling a nearby house to get timber for the makeshift bridge. As it happened, the house was occupied by Grant and his staff, who were asleep, but when they were roused, and told what was going on, they stood by approvingly and watched the proceedings.

Just before ten the artillery barrage was lifted and the assault began to rush forward along the whole Union front. It started out dreadfully. At the appointed hour the Forlorn Hope, carrying their planks and ladders, ran down the aptly named Graveyard road toward a feature in the Confederate bastion known as the Stockade Redan. The Confederates let them come on, right through a steep cut in the road's embankment, then rose up and unleashed a murderous volley that blew away the head of the column. A few Yankees actually got to the trench, and fewer still managed to get across and struggle upon the steep sides of the salient. One of them, Private Howell G. Trogden, of the Eighth Missouri (Union), managed to plant the regimental flag near the top of the slope before sliding back into the ditch with the rest of his comrades. The Confederates defending the Stockade Redan were also Missourians—some of them actually relatives—illustrating as well as anything the fratricidal nature of the war. The Yankee flag remained planted for the rest of the day, while Rebel soldiers ignited five-second fuses on artillery shells and rolled them downhill upon those trapped in the ditch. Fifty-three of the Forlorn Hope were killed or wounded and seventy-eight were awarded the Medal of Honor.*

Similar treatment was in store for the succeeding wave of Union troops. As soon as they came within killing range, so many were shot down that the cut in the Graveyard road became clogged with the dead and dying, making it impossible to get through. When the next wave, consisting of Ohio regiments, arrived on the scene, they were so horrified by what they saw that they either fled or threw themselves down behind what little cover there was. So it went for the better part of the day. According to Sherman's report, the Rebels "rose behind their parapet and poured a furious fire upon our lines; and, for the next two hours, we had a severe and bloody battle, but at every point we were repulsed."

In the midst of all the banging and racketing and gun smoke a fourteen-year-old drummer boy with the Fifty-fifth Illinois named Orion P. Howe was sent to the rear by his regimental commander for more ammunition. As he was leaving the battlefield Sherman noticed that the boy was bleeding.

---

* Established by an act of Congress in 1862, the Medal of Honor was doled out somewhat indiscriminately during the Civil War, including more than eight hundred recipients in a single Maine regiment on the orders of Secretary Stanton. Since the early twentieth century, the medal has been reserved for acts of conspicuous personal gallantry in combat.

Sherman stopped him. "What is the matter?" he asked.

"They shot me in the leg, sir," the boy replied. Sherman told him he should get medical attention, but the boy refused and Sherman had to order him to go to the rear at once, saying that he would tend to the cartridges himself. Afterward Sherman described the incident in a letter to the secretary of war and Howe not only "became celebrated in story and song" but received an appointment to the U.S. Naval Academy at Annapolis. Because of some oversight, it wasn't until thirty-three years later, in 1896, that he was awarded the Medal of Honor.

Private William Chambers had been in the Rebel lines all morning amid the Yankee artillery barrage that shot many of his companions to pieces and the hail of minié balls that tore through flesh and bone. Some men might have gone berserk but Chambers watched Sherman's assault being hurled back and recorded, "The ground in front of our lines [was] literally blue with the dead and wounded Federals. Never before had the idea I once entertained of what a battle was like been so nearly realized as now. The spectacle of perhaps sixty or seventy thousand men *all fighting at once;* with upward of three hundred cannon belching forth their thunder, is a scene I cannot attempt to describe. In these charges the enemy reached our trenches in many places, and desperate hand-to-hand conflicts occurred. A few prisoners were taken, it was those whose trepidity carried them into our works, where they were made captive."

While this was happening, McPherson's corps, which adjoined Sherman to the left in the Confederate north-center, was received in comparable fashion. As his regiment waited for the signal to attack, Sergeant Osborn Oldroyd of the Twentieth Ohio, Logan's division, recalled that the men "were busy divesting themselves of watches, rings, pictures and their keepsakes, which were being placed in the custody of the cooks, who were not expected to get into action."

By 10 a.m. the Federals had formed three lines in front of John Forney's division and, according to Rebel captain J. H. Jones, "began a steady advance upon our works. Their lines were about one hundred yards apart. They came on as rapidly as the fallen timber would permit, and in perfect order. We waited in silence until the first line had advanced within easy rifle range, when a murderous fire was opened from the breastworks," wrote Jones, whose regiment was manning what was called the Great Redoubt. "We had a few pieces of artillery which ploughed their ranks with murderous effect. Still they came bravely on. . . . If any of the first line escaped, I did not see it."

Having witnessed the gory eradication of the first wave, the second wave of McPherson's bluecoats threw themselves into the timber the Confederates had chopped down in their front and waited for a renewal of the Federal artillery barrage that had been lifted as they neared the enemy lines. When this seemed to silence the Confederate positions, the advance was resumed, but only to be met by more of the same treatment. As it had been in Sherman's sector, those Federals who actually reached the Rebel breastworks were shot down as soon as they tried to scale them, and so died in the last ditch.

A tenacious Irish regiment from Missouri plunged forward in a cloud of horrible Celtic profanity and right into a perfect storm of Rebel canister and shot, yet somehow they managed to plant its emerald green flag with a golden harp on the slopes of the Great Redoubt. But that was as far as they got; they had needed scaling ladders at least eighteen feet tall, but the ones they'd been given were only twelve. Along with everyone else who had attained a foothold that far forward, they were compelled to huddle in the ditches below, while the Rebels entertained themselves by heaving the short-fused artillery shells on top of them. Succeeding Union soldiers who witnessed the carnage "found it was foolish to remain any longer."

In the midst of this, Dora Miller had ventured to look out of her cave in Vicksburg to a park near the battlefront where a Rebel reserve regiment was waiting for the call. "I watched the soldiers cooking on the green opposite," she said. "The half-spent [cannon] balls coming all the way from those lines were flying so thick that they were obliged to dodge at every turn."

By now the Federal attack had assumed a spontaneous, bloody momentum all its own. Next into the gristmill was McClernand's corps, opposite the south-center of the Confederate positions defended by General Carter Stevenson's veteran division. Since daybreak McClernand's artillery had pounded the Rebel works with everything it had, and at 10 a.m., with bugles blaring, the blue brigades surged forward astride the Vicksburg–Jackson railroad. Barring their way into the city was a dangerous obstacle known as the Railroad Redoubt, which towered over the tracks and was defended by a single Alabama regiment.

The man chosen to spearhead the Union charge was Michael Lawler, whose brigade of Iowans had cracked the Rebel line at the Battle of the Big Black. Once again in his shirtsleeves, the elephantine Lawler roared, "First Brigade . . . charge!" and, with this inspiration ringing in their ears, the blue wave rushed forward through a hellish gunfire, grappling and scampering their way over the abatis of felled timber until they reached the Rebel trench at the base of the redoubt. There, most of those who had not already been shot down jumped into the trench for cover, but a dozen valiant souls leaped the ditch and began clawing their way up the steep slope of the fort. Nearing the top, at the angle of the salient, they found a breach that the artillery barrage had blown out of the parapet, and these bold men quickly scrambled through it, along the way planting their regimental flag near the top. A ferocious hand-to-hand battle ensued between the Iowans and those Rebels occupying that part of the redoubt. But when Lawler's men were joined by soldiers of two Ohio and Illinois regiments, the Rebels retreated to a second defensive line within the works, where they were reinforced by the five hundred men of Waul's Texas Legion, who had been reserved for just this sort of emergency.

Across the railroad tracks another fierce contest was in progress at a feature that became known as the Second Texas Lunette, a quarter-moon-shaped work manned by the regiment it was named after. Five Yankee regiments attacked this position simultaneously with Lawler's charge on the Railroad Redoubt. As the blue line swelled to the base of the slope guarding the lunette, a Private Brooke exclaimed, "Here they come!" and the Texans rose up and opened fire, causing most of the attacking Illinoisans and Ohioans to plunge headlong into the ditch, dead or alive.

In time, however, a consensus arose within the ditch that, rather than simply cower there while bullets and lighted artillery shells rained down upon them, another attempt should be made to storm the bastion. Accordingly, a number of these men began climbing up the slope and reached the ramparts. One of these was Corporal Thomas Higgins, color-bearer of the Ninety-ninth Illinois, who, when he appeared at the rampart, was unceremoniously snatched into the fort, colors and all, by Rebel soldiers who were so incredulous that he could have survived their fire they accused him of wearing a breastplate—what today would be called a bulletproof vest. Higgins countered that if in fact he had owned such an apparatus, he would have worn it on another part of his anatomy, but a disbelieving Texas captain came up and insisted on feeling his chest, claiming "he never knew his men to fire at a man that close and miss him before."

By then a number of Yankee soldiers had boldly fought their way up to an artillery position on the parapet and, after killing all the gunners, were pouring a murderous fire through the embrasure. When it appeared as if the position might fall, the Texans' commander, Colonel Ashbel Smith, shouted, "Volunteers to clear that embrasure!" Four Rebel soldiers immediately rushed to the wall and blasted the Yankees full in the face, so that they slid back down into the ditch with their friends. Aside from some minor killing for killing's sake, here ended the extent of McClernand's original advance upon his assigned sector of the Confederate line.

And here was where the trouble lay, as it often did with McClernand. By then it was 2 p.m. and the battle had been in progress for four hours. Both Sherman and McPherson had reported to Grant that their attacks had stalled with heavy losses, but two hours earlier McClernand had sent a message to Grant that arrived as he was conferring with Sherman over what to do next. McClernand stated, "We are hotly engaged with the enemy. We have part possession of two forts, and the Stars and Stripes are floating over them. A vigorous push ought to be made all along the line."

According to Sherman, Grant handed him the note with the comment: "I don't believe a word of it."

Sherman may not have either, but he counseled Grant to take it seriously, "because the note was official, and must be credited, and I offered to renew the assault at once with new troops." Grant rode off to give similar orders to McPherson, and thus by three o'clock the fighting had broken out all over again.

The fact was that McClernand's corps did not at any time have even partial possession of anything other than the Railroad Redoubt—and that not for long. The mere sight of Federal regimental flags flying on the outer works was encouraging, but certainly no proof that those positions were occupied.

The afternoon attacks by Grant's army were even less successful than those that morning, since the Confederates had become emboldened by their successes, which is not to say, however, that the fighting was any less brutal or deadly; the whole Rebel salient had turned into a giant killing factory.

Sherman ordered two fresh brigades into the fray, which were duly cut to pieces before the rest beat a hasty retreat, while many of those in the forward echelons were forced to wait until the cover of darkness to make their escape. Among these units was the Eighth Wisconsin, which had carried into the battle its mascot, a full-grown bald eagle named Old Abe, who likely would have been reduced to a handful of feathers if Sherman had not declared early on that "this is murder; order those troops back." News that the attack would be renewed apparently wore hard on Union morale as well. One diarist in McPherson's corps noted of a heavily mauled Illinois regiment that "its officers were almost all of them drunk, their Colonel being carried off the field by 4 men in a beastly state of intoxication."

McPherson's efforts to restart the attack of XV Corps seemed half-hearted and accomplished nothing. However, one of his divisions under Brigadier General Isaac Quinby had been ordered by Grant to support McClernand's troops. But rather than use Quinby's fresh force to launch a shock attack of its own, McClernand broke it up and began sending individual units to prop up his beleaguered forward units. The result of this mismanagement was that the Confederate officers saw an opportunity to inflict further damage and suddenly, with a bloodcurdling Rebel yell, they came barreling out of their fortifications and not only chased the Yankees away from the Railroad Redoubt but routed them back almost from whence they had come.

As the Union tide slowly ebbed away from the Second Texas Lunette, the Rebel colonel Smith reported, "The loss of the enemy was enormous. The ground in our front and along the road, and either side of the road for several hundred yards way to the right, was thickly strewn with their dead. In numbers of instances two and three dead bodies were piled on each other. Along the road for more than 200 yards the bodies lay so thick that one might have walked the whole distance on them without touching the ground."

It had been a bitter day for Grant, made bitterer still by the realization that the last assault had been caused by McClernand's vainglorious duplicity. In a reckless quest for military laurels, he had overstated his true situation in order to persuade Grant to have his two other corps renew the fighting, thereby preventing the Confederates from using their reserves against him. At least that was how the thinking went among most of the senior officers of the Army of the Tennessee after darkness finally closed over the battlefield and the moans and cries of the wounded wafted up in no-man's-land. In the military, there is no greater sin than falsifying or exaggerating a report in the midst of battle.

CHAPTER SEVENTEEN

A Corpse Factory

When morning broke gray and drizzly on May 23, Grant faced sobering facts. So much blood had been spilled the day before that the ground was still soaked with it, and as many as two thousand of his soldiers still lay dead or mangled all along the Rebel front. Aside from having to eat his words about Pemberton's army being "demoralized," he was now forced to the disagreeable conclusion that, at least for the time being, Vicksburg could not be taken by storm. He therefore determined to take it by siege.

A siege is a tactic of battle as old as organized warfare, with protocols all its own that have been refined since prebiblical times. A true siege requires first that the enemy be surrounded or blockaded—the military term is "invested"—such as the Confederates were at Vicksburg, so that he can neither escape nor be reinforced nor resupplied. Next comes the process of getting at the besieged to compel his surrender. The most common method is to "reduce" his fortifications. In olden times, intriguing siege engines were employed, the most familiar being the catapult and its many variations, which worked by fulcrum or counterweight.* Because in ancient times sieges could last many months or even years, the patience of the besiegers often wore thin. In ancient China, for example,

---

* During the siege of England's Warwick Castle in the late 1300s, for instance, a diabolical apparatus known as a trebuchet was constructed just out of bow-and-arrow range of the castle. Tall as a five-story building, the device was used as a sort of giant wrecking ball to hurl enormous rocks at the fortress's three-foot-thick stone walls, ultimately breaching them. A modern replica of the thing has been known to fling a five-hundred-pound grand piano the length of a football field with astonishing accuracy.

it was common practice to catapult the bodies of plague victims into fortresses; other projectiles included severed heads, hornet hives, and wads of human excrement.

If the fortress could not be breached, the tactics of siege warfare called for an "escalade," or attack over walls, which is what Grant had tried unsuccessfully at Vicksburg. If these efforts failed, the besiegers could always resort to a trick or ruse, the most famous example of which is the Trojan horse. Undermining was also an option, in which the attackers would tunnel right up beneath the castle wall, then pull out the tunnel supports and hope that the whole structure would collapse, wall and all.

If none of those methods worked, there was always the alternative of starving out the enemy since, being surrounded, he was unable to replenish his provisions. This had its drawbacks, however, including (1) the besieging army would run out of food first and (2) a friendly army would appear on the scene to relieve the siege.

Most of these elements were in place when Grant concluded to lay siege to Vicksburg. By then, of course, artillery had replaced the catapult as the primary siege engine. Modern warfare had refined the art to include underground works, or "approaches," that would shelter the attackers from rifle and cannon fire while at the same time allowing them to employ these weapons themselves. It also masked tunneling operations in which explosives would be set off beneath the enemy fortifications.

Grant's problem at Vicksburg, however, was that no one really knew much about the conduct of sieges except what they had gleaned from reading books. Sieges had been commonplace in Europe for ages, but the Americans' only experiences had been at Yorktown during the Revolution and at Veracruz in the Mexican War, and neither was protracted.

Nevertheless, within a few weeks, Grant would have set all the textbook solutions into motion: ten Federal divisions along the entire seven miles of Confederate front, working their "mining approaches" or "parallels" forward with varying degrees of success—and not just this, either. Another tactic of siege warfare is never to give the enemy a moment's rest, in hopes of wearing down his resistance. Thus, from sunup to sundown, Sundays included, the artillery would boom and the sharpshooters would ply their grisly trade, until no head could safely appear on either side of the line without risk of being blown apart.

There were other problems. Foremost, Grant needed reinforcements. This was not only because his army had been fought to a frazzle, but also because he was well aware that Joseph Johnston was gathering a relieving army in his rear. In fact, his scouts had figured it at 30,000—an overestimation, but it was still a force to be reckoned with, especially when Grant knew that the Confederacy would send every man it could spare before allowing Vicksburg to be lost. Thus was his sense of urgency; he was working against time. Later he said that this was the reason he ordered the second wave of frontal attacks on Pemberton's positions, even after the discouraging results of May 19.

Grant could call immediately upon his own command for part of the reinforcement. He still had most of Hurlbut's 10,000-man corps back in Memphis. On May 29 he telegraphed Halleck that he had asked Banks to bring his 12,000 men to Vicksburg to join in the siege, adding, "If Banks does not come to my assistance, I must be reenforced from elsewhere."

Halleck, who by now had become aware that his orders for Grant to send his army downriver to Port Hudson to join Banks were superfluous, had already instructed Banks to get up to Vicksburg as soon as possible. During the next few days he bombarded Grant with unhappy queries such as, "Are you in communication with General Banks? Is he coming toward you or going farther off? Is there, or has there been, anything to hinder his coming directly to you by water from Alexandria?"

And again on June 2: "I have sent dispatch after dispatch to General Banks to join you. Why he does not I cannot understand."

When Grant informed Halleck, "I am in communication with [Banks]. He has Port Hudson closely invested," the commander in chief blew his stack. "His separate operation at Port Hudson is in direct violation of his instructions," Halleck wrote. "If possible, send him this dispatch."

Nathaniel Banks was in no more agreeable mood to obey Henry Halleck than Grant had been when the commanding general ordered him to abandon the Vicksburg battle and march on Port Hudson. After dallying around for nearly six months the Massachusetts politician had marched his army all the way from the swamps of the Red River to concentrate on Port Hudson, and he intended to take it. And at this point his reasons made sense. In order to collect the 20,000 men he felt he needed for the job, he'd had to strip New Orleans of troops even with the possibility that the Rebel general Dick Taylor might move in and recapture the city. Thus he wanted at least to be within striking distance of it should that occur. Furthermore, he said later, he did not like the prospect of leaving the enemy army at Port Hudson behind him if he marched on Vicksburg, lest it come up and fall upon him from the rear.

In any case, on May 19, the day before Grant's grand assault at Vicksburg, Banks's army began to invest the fortifications at Port Hudson, engaging in a number of small, vicious fights that finally drove the outnumbered Confederates into their bastion.

The Rebel general Franklin Gardner was caught off guard by the Banks excursion; in fact he'd been bounced around so many times recently he was probably beginning to feel like a billiard ball. Two weeks earlier he'd been ordered by Pemberton to strip the Port Hudson garrison and rush to Vicksburg to help meet Grant's invasion. Then, after Pemberton received urgent instructions from Jefferson Davis that both Vicksburg *and* Port Hudson must be held to the last extremity, he was ordered to return with a majority of the garrison. Then, the day after Grant's first assault at Vicksburg, Gardner received yet another order from Johnston, telling him, "Evacuate Port Hudson forthwith and move with your troops toward Jackson, to join other troops which I am uniting. Bring all your field pieces that you have, with means of transportation."

It is said that Gardner had just put Johnston's order in his coat pocket and was in the process of writing instructions to comply with it when scouts brought word that Banks was closing in.

Following the abortive attack back in March when David Farragut had attempted to run the batteries with his fleet after Banks's army failed to show up, Gardner had wisely used the time to materially reinforce Port Hudson's defenses, on both the water and the land sides. Batteries were strengthened and the engineers built new embrasures, felled trees for abatis, and cleared fields of fire in anticipation of a land attack. Like Vicksburg, Gardner's landward line was shaped in a low arc about seven miles long, anchored at both ends by the hundred-foot bluff overlooking the Mississippi. But unlike Vicksburg, where Pemberton had some 30,000 men to defend it, Gardner could count on only 5,700—1,000 of these being artillerists, which presented him with a tall order to fill. He could do so only by using his interior lines to the fullest extent possible.

During this period he was molested only by those of Farragut's warships that had failed to run the passage on March 13, but this was not without consequences. As they lay downstream and out of range of the Rebel guns, the big 13-inch Yankee mortars were especially frustrating because there was simply no place to hide from them. One soldier recalled their shells "uprooting the earth like a small volcano, and throwing out pieces of roots and other substances which had probably never seen the light of day before." That description was punctuated on the night of May 8 when one of the mortars scored a direct hit on a water battery where a soldier was standing, "driving his body through the wooden battery floor into the ground below and leaving only his feet sticking out." On the brighter side, occasionally one of the monster shells would land and explode in the Mississippi, causing hundreds of stunned fish to float to the surface, and these were gratefully gathered up by the Confederates, who would row out in skiffs before the fish could recover.

Banks's confidence was exceeded only by his lack of military education. With the Rebels at bay, he determined to defeat them with a full-scale assault on May 27. It began as a fiasco and ended the same way. The night before, Banks had called a meeting of his four division commanders: Generals Thomas W. Sherman (no relation to William Tecumseh), Christopher C. Augur, Godfrey Weitzel, and Cuvier Grover—West Point men all. In the course of this conference Banks issued an eleven-part operational order that ended: "Port Hudson must be taken tomorrow."

The order was detailed enough, describing everything from the coordination of the army artillery's fire with that from Farragut's naval guns, to storming parties to cross the eleven-foot ditch in front of the Rebel works, to the positioning of troops. In essence, Banks's concept seemed to be a mirror of Grant's operational tactics at Vicksburg, in which a massive artillery bombardment at sunup would be followed by a simultaneous assault by all four divisions.

On paper, Banks certainly enjoyed an overwhelming advantage. He had nearly a hundred pieces of artillery, plus the guns of Farragut's fleet, compared with between forty and fifty that Gardner could bring to bear. In troops as well Banks outnumbered the Confederates four to one—and they had an almost impossibly long line to defend. But somewhere between "I told him to do it" and "I ordered it done," Banks's instructions broke down, probably due to their vagueness, which left the individual commanders with the widest latitude to "if possible force the enemy's works at the earliest moment"—whatever that was supposed to mean.

·   ·   ·

When the Federal bombardment opened at dawn, the Confederates wisely took to ground. About midmorning Weitzel's division began to move against the northern part of the Rebel salient at Port Hudson. His charge began about a quarter mile from the enemy lines, in a countryside at least—if not more—cut up than that around Vicksburg. Ravines, promontories, creek beds, and swamps were densely overgrown with a forest of huge magnolia trees and tangled with vines, cane, and other underbrush. Rebel skirmishers hotly contested the ground, firing from behind trees, logs, and bushes, but fell steadily back as wave after blue wave moved forward. One Yankee described the action as "a gigantic bush-wack." Unlike the midwesterners who peopled Grant's army, most of Banks's troops had been shipped down from New England, men from Connecticut, Massachusetts, New Hampshire, Vermont, and Maine, and they suffered terribly from the Deep South summer weather.

The Rebels let them come on until they reached the clearings about two hundred yards distant from the fortifications, then let loose with an appalling combination of canister, grape, and rifle fire. Men dropped in the ranks screaming or crying out while the rest tried to pick their way forward through the tangled abatis of sharp pointed logs. Here they were met by "fearful execution" by the Rebel guns and infantry, and Weitzel's attack stalled in its tracks. General Grover's division was likewise repulsed, as was Augur's; only Thomas Sherman's command avoided the death and destruction visited on the other three.

This was because Sherman had waited all morning back at his headquarters while hundreds of his fellow Yankees were being shot down at the Rebel front. When Banks rode over to investigate Sherman's inactivity, he found the general and his staff at lunch in his mess tent. They had not even bothered to saddle their horses. It was said that Sherman had been opposed to the assault from the beginning, but Banks accused him of having "failed utterly and criminally to bring his men into the field." Sherman's position was that he had understood he would be notified when it was his turn to attack, but in any case it became one of the strangest performances in the war.

Finally at about 2 p.m., having been ordered personally by Banks to "carry the works at all hazards," Sherman saddled up and led his division against the Confederate center, along with those elements of Augur's division that had not yet been committed. Their fate was pathetically similar to that which had befallen Weitzel and Grover. As soon as the Federals reached the obstructive abatis several hundred yards out, the Rebels let free with a lethal fire. Sherman was among the first to be hit when a large ball of grapeshot tore through his leg, crushing the bones. The same blast killed his horse and two of his staff officers and wounded another. Sherman was carried from the field crying, "Lead them ahead, straight ahead." He lost the leg, his division was repulsed with heavy loss, and Augur's men likewise fled in terror and disorder—an altogether unsatisfactory conclusion to an otherwise unhappy day.

Meantime, Banks was desperately trying to snatch some kind of victory out of this heap of failures. Late in the afternoon, as the battle alternately raged and sputtered all along the Rebel front, Banks committed two Louisiana regiments, the First and Third Native Guards. Of itself, this might have sounded somewhat unusual—for Louisianans to be fighting in the Yankee army—but these Louisianans happened not only to be black men but were the first ever committed to an attack thus far in the war.

In the summer of 1862 Congress had made provisions for Negroes, or "Coloreds," to be enlisted in the army, but it wasn't until after the Emancipation Proclamation that any major organizing efforts were undertaken. It will be remembered that in the spring of 1862, when Grant was under a cloud of disapproval, Secretary of War Stanton sent two spies to Vicksburg to watch him. One of them, Charles Dana, arrived under the guise of a pay inspector, but the other, the army's adjutant general, Lorenzo Thomas, did not show up at all.

That was because when he reached Memphis Thomas became so enamored by the possibilities of recruiting former slaves that he devoted all of his time to the project and forgot about Grant entirely. Up and down the river Thomas traveled, setting up camps for the recruitment of blacks, developing programs whereby white noncommissioned officers could receive commissions for serving in black regiments, and issuing stern warnings to senior officers who might be prejudiced against the notion of employing blacks in the fighting arm of the forces. One of those in opposition was Tecumseh Sherman, who, when asked "whether a Negro couldn't stop a bullet as well as a white man," replied, "Yes, but a sandbag is just as good." Likewise, while Grant was still stuck on the Louisiana side of the river, Stanton had had to prod him to cooperate in the raising and maintenance of black troops.

Yet more than a year earlier, down in New Orleans, Benjamin Butler had taken it upon himself to raise a Corps d'Afrique from the city's substantial population of "Free Men of Color," who had been a feature of New Orleans for more than fifty years. They consisted of descendants of slaves who had been either freed by their masters or bought their way to freedom, but a great many others were the descendants of former slaves in Haiti who had fled to New Orleans during the great slave rebellion there in the early part of the century. Many of the black enlistees were educated, held property, and were skilled as artisans. These men became the First Louisiana Native Guards and, with the exception of their colonel, they were officered by blacks.

By contrast, the Third Louisiana Native Guards was composed mostly of recently freed slaves and was officered by whites. Together they numbered 1,080 men.

Although many blacks were being taken into the army at that point, they were generally used as teamsters, cooks, laborers, or for other menial tasks, the theory being that they could not be relied upon to fight well in battle. Some months earlier a black detachment had acquitted itself well in defending a post in Kansas, but the skeptics contended that blacks would not stand up exposed to the concentrated enemy fire of a battle charge.

All this did not sit well with the black soldiers, whose pay, equipment, and overall treatment were inferior to that of white troops. Furthermore, most of them had done menial work all their lives and were eager to show their mettle. This was all the more remarkable since official Confederate policy was to treat blacks captured in battle as nothing more than runaway slaves, and to dispose of them accordingly. Unsettling rumors abounded that Confederate soldiers executed blacks taken prisoner, and in horrifying ways at that.

In fact, there were already notions afoot in the South to arm slaves and enlist them into the Confederate army in exchange for their freedom once the war was over. If this could be done promptly and successfully, it was argued, the imbalance of manpower might suddenly be tipped in favor of the South. A leading proponent of this was the Rebel general Patrick Ronayne Cleburne, perhaps the most respected division commander in the western theater. In a lengthy confidential memorandum circulated among high-ranking officers in the Army of Tennessee, Cleburne argued in his lawyer-like manner that arming the slaves was a question of chilling mathematical logic; that even if Confederates killed Yankees by two to one, at the rate things were going they would still run out of soldiers before the war was done. Speaking from the height of personal experience as an Irishman, Cleburne maintained that it was far better for southerners to lose their slaves than to be subjugated by the North. He also contended that such a policy would immediately nullify Lincoln's Emancipation Proclamation, eliminate the Yankee cause of fighting to free the slaves, and quite possibly bring England and France to the side of the Confederacy.

His presentation was greeted at first with silence, then by outbursts of indignation and outrage from several generals who denounced the idea as "monstrous" and "revolting." Some agreed with him, while others were noncommittal, and some months later, when Jefferson Davis got wind of the proposal, Cleburne was ordered to suppress his document and all opinions about it, on grounds that it was too controversial and would lead to dissension in the South. There the matter rested, at least for the time being.

The anxious soldiers of the two black Louisiana regiments checked their muskets, fastened their bayonets, straightened their lines, and prepared to receive their baptism of fire. However, "they had hardly done so," a Federal officer reported, "when the extreme left of the Confederate line opened up on them, and forced them to abandon the attempt with great loss."

They were opposed by about three hundred Confederates of the Thirty-ninth Mississippi, commanded by Colonel William B. Shelby. These hardened men had fought Weitzel's division from morning to afternoon and now had confidence in themselves, as well as the range of the enemy. When the First and Third regiments got within two hundred yards of the Rebel line all hell broke loose. Earlier, Shelby had called on the gun captain of one of the river batteries to provide support with their big siege cannons, which he did most effectively, having preregistered them for just such a purpose. Then Shelby opened fire with three field guns of his own, loaded with grape, canister, and spherical shot that tore into the ranks of the helpless blacks. When the rifle fire of the infantry was added to this, the blue formation broke and fled in spectacular confusion.

Not that anyone could have blamed them, for in those few short minutes the two regiments suffered some 20 percent casualties, which, if nothing else, proved that they were just as brave and just as smart as their white comrades who had earlier departed the field in the same fashion. The Northern press, however, used the occasion to fictionalize the affair for the benefit of its readership, depicting the black soldiers as having scaled the Confederate ramparts and planted their flag there, and being driven off only after a hand-to-hand struggle against overwhelming numbers.

In the end Banks's adjuration that "Port Hudson must be taken tomorrow" fell flat and tragic and—with the loss of 2,000 men to the Confederates' 275—like Grant up at Vicksburg he settled down for a siege. Asked by a newspaper reporter to explain why he had ordered the assault in the first place, Banks gave this impolitic reply: "The people of the north demand blood, sir."

At Vicksburg, the residents were at last getting a taste of hard war. The city's hospitals had long since overflowed with the wounded from the battles at Champion Hill and the Big Black. Military hospitals had also been set up in tents around the town and when these began filling up convalescents were billeted in private homes. As the city's cemetery now lay outside the Confederate lines, the dead had to be disposed of within the confines of the city. The influx of some 30,000 soldiers put an almost unimaginable strain on Vicksburg, which had housed only 4,500 residents before the war. Drinking water became a problem and sanitation a major concern. Food that had been scarce and pricey before the siege now soared in value, when it could be had at all.

Dora Miller, who often remained in her house, watching from the balcony, remembered that "at all those caves I could see from my high perch, people were sitting, eating their poor suppers, at the cave doors, ready to plunge in again. As the first shell flew they dived, and not a human being was visible."

Vicksburg was completely blocked in, and all the produce, grain, and livestock of the rich Yazoo delta were now shut off. If some piece of machinery broke, there was no longer a steamboat or railroad to bring replacement parts; whatever it was stayed broke. Communications—telegraph and mail—were likewise cut off for the duration. Emma Balfour told her diary, "Last night Mrs. Higgins and myself [sat] up until after eleven o'clock making cartridges. We get no help from the outside world now, and have to help ourselves."

Yet all that was mere inconvenience compared with the reign of terror that now descended from the skies on an hourly basis. From the river, Porter's mortar boats kept up a regular bombardment of the city's environs, while from landward Grant's artillery relentlessly threw barrages of shells into the town. The shocking part of it was that much of the naval firing was deliberately aimed at the civilians. Since the frontline trenches were up to two miles from the city, Porter's ships, throwing their 250-pound shells "as big as a full grown hog," were out of range. About the most they could hope for by way of a military target was a chance hit one of the Confederate river batteries, while the rest of the shells simply exploded within the city itself.

Likewise, from Grant's infantry lines in the east, the aim of his guns was theoretically at the top of the Confederate fortifications—their ramparts—where the most damage would be done. But any shell that overshot that point would also invariably land inside the city proper, and most did.

The ultimate discomfort of the Vicksburgians began upon the arrival of Grant's army on the outskirts of town. During the earlier naval bombardment by Farragut a few citizens had excavated caves in the many hills or cuts that formed the area's topography. Lucky they were, too, that the ground upon which Vicksburg lay was composed of a deep silty soil known as loess, which was not only easy to work with but normally firm enough to tunnel into without requiring elaborate timber frames and bracings.

The initial cave shelters were built by either slaves or hired black workmen and were fairly simple affairs, usually dug into an earthen facing such as a road or hillside that was near the home of the cave's occupant, and more or less used as an incidental bomb shelter where a family could huddle when the Yankee navy started throwing shells.

With this new situation, however, the caves began to take on an entirely new dimension. Where before they had merely been scooped-out holes that workers charged about twenty dollars to dig, they now assumed the character of complex engineering projects, housing large families and even multiple families, along with their servants, and could cost as much as a hundred dollars, but were a bargain at any price. A few of the caves were built to hold a hundred persons or more. It was soon discovered to everyone's horror—something most cave-dwelling animals already knew—that a single access point could prove fatal to everyone inside if a shell landed nearby, and alternative escape routes were therefore constructed. Most large caves had arched ceilings and were configured with a kind of "great room" just inside the entrance, with arms branching off for sleeping areas for men and women, partitioned with blankets.

Soon the occupants began dragging in their furnishings to make the caves more comfortable—Persian rugs were laid over bare dirt floors, sofas, easy chairs, beds and bedding, lamps, and tables were arranged around the rooms. Cooking stoves and other kitchen implements were brought in. Paintings, mirrors, even tapestries were hung on the dirt walls. There was a practical aspect to this, too, since so many homes were smashed up by the Federal bombardment that their furnishings most likely would have been ruined anyway. One woman wrote, with no apparent irony, that Vicksburg "was so honeycombed with caves that the streets look like avenues in a cemetery."

Among the new cave dwellers was Emma Balfour, who had spurned the notion until the danger from mortar fire revealed itself. She and her physician husband had become quite friendly with the Rebel general Stephen Dill, a frequent visitor to their home. During Grant's big assault she wrote in her diary, "We have provided ourselves with a cave, as Gen. Lee says there will be no safety elsewhere. Our entrenchments are from a mile and a half to three miles from town, varying with the nature of the country. Of course shells and balls from these will reach any part of town, and the gunboats from the other side can throw to & beyond our entrenchments in many places. When the Gen. asked me if we were provided with a rat-hole, I told him it seemed to me we were all caught in a rat-hole."

The bombardment put a terrific strain on the citizenry, now reduced to the bare, anxious life of some long-forgotten tribe of cliff dwellers. Most maddening was its sheer relentlessness. In accordance with Grant's policy and the dictates of siege warfare, the Federal artillery—some two hundred guns strong—fired regularly at the Rebel positions as long as they were visible, which meant from sunup to sundown, and intermittently after dark. The mortar boats, firing high-trajectory ammunition, had no such restriction because they had preregistered and so could—and would—fire all through the night. The results were, of course, earthshaking, and the people in their caves and tunnels lived in constant dread of being buried alive. Newly-wed Dora Miller, who, along with her husband, was a secret Union sympathizer, wrote in her diary, "We are utterly cut off from the world, surrounded by a circle of fire. Would it be wise like the scorpion to sting ourselves to death?"

Lucy McRae Bell, daughter of the sheriff, was only thirteen or fourteen when she lay down to sleep one night in the cave her parents shared with eight other prominent Vicksburg families, comprising at times some sixty people. "The mortars were sending over their shells hot and heavy," she recalled afterward. "They seemed to have range of the hill, due, it was said, to some fires that a few soldiers had made on a hill beyond us. Everybody in the cave seemed to be alarmed and excited, when suddenly a shell came down on the top of the hill and exploded. This caused a large piece of earth to slide from the side of the archway in a solid piece, catching me under it. Dr. Lord [an Episcopal priest] whose leg was caught and held by it gave the alarm that a child was buried. Mother reached me first, and a Mrs. Stiles, who was partially paralyzed, with the assistance of Dr. Lord, succeeded in getting my head out first.

"The people had become frightened, rushing into the street screaming and thinking that the cave was falling in. Just as they reached the street, over came another shell bursting just above them, and they rushed into the cave again." When Lucy was finally pulled free, "The blood was gushing from my nose, eyes, ears and mouth," she said, but no bones had been broken. "Just here I must say," Lucy concluded in an interview published in 1912, "that during all this excitement there was a little baby boy born in the room dug out at the back of the cave; he was called William Siege Green."

Others were not so lucky. "One afternoon, amid the rush and explosion of the shells, cries and screams arose—the screams of women amid the shrieks of the falling shells," recalled one of the cave dwellers. Upon investigation, "it was found that a negro man had been buried alive within a cave, he being alone at the time. Workmen were instantly sent to deliver him, but when found, the unfortunate man had been dead some little time."

And again: "I was told that a mother had taken a child into a cave about a hundred yards from us, and . . . laid it on its little bed. A mortar shell came rushing through the air and fell with much force, entering the earth above the sleeping child—cutting through into the cave . . . crushing in the upper part of the little sleeping head and taking away the young innocent life without a look or word of passing love to be treasured in the mother's heart. I sat near the square of moonlight, silent and sorrowful, hearing the sobs and cries of a mother for her dead child."

"We were safe at least from shell fragments," Mary Loughborough told her diary, "though no one seemed to think our cave any protection should a mortar round fall on top of the ground above us. We had our roof arched and braced, the supports of the bracing taking up much room in our confined quarters. The earth was about five feet thick above, and seemed hard and compact; yet poor M [Major James Loughborough, her husband], every time he came in, examined it, fearing, amid some of the shocks it sustained, that it might crack and fall upon us."

One day, Mary continued, "a young girl, becoming weary in the confinement of the cave, hastily ran to the house in the interval that elapsed between the slowly falling shells. On returning, an explosion sounded near her—one wild scream, and she ran into her mother's presence, sinking like a wounded dove, the life blood flowing over the light summer dress in crimson ripples from a death-wound in her side, caused by a shell fragment."

When someone asked Mary how she had stood it all, her reply was straight and stark: "After one is accustomed to [it] we do not mind it; but becoming accustomed, that is the trial."

As sieges go, the one at Vicksburg wasn't especially uncomfortable for the Yankee army. So much of modern warfare seems to be fought in steaming jungles, parched deserts, freezing mountains, or the trackless wastes of the Seven Seas that Vicksburg seems almost benign. Here is Charles Dana on the subject. "We were in an incomparable position for a siege as regard the health and comfort of our men," he wrote. "The high wooded hills afforded pure air and shade, and the deep ravines abounded in springs of excellent water, and if they failed it was easy to bring it from the Mississippi. Our line of supplies was beyond the reach of the enemy, and there was an abundance of fruit all about us. I frequently met soldiers coming into camp with buckets full of mulberries, blackberries and red and yellow wild plums."

Well and good so far as it went, but on the immediate hand an obnoxious problem remained from the assaults of May 22—the hundreds of Union dead that still lay baking and bloated in no-man's-land, posing problems of sanitation and morale. Likewise were the "fearful agonies" of the wounded who had also fallen between the lines and were a pitiable thing to listen to, though they grew less frequent each day. A few Rebel soldiers had ventured out at night to bring them water or assist them in some way, but by and large these helpless, wretched people remained untended. Some of the Confederate brigade and division commanders had sent notes to their counterparts across the way suggesting a truce to bury the dead and carry off the wounded, but to no avail. Pemberton himself finally dispatched a note to Grant saying that if the Yankees did not want to perform the disagreeable duty, his soldiers would do it for them, but Grant refused on grounds that it might be interpreted as a sign of weakness on his part.

The disgusted Confederates claimed that the Yankees, having been unable to fight them out of their positions, were now trying to "stink" them out. However, when Federal soldiers also began to complain of the smell and Grant's medical staff told him there might be health and sanitation consequences—cholera notable among them—he relented and the truce was set for 6 p.m., on Monday, May 25. Not having been informed of the agreement, some Yankee soldiers cheered when they saw white flags go up. "It made us happy," recalled Sergeant Oldroyd, "for we fancied it a sign they wanted to surrender—but no such good luck."

During the next two hours the men of both armies came out from their lines and began to mix and mingle. Some played cards, some tried to barter, but the Confederate soldiers had little to offer except tobacco or the occasional war souvenir that they exchanged for Yankee coffee, fat meat, and hardtack. A number had written letters that they asked to be delivered to friends or loved ones on the other side. Some merely engaged in fraternal conversation, occasionally involving opinions on the causes of the war and predictions of its outcome. In a few instances, especially with the Missouri regiments on both sides, there were poignant reunions.

In the southernmost sector a Union general approached the Rebel general Stephen Lee and asked if he would have a drink with him. Lee declined. Trying to make conversation, the Yankee remarked, "Your lines look very strong."

"I think I can hold them," Lee replied.

Still wishing to create a more fraternal atmosphere, the Federal officer began apologizing that the navy's mortar boats had continued to fire into Vicksburg during the truce, insisting that it was "a misunderstanding."

Lee knew this was not so, since the Yankees had a signaling station between Grant and the fleet, whose messages in fact the Confederates had been reading on a regular basis.

The firing was "of no consequence," Lee told the Federal general, since "there was no one in the city but the women and children and the sick and they were accustomed to it."

At the same time, officers of both armies had entered into the no-man's-land in hopes of gathering intelligence on the enemy's dispositions. Samuel Lockett, the Confederate engineer, had been standing on the parapet of the Stockade Redan, examining a Yankee zigzag trench that was being constructed, when a blue-clad orderly approached and told him that General Sherman wished to speak with him. When Lockett found Sherman a couple of hundred yards out in no-man's-land, the Federal commander introduced himself by saying, "I saw that you were an officer by your insignia of rank," and indicating that he had with him "some letters entrusted to me by Northern friends of some of your officers and men. I thought this would be a good opportunity to deliver this mail before it got too old." To which Lockett replied, "Yes, General, it would have been very old indeed if you had kept it until you brought it into Vicksburg yourself." Sherman's response to this impertinence seemed good-natured enough. "So," he asked the Rebel major, "you think then I am a very slow mail route?"

When Lockett replied that indeed he did, considering that the Yankee army seemed to have no other choice than burrowing its way into Vicksburg, Sherman answered, "Yes, that is a very slow way of getting into a place, but it is a very sure way, and I was determined to deliver those letters sooner or later." After this preliminary patter, Sherman invited Lockett to have a seat on a log, where "the rest of the truce was spent in pleasant conversation"—so much so that as Lockett later admitted, "His civility certainly prevented me from seeing many other points in our front that I as chief engineer was very anxious to examine." For his part, Sherman had gotten close enough to the Rebel lines that he was able to write in his memoirs, "I have since seen the position at Sevastopol, and without hesitation I can declare that at Vicksburg to have been the most difficult of the two."*

At 8 p.m. bugles on both sides began to blow and officers started calling the men back to their respective sides. It is a wonder what would have happened if, all at once, everyone had disobeyed them, but in any case they did not, and within moments of the appointed ending of the truce sharpshooters returned to their distasteful work, and the zip and zing of bullets filled the air across the battlefield until the last rays of the sun.

After that, the siege of Vicksburg settled into a relentless kind of monotony of killing, since there wasn't much else to do until either the Confederates were starved out or the Yankee tunneling crews bored close enough to blow breaches in the Rebel fortifications—or, in the

* The yearlong siege at Sevastopol, a Russian port on the Black Sea, was a feature of the Crimean War, which took place a decade before the American Civil War. There, a combined British-French army attacked strong Russian positions, and before emerging victorious in 1855, nearly 70,000 men were lost. The war had started as a dispute over who controlled Palestine and Jerusalem—the Holy Land.

alternative, Joseph Johnston collected enough of an army to launch a successful attack on Grant's rear and ruin his whole enterprise.

Records indicate that about 4,500 Confederates and 550 Federal soldiers were killed or maimed during this period, the overall effect of which was to turn Vicksburg into a great corpse factory that, if nothing else, kept coffin makers busy. Federal troops in the front lines began constructing a maze of trenches with parapets and firing steps from which rows of sharpshooters kept up a constant barrage from sunup to sundown. The Rebels of course had their own version of this. For some on both sides it was a betting game—and sometimes just for laughs—to place a hat on a stick and raise it a few inches above a parapet to see how long it took for an enemy bullet to strike it.

Osborne Oldroyd recorded that the men of his company affixed an army coat with a hat on top to a T-branched stick and elevated it above their trench. "In an instant they were riddled with bullets from the enemy," he reported. A good example of this occurred on June 17, when Brigadier General Isham W. Garrott, infuriated by the sniping at his men, grabbed a rifle from a soldier in the Twentieth Alabama and raised up to fire at a Federal sharpshooter. A Yankee bullet hit him in the heart, killing him instantly. Likewise was the fate of the popular old Brigadier General Martin E. Green of Bowen's division, who was shot in the head and killed on June 27 as he peered over the parapet at a Federal trench being dug some sixty yards away.

The men soon found there wasn't much safety behind the lines either. One morning some Confederates of the First Missouri were sitting around a fire eating boiled rice "when John Harper's spoon was struck while just in the act of putting it into his mouth, by a small piece of shell, which tore a hole in the spoon and spattered the rice all over his face." An officer noted that the soldier remarked (a century before it was "cool" to say so), "That was cool," and continued to finish his breakfast.

As the days wore on and more and more men were struck down in this way, engineers for both sides worked feverishly to correct the problem, building deeper traverses and often covering the trenches with logs. Still, with that many men involved, some—out of carelessness if nothing else—were invariably bound to expose themselves for some brief moment, during which they were subject to sudden death. This was not universally true, however. Over time, in some sectors of the line, a sort of live-and-let-live attitude developed, despite official orders to the contrary, while in others the killing was continuous.* Perhaps it had to do with the very proximity of the armies, which at some points lay as little as fifty yards apart. The men of both sides frequently heard their enemies laughing—or cursing— and smelled their cooking across the no-man's-land. Often at night regimental bands on both sides of the line would play familiar tunes, and singing groups regularly serenaded with sentimental favorites. Compared with the impersonality of sharpshooters' bullets and cannon shots, this lent a strange intimacy to the war.

Then there was the incessant artillery fire, pulverizing the Confederate defenses almost as fast as they could be rebuilt. During these bombardments, Rebel soldiers took refuge in bombproofs or traverses just behind the lines but had to work all night filling sandbags, shoveling dirt, or wrestling timbers to keep their fortifications viable. This of course had a wearing effect as well, for the men were tired all the time from lack of sleep and poor rations, even at the beginning of the siege. By now, the men on both sides—and the citizens of Vicksburg as well—had accustomed themselves to the strange and mournful music of the battlefield. Most of the soldiers already knew the bone-shivering whine of the minié ball, but now they were able to tell the difference between the whooshes, chugs, screeches, or screams emitted by various sizes and calibers of artillery pieces—the "bang" of rifled Parrots, the "crack" of Whitworth guns, the "boom" of 6-pounders and 12-pounders, and the expletive-producing "railroad-train whirr" of one of Grant's big siege guns. Many of the Federal shells were timed to explode right above the Confederate positions, where even the comfort of a trench did not ensure safety. Often men were found dead who had not been visibly marked; the mere concussion produced by a nearby artillery round was sometimes enough to stop a human heart.

Of course if the gun was aimed too high the shells sailed over the Rebel lines and landed in the city, making life miserable there, too. For its part, the Confederate artillery offered little answer to the Union guns, since ammunition was low and Pemberton had ordered it conserved for Grant's next assault, which was anticipated daily. A Rebel

---

* This was particularly true in the northern sector of the line, where Confederate troops had suddenly received 10,000 British Enfield rifles, brand-new in their packing cases. Before the siege had cut the city off, they had been destined for shipment to the trans-Mississippi. The Rebels discarded their dated and worn-out Mississippi muskets for these modern weapons and took delight in trying them out on their foes across the way.

captain complained that if his battery wanted to fire at the enemy, "You almost had to put the reasons for it in writing."

It was during this period that Grant had another encounter with the bottle, which he seemed wont to do when there was leisure time at hand. It began on June 5 when his chief of staff, Rawlins, began to notice a change in his behavior. After some snooping, he discovered that Grant had been drinking wine with one of the surgeons, and then he discovered an entire case of wine outside the general's tent. Grant objected when Rawlins had it taken away, claiming it was there only in order to toast the Union army when Vicksburg fell, but that night the aide wrote his boss a stern letter that began: "The great solicitude I feel for the safety of this army leads me to mention, what I had hoped never again to do, the subject of your drinking." Rawlins, who was a lawyer, laid out his case as in an opening and a closing argument, beginning with a list of particulars such as his discovery of an empty wine bottle in Grant's quarters, his association with prominent drinkers on his staff, and "lack of your usual promptness and decision, and clearness in expressing yourself in writing."

Then Rawlins dropped the anvil. Unless Grant promised never to touch "a single drop of any kind of liquor," he would ask to be relieved of further duty under him. Unfortunately, when Rawlins went to deliver the letter the next morning, he found that Grant had taken off on a steamboat for a trip up the Yazoo River to Satartia, where it was rumored Johnston was gathering his army to relieve Pemberton at Vicksburg. The trip turned out to be a two-day binge.

Charles Dana had gone along with Grant and his escort, consisting of a small troop of cavalry. On the way upriver Grant spied another boat, the *Diligence,* coming down and, being friends with its captain, decided to transfer to it and send it back upriver again. As luck would have it, aboard the *Diligence* was the ubiquitous newspaperman Cadwallader, who had just concluded his own visit to Satartia, where he had found the rumors of Johnston's activity near there to be false.

"I was not long in perceiving that Grant had been drinking heavily, and that he was still keeping it up," Cadwallader wrote many years later, long after Grant was dead. "He made several trips to the bar room of the boat in a short time, and became stupid in speech and staggering in gait. This was the first time he had shown symptoms of intoxication in my presence, and I was greatly alarmed by his condition, which was fast becoming worse."

The only member of Grant's staff who was present was a young lieutenant, and when Cadwallader asked him to somehow get the general into his stateroom the aide demurred. He then went to the boat's captain and asked him to intervene or, at the least, not to allow Grant to be served any more liquor. But the captain likewise refused on grounds that Grant "was the department commander with full power to do what he pleased."

At this point Cadwallader said he threatened to report the captain to Rawlins, who he said would have him "sent out of the department in chains." This finally got the barroom closed and the key to the liquor cabinet "lost in a safe place."

Cadwallader then "enticed" Grant into his stateroom, locked the both of them inside it, "and commenced throwing bottles of whiskey which stood on the table, through the windows into the river." At this, Grant became angry and ordered Cadwallader to leave, but the correspondent "firmly, but good-naturedly declined to obey.

"I said to him that I was the best friend he had in the Army of Tennessee; that I was doing for him what I hoped someone would do for me should I ever [be in] his condition." After a while Grant seemed to settle down and "as it was a very hot day and the stateroom almost suffocating," Cadwallader talked him into taking off his coat, vest, and boots and got him to lie down in his berth, where the reporter "soon fanned him to sleep."

That might have been the end of it but, according to Cadwallader's account, "before he [Grant] had recovered from his stupor we had reached Satartia, when another source of trouble arose." Not far from Satartia, while it was still light, Grant's vessel encountered two naval gunboats, and a navy officer came aboard to warn that the town was not safe; that the Union forces there had retreated and that "the enemy is probably in the town now."

But Grant, apparently still drunk, "was determined to dress and go ashore," Cadwallader said, and ordered his cavalry escort commander to take the horses off the boat and accompany him. By this time it was dark, and all the more dangerous, and the escort officer was in a serious quandary; to take the commanding general of the army ashore under those conditions was foolhardy but, in Cadwallader's words, "to disobey would lead to—he knew not what."

Dana, who was also on board, and who must have been aware of the situation, put it a good deal more tactfully in his memoirs, stating that "Grant was ill and went to bed soon after we had started," adding,

"When I knocked at his door when they reached Satartia to ask whether he still wanted to go ashore, the general was too sick to decide and replied, 'I will leave it with you.' " Dana said he immediately ordered the boat to return to Haines's Bluff, where, next morning, the commanding general was "duly sober" by Cadwallader's recollection, while Dana's account says that "Grant came out to breakfast fresh as a rose, clean shirt and all, quite himself."

"Well, Mr. Dana," Grant said, "I suppose we are at Satartia now." To which Dana replied, "No, General, we are at Haines's Bluff."

At that point Dana departed from the group, but Cadwallader remained with the boat at Haines's Bluff only to become "almost thunderstruck at finding an hour afterward that Grant had procured another supply of whisky from on shore and was quite as much intoxicated as the day before." The reporter again managed to get the drunken general into his cabin, but not before Grant ordered the captain to proceed to Chickasaw Bayou, farther down the Yazoo.

If, however, they had started then, Cadwallader explained, Grant would have arrived at the bayou in midafternoon, when the place would be "filled with officers, men and trains from all parts of the army. To be seen in his present condition would lead to utter disgrace and ruin," the journalist said, so he conspired with the boat's captain to fabricate a story about not being able to get up steam. After a couple of hours had passed, "Grant's impatience at last threatened to burst all restraints," and the captain was forced to get under way. However, a further conspiracy between Cadwallader and the captain landed them on a sandbar, so that they did not reach Chickasaw Bayou until sundown. There, as bad luck would have it, they were told to tie up "next to a steamboat used by 'Wash' Graham, as a headquarters sutler boat," which "kept open house to all officers and dispensed free liquors and cigars generously."

His darkest fears now aroused, Cadwallader climbed over the rail, buttonholed Graham, and "cautioned him against allowing Grant to have any liquor," receiving in return the solemn promise of the sutler that "the General should not have a drop of anything intoxicating on his boat." By the time he returned to the *Diligence,* however, to Cadwallader's mortification, "the general could not be found.

"Suspecting that he had gone aboard Graham's boat," Cadwallader continued, "I went to its office on the bow, but no one had seen Grant." However, after following "a hum of conversation and laughter proceeding from a room opening out of the ladies' cabin," he nudged his way through a crowd of officers only to find "Wash" Graham wreathed with cigar smoke in front of a table "covered with bottled whisky and baskets of champagne, and Grant in the act of swallowing a glass of whisky. I was thoroughly indignant," the reporter said, "and may have shown rather scant ceremony in saying to him that the escort was waiting and that it would be long after dark before we could reach headquarters. He was not very well pleased by my interruption."

A playwright composing slapstick could hardly have come up with a better script, and it gets better. When Cadwallader finally got Grant off the sutler's boat to join the cavalry escort back to army headquarters, it turned out that the horse Grant had brought along for his own use was a creature known as Kangaroo, which he had borrowed from another officer and which had gotten its name "from his habit of rearing on his hind-feet and making a plunging start whenever mounted."

The drunken Grant gave Kangaroo the spur the moment he got on "and the horse darted away before anyone was ready to follow," Cadwallader said. "The road was crooked and tortuous . . . between sloughs and bayous. Each bridge had one or more guards stationed to prevent fast riding or driving over it; but Grant paid no attention to roads or sentries. He literally tore through everything in his way. The air was full of dust, ashes and embers from camp-fires, and shouts and curses from those he rode down in his race."

By the time Cadwallader and the escort had time to mount, Grant "was out of sight in the gloaming," but at least he had escaped impalement from bayonets or being shot down by the road guards. When Cadwallader finally caught up with him, Kangaroo had slowed to a walk, and Grant was "reeling in the saddle." After some minor unpleasantries the reporter got Kangaroo's reins away from the general and led the horse off the road to a clearing, where he helped Grant dismount; then he unsaddled the horse and put the saddle down for a pillow. "He was soon asleep," Cadwallader wrote.

Leaving Grant, the reporter then went looking for the cavalrymen, whom he found "spread out over the bottom for half a mile circling about searching for the general, fully expecting to find him lifeless." Cadwallader hailed one of the men and told him to "proceed directly to headquarters and report at once to Rawlins—and to no one else—and say to him that I want an ambulance and a careful driver, sent to me immediately."

It was totally dark when Cadwallader returned to the clearing where Grant slept, noting that if some "bummer or straggler" should appear, he was fully prepared "to cut off [Grant's] shoulder straps [his insignia of rank] instantly." Before the ambulance came, however, Grant awakened and began to insist on riding Kangaroo back to headquarters. Instead, the journalist "took him by the arm, walked him back and forth, and kept up a lively rather one-sided conversation, till the ambulance arrived."

As if he had not been enough of a trial already, Grant then refused to get into the ambulance and persisted in wanting to ride Kangaroo. He relented only after Cadwallader agreed to ride in the ambulance with him, with their two horses led by an orderly from the cavalry escort.

It was after midnight, the journalist said, when they reached camp, where the furious Rawlins and another staff officer, Colonel John Riggin, were "waiting for us in the driveway." Cadwallader got out first, followed promptly by Grant. "He shrugged his shoulders, pulled down his vest, 'shook himself together' as one just rising from a nap, and seeing Rawlins and Riggin, bid them good-night in a natural tone and manner, and started to his tent as steadily as he ever walked in his life.

"My surprise," Cadwallader recalled, "amounted to stupefaction. I turned to Rawlins and said I was afraid that he would think I was the man who had been drunk. But he replied in suppressed tones through his clinched teeth: 'No, no. I know him. I want you to tell me the exact facts—and all of them—without any concealment. I have a right to know them, and I will know them.' The whole appearance of the man indicated a fierceness that would have torn me into a thousand pieces had he considered me to blame."

Cadwallader proceeded to give Rawlins an account of Grant's magnificent bender, fearing for his own part that when the general woke up in the morning he just might decide to eject the reporter from the department. Rawlins calmed him. "He will not send you out of the department while I remain in it," the chief of staff said, and indeed, according to Cadwallader, from then on Grant treated him as a respected member of the staff.

No one likes to discover that their idols have feet of clay, and several of Grant's biographers have attempted to discount or discredit Cadwallader's account, principally by citing a few known errors in his memoir, which he did not write until 1896, and which even then remained unpublished for another fifty-plus years. But the fact that Cadwallader remained a close and special member of Grant's coterie even after he went back east, and through the end of the war—and that he shared a house in 'Washington's Georgetown with Rawlins after the war was over—seems to speak for itself. By practically all contemporary accounts, notably from other newsmen, Cadwallader was considered a thorough and trustworthy journalist.

Grant's latest improvident behavior had for the most part gone undetected and, more important, there is no indication that it had a significant bearing on any military operations. As previously noted, he simply seemed to have a penchant for going off on the occasional toot when Mrs. Grant or some important military operation was not immediately at hand. Perhaps he thought he had earned it, but in any case the domineering presence of John Rawlins by all accounts formed a bulwark against repeated performances of this sort. According to Charles Dana, Grant, if not in fear of Rawlins, was at least somewhat in awe of him. "Without him," Dana said, "Grant would not have been the same man. I have heard him curse at Grant when, according to his judgment, the general was doing something that he thought he had better not do." The general's drinking, although Dana did not say it outright, was of course one such thing.

Meantime, another thorny problem had been needling Grant ever since the misbegotten assaults of May 22, and that was what should be done with McClernand. The commanding general was angry with the flamboyant Illinoisan for issuing what he believed was a false report that his troops had occupied part of the Confederate line, which indirectly resulted in the death and wounding of hundreds of men. Cadwallader was in Grant's headquarters tent when news was brought that McClernand's force had never conquered any significant part of the Rebel line and the journalist recorded "the grim glowering look of disappointment and disgust which settled down on Grant's otherwise placid countenance, when he was convinced of McClernand's duplicity, and realized its cost in dead and wounded."

The fact that Grant did not fire McClernand forthwith remains something of a mystery; Dana secretly wrote Secretary Stanton that Grant had planned to relieve McClernand right after the May 22 attack, but apparently he changed his mind and decided to wait until Vicksburg fell. On that same day, Grant had telegraphed Halleck about the battle: "Gen. McClernand's dispatches misled me as to the real state of facts and caused much of this loss. He is entirely unfit for the position of Corps Commander both on the march and on the battle field. Looking after his Corps gives me more labor, and infinitely more uneasiness, than all the remainder of my Dept." Yet Grant still took no action. Perhaps it had to do with his own sense of culpability in not having supervised McClernand more closely since, beginning at Fort Donelson, it had become obvious that he was the weakest of Grant's generals. Moreover, there was also the sticky possibility that, should he fire McClernand, the wily politician would find some way to have an official investigation launched of Grant's decision to proceed with the assaults in the first place. After the failure of May 19, the double failure on the twenty-second would be harder to explain—especially to a committee sitting around a table a thousand miles away in Washington. In any case, nothing was done about McClernand, which left some of Grant's closest associates mystified at his forbearance.

Astonishingly, even though McClernand knew that Grant and others were highly displeased over his behavior during the May 22 assault, he continued to cause trouble, and in early June he took it upon himself to provoke an ugly confrontation with Colonel Wilson of Grant's staff, which in itself probably ought to have gotten him fired.

Wilson had ridden to McClernand's headquarters with orders from Grant that the XVII Corps should strengthen its guard on the Big Black River in case Johnston should appear. For some reason McClernand flew into a rage and shouted, "I'll be God damned if I'll do it—I am tired of being dictated to—I won't stand it any longer, and you can go back and tell General Grant!" This in turn infuriated Wilson, who took the fiery general's cursing to be aimed at him and came very close to challenging McClernand to a fistfight. At this, the XVII Corps commander calmed down and apologized. "I am not cursing you," he told the ruffled aide. "I was simply expressing my intense vehemence on the subject matter."

When Wilson indignantly reported McClernand's outburst to Grant, the general seemed more amused than angry, and from then on whenever an officer was overheard cursing—a practice Grant himself disdained—staff members would jocularly remark that the blasphemer was just "expressing his intense vehemence." Privately, however, Grant told Rawlins, "I'll get rid of McClernand the first chance I get."

He didn't have to wait long, thanks to the eagle eyes of William Tecumseh Sherman, who was at first startled, then incensed, when he read a sort of congratulatory order that McClernand had placed in an Illinois newspaper, and which had been picked up by the *Memphis Evening Bulletin*. In it, McClernand styled his corps "the Army of the

Mississippi"—as if it were somehow separate from Grant's army—and lauded his troops for their courage and accomplishments during the attacks of May 22. Worse, he implied that both Sherman and McPherson had prevented his men from achieving victory by not attacking with enough vigor to take the pressure off his own advance.

Sherman immediately sent the clipping to Grant, along with his own scathing appraisal of it, branding it, among other things, "a catalogue of nonsense . . . addressed not to an army, but to a constituency in Illinois." He also directed Grant's attention to an order from the War Department that expressly forbade any publication of official letters or reports, on pain of dismissal from the service.

The first thing Grant did was to ask McClernand if the news story was accurate. Replying that it was, and now fearing that he might be in hot water, McClernand added, "I regret that my adjt [adjutant] did not [send] you a copy promptly as he ought & I thought he had."

That wasn't good enough for Grant. In the small hours of the morning of June 18, Colonel Wilson, dressed in his best uniform, and undoubtedly relishing his assignment, presented himself at McClernand's headquarters and requested that the general be awakened. After a short while he was led in to meet McClernand, who had likewise dressed in his full uniform and was seated at a desk with his sword lying across it. The general unsealed Wilson's envelope, read the contents, and exclaimed, "Well, sir. I am relieved!" He then looked at Wilson directly and said, apparently in reference to Grant, "By God, Sir, We are both relieved!" Next day a furious McClernand was on a steamboat bound for Illinois, but by a long shot it would not be the last that was heard from him. For his part, Grant told Dana that McClernand's departure was "better than 10,000 reinforcements."

Nevertheless, just as a precaution, Grant ordered up 10,000 reinforcements anyway, from his command at Memphis. He had a premonition that something very nasty was brewing to the east, right behind his army.

CHAPTER EIGHTEEN

Martha Says Rats Are Hanging in the Market for Sale with the Mule Meat

Away to the east at Jackson, Joe Johnston was gathering his "Army of Relief," as it had come to be styled. Two weeks after the Battle of Champion Hill he had about 22,000 men, including Loring's errant division, with more expected daily from Bragg's Tennessee army. Still, the Virginian seemed in no great hurry to move on Grant's rear. He complained to Secretary of War Seddon about lacking wagons, artillery, and other military accoutrements, and that many of those under his command were undisciplined and untrained. There probably was some truth in this last, as some who had joined since the siege began were raw militia or home guard troops. As Grant put it, "Johnston is still collecting troops at Canton and Jackson . . . all the country is joining his standard." But the majority of the Confederate army under Johnston were experienced soldiers, and if he intended to do anything with them now was the time.

For six months, all the maneuvering and fighting between the two armies had resembled an elaborately dangerous chess game and now Grant held Pemberton in check, if not quite checkmate, because getting out of it would require almost a miracle. The miracle, however, remained inert, fifty miles away.

On May 20, right before Grant's big assault, Pemberton had sent the following message to Johnston by courier: "An army will be necessary to save Vicksburg, and that quickly. Will it be sent?" And the next day: "The men credit and are encouraged by a report that you are near with a large force. They are fighting in good spirits and their organization is complete."*

On May 23, the day after Grant's second assault, between Pemberton's 29,500 men within the Vicksburg lines and Johnston's force in Grant's rear, the Confederates totaled 51,500, while Grant could muster 51,000—again, considerably better odds than the Rebels were used to. On May 25 Johnston told Pemberton, "Bragg is sending a division. When it comes, I will move to you. Which do you think is the best route?"

That was relieving news, as it were. It was Pemberton's thinking, or so he said later, and so he told Johnston, that the two forces combined could eject the Yankees from the Haines's Bluff lodgment, cutting off Grant's line of supply and forcing him to use the tenuous Grand Gulf base to feed his troops. The notion of "living off the land" had worked well enough for Grant in the beginning, but so far as sustaining a large army in a long siege it would not do.

"My men are in good spirits awaiting your arrival," Pemberton told Johnston. "You may depend on my holding this place as long as possible," he said, adding the next day, "When may I expect you to move, and in what direction?"

But on May 29, four days after Johnston's encouraging message, Pemberton received this from Johnston: "I am too weak to save Vicksburg; can do no more than attempt to save you and your garrison. It will be impossible to extricate you unless you co-operate and we make mutually supporting movements." Just what those movements were, Johnston left up to the discretion of Pemberton, who was stuck inside like a bug on flypaper.

Since Johnston was barely on speaking terms with Jefferson Davis, he was doing all his communicating with Richmond through the secretary of war. On June 4 he repeated to Seddon that his army was still too small to relieve Grant's siege, despite the fact that three days earlier John Breckinridge's combat-tested division had arrived from Tennessee, bringing up his overall strength to approximately 31,000. Johnston, however, kept underreporting his numbers, prompting a

---

* Being a Confederate courier in those days was risky business indeed after Grant had surrounded Vicksburg. Some, familiar with the roads and trails, traveled by night the fifty or so miles it took to reach Johnston's headquarters. Others were known to swim across the Yazoo clinging to a log or use small skiffs at night. Some were captured. Some returned bringing sacks of the precious percussion caps that Pemberton was so desperate for.

lengthy dispute between himself and the Richmond authorities—who were keeping tabs—as to how many troops he actually had on hand. The fact was that during the first week in June, before Grant's reinforcements arrived, the combined Confederate army still outnumbered the Yankees by about 58,500 to 51,000.

The problem was—as some in Richmond continued to point out—that reinforcements would soon be reaching Grant far in excess of anything more the Confederacy could send to counter them. When Seddon suggested that Johnston order more troops from Bragg's army, Johnston testily passed the buck: "To take from Bragg a force which would make this army fit to oppose Grant would involve yielding Tennessee. It is for the Government to decide between this State and Tennessee."

It is here that the authorities in Richmond—in particular Jefferson Davis—probably dropped the ball. They could certainly read maps, and had emphasized on many occasions that the loss of Vicksburg would be catastrophic to the cause, yet now they seemed paralyzed. Even if a substantial diversion of the Army of Tennessee to Vicksburg compelled Bragg to withdraw from Tullahoma to the formidable bastion of Chattanooga, he might easily have held out there while the crisis in Mississippi was disposed of. But this is in retrospect. Besides, Johnston's force, along with Pemberton's, already outnumbered the Yankees, at least for the time being, and the government anticipated that he would do something about it.

Johnston, however, did not seem to see it that way. On June 15 he reported to Richmond, "I consider saving Vicksburg hopeless." The next day he received a stern reply from the secretary of war: "Your telegram grieves and alarms us. Vicksburg cannot be lost, at least without a desperate struggle. The interest and honor of the Confederacy forbid it."

Johnston was unmoved by this plaintive appeal. "I think you do not appreciate the difficulties in the course you direct, nor the consequences of failure," he responded. "Grant's position, naturally very strong, is intrenched and protected by powerful artillery, and the roads obstructed. I will do all I can, without hope of doing more than aid to extricate the garrison."

"Rely upon it," Seddon responded testily, "the eyes and hopes of the whole Confederacy are upon you, with the sentiment that it were better to fail nobly daring than . . . to be inactive. I rely on you for all possible to save Vicksburg."

· · ·

On the morning of May 27 there occurred one bright episode in Rebeldom that most Vicksburgians witnessed firsthand, when the Yankee ironclad *Cincinnati* came around the bend and began lobbing shells at a Confederate battery on the hillside.

The reason for this was that Sherman had complained to Grant that the battery in question was annoying the men of Frederick Steele's division, which anchored his right flank, and he wanted it disposed of by a Union ironclad. Admiral Porter wasn't so sure—at least not enough to risk one of his most powerful gunboats—and he instead began bombarding the Confederate position with his mortar ships. But when this did not produce the desired effect Porter, with certain misgivings, ordered *Cincinnati,* which had already been sunk once, a year ago, above Memphis, to throw her weight into the offending Rebel battery.

Grant and Sherman had assured Porter that the biggest guns had been removed from the battery by the Rebels and hauled to the defensive lines in the rear of the city, and that Sherman's artillery and sharpshooters would keep at bay any Confederates who tried to fire on *Cincinnati* while she did her destruction. They were wrong. The heavy guns were still there, having been masked by lowering them behind the parapets, and as soon as *Cincinnati* came into range she was blasted by everything the Rebel artillery could throw.

Hearing the racket of the battle, the townspeople came out to watch the proceedings, crowding Sky Parlor Hill and any other eminence where a view could be obtained. *Cincinnati* came up bows-on, which was her most protected angle, and whenever the Rebel guns scored a hit the men cheered and the ladies shrieked and fluttered their handkerchiefs.

Unfortunately, the ironclad could not hold her course sideways in the river and as the current began to swing her around she came about, until her vulnerable stern was facing the Vicksburg bluffs. This was where she met her doom. A shot wrecked her stern and started a leak; another went right through her topside and out the bottom; yet another went through her hull below the waterline. The captain told the crew it was every man for himself, and the ship went down with twenty men killed outright by Rebel fire or drowned.

It was a big day in a bad week for the Confederacy, and Emma Balfour, who had been watching from Sky Parlor, told her diary: "There arose a glad shout, 'She is sinking!' There she lies under water except for her chimneys & her horn. I don't think any of them will be so anxious to try our batteries again."

In this, she was correct.

. . .

Behind the Confederate bomb-cratered lines in Vicksburg, Uncle Joe Johnston had of course become the savior incarnate. Vicksburg's *Daily Citizen* advised: "The most agreeable news nowadays is to hear from General Johnston. . . . We have to say to our friends and the noble army here that relief is close at hand. Hold out a few days longer, and our lines will be opened, the enemy driven away, the siege raised, and Vicksburg again in communication with the rest of the Confederacy."

Marmaduke Shannon's *Vicksburg Whig* having been demolished by shell fire, a former member of its staff nevertheless wrote, "All [were] anticipating the defeat and destruction of Grant's army as soon as Johnston arrived with the fifty-thousand men he was reported to have under his command."

Everywhere in the city the rumors flew of Johnston's pending liberation—some said with an army of 50,000, others with 60,000, and still others with 100,000. Some reports placed him at Clinton, others had him already across the Big Black, or at Satartia, scene of Grant's recent dissipation.

On June 3, Sergeant William Pitt Chambers of the Forty-sixth Mississippi had just received the dying words of one of his companions, a litter bearer who was shot in the chest as he walked behind company lines, when near sunset Chambers remembered that "we distinctly heard heavy firing in an easterly direction and conjectured at once that Gen. Johnston was coming at last. *How high rose the hopes of our men! And how eagerly we listened for a renewal of the fight on the morrow. But we heard it no more, and in a day or two the men were as despondent as ever."

Meanwhile, Grant's policy of giving the enemy no respite continued apace. The shelling from both the land and the river was increased mainly to ramp up the terror factor, which produced inconclusive results. Chambers remembered that in the Rebel lines they watched the huge naval mortar shells "streaming across the sky like a flying meteor, describe a great curve and pitch headlong to the earth, gathering momentum as they fell. Sometimes they bursted high in midair with a detonation like thunder, sometimes they exploded near the ground, and they buried themselves in the earth and tore out great holes when the explosion came."

An officer with a New Hampshire regiment that had come downriver to reinforce Grant's army was aboard a transport, waiting to be offloaded. "The boom, boom of the mortar fleet every two minutes," he wrote. "We timed the shells as they left the mortars on their aerial flight and found that it took about 18 seconds for them to land in the city." Another officer recalled that the shells "dropping into every part of the city from over the clouds look[ed] like big potash kettles." A citizen of the town distinctly recalled the queer sensation of being able to see their shadows on the ground as they passed the sun overhead.

The destruction was terrible. It was calculated that about two-thirds of all the artillery shells fired from Grant's lines east of Vicksburg flew over the Confederate fortifications they had been aimed at and landed in town. So far as Porter and his mortar fleet were concerned, they were content "day and night, throwing shells into every part of Vicksburg and its works, some of them even reaching the trenches in the rear of the city."

A Mrs. Groome was once caught in the open and crouched with her mother and her aunt behind some cotton bales when a tremendous concussion showered them with earth and wads of cotton.

"Oh, sister, are you killed?" Mrs. Groome's mother asked her aunt, picking the dirt and lint from her face.

"No, are you?" came the reply.

As the days rumbled past, the outcome was predictable and wretched. William Tunnard of Baton Rouge, a sergeant in the Third Louisiana, told his diary: "Palatial residences were crumbling into ruins, the walks torn up by mortar shells, the flower beds trodden down, the shrubbery neglected. Fences were torn down and houses torn to pieces for firewood. Even the enclosures around the revered dead were destroyed, while wagons parked around the graveyard, horses tramping down the graves, and men using the tombstones as convenient tables for their scanty meals, or a couch for an uncertain slumber. Dogs howled through the streets at night, cats screamed forth their hideous cries, and an army of rats, seeking food, would scamper around your very feet. Lice and filth covered the bodies of the soldiers. Delicate women and little children, with pale, care-worn and hunger-pinched features, peered at the passerby with wistful eyes from the caves."

By mid-June, a month into the siege, the former reporter for the *Vicksburg Whig* wrote that "Vicksburg was in a deplorable condition. There was scarcely a building but what had been struck by the enemy's shells, while many of them were entirely demolished. The city had the appearance of a half-ruined pile of buildings, and on every

street unmistakable signs of the fearful bombardment it had undergone, presented itself to the observer."

Even so, most of the citizens tried to live as normal a life as possible
under the circumstances. On Sundays, many tried to attend church,
although, as Emma Balfour wrote, "The church had been considerable injured, and was so filled with bricks and mortar & glass that it
was difficult to find a place to sit."* Afterward, people dressed in their
Sunday finery would promenade along the streets until the shelling
began again. They had figured out that at about midday the Yankees
on the mortar boats would take an hour or so to eat their lunch, during
which the guns remained silent.

The women, especially, seemed to be a bulwark against pessimism,
no matter how frightened or worried they were in private moments.
Pemberton had made his headquarters next to Emma Balfour's home
and was a frequent visitor. "I laughed at Gen. Pemberton the day
before for being gloomy & told him the ladies were not despondent,"
she wrote. "So he told Col. Higgins [chief of artillery for the river bat-
teries] to tell me he thought things looked brighter now."

In Richmond, the desperation was palpable. Robert Lee had begun
moving his army northward through the Shenandoah Valley toward
his rendezvous with destiny in Pennsylvania, and all the troops that
could be spared from North Carolina and South Carolina, Georgia
and Alabama had already been sent to Johnston. Nobody, Davis and
Johnston included, seemed willing to further weaken Bragg's Tennessee army, and all that was left was to call upon the western forces
across the Mississippi.

This, it will be recalled, had been tried at various times without
success—most notably at Shiloh—for it seemed that the Confederate
government simply could not control its armies west of the river. This
time, however, the feisty General Dick Taylor agreed to see what he
could do. It wasn't Taylor's first choice, though, as he argued to
departmental commander Kirby Smith that, with the Yankee general
Banks gone off to Port Hudson, he was already far along in retaking
New Orleans. But Smith convinced him that under the present emergency it was more critical to beat or disrupt Grant, since, if Vicksburg

---

* She was referring to the Christ Episcopal Church, which had been built in 1826
and consecrated in 1839 by the future bishop and general Leonidas Polk. It survives
today as the oldest public building in Vicksburg.

was lost, New Orleans wouldn't matter much anyway. With that in mind, Taylor gathered up a force of 5,000 Texans, loaded them on steamboats, and headed north through the back bayous of Louisiana.

His principal objects were the Yankee supply depots on the western side of the river at Milliken's Bend, Young's Point, and Lake Providence. If these could be taken, the reasoning went, then Grant's already tenuous line for supplies and reinforcements to Grand Gulf would be severely hampered, if not entirely cut, and the Yankee army might be forced to withdraw.

What Taylor didn't know, however, was that between the time these plans were laid and the time they were to be executed, Grant had already bottled up Pemberton in Vicksburg and was now using Haines's and Snyder's bluffs on the Yazoo as his direct supply depots. The awful truth was that it didn't matter a tinker's damn what happened at Milliken's Bend or Young's Point or anywhere on the Louisiana side of the river, except that that was where Grant was billeting his Negro troops for further training. In fact, these soldiers weren't even getting training, except for some cursory drill instruction, since Grant intended to employ them as laborers.

All this notwithstanding, when Taylor arrived on the scene he determined to go ahead with his attack, if for no other reason than he was there, and so were the Yankees, unprepared as they were.

On June 6, Taylor's men were within striking distance of the Federal encampment at Milliken's Bend, which was located on a levee right beside the river. When everything was said and done, the battle that ensued did not reflect much credit on anyone concerned. First, the Federal commandant of the Milliken's Bend post was under arrest for unspecified complaints. Second, the four regiments of "African descent" that manned it—2,500 strong—had most recently been slaves on nearby plantations and had been issued new Austrian-made rifles that even their officers were barely familiar with. Third, even though they had received adequate forewarning that a large body of Rebels was in the area, their plan of battle seemed to fall to pieces as soon as the shooting started.

Just before sunup on June 7, a 1,400-man brigade of Major General John G. Walker's Texas Division led by Brigadier General Henry McCulloch marched to within shouting distance of the Union lines, when Federal pickets sounded the alarm. McCulloch formed his men in line of battle and sent them forward across a plain of open fields that was bisected by hedgerows. Though the hedgerows provided a good defensive line, the Federal troops seemed to panic and retired back to the first of two natural levees that edged the river.

There, their commanding officer, Colonel Herman Lieb, formed a main line of resistance. The bluecoats were able to get off a volley felling a number of Rebels but were shocked and dismayed when McCulloch's men continued marching forward, and they were in the process of scrambling over the top of the first ten-foot levee when the Confederates fell upon them.

According to witnesses, the Confederates began shouting, "No quarter for the officers. Kill the damn abolitionists. Spare the niggers." This disturbing proclamation caused a number of white Federal officers—including a colonel who was later dismissed for cowardice— to flee over the levees, leaving the blacks to contend with the blood-thirsty Rebels.

What ensued was a brutal hand-to-hand struggle down to and including gouging fingers and strangling hands that finally saw the black troops running for their lives with the triumphant Texans in pursuit. The Confederates' jubilation was soon dampened, however, when they topped the levee and found, staring at them, the ferocious guns of the Union ironclad *Choctaw,* which had been sent upriver as soon as word got out that an enemy force was at hand. One blast from *Choctaw*'s enormous hundred-pounder Parrot swept the levee and sent the Confederates scampering back on the far side, glad to be alive—most of them—and wondering what to do next.

Repeated attempts to storm the levee and finish off the black troops were continuously thwarted by the mutilating fire from the ironclad while the Texans sought guidance from General Walker, whose head-quarters was some distance away. In the meantime Rebel soldiers occupied themselves by plundering the Federal camp, tending their wounded, and finishing off or making prisoners of those who had not escaped. Even before Walker could provide his advice a second Yankee gunboat, the *Carondelet,* was sighted heading toward them, which resolved the question. McCulloch ordered the brigade to withdraw, and with that the episode was closed, or so it seemed.

The Texans had suffered 44 dead, 131 wounded, and 11 missing. The Yankees counted a dismaying 131 dead, 285 wounded, and 266 missing—nearly 25 percent casualties.

Within a short period, Grant received word that the Texans had hanged a number of the black soldiers whom they had taken prisoner. This distressing report prompted him to send a message to General

Taylor in which he more or less threatened to hang one Confederate prisoner for every Union prisoner so disposed of. For his part Taylor denied any knowledge or sanction of such atrocities, and the matter never having been proven was dropped.

Porter arrived on the scene shortly after the fighting ended and reported: "I went up in the *Black Hawk* and saw quite an ugly sight. The dead negroes lined the ditch inside the parapet, or levee, and were mostly shot on the top of the head. In front of them, close to the levee, lay an equal number of rebels, stinking in the sun."

When the result of the battle began to circulate, many southerners found the notion of white troops retreating from a fight with black soldiers hard to swallow. "There must be some mistake," wrote Kate Stone, then in Texas after her flight from Brokenburn, which lay just south of Milliken's Bend. "It is hard to believe that Southern soldiers— and Texans at that—have been whipped by a mongrel crew of white and black Yankees."

McCulloch, a former Indian fighter and commander of the Texas Rangers, had this to say about the battle in his official report: "The charge was resisted by the negro portion of the enemy's force with considerable obstinacy, while the white or true Yankee portion ran like whipped curs almost as soon as the charge was ordered."

General E. S. Dennis, who had been in overall command on the western side of the river, concurred. He told Charles Dana, "It was the hardest fight he had ever seen," and that it was "impossible for men to show greater gallantry than the negro troops in that fight."

If the battle for Milliken's Bend proved anything it was a reaffirmation, after Port Hudson, that black soldiers would fight and, second, that no soldiers of any character whatever could stand up to the close-in firepower of an ironclad warship. Lastly, it ended any hopes Pemberton might have had for reinforcements to appear from across the Mississippi.

As the days wore by the people in and around Vicksburg—citizens and soldiers alike—settled into a grim determination to weather whichever storm was coming their way. In the city, the shelling continued day and night, while the residents hunkered down in their caves or cellars. During Farragut's shelling the previous summer, people had built their caves facing east, away from the river, where the mortar boats were. But now, with Grant to the east, they were catching it from both directions. One aspect of the siege was the sheer relentlessness and volume of the carnage. Between the big mortar shells from the river and the rifle and cannon fire from Grant's lines there seemed to be no peace, only a brief slackening from time to time. It was calculated that, depending on the mood of the Yankees, from five hundred to five thousand artillery shells of every description landed in Vicksburg *each day*. Residents described a constant rain of metal in various ways: it reminded some of hail, others of great handfuls of rocks being showered upon them; still others thought the shrapnel sounded like the rattle of marbles flung down on a metal roof. Mary Loughborough wrote in her diary, "I could have sent out at any time, near the entrance of our cave, and had a bucketful of balls from shrapnel and the Minie rifle, picked up in the shortest possible time."

Even spent shells that were seemingly harmless were often harbingers of death. A Confederate orderly named Henry rode by Mary Loughborough's cave every day taking a general's horse to water, and over time he became friendly with Mary and her two-year-old daughter, sometimes bringing them flowers and other small gifts. One day after prancing the general's sleek, black thoroughbred to the child's delight, Henry and another courier stopped to pick up an unexploded Parrot shell to dismantle it for the powder inside. "In a few moments I heard a quick explosion in the ravine, followed by a cry—a sudden agonized cry," Mary wrote. In turning the set screw the men had inadvertently ignited the fuse and the shell blew up, tearing off both of Henry's hands and laying shrapnel deep in the young courier's brain. Both men died before sundown.

This particular danger wasn't confined to the city either. Out in the battle-ravaged terrain of the Stockade Redan was a great poplar tree, estimated at four feet thick, that "must have been struck by two hundred balls, top to bottom," according to Ephraim Anderson, a Missouri colonel. When it could support its weight no longer, the tree fell, landing in the rear of the Twenty-seventh Louisiana Regiment. One morning a party of Louisianians decided to make a fire of the toppled tree to cook their breakfast, "and were stooping over and around it, frying their meat in the blaze, when a shell [that had long been] buried deep in the wood was ignited, and exploded in their midst," Anderson said. "Many were knocked down and I thought, at the moment, killed." But all got up except two—some with whiskers and hair considerably singed and others slightly scratched. None had been badly hurt.

Between wounds and illness, at any given time about 5,000 of the 30,000-man Rebel army in Vicksburg were in the various hospitals spread about the city, many in private homes; some of them consisted merely of a cluster of tents, and these, despite flying a yellow flag—the precursor to the red cross hospital emblem—were no more immune to artillery fire than any other place. In mid-June Dr. Joseph Alison, a surgeon in the medical corps, wrote in his diary, "Rations very short. We all look for help *one of these days.* Incessant fire. Lieutenant Young was killed on the lines. He was as clever a gentleman as ever lived, and his loss will be long felt by all who know him. He was the last of three brothers. All perished in this cruel war."

William L. Foster, chaplain of a Mississippi regiment, visited Hospital No. 1, and described it as "a beautiful residence," where the sick were housed. The wounded, however, were kept in tents in the protected valleys and hollows nearby. "As I entered one of these valleys," he said, "a most horrible spectacle greeted my eyes. Every tent was filled with the wounded and dying. There they lay, poor, helpless sufferers; some groaning from excessive pain, others pale and silent through loss of blood." At almost every pace through the tent Foster encountered sights that made him recoil: a man burned almost to a crisp when a caisson carrying artillery powder exploded; a boy "not more than seventeen" shot through the eye. And outside each surgery tent the inevitable pile of legs, arms, hands, fingers, and feet. "There is no Sabbath [quiet] here. War knows no Sabbath. How unnatural is war," the chaplain wrote.

It was generally conceded during the war that if a man lost a major limb to amputation he had at best only a 50 percent chance of survival (compared with almost no chance if amputation was not performed). In Confederate Vicksburg, the dead were generally taken to trenches about a quarter mile back from the main lines and laid to rest head-to-foot, in fifty-foot-long trenches, "with a blanket for a winding sheet and in [their] soiled battle-stained garments." Across the lines in the Federal camp, where the food and clothing were plentiful, death proved to be an equal opportunity employer: most of the Yankee dead were buried exactly the same way.

Emma Balfour, who had steadfastly refused to go into a cave but relented after several near misses that shook her house "like a cradle," wrote, "Today a shocking thing occurred. In one of the hospitals where some wounded had just undergone operations, a shell exploded and six men had to have limbs amputated. Some of them that had been taken off at the ankle had to have the leg taken off to the thigh, and one who had lost one arm had to have the other taken off. It is horrible and the worst of it is we cannot help it."

. . .

Not only did the citizens of Vicksburg have their caves or burrows, but the men of both armies did also, in and around the trenches. The Confederates were of course under constant bombardment from Grant's artillery and sharpshooting from the front lines, and the bluecoats could either be picked off at three hundred yards or blasted by cannon fire whenever the spirit moved some Rebel gun captain to do so. Thus all dug in, until the Blue, the Gray, and the women and children— nearly 100,000 of them, now that Grant's reinforcements were arriving—were living much of their lives burrowed mole-like, beneath the ground.

Often in the evenings friends and soldiers would drop by Mary Loughborough's cave, and there would be guitar playing and singing and laughter amid the bursting of the shells. To her "it sounded like the crashing and bitter spirit of hate near the light and grace of happiness. How could we sing and laugh amid our suffering fellow beings— amid the shriek of death itself?"

By mid-June the food shortage had become critical. At first, friends would stop by Mary's cave and bring her treats. "Two large, yellow, ripe June apples, sealed in an envelope. They were as much of a variety to me as pineapples would have been," she wrote. Others brought ham, or pieces of bread, which was becoming very scarce. But as the siege wore on even these meager delicacies began to dry up. "Fruits and vegetables were not to be procured at any price. Everyone felt . . . the fear of starvation."

The men in the Rebel trenches, who once got up with the sun to the welcome smell of bacon, eggs, and grits, had been on half rations since the first of the month, and their bread, known most politely as "pea-bread," was a concoction of ground-up field or "cow" peas with a little yeast for leavening. One Rebel soldier swore that a loaf of the pea-bread was so hard "one might have knocked down a full-grown steer with a chunk of it." By mid-June their meals consisted of two pea-meal biscuits and two pieces of bacon a day. Some men ate it all at once and went hungry the next day, preferring at least "to have one good meal." They also discovered that the tender leaves of the cane that grew so profusely in breaks all around the area could be nourishing— essentially what the Chinese call bamboo shoots.

The men had long been eating the flesh of horses and cattle killed during the bombardment; then the authorities began killing the mules.

Everybody knew they were going to have to eat the mules; it was just a matter of time. At the beginning of the siege, horses not belonging to officers or couriers and most of the army's reserve mules that were not immediately needed for drawing wagons and artillery had been turned out into the countryside on Pemberton's orders, for there simply was not enough food for them within the confines of town. Now, with the cured salt pork nearly gone and men on the verge of starvation, "the ever-faithful mule," as one Rebel officer put it, "was now looked upon with a pitiless eye."

Most of the soldiers understood, and even welcomed it, for a hungry man is a practical man, and since the middle of June they had been further reduced to one-quarter rations—barely enough to sustain life, let alone endure the rigors of combat. Nevertheless, when Federal soldiers would taunt Confederates in the line about having nothing to eat but pea-bread, they would respond, "Don't worry about us, for we have many mules to eat."

Civilians, too, had begun to resort to the practice. Dora Miller wrote, "We are lucky to get a quart of milk daily from a family near who have a cow they expect hourly to be killed. I send five dollars to market each morning, and it buys a small piece of mule meat." Mary Loughborough told her diary, "A certain number of mules are killed each day by the commissaries and are issued to the men, all of whom prefer the fresh meat. There have already been a few cases of scurvy. The soldiers have a horror of the disease. I suppose the mule meat is all the more welcome."* Even Mary thought it would be better than the pitiful allowance of food she was getting, but her husband told her, "No; wait a little longer."

Some joker went so far as to circulate a satirical menu for the fictional "Hotel de Vicksburg," featuring "Mule Tail Soup, Roast Mule Rump Stuffed with Rice, Mule Beef Jerked, Mule Ears Fricasseed, Mule Hide Stewed, Mule Spare Ribs, Mule Liver, with Mule Salad, Mule Hoof Soused, Mule Brains a la Omelet, Mule Kidney and Cold Mule Tongue" on the side. If anybody laughed, so much the better, for life in Vicksburg was no laughing matter.

And if anybody thought that eating a mule was unpalatable, consider the dilemma of the First Missouri. Somewhere in its wide travels the regiment had acquired a camel, one of the last of the beasts that Jefferson Davis had so persistently arranged a decade earlier to be

---

* Mule meat would probably not have had any effect on the prevention of scurvy, which is caused by a lack of vitamin C, a fact discovered by a Scottish physician in the previous century.

brought from Egypt to the South and Southwest as transport animals for the old army. Just as the Yankee Eighth Wisconsin kept an American bald eagle for a mascot, the Rebel Missourians had adopted the camel, described by their commanding officer as "a quiet, peaceable fellow, and a general favorite." But one day a Yankee sniper got him and, under the circumstances, there was nothing else but to carve him up into steaks and eat him.

As the days and weeks passed, the prices for anything edible became positively scandalous. Flour was selling at $5 a pound ($82 in today's money), beef (usually oxen, horses, or milk cows butchered after they had been killed by the shelling) at $2.50 a pound, molasses at $10 a gallon. Thus, only the wealthy could afford these "luxuries." After the first few weeks the army had undertaken to supply citizens with meager rations but, since these were no better than the soldiers' fare, those who could afford it tried to supplement. Some with large families and no funds resorted to begging or stealing. The wealthier citizens formed a committee to help, but not even they could provide enough food to be of significant impact. Even more alarming, where Sergeant Tunnard had remembered "dogs howl[ing] through the streets at night" and "cats scream[ing] forth their hideous cries," Dora Miller now said, "We don't see any more pitiful animals prowling around," and while she speculated that they must have all been killed by the barrage or starved to death, there may have been darker reasons underfoot.

With the exception of the heat of the Southern summer, the sniping, the bugs, and the occasional snakebite, over in the Yankee lines they had it pretty good. Every day steamers from Cairo and Memphis arrived at Haines's Bluff with tons of food and clothing. An Illinois infantryman wrote to his wife, "We have had killed of our Regiment, 5, wounded, 30. We are living very well here. We have good potatoes, pickles and kraut, or rather pickled cabbage, fresh ham as we prefer, dried apples and peaches, and biscuits and good butter." And the Ohio sergeant Osborn Oldroyd wrote: "There is joy in our camp, for Uncle Sam has again opened a clothing store, which we shall patronize, asking nothing about price or quality. The boys cheered lustily when they saw the teams drive in and heard what they were loaded with."

By contrast, Dora Miller said that Confederate soldiers who managed a respite from the front lines "swarm about like hungry animals seeking something to devour. Poor fellows, my heart bleeds for them.

They have nothing but spoiled, greasy bacon and bread made of musty pea-flour." When her cook was making cornbread, Dora said, "they would come to the kitchen and beg for the bowl she had mixed it in. They shake up the scrapings with water, put in their bacon and boil the mixture into a kind of soup.

"When I happen in," she continued, "they look so ashamed of their poor clothes." That same day a sick soldier "crawled upon the gallery to lie in the breeze," and Dora had her cook make him up some corn-meal gruel, and even put in a shake of precious nutmeg. When he ate it, she said he began to cry, and as the tears ran down his cheeks he told her, "Oh, madam, there was never anything so good!"

Meantime, Grant was methodically escalating the violence. Reinforcements were arriving daily—many of them New Englanders from the eastern armies—bringing more artillery with them. By mid-June Charles Dana was able to tell Stanton that "no amount of outside alarm [the threat from Johnston] loosened Grant's hold of the rebel stronghold. Grant soon had eighty-five thousand troops around Vicksburg, and Pemberton's last hope was gone." Even though Dana had overestimated by more than 10,000, still it was the first time the Federal army had significantly outnumbered the Confederates.

Also by mid-June there were no fewer than thirteen "approaches" slouching toward Vicksburg from one end of the Federal lines to the other. Each of these "parallels" was large enough to conceal horses and riders, large bodies of troops, artillery pieces, and, more ominously, wagonloads of black powder kegs. A bit farther back, all along the lines, rows of sharpshooters protected behind head-high, bullet-proof plank fences made sure that nothing showing above the Rebel parapets went unpunished, while the remorseless Federal artillery made life miserable or worse for everything else.

With the situation apparently deadlocked, Grant decided that if he couldn't dislodge the Confederates from their fortifications by human assault he would blow them out of it with his artillery, and he set June 20 as the date for this explosive enterprise. At 4 a.m. the barrage opened when all two hundred guns of the Federal batteries roared awake and for the next six hours blasted away at the Rebel positions. Charles Dana reported that the enemy defenses "were little injured," but he was wrong.

Behind their lines the Rebel commanders were horrified as they saw gun after gun dismounted and wrecked by the Yankee shelling, the tops of parapets blown off, and their glacis collapsed into the ditches in front. If ever there had been a time for a further assault on the Confederate line, that was probably it, but Grant did not order one, though he had the entire army "held under arms from 6:30 a.m. ready to take advantage of any signs the enemy may show of weakness." Perhaps it was because he was unable to see the damage the barrage was doing as a result of all the gun smoke. It was so thick that, as one Union soldier remarked, "the entire Rebel army might have escaped under its cover" and the Yankees would never have known it.

Somehow word had leaked out the day before that there would be a big cannonade and a Rebel officer persuaded Lucy McRae's mother and several other families that they would be safer in a ravine behind the Confederate lines. No sooner had they pitched their tent, Lucy said, than the barrage opened: "Balls were whizzing, cannon booming from the rear, mortars replying in rapid succession." In the midst of all this, she said, "a cannonball that had spent its force on the side of the hill came rolling into the tent. A young lady screamed as it rolled upon her, and in less time than it takes to tell it we were all up and out of the tent." Lucy's mother told her servant, "Rice, take that tent up and let us go to town!" Rice replied, "Yes, ma'am, let us go 'way from dis place before us all is killed."

As the Yankee trenches, or "saps," approached the Rebel lines, overhead coverings had to be fashioned as protection against sharpshooters and the occasional cannon fire. These coverings were known as "sap rollers" and one in particular was keyed on what Grant's engineers had fixed as the crucial point in the Confederate fortifications—the Third Louisiana Redan. This was close to the center of the line near the Jackson road and bulged out in a V-shaped salient. If it could be taken, the Yankees reasoned, the bluecoats could pour in and the whole enemy line would collapse, as it had during the Battle of the Big Black.

The Third Louisiana Redan was in McPherson's sector, and the project fell on Logan's division. The man specifically chosen to implement the approach was Captain Andrew Hickenlooper, an engineer by trade, who began digging operations at the Shirley House, about a quarter mile from the Confederate position. During the truce to bury the dead Hickenlooper had used the opportunity to scrutinize the redan for ways of getting at it, and within a few days he had devised his plan. A mining detail of three hundred men now rotated night and day to push the sap forward, but when they got into rifle range of the Rebel redan they were forced to fabricate a sap roller to shield them from being shot down from above. What they came up with was the frame of an old railroad flatcar that they piled with cotton bales and slowly pushed ahead of the diggers.

By that time the Yankee artillery could thoroughly dominate the Rebel guns wherever it wished, since most of the Confederate cannons were fixed in positions and the Federal artillery could be moved about at will. In McPherson's sector in particular the Third Louisiana Redan had been singled out for such treatment, so that the moment the enemy gunners pushed their piece into the embrasure it became the target for a dozen Yankee cannons. Thus the Confederates were left mostly with the option of rifle fire to stop Hickenlooper's obnoxious sap roller as it inched steadily toward them with each passing day.

Out of exasperation, wrote Sergeant Tunnard, Colonel Samuel D. Russell of the regiment determined to put an end to "the hated object" with a novel invention. He plucked a wad of cotton from one of the bales protecting the gun embrasures, soaked it in turpentine, and thumbed it into the little hollow on the rear end of a minié ball. That same evening Russell dared to poke his head above the parapet, took aim at where he knew the sap roller to have been, and pulled the trigger. According to Tunnard, the powder in the rifle ignited the turpentine-soaked cotton, and this flaming bullet "sped . . . straight to the dark mass of cotton-bales, like the rapid flight of a firefly."

Other men took turns popping their heads above the ramparts and firing similarly altered bullets, but when nothing seemed to happen everybody, disappointed, finally went to bed except the guard. Then, several hours later, one of the sentries cried out, "I'll be damned if that thing ain't on fire!"

Russell's magic bullets had caused the cotton atop the sap roller to smolder before finally bursting into flames, while the Yankee diggers tried to stomp it out. By then the whole Rebel parapet was alive with riflemen who methodically shot down the bluecoats who found themselves backlit by the blaze, and by morning the sap roller was "reduced to ashes and a mass of smouldering embers," with nothing left but its iron wheels and axles.

This halted the sapping operation, but not for long. One morning a few days later another, even stranger-looking contraption appeared above the Federal trench, this one consisting of long, thick flaps of cane wrapped around cotton bales that had been thoroughly water-soaked, and again the Yankee juggernaut moved inexorably forward.

By now life in the Vicksburg trenches had become a remarkable microcosm of the First World War, a half century into the future, when millions of men would be similarly employed. The big Civil War battles up till Vicksburg had been two- or three-day clashes, with the horror coming all at once, and then it was over. But the introduction of trench warfare with its concentrated day-and-night artillery shelling and sharpshooting began to take a toll heretofore unknown on men's psyches. Before long the Union army began to rotate its troops in and out of the trenches on a regular basis, for it was beginning to dawn on the commanders and medical authorities that men who are constantly exposed to fire come to believe they will eventually die from it.

Given rest and time to recuperate their attitudes change; they regain confidence and morale. Grant could easily afford to do this because he had the superior force, and only he knew if, or when, he was going to attack. The Confederates had no such luxury and, for the most part, had to be ready all the time. By the time the First World War rolled around, forty-eight hours was considered the maximum that men could be kept in a frontline trench and still be fit for duty. At the time of the Civil War there was no such term as "shell shock," or "combat fatigue," but medical personnel did recognize an affliction called "neurasthenia," or nervous breakdown, which was precisely the same thing.

With little to do all day but dodge bullets, many men began to create what has come to be called "trench art." In World War I troops on both sides fashioned elaborate decorations of amazing artistry out of the brass shell casings that accumulated by the tens of millions on the battlefields. Some of the vases, pitchers, and other vessels they produced have become prime collector's items. At Vicksburg the men worked mostly with lead, which, because of its low melting temperature and softness, was easy to mold or whittle. The Confederate soldiers particularly enjoyed making figurines for the children of the city.

Mary Loughborough, still enduring the siege in a cave with her two-year-old daughter, wrote, "They amused themselves, while lying in the trenches, by cutting out little trinkets from the wood of the parapet and the Minie balls that fell around them." She particularly remembered a Major Fry, from Texas, "who excelled in skill and ready invention: he sent me one day an arm chair that he had cut from a Minie ball—the most minute affair of the kind I [ever] saw, yet completely symmetrical. At another time he sent me a diminutive plough made from the parapet wood, with traces of lead, and a lead point made from a Minie ball."

Having decided that he could not take the Confederate fortifications by storm, or drive them out of it with artillery, Grant now looked forward to blowing the whole enemy position to kingdom come. In each of the twelve divisions, the progress of the saps was a main topic of conversation.

Two days after the big artillery barrage, Captain Hickenlooper's sap reached the ditch beneath the Third Louisiana Redan when the call went out "for all men having a practical knowledge of coal-mining to report to the chief engineer." On the night of June 22, thirty of these people, armed with drills, short-handled picks, and shovels, began to dig a mine shaft five feet high and four feet wide beneath the Rebel bastion. When they had tunneled in some forty-five feet, they began branching out with lateral galleries into which they intended to place gunpowder—some 2,200 pounds of it in all.

The Confederates had watched these proceedings with growing concern and began countermining operations of their own. Atop the Third Louisiana Redan they sank a vertical shaft about fifty feet deep, intending to beat Grant's miners to the punch by exploding a mine of their own that would foil the Yankee designs. Pemberton's chief engineer, Samuel Lockett, remembered, "It was very difficult to determine distance under ground, where we could hear the enemy's sappers picking, picking, picking, so very distinctly that it hardly seemed possible for them to be more than a few feet distant."

Before the Rebels could explode their mine, however, Hickenlooper touched off his. Grant had turned up for the occasion and ordered the army to be under arms and ready to exploit any advantage that the mine might create. The hour was set for 3 p.m. As the minutes ticked by, an unearthly silence enveloped the battlefield, with everyone waiting for the mine to go off. Behind the front lines, "as far as the eye could reach, to the right and left, could be seen the long winding columns of blue moving to their assigned positions behind the besiegers." Confederate general Louis Hébert naturally suspected that something significant was afoot and told the Third Louisiana to move back from its redan to a line of trenches in the rear. That left six heroic Mississippians who were still down in the countermine, digging away.

As three o'clock came and went and nothing happened, people in the Federal lines began to complain that "someone has blundered." As they waited longer and longer, many were about to give up on the mine, when suddenly the thing went off, exactly half an hour late.

Nobody had ever seen anything like it. The entire redan, it was said, seemed to lift into the air, "gradually breaking into fragments and growing less bulky in appearance, until it looked like an immense fountain of finely pulverized earth, mingled with flashes of fire and clouds of smoke, through which could occasionally be caught glimpses of dark objects, men, gun carriages, shelters, and so on."

Then, out of the seething cauldron came a deep mighty roar that expanded into an almost overwhelming crack, like a thunderbolt right overhead. Men in the Union lines began to recoil as the pile of debris rose up and seemed to lurch toward them. When it finally rained down it was found to contain huge clods of dirt, pots and pans, tents, mess kits, haversacks, ammunition crates, rifles, shovels, articles of clothing, and Rebels and parts of Rebels, including the unfortunate six Mississippi counterminers.

When the smoke and debris finally cleared it didn't look like the same terrain—and it wasn't. True to his intention, Grant had blown the Third Louisiana Redan clear off the face of the earth, with nothing left but a smoldering crater, like the cone of an exploded volcano. The Forty-fifth Illinois had been tapped to exploit the shock and damage caused by the explosion, and even before the dust had settled these men charged through the still-smoking gap that had been breached in the Rebel line. Their ardor was immediately dampened, however, when they were met by a veritable wall of rifle fire from the Third Louisiana, whose men had lain mostly out of harm's way in their trench behind the redan. Now the Yankees found themselves in a trap perhaps worse than if they had simply charged up the face of the redan before the mine exploded. Here they were being shot at like fish in a barrel, and there was little they could do to get back at their tormentors. A number of Illinoisans tried holding their rifles up over their heads and firing blindly over the rim of the crater, but this seemed to do little good. Then the Rebels began throwing lit artillery shells down upon them, and bringing up reinforcements fast. After about two hours of fighting, and with darkness coming on, the Yankees began to withdraw, and that, for the most part, was all that came of the first Third Louisiana Redan mine.

In the ensuing week more Union mines were set off, with greater or lesser degrees of success. Two days after Hickenlooper's first blast, McPherson ordered him to try again, this time off to the right, in hopes of bringing down the rest of the First Louisiana parapet, crater and all. Hickenlooper set to work and four days later had burrowed deep beneath the Confederate ramparts. There, however, his miners reported that they could hear the unmistakable sounds of Rebel countermining, so they decided to set off their mine prematurely.

Having lost the hapless Mississippians in the first countermining attempt, the Confederates were now employing a crew of eight blacks, with a white overseer, and it was these men who were picking away in midafternoon on July 1 when the Yankees detonated their 1,800-pound mine. This explosion actually caused more damage than the first, blowing away a much larger chunk of the parapet and leaving only a giant hole in the ground where the gun ports had been.

When the usual detritus of dirt clods, pots and pans, rifles, and ammo crates came raining down it also rained down, of all things, a live man, who had sailed clear over into the Federal lines. This fortunate soul was one of the black counterminers who had been working deep underground when the mine went off. Aside from being horrified by the experience, he was otherwise unhurt, and when asked by some of the soldiers how high he thought he had been blown he replied, "Dunno, massa, but I t'ink about t'ree mile." A contingent of Iowa soldiers set the man up in a tent and began charging fifty cents for people to take a look at him, but General Logan came to the rescue and the man was brought to headquarters where he performed custodial duties until the end of the siege.

Despite all the Yankee mining and cannonading, no one yet had actually been able to make or hold a significant breach in the Rebel lines, but as the sweltering summer days dawned one after the other it became apparent that the Confederate forces could not keep on much longer. Grant's artillery barrages had all but silenced the Rebel guns, and want of food was causing the southerners to become dispirited, lackadaisical, and even mutinous.

On June 28, the forty-second day of the siege, Pemberton received a letter purporting to represent the sentiments of the men in ranks. Titled "Appeal for Help," after complimenting Pemberton on his stubborn resistance, patriotism, and personal bravery, the letter propounded that "everybody admits that we have covered ourselves in glory but . . . a crisis has arrived in the midst of our siege." It went on at length about the lack of proper food and that the men were required to stay in their trenches day and night. "Men don't want to starve, and don't intend to, but they call upon you for justice, if the commissary department can give it; if it can't, you must adopt some means to relieve us very soon.

"If you can't feed us, then you had better surrender us, horrible as the idea is, than suffer this noble army to disgrace themselves by desertion," the letter said. "I tell you plainly, men are not going to lie here and perish, [even] if they do love their country terribly. You had better heed a warning voice, though it is only the voice of a private soldier."

What reaction Pemberton had to this, if any, is lost to history, but he, among all of them, knew how desperate their situation was, yet he hung on, still hoping for his miracle.

Despite all the doomsaying and procrastination, Johnston had finally been vexed to movement by the repeated haranguing of the secretary of war, but still he promised no hope of actually raising the siege. He would only provide enough of a diversion to give Pemberton a chance to march his army out of the city and escape southward.

However, instead of moving promptly, Johnston delayed with the usual excuses, not enough supplies, artillery, wagons, equipment, etc. And once he got going his movements were badly coordinated and he kept stopping to reconnoiter, when he might have had his cavalry doing that all along. In the meantime, Pemberton inquired of his division commanders whether or not they felt their troops were healthy enough for the rigors of a breakout—the hard marching and fighting that would inevitably ensue once Grant discovered they were trying to escape. Not one of them did. At that point Pemberton sent a messenger to Johnston asking if he would make overtures to Grant, in essence surrendering Vicksburg in exchange for Grant's allowing Pemberton's army "to pass out, with all its arms and equipages."

Johnston, however, was unwilling to do this—even though he was the highest officer on the scene—for the last thing he wanted was the stain on his reputation for having been the man to surrender Vicksburg. "Negotiations with Grant for the relief of the garrison, should they become necessary, must be made by you," he replied to Pemberton. "It would be confession of weakness on my part, which I ought not to make. When it becomes necessary to make terms, they may be considered as made under my authority."

So if someone was going to swing for the fall of Vicksburg, it would have to be Pemberton alone. Johnston wanted no part of it, even though at the time he commanded a fresh army that by now consisted of 32,000 men.

As the siege dragged on and food became more alarmingly scarce, there were reports that some desperate people were eating rats. "Martha says rats are hanging dressed in the market for sale with mule meat," Dora Miller told her diary, referring to her cook, whom she had sent into town. "There is nothing else." There were also stories of soldiers in the trenches eating rats, in particular the Louisianans.*

In her notebook, Mary Loughborough recorded this sad story. "We were now nearing the end of our siege life. The rations had nearly all been given out. My little one swung in her hammock, reduced in strength, with a low fever flushing her face. A soldier brought up one morning a little jaybird as a plaything for the child. After playing with it for a short time, she turned wearily away.

" 'Miss Mary,' said the servant, 'she's hungry; let me make her some soup from the bird.'

"At first I refused; the poor little plaything should not die; then, as I thought of the child, I half consented. With the utmost haste, Cinth disappeared; and the next time she appeared, it was with a cup of soup and a little plate, on which lay the white meat of the poor little bird."

Where at the beginning some of the cave dwellers had marveled at the comfort and decor of their caves, after nearly seven weeks the constant shelling and the dark, suffocating dankness were wearing very thin. And there were worse things, too, as Mary Loughborough found out.

"As I was passing through the cave I saw something stirring at the base of one of the supports of the roof: taking a second look, I beheld a large snake curled between the earth and the upright post. I went out and quickly sent one of the servants for [Major Loughborough] who, coming up immediately, took up his sword and fastened one of the folds of the snake to the post. It gave one quick dart toward him, with open jaws. Fortunately, the length of the sword was greater than the length of the upper body; and the snake fell to the earth a few inches from [her husband], who set his heel firmly on it, and severed the head from the body with the sword. I have never seen so large a snake; it was fully as large round the body as the bowl of a good-sized glass tumbler, and over two yards long."†

Between the shelling, the hunger, and their caveman existence, the

---

* The distinguished Vicksburg historian Edwin Bearss believes the rats referred to in connection with the Louisiana troops might have been muskrats, which the Acadians, or Cajuns, had long found palatable. It seems unlikely, however, that there was a significant enough muskrat population within the lines to make many meals, while the trenches were said to have been overrun by the regular type of rats.

† From her description, the snake was likely an eastern diamondback rattlesnake, which is the largest and most dangerous poisonous reptile in North America. But since she did not indicate the color of the snake, it may also have been an indigo snake, bull snake, or possibly some other large snake that inhabited that area a century and a half ago.

citizens of Vicksburg were enduring hardships beyond any previously known in the history of the country. Yet somehow still they soldiered on with the men in the trenches. The Vicksburg *Daily Citizen,* having run out of newsprint and now being published on long strips of flowery wallpaper, ran a box on its front page in response to Yankee taunts that Grant would soon be eating his dinners in Vicksburg. "Ulysses must get into the city before he dines in it," an editorialist observed. "The way to cook a rabbit is, 'first to catch the rabbit.' "

CHAPTER NINETEEN

The Father of Waters Again Goes Unvexed to the Sea

W hile the citizens of Vicksburg proper were undergoing their ordeal, residents in the outlying areas within the Yankee lines were faced with trials of their own. At first food was plentiful, especially on the larger plantations. They had always set aside enough corn, grain, pork, beef, and vegetables put up in jars to supply the families and the slaves, while sending the rest to market in the city. But as Grant's armies came on his men had taken as much as they needed—which is to say most of it—for the campaign to Jackson and thence to Vicksburg. When the matter settled down into a siege, though, and there were some 70,000 Yankee soldiers occupying the countryside, a goodly number of the Union soldiers treated the farmers at worst as enemy combatants and at best as enemy agents and raided not only their foodstuffs but their valuables, furnishings, and livestock as the spoils of war. It is hard to blame them, since they did not wish to be there in the first place, and when they came across southerners who almost universally despised them the inevitable occurred: heavily armed young men going up against unarmed hostiles will have their way when they will, and answer for it later if necessary.

Despite orders against random "foraging," it continued on a regular basis, as it had earlier on the Louisiana side of the river, until practically every southerner in the affected area had a horror story to tell. The pattern seemed to be the same in the many recorded instances: a party of Federal soldiers would arrive at a home on the pretext of searching for weapons. The proprietor, usually a woman, would deny having any, or produce whatever hunting guns that were in the home. The soldiers would then decree that a further search was necessary and in going through the house everything became fair game. Of particular interest was ladies' jewelry and of course the family silver, which had usually been buried or hidden by that time. They would also "search" the smokehouses and cellars for guns and other contraband, helping themselves to hams, put-up vegetables, corn, and so forth in the process.

At that point, the property owner would usually go to the commanding general of the sector of the Federal line in which the home was located and apply for protection. Most times, this involved taking an oath of loyalty to the Union. On one occasion, a Mrs. Booth went to General McClernand, but was told that "he could not protect her because she had two sons fighting against the U.S." The security offered normally consisted of a letter from the commanding general that the owner could present to foraging parties, stating that the property was not to be molested. In some instances an actual military guard was supplied. Neither of these measures was particularly effective. Sometimes the foragers would ask to see the letter of protection, then pocket it, or tear it up before the owner's eyes and proceed with the looting.

This continued all through the siege, and some diarists began to record the number of daily visits they received from "Yankee scum." Emilie McKinley, a Philadelphia-born tutor who lived on one of the plantations about seven miles out from Vicksburg and was vehemently pro-South, wrote on May 29, "The Yankees found the silver last Monday evening. We have seen but one or two Yankees today. A terrible fight is going on this evening."

As the days passed, different foraging parties would arrive to search the house for firearms. When it became apparent that the silver, jewelry, china, and other sought-after items were gone, they went after other things. Horses were a big favorite. Men's clothes and appurtenances also attracted unwanted attention, as did furniture: chairs, sofas, pianos, and elegant dining tables often disappeared down the road, strapped onto Federal wagons. One man even had the cooking stove stolen out of his kitchen and taken to a Yankee encampment.

On many occasions a foraging party would appear at the door and demand to be served dinner. Not to do so was to invite trouble. Weapons were often produced. Men were beaten and women roughly handled. "Two Yankees have just arrived and asked for dinner," wrote Emilie McKinley. "They have eaten. After stealing all we have to eat, they have the presumption to come for dinner." "Their impertinence," she said later, "is unparalleled."

On another occasion she recorded, "The other day Mrs. Downs told a Yankee officer who was eating his dinner at her house, while his men were rushing furiously around the house shooting the poultry, that these were terrible times to live in.

"Yes, they are rather uncomfortable," was his reply.

"Uncomfortable!" exclaimed Mrs. Downs. "That word does not give any idea of the times at all!"

As the weeks went by and the foragers found there was nothing left worth taking at some plantations, they often engaged in wanton destruction, dragging women's clothes out of their closets and chests and donning them for play, tearing or cutting them up, or strewing them along roads. Family portraits and other paintings were slashed, mirrors smashed, yards and gardens trampled or dug up, wallboards pried off, or plaster wrecked. Crystal chandeliers were singled out for particular abuse.

Worse, from the southerners' point of view, the Federal soldiers disturbed their slaves, enticing the men to run away and employing the women as cooks or camp servants. In general they made the slaves feel that they had been freed, but most of the bondsmen, who had known nothing in their lives but slavery and life on the plantations, had, in fact, nowhere to go, and no way to live, and in some cases were known to turn on their former masters with dire consequences for both races.

Much of the trouble was caused by Sherman's corps after it was detached from the besieging army and moved east to the Big Black to set up defenses against Johnston's anticipated attempt to cross over and relieve Vicksburg. As a "hard war" man, Sherman's military principles in no way included "winning the hearts and minds of the people." In fact, his philosophy was quite the opposite, as he stated succinctly in a letter to Halleck, who had asked for his confidential thoughts on how the war should proceed.

Couched in language that would shock and dismay modern experts in counterinsurgency, and foreshadowing his controversial "war is hell" decree to the people of Atlanta the following year, Sherman replied, in essence, that the South must be subjugated and made to understand that "we will remove & destroy every obstacle, if need be take every life, every acre of land, every particle of property, every thing that to us seems proper, and we will not cease till the end is attained, that all who do not aid [us] are enemies, and we will not account to them for our acts. If the People of the South oppose [us] they do so at their peril, and if they stand by, mere lookers on the domestic tragedy, they have no right to immunity, protection or share in the final Result. . . . I would not coax [the South] or even meet them half way," he said, "but make them so sick & tired of war that Generations would pass before they would ever again appeal to it."

Thus had Sherman laid it out on paper for Halleck, and to the Southern citizenry around Vicksburg he laid it out in spades, for he was a man who practiced what he preached. The peculiar thing was that Sherman—who was among the most erudite officers in the Union army—on more than one occasion raised his voice in anger over just the kind of practices he seemed to condone. "The amount of burning, stealing & plundering done by our army makes me ashamed of it," he told John Rawlins in a letter involving the court-martial of an officer caught burning a cotton gin near Vicksburg. "I would quit the service if I could, because I fear that we are drifting to the worst sort of vandalism." In any case, the Mississippians caught between the lines during this period got a healthy dose of Sherman's type of warfare, and they weren't likely to forget it.

Be that as it may, Sherman soon found himself under the scrutiny of the evil eye. One day while waiting to see if Johnston would turn up, Sherman got word that a Mrs. Wilkerson, whose son had been a cadet at the Louisiana Military Academy when Sherman was superintendent, was staying at a house nearby. Accompanied by his staff and a cavalry escort, Sherman rode over to the place and into the yard where he found "quite a number of ladies sitting on the porch." When he inquired after her son, Mrs. Wilkerson replied that he was an artillery captain, now besieged inside Vicksburg. But when Sherman asked about her husband, whom he had also known, "she burst into tears and cried out in agony, 'You killed him at Bull Run, where he was fighting for his country.' " Taken aback, Sherman later wrote, "I disclaimed killing anybody at Bull Run; but all the women present burst into loud lamentations, which made it most uncomfortable for me, and I rode away."

Back in Vicksburg, Pemberton was confronted with what was easily the most wrenching decision of his career. Johnston's last message said he was on the way, but Pemberton had no way of knowing if it was really true. The last messenger he sent had been captured by McPherson's forces. His troops, if not actually starving, were certainly on the verge of it. And trying to fight their way out of the encirclement with barely 20,000 to 25,000 fit for duty against Grant's 75,000 would be suicidal. Vicksburg, to his mind, and to everyone on his staff, was as good as lost.

He had even considered a weird suggestion by Johnston that the army might escape across the river, and in fact had begun building flimsy skiffs from the boards of demolished buildings, until the folly of it became apparent. Even if they could have constructed a hundred such boats carrying ten men apiece it would have taken each boat twenty-five round-trips across half a mile of water in the face of Porter's naval fleet and the Union artillery on the opposite shore. Pemberton might as well have told the army to swim across.

The one remaining hope was to save the army, and the way to do it was to confront Grant with terms; else the fighting and killing would go on. The terms Pemberton envisioned were unrealistic. As he had told Johnston, he believed he could convince Grant to allow the men to march proudly out of the city, carrying their arms and with their banners waving, and go on about their business. Anybody who believed Grant would permit such a thing would believe that pigs could fly, but Pemberton was willing to take a stab at it.

Even though none of Pemberton's four division commanders believed their men could withstand the rigors of a breakout, one, Carter Stevenson, felt that rather than being captured his men would be willing to try. John Forney reported that although his troops also were in no condition for a forced march they would "cheerfully continue to bear the fatigues and privations of the siege" in place of surrender. Martin Smith said likewise but thought it best "to propose terms of capitulation before forced to do so from want of provisions." Ironically, John Bowen, unquestionably the army's most combative division commander, felt it was time to call it quits.

On July 2, Pemberton called another council of war—or a council of peace, as it were—where the majority of his officers concurred that surrender was the only practical option. With a heavy heart he penned a letter to Grant in which he suggested that the two of them appoint three commissioners apiece to arrive at suitable terms of surrender. Had he known—which he probably did—of Grant's response to a similar proposal at Fort Donelson the previous year he might not have bothered.

Next morning, July 3, Bowen, who was deathly ill with dysentery, put on his dress uniform and, along with Pemberton's adjutant, Colonel Louis Montgomery, rode out of the Rebel fortifications toward Grant's line carrying a white flag. At least Bowen had thought so; when a hail of bullets whirred around them he turned to discover that Montgomery had forgotten to unfurl the flag, which nearly led to a most unfortunate misunderstanding.

With the truce symbol properly displayed, Bowen entered Federal lines and asked for a meeting with Grant. Bowen had been selected as the messenger—or perhaps he suggested it—because he and Grant had been neighbors and friends back in St. Louis before the war. Grant, however, replied in a letter that he would not meet with Bowen nor, he said, was he interested in appointing peace commissioners concerning terms of surrender. The only terms, Grant said, would be unconditional. Confronted with this aces-up poker hand, Bowen then asked if Grant would agree to see Pemberton personally, and word came back that in fact he would.

When Bowen brought Pemberton Grant's disagreeable response, the commander became incensed and declared that the fighting would go on. But when Bowen said that Grant would like to meet with him personally, it put a different complexion on the matter. At three that afternoon Pemberton, wearing his best new uniform, Bowen, and Montgomery rode out to meet the Union chief, who had brought with him an entourage consisting of McPherson as well as McClernand's replacement as corps commander, Major General E. O. C. Ord, and division commanders A. J. Smith and John Logan.

The interview did not go well. Pemberton seemed "much excited," according to Charles Dana, which was another way of saying that he was rude and snappish with the leader of the Yankee army. Pemberton had hoped, he wrote later, that a private meeting with Grant would produce some terms other than unconditional surrender, but that had not been on Grant's agenda. Still, it was not as though Grant had merely invited Pemberton out for a friendly chat; his desire was to impress upon his adversary that it would be in the best interests of all concerned for the Rebels to lay down their arms and give up now to avoid, in the argot of the day, "the further useless effusion of bloodshed."

Pemberton's reaction to this was unfavorable, and in fact startled Grant. "I can assure you, sir, you will bury many more of your men before you will enter Vicksburg," he told the Union commander.

With the proceedings thus stalled, Grant suggested that the two of them step aside and continue their talk, while McPherson, Smith, Bowen, and Montgomery got together and tried to work something out. Now it was Pemberton's turn to be startled, because it suddenly seemed that Grant was acquiescing to his original proposal of a peace commission.

Grant and Pemberton retired to the shade of a large oak tree, with Grant chewing on an unlit cigar and Pemberton munching on a straw, and neither of them saying very much.*

Meantime, Bowen opened the discussion with the Federal officers by offering a settlement along the lines of Pemberton's initial proposal that the Confederate army be allowed to march out of the city with their arms but leaving behind all artillery and other "public property," except what food was available to sustain them and wagons to carry it in. When the officers brought this proposition to Grant he rejected it out of hand. As the prospective victor, he felt the terms were his to dictate.

Pemberton then told Grant that since he had refused to consider the proposal, it was up to Grant to come up with a counteroffer. To this Grant agreed, and said he would send his decision by letter to Pemberton no later than ten that evening, and called for a general cease-fire on both sides until then.

With that the men parted, and the eerie and emotional quiet continued over the battlefield as the soldiers on both sides wandered out into no-man's-land to wonder over the meaning of the truce and to swap Yankee coffee for Rebel tobacco. In fact, the cease-fire suggestion had been a slick ploy of gamesmanship on the part of Grant, who had already told his commanders to get the word to the Yankee soldiers to say that, if a surrender occurred, the Rebels would all be paroled and free to go home to their families.

How much effect this psychological warfare had on the Confederate troops is unrecorded but, good to his word, at ten o'clock Grant's letter reached Pemberton's headquarters, offering exactly those terms. To Pemberton, Grant's conditions were about as good as he could expect under the circumstances; at least his army would not be packed into steamboats bound for a Yankee prison camp. When the proper paperwork was done, they could be reconstituted to fight again

* Afterward, the tree was hacked down by Union souvenir hunters "into more pieces," Grant said later, "than the True Cross."

another day, and disastrous as losing Vicksburg was Pemberton had not lost the army, which was how he saw it at the time.

He immediately called a council of his generals and asked them to vote on whether to agree to a surrender or not. Only Stephen Dill Lee and William E. Baldwin, both brigade commanders, voted to continue fighting. Pemberton then arose to make an unhappy speech, in which he regretted the avalanche of opprobrium he knew would cascade upon him, as soon as word of surrender got out. He told his officers that his personal preference would have been to place himself at the head of the army and fight his way out of Vicksburg, dead or alive, rather than face "the shame and disgrace" that would soon be heaped over his name. Instead, he announced, "It is my duty to sacrifice myself to save the army, and I therefore shall offer to surrender this army on the 4th of July."

At this there was a commotion among some of the audience at the thought of giving up on the Fourth of July, which by then had become a symbol of celebration of independence for the Yankee nation— though not the Southern Confederacy. To these men it would constitute a double humiliation.

Pemberton, however, quieted them with the revelation of some psychological warfare of his own. "I am a Northern man," he said, "and I know my people. I know their peculiar weaknesses and their national vanity; I know we can get better terms from them on the 4th of July than any other day of the year. We must sacrifice our pride to these considerations."

Repulsive as the notion was, the objecting officers could see the logic in his rationale, and the matter was dropped. Pemberton thus accepted his fate and sat down to compose a response to Grant's terms, asking that his soldiers be allowed to march out of the fortifications bearing their arms and banners before the Federal army marched in. It was an important reservation, for Pemberton's men had sworn that so long as they manned the ramparts at Vicksburg no Yankee would gain its heights unpunished. After the army had marched a considerable distance, Pemberton said, it would stack its arms and colors and the Yankees could have the place. Surprisingly, Grant agreed to this, as well as to a proposal that the Confederate officers could keep their swords and pistols and personal property (mainly their horses). However, Grant said, once the arms had been stacked, the Rebel army would be required to march back into town to be officially paroled.

An interesting aspect of the terms of surrender was revealed years later in an article written in 1887 for *Century Magazine*'s "Battles and Leaders of the Civil War" series by Confederate chief engineer Samuel Lockett. At the time of the capitulation, many in the North wondered why Grant, who had outlawed the paroling of prisoners when he became commander in chief of the Federal armies, would have agreed to set free an entire Rebel army of nearly 30,000, knowing that many of them would take up the cause again. "During the negotiations," Lockett wrote, "we noticed that General Grant and Admiral Porter were communicating with each other by [flag] signals from a tall tower on land and a mast-head on Porter's ship [the *Black Hawk*]. Our signal-service men had long before worked out the Federal code on the principle of Poe's 'Gold Bug,' and translated the messages as soon as sent.

"We knew that General Grant was anxious to take us all as soon as possible to Northern prison-pens. We also knew that Porter said that he did not have sufficient transportation to carry us, and that in his judgment it would be far better to parole us and use the fleet in sending the Federal troops to Port Hudson and other points where they were needed. This helped to make General Pemberton more bold and persistent in his demands, and finally enabled him to obtain virtually all the terms of his original proposition."

When Pemberton's letter of capitulation had reached Grant it was well past midnight, but the Union commander remained awake and at his desk. Freddie Grant had been sitting on a cot in his father's headquarters when Pemberton's reply arrived and recorded that "he gave a sigh of relief and said, 'Vicksburg has surrendered.' " No shouting or histrionics. It was pure Grant.

On the morning of the Fourth of July, white flags appeared up and down the Rebel lines. At exactly 10 a.m. the tattered Rebels marched out of their fortifications in files. There was no talking. The only sounds were muffled orders given by the officers, reminding one Confederate regimental commander of "a funeral *cortage* of some renown[ed] chieftan." Most of the men, said a Union observer, "had a downcast look" as they stacked arms in front of the shattered ramparts. "Most of the officers," said Charles Dana, "had the look of men who had been crying all night," and one old Rebel major began to sob as the men laid their regimental battle flag atop the stack of rifles. At last the storms were over. They had defended the place for nearly seven weeks in the blood and the mud and the heat and the tears, and that counted for something. At least they had that to take with them.

The Union soldiers also stood by mutely, as if at a funeral. There was no jeering, and one Yankee division even gave a hearty cheer. They had to hand it to them, and they did. Once the somber ritual was completed the Rebel army, "some without shoes, some with tattered garments," marched back into the city to receive their paroles.

The citizens of Vicksburg were stunned—many of them were grieved—but no one could feel anything but relief that the fighting had ended. They came out of their caves and squinted into a bright summer sun without all the banging and racketing and the air free of missiles for the first time in forty-seven days.

Margaret Lord, wife of the Episcopal priest, wrote, "Our poor soldiers came in a continuous stream past the house, so pale, so emaciated, and so grief stricken, panting with the heat and Oh! The saddest of all, without their colors and arms. We all congregated on the piazzas with buckets of water to quench their thirst and their 'God bless you, ladies,' and 'nothing but starvation whipped us,' could be heard on all hands."

Mary Loughborough was still standing in the entrance to her cave after seeing her husband off to the surrender ceremony when an old Rebel soldier passing by tipped his hat and said, "It's a sad day this, madam; I little thought we'd come to it, when we first stopped in the entrenchments. I hope you'll yet be happy, madam, after all the trouble you've seen." All she could manage to say was "Amen."

"While this gloom hung over the Confederate forces," wrote Lucy McRae Bell, "a glance over the hills to the north and east of the city brought into view the bright shining bayonets of the mighty host approaching the city." Colonel Robert Bevier of the First Missouri saw it too: "Winding around the crests of hills—in ditches and trenches hitherto undreamed of by us—one long line after another started into view, looking like huge blue snakes coiling around the ill-fated city."

A Yankee chaplain in McPherson's corps wrote, "It was our nation's birthday, and we felt it. We sympathized with it as never before. The oppression of the day and night had given place to light feeling. We seemed to tread on air. . . . It was so strange to stand up straight whenever we chose." Then, he continued, "the brigade band burst out with 'Hail Columbia,' " and the brigade marched forward, "past the rebel gun stacks, over the works, with our field bands playing, through the gazing Johnnies, right down the Jackson Road we went, the 45th leading. Not a dog barked at us, not a cat shied round a corner. Poor things, they had all been eaten in the straitness of the siege."

Out on the river another spectacle was unfolding, as Porter's war-ships, decorated with all their signal pennants, fired broadside after broadside in celebration, while dozens of Yankee steamers pulled up to the city wharfs. Many of these had been leased by Northern specu-lators who hoped to cash in by selling foodstuffs and other hard-to-find items. One carried a load of metal caskets that aggrieved parents might purchase to bring the bodies of their dead sons home for rein-terment.

On into the city the Federals came, led by Black Jack Logan's divi-sion, an army of banners, their bands playing "Yankee Doodle" and other favorite Northern tunes, which went unappreciated by the Southern populace. "You may be sure that none of us raised our eyes to see the flag of the enemy," wrote Margaret Lord. "Every house was closed and every house filled with weeping inmates and mourning hearts."

At the stroke of noon a large Union flag was raised over the Federal courthouse, the highest peak in town, where the Confederate Stars and Bars had flown since the beginning of the war. By this time the sol-diers of both armies had begun to mix and mingle and the Northern men, seeing the emaciation of their former enemies, began to share their provisions. In his memoirs, written long after the war, Grant wrote, "I myself saw our men taking bread from their haversacks and giving it to the enemy they had so recently been engaged in *starving* out. It was accepted with avidity and thanks."

There was, of course, some looting and stealing, but it did not last long after Grant posted provost guards throughout the city. As the day wore on many of the men "began fraternizing and swapping yarns over incidents of the long siege," said Samuel Lockett, who recalled that as he sat on the little white pony he had ridden every day in the lines a Yankee soldier exclaimed, as he walked past, "See here, Mister—you man on the little white horse! Danged if you ain't the hardest feller to hit I ever saw. I've shot at you more'n a hundred times!"

The fraternizing went on until late that night, becoming even more convivial when Confederates pointed out to the Yankee soldiers sev-eral large stores of whiskey that had been hoarded by speculators dur-ing the siege. The exhausted veterans would have had even more to talk about had they known that on this same Fourth of July, a thousand miles away at Gettysburg, Pennsylvania, Robert E. Lee had at last con-ceded defeat and started his army on its final, tortured march back to Virginia.

•   •   •

Two other items remained on Grant's agenda to wrap up the Vicksburg campaign into a neat Independence Day present for Abraham Lincoln's government. First was to dispose of the obstinate Confederate presence at Port Hudson and second was the disposal of Johnston's army in the Mississippi Valley.

To the latter end, Sherman sent his reinforced corps lunging across the Big Black at daybreak on the Fourth of July to find and attack Johnston's army before it could escape. Now that Vicksburg had fallen, Grant had provided Sherman six more divisions to add to the seven he already had, enough to cope with Joe Johnston's measly four divisions. But the redheaded Ohioan didn't even wait for these new troops to arrive; instead he had his leading elements on the east side of the Big Black before noon on the Fourth, headed for Jackson, Canton, or anywhere else that the Rebel "army of relief" might be found.

For his part, Johnston wasn't about to stick around and fight it out. He had already heard distressing rumors that Vicksburg was "gone up," or soon would be. As early as July 3 he went on the defensive, the position in which he felt most comfortable, keeping his army encamped near the gloomy Champion Hill battlefield, while he and his generals spent the entire day going over maps and asking locals for information. "The meeting was adjourned without reaching any decision," said a division commander, Samuel French.

Next morning, there was an ominous silence from the direction of Vicksburg, and Johnston's people began to suspect the worst. "The Fourth passed off very quietly with us," wrote a private from Tennessee, "there being an order against making any loud noise." Later, he said, "We have just received orders to march at three o'clock tomorrow morning with this additional injunction: 'On this march there is to be no loud hallooing, firing of guns, or cutting of large trees. The men are to march in their files, and company officers are to see that this order is enforced, or they will be cashiered. Penalty for the disobedience of this order is death.' " It was signed by Johnston himself.

With Vicksburg gone, and nothing left to rescue, there was little else for Johnston to do but save his army. He made the decision to fall back on the defenses at Jackson and await developments, and when these developments indicated that Sherman was coming after him he evacuated that place, too, and went northwest, keeping just far enough out of reach to make Sherman see it was going to be a long chase. Finally, on July 16, satisfied that Johnston was no longer a factor in the Mississippi Valley equation, Sherman took his troops back to the Big Black for a well-deserved rest. But not before burning Jackson one more time, just in case he had missed anything, converting it, as he wrote later, into "one mass of charred ruins."

The Port Hudson question also resolved itself in the Yankees' favor when, on July 9, General Gardner surrendered the city after learning the fate of Vicksburg. But not before an ugly and defiant confrontation.

There, too, the Rebels had been clinging like bats to a cliff in the face of bombardment and starvation at least as agonizing and violent as the siege of their comrades upriver. If anyone thought that General Nathaniel Banks was joking when he'd said that the miserable failure of his May 27 attack on Port Hudson was "because the people of the North demand blood, sir," they had another think coming. On June 14 the stylish Massachusetts politician ordered another full-scale assault, with equally gruesome results.

It began with an artillery barrage at 3:30 a.m. but a pea soup fog rolled in off the river and obscured the targets. The attack got under way at four when General Halbert Paine's division marched on the northern end of the Confederate line anchored by an imposing Rebel position known as the "Priest Cap." The Yankees waded through a cotton field to within a few hundred feet of the place when defenders from the First Mississippi rose up and delivered a brutal volley that cut down the bluecoats in windrows. One of the shots broke Paine's leg clean through, and the troops were thrown into confusion.* The fighting at the Rebel works became a savage hand-to-hand melee, but in the end the Confederates refused to be dislodged.

Next the Fourth Division made its bid against the Priest Cap, with the same unfortunate results. Accounts of the battle report that a Private Samuel Townsend of the Ninety-first New York, while trying to plant the Union flag on the Confederate ramparts, was shot down by his own brother, a member of the Mississippi regiment.

It was the same up and down the line. General Augur's division failed to make any appreciable gains in the Confederate center, while General William Dwight's division bogged down in a ridiculous scheme to take Port Hudson by a ruse straight out of the Arabian

* General Paine lay all day in the broiling sun between two rows of cotton, unable to move or even shade his eyes, lest he attract Rebel gunfire. Several courageous Union volunteers repeatedly tried to retrieve him but were shot down, before, late in the afternoon, one of his soldiers managed to drag him out of harm's way.

Nights. Two regiments were to somehow sneak under the great bluffs and assail the fort from the rear and take Gardner's headquarters house, whereupon a rocket would be fired to signal yet another force to rush up some steps and get inside the citadel and open the gates. Then a cavalry squadron led by Colonel Benjamin Grierson, hero of the Great Mississippi Raid, would gallop through the gates, cut down Rebel gunners and riflemen with their sabers, and take the place from the inside. Nothing went right; the two infantry forces were immediately turned back and Grierson wisely refused to participate.

In the end, nearly 1,500 dead and wounded Federal soldiers lay baking in the sun outside Port Hudson's walls. When the Confederates tried to go out and help the wounded they were shot at on Banks's orders, and when Gardner asked Banks for a truce to bury the Union dead the Yankee commander replied that he had no Union dead. Meantime, individual Confederate officers communicated with their Federal counterparts across the way in an effort to clear the battlefield. These were met with mixed results. Several Union commanders allowed the truce and the dead were buried and the wounded removed. In the Second Division's sector, however, Dwight stated to an officer who approached him on the subject: "No, sir, its all a stratagem of the enemy to get the dead carcasses carried away from their works. No, sir, I'll stink the rebels out of the citadel with the dead bodies of these damned volunteers if I cannot make the cowards take it by storm, as I have ordered them to do." Accordingly, the dead of Dwight's division continued to decompose in the sun, leaving bleached bones and vulture-picked flesh poking through their rotted uniforms until the end of the siege.*

Having at last absorbed an instructive lesson from the futility of his assaults Banks, like Grant at Vicksburg, settled down to a siege. It was the usual "killing for killing's sake," with starvation as the ultimate backup. Banks now had about 12,000 men and Gardner about half that many, and the Confederates were outgunned ten to one. Bad as

* William Dwight was not a man especially beloved by his troops or his superiors. Although he told people he had "resigned" from West Point, he had in fact flunked out. During his service under Banks it was understood that "his principal interest was in flushing out stores of cotton for shipment to Massachusetts mills." In 1864 Dwight was placed under arrest on charges that he had "retired to a place out of gunshot to take his lunch" during the battle at Winchester, Virginia.

those odds seemed, the Rebels gave as good as they got, particularly when they took one of the enormous 10-inch columbiads from the river battery and mounted it on a railcar, allowing them to run it up and down the tracks and fire at will on different Yankee positions.

For their part, the Yankees baptized this formidable weapon the "Demoralizer," and were especially alarmed by the unearthly sounds that emanated when its load passed overhead. It did not take long for them to discover the cause of these peculiar noises after a Federal officer was struck in the mouth by a shard from an old French bayonet that sliced his tongue in two. The Rebels, it seems, being short of cannon shot, were ramming anything they could find down the barrel of the gun, including "flatirons, ball-bearings, nails, railroad spikes, nuts and bolts, hatchet-heads, rocks, sugarcane knives," and, of course, broken pieces of bayonets.

Aside from these wicked aerial missiles and the incessant sharp-shooting by both sides, death came in various other ways, most especially for the vulnerable New Englanders who had never experienced a summer in the Deep South. Sunstroke killed any number of men, some of them merely lying down in their entrenchments and never rising again. Disease, as well, was responsible for many deaths, particularly the myriad fevers common to that section of the country.

Still both sides fought on with grim determination, even when an outbreak of scurvy threatened to decimate the Rebel camp and mule meat became the entrée of last resort, until, on July 7, word came by river steamer of the fall of Vicksburg. On that morning, the Rebel soldiers were shocked and bewildered by the roar of unrestrained cheering from their opposite numbers and the sudden delirious music of Yankee regimental bands from one end of the line to the other. A Federal officer wrapped a newspaper story of Vicksburg's surrender around a rock and flung it into the Rebel trenches, whereupon a Confederate officer hollered back, "This is another damned Yankee lie!" But when an official copy of the report arrived under Grant's signature, Gardner—who was said to have been "seated on the portico of his headquarters smoking a pipe of dried magnolia blossoms"—decided it was time to act. A hastily called council of war reached the inevitable conclusion and a surrender conference was arranged for the following day.

For some reason Banks chose not to attend the ceremony but sent instead his chief of staff, General George L. Andrews, who declined to accept Gardner's sword when it was offered. "I return your sword as a proper compliment to the gallant commander of such gallant troops," Andrews told the Confederate general, adding that said gallantry "would be heroic in any other cause."

"This is neither the time nor the place to discuss the cause," Gardner sharply told the Yankee officer as he returned his sword to its scabbard.

As Grant had done at Vicksburg, Banks paroled the soldiers but decided to keep the officers under arrest, promising that they, too, would be paroled in a few days. He changed his mind, though, and had the officers shipped off to prison, most of them to the infamous Johnson's Island camp in Ohio.

If casualties alone had been the measure of victory, the Confederates would have won the Battle of Port Hudson hands down. During their forty-six days of investment they recorded a loss of 188 men killed, 483 wounded, and a couple of hundred others who had died from sunstroke or disease. Banks's army, however, sustained 978 killed, 3,228 wounded, and 418 missing, plus a substantially large but uncounted number who had died from sickness.

This episode concluded the final chapter of Rebel domination of the Mississippi River valley and, with it, any realistic chance of a separate Southern nation.

For Ulysses Grant and the Union navy it had been a magnificent campaign. From a faulty start two years earlier at the Battle of Belmont below Cairo, Illinois, it had been one long, slow, bloody grind southward: Forts Henry and Donelson, Island Number 10 and Fort Pillow, Memphis, Shiloh, Corinth, Holly Springs, Chickasaw Bluffs, Arkansas Post, Grand Gulf, Raymond, Jackson, Champion Hill, and finally Vicksburg and Port Hudson. Abraham Lincoln summed it up serenely by declaring, "The Father of Waters again goes unvexed to the sea."

It came with a high price, for the casualties at Vicksburg and Port Hudson exceeded those of any Civil War battle except Gettysburg, in which far more troops were involved; the difference was that most of the other battles were fought over several days, while Vicksburg was fought over six months—not that this made much difference to the grieving families of the dead.

Beginning with Sherman's ill-fated attack on Chickasaw Bluffs and ending with the surrender, Federal losses in the Vicksburg campaign totaled 2,827 killed, 12,437 wounded, and 1,946 missing for a total of 17,210. The Confederate bill for the same period was 3,068 killed, 6,042 wounded, and 4,400 missing for a total of 13,510. Combined casualties of both armies—not including Pemberton's 29,500 who were surrendered at the end—were 30,720. In addition, the Rebel army lost four generals killed, sixty thousand rifles, and more than three hundred pieces of artillery that the South would never come close to replacing.

The victory had far-reaching consequences. Not only could Federal warships travel freely from St. Louis to the Gulf of Mexico, the states of the middle West were now able to resume their vital commerce and foreign trade, relieving much of the discontent in that section of the Union. Though the Rebels still maintained some clandestine traffic across the river, the vital stream of Texas beef, corn, and grains that fed the armies of Lee and Bragg was reduced to a trickle, and any notion of reinforcing armies from one side to the other was out of the question. Lincoln had put his finger on it early in the war when he told Admiral Porter that Vicksburg was the key to ultimate victory. "The war can never be brought to a close," the president said, "until that key is in our pocket." To Henry Halleck's pronouncement that the conquest of Vicksburg was "worth forty Richmonds," he might have added "forty Gettysburgs" as well. Momentous as that bloody encounter was, it was basically a large raid, and aside from the appalling casualties that the South could ill afford to lose Gettysburg had settled nothing, since Lee had retired with his army intact.

Union men in high places concurred. Grant, for one, wrote afterward that "the fate of the Confederacy was sealed at Vicksburg," and Sherman, with habitually pungent prose, declared that the results of Vicksburg and Gettysburg "should have ended the war; but the rebel leaders were mad, and seemed determined that their people should drink of the very lowest dregs of the cup of war, which they themselves had prepared."

Sherman was right, of course, but his remarks were made in retrospect. The past is littered with "what if" questions that professional historians habitually insist have no place in history—just before, that is, they go on to ask them anyway. In this case, the implications of Vicksburg's loss to the Confederacy poses a "what if" question that might in fact be instructive, as well as interesting, since the events of the next ten months of the war were so dreadful, and the consequences to the South in the decades to come so far-reaching.

In the early days of July, with Lee off in Pennsylvania and Grant tightening the noose around Vicksburg, Jefferson Davis became so anxious that he had to be put to bed, and his physicians expressed concern that he might even die. But then on July 6 he rose and sent a telegram asking to be informed about the situation in Mississippi. Next day Secretary of War Seddon sent him the official report, which had just come in, with a covering letter that began: "With the deepest regret at being compelled to inflict the pain of such disastrous intelligence . . ." The Confederate president had only two days to absorb that shocking news when a letter from Lee reached him, saying that the Army of Northern Virginia had been forced to retire from Gettysburg with heavy losses.

Not only that, but further reports arrived warning that the Union armies were taking full advantage of the situation, with Rosecrans now moving against Bragg in Tennessee, and Bragg in full retreat, and Federal troops suddenly landing in force on the barrier islands off the coast of Charleston. There was also news of the fate of Port Hudson and, worse, that Robert E. Lee wanted to resign.

A lesser man might have gone back to bed and pulled the shades but Davis did no such thing. While he acknowledged that "we are now in the darkest hour of our political existence," he also seemed strangely relieved, and sought to put the best face on things by telling his cabinet that the loss of territory, lamentable as it might be, also meant that there was that much less territory to defend. Hence, by his new way of thinking, soldiers who had been tied down in fixed positions such as Vicksburg and Port Hudson were now free to concentrate against Federal armies in the open field and defeat them (forgetting, apparently, that those troops were still on parole and could not, under penalty of death, resume the fight until—and if ever—they were properly exchanged).

Now Davis had come full circle from his ham-handed dictum at the beginning of the war that the Confederacy must contest and defend every square inch of Southern soil. Accordingly, he wrote a series of letters to the governors and military commanders of the now severed Western Department urging them to even greater exertions and to develop a new sense of self-sufficiency.

To Major General Kirby Smith, military commander of the department, Davis intimated that the fall of Vicksburg and the loss of the Mississippi actually created new and exciting opportunities that would allow him to "assume the offensive." These included the recommendation that Smith begin building factories to manufacture shoes, clothing, munitions, and even a steel-rolling mill that could turn out gunboats.

But no matter how receptive these officials may have been to Davis's letters, it was an inescapable fact that those same communications now had to be sneaked across the Mississippi River, likely in the dark of night, an embarrassment that was lost on no one.

If Davis's picture of the South's prospects seemed rosy, it was not reflected in the thinking of many of his senior commanders. For example, General John B. Gordon, a hero of Gettysburg, said, "The shock of Vicksburg was felt from one end of the Confederacy to the other," while General James Longstreet, Robert E. Lee's "Old War Horse," wrote afterward of the surrender, "For myself, I felt that our last hope was gone, and that now it was only a question of time with us." Colonel Josiah Gorgas, the highly respected chief of ordnance for the Confederate army, secretly told his diary, "One brief month ago we were apparently at the point of success. Lee was in Pennsylvania threatening Harrisburg, and even Philadelphia. Vicksburg seemed to laugh at all Grant's efforts to scorn. All looked bright. Yesterday we rode on the pinnacle of success—today absolute ruin seems to be our portion. The Confederacy totters to its destruction."

It was indeed as bad as that, and worse. Worse because, fatally wounded as it was, the Confederate army was still extremely dangerous, and leaders like Davis knew it. Their sense of reality had been clouded by the succession of feeble Northern generals such as Irvin McDowell, who got whipped at Bull Run; George McClellan, who had lost the Peninsula Campaign; John Pope, so badly mauled at Second Bull Run; Ambrose Burnside, humiliated at Fredericksburg; and Joseph Hooker, who got snookered by Lee at Chancellorsville. There was dissidence against the war in the North and cries for making peace. If the Confederacy could hold on only until the presidential election in November 1864—and with a few more spectacular victories such as Lee had been able to deliver—there was a good chance that Lincoln and the Republicans would be turned out of Washington and a new administration persuaded to let the South go its separate way. At least that was Davis's thinking, as well as many of those around him.

What they did not count on was the likes of a Ulysses Grant, whose military philosophy defied anything that had been seen so far in the war or, for the most part, in modern military history. Here was a general who rejected out of hand the notion that "he who fights and runs away lives to fight another day," substituting instead the tactics of a pit bull, which, once in close quarters with an opponent, will hang on till-death-do-us-part. Grant's willingness to sustain losses that would have been unthinkable in the early years of the conflict now seemed to present the North's best chance of winning the war quickly, and Lincoln was not hesitant to say so ("I can't spare this man—he fights"). Despite the bloody draft riots that paralyzed New York and Chicago in the summer of '63, the Federal armies were growing stronger every day while the Confederacy was growing weaker. Its high points had been reached at Gettysburg and at Vicksburg, though no one on either side had any sure way of knowing it. Such was their blind hatred of the North that for Davis and those surrounding him there was nothing left but to hope for the best and fight it out till the last dog died. And that would not be a long time in coming, for after Vicksburg Lincoln brought Grant east to face the indomitable Robert E. Lee.

In both tone and substance, Lincoln's year-end message to Congress was conciliatory toward the South and, like his Emancipation Proclamation from the year before, it contained both the carrot and the stick. He realized that the Confederates were suffering and tried an appeal to their sense of reason. The carrot was contained in a document entitled "A Proclamation of Amnesty and Reconstruction," which offered a full presidential pardon to all soldiers and employees of the Confederacy who would lay down their arms, take the loyalty oath, and accept the Emancipation Proclamation. The stick, by implication, was that otherwise all bets were off, although no deadline was specified.

The southerners, however, were treated to a demonstration of things to come less than two months later, when the North unleashed William Tecumseh Sherman on a rampage across the state of Mississippi. Ostensibly planned as a mission to destroy Confederate supplies, the operation soon turned into little more than a punitive raid. With a force of 15,000 Sherman cut a pitiless swath of devastation ten miles wide and 150 miles long, in which he refined and perfected his hard-war techniques that would later be used in Georgia and the Carolinas during his infamous "march to the sea." Little or no property was spared, public or private; looting and burning were the order of the day, as Sherman warmed up for the big finale that would begin next fall in Atlanta, where he informed that city's mayor, "War is cruelty; you cannot refine it." When Sherman was finished, little was left among the smoking ruins from Vicksburg to Meridian but a bewildered and miserable population of women, children, and old men—living testimony, at least to Mississippians, of the terrible consequences of rejecting the president's amnesty program.

However, if Lincoln's magnanimous gesture had any chance of success, it was probably doomed in the fine print, which excluded from pardon all officials of the Confederate government, army generals, former U.S. congressmen and federal judges, and high-ranking naval officers—in other words, everybody in a position to actually bring the war to a close. Thus, what Lincoln thought of as an act of reconciliation might actually have worked in the reverse. A corollary to Samuel Johnson's superb observation that "the prospect of hanging concentrates the mind wonderfully" might read, "Few things cause a man to struggle on more than the notion of a noose around his neck."

For their part, the Rebel leaders weren't about to be reconciliated, let alone reconstructed, as Jefferson Davis's message to the Confederate Congress, which happened to be delivered the same day as Lincoln's, made abundantly clear. After admitting that "grave reverses" had befallen the Southern armies, Davis went on to denounce Lincoln as "a despot" and the Yankee armies as "criminals" and "savages," while reiterating the Confederate theme that an "impassable gulf" divided the two sections of the country.

The Confederate legislators, finding themselves likewise unpardonable, fully concurred with the president and in a joint resolution declared Lincoln's offer nothing more than a sham to provoke desertions within the Rebel armies. Their decree, styled, "Address of Congress to the People of the Confederate States," informed Southern citizens that the Lincoln amnesty proposal was "only to delude and betray" and would ultimately lead to "your subjugation, destruction of your political and social fabric," and, in the end, "public degradation and ruin." In short, the document concluded, "It is better to be conquered by any other nation than the United States."

The Southern press, while not formally excluded from the amnesty, weighed in with even stronger denunciations of Lincoln's gesture than those of either the Confederate president or Congress, probably on the assumption that, should the South concede, their heads would likely be among the first to roll.

Such was the reaction of the Confederate leadership to their tragic summer that saw the whole complexion of the war turn against them. Defeat at Gettysburg was one thing, but if Vicksburg had held firm there might have been hope. The brilliant Lee with his unimpeachable Army of Northern Virginia might yet again have pulled off some exquisite battlefield victory. But the loss of Vicksburg was simply too great to overcome, and there was no way to redeem it, or the Mississippi River valley.

Soberer men might have looked to their maps and reflected on these things, but from Jeff Davis on down the Southern leadership appeared seduced by the poisonous cocktail of hatred, pride, arrogance, and fear. Still, anybody with a brain ought to have seen it: the Confederate Treasury was nearly bankrupt—$600 million in debt—and so awash in paper money that a barrel of flour cost four months' wages for the average earner. When the war began, a paper dollar issued by the Richmond mint was presumed to be worth a dollar of gold. Two years later it took three paper "shinplasters" to buy one gold dollar and, after Vicksburg and Gettysburg, it took twenty. People of wealth had begun selling their silver, jewelry, paintings, and other family treasures to questionable "auctioneers"—often from Europe—in exchange for gold enough to buy food, clothing, and fuel for heat. The poor, as usual, often went without. The Richmond government couldn't pay its debts, nor could it pay its army, which didn't matter too much anyway, since its money was becoming worthless.

Whereas before the twin disasters of the Fourth of July Confederate diplomats abroad had been received at least cordially—even if the results were not satisfactory—now their British and French counterparts became coolly civil, and sometimes not even that.

Of the territory the Southern Confederacy laid claim to in 1861 nearly half was now gone: all of Kentucky, Missouri, Maryland, and Oklahoma, as well as most of Tennessee, Mississippi, Louisiana, and Arkansas and parts of North Carolina, Florida, Alabama, Texas, and New Mexico. Rebel armies in the field were now outnumbered at least two to one, which might have been considered fair odds in the old days but the old days were gone and Lincoln had just put out a call for a new draft of 500,000—more than were serving in all Confederate armies combined.

Clearly, the handwriting was on the wall, and yet the prevailing powers in the Richmond government refused to read, or refused to accept, the message it told. Margaret Mitchell in her Civil War novel had it just right when she created Scarlett O'Hara, whose defining philosophy was "I won't think about that! I just won't think about it! Tomorrow is another day!"

It would take a phalanx of modern psychiatrists to unravel the peculiar psychology that infected the Southern leaders—or perhaps not even that; to paraphrase Freud's ungenerous opinion of the Irish, the southerners seemed to be "a race of people for whom psychoanalysis would be of no use whatsoever." One thing for certain is that these were not impressionable eighteen-year-old girls like Scarlett O'Hara but for the most part mature, well-educated men, many of whom *did* in fact see the handwriting and yet, like Colonel Gorgas, chose to consign their opinions to private diaries or, like Longstreet, simply kept their conclusions to themselves. But in most cases these people simply ignored facts that they knew to be true, and therein rests the tragedy.

Six hundred and fifty thousand Americans died fighting in the Civil War, and hundreds of thousands more were wounded and maimed*— as many as half of them in battles fought after the fall of Vicksburg.† Moreover, the period between the conquest of Vicksburg and the end of the war saw by far the worst of the destruction visited upon the South: the burning of Atlanta, Philip Sheridan's ruthless campaign in the Shenandoah Valley, Sherman's Meridian raid and his March to the Sea, the burning of Columbia, South Carolina, and other places.

By war's end the South was utterly and dismally prostrated, its infrastructure of railroads and communications wrecked, much of its commercial and private property destroyed, its fields fallow, and its livestock decimated. With the agricultural economy in ruins, its millions of former slaves became wretched, for the system of feeding and clothing them was broken. Even if it had been possible to employ them, there was little money to do it, for in the intervening years of the war the textile mills of England and France had found other sources of cotton, or switched to other fibers.

The disenfranchisement of former Confederate soldiers and officials left a leadership vacuum that was filled in many cases by incompetents and malfeasants or, under the harsh terms of Reconstruction, left up to the occupying Union army, which was there mainly to keep order.

It would have been smarter if Davis, above all others, had looked reality in the eye in the days following July 4, 1863. What would have stared back at him was the inescapable truth that, as a practical matter, there was by then no way the Confederacy could win the Civil War militarily. Politics was the sole remaining hope, the possibility, however remote, that the Republican administration would be defeated in

---

* In the years immediately following the war, for instance, a lion's share of the state budget of Mississippi went to buy artificial limbs for Confederate veterans.

† It is a practical impossibility to arrive at precise casualty figures for the war. Many Confederate records were destroyed, and many reports were not made at all. Further, some authorities lump into the casualty figures the troops who were captured, such as entire armies that were made prisoners (but later paroled) at Fort Donelson and Vicksburg.

the next year's elections and, remoter still, that whatever new administration came to power would see fit to agree to split the country into two separate nations.

It can always be argued that the war should never have been started in the first place. But it was, because neither side understood the military capabilities of the other. Few public figures except for Jefferson Davis and William Tecumseh Sherman thought the conflict would last more than six months. As a rule, northerners supposed that the Confederate army was little more than "an armed mob led by lawyers" that would run away at the first taste of battle, while the South assumed that, once the Union invaded the South and got badly mauled, it would soon come to the bargaining table. After July 4, 1863, though, the strategic situation was clear enough. The leading Confederates, however, had managed to equate the arrogance of pride with dignity, which made hatred seem respectable, while many Northern politicians had become hell-bent on reducing the South to the status of a fiefdom.

The often-cited World War I British military historian General J. F. C. Fuller was an eccentric, and to some even a crank, but he made an admirable case when he declared that "1917 would have been an excellent time to stop the war." Considering the millions of men in France and Belgium who died in the trenches after then, while little or nothing was gained by either side, he was of course correct. The kink in Fuller's theory lay in how to accomplish the sensible. Neither of the belligerents—the British and French on the one side and the Germans on the other—was willing to settle for anything besides ultimate victory. By 1917 too much blood had been spilled for that.

Yet the men who actually manned the trenches in Europe bore no great animosity toward their enemies. As at Vicksburg, they held occasional truces, fraternized, and wanted nothing more than to go home in one piece. The problem lay with the governments, which produced the strange psychology of the battlefield in which a man might toss a friendly apple or an orange into the enemy trench one moment and a hand grenade the next, but this never fazed the leadership in that most brutal of wars. This was just as true in the Confederacy, which didn't in fact stand even half the chance of winning that the Central Powers did in 1917, especially after Russia quit the war and the Germans suddenly had a million more men to send to the Western Front.

The problem with the Rebel leaders was that they simply did not trust Lincoln and the Yankees. After all, hadn't Lincoln promised from the beginning that he had no intention of "disturbing slavery in the states where it existed" but then issued the Emancipation Proclamation? Once they laid down their arms, the Confederates reasoned—Davis and the Congress foremost among them—what was to keep the Northern monster from descending wolf-like upon them?

There were, to be sure, those who proposed to do just that. The Massachusetts senator Charles Sumner advocated breaking the seceded states into military districts to be ruled "indefinitely" by a single Republican "czar" in Washington, who could do with them as he pleased without concern of opposition, political or otherwise, including the resettlement of the population.* Sherman thought along similar lines, proposing that any southerner—man, woman, or child—who did not readily accept Federal authority should be "banished" from the country and "become a denizen of the land," whatever that meant. He even used for illustration the British policy of forcibly repopulating Northern Ireland with Scottish settlers.

Contributing heavily to the tragedy was that the Richmond leadership would not, or could not, understand that Abraham Lincoln was the best friend they had among those holding the power in the U.S. government. Instead, they had demonized him to such a degree that whatever he said or did was instantly taken as yet another example of his mendacity.

It is unfortunate that the Confederates did not adopt the English model as their diplomatic paradigm, for however shrewd and shifty British diplomacy had become over the centuries, it was above all else *rational.* The deliberate approach of that most rational of nations was always to ask at some point, "But what is best for Great Britain?" and if compromise was best, then compromise it was. Hence after Yorktown they conceded the sovereignty of the United States, and did likewise in the War of 1812. The notable exception occurred at the outset of World War II when the British might easily have made a separate peace with Germany and, quite possibly, been let alone, so long as they behaved themselves. But after being duped more than once by Adolf Hitler they wisely, if reluctantly, chose to fight, though they soon found themselves in a struggle for their very existence.

The difference between the Confederates in 1860 and the British eighty years later was that the British were finally able to distinguish between a tyrant and a man who meant them no real harm, whereas the

---

* Sumner was the senator who had been so severely beaten by a South Carolina congressman in 1856 that he did not return to his post for three years.

southerners failed to do so; in the end they were deluded by their own party line. Had Davis and the others been able to see through their fog of hatred, they might have reached the same conclusion that J. F. C. Fuller would regarding the year 1917: that the summer of 1863 was "an excellent time to end the war."

First off, their bargaining position was infinitely better than it would be afterward. The war had become so bloody, and the casualties so horrendous, that Lincoln himself some months before the election of 1864 drew up an extraordinary document in which he stated, "This morning, as for some days past, it seems exceedingly probable that this administration will not be re-elected. Then it will be my duty to so cooperate with President-elect as to save the Union between the election and the inauguration, as he will have secured his election on such ground that he cannot possibly save it afterward." The despondent president then showed the document to each of his cabinet members and had them sign the back of it as witnesses, then put it away for future use, if necessary.

Equally as extraordinary, Lincoln drafted yet another secret document in his own "peculiar style," so he said, proposing that a "peace commission" be appointed to see on which terms the Confederates would agree to a restoration of the Union. Though nothing came of it, clearly this showed that the president's frame of mind was in a receptive mood for any honest and reasonable solution that would bring the country back together.

What Lincoln had in mind of course was not simply a cessation of hostilities and return to business as usual. The slavery issue was extremely tricky for him and any approach to the Richmond government would have been in the nature of a "feeler." But with an election looming he didn't have to be reminded that there were four slaveholding states still in the Union whose vote would turn on every perceived nuance in regard to the subject. How the president would have handled the question of slavery if the peace commission had gone forward is anybody's guess, but at least it would have got the two sides talking.

The issue here, though, is not about Lincoln's predisposition to treat with the southerners, for he had been making public overtures to them since the war began. It was only in the opening days, when he was fairly certain the war could be won, that he rebuffed Southern envoys, and in the closing days when he was certain that it *had* been won, and on his terms, that he rejected their pleas. But suppose that in the summer of 1863 Jefferson Davis had convened a "peace commission" of his own to approach Abraham Lincoln on the subject of restoration? Who might have composed such a body is almost as interesting as the notion itself. Robert E. Lee, for instance, would have carried great weight, being highly, if begrudgingly, respected in the North. On the other hand, soldiers often don't make good diplomats—or, for that matter, good politicians, as Grant himself proved in years to come.

In any case, it is almost a certainty that if the Confederates had shown a willingness to rejoin the Union after the fall of Vicksburg they would have received a far better deal than what they got, which was just a step or so above becoming Sherman's "denizens of the land." Slavery of course would have been abolished, but a great many southerners—Davis foremost among them—knew that the institution was eventually doomed, with or without war; their main concerns would have been what to do with all the freed slaves and, second, how to account or compensate for the financial loss of what they referred to as property.

(Considering that the value of the slaves in the Confederate states was approximated as $6 billion total, while the financial cost of the war to the Federal government was running approximately $6 billion per year, the rational solution ought to have been apparent. Compensating the southerners would have been worth it at twice the cost. Unfortunately, by then, the Southern mind, or at least the Southern leadership, had gone far beyond "property.")

Lincoln's concerns at seeing the nation restored necessarily would have included secure agreements from the Confederate leadership, as well as agreements state by state, that henceforth the South would abide by the laws of the land as enacted by the U.S. Congress—to which it could send representatives, as in the old days. Dissolution of the Rebel government and disarmament of its military would of course have been part of this equation, although given Southern mistrust it doubtless would have presented another tricky subject.

To speculate on the particulars of any such peace accord is beyond the scope of this hypothetical essay—or argument, as it were—but it is by no means idle conjecture that if the Confederacy had sought to make peace after the fall of Vicksburg, then tens of thousands of lives would have been spared, and place-names such as Chickamauga, Atlanta, the Wilderness, Spotsylvania, and Cold Harbor would not still conjure up the images of death and terrible suffering that they did then, and do today.

If cooler and more reasonable heads had prevailed in the Confederacy after the misfortunes at Vicksburg and Gettysburg, the Union would have been restored, slavery abolished, and the South could have retired from the field with honor and with its economy more or less intact, instead of the bankruptcy, humiliation, and ruin that attended its ultimate surrender. That this solution was not possible remains unfortunate.

Grant himself was quite surprised and then disappointed at the outcome of his victory. "The fall of Vicksburg," he wrote his father, "now will only result in the opening of the Mississippi and demoralization of the enemy.

"I intended more from it," he said.

CHAPTER TWENTY

They'd All Be Dead Anyhow

For a few days after the surrender, life in Vicksburg devolved into a turbulence that was almost surreal as Grant permitted his Federal army to visit the place that had been the object of so much consternation. The citizens, most of whom would rather have shut themselves up inside their houses, were instead forced to go out for food, the principal supplier of which, to their eternal disgust, was the Yankee army. Those who could afford it went down to the wharfs to purchase meat and groceries from the steamboats, but those who couldn't—and these included most, since Confederate money was nearly worthless—had to rely on the largesse of the enemy when the Rebel army ceased to exist.

After the Confederate soldiers received their paroles, which took about a week, they left the city and marched east toward Alabama, carrying enough food from Grant's commissaries to take them across the state to a camp where Pemberton hoped to reorganize them, or at least hold them together. Jefferson Davis was keen on this last, and opposed the granting of leaves so the men could visit their homes, but Pemberton disagreed. After all his men had been through, he said, if there was any hope of putting the army back in fighting shape the men needed some time at home. In the end he won his point. When he himself finally walked up to the house in Gainesville, Alabama, where his wife, Pattie, and their children had been staying, he had aged so much during the siege that his hair had turned stone gray, and his own daughter didn't recognize him and shrank from his embrace.

Also, on the long march away from Vicksburg, Pemberton finally encountered Johnston's army encamped on the far side of the state, and he found the commanding general "sitting on a cleared knoll on a moonlit night." According to a biography written by Pemberton's grandson, Johnston stood up and offered his hand saying, "Well, Jack old boy, I am certainly glad to see you."

Pemberton refused the hand and instead raised his own in a formal "punctilious" salute, informing Johnston that " 'according to the terms of parole prescribed by General Grant, I was directed to report to you.' Both men stood motionless and in silence," the grandson wrote, until Pemberton "saluted once more and turned away. It was the last meeting between these two," which was regrettable, since early in the war they had been friends and Pemberton had served on Johnston's staff.

At Pemberton's request, a court of inquiry was called in Richmond to determine what and who had been responsible for the loss of Vicksburg. Pemberton had offered to resign but Davis would not hear of it—and yet, owing to his high rank, there was simply no position available in the Confederate army in which to place him. In the end Pemberton resigned anyway. He accepted a commission as a colonel of artillery, in which he fought credibly and bravely during the final campaigns of the war.

As Pemberton had predicted, shortly after the fall of Vicksburg, it seemed that everyone in the Confederacy was clamoring for his head, except Jefferson Davis.

Some of the more scurrilous barbs pilloried Pemberton for having surrendered the fortress on the Fourth of July, intimating that it was done deliberately to give aid and comfort to the enemy. Also, word got around that he had agreed to give up Vicksburg for a million dollars in Yankee gold.

One of the most damning condemnations came from Johnston—or from his surrogates—not long after the surrender. Using documents that could have been obtained only from Johnston's files, anonymous letters began to appear in Southern newspapers accusing Pemberton of disobeying Johnston's orders to attack Grant when he first crossed the river, and again when Pemberton did not abandon Vicksburg and march his army toward Johnston at Canton, or near there, right before the Battle of Champion Hill.

Pemberton responded to none of it. "I am content to wait for the vindication of my military reputation," he wrote to a friend, "until the country shall be at rest, and my public defense shall have been successfully accomplished." However, that day would never come, for there would be no "public defense," as Pemberton alluded to the court of inquiry. As the Union armies pressed relentlessly southward, all senior officers who might have served on such a court were needed elsewhere in the field, and so the matter was dropped.

Like many Confederates after the war, Pemberton found himself in dire straits, except that he didn't have family in the South to help him out, and his family in Philadelphia had disowned him—or so he thought. Vilified in both North and South as a traitor, there were few options if he wanted to live on American soil. But as it turned out Pemberton's aged mother, Rebecca, unexpectedly bought him a small piece of farmland near Warrenton, Virginia, complete with a dilapidated house and barn. There, in the summer of 1866, and with no experience whatever, he set out to become a farmer. He named the place Harleigh, after an estate in Pennsylvania that had been owned by an ancestor.

For the next ten years Pemberton, Pattie, and the five children lived an idyllic, if austere, life trying to make ends meet in an economy that remained stagnant. At night there would be piano recitals and family singing and Pemberton would read to the children from Dickens, Thackeray, Dumas, and Mark Twain, who was all the rage in America. In the end, however, Pemberton simply couldn't make it work.

By then he had reestablished relations with two of his brothers (another two had fought for the Union and remained distant) who convinced him to return to Philadelphia, which he did in 1875. But Philadelphia turned out not to offer much in the way of lucrative employment for an ex-Rebel general, and within a year he moved the family to Allentown, Pennsylvania, where he became associated with a furnace company related to the prosperous steel industry. As a former U.S. Army officer who had sided with the Confederacy, he was still, by law, no longer an American citizen, and it was not until 1879, when Congress began to dismantle the Reconstruction Acts, that Pemberton ceased being one of Sherman's so-called denizens of the land and was finally allowed to vote.

In 1881 his health began to fail and he again moved to Philadelphia, but a few months later he died, at the age of sixty-seven. While the other lieutenant generals of the Confederacy such as Lee, Johnston, Beauregard, and Bragg were beginning to attain almost god-like status, Pemberton remained virtually ignored.

. . .

Following Vicksburg, Joseph Johnston took most of his army of relief to join Bragg, and after Bragg failed at Chattanooga he was given command of the Army of Tennessee. From there, true to form, Johnston conducted a long and agonizing retreat that ended in Atlanta, when Davis finally fired him in the summer of 1864. The next year, after the calamity at Nashville, Johnston was again put in charge of what was left of the Army of Tennessee, but it was his last command, and he surrendered to Sherman in Goldsboro, North Carolina, a week after Lee had capitulated to Grant.

After the war, Johnston worked briefly for a railroad but soon became a highly successful insurance manager for a London-based company that thought his name recognition might draw customers. It did, especially after Johnston recruited a number of other well-known former Confederate officers. He might have left well enough alone and enjoyed his wealth and reputation as a Southern hero, but instead he decided to throw a dungbomb at his old enemy Jefferson Davis, which in turn spattered him from head to toe.

This came in the form of a memoir he published under the title *Narrative of Military Operations Directed During the Late War Between the States,* which amounted to little more than a screed against Davis. As well, Pemberton and General John Bell Hood, who had replaced Johnston right before the Battle of Atlanta, were tarred with the same brush.

Published in 1874, the *Narrative* was a financial failure but it touched off a "war of the words," or "battle of the books," that lasted a decade. One of those it especially infuriated was farmer Pemberton, who, having been denied the court of inquiry he believed would have vindicated him, now sat down to refute the unexpected catalogue of charges by Johnston. Until then, Pemberton had been content to let matters rest, but the new round of accusations hurt him deeply since, in order to discredit Jefferson Davis, Johnston had insinuated that the former president's promotion of Pemberton was made not on merit but out of stupidity, thus turning an argument over strategy and tactics into a personal insult.

Throughout his remaining time on the Virginia farm and into his later years in Pennsylvania, Pemberton worked on his refutation, laboriously collecting statements from his officers as to their appreciation of the matters in dispute. He worked, in fact, right up until his death, but apparently he never felt he had got his manuscript quite right. In 1883, two years after Pemberton had died, Pattie sent the pages to the former Rebel general Marcus Wright, who was compiling the Confederate account of the war for the 128-volume U.S. government–published *Official Records of the Union and Confederate Armies.*

Wright did not find Pemberton's 150-page essay appropriate for inclusion in the *Official Records,* but apparently he kept it for a souvenir until his death in 1922, whereupon it remained in his estate for more than seventy years, when it finally resurfaced in the 1990s at an Ohio flea market. There, it was spotted by a Civil War buff and was finally published in 1999 under the title *Compelled to Appear in Print.*

Both Johnston's *Narrative* and Pemberton's *Compelled to Appear* rehash the old questions: Should Pemberton have left Vicksburg and Port Hudson uncovered and put his entire force in the field to attack Grant when he first landed at Bruinsburg? Should he likewise have employed the entire army as Grant moved inland and brought him to battle? After the fall of Jackson, should Pemberton have acted sooner to effect a linkup with Johnston's forces at Canton? And finally, should he have gone to extraordinary lengths *not* to move the army back into the Vicksburg defenses after the failure at Champion Hill?

On the other hand, should Johnston have sent away all the reinforcements that had arrived on the outskirts of Jackson and abandoned the city instead of fighting for it? Should he, when he had 22,000 men, have attacked Grant's rear soon after Champion Hill? And when he had an army of 33,000, should he not have found some way to relieve Pemberton at Vicksburg?

One answer to this last question is framed interestingly in a letter written in 1941 to Pemberton's grandson, who was also his namesake, which appears in a footnote in the biography of his grandfather. The author of the letter, an army colonel and evidently a military historian, postulates that Grant's behavior at Vicksburg "depended upon an absolutely supine attitude in Joe Johnston—who by every standard ought to have pitched into him. But Johnston wasn't a fighter . . . I've never been able to account for the high reputation he enjoyed. If Jackson, or Lee, or even Longstreet—any of the killers—had been sent out there Grant wouldn't have been free to starve out fortresses."*

But Grant was free to do so, and he did starve them out, and the answers to all these questions and many, many more remain obscured not so much by the fog of war as by the fog of time, when one can only ponder over documents and records and correspondences and books

---

* He might also have included Nathan Bedford Forrest in his list.

and reach conclusions that would doubtless be a far cry from the perspective of the man standing on the ground in that long-ago time.

Johnston, in any case, did not serve his reputation well by publishing his *Narrative,* which appeared in parts yet again in the widely popular *Century Magazine* series in the 1880s. His friends had warned him against writing it in the first place, but Johnston apparently could not resist the temptation; in the end his reputation came to be more tarnished than polished by its publication.

Still, Johnston was able to maintain his financial success, as well as a political career, serving a stint as a Democratic congressman and the U.S. commissioner of railroads. Although he had publicly stated that the South was better off for the end of slavery, when the Republicans won the presidential election of 1888 he declared that "the consequences to the south of . . . Gettysburg were small compared with the effect of Negro supremacy which the Republican party will inevitably establish in all the former slave states."

His vitriol against Jefferson Davis did not abate with time, and on one occasion in his later years he intimated to a newspaperman that the former president, on his flight south from Richmond, might have absconded with millions of dollars in gold from the last of the Confederate Treasury. This fiction was disproved nearly twenty years after the war when the last acting Confederate treasurer gave his account, with full documentation, of the ultimate disposition of all the remaining Confederate assets.

Johnston had remained friends with many former Confederate officers as well as old enemies who had stayed with the Union, and when William Tecumseh Sherman died in 1891 he went to New York to serve as an honorary pallbearer at the funeral. It was a cold, damp winter day, and at the graveside Johnston stood hatless, exposing his bald head to the rain and cold. When someone suggested that he put on his hat he responded, "If I were in his place and he were standing in mine, he would not put on his hat." Three weeks later, at the age of eighty-four, Joseph E. Johnston was dead of pneumonia.

Jefferson Davis continued to vent his spleen against the North until the bitter end, which occurred, for all practical purposes, on April 9, 1865, at Appomattox Court House, Virginia, when Robert E. Lee surrendered the Army of Northern Virginia to Ulysses S. Grant. Even if there had been some slight reason to prolong the fighting after the loss of Vicksburg and the debacle of Gettysburg, it had certainly vanished with the fall of Atlanta and Sherman's devastating rampage across the interior of the Southern states. A desperate campaign by John Bell Hood to retake Nashville had ended in one of the worst disasters ever to befall a Confederate army, while Lee's soldiers were dying literally in the last ditch up at Petersburg, Virginia, where Grant had finally cornered them.

By that time Davis's revulsion at the Union seems to have become an obsession, and it does not appear that he was operating as an entirely rational man. The favorable peace conditions that he probably could have secured from Lincoln after Vicksburg were now, a bloody year and a half later, the only good reason that he had for fighting on, and even those terms were now in serious jeopardy as the Radical Republicans concocted ever-harsher schemes for punishing the South.

Ironically, one concession Davis did make concerned the explosive question of turning slaves into Confederate soldiers. After dismissing as "too controversial" the entreaty by General Patrick Cleburne that slaves be armed and enlisted to fight for the South, Davis finally embraced the notion very late in the game. The Confederate Congress began debating the issue in the early months of 1865, creating a starburst of vituperation in Richmond. The bombastic old General Howell Cobb of Georgia roared, "If slaves will make good soldiers, our whole *theory* of slavery is wrong!" Davis rebuked him this way: "If the Confederacy falls, there should be written on its tombstone, 'Died of a Theory.' " In the end, less than a month before Lee's surrender, the Confederate Congress approved a bill providing for the partial emancipation and enlistment of slaves in the Confederate armies. The lawyer in Cleburne might have found the debate interesting had he lived to see it, which he did not. He was slain leading his division during Hood's charge on Franklin, Tennessee, in November 1864.

After the war, Davis was put into prison at Fort Monroe, Virginia, and shackled in chains while the Federal authorities decided what to do with him. Hanging was a very real prospect, but in the end he was released lest he become a sort of supermartyr.

As Davis languished in prison, the ownership of Davis Bend and Brierfield dangled in a legalistic limbo after the Federals occupied that part of Mississippi. For the first two years, the four-thousand-acre property belonging to both Davis and his brother Joseph came under the purview of the Freedmen's Bureau, which had set the former slaves to planting corn, beans, wheat, and, of course, cotton. By then Davis's home had been looted and desecrated by Northern soldiers and Hurricane, the palatial home of Joseph Davis, had been burned to the ground, but with Jefferson still incarcerated the elderly brother began proceedings to get the property back.

He knew he had to work fast, because by early 1867 the Radical Republicans had begun to enact severe Reconstruction measures designed to divest many southerners of their property. By forcing his claims, including a direct appeal to the new president, Andrew Johnson, Joseph Davis was able to resecure tentative title to the land, and immediately he sold it to, of all people, Jefferson's former slave Ben Montgomery, who was routinely described in the argot of the times as "an intelligent negro," and who, in 1861, had been the one to row Jefferson Davis out to the steamboat for his trip to Montgomery as the Confederacy's first and only president.

The selling price was $300,000, or $75 per acre, financed by Joseph at 6 percent interest, with no down payment. It was the hope of the Davis family that Montgomery and his people could farm the place for enough profit to pay the $18,000 per year interest rate as well as the payments on the principal. It was an amicable agreement all around, because both Davises had a warm respect for Montgomery, and he for them. In Ben's case, he had gone from the utter poverty of slavery to ownership of a four-thousand-acre plantation, and as for the now impoverished Davis brothers they hoped the sale would produce an annual stipend that would keep them afloat in troubled times.

It didn't work out that way. First, the unpredictable Mississippi River experienced an unusually severe flood in 1867 that cut through the neck of Davis Bend, flooding all the planting fields and rendering the property—at least for the foreseeable future—into Davis Island. At that point Jefferson, who had just been released from Fort Monroe, forgave Ben Montgomery the first year's interest and principal on the sale, and even found enough money in his own savings to provide for some of his former Davis Bend slaves.

In 1874, however, Montgomery defaulted on Davis Bend. A combination of weather, insects, and a lack of sophisticated management skills had convinced him he would never make a profit. By then, however, Radical Republican Reconstruction measures were in full swing and the local courts were packed with Northern Republican judges and justices, and Jefferson Davis's ownership again came into question. Entering a fifteen-year-long maze of antagonistic legal battles, Davis somehow emerged with his title to Brierfield intact. During his remaining years Davis leased Brierfield for farming, with mixed results. The river, having cut off the original bend, was now far more prone to overflow and ruin crops, but at least he had kept title to the place, and every so often there was enough to pay the taxes and even make a profit.

In the meantime, Davis had begun work on his own two-volume memoir of the war, which was finally published in 1881 and entitled *The Rise and Fall of the Confederate Government.* It was, as might be expected, a 1,200-plus-page justification of secession and his conduct of the war. Singled out for special attention, as also might be expected, was his old West Point classmate Joseph E. Johnston.

By then, Davis and his wife, Varina, were living in an elegant beachfront home called Beauvoir, situated on the Mississippi Gulf Coast at Pass Christian, which had been the gift of a wealthy admirer, a Mrs. Sarah Dorsey. In the winter of 1889 Davis journeyed alone to Brierfield, where he became ill with a cold, bronchitis, and fever. In a last letter to Varina he confided his unhappiness: "Nothing is as it should be, and I am not able even to look at the place."

Next day Jefferson Davis boarded the paddle wheeler *Natchez*—the same boat that twenty-eight years earlier had carried him from Davis Bend into the most turbulent era in American history—and steamed downstream to New Orleans, where he died on December 6, 1889, at the age of eighty-one.* In 1931 Brierfield, still owned by the Davis family, burned in an accidental fire, leaving only the chimney posts and foundation. The land has since passed into other hands.†

Grant naturally became the hero of the hour after conquering Vicksburg and opening the Mississippi River. He proposed at once to take his splendid army deep into Confederate territory and capture Mobile—the Confederacy's last important Gulf Coast port—or even Atlanta, but the ever-timid Halleck vetoed the plan, instead breaking up part of Grant's army for other duties.

Then, in September 1863, General Rosecrans got in over his head with Braxton Bragg's army at the Battle of Chickamauga and found

---

*Jefferson Davis's funeral cortege in New Orleans is said to have been attended by one of the four largest crowds ever to assemble in the South for a burial procession. The other three were those of Martin Luther King Jr., Elvis Presley, and Alabama football coach Paul "Bear" Bryant.

† Beauvoir, which had withstood 150 years of Gulf Coast storms, was practically demolished in 2005 by Hurricane Katrina; little was left but a hollow shell, though the building has been now restored with the aid of charitable contributions.

himself defeated and under siege at Chattanooga, and Grant was sent to straighten things out. It was a thorny situation, since Bragg's Rebel army was then in the process of starving Rosecrans out just as Grant had starved out Pemberton.

By then Grant had been promoted to theater command, composed of the Union armies of the Ohio, Cumberland, and Tennessee, and Sherman now became the commanding general of the last.

When Sherman reached Chattanooga in the late autumn of 1863, he was astonished to behold the rocky brow of Lookout Mountain frowning down above the city, "with its Rebel flags and batteries. I had no idea how bad things were," Sherman said. "Rebel sentinels, in a continuous chain, were walking their posts in plain view, not a thousand yards off."

"Why, General Grant, you are besieged!" Sherman exclaimed, with not a little irony, to his cigar-chomping riding companion.

"It is too true," was Grant's solemn reply.

Immediately Grant began to bring reinforcements to Chattanooga, and within two weeks an attack was launched that broke the Confederate army and sent it reeling into northern Georgia, where Sherman's combined army would begin its ruthless grind southward toward Atlanta. Before he left, Sherman briefly suspended his feud with the press to publish an open letter to the people of the South, in which he warned them "to prepare for my coming."

In March 1864 Congress passed a law reviving the rank of lieutenant general, highest post in the army, and the first recipient was Ulysses S. Grant, who was promptly ordered to come to Virginia to see what he could do about Robert E. Lee.

Grant had no grandiose tactical schemes in mind other than overwhelming Lee with blunt, brute force, which the Federal army—more than twice Lee's size—could deliver. In May 1864, Grant marched the Yankee host against Lee in the Battle of the Wilderness, in which he incurred staggering casualties while Lee slipped off to fight another day. However, instead of pulling back as had so many previous Union commanders, Grant hugged Lee's army vise-like to Spotsylvania, where the bloodshed became ever more unspeakable, and yet again to Cold Harbor, which gave even Grant pause at the carnage his soldiers were enduring.

Federal losses during this period exceeded the entire strength of Lee's army, and when casualty lists began to appear in Northern newspapers many people came to regard Grant as a "butcher," unable or unwilling to conceive of anything beyond using his force as a bludgeon. There was some truth in this, but it was born of a deliberate and considered decision to never give Lee a chance to strike and humiliate him as he had done with so many previous Yankee commanders. In a nutshell, Grant's theory was that the time for the niceties of military science had passed, and the quickest way to win the war was to press Lee at every extremity. In the summer of 1864 he at last brought Lee to bay at Petersburg, Virginia, just below Richmond, and there, as with Pemberton at Vicksburg, Grant forced the Confederate army into the ordeal of a siege. From then on it was simply a matter of time.

Grant was as magnanimous as possible with the terms of surrender at Appomattox the following spring, allowing Lee's army, after being disarmed, to go home. In the months and years that followed he became a celebrated hero figure, lauded nationally and internationally as the greatest general of his time. Persuaded by friends that he ought to go into politics, Grant was elected the eighteenth president of the United States in 1868. He served two terms before his administration was turned out in 1877, marked by unprecedented scandal and corruption. Although Grant was personally honest, he had allowed cronies to control him and the Reconstruction measures in the South went far beyond the punitive into the purely dishonest.

Afterward Grant traveled abroad with Julia and was feted by kings and emperors, returning in 1880 to form a brokerage business. Despite his fame and reputation it failed, and he was thrown into personal bankruptcy and forced to give up his trophies, swords, and souvenirs for unpaid loans. He obtained an army pension but remained so deeply in debt that, with the encouragement of Mark Twain, he went to work on the story of his military experiences, published in 1885 as *The Personal Memoirs of U. S. Grant.* It was one of the most phenomenal successes in the history of publishing, earning some $450,000 (nearly $10 million in today's money).

Yet Grant never lived to enjoy it. A year earlier he had been diagnosed with throat cancer likely brought on by a smoking habit that was said to be upwards of twelve cigars a day. Toward the end, the disease rendered him speechless and he was reduced to writing notes to communicate with his editors on the memoirs project. He died on July 23, 1885, and his remains, along with Julia's, lie in a mausoleum that is still a prominent landmark high above New York's Hudson River.

After Vicksburg, William Tecumseh Sherman took the Army of the Tennessee from Chattanooga to Atlanta, and thence on his notorious March to the Sea, during which he apparently suspended any allegiance he might have felt toward the Sermon on the Mount. His two-month rampage left a swath of rubble and blackened chimneys across Georgia and South Carolina, many of which remained well into the twentieth century.

Afterward, at Goldsboro, North Carolina, Sherman accepted the surrender of Joseph Johnston, who commanded the last sizable Confederate army, but his lenient terms created such an outrage among Northern radicals that Sherman was not only overruled, he was nearly court-martialed. A week earlier Lincoln had been assassinated and the radicals were out for blood. Sherman's terms to Johnston were that the Rebels should agree to cease making war and return to their state capitals, where they would turn in their arms to the states' arsenals, after which they were free to go, with Sherman's promise that they would remain unmolested by the Federal government. He also pledged that Southern state legislatures would be free to operate again once a loyalty oath was taken and, further, that "the rights of person and property" would be restored to the Confederate soldiers. Sherman's antagonists—but not Sherman himself—interpreted the "property" part as meaning the return of slaves to slavery.

About everybody in the administration in Washington was horrified when these stipulations became known, and Grant was sent to North Carolina at once to reverse Sherman's proposed agreement. Worse, Henry Halleck became so incensed that he leaked to the newspapers what had up to then been an administrative matter, confiding in a letter to a friend that Sherman "must have some screw loose again." And if Halleck was incensed, the infuriated Edwin Stanton wrote an abusive letter to the press disavowing Sherman's action. The newspapers had about as much love for William Tecumseh Sherman as he had for them, and many newspapermen launched into a tirade against the mercurial Ohioan, not only calling into question the usual issue of his sanity but accusing him of insubordination and even treason.

For his part, Sherman responded with the observation, "The South is broken and ruined, and appeals to our pity. To ride the people down with persecutions and military exactions would be like slashing away at the crew of a sinking ship. I will fight as long as the enemy will fight, but when he gives up and asks quarter, I will go no further." It is notable that when Sherman led his 60,000-man army in the grand victory parade in Washington the following month, not a soldier's head was turned toward, nor a salute given, to Halleck's reviewing stand, and when Stanton tried to shake hands Sherman refused.

With peace finally achieved, Sherman was sent west to supervise fighting the Indians, whose suppression had been neglected during the war, but after Grant became president Sherman was made general in chief of the army, a post he held for the next fourteen years. When he saw his good friend Grant falling into the hands of unscrupulous politicians Sherman tried to warn him, but to no avail, and over time relations between them became strained. Still he retained an abiding fondness for his old wartime companion, and once remarked that "Grant stood by me when I was crazy and I stood by him when he was drunk."

In 1875 he published his autobiography, entitled *The Memoirs of General William T. Sherman, by Himself.* A few months earlier, he had told his brother John, the senator, "You may be surprised, and maybe alarmed, that I have at last agreed to publish in book form my Memoirs." As might be expected, the book was controversial, since Sherman was notoriously unable to be anything other than plain-spoken. The memoirs appeared in two volumes and was made available, as was the custom of the time, through subscription. Twenty-five thousand copies were sold at $7 a set, for which Sherman received $25,000.

Following his retirement from the army in 1884 Sherman moved to New York City, where he kept up a lively social life and was guest of honor at countless reunions of the Grand Army of the Republic, as the Union veterans had styled their organization. His wife, Ellen, died in 1888, and he followed her two and a half years later. Of all his pithy comments, perhaps the one Sherman is best known for was his response to a group of politicians who were badgering him to run for president: "If nominated, I will not run, if elected, I will not serve."

Of McClernand and McPherson, the two other principal Union commanders under Grant at Vicksburg, the former lived up to his reputation for troublemaking while the latter was short-lived, period.

Immediately upon returning home to Illinois, McClernand began to bombard Lincoln with letters that lambasted Grant for his personal vindictiveness and called for a public investigation of his own removal from command. When these demands were ignored, he began clamoring for an investigation of Grant for incompetence, but nobody paid any attention. Finally, as if to shut him up, Washington assigned McClernand to command of his old XIII Corps, which was now widely dispersed in Texas, mainly near the Mexican border. He spent a year there putting out small Confederate fires before contracting

malaria and turning the corps over to the behemoth Irishman Mike
Lawler, who had risen to division commander.

In the spring of 1864 he returned to Springfield and resigned from
the army but remained active in Democratic politics. After the war he
fought long and hard against Radical Republican suppression of the
South. In 1887, with the Democrats back in power, McClernand was
named U.S. commissioner for the Utah Territory, where he had to confront the thorny problem of polygamy among the Mormons.* At the
end he wound up financially broke, but shortly before his death, which
occurred on September 20, 1900, Congress passed a bill giving him a
hundred-dollar-a-month pension. McClernand is buried close by his
friend and longtime political opponent Abraham Lincoln.

The career of James Birdseye McPherson, whom both Grant and
Sherman thought would "go all the way" to command the U.S. Army,
was cut short at the Battle of Atlanta on July 22, 1864, fulfilling Sherman's grim caveat, "If he lives." By then McPherson was commanding
the Army of the Tennessee under Sherman when Hood launched his
first massive attack on the Federal left. As McPherson rode to the
sound of the firing with only an aide to accompany him, he was surrounded by Confederate skirmishers. Ordered to halt, McPherson
instead tried to ride away but was shot down. Sherman was brought to
tears when the body of his friend was carried into his headquarters,
and a newspaper correspondent wrote that Grant was similarly moved
when he received a telegram with the news.

Admirals Farragut and Porter, foster brothers in civilian life, adversaries in war, went their separate ways after Vicksburg fell. To the disgust of Porter, Farragut gained command of the fleet assigned to take
Mobile, where he made his famous declaration, "Damn the torpedoes,
full speed ahead!" during the Battle of Mobile Bay. After the war he
was given command of the European Squadron until his retirement,
and he died in 1870 at Portsmouth, New Hampshire, aged sixty-nine.

David Dixon Porter went on to command the North Atlantic
Blockading Squadron until the end of the war, when he was promoted
to vice admiral and made superintendent of the U.S. Naval Academy
in 1870. Following his retirement he became a novelist until his death
in 1891 in Washington, D.C. He is buried in Arlington National
Cemetery.

After overseeing the fall of Port Hudson, Major General Nathaniel

---

* Utah was finally admitted to the Union in 1896 after the Mormons formally
renounced multiple marriages.

Banks took his army on an ill-advised and ill-conceived expedition up the Red River to capture Shreveport, Louisiana. Grant had opposed the operation from the start, desiring instead to send Banks's army against Mobile, but true to form Halleck was against it. The expedition became a monumental waste of life, time, and money and in the end Banks's 30,000-man army was defeated and forced to withdraw by 6,000 Confederates under the ever-resourceful Richard Taylor. For twenty-five years after the war Banks served in Congress alternately as a senator or a representative from Massachusetts, until his death in 1894. Notably, Banks was the key player in Congress who shepherded the controversial purchase of Alaska from the Russians in 1867.

After Grant was promoted to general in chief of the Federal armies, Henry Halleck, whom the soldiers knew as "Old Brains" and to whom Lincoln once referred as "little more than a first rate clerk," was demoted to become Grant's chief of staff, in which he served quite harmoniously. After the war he was sent to California, which might or might not have had to do with his set-to with Sherman in the wake of the Sherman surrender controversy. In 1871 Halleck was brought back east to administer military affairs at Louisville, Kentucky, where he died the following year. He was buried in New York City.

Benjamin Grierson, who led the famous cavalry raid, was sent off with Banks for a time, until he was recalled by Grant to lead cavalry in Mississippi. He was soon promoted to major general and decided to make the army a career. After the war he went west to fight the Indians, which he did by organizing the Tenth Cavalry, consisting of twelve companies of black troopers with white officers. These became the famed "Buffalo soldiers," but Grierson quickly found himself the subject of a whispering campaign by his fellow officers for trusting in his blacks to perform well in what had always been a "white" branch of the service. He lived until 1911 when he died of complications from a stroke suffered a few years earlier. He is buried in Jacksonville, Illinois.

John Rawlins, Grant's long-suffering chief of staff, took time off from the occupation of Vicksburg to marry a governess of a local family, who was originally from Connecticut. For the remainder of the war he continued to serve Grant and keep him on the straight and narrow. It was said by some that Rawlins was in fact the brains behind Grant, but there is no evidence of this. Just having Rawlins as a first-class staff man would have been enough.

When Grant took over the army in 1864 Rawlins became the army's chief of staff, and when Grant was elected president he became, for a time, secretary of war. Unfortunately, Rawlins had been plagued by tuberculosis for several years and passed away in 1869, at the age of thirty-eight. He is buried in Arlington National Cemetery.

James H. Wilson, Grant's engineer during the Vicksburg campaign, had one of the more colorful careers among former Civil War officers. After Vicksburg he was promoted to brigadier general and switched to the cavalry, in which he served under Sherman throughout the Battle of Atlanta. Afterward, when Sherman went east on his March to the Sea, Wilson went north to the Battle of Nashville, then returned south into the interior of Alabama, where he shamelessly burned all the buildings at the university except the president's mansion, which he spared because of its exceptional beauty. Afterward, Wilson at last brought Nathan Bedford Forrest to bay near Selma, Alabama, and proceeded to destroy much of that city, which had become a Confederate industrial center.

After the war he engaged in railroad engineering enterprises but when, in 1898, the Spanish-American War broke out, he volunteered for duty at the youthful age of sixty-one. Recommissioned a major general of volunteers, he took part in the American capture and occupation of Cuba and Puerto Rico. Not content with this, at the outbreak of the Boxer Rebellion in China in 1900, he volunteered again and led American and British troops against the gates of the Forbidden City.

Wilson wrote a number of books, including his autobiography, and his last official duty came in 1901 when he became the U.S. representative at the coronation of King Edward VII of England, but he lived on until 1925, when at the age of eighty-eight he died in Wilmington, Delaware.

Charles Dana, the former newspaperman who had been sent west to spy on Grant and then became Grant's great friend and confidant, stayed with the army through the Chattanooga and Chickamauga campaigns. It was he who had recommended to Stanton and Lincoln that Grant be made general in chief of the army.

After the war Dana became editor and part owner of the *New York Sun* and turned it into one of the nation's most influential papers, supporting Grant for president in 1868. But Dana broke with Grant as the magnitude of corruption in his administration became known, and his paper backed Grant's opponents thereafter. Dana spent his later years editing and learning Russian. He allowed his memoirs to be ghostwritten by the muckraking journalist Ida Tarbell and they were serialized in *McClure's* magazine beginning in 1897, which was also the year of his death, in New York City.

Sylvanus Cadwallader, who had accompanied Grant on his great bender, stayed with the army through all the big battles in Virginia, enjoying a special place in Grant's entourage. After the war he remained in Washington as the *New York Herald*'s bureau chief, then went home to Wisconsin, where he became assistant secretary of state.

In the 1880s Cadwallader decided to move to California and raised sheep on a ranch near Mount Shasta, in the remotest part of the state. There he began work on his reminiscences, which he did not finish until 1896. He sent the manuscript to Wilson, who vetted it and vouched for its accuracy, but for some reason it remained unpublished for the next half century, until the historian Benjamin P. Thomas brought it to the attention of Alfred A. Knopf. It was finally published in 1955 as *Three Years with Grant.* No record has been found regarding Cadwallader's death, but at the time work on the memoir was completed he was in his seventies.

Among the prominent Confederates of the Vicksburg campaign, General John S. Bowen, the longtime friend of Grant who had fought against all odds at Port Gibson and helped convince Pemberton to surrender, lived less than two weeks after being paroled. Weakened by dysentery in the last days of the campaign, he succumbed to the illness on July 13, 1863, near Raymond, and is buried in the Confederate cemetery at Vicksburg.

After Vicksburg, practically all of the other Confederate generals went on to fight with Johnston's—later John Bell Hood's—army at Atlanta, and then to the final fiasco of the Nashville campaign, including Stephen Dill Lee, who had defended against Sherman's disastrous attack at Chickasaw Bluffs. Lee became a corps commander and, after the war, a Mississippi state senator and later president of what is now Mississippi State University. He died in 1908 at the age of seventy-five and is buried in Columbus, Mississippi.

General William Wing "Old Blizzards" Loring, whose disappearance from the Battle of Champion Hill caused so much consternation, took his division with Hood's army to the battle at Franklin, Tennessee, where, on November 30, 1864, no less than five Confederate generals were killed.* At the height of the carnage, while his men were trying to pick their way through a hedge of thornbushes to get at the enemy, a witness described the one-armed Loring seated on his horse,

---

* Among these were Patrick Cleburne, who had suggested giving slaves freedom in exchange for fighting for the Confederacy. Three others, States Rights Gist, Hiram Granbury, and John Adams, served in Johnston's "army of relief" at Vicksburg. The fifth was a Tennessean by way of Ohio, Otho French Strahl.

facing the Federal firestorm, and roaring, "Great God! Do I command cowards?"

After the war Loring secured a job from the khedive of Egypt to command an infantry division, which he did for ten years until 1879, when he returned to the United States. He died in New York City in 1886 and was buried in his boyhood home of St. Augustine, Florida.

Of the other characters in the drama, diarist Mary Loughborough waited until her husband, James, marched away with the rest of the Rebel army, then, with her two-year-old daughter, caught a steamboat for Arkansas, where she waited out the rest of the war. As she and her daughter stood on the deck she watched the city recede in the distance and later wrote: "Vicksburg, with her terraced hills—with her pleasant homes and sad memories, passed from my view in the gathering twilight—passed, but the river flowed on the same, and the stars shone out with the same calm light."

With the encouragement of friends, Mary's diary was published in 1864 as *My Cave Life in Vicksburg* and became a best seller in the North. James survived the war and joined her in Little Rock where he became the Arkansas land commissioner and a delegate to the Democratic convention. He died in 1876, while Mary went on to found the popular *Arkansas Ladies Journal,* which promoted women's suffrage. When someone suggested that politics was too dirty for women, she wrote, "Why wouldn't it be a good idea to change politics so it shall be fit for women?" She died in 1887, but her daughter, Jean, who had survived the siege on a diet of jaybird soup, became a well-known newspaper and magazine writer and designed the Arkansas building at the 1893 World's Columbian Exposition in Chicago.

After nearly two years as refugees in Texas, Kate Stone and her mother and younger brothers returned to Brokenburn in November 1865, seven months after the war ended. "It does not seem the same place," she reflected. "The bare rooms, the neglect, the defacement . . . all the furniture was divided up between the Yankees and the Negroes . . . the gardens, the orchards, and fences are mostly swept away."

A former slave called "Uncle Bob," who had remained at the plantation as a self-appointed caretaker, had managed to save the family silver from the Yankees by hiding it in his cabin. After the Stones left, he had begun planting cotton on the land when it was fetching $1 a pound (about $500 per bale). "He has done the best he could to care for things," Kate wrote. "Every now and then he brings us presents of candy, raisins and nuts."

Bob asked to rent a piece of the Stone property to plant cotton but Kate's mother let him have it rent-free. Meantime, she and Kate's older brother William prepared to put in their own cotton crop; Mrs. Stone obtained an "advance," or loan, from a New Orleans cotton broker, while William hired a number of black ex-soldiers as field hands. The cotton survived a river flood, but just as the bolls began to burst they were attacked by the dreaded boll weevil, which by then had made its way up from Mexico through Texas and into Louisiana and Mississippi. "When it was looking as luxuriant and promising as possible, the worms came," Kate wrote. "In a few days the fields were blackened like fire had swept over them."

They made only twenty bales that year, which brought in about $10,000, but it had cost them $25,000 in labor. The economics of growing cotton had been forever changed by the war, and would remain so well into the next century, until the development of mechanized farm equipment. Between the floods and the weevil, the Stones eventually abandoned Brokenburn and moved to the Mississippi side of the river, but shortly afterward their house burned and the family moved in with William Stone.

In 1869, at the age of twenty-nine, Kate married Henry Bry Holmes, a former lieutenant in the Confederate army, who became the sheriff of Tallulah, Louisiana. They had four children, two of whom lived to adulthood. Kate died in 1907. Her diary was discovered and edited by the Texas A & M historian John Q. Anderson and published in 1955 as *Brokenburn: The Journal of Kate Stone, 1861–1868.*

Of Emilie McKinley, who wrote about life behind Union lines during the siege, little is known except that she kept her diary, which eventually wound up in the hands of her nephew, who was the librarian of the St. Louis Public Library. In the 1990s it came to the attention of Gordon A. Cotton, former director and curator of the Old Courthouse Museum in Vicksburg, who edited and annotated it and saw it through publication in 2001 as *From the Pen of a She Rebel.*

After the surrender of Pemberton's army, General James B. McPherson took over the Balfour house as his headquarters and Emma Balfour moved to a rented home in Demopolis, Alabama, where her sister-in-law lived. After the war the Balfours moved back into their home and Emma resumed her civic and social activities until her death in 1886. Her original diary is in the collection of the Mississippi

Department of Archives and History and was edited and published in 2006 by Gordon A. Cotton.

Dora Miller, the pro-Union wife of lawyer Anderson Miller, moved with her husband to New Orleans after Vicksburg fell and taught school after her husband died. There she met the author George Washington Cable, who persuaded her to reconstruct her notes about the siege for *Century Magazine,* which published her account in the 1880s—anonymously, since it would have been social suicide in New Orleans for anyone to admit that they had sided with the Yankees.

When Vicksburg fell Dr. William Wilberforce Lord, rector of the Christ Episcopal Church, his wife, Margaret, and their children received permission from Grant to leave the city. A week after the Yankees marched in and the Confederates marched out, the Lord family boarded a steamboat packed with hundreds of wounded Rebel soldiers that was bound for Mobile.* From Mobile, the Lords went to South Carolina, where they remained for the duration, returning to Vicksburg after the surrender where Dr. Lord once again presided over his flock.

The Rebel sergeants William Chambers and William Tunnard both became writers after the war, Tunnard as editor of the *Shreveport Times* and Chambers as a Mississippi poet.

The Yankee sergeant Osborn Oldroyd returned to Springfield, Illinois, and, for the next sixty-five years, became an inveterate collector of Lincoln memorabilia. The collection grew so large that he rented Lincoln's old house in the city until, in 1893, the home was donated to the state. Then he moved his collection into the William Petersen house in Washington, D.C., where Lincoln had died after being shot at Ford's Theatre, across the street. Oldroyd turned the place into a paying museum of Lincoln artifacts, including rare books, letters, original furniture, manuscripts, portraits, photographs, and other mementos. In 1926 the federal government gave Oldroyd $50,000 for his collection, a sizable sum for the time. He died in 1930 at the age of eighty-eight.

Vicksburg was forever changed by the war and its aftermath. Soon after the surrender a deluge of freed slaves—some said as many as

---

* These soldiers were probably taken to the Confederate hospital at the Grand Hotel in Point Clear, on the eastern shore of Mobile Bay. It is therefore likely that some among their number are buried in the little cemetery called Confederate Rest behind my home.

25,000—who had nothing to eat and nowhere to go swamped the town and they looked to the Federal government for food and shelter. In time, when the plantations began running again, the field hands returned to the countryside, but most of the former house servants remained in town.

The military occupation soon turned harsh. Citizens who refused to sign the loyalty oath often had their homes confiscated and in some cases were exiled. In one case, five women who walked out of a church service when the minister offered a prayer for President Lincoln found themselves "banished" from the city for "behavior disrespectful of the President or the United States flag." A rash of murders of whites by black troops or recently freed slaves brought the population to near panic until the Union commander court-martialed and hanged nine soldiers for murdering the wife of a white plantation owner. That seemed to put an end to much of the violence.

Under martial law people doing business in the city were required to have government licenses, and only persons who had taken the oath were eligible. Corruption inevitably set in and native Vicksburgians soon found that outsiders from the North—so-called carpetbaggers— had obtained the precious trade licenses with bribes. The strain was eased somewhat when the Federal army at last began moving off to fight new battles, and the citizens started slowly to repair and reconstruct their battered homes and public buildings.

The occupation did not stop with the end of the war, however. Reconstruction measures kept Vicksburg and much of the rest of the South under military rule for a decade longer and, in effect, bankrupted the city. Disenfranchised former Confederates could only watch helplessly as corrupt carpetbagger politicos or their stooges ran up the city's debt from $13,000 in 1869 to $1.4 million by 1874, and saw their taxes raised more than 500 percent in the same period. During much of the era, governors and other officials of Southern states were not elected but appointed by the Republican administration in Washington, and many of these office seekers saw opportunities to enrich themselves through the political cronyism that marked Grant's eight years in office.

At the same time many Northern entrepreneurs also arrived in the area, hoping to cash in on the southerners' newfound poverty. They bought up plantations at cut-rate prices or leased them for a pittance to try their hand at growing the "white gold" that had made so many of the natives wealthy. Almost to a man they failed, either because they didn't understand how cotton was grown or because of the floods, or the boll weevil, or that it was an entirely different game now that field labor had to be paid for.

In time they too left, along with the U.S. Army, as the 1870s drew to a close and some sense of normalcy began to return, but not before a calamitous racial encounter set the stage for white supremacy for the next hundred years.

At the time of the 1874 midterm elections the majority of Vicksburg's city and county officials were both Republican and black, save for the mayor, who though white was at the time under indictment for more than a dozen criminal offenses. A group of white citizens calling itself the Taxpayers League decided it was time for a change and installed some three hundred itinerant river rats at a waterfront boardinghouse for the required three months before the election. Their vote carried the day and the Republicans were swept from office—except that they refused to go. The confrontation occurred when Peter Crosby, the black sheriff, appealed for help from his constituents and a mob of armed blacks and whites met on December 7, 1874, resulting in the deaths of as many as three hundred blacks and twenty-nine whites. The event inspired similar movements throughout the South, and in due time the Republican stranglehold was broken, only to be replaced by a new and sinister political system.

It was a tragic commentary on race relations. After slavery had been abolished there was an obvious need for both blacks and whites to redefine their traditional roles in the social order in some harmonious fashion. Instead, whites clung to their notion of the inferiority of the black race, and, in the beginning, the newly empowered blacks understandably tended to flaunt their enhanced status until a gulf began to widen between the races that is only now, well over a century later, beginning to narrow.

Then in 1876 a monumental natural disaster convulsed Vicksburg, when Old Man River at last accomplished on his own what Grant's engineers could not. On April 26, the Mississippi River, just as it had a decade earlier at Davis Bend, suddenly cut a new channel several miles above where Grant had tried his canal. It immediately turned DeSoto Point into DeSoto Island, leaving Vicksburg stranded high and dry, no longer the port that had always been the city's main purpose for existing.

The city appealed to Congress for help, but it was only after proving that the calamity would cost the government in Washington tax income, and that the cutoff endangered access to the thousands of Union soldiers' graves on the battlefield, that authorities agreed to act. Money was appropriated to construct a canal from Vicksburg to the Yazoo River to reconnect the city with Mississippi trade, but floods, epidemics, freezes, and government bureaucracy delayed the project for thirty years, until its completion in 1903.

Since that time, the city on the bluffs has gone somewhat downhill, so to speak, from its promise as a center of Southern commerce that would rival New Orleans, Memphis, or St. Louis. Where Vicksburg was once Mississippi's second largest city, with its current 27,000 residents it doesn't even rank in the top ten, and 20 percent of the population lives below the poverty line. Many of the lovely old homes and buildings remain, their owners proudly pointing out a Union cannonball or two still in the walls. Some have been turned into bed-and-breakfast inns of the "Grant slept here" variety. One of the most lucrative businesses in town has been the recent introduction of "riverboat" gambling casinos that pump about $20 million annually into the city and county economies.

"Old times there are not forgotten" in Vicksburg, however, owing to preservation of what may be the most magnificent national battlefield park in the United States.

As the years passed and the veterans of the battle got older, many desired to return to the scene of their great confrontation. By steamboat or rail it wasn't a difficult trip, since the Northern soldiers had come mostly from states with easy access to the river and, with the exception of the Texans, the Southern boys had lived in either Mississippi or surrounding states.

By 1890, a quarter century after the war, a group of these men decided that the battlefield should be made into a memorial park before it was plowed under for farming or subdivisions or otherwise erased from place and memory. That had happened with the hundreds of caves in which the people had huddled during the bombardment: a year after the surrender the Federal commandant had decreed that they posed a health hazard and ordered them filled in. Likewise, on some parts of the battlefield farmers had filled the trenches and leveled defensive embankments to make room for crops. It had begun to become clear to former soldiers from both sides that the great and terrible events needed to be enshrined so that future generations might better appreciate them.

By the late 1890s the Vicksburg National Park Association had been formed and, after unraveling the usual red tape in Washington, President William McKinley, himself a Civil War officer, signed the act that funded the project, which was to be administered by the War Department.

Former Confederate major general Stephen Dill Lee was named to head the commission to oversee the park. Along with the federal appropriations, local donations of land allowed the commission to acquire eighteen hundred acres that included the Confederate and Union lines in their original seven-mile arc east of town. By then it was thirty-seven years after the battle and not only were memories fading but veterans were dying off.

Forests and undergrowth had reclaimed much of the battlefield not utilized by farmers so that simply relocating the old lines accurately became an arduous undertaking. Military maps were consulted in order to square them with the changed topography. Former soldiers, many quite aged, were enlisted and asked to walk the rough, up-and-down landscape, jogging their memory for such details as the precise location of artillery batteries, rifle pits, trenches, paths of assault, parallels and laterals, various headquarters, and other historical points. Most had little trouble locating the Third Louisiana Redan, where the mine had gone off.

States were invited to build commemorative monuments, and build them they did, in marble, granite, and bronze. In 1906 the Illinois monument was unveiled, a huge marble and granite affair that resembles the Jefferson Memorial in Washington, D.C., and cost a whopping $194,423—nearly $5 million in today's money. Inside the dome are inscribed the names of 36,325 Illinois soldiers who fought at Vicksburg. Local historians like to point out two of the names carved in stone that have drawn particular interest. One is that of Fred Grant, who as a twelve-year-old served honorifically as his father's "aide-de-camp" and received a minor leg wound during the Battle of the Big Black. The other is Private Albert D. J. Cashier, a solitary, nineteen-year-old, hard-marching, hard-fighting, pipe-smoking Irishman known around camp as "Little Albert." After the war he returned to Illinois and worked at several jobs before retiring on a veteran's pension, only to have it discovered—in his seventieth year, during a trip to the hospital after being struck by an automobile—that he was in fact a woman, whose real name was Jennie Hodgers. Thus unmasked, authorities committed her to an insane asylum, where she died in 1915.

Right next to the Illinois monument is the Shirley House, which served as an observation platform and headquarters for various Union generals. The famous tree beneath which Grant and Pemberton sat before the surrender was located on the Shirley property. An outstanding example of antebellum river architecture, it was allowed to become dilapidated over time and was nearly torn down before restoration was completed in the late twentieth century. A photograph of the Shirley House, taken at the time of the battle and depicting the Federal soldiers' encampments around it, is perhaps the most remembered picture of the event.

Other spectacular monuments were built along the new roads that wound along the puzzling, tortuous terrain the Yankees had had to face back in '63, hills, valleys, folds, dead-end gulches, dipping, rising, and rolling as if the waves of a great, chaotic ocean storm had somehow been frozen in time. The Wisconsin monument, dedicated in 1911, features a six-foot-tall bronze statue of Old Abe, the revered bald eagle mascot of the Eighth Wisconsin. (The original Old Abe, who survived the war perched on a music stand during battles, died of smoke inhalation in a fire where he was kept in the Wisconsin state capitol in 1881. His body was then stuffed and put on display until, in 1904, another fire at the capitol consumed him entirely. Since 1915, a replica of Old Abe has been on exhibit in the new capitol building.)

The park now contains monuments representing all the twenty-eight states whose soldiers fought in the battle—nearly four hundred in all—some great, some small. Because of the South's impoverished condition after the war, the Confederate monuments are noticeably less grandiose than their Northern counterparts, many of them consisting of smaller bronze tableaux that are no less moving because of the pathos of their artistry: a dying soldier reaching up with outstretched arms; another succored by a drink of water from a comrade. In 1962 Texas, then flush with oil money, unveiled a splendid red granite monument of the amphitheater type, complete with yucca plants.

The Missouri monument, unveiled in 1917, is unique among the others since it is dedicated to the soldiers of *both* sides who fought in the battle, juxtaposing the twenty-eight Yankee Missouri regiments against the fifteen Rebel Missouri regiments that were defending Vicksburg, brother against brother and friend against friend.

By far the most interesting exhibit in the park is the raised hulk of the ironclad *Cairo*, which was sunk by Confederate mines in 1862 and exhumed from the Yazoo River in 1964, a true labor of love by former

Park Service historian Ed Bearss and his dedicated crew. After locating the ship in 1956, Bearss relentlessly and successfully pursued local, state, and national politicians for funding to recover and preserve the gigantic historic relic, which was finally put on display in 1977. Since then, the 175-foot vessel has undergone extensive restoration and, with its accompanying naval museum, is by far the most popular exhibit for the million or more people who visit the park each year. And towering right above it, almost as a punctuation point, is the twenty-story-tall granite United States Navy obelisk, fashioned after the Washington Monument, inscribed with the names of Admirals Farragut, Porter, Foote, and Davis to remind people that without the navy the battle might not have been won.

Adjacent to Battlefield Park is the Vicksburg National Military Cemetery, which contains the graves of 17,000 Union soldiers. These include not only those who were killed or died of disease in the Vicksburg battle but others who were disinterred after the war from nearby places. It is the largest repository of Union dead in the nation, including that of Arlington National Cemetery. No Confederate soldiers are buried there, however; 1,600 who died at Vicksburg are interred nearby at Confederate Rest in Greenwood cemetery, provided by the city. The others are presumed to have been carried away by their families or remain in the ground where they were originally placed.

A friend liked to tell the story of the time years ago when as a small boy he was walking over the battlefield with his great-aunts and his grandmother, whose father had fought at Vicksburg during the war. Standing at the edge of the magnificent cemetery with its white marble tombstones stretching as far as the eye could see, he asked one of the women, "But why did they do it, Bamaw? Why did they die?" to which the old lady replied wearily, "Oh, I don't know, son. I suppose they'd all be dead by now anyhow."

In time, the soldiers who had survived gradually vanished like the dinosaurs. They were not gods, nor were they saints, but in their time they were giants who ruled the earth, and they feared not. No army as yet assembled could have matched them. For all of them, black and white, North and South, the war had been a defining epic, a time when lives had changed forever. Most of them had seen horrific things— perhaps even *done* horrific things—and after it was over some few went around like the Ancient Mariner, telling their story to anyone who would listen, while others kept a stony silence and never told a soul.

The Yankees went home to enjoy the prosperity that continued to grow in the North, while the Rebels went back to rebuild and come to terms with what had happened and wonder where it had gone wrong. Of the half million or more who had been wounded, many eventually died of complications from their wounds, while others simply hoped for a day when they felt well enough to be wheeled out into a garden to sit in the sun.

A number of them lived on to see the age of automobiles, airplanes, radio, skyscrapers, and world wars on an almost unimaginable scale. Whether they knew it or not, after they were gone their dust would enrich the soil of a better, stronger nation, forged in the crucible of their blood, alloyed with their sweat, and tempered with their tears.

Acknowledgments and Source Notes

Any acknowledgment is incomplete without paying homage to all the dogged historians who have gone before to help provide context, insight, and references on the Civil War in general and the Battle of Vicksburg in particular. My thanks to them is profound and heartfelt. In undertaking this study, one of the things that struck me yet again is the sheer volume of official Civil War information as well as private accounts of the era. My previous book concerned the Battle of New Orleans in the War of 1812 and there was hardly a shred of formal documentation other than some federal court records and the report of the commanding general, Andrew Jackson, which was only a few pages long. Yet during the fifty years between then and the Civil War, the proliferation of bureaucracy and the impulse to converse by letters is positively startling. Everybody who was anybody made reports, in triplicate, and those who weren't kept diaries or wrote memoirs. In most ways it is a historian's dream but in others a nightmare, being confronted with such an avalanche of information. Nevertheless, one takes it as one finds it, with gratitude, trepidation, or both.

I relied first on core records and documents and accounts by participants. Foremost among these is *War of the Rebellion: A Compilation of the Official Records of the Union and Confederate Armies.* Known as the *Official Records,* this monumental work, gathered, organized, and published by the U.S. government between 1880 and 1902, is composed of 128 volumes containing more than a hundred thousand pages of official battle and campaign reports, correspondence, telegraphic messages, letters, tables of organization, statistics—every pertinent scrap of paper generated by the Union and Confederate armies that could be located. It provides the blueprint for any historical study of the various aspects of the war.

Also very useful was the series *Battles and Leaders of the Civil War,* in this case volume 3. It is a compilation of articles by prominent soldiers, both Union and Confederate, published by *Century Magazine* between 1884 and 1887. Here are the voices of the leaders, recounting firsthand experiences of the great battles. Likewise, of solid help were the forty bound volumes of *Confederate Veteran,* a magazine published in the South—but with many contributions from Northern veterans—from 1893 until 1933, when the last of the soldiers were dying away. In addition, the *Southern Historical Society Papers,* now in the possession of the Virginia Historical Society, contain many fascinating memoirs and accounts of the war and the era. This fifty-two-volume set, comprising thousands of pages, was compiled between 1876 and 1953, and was edited during its last decade by the historians Douglas Southall Freeman and Frank Vandiver.

Until recently, copies of these important resources could be found only at major libraries, but in our electronic age all are now available on CDs at a fraction of the price one would have had to pay to have the actual books and can be stored in a small box on a desk instead of taking up a entire wall of bookshelves.*

On the particular subject of the Battle of Vicksburg, the definitive postwar study is a three-volume, two-thousand-page study by Edwin Bearss, who has been previously noted here as the former Park Service historian instrumental in raising the *Cairo.* His is by far the most detailed and comprehensive narrative of the battle, published in 1985–86 by the Morningside Press of Dayton, Ohio, which in addition offers a veritable gold mine of Civil War literature, particularly about the war in the West. Two other practical, scholarly accounts of the battle are worthy of prominent mention. They are *Ninety-eight Days: A Geographer's View of the Vicksburg Campaign,* by Warren E. Grabau, and *Guide to the Vicksburg Campaign,* edited by Leonard Fullenkamp, Stephen Bowman, and Jay Luvaas. Anyone wishing to visit the site of the battle would do well to absorb these books.

Dee Alexander Brown's *Grierson's Raid* and Timothy B. Smith's *Champion Hill: Decisive Battle for Vicksburg* illuminate those aspects

* For example, a reproduction of the *Southern Historical Society Papers* in book form retails for approximately $1,500, whereas the CD set sells for about $50.

of the campaign. As for the navy's role, solid perspective can be found in Allen H. Gosnell's *Guns on the Western Waters: The Story of River Gunboats in the Civil War*, Fletcher Pratt's *Civil War on Western Waters*, Chester G. Ahern's *Ellet's Brigade: The Strangest Outfit of All* and *Naval Battles of the Civil War*, and John D. Milligan's *Gunboats down the Mississippi*.

There are many excellent biographies and autobiographies of the major players in the drama; foremost are the personal memoirs of Grant and Sherman, Sherman's selected letters, and the account of the war by Jefferson Davis. Among the recent books are *Grant and Sherman: The Friendship That Won the Civil War* by Charles Bracelen Flood, who was for a while my companion in a lonely outpost during Vietnam War days, and *Grant: Triumph over Adversity* by Brooks D. Simpson. Also highly recommended are *Jefferson Davis: The Man and His Hour* by William C. Davis and Stephen Woodworth's *Jefferson Davis and His Generals: The Failure of Confederate Command in the West*, along with *Jefferson Davis: Tragic Hero*, written by my former college professor Hudson Strode.

Stephan Oates's *With Malice Toward None* and Carl Sandberg's two-volume opus *Abraham Lincoln* reveal much of the character and trials of that great American. The lives of Generals McClernand, Van Dorn, and Johnston are well chronicled in *Major General John A. McClernand* by Richard L. Kieper, *The Tarnished Cavalier* by Arthur B. Carter, and *Joseph E. Johnston: A Civil War Biography* by Craig L. Symonds.

Pemberton: The General Who Lost Vicksburg, by Michael B. Ballard, and *Pemberton: Defender of Vicksburg*, by his grandson John C. Pemberton, as well as *Compelled to Appear in Print: The Vicksburg Manuscript of General John C. Pemberton*, edited by David M. Smith, form an excellent picture of that luckless commander.

For biographical material on the various subordinate generals in the contest, Ezra Warner's indispensable two-volume work *Generals in Blue* and *Generals in Gray* is among the most commendable examples of historical research. Over a period of years, Warner researched, compiled for the record, and published the biographies and photographs of every Union and Confederate general officer in the Civil War, of which there were more than a thousand. These books represent a historical labor of love.

In addition to the memoirs and recollections noted in the final chapter of this book, for personal accounts of soldiers and citizens during the Vicksburg campaign and siege I have relied on an abundance of information from books, diaries, letters, magazine and newspaper stories, and other commentary and written accounts by the participants. A particularly good compilation of the life of Vicksburgians during the conflict is *Vicksburg: A People at War, 1860–1865* by Peter F. Walker, as are Gordon Cotton's *Vicksburg: Stories of the Siege* and *Vicksburg and the War.*

For Mississippi politics, economics, and society John K. Bettersworth's *Confederate Mississippi* is invaluable, as are his *Mississippi in the Confederacy: As They Saw It* and James W. Silver's *Mississippi in the Confederacy: As Seen in Retrospect,* the latter two volumes being recollections by various players and observers during the war and its aftermath. Much of my appreciation of Brierfield comes from Frank Edgar Everett Jr.'s *Brierfield: The Plantation Home of Jefferson Davis.*

Finally all due credit and a debt of thanks must be given to the historians Bruce Catton and Shelby Foote for their epic works on the Civil War. Their dazzling narratives give shape, dimension, and perspective to what is arguably the most complex subject in American history, and I would be lost without them.

Index

Page numbers in *italics* refer to maps.

Louisiana, CSS, 118, 153
Louisiana Seminary of Learning and
    Military Academy, 86–7, 408
Louisville, USS, 58, 276
Lovell, Mansfield, 111, 118, 134, 173

McClellan, George B., 38, 42, 47, 50,
    82–4, 90, 132, 147, 148, 162, 177, 191,
    226, 320, 423
McClernand, John A., 56, 76, 78–9, 90,
    94, 96, 101–2, 184, 238; Big Black
    battle and, 331–2; Champion Hill and,
    323, 324, 326, 329, 340; Grant and,
    185–8, 198, 220, 235–6, 263, 274, 306,
    350–3, 377–9, 445; Grant's firing of,
    377–9; Lincoln and, 185–6, 188,
    224–5, 235*n*, 236, 263, 445, 446;
    second Vicksburg assault and, 350–2;
    Sherman and, 226, 227–9, 235*n*, 263,
    274, 378–9; Vicksburg campaign and,
    240–2, 263, 274, 275, 279, 286–7, 290,
    292–4, 293*n*, 297, 298, 305, 306, 310,
    312*n*, 314, 317, 331–2, 377–9, 406
McClernand, Minerva, 286, 292
McClure's, 448
McCormick, Cyrus, 28
McCulloch, Henry, 387–9
McDowell, Irvin, 423
McKinley, Emilie, 406–7, 451
McKinley, William, 456
McNair, Evander, 318
McPherson, James B., 56, 244–5, 252,
    274, 297, 298, 305, 317, 340, 451;
    Champion Hill and, 323, 327, 330,
    340; death of, 446; Jackson assault
    and, 312, 312*n*, 313, 315, 316; Raymond
    battle and, 310, 311; second Vicksburg
    assault and, 349–50, 352–3, 379;
    Vicksburg siege and, 396, 400, 409,
    410, 411
McRae, CSS, 116
Mallory, Stephen, 152
Manassas, CSS, 108, 114, 116
Martin, Anne, 311–12
Maryland: agriculture in, 25; Lee's
    invasion of, 172, 319–20; secession
    issue and, 33; slavery issue and, 37*n*

Maury, Dabney H., 165
Maxey, Samuel B., 317–18
Medal of Honor, 348–9, 348*n*
medicine, 28–9
*Memoirs of General William T.
    Sherman, by Himself* (Sherman), 445
Memphis, Tenn., 72, 102, 107, 123, 130,
    144–6, 147, 148, 194, 274; Sherman
    and, 181–3, 184, 196, 203, 246
Memphis Evening Bulletin, 378–9
Methodists, 34, 127
Mexican War, 32, 44–6, 63, 67, 75, 85,
    99, 175, 190, 214, 268, 317, 355
Mexico, 44
Michigan, 28
Michtom, Morris, 299*n*
Miller, Anderson, 452
Miller, Dora, 35, 350, 363, 393, 394–5,
    403, 452
Milliken's Bend, Battle of (1863), 387–9
Mill Springs, Battle of (1862), 72, 75,
    172*n*
Mingo, SS, 59
minié balls, 10
Minnesota, 28
Mississippi, 26, 81, 246; Civil War's
    impact on, 39; Davis's message to
    legislature of, 208–12; Grant's
    advance into, 183–8, 195, 196–202,
    203–4, 214, 226, 231; secession of, 69;
    Sherman's march through, 424, 427;
    terrain of, 299
Mississippi, CSS, 118, 153
Mississippi, USS, 268, 269, 270, 271
Mississippi Central Railroad, 184, 198,
    237, 239
Mississippi River: British blockade of,
    53*n*; cotton trade and, 26, 27, 65;
    Grant's crossing of, 17, 272–8, 281–7,
    292–4; Island Number 10 in, 72,
    102–6, 111, 132; rechanneling at
    Vicksburg of, 454–5; strategic
    importance of, 23–4, 38, 53
Missouri, 154*n*; Grant's campaign in,
    51–60; secession issue and, 33
Missouri Compromise (1820), 32, 68
Missouri Orphan Brigade, 154